Environmental Valuation
in South Asia

Edited by

A.K. Enamul Haque, M.N. Murty and Priya Shyamsundar

CAMBRIDGE UNIVERSITY PRESS
Cambridge, New York, Melbourne, Madrid, Cape Town,
Singapore, São Paulo, Delhi, Tokyo, Mexico City

Cambridge University Press
4381/4, Ansari Road, Daryaganj, Delhi 110002, India

Published in the United States of America by Cambridge University Press, New York

www.cambridge.org
Information on this title: www.cambridge.org/9781107007147

© A.K. Enamul Haque, M.N. Murty and Priya Shyamsundar 2011

First published 2011

Printed in India at Replika Press Pvt. Ltd.

A catalogue record for this publication is available from the British Library.

Library of Congress Cataloguing in Publication data
Environmental valuation in South Asia / edited by A.K. Enamul Haque, M.N. Murty, and
Priya Shyamsundar.
     p.   cm.
     Includes bibliographical references and index.
     Summary: "Provides an overview of different environmental problems in South Asia
and examines how economic valuation techniques can be used to assess these
problems"--Provided by publisher.
     ISBN 978-1-107-00714-7 (hardback)
     1. Environmental economics--Asia, South. 2. Environmental quality--Asia, South.
     I. Haque, A. K. Enamul. II. Murty, M. N. (Maddipati Narasimha), 1942- III.
Shyamsundar, Priya, 1964- IV. Title.

     HC430.6.Z9E5425 2011
     333--dc22   2010040402

ISBN 978-1-107-00714-7 Hardback

Contents

List of Figures

List of Tables

List of Appendices

List of Contributors

M. Jahangir Alam
Department of Economics and
Social Sciences
BRAC University
Dhaka, Bangladesh

Shrinivas Badiger
Centre for Environment and
Development
Ashoka Trust for Research in
Ecology and the Environment,
Bangalore, India

Avishek Banerjee
Institute of Economic Growth
Delhi University Enclave
Delhi, India

Caroline van den Berg
World Bank
1818 H. Street NW
Washington DC, USA

Cyril Bogahawatte
Department of Agricultural
Economics
University of Peradeniya
Peradeniya, Sri Lanka

Saudamini Das
Institute of Economic Growth
University of Delhi Enclave
Delhi, India

Santadas Ghosh
Department of Economics and
Politics
Visva-Bharati
Santiniketan, West Bengal, India

Indrila Guha
Department of Economics
Vidyasagar College for Women
Kolkata, West Bengal, India

S.C. Gulati
Institute of Economic Growth
Delhi University Enclave
Delhi, India

Herath Gunatilake
South Asia Department
Asian Development Bank
6 ADB Avenue,
Mandaluyong City 1550,
Metro Manila, Philippines

Usha Gupta
Department of Business Economics
Bhim Rao Ambedekar College
University of Delhi
Main Wazirabad Road
Delhi, India

A.K. Enamul Haque
Department of Economics
United International University (UIU)
Satmasjid Road, Dhanmondi
Dhaka, Bangladesh

K. Omar Hattab
Department of Soil Science and
Agricultural Chemistry
Pandit Jawaharlal Nehru College of
Agriculture and Research Institute
Puducherry U.T., India

Janaranjana Herath
Department of Agricultural
Economics and Business
Management
Faculty of Agriculture
University of Peradeniya
Peradeniya, Sri Lanka

Md. Zakir Hossain
Transparency International
Bangladesh
Dhaka, Bangladesh

Ratna Kumar Jha
District Agriculture Development
Office, Bhaktapur
Department of Agriculture , Nepal

Himayatullah Khan
Institute of Development Studies

NWFP Agricultural University
Peshawar, Pakistan

Rajeeva Kumara
Sobaganahalli, Kothigere Post
Kunigal Taluk
Tumkur District, Karnataka, India

Sharachchandra Lele
Centre for Environment and
Development
Ashoka Trust for Research in
Ecology and the Environment
Bangalore, India.

S. Madheswaran
Centre for Economic Studies and
Policy
Institute for Social and Economic
Change
Bangalore, India

Ajit Menon
Madras Institute of Development
Studies
andhinagar, Adyar
Chennai
Tamil Nadu, India

M. N. Murty
Institute of Economic Growth
Delhi University Enclave
Delhi, India

P. Nasurudeen
Department of Agricultural
Economics and Extension
Pandit Jawaharlal Nehru College of
Agriculture and Research Institute

Karaikal
Puducherry U.T., India

Min Bikram Malla
Practical Action Nepal Office
Pandol Marg, Lazimpat
Kathmandu, Nepal

Iswaragouda Patil
Head Post Kunnur
Shiggaon Taluk
Haveri District
Karnataka, India

Subhrendu Pattanayak
Sanford School of Public Policy
and Nicholas School of the
Environment
Duke University
Durham, NC, USA

Adhrit Prasad Regmi
Centre for Rural Development
and Self-help
Dallu Residential Area, Chhuni
Kathmandu, Nepal

W.R. Rohita
No. 56, Darshanapura
Kundasale, Sri Lanka

K. R. Shanmugam
Madras School of Economics
Gandhi Manadapam Road, Kottur
Chennai, India

Priya Shyamsundar
South Asian Network for
Development and Environmental
Economics
32/25 Sukhumvit Soi 67
Bangkok, Thailand

P. Selvaraj
Fisheries College and Research
Institute
Chidambaranagar
Thoothukudi
Tamil Nadu, India

L. Umamaheswari
Department of Agricultural
Economics
Pandit Jawaharlal Nehru College of
Agriculture and Research Institute
Karaikal
Puducherry U.T., India

Jeffrey R. Vincent
Nicholas School of the
Environment
Duke University
Durham, NC, USA

Jui-Chen Yang
Research Triangle Institute (RTI)
Research Triangle Park, USA

Preface

Applied research in environmental economics has gained momentum in recent times and is viewed as a means to aid environmental management. The South Asian Network for Development Economics and Environment (SANDEE) has contributed to this momentum in South Asia, a region with a vast and growing ecological footprint. During the last ten years, SANDEE has sponsored research on several aspects of environment and development. It has also organized numerous workshops to meet training needs.

SANDEE uses innovative strategies to build capacity in environmental economics. Researchers and managers from universities, governments and NGOs are provided with repeated opportunities to improve their skills. The process for an economist to produce a useful piece of research is detailed. It involves his/her attending a teaching workshop, writing a research proposal related to an environmental problem in his/her country, presenting ongoing research to receive comments, receiving guidance from a SANDEE advisor and writing a manuscript. The final research output is peer-reviewed by an international expert. Thus, SANDEE research is grounded in the realities of local problems but benefits from the advice of scholars from around the world.

This book contains contributions from SANDEE researchers and advisors. The papers in the book are on environmental valuation in South Asia and provide information for designing sustainable development policies. They constitute detailed micro case studies of air, water, land and forest resources from the region.

The studies in this book have benefited from comments from many experts including Kenneth Arrow, Partha Dasgupta, Jean-Marie Baland, Kanchan Chopra, Herath Gunathilake, K. G. Maler, Subhrendu Pattanayak, E. Somanathan, Rehana Siddiqui and Jeff Vincent, to name a few. Many chapters have also been anonymously peer-reviewed. The editors have acted as advisors on specific projects and worked with several researchers from the beginning to the final culmination of this book.

The credit for producing the research presented in this book also goes to the highly motivated team at the SANDEE Secretariat. Manik Duggar, Pranab Mukhopadhyay, Kavita Shresta, and Anuradha Kafle, who were at SANDEE when these studies were done, have made the development of these projects possible. Current staff, including Mani Nepal and Krisha Shresta, has continued to work with the same spirit.

The task of preparing this book from SANDEE projects was entrusted to the Institute of Economic Growth (IEG) with M. N. Murty as coordinator. The IEG organized three book-related workshops and brought together contributors so that they could further develop their chapters. The former Director, Kanchan Chopra and several IEG faculty and staff provided intellectual and administrative support. We express our thanks to them.

Finally, we are thankful to SANDEE'S donors – IDRC (International Development Research Center), Sida (Swedish International Development Cooperation Agency), NORAD (Norwegian Agency for International Cooperation) and the World Bank for their financial assistance, and, to the staff who represent these agencies on SANDEE's Board for their advice and support.

Enamul Haque, M. N. Murty and Priya Shyamsundar

1

Introduction

1.1. About the book

This book is about the valuation of environmental services in South Asia. It brings together, for the first time, multiple case studies on valuation undertaken by economists and environmental scientists from Bangladesh, India, Pakistan, Nepal and Sri Lanka under the aegis of the South Asian Network for Development and Environmental Economics (SANDEE). The book provides an over-view of different environmental problems in South Asia and examines how economic valuation techniques can be used to assess these problems. It seeks to offer robust evidence of the monetary benefits of resource conservation and the costs of a decline in environmental quality as South Asian economies grow rapidly.

As elsewhere, markets for many environmental goods are absent in South Asia and the prices of these resources are unknown. Therefore, the chapters in this book discuss various methods for generating information on the prices of environmental goods and services. Another feature of the book is its exposition of the use of environmental and economic data and analytical techniques under circumstances when data are difficult to obtain. Thus, the book seeks to address some of the challenges of valuing environmental changes that are unique to developing countries. The book is also designed to serve as a work book for students and practitioners of environmental valuation. Each chapter offers a description of an environmental problem and the valuation strategy used. This is followed by a discussion of methods of estimation and results.

1.2. Environmental valuation in South Asia

Environmental resources constitute the core of life supporting systems on earth. They offer a number of services for human well-being, which are ordinarily not accounted for in regular market transactions. Many of these services are public goods or external benefits from conserving resources. In other cases, human activity results in pollution, with tangible costs that need to be accounted and assessed. Because the benefits from environmental services and costs of pollution are not always immediately obvious or because they are not priced and exchanged, they tend to be ignored with serious consequences for human health, income and well-being.

Economists consider the problem of valuing environmental services as a result of market failure and have tried to develop special tools and methods of valuation. In fact, valuation of environmental services now occupies a central place in the environmental economics literature. Its increased prominence is largely because it provides information that can be used for (a) designing policies for the sustainable use of environmental resources, (b) making investment choices with a due consideration given to environmental impacts and risks of projects, and (c) accurately measuring a country's Gross Domestic Product/Net National Product (GDP/NNP) after accounting for the contribution of natural resources.

In the developed world, valuation has entered the mainstream of policy and legal frameworks. Numerous valuation exercises are routinely undertaken to make policy choices about air quality standards or to settle legal disputes about oil spills or wetland loss, for example. Developing countries in Asia, Africa and Latin America, especially the emerging economies of China, India, Brazil and Russia, are now witnessing environmental degradation of formidable proportions. However, in these countries, there are fewer assessments of the true value of environmental services. While there are now requests from parliamentarians and the judiciary for evaluations of the price of environmental goods and services, there are very few studies that can be readily presented for public review. Thus, there is an urgent need to undertake environmental valuation exercises in these regions of the world. Such studies can identify the importance of environmental conservation as a path for sustainable development. Well done studies can also reduce methodological uncertainties about how to undertake this kind of research in the developing world.

Recognition of the need for environmental valuation came rather late to South Asia with some empirical studies start appearing only during the late 1990s. The initial cohort of studies included books that value water quality (surface and ground water) – prominent amongst these are Markandya and Murty (2000) on cleaning the Ganges, and Murty, Mishra and James (1999) on the economics of water pollution. Another dominant trend included studies focused on bio-diversity conservation and eco-tourism[1]. Interestingly, valuation in South Asia initially saw a number of contingent valuation studies[2]. The enthusiasm found in West for contingent valuation clearly had an influence on the first set of valuation studies done in the region. There was also interest in estimating pollution abatement cost functions in order to assess the possibility of using economic instruments such as taxes to reduce pollution[3].

In more recent years, there has been an upsurge in studies that have examined the health impacts of water and air pollution[4]. A good part of this literature took its cue from an earlier study done by (Cropper et al., 1997) on the health benefits of air pollution control in Delhi. Another strand of this literature, responding to demand from development agencies such as the World Bank, used valuation methods to examine willingness to pay for water service delivery[5].

The above is the context for the chapters presented in this book. Whereas most of the previous valuation studies in the region have been from India, this book is unique in that it brings together studies from across South Asia. Another area of interest in organizing this book was to see how varied valuation numbers may be across South Asia. Interestingly, as will be shown later, the valuation numbers for similar issues are comparable in the different countries. This suggests that the benefit transfer approach which applies valuation numbers from one country to another, can be used. This book can also contribute as a teaching tool. Many colleges and universities now teach environmental economics. Thus, the varied chapters in the book can serve as examples of how to apply a valuation method to

---

[1] Some of these are Hadker et al. (1997), Murty and Menkhaus (1998), Chopra (2004), and Santa Kumar, Haque and Bhattacharya (2005).

[2] World Bank (1993), Misra (1997), Hadker (1997), Venkatachalam (2000), Markandya and Murty (2000).

[3] Mehta (1995), Pandey (1998), Murty, James and Mishra (1999), and Murty and Kumar (2004).

[4] Kumar and Rao (2001), Lvovsky et al. (2002), Murty, Gulati and Chettri (2003), Dasgupta (2004), Goldar et al. (2005), and Gupta (2008).

[5] Chowdhury (1999), Whittington et al. (2002), and McKenzie and Ray (2004).

different contexts, what kinds of data are required, and what challenges are likely to be faced.

1.3. Valuation methods

Environmental economists describe environmental values as use values, option values and non-use values. The literature further categorizes the methods for measuring these values as revealed and stated preference methods. Revealed preference methods provide methodologies for estimating environmental values in the context of consumers and producers making consumption and production choices in market. Stated preference methods rely on values that are expressed by consumers and producers in the context of hypothetical markets scenarios. Chapters 2 and 3 of the book provide a succinct review of these methods.

Environmental degradation has unfortunately become a by-product or an externality associated with economic development. Most often, the many environmental externalities of production in agriculture and industry are ignored. Several case studies presented in this book examine the costs of these ignored externalities. A common approach taken is to estimate production functions, treating the environment as an input in the production of a marketable good. Any decline in the quality of the environmental input is expected to affect output. Because several case studies use this approach, we have dedicated an entire chapter (Chapter 3) to describe this method in detail.

Two chapters in this book use the production function approach to analyze externalities related to shrimp farming. Chapter 4 shows how shrimp production affects paddy cultivation in southern India, while Chapter 5 examines the effect of lagoon water pollution on shrimp production in Sri Lanka. These studies value the external costs of shrimp farming, which contributes to water and soil salinity, thereby leading to a decline in fish or rice yields.

An interesting variant of the production function method is used in estimating the contribution of pesticides to vegetable farming in Nepal (Chapter 6). Here the story is slightly different. Pesticides are used as damage control agents – they don't increase or decrease output directly. Rather, increased use of pesticides is expected to decrease the impact of pests and thus indirectly contribute to reducing yield losses. This case study shows that pesticides are used in quantities larger than optimal in vegetable farming in Nepal. Thus, reducing pesticide use is likely to be both economically efficient and environmentally appropriate.

Chapters 7 and 8 focus on the regulating services of eco-systems. Chapter 7 aims to measure the benefits of forest re-generation by examining the links between stream flow, agricultural water use and economic returns to agriculture in the Western Ghats. The counter-intuitive results from this case study are discussed in greater detail later. Chapter 8 estimates storm protection benefits from conserving mangroves in the north-eastern coast of India. Both these chapters provide examples of techniques for estimating eco-system services.

Two chapters use the travel cost method to estimate demand functions for recreation. The travel cost method is a well-honed technique that uses the costs that visitors bear in traveling to a recreational site for estimating the demand curve for recreation. Chapter 9 discusses urban parks near Islamabad, Pakistan and Chapter 10 examines a remote rural protected area in the Indian Sunderban. While the Pakistan chapter follows the individual travel cost approach, the Indian study uses the zonal travel cost approach because of infrequent multiple visits to the site.

There are several studies in this book that estimate health production functions. Conceptually, health is an outcome that is a result of exposure to pollution. Health status is also affected by a number of other variables such as income, health stock, conditions of living or lifestyle, and adaptive behaviour. Environmental economic studies that seek to understand the health impacts of pollution generally follow two approaches. The first approach is to estimate a full health production function using a systems approach because many household decisions are inter-related. This approach jointly estimates a dose-response function, which provides an estimate of probability of a person falling sick due to exposure to pollution, along with a mitigating or medical costs function and an avertive expenditures function. This allows researchers to establish an individual agent's Marginal Willingness to Pay (MWTP) to reduce pollution.[6] A second linked approach is to estimate the dose-response function and a mitigating cost function separately and use the estimates from these regressions to obtain the MWTP. Several studies (Chapters 11 to 15) in this book follow this approach to estimate the health effects of indoor and outdoor air pollution and arsenic contamination of water.

---

[6] MWTP should also include the disutility from sickness but this factor is often ignored because of difficulties in estimation.

Another methodological technique illustrated in this book is the use of the Hedonic Price approach. This method evaluates changes in the value of an environmental good by assessing changes in the prices of a marketed good or service in a surrogate market. Chapter 16 in this book examines housing markets and prices in Delhi and Kolkata to estimate the benefits from reducing air pollution. Chapter 17 uses wage data from industrial workers to estimate the value of statistical life. The interesting issue here is whether the markets of linked goods are sufficiently robust to allow one to estimate the value of environmental changes. Our case studies suggest that this is indeed true and the hedonic approach can be applied to developing countries.

Finally, Chapter 18 illustrates the use of the Contingent Valuation Method (CVM). In contingent valuation, the preferences of economic agents and their willingness to pay for environmental changes are directly gauged by asking survey questions. This stated preference method is particularly useful when revealed preference methods are unavailable. This Chapter provides a step-by-step account of the procedures used to implement a contingent valuation survey in the context of a water supply and sanitation project in Sri Lanka.

In the following sections, some of the findings of the case studies in this book are discussed. An attempt is made to show how these valuation studies can be used by placing them amidst the environmental challenges faced by South Asia.

1.4. Implementing full cost pricing in agrarian settings

Agrarian losses from ignoring the environment are a key problem faced in South Asia. The food production and quality of our environment are closely linked. As a result, loss in production due to deteriorating environmental conditions might lead to increased poverty. During the last decades, economic growth has lead to significant poverty reduction – 16 per cent in Bangladesh (1999–2004) and around 17 per cent in India (1984 –2004)[7]. Part of this reduction in poverty can be attributed to agrarian changes and the green revolution. However, even as the importance of improved agriculture is recognized, there are many counter examples of environmental damage as a result of over-zealous agricultural practices, for example, pesticide pollution, forest degradation and water use. One of

---

[7] Planning Commission, Government of India.

the main reasons why such environmental problems are faced is because of a complete failure to account for the price of the environment.

The failure to undertake 'full cost' pricing is well illustrated by two SANDEE research studies that have looked at shrimp farming in India and Sri Lanka. The shrimp industry is a very lucrative industry and brings in considerable foreign exchange. In India, it brings in about two billion US $ in a regular year. However, depending on how intensively the farming is done, it can cause surface and ground water pollution and salinization of agricultural lands.

The first study reported in Chapter 4 examines the salinization of paddy lands by adjacent shrimp farms in South India. Soil data shows that soil salinity was in the normal range before shrimp farms arrived 15 years ago. By examining two similar villages one closer to shrimp farms than the other, the study has shown that the costs to farmers from the salinization externality ranges from INR 1000 to INR 5000 per hectare – a significant cost because the average returns to paddy in this area are about INR 6000 per hectare.

In Sri Lanka, the situation is somewhat different. Shrimping is a major industry in the Dutch canal lagoon with over 1300 farms occupying various tracts. Unfortunately, they have had many episodes in the last decade of disease outbreaks – the main reason is that the pollution created in the lagoon by the waste discharged by the farms themselves, has a negative feedback impact on the farms. The study reported in Chapter 5 shows that reduction in lagoon pollution to safe levels would increase yields by about seven per cent. So in the former case, it is a direct one-sided externality and in the later case, we have a reciprocal externality with an open access coordination problem.

The question is how can these be rectified? The two obvious courses are government and community action. In terms of government action, there are laws in India that limit the type and geographic prevalence of shrimp farming, however, these laws are not always well implemented. In Sri Lanka, a project to clean up the basin has been in the books for years but the question is should the public sector subsidize the private sector for its own inaction? Arguably, an effluent tax would be a way forward if the regulatory framework to impose such a tax exists.

In terms of community action, in the Indian case study, a second nearby village escaped the impact of the shrimp farms because villagers coalesced together under a farmers' organization. There are many attempts to scale up such community-based efforts through watershed management programmes in South Asia. This example suggests that such efforts are critically needed for managing agrarian areas where full cost pricing is difficult to implement.

1.5. Accounting for linked ecological and social systems

Any environmental resource transformed into a flow that is valuable to us is a service that ecosystems provide. Ecosystems provide many valuable services to human beings. Arguably, the entire life support system that we are dependent on for the continuation of the human species is an eco-system service. However, this over-arching service is better understood if further categorized. Some commonly identified eco-system services are – climate regulation, pollination, pest control, ground and surface water maintenance, filtering and water purification, biodiversity provision, food and shade provision, waste absorption and so on (Millennium Ecosystem Assessment, 2005).

Scientific understanding of eco-systems services has grown over time. However, the long time it has taken to get to the current understanding of climate change and its determinants suggests that the complexities of ecological and bio-physical interactions are enormous. Measuring changes in eco-system services, valuing these changes, and establishing the right institutions to regulate these changes are looming challenges.

This book provides two good examples of the complex nature of ecological interactions, especially when overlaid with human enterprise. The first example is provided by a study in Chapter 7. This study examines the hydrological services provided by forests in the Western Ghats of southern India. In the study area, there is an interesting water management strategy that has been used for many years. Here, agriculture is either rainfed or irrigated through the use of water from storage tanks. For example, in the study village, if the tank fills up during the Rabi/Summer season, water is released and farmers grow paddy. If the tank does not fill up, none of the farmers get water and they switch to a rainfed crop.

Chapter 7 compares run-off/rain ratio in two nearby forests and concludes that the ratio is much higher in un-conserved and relatively degraded forests and less in dense and conserved forests. Therefore, conservation of forests means less water for surface or tank irrigation and more water for ground water or well irrigation. Farmers could potentially be better off by conserving the forest if they used ground-water for irrigation. But, because of the unique and collective way decisions are made to use surface water for growing crops, more forests would actually mean a significant reduction in average expected annual income to farmers. So, here is an interesting situation, where the local institutional arrangement for water management works in harmony with degraded forests.

The second example in Chapter 8 looks at the cyclone of 1999 that killed around 10,000 people along the coast of Orissa. In this chapter, Saudamini Das asks if the presence of mangroves provided any storm protection to households and their assets during the storm. By combining GIS data with census information, she examines the mangrove mediated effects on residential property in Kendrapada district of Orissa and concludes that mangrove forests, by reducing the velocity of storm surge, offered protection. In the absence of mangroves, the number of houses that fully collapsed would have increased by some 23 per cent.

Das's work suggests that the mangrove forests can act as a natural barrier during storms. This assessment is important because climate change is likely to increase the frequency and intensity of storms in South Asia. So should mangroves be conserved in Orissa? While, the opportunity costs of land are higher than the protective value mangroves provide to residential property, the overall protective values of mangroves are high enough to promote conservation.

The sustainable development challenges are here clear – a) careful economic analyses of the multiple services of forests is needed – even in the case of Chapter 7, the conclusion is not to allow forests to degrade but to recognize that there are some costs associated with conservation; b) the data needs for undertaking this kind of analyses are immense and methods inter-disciplinary. Therefore it is required to teach ourselves, more so than before, the language of scientists; and c) as evident in so many instances, the institutional arrangement matters tremendously. This is obvious in the case of hydrological services in the Western Ghats. In the case of the mangroves in Orissa, it is interesting that much of the degradation of mangroves took place after 1952, when new Government rules transferred mangrove forests from local *Zamindars* (the feudal landowners) to the government. Moving forward to fix this problem will require both public investments in mangrove restoration and new public-private arrangements to get communities involved in mangrove conservation.

1.6. Improved health outcomes

The ambient air and water pollution in South Asia on an average is much higher than safe standards. The World Health Organization (WHO) standard for annual PM_{10} concentration, small particles that can enter the respiratory system, is 50 µg/m^3. However, in Dhaka, the annual average PM_{10} concentration was estimated to be 133 µg/m^3 in 2003 (World Bank 2006) and this number was 194 µg/m^3 in Karachi in 2003 (World Bank 2006). In India, in 2007, over 50 per cent of 304 monitoring stations registered PM_{10} concentrations higher than the levels prescribed by the National Air Quality Standards (CPCB, 2008). In fact, 51 per cent of the residential stations had PM_{10} levels that were considered 'critical'; interestingly only 14 per cent of the industrial stations were in the critical status. In terms of water pollution, organic pollutants tend to be the most important source of pollution. In India alone, some one million children are estimated to die annually as a result of water related diseases such as diarrhoea (Parikh et al., 1999). Thus, reducing pollution of surface and ground water and indoor and outdoor air pollution is a huge environmental challenge for policy makers.

A number of studies reported in this book are eye opening in terms of the magnitude of damage pollution causes and the challenges the governments and communities face in reducing pollution. The studies suggest that the costs of outdoor air pollution per person per year in terms of morbidity effects are approximately INR 100 in India (Chapter 11) and LKR 699 in Sri Lanka (Chapter 14). To get a better understanding of these numbers, it is useful to compare these to annual income. The annual per capita income in Sri Lanka was LKR 77,556 per year in 2006–2007 (HIES, 2008). Thus, conservatively, the costs of air pollution are close to one percent of per capita income in Sri Lanka. In Kanpur, the per capita income in the sample studied was approximately INR 15000 per year. This places morbidity costs of ambient air pollution in the same range of less than one percent of per capita annual income. Chapter 16 estimates the total annual damages, including morbidity and mortality effects, from air pollution in the cities of Delhi and Kolkata to be INR 54,833 and INR 37,026 million respectively.[8] The Kanpur study in Chapter 11 estimates that the annual health damages from morbidity effects alone for people in this city as INR 310 million per

---

[8] Reducing air pollution to meet current safe standards would provide a representative household an annual benefit of INR 23,354 (US $486.54) in Delhi and INR 11,727 (US $244.31) in Kolkata.

year. From this and from the relative sizes of the city, an assessment that mortality costs dwarf morbidity effects on households can be made.

It is known that investments to reduce air pollution are not cheap. Gupta (2007) estimates elsewhere that the cost of converting different categories of vehicles in Kanpur to run on CNG, which would reduce PM_{10} concentration by about 25 per cent, would be INR 590 million per year. The costs would outweigh the benefits from health gains if only the morbidity effects are considered; however, if mortality benefits are taken into account, then economic analyses would suggest that the city should be cleaned up (Gupta, 2007). The valuation studies suggest that it may be timely to consider air quality clean-up investments in South Asian cities, however, both costs and benefits of clean up need to be carefully analyzed.

A silent menace, but less well known than ambient air pollution, is indoor air pollution. Because of their dependence on biomass for cooking and the lack of proper ventilation and stoves, scores of women and children in South Asia face high health risks from bad indoor air.[9] According to the WHO (2007), for example, some 7500 Nepali deaths in 2002 can be attributed to indoor air. In this book, Chapter 15 examines solutions to indoor air pollution in the form of improved stoves and chimneys. It finds that in rural Nepal, 80 per cent of children in households with traditional kitchens had a cough, two weeks prior to the survey, while the same number dropped to 20 per cent in similar households with improved kitchens. This chapter shows that small interventions such as improved stoves and smoke hoods actually reduce indoor air pollution (PM_{10}) by some 66 per cent[10] and an investment of NPR 5150 for improved cooking stoves could bring significant health benefits. The annual costs-of-illness to rural Nepalese households from IAP is about four per cent of household income, which is higher than morbidity costs from outdoor pollution in neighboring countries. This suggests that indoor air pollution needs to become a higher priority for policy makers.

The quality of surface and ground water are another source of concern in South Asia. This book has several water pollution related studies covering a range of issues such as agro-production related pollution, arsenic contamination and water polluted by human and other waste. These studies

---

[9] Pant (2008), Lvovsky et al. (2002).

[10] Malla finds that the 24 hour average levels of PMresp (respirable particulate matter) were 764 μg/m³ when there were no improvements made to the kitchen relative to levels of 255 μg/m³ in kitchens with improvements.

are useful because estimates of benefits of improved water quality for household use can provide inputs for designing policies for the supply of safe clean water. A case in point is the study on provision of clean water in Sri Lanka (Chapter 18). Two case studies from Bangladesh suggest that households spend from 0.6 to 1.3 per cent of annual income on coping with childhood diarrhoea and the related number for exposure to arsenic contamination in water is 0.7 per cent.

1.7. Micro to macro: valuation and better measures of sustainable development

The World Bank (2006) estimates that the costs imposed on people due to environmental changes result in loss of four per cent of GDP in Bangladesh. Such numbers provide a window into understanding the value of environmental goods in a country but do not form a core aspect of Bangladesh's income accounts. This is because Bangladesh, like most other countries, does not measure its GDP accurately and ignores environmental externalities. The valuation studies reported in this book along with other available studies provide the micro foundations for extending national income accounts to measure green GDP or the 'comprehensive' wealth of a country.

Focusing on strategies to green GDP, it is useful to note that the UN methodology of integrated environmental and economic accounting (UN, 1993) prescribes creating satellite physical and monetary accounts of environmental changes. Developing these satellite accounts requires an aggregation of changes in natural resource stocks at the micro (firms and household) level to arrive at changes at the level of sectors and from sectors to the national level. The UN methodology, however, does not explain how aggregation of changes in natural resources or environmental stocks can be done. There are many difficulties in measuring aggregate changes in environmental stocks such as water quality, air quality and forest cover, while this can be more easily done for stocks of exhaustible resources.[11] In the case of environmental stocks, depletion and its monetary valuation need to be firm or region-specific. For example, in the case of ambient air quality (measured in PM_{10}), pollution levels need to be understood in the

---

[11] Production and use accounts at the sector or macro level can be prepared by simply adding the firm-level production and uses of fossil fuels or minerals or ores. The market determined resource rents can be used to prepare monetary accounts of depletion of exhaustible resources.

context of a specific airshed, and in the case of water quality [measured in Biological Oxygen Demand (BOD)], changes should be measured within a watershed. The valuation of environmental quality changes needs to also be region or site-specific because these numbers can vary from area to area[12].

Various chapters in this book provide case studies that can be useful for developing region or project specific physical and monetary accounts of changes in environmental stocks. For example, Chapter 16 shows that the two urban airsheds of Delhi and Kolkata differ with respect to number of households, air pollution levels and household valuations of a unit of pollution. Damages caused by a tonne of particulate matter pollution in Delhi are much higher than in Kolkata. Therefore, we need to know these kinds of monetary values and how they differ in different airsheds in order to slowly build up the aggregate monetary accounts required for estimating green GDP.

Finally, a significant problem with the current environmental policy regime in South Asia is the absence of a link between the ambient and source standards (Mehta, Mundle and Sankar, 1995). Hence, it is quite possible that the quality of the environment could continue to deteriorate despite high degree of compliance among individual polluters. For developing sectoral and region specific physical accounts of pollution, a clear understanding and modeling of the relationship between pollution loads at sources and ambient pollution is needed. This is an area of further research for environmental accounting in South Asia. These studies, in combination of valuation studies reported in this book, could provide the necessary inputs for estimating Green GDP in these countries.

1.8. Increasing revenues through better valuation

Several economic instruments can provide an incentive for improving the environment and can also be used to finance environmental management. The commonly discussed instruments are taxes, charges, payments for ecological services and tradable permits. Furthermore, there are many variants of these or alternate instruments that have evolved in different countries.[13]

There are many opportunities for financing environmental improvements. The first step toward this is to understand how individuals and households

---

[12] The benefit transfer approach can be used in comparable areas when site specific information is not available.

[13] See Sterner (2003); OECD (2009).

value these improvements. There are many studies worldwide of willingness to pay for clean water, for instance. Chapter 18 presents a case study that examines a Water Supply and Sanitation (WSS) project in Sri Lanka and shows how estimates of WTP can be used in designing WSS projects.

One area where there is huge scope for financing conservation is with recreational services. All over South Asia we see a surge in domestic tourism as incomes have grown. But the prices people pay to visit parks and protected areas are still minimal. A study from Pakistan in Chapter 9 suggests that the government could earn revenues to the extent of PKR 4.3 million per year from increasing park fees PKR (Pakistani rupees). We have a similar story in the case of the Indian Sunderban National Park. This is home to the Royal Bengal Tiger and makes up, along with the Bangladesh Sunderban, the largest contiguous mangrove forests in the world. The current entry fees to visit the Sunderban are very low and park authorities are able to capture less than ten per cent of consumer surplus. If the fees are increased from the current value of INR 15 to INR 154 per visitor per day, total revenues can be increased by more than 300 per cent, bringing nearly INR five million per year to the park. Thus, revenue generation through higher user fees in natural areas may be one of the more obvious ways to finance environmental protection.

1.9. Challenges to environmental valuation in developing countries

There are some interesting challenges to undertaking studies, valuation and otherwise, in developing countries. Many of the researchers who have contributed to this book have dealt with these challenges through sheer hard work and through some smart thinking. Some of these issues have been outlined here.

Environmental economics studies often combine primary data collection with secondary sources of data. Gathering secondary information can be difficult in South Asia unless these are well published data available in the public domain. In most cases, usable secondary data often lies in government offices. However, persistence can prevail and a good example of this is the super cyclone study presented in Chapter 8. When asked about how she collected secondary data on cyclone damages, Saudamini Das reported in the following manner.

"I made 4 trips to Orissa and travelled to 3 districts covering 100s of kilometers. I visited at least 20 offices and went at least 3 to 4 times to each office. All this effort was only to get permission for my research associate to copy data. All had a standard reply – that the data (probably) do not exist. One guy said the files got burnt, another said it got damaged in the last monsoon flood, another said there was a theft and the super cyclone file was stolen. One officer told me that he has joined the office few months back and his predecessor has kept the files somewhere that nobody in the office is able to trace. Then he sent me to the store with his PA and said very nicely if I can spare little time and can help trace the file with his PA's help? But to my horror I found some 20 near open almirahs with piles of paper here and there. This was the experience in almost every office, but I never gave up."

Saudamini eventually used every network she had and brought to bear some political influence to get government officials to allow her to access the data. There are several similar stories that suggest that collecting secondary data in South Asia means convincing the government officials, but the rewards are high.

A second issue that often crops up is about the methodological and data problems involved in matching household and environmental data. Environmental economics studies frequently involve collecting household specific socio-economic information but this needs to be matched with environmental data on air or water quality, mangrove loss, soil salinity and so on, which is usually not available at the household or firm level. Thus, valuation studies require economists to identify the scientific data they need, learn about how this data are measured and collected, understand methodologically the link between changes in the environmental variables and welfare outcomes and then figure out how to show this link empirically. In the shrimp salinity study described in Chapter 4, for example, Umamaheshwari indicates that she first collected household data on farm production and then matched this to farm soil salinity levels. She collected soil data by identifying plots with the help of village leaders and by using existing land records. She then used maps and went back to each household to confirm the location of their plots. So after several rounds of data collection, she had her full set of information. A slightly different approach is taken in the air pollution studies. The starting point for these studies is environmental data. A common approach is to draw circles of varying distance around existing air quality monitoring stations and then identify a set of sample households within these concentric circles for the household survey. In general, the case studies in this book offer a diverse set of strategies for data collection, mapping and analyses.

Some challenging issues emerged from the extreme circumstances that some researchers faced in their work. The Sunderbans, where the travel cost study in Chapter 10 was undertaken, for example, is a remote, fragile and watery land, with no electricity, difficult transportation options and is home to amongst the poorest people in South Asia. The researchers had to win the trust of the people slowly by spending large amounts of time listening to their stories before embarking on their survey. Arguably, this forced the researchers to really comprehend the situation they were trying to study. The situation is not that different when working with the urban poor – building trust by listening to their narratives, helping with small difficulties and providing medicine occasionally were all part of the research endeavour. Given illiteracy among the poor, new strategies had to be adopted in other ways – for example, health diaries could not be left behind for households to fill on their own, leading to weekly visits to homes to collect data (Chapter 11).

References

CPCB (Central Pollution Control Board), 2007, National Ambient Air Quality Status, Series: NAQMS // 2008–2009, Ministry of Environment and Forests, New Delhi.

Chopra, K., 'Economic Valuation of Bio-diversity: A Case of Keolodev National Park in G.K. Kadekodi', (New Delhi: Oxford University Press, 2004).

Cropper, M.L., Simon, A.M., Alberrini, A. and Sharma, P.K., 'The Health Benefits of Air Pollution Control in Delhi', *American Journal of Agricultural Economics* 79(5), (1997), 1625–1629.

Chowdhury, N.T., 'Willingness to Pay for Water in Dhaka Slums: A Contingent Valuation Study', Ahmad, Q.K., Nishat, A., Chowdhury, Q.I., Haque, A.K.E., and Rahman, A. (eds.), *Environmental Economics in Bangladesh*, IUCN, Dhaka, (1999), 105–116.

Dasgupta, P., 'Valuing Health Damages from Water Pollution in Urban Delhi, India: A Health Production Function Approach, *Environment and Development Economics*, 9, (2004), 83–106.

Ahmad, J.K., Goldar, B.N., and Misra, S., 'Value of Arsenic-free Drinking Water to Rural Households in Bangladesh', *Journal of Environmental Management*. 74 (2), (2005),173–185.

Kadekodi, G.K. (eds.), 'Environmental Economics in Practice', (New Delhi: Oxford University Press, 2004).

Kumar, S. and Rao, D.N., 'Valuing Benefits of Air Pollution Abatement Using Health Production Function: A Case study of Panipat Thermal Power Station, India', *Journal of Environmental & Resource Economics*, (2001).

Lvovsky, K., Akbar, S., Alam, S., Balasubramanian, Barnes, D., Kojima, M., Kumar, P., 'India: Household Energy, Indoor Pollution, and Health, ESMP, the Netherlands, BNPP Publications, World Bank, 2002.

Gupta, U., 'Valuation of Urban Air Pollution – A Case Study of Kanpur City', *Environmental and Resource Economics*, 41(2008), 315–326.

Gupta, U., 'Valuation of Urban Air Pollution: A Case Study of Kanpur Nagar, Utterpradesh, India', PhD Thesis, University of Delhi, 2007.

HIES (Household Income and Expenditure Survey), 2006–07, Final Report, Ministry of Census and Statistics, Ministry of Finance and Planning, Sri Lanka, 2008.

Hadker, N., Sharma, S., David, A., Muraleedharan, T., 'Willingness to Pay for Borivili National Park: Evidence from Contingent Valuation', *Ecological Economics,* 21, (1999), 105–122.

Millennium Ecosystem Assessment, 2005, 'Ecosystems and Human Well-being: A Framework for Assessment'.

Mc Kenzie, D. and Ray, I., 'Household Water Delivery Options in Urban and Rural India', Working Paper No. 224, Stanford Centre for International Development, (USA: Stanford University, 2004).

Markandya, A. and Murty, M.N., *Cleaning Up Ganges: The Cost Benefit Analysis* (New Delhi: Oxford University Press, 2000).

Mehta, S., Mundle, S. and Sankar, U., *Controlling Pollution: Incentives and Regulation* (New Delhi: Sage Publications, 1995).

Misra, S., 'Measuring Benefits from Industrial Water Pollution Abatement: Use of Contingent Valuation Method in Nandesari Industrial Area of Gujarat in India', Working Paper No. E/185/97, Delhi, Institute of Economic Growth, 1997.

Murty, M.N. and Menkhaus, S., 'Economic Aspects of Wildlife Protection in Developing Countries: A Case Study of Keoladev National Park, Bharatpur, India, *Valuing India's Natural Resource',* (New Delhi: SPWD, 1998).

Murty, M.N., James, A.J., and Misra, S., *'Economics of Water Pollution : The Indian Experience',* (New Delhi: Oxford University Press, 1999).

Murty, M.N., Gulati, S.C., and Chettri, P., 'Valuation and Accounting of Urban Air Pollution in the Indian Subcontinent', Monograph, *South Asian Network of Economic Institutions (SANEI), 2003.*

Murty, M.N. and Kumar, S., *Environmental and Economic Accounting for Industry,* (New Delhi: Oxford University Press, 2004).

Murty, M.N., *Environment, Sustainable Development and Well-being: Valuation, Taxes and Incentives,* (Delhi, India: Oxford University Press, 2009).

OECD, 2009. OECD / European Environment Agency Instruments Database, http://www2.oecd.org/ecoinst/queries/index.htm

Pandey, R., 'Pollution Taxes for Industrial Water Pollution Control', *Mimeo,* (New Delhi: National Institute of Public Finance and Policy, 1998).

Pant, K.P., 'Estimating Health Benefits when Behaviours are Endegenous: the Case of Indoor Air Pollution in Rural Nepal, SANDEE Working Paper No. 34–08, 2008.

Parikh, K. S., Parikh, J., Hadkar, N. and Muraleedharan, T., 'Economic Valuation of Air Quality Degradation in Chembur', Bombay, IGIDR Project Report, 1994.

Parikh, K. S., Parikh, J. and Raghu Ram, T.L., 'Air and Water Quality Management: New Regulations Needed', in K. S. Parik (ed.) *India Development Report* (New Delhi: Oxford University Press, 1999).

Sterner, T., *Policy Instruments and Natural Resource Management, Resources for Future*, (Washington DC: Resources for the Future Press, 1999).

Venkatachalam, L., 'Economic Valuation of Water Used in the Household Sector: A Contingent Valuation Approach in a Developing Country Context' Thesis Submitted for the Degree of Doctor in Philosophy in Economics, University of Madras, Channai, 2000.

UN: *Integrated Environmental and Economic Accounting,* Interim version (Sales No. E93 XVII 12), United Nations, New York,1993.

World Bank Water Demand Research Team, 'How Reliable are Contingent Valuation Studies in Developing Countries? Evidence from a Multi-Country Study', *The World Bank Research Observer*, Vol. 8, No.1, 1993.

World Health Organization, 'Indoor Air Pollution: National Burden of Disease Estimates', WHO Press, World Health Organization, 2007.

Whittington, D., Pattanayak S.K., Yang J.C., and Kumar, B., 'Do Households Want Improved Piped Water Services? Evidence from Nepal', *Water Policy* 4(6), (2002) 531–556.

2

Environmental Valuation: A Review of Methods

A.K. Haque, M.N. Murty and *P. Shyamsundar*

2.1. Environmental resources and economic valuation

Environmental resources provide a number of benefits that allow us to live on and enjoy this earth. As identified by Freeman (2003), these flows can generally be classified into:

(a) Inputs into production process whether it is the use of oil to run all forms of economic activity, or top soil for agriculture, or life support services provided by water, the atmosphere etc.;

(b) waste absorption services in terms of the ability of the earth and the living atmosphere to mitigate pollution; and

(c) amenity services and non-use benefits that allow us to appreciate the world that we live in.

While the services provided by the environment are immensely valuable, as economists, our interest is in valuing incremental changes in the flow of these services. Every day, we make choices that change the flow of environmental resources. Unfortunately, since we live in a world characterized by scarcity, there are always trade-offs to be made between the uses of different resources. These decisions will be flawed if they are not based on an understanding of the relative value of these resources.

In general, economic activity is based on numerous decisions about goods and services that are bought and sold in markets, which assign value to these goods through market equilibrium prices. Prices also signal scarcity, allowing limited resources to be efficiently used. This is true for many regularly traded goods such as tables and chairs as well as natural resources such as iron and gold. However, the vast majority of environmental goods are not traded in markets and do not come with a handy price tag. Many environmental resources, the global climate regime for example, are public goods. People cannot always be excluded from consuming these goods, changes in them cannot be reversed in short order, and the extent and implications of changes are uncertain. Thus, existing markets are unable to capture the true economic value of changes in many public goods such as the global climate. Other renewable resources such as forests or aquifers in many countries have ambiguous property rights, making it difficult for markets to provide the right signals. In this context, it is useful to have a set of tools to enable one to understand and estimate the value of changes in different non-market goods and services.

2.2. Environmental values

Environmental values are often classified into use values and non-use values. Use values refer to current direct and indirect ways in which people make physical use of an environmental good. For example, the value a farmer gets from using publicly available water or the benefit trekkers obtain from a view of the Himalayas are considered use values. The indirect use benefits from environmental goods are associated with the many services that they provide. For example, forests provide carbon storage, hydrological services, biodiversity conservation and so on. These are useful and protective services that provide a variety of indirect benefits.

People also obtain utility from environmental resources even if they do not personally use them. Krutilla (1967) introduced the idea of existence values, or the benefits that people obtain from simply knowing about the existence of the Amazon rain forest, for example. Later, Krutilla and Fisher (1975) suggested that the bequest motive may be one possible explanation for existence values, while McConnell (1983) suggested that altruistic attitudes toward other people's use of a resource could also explain existence values. Voluntary contributions amounting to millions of dollars made by members of environmental groups to protect wild life, forests and bio-diversity in different parts of the world and the willingness of environmental activists to volunteer their time to lobby for environmental legislation provide evidence of existence values.

There is yet another category of environmental value that is referred to as option value (Wiesbrod, 1964). Option values accrue to economic agents when there is uncertainty about supply and/or demand for an environmental good. For example, on the demand side, even if people are unsure whether they ever want to use an aquifer in future, they may still like to retain the option of doing so. On the supply side, people may be unsure of the supply of environmental services. For example, they may want to preserve the option of saving a fish species because they are unsure if a particular river cleaning programme would achieve its goals in the future. The literature further distinguishes between two types of option values.

The first, known as the 'timeless' option value approach[1], treats option value as the amount that people will pay for a contract that guarantees them the opportunity to purchase a good for a specified price at a specified point in the future. This is like a risk premium to compensate for uncertainty about future taste, income, or supply. The second is known as 'time sequenced' or the 'quasi-option value approach.[2] Quasi-option value is regarded as a risk premium people may pay to delay a decision on the development or use of an environmental resource, which if undertaken, might foreclose the possibility of making a better informed decision of resource conservation later. Figure 2.1 provides a simple summary of how different environmental values are often categorized.

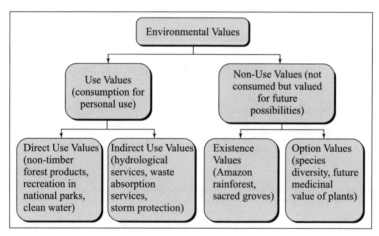

Figure 2.1.   Different categories of environment values

Source: Modified from Gunatilake H. M. (p. 5) 2003. Environmental Valuation: Theory and Applications.

---

[1] Cicchetti and Freeman, 1971; Krutilla et al. 1972; Schmalencee, 1972; Bohm, 1975; Anderson, 1981; Graham, 1981; Bishop, 1982; V.K. Smith, 1983,1984.1987; Mendelsohn and Strang, 1984; Freeman, 1984, and Plummer and Hartman, 1986.
[2] Arrow and Fisher, 1974; Henry, 1974; Krutilla and Fisher, 1975; Conrad, 1980; Freeman, 1984, Miller and Lad, 1984; Fisher and Hanemann, 1985a, 1985b,1986,1987; Grham-Tomasi, 1986.

2.3. Measuring environmental values and policy changes

The environmental values described thus far have to be measured in order to make reasonable decisions about environmental changes taking place in any economy. In order to estimate these values, an inter-disciplinary approach involving social scientists, ecologists, health experts, and engineers, in addition to economists is needed. Any valuation has to be preceded by robust measurements of changes in the bio-physical environment.

A situation can be considered where the Government of Nepal decides to introduce new vehicular standards to reduce air pollution in Kathmandu. It is useful to ask what the benefits of this new reform are relative to the costs to citizens as well as the government. In order to value the benefits, a three stage process as explained in Table 2.1 (Freeman, 1992) is required.[3]

Table 2.1. How to evaluate environmental policy changes

Bio-physical and behavioural relationships	
$Q = Q[S, R(S)]$	(Stage 1)
Q: Environmental quality.	
S: Environmental policy change.	
R: Economic agents' responses to environmental policy changes.	
$E = E(Q, M, A)$	(Stage 2)
E: Effect on human, plant and animal life.	
M: Mitigating activities of users	
A: Averting activities of users.	
$V = V(E)$	(Stage 3)
V: Monetary value of effects of environmental policy changes.	

In the first stage, the bio-physical relationship between environmental policy changes and environmental quality needs to be clearly established. New regulations such as introduction of new Euro vehicular standards or adoption of lead free gasoline or increased parking fees will change how economic agents use cars or the types of cars they buy. This is then expected to lead to reductions in particulate matter in the air. This relationship between changes in a regulation, human response to the regulation and ultimate changes in ambient air quality is the first step in evaluating the impacts of regulatory policy changes.

---

[3] See also Murty and Kumar (2004) for a similar description.

In the second stage, a relationship between the environmental quality changes and human impacts and use has to be identified. In the Kathmandu case, a reduction in air pollution is expected to improve human health – acute respiratory infections could decrease, for instance, and asthma and heart attacks may be reduced. So the next stage involves an assessment of changes in health. At this point, the help of doctors or epidemiologists may be required.

In the first two stages it is mainly the job of environmental scientists, engineers and ecologists to identify and estimate the relationship between policy changes and the environmental quality and the relationship between the environmental quality changes and human impacts. But there is a role for social scientists – for example, the health effects of air or water pollution depend upon the mitigating and averting activities of people to minimize health damages. Thus, in assessing the impact on human health, we need to take these responses into account.

In the final stage, economists will be required to undertake a monetary valuation of environmental policy changes. This general approach forms the basis for developing various methods of valuation described in the environmental economics literature.

2.4. Valuation methods

Economists have identified a variety of tools to value changes in environmental goods and services. These valuation techniques can generally be classified into observed and hypothetical methods. In the case of observed methods, the benefits or damages from a change in the supply of environmental good is measured by observing the behavior of users either in regular or simulated markets for environmental goods or in markets for related private goods. Thus, these methods ascertain value for the environment based on the 'revealed preferences' of economic agents. Most of the chapters in this book present varying examples of 'revealed preference' methods.

There are many situations, however, where markets are not available to establish the number of individuals willing to pay for a good or service. People, who may never see the Bengal Tiger, may value its existence but it is hard to understand how much they value the tiger's existence without actually directly asking them. Thus, economists have devised a number of techniques to value non-market goods that involve the creation of hypothetical markets or which ask economic agents to 'state' their preferences. A specific and detailed example of this technique is presented in Chapter 18.

Table 2.1 presents a summary of the different valuation techniques, which are further discussed below. This is an illustrative and not an exhaustive list of techniques. Also subsumed in some of this discussion are some other direct market approaches such as the replacement cost approach, which establishes the value of an environmental good by the market value of something that may replace it or the opportunity cost approach that establishes value by identifying the value of the next best alternate use of a resource. Direct market approaches for environmental valuation can be only used in cases where a marketable good can replace an environmental good, for example compensating afforestation to replace certain forest species lost due to a development project. However, these methods cannot be used if the forest species lost are unique and therefore not replaceable.

Table 2.2. Valuation techniques

Valuation Methods		
	Revealed Preference	**Stated Preference**
A	*Environment as an input into a production process* Productivity changes Health production function Travel cost method	*Direct techniques* Contingent valuation
B	*Environment as a characteristic of a market-based good* Hedonic property price approach Hedonic wage methods	*Indirect techniques* Contingent ranking Hypothetical travel cost

In the sections below the different valuation techniques used in this book are briefly summarized.

2.4.1. Production function approaches

Air, land and water quality are often inputs into the production of goods and services as other conventional inputs. Damage to the environment reduces the supply of these inputs, and as a result production falls. Examples for this are increased salinity of land due to shrimp farming reducing the productivity of paddy farms and water pollution causing output losses to industry and agriculture. Conversely, programmes to improve environmental quality can benefit environmentally sensitive forms of production by raising the supply of such inputs. Chapter 3 of this book explains how production, cost and profit functions can be used to estimate the value of the environment as an input in production. Thus, this method is not discussed here – but several studies, for example, Umamaheshwari, Rohita and Jha, use this approach in their chapters. A variant of this approach, the health production function is discussed below.

2.4.2. The household health production function model

The household health production model can be used to estimate the value households place on reduced morbidity and mortality due to reduction in air or water pollution. The health production function model was first developed by Grossman (1972) and early papers include Cropper (1981), Gerking and Stanley (1986) and Harrington and Portney (1987). The idea underlying this model is that households use health as an input into productive activity. When health changes occur as a result of environmental factors, the change in the productive activity can be measured and valued.

Consider a general model in which environmental quality Q, such as clean air, and other variables such as mitigating activity, M, which would include doctors visits, avertive activity, A, such as installing of chimneys or air-conditioners, the stock of health capital, K, and stock of social capital, S (for example, education) are inputs into a health production function, H. H is generally represented by a variable such as the number of sick days.

$$H = H(Q, M, A, K, S) \tag{1}$$

Pollution affects individual utility indirectly through the health production function and directly by affecting outdoor recreation and other amenity services. If an individual's utility function is defined as:

$$U(X, H, Q, L, I) \tag{2}$$

where X is a private good consumed by the individual, and L and I are leisure and income. If the private good X is taken as a numeraire, the individual's budget constraint is given as:

$$I = I^* + w(T - L - H) = X + P_m M + P_a A \tag{3}$$

Given the environmental quality level Q, health capital, K, and human resource capital, S, income I, and prices w (wages), P_m (price of mitigating actions) and P_a (price of avertive actions), the individual maximizes (4) with respect to X, M, A, and L. I^* refers to exogenous income.

$$MaxG = U(X, H, Q, L, I) + \lambda[I^* + w(T - L - H) - X - P_m M - P_a] \quad (4)$$

After solving this problem one can obtain the marginal willingness to pay for environmental quality changes as (Freeman, 2003)

$$\frac{dI}{dQ} = w\frac{dH}{dQ} + P_M \frac{\partial M}{\partial Q} + P_A \frac{\partial A}{\partial Q} - \frac{\partial u/\partial Q}{\lambda}\frac{dH}{dQ} \quad (5)$$

where

$H = H(Q, M, A, K, S)$, the health production function

$M = M(w, P_M, P_A, Q, I, K, S)$, the mitigation action function   (6)

$A = A(w, P_M, P_A, Q, I, K, S)$, the avertive action function

constitute a system of simultaneous equations corresponding to optimum values. Several chapters (for example, Gupta, Hussain and Haque, Bogahawatte and Herath) in this book estimate willingness to pay using different variants of this model.

2.4.3. Travel cost methods

The travel cost method is used primarily to value the recreational benefits of various parks and natural areas. The assumption here is that there is weak complimentarity between the demand for environmental good, say visits to a wetland to watch birds or a tiger reserve, and the private good, travel.

In this method, the individual traveler's utility depends on the total time spent at the site, the quality of the site, and the quantity of a composite private good (other than travel). With the duration of a visit fixed for simplicity, the time spent on the site is represented by the number of visits.

The individual maximizes the following utility function:

$$U(X, r, Q) \quad (7)$$

Subject to monetary and time budgets

$$M + p_w t_w = p_x X + cr \quad (8)$$

$$t^* = t_w + t\,r \quad (9)$$

Substituting the time constraint (9) into the monetary budget constraint (8) yields:

$$M + p_w t^* = p_x X + p_r r \quad (10)$$

where p_r is the full of price of a visit given by:

$$p_r = c + p_w t$$
$$= f + p_d d + p_w t \qquad (11)$$

where

X: the quantity of private good other than travel consumed by a person

p_x: price of the private good

r: number of visits to the recreation site,

Q: environmental quality at the site,

M: exogenous income,

p_w: wage rate,

c: monetary cost of a trip,

t^*: total discretionary time,

t_w: hours worked,

t: round-trip travel time, and

f: admission fees

d: distance in kms covered in the trip, and

p_d: cost of travel per km.

Equation(11) shows that the full price of a visit consists of three components – the admission fee, the monetary cost of travel to the site, and the time cost of travel to the site. The cost of time spent at the site is also sometimes added. On the assumption that individuals are free to choose the number of hours worked at a given wage rate, the time costs are valued at the wage rate.

Maximization of equation (7) subject to the budget constraint in equation (10) yields the individual's demand function for visits:

$$r = r(p_r, p_x, M, Q) \qquad (12)$$

The travel cost method can be used to estimate the demand for the recreational services offered by a natural site. It can also be used to estimate the consumer surplus or recreational value from a protected area and to set park entry fees. Two chapters in this book, Khan, and Ghosh and Guha, follow this approach.[4]

2.4.4. Hedonic price methods

The price of a commodity is a function of the characteristics it possesses. Land, for example, has different characteristics in terms of location, size,

---

[4] Recently, more general travel cost models, called hedonic travel cost models, estimate demand for specific environmental attributes of resource sites by making use of data for a number of sites. This book does not carry these examples.

and local environmental quality. Similarly, different jobs have different characteristics in terms of risk of on-job accidents, working conditions, prestige, training and enhancement of skills, and the local environmental quality at the work place. By observing changes in the prices of a product with respect to changes in these characteristics, the premium or the price the consumer pays for particular characteristics can be found. This is the logic underlying hedonic methods, which build on the fact that environmental characteristics like air or water quality affect the price of a good such as land. Ridker (1967) and Ridker and Henning (1967) provided the first empirical evidence that air pollution affects property values. Thaler and Rosen (1976) were the first to suggest that labour market could be viewed as hedonic market.

2.4.5. Hedonic property value model

The hedonic property values method is now widely used for finding the value people place on urban environmental quality[5]. Let the price of ith residential property (P_i) be a function of structural (S_i) features including the number of rooms, size of the property etc., neighbourhood (N_i) characteristics such as parks and roads and environmental characteristics (Q_i) such as clean air, a view of the ocean and so on.

$$P_i = P(S_i, N_i, Q) \qquad (13)$$

Consider the utility function of the individual who occupies house i:

$$U(X, S_i, N_i, Q) \qquad (14)$$

where X represents a composite private good that is taken as a numeraire. Assume that preferences are weakly separable in housing and its characteristics. The individual maximizes (14) subject to the budget constraint:

$$M = X + P_i \qquad (15)$$

---

[5] Ridker (1967) and Ridker and Henning (1967) provided early empirical evidence that air pollution affects property values. The early studies include Freeman, (1974a;1974b) Anderson and Crocker (1971;1972), Lind (1973), Pines and Weiss(1976), Polinsky and Shavell (1976), Nelson (1978), Portney (1981), Gerking et al. (1986), Horowitz (1986), Dennis (1987), Murdoch and Thayer (1988), and Kanemoto (1988). The most recent studies are McClelland et al. (1990), Michaels and Smith (1990), Parsons (1992), Lansford and Jones (1995), Kiel (1995), Kiel and McClain (1995), Dass and Taff (1996), and Mahan, Polasky, and Adams (2000).

The first order condition for the choice of environmental amenity q_j is given by:

$$\frac{\partial u / \partial q_j}{\partial u / \partial x} = \frac{\partial P_i}{\partial q_j} \tag{16}$$

The partial derivative of (14) with respect to one of the environmental quality characteristics q_j, such as tree cover or clean air quality gives the implicit marginal price of that characteristic. The implicit marginal price is the additional amount paid by any household to choose a house with the additional amount of that characteristic, other things being equal. The idea is that individuals choose the level of a characteristic at which their marginal willing to pay for that characteristic is equal to its implicit marginal price.

The analysis described above provides a measure of price or the marginal willingness to pay for a house at a particular location. But it does not provide a marginal willingness to pay function for the housing characteristic. In the second stage, marginal willingness to pay for environmental quality is expressed as a function of q_j given S_i, N_i, and a vector of other environmental characteristics Q_i^* and socio-economic characteristics (G_i).

$$b_{ij} = b_{ij}(q_j, Q_i^*, S_i, N_i, G_i) \tag{17}$$

Equation (17) gives the individual's marginal willingness to pay for the improvement in the environmental quality q_j. Assuming that the individual's utility function is weakly separable with respect to housing characteristics, welfare changes for large changes in q_j can be estimated. If there is an improvement in the environmental characteristic from q_j^0 to q_j^1, the value individuals place on such an improvement (B_{ij}) can be estimated by integrating (17) with respect to q_j.

$$B_{ij} = \int_{q_j^0}^{q_j^1} b_{ij}(q_j, Q_i^*, S_i, N_i, G_i) \partial q_j \tag{18}$$

The estimation of marginal willingness to pay for a housing characteristic using the above described model requires a two-stage estimation process (Rosen, 1974). In the first stage, the hedonic property price equation (13) is estimated and the implicit marginal prices for a given characteristic are computed for all the observations in the sample (given the mean values of the rest of the characteristics). In the second stage, taking the calculated implicit marginal price as an endogenous variable, the marginal willingness to pay function (17) is estimated. This approach is used in Chapter 16 by Murty et al. to value air quality in Delhi and Kolkata. There are, however, problems of identification of the marginal willingness to pay function and endogeniety of characteristics and the implicit price that need to be addressed in this class of models (Rosen, 1982, Mendelsohn, 1987).

2.4.6. Hedonic wage model

The main idea behind the hedonic wage model is that jobs can be classified with respect to various risk characteristics they possess and that workers understand these risks. The differences in wages, therefore, reflect workers' marginal valuation of differences in the risks on job. Hedonic wage models are used to value willingness to pay for risk and to value environmental amenities that vary across regions. Chapter 17 by Shanmugam and Madheswaran in this book examines labor market data from Chennai (India) to understand the relationship between jobs, wages and risks.

Suppose an individual chooses a job to maximize expected utility from the consumption of a composite commodity X and from a vector of job characteristics, J_j. In addition to J_j each job is characterized by the risk of accidental death μ_j. Individuals face a hedonic wage function, a locus of points at which firms' marginal wage offers equal workers' marginal acceptance wages, given by:

$$w = w(\mu_j, J_j) \tag{19}$$

where w is the wage rate per day or a week. The individual chooses a specific job to maximize expected utility, subject to the wage constraint:

$$MaxE[u] = \pi U(X, J_j) + \lambda[w(\mu_j, J_j) - X] \tag{20}$$

where π is the probability of surviving the period and $\pi = 1 - \mu$ and $U(X, J)$ is the individuals' utility function.

The utility maximizing conditions for the choice of X and the job risk μ_j are:

$$\pi \partial U / \partial X = \lambda \tag{21a}$$

$$U(.)/\lambda = \partial w./\partial \mu \tag{21b}$$

$$\frac{\pi \partial U / \partial J_j}{\lambda} = -\partial w / \partial J_j \tag{21c}$$

for all the job characteristics J_j. Equation 21b shows that the marginal willingness to pay for an increase in the probability of surviving the job risk must equal its marginal implicit price. Equation 21c requires that the marginal willingness to pay for each job characteristic equals its marginal implicit price. The estimation of the marginal willingness to pay function for each job characteristic follows the same two-step procedure previously identified in the case of hedonic property value model. There are numerous empirical studies that use the hedonic wage models,[6] but, here again there are concerns related to the identification of the marginal bid function.

2.4.7. Contingent valuation

It has been previously noted that observed hypothetical methods are classified as direct and indirect. The direct hypothetical methods try to elicit the value people place on the change in supply of environmental goods by asking a direct question to the beneficiary of the change. These methods, which include contingent valuation, posit links between amenity levels and individual behaviour (Smith and Krutilla, 1982). In indirect hypothetical methods, people are asked to respond to hypothetical markets, but their responses are indirectly related to valuing the environmental good. Examples of these methods are contingent ranking and hypothetical travel cost methods.[7]

The Contingent Valuation Method (CVM) is a survey-based tool. The survey instrument seeks to create a hypothetical market and the response to this market allows researchers to estimate respondents' values associated with an environmental good. The survey instrument, which is crucial in CVM, generally has the following three components – (a) a description of the choice setting in which the respondent imagines himself or herself; (b) the question from which values will be inferred; and (c) questions about the respondent. Components (a) and (c) are common for all survey instruments. Component (b) identifies whether the survey is trying to solicit either Willingness to Pay (WTP) for an environmental improvement (compensating surplus) or to avoid loss (equivalent surplus) or Willingness

---

[6] Thaler and Rosen (1976), Viscusi (1978, 1979, 1981), Brown (1980), Olson (1981), Arnold and Nichols (1983), Viscusi and O'Connor (1984), Gerking et al. (1988), and Moore and Viscusi (1988). Some of the most recent studies are by Gegax et al. (1991), Knieser et al. (1991), and Liu et al. (1998). There are two recent studies using data from India, one by Shanmugam (1997) and another by Simon et al. (1999).

[7] In the contingent ranking method, individuals are asked to rank the alternatives according to their attributes. In the hypothetical travel cost method, respondents are asked about how their choices are affected if the level of public supplied at the site is increased.

to Accept Compensation (WAC) to accept loss (compensating surplus) or to forgo a gain (equivalent surplus). The choice between WTP and WAC question formats depends on the property right to the environmental good in question. However, for a number of practical reasons, most CVM studies obtain estimates of WTP.

There are a number of biases that need to be overcome in undertaking good CVM studies. The revealed WTP may be different from the true WTP due to various reasons such as strategic bias, starting point bias, anchoring, and so on. There is a large amount of work done on reducing these biases and CV studies need to carefully follow these strategies (Mitchell and Carson, 1989). Chapter 18 undertakes a contingent valuation study related to water supply and sanitation services in Sri Lanka and explains the methods for avoiding some of these biases.

2.5. Conclusion

This chapter sought to provide a brief introduction to the different methods of environmental valuation used in detail in subsequent chapters. The next chapter provides a detailed discussion on the theory of production and its use in environmental valuation. Each case study in the book also provides a description of the method of valuation, data requirements and estimation methods used.

As should be clear from discussions in this and subsequent chapters, the choice of the method of valuation in case studies depends upon the type of environmental service valued and the context in which it is valued. Take, for example, the valuation of urban air quality attempted in some chapters. Two methods of valuation – the household health production function in the context of measuring health benefits alone, and hedonic prices, in the context of measuring total benefits including health, amenity services etc., are used. For measuring recreational services of an environmental resource, the choice is between the travel cost, hedonic prices and CV methods and two chapters dealing with this problem have used the travel cost method.

In any environmental valuation study, one has to first choose between revealed and stated preference methods. Revealed preference methods use data observed in real markets and can provide more reliable estimates of environmental values. However, they are context specific and cannot be used to estimate non-use values. In contrast, CV methods can be used to estimate both use and non-use values.

References

Cicchetti, C.J., and Freeman, A.M. III, 'Option Demand and Consumer's Surplus: Further Comment', *Quarterly Journal of Economics,* 85, (1971), 528–539.

Doss, C.R., and Taff, S.J., 'The Influence of Wetland Type and Wetland Proximity on Residential Property Values', *Journal of Agricultural and Resource Economics,* 21, (1996), 120–129.

Freeman, A.M. III, Air Pollution and Property Values: A Further Comment, *Review of Economics and Statistics,* 56, (1974a), 454–456.

Freeman, A.M. III, 'On Estimating Air Pollution Control Benefits from Land Value Studies', *Journal of Environmental Economics and Management,* 1, (1974b), 74–83.

Freeman, A.M. III, *The Benefits of Environmental Improvement: The Theory and Practice,* (Baltimore, Md: Johns Hopkins University Press for Resources for Future, 1979).

Freeman, A.M. III, 'The Quasi-Option Value of Irreversible Development', *Journal of Environmental Economics,* 2, (1984a), 292–295.

Freeman, A.M. III, 'The Size and Sign of Option Value', *Land Economics,* 60, (1984b), 1–13.

Freeman, A.M. III, *The Measurement of Environmental and Resource Values: Theory and Methods,* (Washington D.C.: Resources for the Future, 1993).

Gerking, S. and Stanley L.R., 'An Economic Analysis of Air Pollution and Health: The Case of St. Louis', *Review of Economics and Statistics,* 68, (1986), 115–121.

Graham-Tomasi, T., and Wen F., 'Option Value and the Bias for Ignoring Uncertainty', (Mimeo., School of Natural Resources: University of Michigan, 1987).

Hanemann, W.M., 'Welfare Valuation in Contingent Valuation Experiments with Discrete Responses', *American Journal of Agricultural Economics,* 66, (1984), 332–341.

Hanemann, W.M., 'Welfare Evaluation in Contingent Valuation Experiments with Discrete Response Data: Reply', *American Journal of Agricultural Economics,* 71, (1989), 1051–1061.

Hanemann, W.M., 'Willingness to Pay and Willingness to Accept: How Much They Can Differ?', *American Economic Review,* 81, (1991), 635–647.

Hanemann, W.M., 'Valuing the Environment through Contingent Valuation', *Journal of Economic Perspectives,* 8, (1994), 19–43.

Knieser, T. and Leeth, J.D., 'Compensating Wage Differentials for Fatal Injury Risk in Australia, Japan and the United States', *Journal of Risk and Uncertaint,* 4, (1991), 75–90.

Krutilla, J.V., 'Conservation Reconsidered', *American Economic Review,* 57, (1967), 777–786.

Krutilla, J.V., Cicchetti, C.J., Freeman, A.M. III, and Russell, C.S., 'Observations on the Economics of Irreplaceable Assets,' in Kneese, A.V., and Bower, B.T.

(eds.), *Environmental Quality Analysis: Theory and Method in the Social Sciences* (Baltimore: The Johns Hopkins University Press for Resources for the Future, 1972).

Krutilla, J.V. and Fisher A.C., *The Economics of Natural Environments, Resources for the Future*, (Baltimore: The Johns Hopkins Press, 1975).

Kumar, S., 'Economic Evaluation of Development Projects: A Case Analysis of Environmental and Health Implications of Thermal Power Projects in India', a Ph.D. thesis submitted to Jawaharlal Nehru University, New Delhi, 1999.

Kanemoto, Y. 'Hedonic Prices and the Benefits of Public Projects', *Econometrica*, 56, (1988), 981–989.

Mendelsohn, R., 'Identifying Structural Equations with Single Market Data', *Review of Economics and Statistics*, 67, (1985), 525–529.

Mendelsohn, R. and J. Strang, W., 'Cost-Benefit Analysis Under Uncertainty: Comment', *American Economic Review*, 74, (1984), 1096–1099.

Mendelsohn, R., 'A Review of Identification of Hedonic Supply and Demand Functions', *Growth and Change*, 18, (1987), 82–92.

Mitchell, R.C. and Carson, R.T., 'Using Surveys to value Public Goods: The Contingent Valuation Method', (Washington D.C.: Resources for the Future, 1989).

Murty, M.N. and Kumar, S., *Environmental and Economic Accounting for Industry*, (Delhi: Oxford University Press, 2004).

Polinsky, A.M., and Shavell, S., 'Amenities and Property Values in a Model of an Urban Area', *Journal of Public Economics*, 5, (1976), 119–129.

Portney, P.R. (1994), 'The Contingent Valuation Debate: Why Economists Should Care', *Journal of Economic Perspectives*, 8, (1976), 3–17.

Portney, P.R., 'Housing Prices, Health Effects and Valuing Reduction in Risk of Death', *Journal of Environmental Economics and Management*, 8, (1981), 72–78.

Portney, P.R. (ed.), *Public Policies for Environmental Protection*, (Resource for the Future: Washington D.C.).

Rosen, S., 'Hedonic Prices and Implicit Markets: Product Differentiation in Perfect Competition', *Journal of Political Economy*, 82, (1974), 34–55.

Ridkar, R.G. and Henning, J.A., 'Determinants of Residential Property Values with Special Reference to Air Pollution', *Review of Economics and Statistics*, 49, (1967), 246–257.

Ridkar, R.G. and Henning, J.A., 'Determinants of Residential Property Values with Special Reference to Air Pollution', *Review of Economics and Statistics*, 49, (1967), 246–257.

Ridker, R.G., *Economic Costs of Air Pollution: Studies in Measurement*, (New York: Praeger, 1967).

Schmalenesee, R., 'Option Demand and Consumer Surplus: Valuing Price Changes Under Uncertainty', *American Economic Review*, 62, (1972), 813–824.

Shanmugam, K.R., 'Compensating Wage Differentials for Work Related Fatal and Injury Accidents', *The Indian Journal of Labour Economics*, 40, (1978).

Thaler, R. and Rosen, S., 'The Value of Life Savings', Terleckyi, N. (ed.) *Household Production and Consumption*, (New York: Columbia University Press, 1976).

Viscusi, W.K., 'Labour Market Valuations of Life and Limb: Empirical Evidence and Policy Implications', *Public Policy*, 26, (1978), 359–386.

Viscusi, W.K., *Employment Hazards: An Investigation of Market Performance*, (Cambridge, Mass: Harvard University Press, 1979).

Viscusi, W.K., 'Occupational Safety and Health Regulation: Its Impact and Policy Alternatives' Crecine, J. (ed.), *Research in Public Policy Analysis and Management*, 2, (1981), Greenwich, Conn.: JAI Press.

Viscusi, W.K. and O'Connor, 'Adaptive Responses to Chemical Labeling: Are Workers Bayesian Decision Makers?', *American Economic Review*, 74, (1984), 942–956.

Viscusi, W.K. and Moore, M., 'Rates of Time Preference and Valuation of the Duration of Life', *Journal of Public Economics*, 38, (1989), 297–317.

Weisbrod, B.A., 'Collective Consumption Services of Individual Consumption Goods', *Quarterly Journal of Economics*, 78, (1964), 471–477.

3

Valuing the Environment as a Production Input

Jeffrey R. Vincent

3.1. Introduction

Most research on the value of changes in environmental quality focuses on values from the standpoint of individual consumers. Three valuation methods dominate this research – contingent valuation, hedonic pricing, and travel cost models[1]. These are sometimes the only methods considered in references on valuation methods. One example of this is the excellent primer by Champ et al. (2003). Yet, environmental quality can also affect production. For example, infiltration of saline water from shrimp farms can damage harvests on neighbouring rice farms, the loss of spawning grounds when mangroves are cut down can reduce fish catch, and damage from acid rain and other forms of air pollution can reduce timber harvests. This chapter focuses on the valuation of these sorts of effects.

In these cases, environmental quality is acting as a non-market, or unpriced, production input. Damage to the environment reduces the supply of this input, and as a result production falls. Conversely, programmes to improve environmental quality can benefit environmentally sensitive forms of production by raising the supply of such inputs. These production-related benefits can be among the most important benefits generated by environmental improvements. This is especially likely to be the case in developing regions of the world such as South Asia, where agriculture accounts for a larger share of GDP than in higher-income regions and renewable resources such as forests and fisheries underpin local economies.

---

[1] There are other chapters in this book providing detailed case studies from South Asia using these methods of environmental valuation. Chapter 1 provides a brief description of these methods.

In principle, the valuation of changes in environmental quality that affect production is straightforward – one needs to estimate the change in profit caused by the environmental change. There are several ways to estimate the change in profit, however, and one might not have the data necessary to use all of them. Understanding the relationships among the different approaches, and the conditions under which they are valid, is thus important. Moreover, sometimes one might only be able to estimate a component of the change in profit, such as the change in revenue or the change in cost. A question that arises is whether partial measures such as these can be used to value environmental changes.

This chapter examines these and related aspects of the valuation of the environment as a production input. It reviews the relationships among three key functions in production economics – production functions, cost functions, and profit functions – and explains how they can be used to value changes in environmental quality. Sections 3.2–3.4 are purely conceptual.[2] They illustrate the relationships among the three functions by referring to a specific type of production function, the Cobb-Douglas function. This is the most common production function used in applied economic analysis. Section 3.2 reviews how a production function can be used to value changes in environmental quality, while sections 3.3 and 3.4 review how cost and profit functions can be derived from a production function and used to perform the same valuation. Use of a production function is typically called the primal approach, while use of cost and profit functions is typically called the dual approach.

Although sections 3.2–3.4 refer to the specific case of Cobb-Douglas technology, the intention is to provide intuition about fundamental points that are generally relevant, not points that are unique to that technology. Issues that arise if certain assumptions made in those sections do not hold are discussed in section 3.6, and implications for empirical work are discussed in section 3.5. The material in sections 3.2–3.6 should prepare one to read more advanced material on production economics, such as Chambers (1988), Just and Pope (2001), and Mundlak (2001), and more advanced material on the valuation of the environment as a production input, such as Point (1995), Huang and Smith (1998), Freeman (2003), and McConnell and Bockstael (2005).

---

[2] I thank Rick Freeman for carefully reviewing the first part of the chapter. Any remaining error is mine.

The seventh and final section of the chapter presents an applied example. It illustrates how production and profit functions can be used to value environmental inputs to agriculture.[3] The specific case considered is rice production in India. Research by atmospheric scientists indicates that air pollution has reduced rainfall in South Asia in recent decades (Ramanathan et al., 2005). In section 3.7, econometric methods are applied to farm-level data for 1994–1999 to estimate production and profit functions for rice. Those functions are then used to estimate the economic benefits – increased farm profits – that would result from hypothetical pollution reductions that reversed the decline in rainfall. Applications presented in other Chapters of this book are also refered at various points.

3.2. Production function

The focus in this section and sections 3.3–3.5 is on a private firm that produces a single output, which it sells in a competitive market. To produce this output, the firm uses a single, variable input, which it buys in a competitive market. So, both the output produced by the firm and the input that it uses are priced, and the prices are not affected by the firm's supply of the output or its demand for the input. A simple static setting is considered and dynamic issues related to risk or fixed inputs (investment, depreciation) are ignored. The implication of these various assumptions is that the change in the profit of the firm equals the welfare impact on the owner of the firm, as it gives the change in the owner's income.

In addition to the priced input that is under the control of the owner, output is affected by environmental quality, which is a public good that is beyond the control of the owner. Implicitly, therefore, environmental quality represents a second production input. This question will be considered from three vantage points: the production function (this section), the cost function (section 3.3), and the profit function (section 3.4). To make a connection to the empirical analysis in section 3.7, one can think of the firm as a farm, the output as rice, the priced input as farm labour, and environmental quality as climate, measured by rainfall.

---

[3] Chapters by Umamaheswari et al. and Jha and Regmi in this book provide detailed case studies of evaluating production externalities in agriculture using production functions. The chapter by Rohita provides a case study of evaluating a water-pollution externality of shrimp farming, again using the production function approach.

3.2.1. Variables and assumptions

A production function is a technical relationship that relates physical quantities of outputs to physical quantities of inputs. For a firm that produces a single output q, uses a single variable input x, and is affected by environmental quality E, the Cobb-Douglas production function is

$$q = ax^{\beta} E^{\gamma}$$

where

q = output

x = variable input

E = environmental quality

α, β, γ = parameters.

The variables q, x, and E are all assumed to be positive (> 0). As can be seen, the Cobb-Douglas production function indicates that the two inputs interact in a multiplicative way and are both essential to production – if either $x = 0$ or $E = 0$, then $q = 0$ too. It is assumed that production is 'well-behaved' in the senses that $\alpha > 0$, which is necessary if q, x, and E are all positive, and $0 < \beta < 1$ and $0 < \gamma < 1$, which imply that production is increasing in both inputs but has diminishing returns.

The top panel of Figure 3.1 depicts this production function at two levels of environmental quality, E_0 (lower quality) and E_1 (higher quality). The vertical axis shows level of output (q), while the horizontal axis shows the level of the variable input (x). The production function slopes upward because it is increasing in the variable input ($0 < \beta$), but its slope becomes smaller as the variable input increases, due to diminishing returns ($\beta < 1$). The fact that the slope is positive but diminishing can be verified by taking the first and second derivatives of the production function with respect to the variable input:

First derivative:　$\dfrac{\partial q}{\partial x} = \alpha\beta x^{\beta-1} E^{\gamma} > 0$

Second derivative:　$\dfrac{\partial^2 q}{\partial x^2} = \alpha\beta(\beta - 1)x^{\beta-2} E^{\gamma} < 0$

All the terms in the first derivative are positive, so the derivative is positive too. This derivative gives the *marginal product* of x – the incremental output that is produced if one more unit of the variable input is used. All the terms in the second derivative are positive except one, $\beta - 1$, which is negative because $0 < \beta < 1$, and so the derivative is negative.

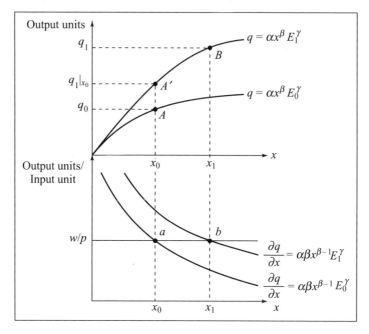

Figure 3.1.   Modeling an environmental improvement: production function

3.2.2. Deriving the input demand function

The production function with the higher level of environmental quality (E_1) is above the one for the lower level (E_0) because production is increasing in environmental quality $(0 < \gamma)$ – for a given level of the variable input, output is higher if environmental quality is higher. How does this change affect the firm's profit? To answer this question, another function needs to be brought into the picture – the *input demand function* for the variable input. The input demand function gives the profit-maximizing level of x: the choice of x that maximizes the firm's profit for a given level of E. To derive this function, one first needs to define the firm's profit, which equals the difference between the revenue from selling the output and the expenditure on the variable input. If one defines

p = price of output
w = price of variable input,

then profit, π, is given by

$$\pi = pq - wx.$$

If the production function is substituted for q, then this expression becomes

$$\pi = p\left(\alpha x^\beta E^\gamma\right) - wx.$$

Profit-maximizing use of x occurs where the first derivative of this expression equals zero. The first derivative is:

$$\frac{\partial \pi}{\partial x} = p\left(\alpha \beta x^{\beta-1} E^\gamma\right) - w.$$

If the derivative is equated to zero, then one obtains:

$$w = p\alpha\beta x^{\beta-1} E^\gamma.$$

The right-hand side of this new expression is the *marginal value product* of the variable input – the price of output, p, multiplied by the marginal product of the input $\left(\partial q / \partial x\right)$, $\alpha\beta x^{\beta-1} E^\gamma$. It gives the firm's marginal willingness to pay for the input and can be interpreted as the *inverse input demand function*. The expression thus says that the firm should use x up to the point where its marginal value product (demand) equals its price, w (supply). Using x beyond this point would generate additional revenue, but the incremental revenue would be less than the cost of the additional amount of x.

A slight rearrangement of this expression is convenient for graphical purposes:

$$\frac{w}{p} = \alpha\beta x^{\beta-1} E^\gamma.$$

This is the profit-maximizing condition expressed in physical terms instead of monetary terms. The right-hand side, which is the marginal product of the variable input, is the inverse input demand function expressed in physical terms. The left-hand side is also in physical terms because it is a price ratio, and the monetary units cancel out. For example, if the input price w is in Rs. per day and the output price p is in INR per kilogram, then the units of the price ratio w/p are kilograms per day. So, profit maximization occurs where the marginal product of the variable input equals the ratio of input price to output price.

If the profit-maximizing condition is solved for x instead of for the price ratio, then the input demand function in standard (not inverse) form can be obtained:

$$x^* = \left(\frac{p\alpha\beta E^\gamma}{w} \right)^{\frac{1}{1-\beta}}.$$

The level of the variable input is denoted by x^* to indicate that it is the profit-maximizing value. Note that the input demand function includes only prices (p, w), environmental quality (E), and parameters from the production function (α, β, γ). It does not include the physical quantity of output (q). Given that $0 < \beta < 1$, the exponent is positive, and so the function is increasing in output price and environmental quality but decreasing in input price. Given that the output and input prices appear as a ratio, if both prices change by the same factor – for example, if p becomes λp and w becomes λw – then the optimal level of the input does not change. There is no 'money illusion.' In other words, the input demand function is homogeneous of degree 0 in prices. The inverse input demand function will be used in the rest of this section, but the input demand function in standard form will be used again when the profit function is analyzed in section 3.4.

3.2.3. Change in profit, without and with input adjustment

The lower curve in the bottom panel of Figure 3.1 shows inverse demand for the variable input in physical terms (i.e., marginal product) at the lower level of environmental quality:

$$\frac{\partial q}{\partial x} = \alpha\beta x^{\beta-1} E_0{}^\gamma.$$

Profit-maximization occurs at x_0, where marginal product equals the price ratio (point a in the bottom panel) and output is at q_0 (point A in the top panel). This is the profit-maximizing combination of x and q, given that environmental quality is at E_0:

$$\pi_0^* = pq_0 - wx_0.$$

If environmental quality improves from E_0 to E_1, then output at x_0 rises to $q_1|_{x_0}$ (point A′ in the top panel): output is now determined by the higher production function. (Read $q_1|_{x_0}$ as 'output when E is at E_1 but x is at x_0.') Profit rises too, to

$$\pi_1\big|_{x_0} = pq_1\big|_{x_0} - wx_0 \,,$$

with the change in profit, $\pi_1\big|_{x_0} - \pi_0^*$, thus being given by just the increase in revenue,

$$p\big(q_1\big|_{x_0} - q_0\big).$$

It is important to recognize that this expression does not equal the full change in profit that results from the environmental improvement. The expression fails to account for the fact that the environmental improvement causes not only the production function to shift but also the inverse input demand function. The upper curve in the bottom panel of Figure 3.1 shows that the inverse input demand function shifts upward when E_0 is replaced by E_1: the environmental improvement causes the marginal product of the variable input to rise. Profit-maximization now occurs at x_1 (point b in the bottom panel), which is greater than x_0, and so output rises to q_1 (point B in the top panel). Hence, after allowing for the adjustment in the variable input, maximum profit is given by

$$\pi_1^* = pq_1 - wx_1 \,.$$

This, not $\pi_1\big|_{x_0}$, is the correct expression for maximum profit at E_1. The change in profit,

$$\pi_1^* - \pi_0^* = p(q_1 - q_0) - w(x_1 - x_0),$$

is now not just a change in revenue: it also includes the change in expenditure on the variable input. Although expenditure on the input rises by $w(x_1 - x_0)$, revenue rises by an even greater amount, $p\big(q_1 - q_1\big|_{x_0}\big)$, because the marginal product of the variable input is greater than the price ratio up to point b. Profit thus rises too: $\pi_1^* > \pi_1\big|_{x_0}$. If one calculates the increase in profit as just the increase in revenue at the initial level of the variable input (i.e., as $p\big(q_1\big|_{x_0} - q_0\big)$), then one understates the benefit of improved environmental quality.

3.2.4. Magnitude of the change in profit

How big is the increase in profit, $\pi_1^* - \pi_0^*$? This can be depicted in two ways. Both are shown in Figure 3.2. Compared to Figure 3.1, the upper panel of

Figure 3.2 includes two additional line segments, which are tangent to the production functions at points x_0 and x_1.[4]

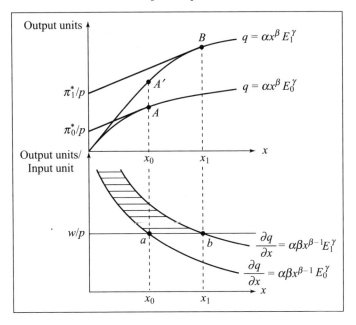

Figure 3.2.   Valuing an environmental improvement: production function

The intercept of each tangent shows the profit associated with the corresponding production point, expressed in physical units instead of money. From above, maximum profit at point A (i.e., for E_0) is given by

$$\pi_0^* = pq_0 - wx_0,$$

which solved for q_0 yields

$$q_0 = \frac{\pi_0^*}{p} + \frac{w}{p}x_0.$$

The equation for the tangent at point A is thus

$$q = \frac{\pi_0^*}{p} + \frac{w}{p}x.$$

---

[4] I am grateful to Subhrendu Pattanayak for suggesting the addition of these tangents.

Its slope, w/p, equals the slope of the production function at point A. The slope of the production function is by definition the marginal product of the variable input, and so the tangency simply reflects the profit-maximizing condition,

$$\frac{w}{p} = \frac{\partial q}{\partial x}.$$

The equation for the tangent to the higher production function (i.e., the one at E_1) at point B using the same logic can be derived by:

$$q = \frac{\pi_1^*}{p} + \frac{w}{p}x.$$

The difference between the intercepts of the tangents,

$$\frac{\pi_1^*}{p} - \frac{\pi_0^*}{p},$$

gives the increase in profits in physical terms. The figure does not show the line passing through point A′, which would cross the production function with E_1 instead of being tangent to it (because the profit-maximizing condition does not hold at A′) and have an intercept between those of the two tangents (because profit at point A′ is higher than at point A but lower than at point B).

In the bottom panel, the increase in profit is shown by the cross-hatched area between the two inverse input demand functions. The cross-hatched area equals the change in *consumer surplus for the variable input*, where the 'consumer' is the firm. This is easily demonstrated. Consumer surplus is the area under an inverse input demand function and above the price line. The expression for this in the case of E_1 is

$$\int_0^{x_1} \left(\alpha\beta x^{\beta-1} E_1^{\gamma} \right) dx - \frac{w}{p}x_1,$$

which simplifies to

$$q_1 - \frac{w}{p}x_1,$$

which in turn is the same as profit in physical terms, $\dfrac{\pi_1^*}{p}$. Parallel analysis for the inverse input demand function that includes E_0 yields consumer surplus equal to $\dfrac{\pi_0^*}{p}$. The change in consumer surplus is thus exactly the same as the difference between the intercepts in the top panel, $\dfrac{\pi_1^*}{p} - \dfrac{\pi_0^*}{p}$.

3.3. Cost function

3.3.1. Definition and characteristics

A cost function is an economic relationship that relates the minimum cost of production to the quantity of output, the prices of variable inputs, and the quantities of fixed inputs, including environmental inputs. In the case considered above, the cost of production is just the firm's expenditure on the single variable input x:

$$C = wx.$$

The objective is to determine the quantity of x that minimizes C for a given level of output:

$$\min_{x} wx \ \text{ subject to } q = \alpha x^{\beta} E^{\gamma}.$$

If q is given and E is not under the control of the firm, then there is only a single quantity of x that satisfies the 'subject to' production constraint, and this quantity must necessarily equal the cost-minimizing value. This quantity can be determined by solving the constraint for x:

$$x = \left(\frac{q}{\alpha E^{\gamma}}\right)^{\frac{1}{\beta}}.$$

This is the *conditional input demand function*. It is 'conditional' because it depends on the quantity of output, q, unlike the input demand function derived in section 3.2.2, which depends only on exogenous variables (prices and environmental quality). If the cost-minimizing quantity of x is denoted by x^*, then the cost function, $C^* = wx^*$, is given by

$$C^* = w\left(\frac{q}{\alpha E^{\gamma}}\right)^{\frac{1}{\beta}}.$$

Note that the cost function includes only the quantity of output (q), the price of the variable input (w), and environmental quality (E), along with the parameters from the production function. Written in implicit form, without any of the functional detail, the cost function is $C^*(q, w, E)$.

Three important characteristics of the cost function are:

(a) It is increasing in output: $\dfrac{\partial C^*}{\partial q} = \dfrac{w}{\beta}\left(\dfrac{1}{\alpha E^\gamma}\right)^{\frac{1}{\beta}} q^{\frac{1-\beta}{\beta}}$, which is positive.

An increase in output raises production cost.

(b) It is increasing in the price of the variable input: $\dfrac{\partial C^*}{\partial w} = \left(\dfrac{q}{\alpha E^\gamma}\right)^{\frac{1}{\beta}}$,

which is positive. An increase in the price of the variable input raises production cost.

(c) It is decreasing in environmental quality: $\dfrac{\partial C^*}{\partial E} = -\dfrac{\gamma w}{\beta}\left(\dfrac{q}{\alpha}\right)^{\frac{1}{\beta}} E^{\frac{-\gamma-\beta}{\beta}}$,

which is negative. An increase in environmental quality reduces production cost.

Note in the second point that when we differentiate the cost function with respect to input price, we get back the conditional input demand function,

$$\frac{\partial C^*}{\partial w} = \left(\frac{q}{\alpha E^\gamma}\right)^{\frac{1}{\beta}} = x.$$

This result is known as *Shephard's lemma*.

3.3.2. Cost function for a production function with two variable inputs

The simplicity of the single variable input model obscures the role of minimization in deriving the cost function, as there is only one value of x that satisfies the production constraint. To make the mathematics of minimization more explicit, a production function with more than one variable input must be analyzed. Consider a Cobb-Douglas production function with two variable inputs, x_1 and x_2:

$$q = \alpha x_1^{\beta_1} x_2^{\beta_2} E^\gamma .$$

(The subscript 1 now refers to a type of input, not to the level of environmental quality.) The cost-minimization problem for this function is:

$$\min_{x_1, x_2} w_1 x_1 + w_2 x_2 \text{ subject to } q = \alpha x_1^{\beta_1} x_2^{\beta_2} E^\gamma .$$

To determine the cost-minimizing values of the two inputs, the production constraint is first solved for x_2,

$$x_2 = \left(\frac{q}{\alpha x_1^{\beta_1} E^\gamma} \right)^{\frac{1}{\beta_2}},$$

and then is substituted into the cost expression to obtain

$$w_1 x_1 + w_2 \left(\frac{q}{\alpha x_1^{\beta_1} E^\gamma} \right)^{\frac{1}{\beta_2}}.$$

Note that the number of choice variables in the cost-minimization problem has been reduced from two (x_1, x_2) to one (x_1). The cost-minimizing value of x_1, x_1^*, can be determined by differentiating this expression with respect to x_1, setting the result equal to zero, and solving the resulting first-order condition for x_1. If this is done, then one obtains:

$$x_1^* = \left(\frac{q}{\alpha E^\gamma} \right)^{\frac{1}{\beta_1+\beta_2}} \left(\frac{\beta_1 w_2}{\beta_2 w_1} \right)^{\frac{\beta_2}{\beta_1+\beta_2}}.$$

This is the conditional input demand function for x_1. Unlike the conditional input demand function for x in the single input production function, this one includes input prices and not just the physical levels of output and environmental quality.

By symmetry, the corresponding conditional input demand function for x_2 is:

$$x_2^* = \left(\frac{q}{\alpha E^\gamma} \right)^{\frac{1}{\beta_1+\beta_2}} \left(\frac{\beta_2 w_1}{\beta_1 w_2} \right)^{\frac{\beta_1}{\beta_1+\beta_2}}.$$

The cost function, $w_1 x_1^* + w_2 x_2^*$, is therefore,

$$C^* = w_1 \left(\frac{q}{\alpha E^\gamma} \right)^{\frac{1}{\beta_1+\beta_2}} \left(\frac{\beta_1 w_2}{\beta_2 w_1} \right)^{\frac{\beta_1}{\beta_1+\beta_2}} + w_2 \left(\frac{q}{\alpha E^\gamma} \right)^{\frac{1}{\beta_1+\beta_2}} \left(\frac{\beta_2 w_1}{\beta_1 w_2} \right)^{\frac{\beta_1}{\beta_1+\beta_2}}.$$

This resembles the cost function for the single input production function by including the quantity of output (q), prices of the variable inputs (w_1, w_2), and environmental quality (E), along with the parameters from the production function.

Shephard's lemma still applies: if the cost function is differentiated with respect to w_1 (or w_2), then the conditional input demand function for x_1 (or x_2) is obtained. Note that the input prices appear in the conditional input demand functions as ratios. The conditional input demand functions are thus homogeneous of degree 0 in prices – use of the inputs does not change if both input prices change by the same multiplicative factor. This condition holds trivially when there is just a single variable input because, as has been seen, the conditional input demand function in that case does not include input prices:

$$x = \left(\frac{q}{\alpha E^\gamma}\right)^{\frac{1}{\beta}}.$$

In contrast, if both input prices change by λ times, then cost changes by λ times too – the cost function is homogeneous of degree one in prices. This can be seen by considering the summary expression for the cost function,

$$C^* = w_1 x_1^* + w_2 x_2^*.$$

If both input prices change by λ times, then x_1^* and x_2^* do not change (because they are homogeneous of degree 0), but w_1 and w_2 become λw_1 and λw_2, and so cost becomes λC^*:

$$(\lambda w_1) x_1^* + (\lambda w_2) x_2^* = \lambda C^*.$$

Analogous reasoning can be used to demonstrate that the cost function for the single variable input case is also homogeneous of degree 1 in prices. So, the cost function is not merely increasing in input prices; it increases proportionately.

3.3.3. Deriving the marginal cost function

Returning to the cost function for the production function with a single variable input, the upper curve in the top panel of Figure 3.3 depicts the cost function at the initial (lower) level of environmental quality, E_0. The horizontal axis shows level of output (q), while the vertical axis shows the minimum cost of production (C^*). The cost function slopes upward because it is increasing in output, and its slope becomes steeper as output increases due to diminishing returns: $\beta < 1$ implies that $1/\beta$, the coefficient on q in the cost function, is greater than one, so cost increases exponentially as output rises.

The cost function can be used to determine how an improvement in environmental quality affects the firm's profit. As in the case of the production function, another function needs to be brought into the picture – the *marginal cost function*. This function gives the minimum cost of producing an incremental unit of q. Deriving it is easy, as the cost function simply must be differentiated with respect to q. This was done above, when demonstrating that the cost function is increasing in output:

$$\frac{\partial C^*}{\partial q} = \frac{w}{\beta}\left(\frac{1}{\alpha E^\gamma}\right)^{\frac{1}{\beta}} q^{\frac{1-\beta}{\beta}}.$$

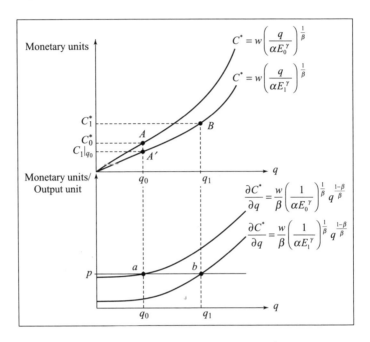

Figure 3.3. Modeling an environmental improvement: cost function

Marginal cost thus equals the slope of the cost function. This parallels the relationship between the inverse input demand function and the production function; as discussed earlier, the inverse input demand function is related to the marginal product of the input, which equals the slope of the production function.

The upper curve in the bottom panel of Figure 3.3 shows the marginal cost function at E_0.[5] The function is upward-sloping, which reflects the fact that the slope of the cost function becomes progressively steeper as output increases. This can be demonstrated by differentiating the marginal cost function with respect to q:

---

[5] Drawn correctly, the marginal cost functions in this figure and Figures 3.4 and 3.7 would pass through the origin. They are drawn differently in order to spot some features easily.

$$\frac{\partial^2 C^*}{\partial q^2} = \frac{w}{\beta}\frac{1-\beta}{\beta}\left(\frac{1}{\alpha E^\gamma}\right)^{\frac{1}{\beta}} q^{\frac{1-2\beta}{\beta}}.$$

This expression is positive because $\beta < 1$ implies that $1 - \beta > 0$.

3.3.4. *Change in profit, without and with output adjustment*

In the case of the production function, the inverse input demand function was used to determine the profit-maximizing output level. Now, the marginal cost function is used to do this. The implicit form of the cost function, $C^*(q, w, E)$, can be used to rewrite the firm's profit,

$$\pi = pq - wx,$$

as

$$\pi = pq - C^*(q, w, E).$$

The profit-maximizing output level occurs where the first derivative of this expression with respect to q equals zero. The first derivative is

$$\frac{\partial \pi}{\partial q} = p - \frac{\partial C^*}{\partial q}.$$

If the right-hand side is equated to zero, then the following is obtained:

$$p = \frac{\partial C^*}{\partial q}.$$

Profit-maximizing production occurs where output price equals marginal production cost. Written explicitly, this expression is:

$$p = \frac{w}{\beta}\left(\frac{1}{aE^\gamma}\right)^{\frac{1}{\beta}} q^{\frac{1-\beta}{\beta}}.$$

The bottom panel of Figure 3.3 illustrates that q_0 is the profit-maximizing level of output at the lower level of environmental quality. The firm produces at point a, where output price equals marginal production cost. Producing beyond this point would generate additional revenue, but the incremental amount would be less than the incremental production cost. In the top panel, this yields a total (minimized) cost of C_0^* (point A).

If environmental quality improves from E_0 to E_1, then the cost function shifts downward, because cost is decreasing in environmental quality. The cost of producing q_0 falls to $C_1|_{q_0}$ (point A′ in the top panel). Profit thus rises, to

$$\pi_1|_{q_0} = pq_o - C_1|_{q_0}.$$

The change in profit if output is held constant at q_0, $\pi_1|_{q_0} - \pi_0^*$, is given by just the decrease in cost,

$$C_0^* - C_1|_{q_0}.$$

As in the case of the comparison of profit at points A and A′ in Figure 3.1, this expression does not equal the full change in profit that results from the environmental improvement. It fails to account for the fact that the environmental improvement causes not only the cost function to shift but also the marginal cost function. As a result, it understates the increase in profit because it ignores the firm's output supply response. In the bottom panel of Figure 3.3, the marginal cost function shifts downward when E_0 is replaced by E_1 – the environmental improvement causes marginal production cost to fall. Profit-maximization now occurs at q_1 (point b in the bottom panel), which is greater than q_0: output rises. Total cost is now C_1^* (point B in the top panel).

After allowing for the adjustment in output, profit is given by

$$\pi_1^* = pq_1 - C_1^*,$$

and the change in profit,

$$\pi_1^* - \pi_0^* = p(q_1 - q_0) - (C_1^* - C_0^*),$$

is not just a change in cost; it also includes a change in revenue. Given that $C = wx$, this can also be written as:

$$\pi_1^* - \pi_0^* = p(q_1 - q_0) - w(x_1 - x_0).$$

This is exactly the same as the final expression for the change in profit in the case of the production function analysis. Two approaches have been used to arrive at the same result.

3.3.5. Magnitude of the change in profit

As in Figure 3.2, the increase in profit can be depicted in two ways. Both are shown in Figure 3.4.

Compared to Figure 3.3, the top panel of Figure 3.4 includes two additional tangents. The intercept of each tangent on the horizontal axis shows the profit associated with the corresponding production point, expressed in physical terms instead of money. From above, profit at point A (i.e., for E_0) is given by,

$$\pi_0^* = pq_0 - C_0^*,$$

which solved for q_0 yields

$$q_0 = \frac{\pi_0^*}{p} + \frac{1}{p}C_0^*.$$

The equation for the tangent at point A is thus

$$q = \frac{\pi_0^*}{p} + \frac{1}{p}C.$$

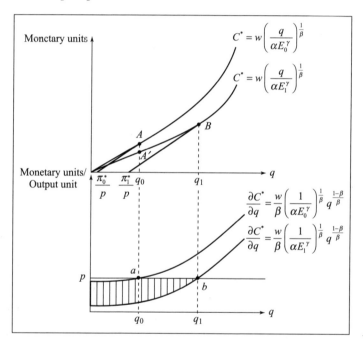

Figure 3.4.   Valuing an environmental improvement: cost function

From the profit-maximizing condition, the inverse slope of the tangent, p, equals the slope of the cost function (= marginal production cost). The equation for the tangent to the lower cost function (i.e., the one with E_1) at point B can be derived by using the same logic:

$$q = \frac{\pi_1^*}{p} + \frac{1}{p}C.$$

The increase in profits is the difference between the intercepts on the horizontal axis,

$$\frac{\pi_1^*}{p} - \frac{\pi_0^*}{p},$$

which is the same result as in the top panel of Figure 3.2. The figure does not show the line passing through point A′, which would cross the cost function for E_1 instead of being tangent to it (because the profit-maximizing condition does not hold at A′) and have an intercept on the horizontal axis between those of the two tangents (because profit at point A′ is higher than at point A but lower than at point B).

In the bottom panel, the increase in profit is shown by the cross-hatched area between the two marginal cost functions. The cross-hatched area equals the change in *producer surplus*. This is easily demonstrated. Producer surplus is the difference between total revenue and total variable cost, which in the figure is the area below the output price line and above the marginal cost function. The expression for this area in the case of E_1 is:

$$pq_1 - \int_0^{q_1} \frac{w}{\beta}\left(\frac{1}{\alpha E_1^{\gamma}}\right)^{\frac{1}{\beta}} q^{\frac{1-\beta}{\beta}} \, dq,$$

which simplifies to

$$pq_1 - w\left(\frac{q_1}{\alpha E_1^{\gamma}}\right)^{\frac{1}{\beta}},$$

or simply $pq_1 - C_1^*$: profit at the higher level of environmental quality, π_1^*. Parallel analysis for the marginal cost function that includes E_0 yields producer surplus equal to profit at the lower level of environmental quality, π_0^*. The change in producer surplus is thus exactly the same as the monetary change in profit, $\pi_1^* - \pi_0^*$.

3.4. Profit Function

3.4.1. Definition

Like the cost function, the profit function is an economic relationship, not a technical relationship. It relates maximum attainable profit to output price (not output quantity, as in the cost function), the prices of variable inputs, and the quantities of fixed inputs, including environmental inputs. It is the solution to the problem,

$$\max_{x} pq - wx \text{ s.t. } q = \alpha x^{\beta} E^{\gamma}.$$

3.4.2. Deriving the output supply and profit functions

The unconditional profit-maximizing input demand function, derived in section 3.2.2, is

$$x^{*} = \left(\frac{p\alpha\beta E^{\gamma}}{w} \right)^{\frac{1}{1-\beta}}.$$

If this is substituted for x in the production function, then the profit-maximizing level of output is obtained:

$$q^{*} = \alpha \left(\frac{p\alpha\beta E^{\gamma}}{w} \right)^{\frac{\beta}{1-\beta}} E^{\gamma}.$$

This expression is termed the *output supply function*. Recall that the profit-maximizing condition in the analysis of the cost function was that output price equals marginal production cost:

$$p = \frac{w}{\beta} \left(\frac{1}{\alpha E^{\gamma}} \right)^{\frac{1}{\beta}} q^{\frac{1-\beta}{\beta}}.$$

If this condition is solved for q, then the following is obtained:

$$q = \alpha \left(\frac{p\alpha\beta E^{\gamma}}{w} \right)^{\frac{\beta}{1-\beta}} E^{\gamma},$$

which is just the output supply function. The output supply function and the marginal cost function are thus two versions of the same supply relationship. Indeed, marginal cost functions are often called 'supply curves.' Like the unconditional input demand function, the output supply function is homogeneous of degree 0 in prices, increasing in output price and environmental quality, and decreasing in input price.

The profit function is obtained by substituting the output supply function for q and the unconditional input demand function for x into the basic expression for profit, $\pi = pq - wx$:

$$\pi^* = p\left(\alpha\left(\frac{p\alpha\beta E^\gamma}{w}\right)^{\frac{\beta}{1-\beta}} E^\gamma\right) - w\left(\frac{p\alpha\beta E^\gamma}{w}\right)^{\frac{1}{1-\beta}}.$$

This is more complex than the cost function because it incorporates adjustments in both the input x and the output q, not just the former. Like the cost function, it is homogeneous of degree 1 in prices: profit increases by λ times if output price and input price both increase by λ times. Unlike the cost function, it is increasing in environmental quality – an improvement in environmental quality reduces cost but raises profit. This can be verified by differentiating the profit function with respect to E, $\partial\pi^*/\partial E$.

If the profit function is differentiated with respect to input price w and the result is multiplied by -1, then the unconditional input demand function is obtained,

$$-\frac{\partial\pi^*}{\partial w} = \left(\frac{p\alpha\beta E^\gamma}{w}\right)^{\frac{1}{1-\beta}} = x^*,$$

while if it is differentiated with respect to output price p, then the output supply function is obtained,

$$\frac{\partial\pi^*}{\partial p} = \alpha\left(\frac{p\alpha\beta E^\gamma}{w}\right)^{\frac{\beta}{1-\beta}} E^\gamma = q^*.$$

These results are known as Hotelling's lemma, which is the profit-function analogue to Shephard's lemma.

In the analysis of the cost function, the corresponding derivations were repeated for the case of two variable inputs. The same will not be done here as the derivations above show explicitly how the profit function results from the solution to an optimization problem.

3.4.3. Change in profit

In Figures 3.2 and 3.4 the production and cost functions were plotted against the physical variables x and q, respectively, and bottom panels were added to account for changes in these variables in response to the improvement in environmental quality. In contrast, the profit function can be plotted against environmental quality E, and the impact of the environmental improvement on profit can be read directly off of this plot.

Figure 3.5 illustrates this.

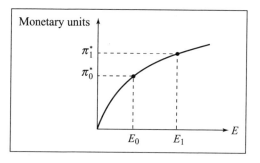

Figure 3.5.   Valuing an environmental improvement: profit function

For given prices, the environmental improvement results in movement along the profit function, not a shift in the function. The function slopes upward (profit is increasing in environmental quality), but the slope diminishes. The latter reflects the diminishing returns to environmental quality in production ($\gamma < 1$). The proof of this, which requires checking that the sign of the second derivative $\partial^2\pi^*/\partial E^2$ is negative, is left as an exercise to the reader. The improvement in environmental quality from E_0 to E_1 on the horizontal axis results in an increase in profit from π_0^* to π_1^* on the vertical axis. If the profit function is known, then we can value the environmental improvement in one step, unlike the two steps that are required if we use either the production function or the cost function.

3.5. Empirical implications

Although the preceding analysis has been purely theoretical, it contains a number of important lessons for empirical analysis. They can be summarized as follows:

3.5.1. *Three types of individual functions – input demand, marginal cost (or output supply), and profit – can be used to estimate the change in profit resulting from an environmental change*

As emphasized throughout the preceding sections, change in profit is the proper measure of the impact of an environmental change on a firm. Change in profit can be calculated by estimating and manipulating any of three individual functions:

(a) If the input demand function is estimated, then it can be used to calculate the change in consumer surplus between one level of environmental quality and another, and that change equals the change in profit.

(b) If the marginal cost function is estimated, then it can be used to calculate the change in producer surplus between one level of environmental quality and another, and that change equals the change in profit. The same holds for the output supply function, which as seen is closely related to the marginal cost function.

(c) If the profit function is estimated, then it can be used directly to calculate the change in profit between one level of environmental quality and another.

Our analysis assumed a single input and a single output. If there are multiple inputs or outputs, then sets of input demand or marginal cost (or output supply) functions must be used instead of individual ones. This point is elaborated in section 3.6.

3.5.2. *Use of full information requires estimating a system of equations, not just a single one*

Although the change in profit can be calculated using individual functions, each of the three approaches presented in sections 3.2–3.4 involves a system of interrelated functions – a production function plus an input demand function, a cost function plus marginal cost and conditional input demand functions, and a profit function plus input demand and output supply functions. If one wishes to use full information related to any of these approaches, then one must estimate a system of equations instead of an individual equation. The estimation of a system of equations is demonstrated in section 3.7.

Compared to estimating an individual equation (i.e., an input demand, marginal cost or output supply, or profit function), estimating a system of equations is more data-intensive, but it can yield statistically more efficient results. The gain in statistical efficiency is usually smaller, however, if the number of observations is smaller or if variables that can be excluded when an individual equation is estimated contain relatively more measurement error. Estimating a system of equations is thus not always more desirable. If data are incomplete, then it might not even be possible. In that case, one must rely on the estimation of individual equations (Huang and Smith, 1998).

3.5.3. *Endogeneity: a potential source of bias in estimating all three functions, especially the production function*

The Cobb-Douglas production function in section 3.2 was written as a deterministic relationship:

$$q = \alpha x^\beta E^\gamma.$$

In practice, this function is not known to the econometrician, who must instead estimate it. The standard estimation procedure for a Cobb-Douglas function is to gather data across a set of firms, take the natural logarithm of each side of the function, add a stochastic error term to it (to account for unobserved factors that affect output and for measurement error in the output data), and then use regression methods to estimate the resulting log-log equation,

$$\ln q_i = b_0 + b_1 \ln x_i + b_2 \ln E_i + \varepsilon_i.$$

i denotes firm, and ε is the error term. The regression coefficients b_0, b_1, and b_2 provide estimates of $\ln \alpha$, β (not $\ln \beta$), and γ (not $\ln \gamma$), respectively.

If one uses Ordinary Least Squares (OLS) to estimate this equation, then one likely obtains biased estimates of the regression coefficients. This is because the variable input, x, is an endogenous variable. Unlike E, it is chosen by firms. As a result, it is likely to be correlated with the error term ε. This is easiest to see by considering the conditional input demand function,

$$x = \left(\frac{q}{\alpha E^\gamma}\right)^{\frac{1}{\beta}}.$$

Note that this function includes output, q. If some unobserved factor generates a shock ε that affects q through the production function, then x will be affected too through the conditional input demand function. The variable input in the production function is thus correlated with the error term in the production function. This correlation has long been known to lead to biased estimates of the coefficients in a production function (Hoch 1958).

To reduce this bias, one must use an estimator other than OLS, such as two-stage least squares. But successful application of two-stage least squares requires one or more *instrumental variables* that are valid and strong. These are variables that are highly correlated with the endogenous explanatory variable but are not correlated with the error term and are not included in the original equation (the production function in this case). Obtaining such variables can be difficult, and using instruments that are invalid or weak can create statistical problems that are worse than the endogeneity problem that one is trying to use them to solve (Murray, 2006).

Endogeneity affects the cost and marginal cost functions, too. Recall that these functions are given by

$$C^* = w\left(\frac{q}{\alpha E^\gamma}\right)^{\frac{1}{\beta}}.$$

$$\frac{\partial C^*}{\partial q} = \frac{w}{\beta}\left(\frac{1}{\alpha E^\gamma}\right)^{\frac{1}{\beta}} q^{\frac{1-\beta}{\beta}}.$$

Both include q as an explanatory variable, which is endogenous because the firm influences it through the choice of x. In the case of agriculture, the argument is sometimes made that output is only weakly endogenous with variable inputs, because the latter are applied toward the start of the growing season. It is argued that the gap in time between the start of the season and harvest reduces the feedback from output shocks to input demand. This argument should always be supported by additional evidence that the shocks do not in fact occur at points in the growing season when farmers respond to them through input adjustments, or, if they occur later in the season, that farmers do not respond to forecasts related to them.

If this argument does not hold, then one must again use instrumental variables in estimating these functions. A variable that is not included in the cost or marginal cost functions is output price, p. This is a promising instrument, as it is likely to be exogenous (more on this in a moment). But if one has data on output price, then one likely has the option of avoiding the cost-function approach altogether and using instead the profit-function approach, which is less prone to endogeneity bias. The profit function and the two functions associated with it, the input demand and output supply functions, do not include any choice variables on their right-hand sides. The only explanatory variables in them are prices (p, w) and environmental quality (E). Assuming that E is determined by the actions of economic agents other than the affected firms (e.g., deforestation by households in upland areas affects baseflow received by farmers downstream), then it is clearly exogenous. If microdata are used to estimate these functions, then input and output prices are also likely to be exogenous. An exception is when one or more firms have market power, which is discussed in section 3.6. If aggregate industry-level data are used to estimate the profit function, then prices are unlikely to be exogenous, and one must again use instrumental variables to correct for the resulting bias. Obtaining valid instruments generally becomes more difficult as data become more aggregated.

Other problems can also occur even when microdata are used. For example, if the firms are located in the same region, then prices might not vary much across them, and this can preclude the estimation of coefficients on the price variables. If the purpose of the analysis is to measure the impact of a change in environmental quality, however, then this is not necessarily a problem. Mundlak (1996) also notes that firms often make decisions on the basis of expected prices, not the market prices observed by econometricians. He demonstrates that there can be a substantial loss of statistical efficiency if one uses market prices as proxies for expected prices when estimating a profit function, and he argues that this statistical inefficiency can be a more serious problem than the endogeneity bias associated with estimating a production function. The most serious problem is when one or more markets are missing and thus complete price data do not exist. This problem is discussed in section 3.6.

3.5.4. Change in revenue: a biased measure of change in profit

If one estimates a production function, then one can use it to predict output with and without an environmental change. One can then predict the change in revenue by multiplying output price by the change in output (= output with the change – output without the change). There are two such predicted changes in revenue, one partial and one complete, depending on whether or not one also estimates the input demand function.

If one does not estimate the input demand function, then one predicts the change in revenue using only the production function. This corresponds to $p\left(q_1|_{x_0} - q_0\right)$ in Figure 3.1. This is a partial change in revenue because it fails to account for adjustments to input use, which affect output. When environmental quality improves, this partial change in revenue understates the increase in profits, as discussed in section 3.2.3. When environmental quality deteriorates, the opposite is true – the partial measure of the loss in revenue overstates the loss in profits. This is illustrated in Figure 3.6, which looks just like Figure 3.1 except that the subscripts 0 and 1 have been reversed to indicate that the change is from better environmental quality to worse. The reduction in revenue associated with the drop from point A to point A' overstates the decrease in profits because it ignores the reduction in costs as input use falls from x_0 to x_1. Using a production function to estimate the negative impact of environmental degradation is commonly called the *damage function approach*. The fact that this approach tends to exaggerate loss of profit is unfortunately often overlooked.

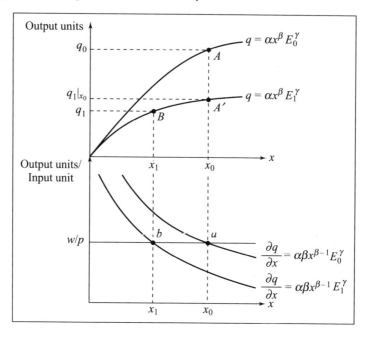

Figure 3.6. Modeling environmental degradation: production function

If one also estimates the input demand function, then one can account for the input adjustment and thus predict the complete change in revenue. This corresponds to $p(q_1 - q_0)$ in Figures 3.1 and 3.6. The complete change in revenue overstates the increase in profits when environmental quality improves (Figure 3.1), because it fails to account for the cost of increased input use, $w(x_1 - x_0)$. It also overstates the decrease in profits when environmental quality deteriorates (Figure 3.6), because it similarly fails to account for cost savings as the firm reduces input use. In the latter case (environmental deterioration), the complete change in revenue is more biased than the partial change. This can be seen easily in Figure 3.6, where the complete change in revenue is associated with the drop from point A to point B, which exceeds the partial reduction associated with the drop from point A to point A'.

If one estimates not only the production function but also the input demand function, then there is no reason to predict a change in revenue – one can instead predict the change in profit, which is (or should be)

the objective of the analysis. Use of the change in revenue as a proxy for the production impact of an environmental change is thus pertinent only when one estimates only the production function and thus predicts the partial change in revenue. The fact that the partial change in revenue is a biased measure of the change in profit does not mean it has no value for economic analysis. For example, suppose that the purpose of the analysis is to determine whether a prospective programme to improve environmental quality is economically justified. If the predicted partial change in revenue exceeds the cost of the programme, then one can be confident that the programme is justified, because a conservative (downwardly biased) measure of the benefits has been used. By the same token, however, if the predicted partial change in revenue does not exceed the cost of the programme, then one cannot say whether or not the programme is justified – perhaps the predicted benefits would have exceed the programme cost if the conceptually correct benefit measure, the change in profit, had been used instead of the partial change in revenue. The partial change in revenue can thus be used to construct one-sided benefit-cost tests.

3.5.5. Change in cost: a biased measure of change in profit

Analogous points can be made about the bias associated with using the change in cost as a proxy for the change in profit. When environmental quality improves but output is held at the initial level, q_0, the resulting reduction in cost, $C_0^* - C_1|_{q_0}$, understates the positive impact of the environmental improvement on the firm. This point was made in section 3.3.4. It is the mirror image of the downward bias that occurs when the variable input is held at the initial level x_0 and the change in revenue, from the production function, is used to measure the change in profit. When environmental quality deteriorates but output is held at the initial level, the bias is in the opposite direction – the increase in cost overstates the damage to the firm. This illustrated in Figure 3.7, which looks like Figure 3.3 except that the subscripts 0 and 1 have been reversed. The cross-hatched area in the bottom panel indicates the amount by which the increase in cost overstates the loss of producer surplus, which has the same shape as in Figure 3.4.

Figure 3.7 can also be used to illustrate the bias associated with using the *replacement-cost method* to value environmental damage. If a firm attempted to restore output to the initial level q_0, then it would incur costs equal to the area given by the approximately trapezoidal area $q_1 ba'q_0$ in the bottom panel. This area exceeds the loss of producer surplus, and so the replacement cost overstates the loss of profit. The problem with the replacement-cost method is clear – only an irrational firm would attempt to restore output to the initial level q_0 after environmental quality has deteriorated, because the marginal cost of producing beyond the new profit-maximizing output level q_1 exceeds the marginal benefit, which is given by the output price p. Simply put, the replacement cost does not generate benefits of equivalent value.

The results in this section and section 3.5.4 illustrate the importance of accounting for adjustments firms make in response to environmental changes. The failure to account fully for these adjustments is the reason why partial or approximate measures of economic impacts, such as revenue-based damage costs or cost-based replacement costs, provide biased measures of welfare impacts.

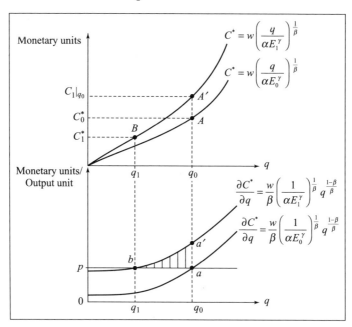

Figure 3.7. Modeling environmental degradation: cost function

3.6. Implications of relaxing key assumptions

3.6.1. Multiple firms

All the preceding analysis assumed a single, price-taking firm. If the environmental change affects multiple firms but does not affect input or output prices, then the sum of changes in profits across firms, where the changes are calculated at fixed prices, is a valid measure of the welfare impact on the set of firms. If the environmental change affects a large share of the firms in an industry, however, then it probably affects prices too. For example, an environmental improvement that affects an entire industry would be expected to reduce output price, due to the increased supply of the output (assuming a downward-sloping demand function for the output), and to raise input price, due to the increased demand for the input (assuming an upward-sloping supply function for the input). Deterioration in environmental quality would be expected to have the opposite effects. The welfare impact on the set of firms is still given by the sum of profit changes across the firms, but now the latter must account for the price changes. Moreover, the price changes create additional welfare impacts on consumers of the output and suppliers of the input, which must be taken into account if the objective is to measure the overall social welfare impact (see Freeman 2003).

Just et al. (1982)[6] deal with these sorts of aggregation issues. A sufficiently large environmental change – for example, global warming – could have economy-wide effects, in which case the impacts would need to be measured using a Computable General Equilibrium (CGE) model. General-equilibrium impacts of environmental changes, or policies to address them, can differ substantially from partial-equilibrium impacts (Hazilla and Kopp, 1990). Bergman (2005) reviews the application of CGE models to environmental issues.

3.6.2. Noncompetitive markets

Issues similar to the ones just discussed occur if the firm is large and faces either the demand function for the output it produces or the supply function for the input it consumes. The firm then has market power and can earn above-normal profits by acting as a monopolist and forcing output prices up or a monopsonist and forcing input prices down. One must again account for such price changes when measuring the impact of the environmental change on the firm's profits (Just et al., 1982; Freeman, 2003). One should also be aware that a welfare gain (or loss) for the firm now does not necessarily equal the corresponding welfare gain (or loss) for society, given the distortions created by the firm's manipulation of market prices.

---

[6] A new edition of this book has been published (Just et al. 2004).

3.6.3. Market distortions

Market power is one source of distortions that can cause market prices to deviate from marginal benefits and costs measured in social terms. Such distortions can also result from taxes, subsidies, regulations, and environmental externalities other than the ones that are the focus of a particular analysis (Freeman, 2003). When analyzing the impacts of an environmental change on producers, one must therefore be clear about whether the objective is to measure the impacts in private terms or social terms. If the objective is the former – that is, if the objective is to measure impacts at market prices – then one can ignore the distortions. The objective of economic analysis is usually to measure impacts in social terms, however, and in that case one must use shadow prices to adjust for the distortions. Belli et al. (2001) contains lucid explanations of shadow-pricing techniques for various distortions.

3.6.4. Missing markets and household production

Production in developing countries is often by households, as in the case of smallholder farms. If the household faces complete markets for inputs and outputs – that is, if it can buy as much of an input or sell as much of an output as it desires at the prevailing market prices – then, leaving aside the issue of risk preferences (discussed in the next section), the change in profit in the productive activity is the correct measure of the welfare impact of an environmental change that affects the household through that activity. The existence of complete markets makes production decisions *separable* from other household decisions, in particular the household's consumption decisions (including the labour-leisure tradeoff). One can then use a profit function for the productive activity to measure the welfare impact of the environmental change on the household. This is obviously a very convenient situation for economic analysis – one does not need to worry about the characteristics of the household's utility function, which is inherently more difficult to measure than its productive activities and their profitability.

Unfortunately, markets are often missing for households in developing countries, especially in rural areas (de Janvry et al., 1991). For example, households might face restrictions on the amount of labour they can buy or sell. When markets are missing, the household's production decisions are no longer separable from its consumption decisions, and the monetary change in profit from its productive activities no longer provides a valid welfare measure. One must instead calculate the change in profit by using shadow or *virtual prices*, which account for nonmarket utility effects. Unlike market prices, virtual prices are endogenous to the household – they are not determined solely by external factors – and they are unobserved. It is possible to test for the completeness of markets and thereby determine whether adjustments using virtual prices are necessary. See, for example, Pattanayak and Kramer (2001).

3.6.5. Risk

The analysis assumed that prices are known with perfect certainty and that the firm's owner is risk neutral. If prices are not known with perfect certainty when production decisions are made (e.g., as in the case of agriculture) but the risk neutrality assumption still holds, then impacts on the firm can be measured in terms of the *expected change in profit*. For example, a set of alternative price scenarios could be prepared, probabilities could be attached to each, the change in profit could be calculated for each, and then the expected change in profit could be calculated by multiplying the change in profit for each scenario by the corresponding probability and summing across the scenarios. Analogous procedures can be used if the magnitude of the environmental change is not known with perfect certainty.

The situation is more complex if the firm's owner is not risk neutral. Then, the owner's risk preferences must be taken into account. The expected change in profit no longer provides a valid measure of the impact of the environmental change on the owner's utility. In effect, the expected change in profit must be adjusted for risk premia (Just et al., 1982).

3.6.6. Fixed inputs

This analysis ignored fixed inputs. It included just a single input, which was a variable one. Fixed inputs are in fact a critical feature of the analysis of producer impacts of environmental changes. If there are no fixed inputs, then under standard assumptions, such as constant returns to scale and free entry and exit of firms, firms should not earn a profit in the sense of a payment over and above the costs of the inputs (including managerial effort) they employ. The existence of such profits should immediately attract new firms into the industry, which would result in the profits being competed away (driven to zero). Total revenue minus total costs, where the latter includes only variable costs, should equal zero at all times.

If production requires a fixed input that is owned by the firm, and if the input varies in quality across firms, then persistent differences in economic surpluses can exist across firms. A good example is agricultural land. Land of higher quality is more productive, which increases the economic surplus of the farm that owns it. The higher surplus simply reflects the greater return generated by the land – although total revenue minus total variable costs is positive, total revenue minus total costs, where the latter includes an implicit payment for the land, would again equal zero. There is a non-zero *quasi-rent* (total revenue minus total variable costs; producer surplus) but a zero economic profit (total revenue minus total costs). Indeed, if the farmer were a tenant who literally rented the land, then he would pay a rent equal to the quasi-rent and would consequently earn zero profits. The landowner would be the one who benefited economically from the land's higher quality. Because fixed costs are fixed, a change in quasi-rent equals a change in profit. The ownership of fixed inputs thus affects the distribution of the production impacts of environmental changes – whether the impacts appear as changes in the firm's profits, which occurs if the firm owns the fixed input, or the income of the owner of the fixed input, which occurs if the owner is different from the firm.

If there is no variation in the quality of the fixed input, then there should not be persistent differences in economic surpluses across firms as long as there is free entry and exit – that is, there should be zero profits in the long run. In the short run, however, environmental changes can affect quasi-rents. If environmental quality improves, then the existing firms in an industry earn above-normal returns during the transition period when new firms, attracted by the above-normal returns, are making the investments necessary to enter into production. These above-normal returns vanish once the new firms begin producing. Conversely, if environmental quality deteriorates, then the existing firms earn below-normal returns during the transition period when they depreciate their fixed inputs and scale back production. The key point here is that the change in an affected firm's profits reflects a change in quasi-rents and is temporary, converging to zero as the level of fixed inputs across firms adjusts to a new competitive level at the new level of environmental quality.

The issues of imperfect knowledge about future prices or the future magnitude of an environmental change, discussed in the previous point, also affect a firm's investment decisions. These effects can be complex, especially when the environmental change is irreversible. See Mäler and Fisher (2005) for more details.

3.6.7. Multiple outputs

Introductory expositions of producer theory usually assume that a firm makes a single output. In fact, firms often make more than one output. A farm that grows several crops is a good example. The theory of production by multi-output firms is well-developed (Chambers, 1988), as is the theory of welfare measurement for such firms (Just et al., 1982). The most natural way to measure the welfare impacts of an environmental impact on a multi-output firm is to use a multi-output profit function. This is the approach used by Pattanayak and Kramer (2001) in their study of the impacts of changes in baseflow on Indonesian farms that produce rice and coffee. It is also possible to add up changes in producer surpluses across the set of outputs, or consumer surpluses across the set of inputs, that are affected by the environmental change. However, certain technical requirements must be satisfied to do this. One must also take care to ensure that these changes are added correctly, as they are interrelated. For more details, see Huang and Smith (1998), Freeman (2003), and McConnell and Bockstael (2005).

3.6.8 Multiple inputs

The assumption of a single non-environmental input was extreme and was done to simplify the graphical exposition of the three approaches (production, cost, and profit functions). Assuming that the firm makes a single output, there is little difference between the single-input and multi-input cases when using a profit or marginal cost function to measure the impacts of an environmental change. One simply must make sure that all the relevant input prices are included in the profit or marginal cost function and the other functions that are associated with it (output supply and input demand, or cost and conditional input demand), if those functions are also estimated. Additional complications arise when changes in consumer surpluses for inputs are used to measure the impacts. As in the case of multiple outputs, one must check some technical conditions and add up carefully (Huang and Smith 1998; McConnell and Bockstael, 2005). The technical conditions are analogous to the conditions for *weak complementarity* identified originally by Mäler (1974) for using inputs, such as travel expenditures, to measure the benefits of environmental improvements to consumers, such as the availability of outdoor recreation sites. An input is weakly complementary to environmental quality if two conditions hold – (a) demand for the input increases when environmental quality improves, and (b) a change in environmental quality has no impact on the affected party (the consumer or the firm) if demand for the input equals zero, which occurs when the price of the input exceeds the choke price.

3.6.9. Nonconvexities

Our analysis assumed that environmental quality enters production in a 'well-behaved' manner. For example, it was assumed that the production function is continuously differentiable (the derivatives $\partial q/\partial E$ and $\partial^2 q/\partial E^2$ exist) and concave ($\partial q/\partial E > 0$, $\partial^2 q/\partial E^2 < 0$) with respect to environmental quality. These assumptions were convenient ones, but they do not necessarily hold in reality. The production set could instead be nonconvex. A simple example is a threshold effect, such as catastrophic crop loss if the amount of rainfall is below a minimum level. Although a production, cost, or profit function that ignores such a threshold could provide accurate predictions as long as environmental quality stays within the well-behaved production region, it would likely provide very misleading ones if the threshold were crossed. Moreover, decisions that make a threshold more likely to be crossed have a cost, a loss of resilience, that is not reflected in normal accounting procedures (Mäler et al., 2007) and thus not in data on profits and costs. The economic analysis of nonconvex production systems is an active area of research. For a good introduction, see Dasgupta and Mäler (2004).

3.7. Example: rainfall and rice in India

The example in this section concerns the impact of rainfall on rice yields in India. This is an environmental issue in the sense that air pollution evidently contributed to a drying trend in India during the latter half of the twentieth century. The pollutants involved are aerosols – tiny particles generated by the burning of fossil fuels and biomass. The link between aerosols and reduced rainfall is described in Ramanathan et al. (2005). The reduction in rainfall is most pronounced during the southwest, or summer, monsoon. Ramanathan et al. estimated that aerosol pollution caused a roughly five per cent decrease in monsoon rainfall during 1960–1998. In a subsequent study, Auffhammer et al. (2006) estimated that if this reduction had not occurred, then mean annual rice harvest in India during 1985–1998 would have been 10.6 per cent higher than it actually was, due to the combination of an increase in yield (2.1 per cent) and an increase in area harvested (8.5 per cent).

Auffhammer et al. analyzed state-level data on rice production in predominantly rainfed regions of the country. In contrast, the example in this section uses household-level data for irrigated farms in Tamil Nadu. Another difference is that the season examined is not the summer monsoon but rather the northeast monsoon. The rice crop in Tamil Nadu during the northeast monsoon is established in late September-mid October and harvested in January–February. The impact of aerosol pollution on rainfall during the northeast monsoon is not as clear as the impact on the summer monsoon. This section simply assumes that a hypothetical pollution-reduction programme would raise rainfall during the northeast monsoon by five per cent. The focus of the analysis is on the use of production and profit functions for estimating the change in profits that occurs as a result of the hypothetical increase in rainfall, not on the link between pollution and rainfall.

Unlike the analysis by Auffhammer et al., the analysis here focuses solely on impacts due to changes in yield. It ignores potential adjustments in rice area. This is one reason to expect the impacts estimated by this analysis to be smaller than those reported by Auffhammer et al. Another and perhaps more important reason is that the farms are all irrigated, which makes them less dependent on rainfall.

3.7.1. Data

Data for the analysis were drawn from the Reaching Towards Optimal Productivity project conducted by the International Rice Research Institute (IRRI) in the 1990s. This study is described in Dobermann et al. (2004). It covered multiple countries in Asia, not just India, and involved the collection of repeated data from hundreds of households during 1994–1999. The analysis presented here used only data for 37 households in Tamil Nadu that harvested rice during the northeast monsoon season. These data were collected by IRRI in collaboration with the Tamil Nadu Rice Research Institute. Data were available for four crop years, 1994/95–1995/96 and 1997/98–1998/99, with many missing observations. Complete data for all four years were available for just 17 households, while 18 households had only one or two years of data. The data were thus an unbalanced panel. The total number of observations was 105.

IRRI collected extremely detailed data on farm inputs, such as the amounts of various pesticides, herbicides, and fertilizers applied, labour used in each activity, and input costs. It also collected data on crop-establishment and harvest dates, yield, and daily weather data (rainfall, minimum and maximum temperatures, solar radiation). To parallel the theoretical models presented in sections 3.2–3.4, the analysis here considers just one variable input, labour (person-days aggregated across all activities, excluding harvest, threshing, hauling, cleaning, and drying), and one environmental input, rainfall (total millimeters from crop establishment until one month before harvest). Labour accounts for most of farming costs in the sample (roughly 60 per cent, excluding the opportunity cost of land). Other variables included in the analysis are yield (kilograms per hectare), the price of rice 'in the field' (i.e., net of harvest, threshing, hauling, cleaning, and drying costs; INR per kilogram), and the farm-specific wage rate (INR per person-day). Prices were not deflated, because the time period was short and because the homogeneity assumptions of the profit, output supply, and input demand functions were imposed during estimation.

3.7.2. Production function

As in section 3.2, the production function was assumed to be Cobb-Douglas:

$$q = \alpha x^{\beta} E^{\gamma},$$

where

q = yield
x = labour
E = rainfall.

This function was estimated by converting all variables to natural logarithms:

$$\ln (q) = \alpha' + \beta \ln (x) + \gamma \ln (E),$$

where $\alpha' = \ln(\alpha)$.

Although the data have a panel structure, ordinary least squares regression was used instead of a fixed- or random- effects panel estimator in view of the large number of households with only one or two observations. The econometrics programme Stata was used to estimate this equation and the ones described in section 3.7.3.

Table 3.1. Estimation of Cobb-Douglas production function for irrigated rice farms in Tamil Nadu during northeast monsoon.

Parameter	Estimate (Standard error)
α'	7.847 (0.467)***
β	0.092 (0.087)
γ	0.039 (0.024)
R^2	0.029
$F(2,102)$	1.54
Number of observations	105

Note: Significance levels for parameter estimates and *F* statistic: *** = 1%, ** = 5%, * = 10%.

Table 3.1 presents the regression results. As expected, the coefficients on both labour and rainfall are positive. However, neither coefficient is significantly different from zero at a five per cent level, nor is the overall equation (as indicated by the insignificance of the *F* statistic). This lack of significance reflects the poor fit of the equation ($R^2 = 0.029$), which is not surprising in view of the fact that we have ignored all inputs other than labour. It could also indicate that the Cobb-Douglas function does not provide a good representation of the farming technology.

The estimate of the coefficient on labour (β) is especially imprecise. In view of this, the production function estimates will not be used to predict the impact of increased rainfall on profit, which would entail using them to construct the input-demand function for labour. Instead, the production function will be used in the way that it is most commonly used in the literature, namely to predict the partial change in revenue described in section 3.2.3, $p\left(q_1|_{x_0} - q_0\right)$. For a five per cent increase in rainfall, this quantity is given by

$$p\left(\hat{\alpha}(1.05E)^{\hat{\beta}} x^{\hat{\gamma}}\right) - p\left(\hat{\alpha} x^{\hat{\beta}} E^{\hat{\gamma}}\right),$$

where p is rice price and the 'hats' over the parameters signify that the estimated values from the regression are being used. Plugging the observed values of p, x, and E into this expression yields a mean value of INR 32 per hectare. This compares to a mean profit of INR 13,692 per hectare, calculated as $pq - wx$. (Deducting the costs of variable inputs besides labour reduces the mean profit to INR 11,013 per hectare.) A five per cent increase in rainfall evidently would not increase profits much. And as noted earlier, the coefficient on rainfall used in this calculation is not significantly different from zero, so it is safest to conclude that the hypothetical increase rainfall would have no impact. Confidence in the estimates in Table 3.1 is also undermined by the fact that instrumental variables were not used to address the endogencity of labour (see section 3.5.3).

3.7.3. Profit function

The profit function was derived for the Cobb-Douglas production function in section 3.4.2. Economists typically do not posit a production function and then derive the profit function for it. They typically assume a *flexible functional form* for the profit function and analyze it instead of the specification that is unique to a particular production function. A flexible functional form is one that provides a good approximation to the actual function, regardless of the shape of the actual function, which is not directly observed by the econometrician. Flexible functional forms include interaction terms (variables multiplied by each other) and higher-order terms (variables raised to powers). Due to these characteristics, they have non zero first and second derivatives.

It was assumed that the profit function has the following specification:

$$\pi = \beta_p p + \beta_w w + \beta_{pw} 2 (pw)^{0.5} + \beta_{pE} pE + \beta_{wE} wE,$$

where w is the wage rate. Application of Hotelling's lemma (see Section 3.4.2) generates the corresponding output-supply and input-demand functions:

$$q = \beta_p + \beta_{pw} (w/p)^{0.5} + \beta_{pE} E$$

$$x = -\beta_w - \beta_{pw} (p/w)^{0.5} - \beta_{wE} E$$

Note that the profit function is homogeneous of degree one in prices, while the other two functions are homogeneous of degree 0. Also note that the same parameters appear in the different equations. For example, β_p multiplies p in the profit function and is the intercept in the output-supply function. β_{pw} is expected to be negative, so that an increase in wage relative to rice price reduces the supply of rice and the demand for labour.

The profit function was first estimated on its own, without the output-supply and input-demand functions and using ordinary least squares. The first column of Table 3.2 shows the results. As with the production function, none of the coefficient estimates are significantly different from zero, and the coefficient on β_{pw} does not have the expected negative sign. The profit function was then estimated as part of a system of three equations that also included the output-supply and input-demand functions. The seemingly unrelated regression command in Stata was used to do this, with cross-equation constraints to ensure that the parameters had identical values across the equations. The second column of Table 3.2 shows the results. Incorporation of the additional information contained in the output-supply and input-demand functions results in much more efficient estimates. Now, all coefficients except β_w are significantly different from zero, and β_{pw} has the expected negative sign. Both coefficients related to rainfall (β_{pE}, β_{wE}) are significantly different from zero, and both are positive.

As per the discussion in section 3.4.3, the impact of increased rainfall on profit is given by the difference in profit at higher and lower rainfall levels,

$$\pi_1 - \pi_0 = \left(\hat{\beta}_p \, p + \hat{\beta}_w \, w + \hat{\beta}_{pw} \, 2(pw)^{0.5} + \hat{\beta}_{pE} \, p(1.05E) + \hat{\beta}_{wE} \, w(1.05E) \right)$$
$$- \left(\hat{\beta}_p \, p + \hat{\beta}_w \, w + \hat{\beta}_{pw} \, 2(pw)^{0.5} + \hat{\beta}_{pE} \, pE + \hat{\beta}_{wE} \, wE \right)$$

which simplifies to

$$\pi_1 - \pi_0 = \left(\hat{\beta}_{pE} \, p + \hat{\beta}_{wE} \, w \right) 0.05E \,.$$

Table 3.2. Estimation of profit function for irrigated rice farms in Tamil Nadu during northeast monsoon.

Parameter	Estimated as single equation	Estimated as part of system
β_p	3241.8	5737.3
	(6354.7)	(267.5)***
β_w	−590.1	−21.8
	(690.6)	(24.3)
β_{pw}	1029.6	−323.5
	(2085.3)	(72.0)***
β_{pE}	−2.259	0.663
	(1.783)	(0.230)***
β_{wE}	0.258	0.023
	(0.157)	(0.008)***
R^2	0.965	0.963
$F(5,100)$	552***	−
χ^2	−	8483***
Number of observations	105	105

Note: Standard errors are shown in parentheses under he parameter estimates. Significance levels for parameter estimates and F statistic: *** = 1%, ** = 5%, * = 10%.

The mean value of this expression is INR 94 per hectare, which is three times larger than the partial change in revenue predicted by the production function. This value remains much smaller than mean farm profits, however.

Though simple, this example illustrates several important points made in this chapter. The broadest two are that the change in profit is the appropriate production-related measure of the impact of an environmental change, and that more than one approach can be used to estimate the change in profit. Of the two approaches used in this example, one (the production function) was partial, and, consistent with points made in sections 3.2.3 and 3.5.4, it understated the value of the environmental improvement. Another point is that the use of full information on the impact of an environmental change on profits requires estimating a system of equations, and it has been seen here that doing so greatly improves statistical results. A final point is that there is no guarantee that an environmental change necessarily has a big impact on production. The estimated impact of increased rainfall presented here is much smaller than the impact reported by Auffhammer et al. But this is not surprising, given that the farms analyzed here were irrigated and thus less dependent on current-season rainfall as a water source, and that potential impacts of rainfall on rice area have been ignored. The impacts presented here reflect only the impact on yield.

References

Auffhammer, M., Ramanathan, V. and Vincent, J. R., 'Integrated Model Shows that Atmospheric Brown Clouds and Greenhouse Gases have Reduced Rice Harvests in India', *Proceedings of the National Academy of Sciences*, 103(52), (2006), 19668–19672.

Belli, P., Anderson, J. R., Barnum, H. N., Dixon, J. A. and Tan, J. P., '*Economic Analysis of Investment Operations: Analytical Tools and Practical Applications*', (Washington DC: The World Bank, 2001).

Bergman, L., 'CGE Modeling of Environmental Policy and Resource Management', Mäler K. G. and Vincent J. R., (eds.), *Handbook of Environmental Economics, Volume 3: Economywide and International Environmental Issues*, (Amsterdam: North-Holland, 2005).

Chambers, R. G., *Applied Production Analysis*, (Cambridge: Cambridge University Press, 1988).

Champ, P. A., Boyle, K. J. and Brown, T. C. (eds.), *A Primer on Nonmarket Valuation* (Boston: Kluwer Academic Publishers, 2003).

Dasgupta, P. and Mäler, K. G. (eds.), *The Economics of Non-Convex Ecosystems* (Dordrecht: Kluwer Academic Publishers, 2004).

De Janvry, A., Fafchamps, M. and Sadoulet, E., 'Peasant Household Behaviour with Missing Markets: Some Paradoxes Explained', *Economic Journal*, 101, (1991), 1400–1417.

Dobermann, A., Witt, C. and Dawe, D. (eds.), *Increasing Productivity of Intensive Rice Systems through Site-Specific Nutrient Management*, (Los Baños, Philippines: Science Publishers, Enfield, New Hampshire, and International Rice Research Institute, 2004).

Freeman, A. M., *The Measurement of Environmental and Resource Values: Theory and Methods*, (Washington DC: RFF Press, 2003), 276–283.

Hazilla, M., and Kopp, R. J., 'Social Cost of Environmental Quality Regulations: a General Equilibrium Analysis', *Journal of Political Economy*, 98, (1990), 853–873.

Hoch, I., 'Simultaneous Equations Bias in the Context of the Cobb-Douglas Production Function', *Econometrica*, 2, (1958), 566–558.

Huang, J. C., and Smith, V. K., 'Weak Complementarity and Production', *Economics Letters*, 60, (1988), 329–333.

Just, R. E., Hueth, D. L. and Schmitz, A., *Applied Welfare Economics and Public Policy* (New Jersey: Prentice-Hall, Englewood Cliffs, 1982).

Just, R. E., Hueth, D. L. and Schmitz, A., *The Welfare Economics of Public Policy: A Practical Approach to Project and Policy Evaluation* (Massachusetts: Edward Elgar, Northampton, 2004).

Just, R. E., and Pope, R. D., 'The Agricultural Producer: Theory and Statistical Measurement', in Gardner, B. L. and Rausser, G. C. (eds.), *Handbook of Agricultural Economics, Volume 1: Agricultural Production* (Amsterdam: North-Holland, 2001).

Mäler, K. G., *Environmental Economics: A Theoretical Inquiry* (Baltimore: Johns Hopkins University for Resources for the Future, 1974).

Mäler, K. G., and Fisher, A., 'Environment, Uncertainty and Option Values', K. G. Mäler, and Vincent, J. R. (eds.), *Handbook of Environmental Economics, Volume 2: Valuing Environmental Change* (Amsterdam: North-Holland, 2005).

Mäler, K. G., Li, C. Z. and Destouni, G., 'Pricing Resilience in a Dynamic Economy-Environment System: a Capital-Theoretical Approach', Beijer Discussion Paper No. 208, (Stockholm, Sweden: Beijer Institute of Ecological Economics, 2007).

McConnell, K. E., and Bockstael, N. E., 'Valuing the Environment as a Factor of Production', Mäler, K. G. and Vincent, J. R. (eds.), *Handbook of Environmental Economics, Volume 2: Valuing Environmental Changes* (Amsterdam: North-Holland, 2005).

Mundlak, Y., 'Production Function Estimation: Reviving the Primal', *Econometrica*, 64, (1996), 431–438.

Mundlak, Y., 'Production and Supply', Gardner, B. L., and Rausser, G. C., (eds.), *Handbook of Agricultural Economics, Volume 1: Agricultural Production,* (Amsterdam: North-Holland, 2001).

Murray, M. P., 'Avoiding Invalid Instruments and Coping with Weak Instruments', *Journal of Economic Perspectives* 20, (2006), 11–132.

Pattanayak, S. K., and Kramer, R. A., 'Worth of Watersheds', *Environment and Development Economics,* 6, (2001), 123–146.

Point, P., 'The Value of Non Market Natural Assets as Production Factors', Pettig, R. (ed.), *Valuing the Environment: Methodological and Measurement Issues* (Kluwer: Dordrecht, 1995).

Ramanathan, V., Chung, C., Kim, D., Bettge, T., Buja, L., Kiehl, J. T., Washington, W. M., Fu, Q., Sikka, D. R., and Wild., M., 'Atmospheric Brown Clouds: Impacts on South Asian Climate and Hydrological Cycle', *Proceedings of the National Academy of Sciences,* 102, (2005), 5326–5333.

4

Should Shrimp Farmers Pay Paddy Farmers?: The Challenges of Examining Salinization Externalities in South India

L. Umamaheswari, K. Omar Hattab, P. Nasurudeen and P. Selvaraj[1]

4.1. Introduction

Shrimp farming is an important socio-economic enterprise in a number of coastal regions of India. According to the Marine Products Export Development Authority (MPEDA), India's nodal agency for the promotion of seafood exports, shrimp accounts for about two-thirds of marine product exports by value, and in 2004–2005 the sector earned foreign exchange worth INR 8,348 crore (US $1.61 billion)[2]. Shrimp is cultivated in an area of almost 200,000 hectares largely in the states of Andhra Pradesh, West Bengal, Kerala, Orissa, Maharashtra and Tamil Nadu (MPEDA, 2005) and exported in diversified forms to Japan, USA, Europe and elsewhere. Shrimp production grew steadily between 1990–1991 to 2001–2002 (Kumar et al., 2004) with scientifically managed shrimp farming expanding in acreage by 8.7 per cent per year and in production by 8.4 per cent per year.

[1] The author is thankful to Jeffrey Vincent for meticulous guidance provided during the study. The author is greatly indebted to Priya Shyamsundar, M. N. Murty, Enamul Haque and S. Madheswaran for their critical suggestions and encouragement that enabled the successful completion of the project. Thanks are due to Sir Partha Dasgupta, David Glover, Kanchan Chopra and Herath Gunatilake for their guidance in the early stages of the study; and to Pranab Mukhopadhyay and Manik Duggar for their support and encouragement. The services of Senior Research Fellows Ravirajan K., Satheesh J. and Gopi S. in the collection and compilation of data; to A. Raja in the collection and analysis of soil samples and S. Ravichandran are gratefully acknowledged.
[2] 1 US $ = 51.735 INR

The short-term financial returns from shrimp farming are high but the intensive approach of shrimp farming does have an environmental impact which extends beyond the immediate farming zone. The use of sea water along with freshwater for shrimp culture can cause salinization of land and groundwater and affect the productivity of agricultural crops and quality of groundwater. For coastal communities, which depend on a mix of agricultural activities, intensive and semi-intensive shrimp farms carry with them a high risk of crop failure. Legislation whose objective is to reduce the adverse impact of shrimp farming exists in India but only rarely has it been enforced. Of current concern to many environmentalists is the Aquaculture Authority Bill, which is designed to regulate coastal aquaculture activities. If approved, the bill will give legal status to the industry and promote large-scale growth of shrimp farming in India.

The salinization of rice-growing lands and groundwater in India by shrimp farms have been well documented (Primavera, 1997), but estimates of the costs of shrimp salinity that integrate economic and soil aspects are not available. Studies from elsewhere, such as Flaherty et al. (1999), have found that the salt load introduced per hectare for cultivation of one crop of shrimp is as high as 3,048 kg in rural Thailand. Thanh et al. (1999) estimate that the salinization costs of shrimp farming in Vietnam in the form of lost paddy production, dike construction cost and delayed cost of planting is US $0.15 per hectare in the Mekong delta.

In another study, Battacharya et al. (1999), report a production loss of 146,160 metric tonnes of rice due to salinization of agricultural lands caused by semi-intensive methods of shrimp culture in Bangladesh. This study examines similar issues and asks whether there are major environmental externalities associated with shrimp farms. In particular, the study asks, What is the external cost of shrimp farm-induced salinization of land on paddy productivity? This question is answered by carefully comparing paddy yields in two similar villages in southern India, one affected by shrimp farms and the other located further away from shrimp farms.

4.2. Study area

Shrimp farming in areas that were previously used as cropland has become a vexing issue in districts of the Kaveri river delta in South India, particularly in Nagapattinam district (in the state of Tamil Nadu) and its adjoining areas (Naganathan et al., 1995). Paddy is the major crop cultivated in the region during the 'samba'[3] season (October–February). The district of Nagapattinam accounts for 38 per cent of total shrimp production of Tamil Nadu and the Union Territory of Puducherry. This district was also reported (Ahmed, 2005) to contain 146 illegal shrimp farms. For these reasons, this district and the adjoining district of Karaikal (in Puducherry) was chosen for this study.

Shrimp is cultivated during the summer (February–June) and during monsoons (October–January). Summer is the major growing season, with production high because of higher salinity levels. The second shrimp crop coincides with the northeast monsoon and production is relatively lower as rains dilute the salinity in shrimp ponds. This is the time when both sea water and fresh water are pumped into shrimp farms to reach the desired level of salinity. This leads to the intrusion of soluble salts into aquifers and salinity gradually builds up in the soil[4]. Currently, the modified extensive and semi-intensive methods[5] of shrimp farming are practiced in this area. Over the last two decades the region has seen several changes in shrimp farming methods in response to multiple disease outbreaks.

To identify the study villages, the help of a local NGO was taken to traverse the coastal stretches of Nagapattinam and Karaikal, which together form a major shrimp farming belt on the Coromandel coast. The village of Chandrapadi in Nagapattinam was chosen as the 'shrimp' study village. There are 14 shrimp farms clustered in the north-eastern part of this village along the Nandalaru tributary and these have a combined pond area of 65 hectare. This area was chosen because – (a) paddy fields are located nearby; (b) the shrimp cluster has been in use for a long period; (c) there are no other shrimp farming clusters in the neighbourhood which removes the possibility of overlapping salinity effect on paddy fields; and (d) time-series data on soil characteristics and cropping details are available.

The shrimp farms in Chandrapadi are located on the Tamil Nadu-Puducherry boundary. The adjacent 'paddy' villages are Poovam, followed by Thiruvettakudy. These two villages were chosen as the treatment and control villages for this study to examine the effect of shrimp farming induced salinity on paddy. These are homogenous villages with an average annual rainfall of 1,350 mm, 70 per cent of which is delivered by the north-

---

[3] Samba denotes second crop season.
[4] The salinity level required for culture is 25–30 ppt whereas seawater has a salinity level of 30–35 ppt.
[5] Modified extensive method has a stock of ten animals/sq ft and semi-intensive method has a stocking density of 20–50 animals/sq ft.

east monsoon, which coincides with the second season ('samba'). Paddy is the major crop cultivated during 'samba' and is rotated with gingelly or black gram. Paddy farmers from both villages depend on canal water as the major source of irrigation, although the supply from the canal is very erratic as both villages are located at the tail end of the deltaic zone. In this region, soil texture varies from sandy to sandy clay and the sub-surface texture is sandy throughout.

In order to understand the effects of salinization (from shrimp farms chandrapadi) on crop yields, farmer surveys in Poovam and Thiruvettakudy were undertaken. All farm households that had cultivated paddy during 2005 rabi were surveyed. Thus, 55 farm households in Poovam and 110 farm households in Thiruvettakudy were surveyed. This data forms the main basis of this study.

Poovam village has a population of 1,264 and the literacy rate is 67 per cent. Out of 200 households, 85 are farm households and others are wood traders and agricultural labourers with a number of households depending on work at brick kilns. The survey of 55 farm households revealed that during 'samba' 2005, paddy was cultivated in 49.36 hectares. The land holding per household is 1.27 hectare and fallow land area accounts for 29 per cent of the total land area of 70 hectare. The village has three sluice gates, one of which is defunct, and the other two are used to drain excess water out of the fields during heavy rains.

The survey of 110 farm households in Thiruvettakudy revealed that land holding per household is 2.08 hectare and the total land area is 228.84 hectare. The population is 2,918 and the village's literacy rate is 60 per cent. Paddy accounts for 88 per cent of the gross cropped area in the village, which is 218 hectares. Thiruvettakudy's farmers are all members of the Farmer's Irrigation Society (FIS) whose responsibility is to maintain canals and temple ponds, to operate sluice gates that regulate canal water supply and to adjudicate disputes between farmers. There is tension over land use between paddy farmers and the private sector shrimp farming industry. When in 1994–1995 about 88 hectare of land was bought by a private firm to set up shrimp farms, the FIS opposed their project. Shrimp farming could not proceed, but this parcel of land has since remained fallow.

4.3. Data

This study uses secondary data and survey data. Secondary data on agro-climatic features, land use and cropping characteristics of the study villages during the period 1990–1991 to 2003–2004 were collected from the Directorate of Economics and Statistics (village annual crop abstracts) at Karaikal to confirm the homogeneity of the two paddy villages prior to the establishment of shrimp farms. Secondary data on soil salinity in Poovam and Thiruvettakudy were collected from the Soil Testing Laboratory at Karaikal to record the salinity during the pre-shrimp period (1994–1995). Soil salinity data for the post shrimp period of 2002–2003 for Thiruvettakudy were collected from the National Agricultural Technology Project (an Indian Council of Agricultural Research programme).

Primary data from paddy farmers in the two paddy villages was collected using a pre-tested interview schedule with questions on socio-economic profile, input use, cost and returns from paddy cultivation, and attitude towards shrimp farming. Data pertaining to paddy cultivation are for the year 2005 rabi season (October 2005–February 2006). There exist variations in the variety sown, technology adopted (transplanted/direct sown paddy) and consequently input use in different fragments operated by the same farmer. Fragments are parcels of land that are owned/leased in by a farmer at various locations in the same village. A fragment may include one or more contiguous plots. A plot – treated as a sampling unit in soil science terminology – is an area of land enclosed by bunds on all four sides. This meant that data on paddy cultivation aspects had to be collected for individual fragments. The final sample size includes 165 paddy households covering 257 fragments. Of the total sample, 55 farms and 48 fragments are from Poovam and 110 farms and 209 fragments are from Thiruvettakudy.

Soils data were also collected from the two villages. Surface soil samples (up to a depth of 30 cm) were taken from cultivated lands, current fallows and permanent fallows and also from agricultural land 30 and 60 metres away from shrimp farms to ascertain the intensity and spread of soil salinity in Poovam. In the control village of Thiruvettakudy, soil samples were taken only from paddy lands. Soil samples were taken from land fragments at the start of the paddy season during the months of September and October 2006. For easy management, farmers divide their fragments into plots. From each plot, soil samples were taken from three different locations, and mixed to get a representative soil sample for that plot. A total of 314 and 577 soil samples were collected from Poovam and Thiruvettakudy, respectively. The samples were air dried to remove moisture content and then processed, inert material was removed, the soil was pulverized and a soil solution was prepared for analysis. Thereafter the salinity indicator, electrical conductivity, was measured.

4.4. Homogeneity of paddy villages

Poovam is immediately adjacent to shrimp farms whereas Thiruvettakudy is physically separate from them. The secondary data on land use, irrigation and crop cultivation and soil data for the pre-shrimp period were collected and analyzed to establish that the two villages were identical with respect to agro-climatic and cropping characteristics and soil salinity status before the introduction of shrimp farms.

Table 4.1 contains details about agriculture in Poovam and Thiruvettakudy for both periods, before and after the operation of shrimp farms.

In the period before shrimp farming was brought to the region, Poovam and Thiruvettakudy had 70 per cent and 81 per cent respectively of village lands under crops. Poovam had approximately 48 per cent of its Gross Cropped Area (GCA) under paddy while the proportion for Thiruvettakudy was nearly 59 per cent under paddy. Their cropping and irrigation intensity were similar and so was the ratio of net sown area to total land. Thus, although Thiruvettakudy is nearly twice the size of Poovam, in terms of cropping pattern the two villages were homogenous.

In the post-shrimp farming period, area under paddy as a percentage of GCA remained stagnant in Poovam, while it increased to 83 per cent in Thiruvettakudy. Given the agricultural histories of both villages and their crop growing patterns, it is inferred that this difference has been caused by rice farmers in Poovam encountering greater levels of soil salinity than their counterparts in Thiruvettakudy. There was, however, a decline in GCA in both the villages, mainly due to problem of water scarcity[6].

4.5. Soil characteristics

The soil testing laboratory maintains a register in which electrical conductivity (EC: a measure of salinity), pH (its acidic or alkaline value) and nutrient status of soil samples brought in by farmers are tested and recorded. The test results are used to prescribe use of fertilizer to farmers. The EC data of the soils is summarized in Table 4.2.

---

[6] A sharp increase in fallow lands (other fallows and cultivable waste) by 29.16 per cent and 27.06 per cent was observed in both Poovam and Thiruvettakudy, respectively during 1990–2003. This is reflected in a decline of Net Sown Area (NSA) in these villages. A large area is left fallow (203.18 ha) in Thiruvettakudy mainly for use as house plots and for construction of institutions. Further, the problem of seawater intrusion in the tract of land adjoining Poovam and Thiruvettakudy during heavy rains in the north-east monsoon season is another cause for the presence of fallow lands. But, the discussions with farmers indicated that historically seawater intrusion has not been a major problem in Poovam village itself.

Table 4.1. Land use and cropping characteristics of paddy villages (in hectares)

S. No.	Particulars	Before shrimp farming (1990–1992)		Shrimp farming period (1993–1995)		After shrimp farming (2001–2003)	
		Poovam	Thiruvettakudy	Poovam	Thiruvettakudy	Poovam	Thiruvettakudy
1.	Geographical area	207.40	549.00	217.89	558.00	217.89	558.00
2.	Current fallows	31.40 (15.14)	62.27 (11.34)	45.23 (20.75)	131.30 (23.53)	15.66 (7.18)	18.23 (3.26)
3.	Other fallows	10.23 (4.93)	14.80 (2.69)	8.83 (4.05)	13.37 (2.39)	24.68 (11.33)	33.18 (5.94)
4.	Cultivable waste	7.17 (3.46)	36.53 (6.65)	6.90 (3.17)	38.67 (6.93)	57.12 (26.22)	170.0 (30.46)
5	Net sown area (NSA)	121.93	347.00	107.83	278.50	66.70	222.29
6.	Gross cropped area (GCA)	146.07	445.40	121.37	326.53	66.73	230.52
7.	Paddy area	70.50	265.63	60.13	223.60	32.37	192.29
8.	Per cent of paddy area to GCA	48.26	59.64	49.54	68.47	48.50	83.41
9.	Per cent of NSA to total area	58.78	63.20	49.48	49.91	30.61	39.83
10.	Per cent of GCA to total area	70.42	81.12	55.70	58.51	30.62	41.31
11.	Cropping intensity (%)	119.79	128.35	112.55	117.24	100.04	103.70
12.	Irrigation intensity (%)	100.14	101.41	100.00	100.61	100.00	100.32
13.	Productivity of paddy (Kg ha^{-1})+	4000–4500	4000–4500	–	–	–	–

Source: Village Annual Crop Abstracts, Directorate of Economics and Statistics, Karaikal (Data was not available for the period 1996 to 2000).

+As told by farmers through recall and figures in parentheses indicate percentage to village panchayat, or local self-government, area.

Pre-shrimp period denotes average for the triennium ending 1992–1993. Shrimp period and post-shrimp periods denote averages for triennium ending 1995–1996 and 2003–2004, respectively.

Table 4.2. Soil salinity during pre-shrimp farming period (1994–1995)

Soil status	Soil EC (dS m⁻¹)			
	Min	Max	SD	Mean+
Poovam	0.1	0.4	0.125	0.23
Thiruvettakudy	0.1	0.7	0.136	0.23

Source: Soil Testing Laboratory, Karaikal
+t test : P value = 0.461
EC: Electrical Conductivity in deci Siemens per metre.

An EC value of less than 1 (EC < 1) indicates that soils are highly suitable for cultivation, whereas an EC in the range of 1–3 is injurious to crop growth. EC values between 3 and 4 will definitely cause yield reduction and soils with an EC value more than 4 (EC ≥ 4) are designated as saline soils and need reclamation to restore them for cultivation. In the pre-shrimp farming period, salinity levels were below one in both villages. Furthermore, the point estimates of means are the same, which provides evidence that the selected paddy villages were similar with regard to soil salinity at this time. In Thiruvettakudy village, for the 577 soil samples taken from 209 fragments, EC values ranged from 0.01 to 0.96, implying normal soils (Table 4.4).

Table 4.3. Range of EC values for Poovam soil samples

S.No.	Category of land	Soil samples (no.)	EC range (dS m⁻¹)
1.	Cultivated lands	215	0.02–2.13
2.	Current fallows	36	0.20–3.90
3.	Permanent fallows	17	1.70–6.60
4.	Near shrimp farms		
a)	Distance of 100 ft	18	5.64–15.89
b)	Distance of 200 ft	28	4.95–11.09
	Total soil samples	314	0.02–15.89

Source: Soil data collected by the author, 2006.

Having shown that soils in both control and treatment villages were not saline in the pre-shrimp period, the next step in this analyses was to compare pre-shrimp farming soil salinity with current salinity in the two villages. The soil samples taken from cultivated lands and fallow lands in Poovam in 2006 show EC values in the range of 0.02 to 6.60. In areas adjacent to the shrimp farm, EC levels were very high ranging from 4.95–15.89. In the cultivated lands, the EC ranged from 0.02–2.13 (Table 4.3).

Table 4.4. Range of EC values for Thiruvettakudy soil samples

Soil salinity indicator	Range
EC in dS m⁻¹	0.01–0.96
Total soil samples	577

Source: Soil data collected by the author, 2006.

4.6. Comparing paddy cultivation

The chief difference between the paddy economics of the two villages is seen in the net returns figures – per hectare net returns for Transplanted Paddy (TP) is INR 6,265 for Thiruvettakudy's farmers versus a loss of INR 5,400 per hectare for Poovam's farmers. Although the variable cost per hectare is higher in Thiruvettakudy (INR 19,000 as against INR 16,784 in Poovam) it is the large gap in the productivity between the two villages that makes a significant difference. In Thiruvettakudy, yield is 3,973 kg per hectare, which is 87 per cent more than Poovam's 2,124 kg per hectare. In the case of direct sown paddy (DS) the net returns per hectare are INR 4328 in Thiruvettakudy, against a loss INR Rs 4743 in Poovam. The details on input use, productivity, cost and returns from TP and DS along with the descriptive statistics of variable inputs obtained from survey of farm households are furnished in Tables 4.5 and 4.6.

Table 4.5. Descriptive statistics for transplanted paddy

S.No.	Items	Poovam (n=23)		Thiruvettakudy (n=110)		t test
		Mean	CV %	Mean	CV %	p-value
1.	Seeds (Kg ha⁻¹)	141.29	45.66	124.54	12.54	0.228
2.	Organic manure (Kg ha⁻¹)	9153.18	123.74	6619.52	39.38	0.298
3.	Urea fertilizer (Kg ha⁻¹)	303.41	126.57	380.58	99.06	0.386
4.	DAP fertilizer (Kg ha⁻¹)	85.99	122.01	121.71	71.29	0.138
5.	MOP fertilizer (Kg ha⁻¹)	115.76	167.02	31.71	220.03	0.051
6.	Plant protection cost (Rs ha⁻¹)	434.26	124.66	117.04	344.56	0.013

(Contd.)

(*Contd.*)

S.No.	Items	Poovam (n=23)		Thiruvettakudy (n=110)		t test
		Mean	CV %	Mean	CV %	p-value
7.	Human labour (Rs ha^{-1})	8546.01	36.03	9617.11	27.20	0.131
8.	Machinery charges(Rs ha^{-1})	1955.39	56.30	2614.72	54.77	0.018
9.	Variable cost (Rs ha^{-1})	16784.98	39.11	19000.43	25.53	0.137
10.	Productivity of paddy (Kg ha^{-1})	2124.77	44.31	3973.06	47.98	0.000
11.	Price (Rs kg^{-1})	5.37	7.41	6.30	11.15	0.000
12.	Gross returns (Rs ha^{-1})	11384.22	44.03	25266.03	53.96	0.000
13.	Net returns (Rs ha^{-1})	−5400.77	170.37	6265.60	196.34	0.000

CV % = Standard Deviation/ Mean × 100
Source: Farm Survey 2005–06.

In general, TP is more input intensive and hence the cost of cultivation is high as compared to DS farms. Also productivity is significantly higher for TP farms. In Poovam the average yield was higher for TP at 2,124 Kg ha^{-1} as compared to only 1,670 Kg ha^{-1} for DS. Similarly, TP farms in Thiruvettakudy recorded a higher average yield of 3,973 Kg ha^{-1} while in DS farms yield was 3,016 Kg ha^{-1}.

4.7. Estimation of externality cost

An externality exists when the consumption or production choices of one person or firm enters the utility or production function of another entity without that entity's permission or compensation (Kolstad, 2000). Shrimp farming in agricultural lands causes two kinds of externalities – (a) An intra-generational externality borne by the current generation due to decline in crop yields caused by increasing salinization of land and water resources and the associated adverse socio-economic effects in the region. By adopting reclamation measures and better water management, this salinity can be reversed or minimized; (b) An inter-generational externality that will be borne by future generations because of environmental damage to land and groundwater resources. In this study, the intra-generational externality cost of salinization of land is valued.

Table 4.6. Descriptive statistics for direct sown paddy

S.No.	Items	Poovam (n=25)		Thiruvettakudy (n=99)		t test
		Mean	CV %	Mean	CV %	p-value
1.	Seeds (Kg ha^{-1})	137.50	33.35	130.30	17.01	0.452
2.	Organic manure (Kg ha^{-1})	9072.73	60.83	4455.82	89.18	0.000
3.	Urea fertilizer (Kg ha^{-1})	185.15	70.74	211.84	62.14	0.369
4.	DAP fertilizer (Kg ha^{-1})	52.26	119.56	115.76	108.05	0.000
5.	MOP fertilizer (Kg ha^{-1})	54.39	94.47	54.69	273.25	0.987
6.	Plant protection cost (Rs ha^{-1})	146.99	131.76	47.31	273.21	0.021
7.	Human labour (Rs ha^{-1})	6571.20	47.00	7829.59	39.37	0.077
8.	Machinery charges (Rs ha^{-1})	1818.69	69.18	2109.25	51.14	0.297
9.	Variable cost (Rs ha^{-1})	12966.81	36.43	14630.63	47.33	0.162
10.	Productivity of paddy (Kg ha^{-1})	1670.71	53.59	3016.15	28.02	0.000
11.	Price (Rs kg^{-1})	5.47	8.81	6.25	11.70	0.000
12.	Gross returns (Rs ha^{-1})	8223.07	63.46	18959.29	29.82	0.000
13.	Net returns (Rs ha^{-1})	−4743.75	−116.44	4328.66	205.97	0.000

CV % = Standard Deviation/ Mean × 100
Source: Farm Survey 2005-06

The externality effect of a decline in soil quality is depicted in Figure 4.1. Given the market price P_0 and MC, the marginal cost of production (i.e. the supply curve), TR is the total revenue obtained from sale of the main produce of paddy. TVC is total variable cost, which includes costs of seeds, manures, fertilizers, plant protection chemicals, human labour and machinery. Output is Q_0; OP_0EQ_0 is TR; $OAEQ_0$ is TVC; AP_0E is producers' surplus, which equals the sum of fixed costs and profit. With an externality, MC shifts to MC output falls and Q_1BEQ_0 is the loss in TR; ABE is both loss in profit and loss in producer surplus, because fixed costs are fixed.

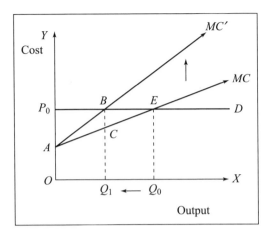

Figure 4.1. Externality effect of decline in soil quality.

The externality cost ABE caused by salinity is valued using the change in productivity method by a comparison of salinity affected and unaffected paddy villages. In the next section, a production function for paddy is estimated and examined to see whether and how soil salinity affects yields in the control and treatment villages.

4.8. Factors causing soil salinity

What is the link between salinity in soil and shrimp farming? Finding answers scientifically help decide whether salinity is primarily caused by shrimp farming or whether other factors too are responsible. In general, the intensity of salinity is influenced by factors like soil type, topography and location of fields. In the study area, the soil type varies from sandy to sandy clay but the sub-surface texture is sandy throughout. There are no variations in slope and therefore for this analysis the location of fields was the most important factor. The location of paddy farms was identified by measuring the vertical distance from key hydro-geological structures in the village – the tertiary canal, shrimp farms and drainage shutters – to the mid-point of each farm fragment in the sample.

Each fragment in the dataset is comprised of a number of plots which ranged between one and five in Poovam and tended to be slightly more in Thiruvettakudy. To examine the link between soil salinity in the farm fragments and shrimp farms, mean EC was regressed on distance variables and a village dummy. Linear, log-log and semilog models were attempted. The log-log form is reported in Table 4.7, which was chosen taking into account the signs and significance levels of the coefficients of explanatory variables.

Table 4.7. Estimated Log-Log function of salinity on distance parameters (Dependent variable Log of mean EC in dS m⁻¹)

Variables	Regression coefficients	Standard error
Intercept	−2.968***	0.128
DIS SHR	0.032*	0.019
Village dummy	1.211***	0.137
R²	0.241***	
Adj R²	0.235	
F	40.28	
N	257	

Note: *** , * denote significance at 1 per cent and 10 per cent level respectively.

All the distance variables were highly collinear, hence, in the final model, all distance variables were dropped other than distance to shrimp farm. The salinity regression analysis shows that mean EC is positively and significantly influenced by distance from shrimp farms (DIS SHR) and the village dummy (Poovam = 1). The significance of the dummy variable for Poovam suggests farms in Poovam are more saline than farms in Thiruvettakudy. This supports the hypothesis that Poovam is affected by shrimp farms given that both villages had the same salinity in the period before shrimp farming was introduced to the region and given that Thiruvettakudy is actually a bit closer to the sea. However, in terms of the significance of the shrimp farm distance variable, there is a caveat to be recorded. The coast runs almost parallel to the shrimp bund and therefore the variable measuring distance from the shrimp bund is highly correlated with distance from the coast. Hence, part of what the distance from shrimp farms variable may be picking up is distance from saline sea waters.

4.9. Production function analysis

In order to assess the salinity externality on paddy yields, a paddy production function was estimated with soil salinity as one of the independent variables affecting paddy cultivation.

$$Y = \alpha X_1^{\beta_1} X_2^{\beta_2} X_3^{\beta_3} X_4^{\beta_4} e^u \tag{1}$$

where,

Y = Paddy yield (Kg ha^{-1})

X_1 = Human labour cost (Rs ha^{-1})

X_2 = Machinery cost (Rs ha^{-1})

X_3 = Quantity of Urea + DAP (Diammonium Phosphate in Kg ha^{-1})

X_4 = Mean EC (dS m^{-1})

e^u = error term

βs are regression coefficients of respective variables.

Table 4.8. Descriptive statistics of affected farms

Variable	Observation	Mean	Std Deviation
Yield	48	1888.281	936.4028
Urea DAP	48	310.2431	307.8608
MeanFC	48	.4397917	.6329044
Labcst	48	7517.462	3209.589
Machcst	48	1884.2	1174.844

Table 4.9. Descriptive statistics of unaffected farms

Variable	Observation	Mean	Std Deviation
Yield	209	3519.79	1571.638
Urea DAP	209	419.6686	342.6793
MeanEC	209	.0866986	.1093913
Labcst	209	8770.385	2977.17
Machcst	209	2375.286	1298.826

Table 4.10. Descriptive statistics of combined sample

Variable	Observation	Mean	Std Deviation
Yield	257	3215.073	1604.298
Urea DAP	257	399.2312	338.5818
MeanEC	257	.1526459	.3198046
Labcst	257	8536.376	3054.878
Machcst	257	2283.566	1288.731

In order to estimate the production function, pooled regressions of paddy yield in both control and treatment villages on the input variables were used. In these regressions, yield is measured as kg of paddy per hectare. The variable inputs – urea and DAP fertilizer are expressed in physical units as Kg ha⁻¹. For labour input, wages are the same for a particular operation in all farms, while transplanting and weeding are done on a contract basis. Thus, labour cost are calculated per hectare (Labcst). In the case of machinery, the unit cost of machinery per ploughing per acre is the same for all farms in a village and so total machinery cost per hectare (Machcst) was included based on number of hours of machinery used.

Three different specifications are used to test the hypothesis that salinity has a significant effect on paddy yield. Model I estimates a Cobb-Douglas production function and includes all the variable inputs identified in equation 1 in log form. Also included is a village dummy, which is defined as being equal to 1 if the farm is a Poovam (shrimp-affected) farm and 0 if the farm is from Thiruvettakudy. Model II includes all the variables used in Model I as well as an additional interaction term of the log of the fertilizer variable interacted with log mean EC. This model tests whether there is a synergistic effect between fertilizer use and salinity, i.e. if increased salinity in combination with fertilizer use contributes to increased productivity. Model III takes into account a possible exponential relationship between salinity and paddy production. Thus, in this regression mean salinity is not logged.

The results of estimated pooled production functions for paddy farms are given in Table 4.11.

In model I, the elasticity of output with respect to variable inputs, human labour and fertilizer are positive and significant. The coefficient of mean EC is −0.0628 and significant at the 5 per cent level. This suggests that a one per cent increase in salinity *ceteris paribus* reduces paddy yield by 0.06 per cent.

In model II, the coefficient of the interaction variable of fertilizer x mean EC is positive but not statistically significant, which indicates that increased fertilizer use does not counteract salinity, and that fertilizer use in combination with salinity does not affect yield. The coefficients of the other variables are similar in sign to those obtained in model I. Model III assumes an exponential relationship between salinity and yields and the coefficient of salinity is significant at the five per cent level. The other variables behave in a manner similar to Model I.

All three models show that there is a significant effect of salinity on paddy yield. Using different specifications simply strengthens the robustness of the analyses. The estimates show that there is non-linear relationship between salinity and land productivity explained by either logarithmic or exponential functions.

Table 4.11. Estimates of production function for paddy farms

Dependent variable LnY Independent variable	Model I Coefficient	Model I T Statistics	Model II Coefficient	Model II T Statistics	Model III Coefficient	Model III T Statistics
$Ln\,X_1$	0.1372*	1.827	0.1340*	1.788	0.1343*	1.790
$Ln\,X_2$	0.0949	1.424	0.1086*	1.613	0.1094*	1.629
$Ln\,X_3$	0.1422***	3.986	0.1838***	3.894	0.1305***	3.517
$Ln\,X_4$	−0.0628**	−2.031	−0.1952*	−1.889	—	—
D	−0.4860***	−6.297	−0.4765***	−6.158	−0.4953***	−6.600
X_4	—	—	—	—	−0.1981**	−2.084
$X_5 = Ln\,X_3 * Ln\,X_4$			0.0244	1.343	—	—
Constant	5.1194	7.414	4.829	6.683	5.294	7.670
R^2	0.3963		0.4007	0.3968		
Adjusted R^2	0.3843		0.3863		0.3848	
F	32.957		27.853		33.029	
N	257		257		257	

Note: ***, ** and * denote significance at 1 per cent level, 5 per cent and 10 per cent levels respectively.

Y = Paddy yield (Kg ha⁻¹)

X_1 = Human labour cost (Rs ha⁻¹)

X_2 = Machinery cost (Rs ha⁻¹)

X_3 = Quantity of Urea + DAP (Kg ha⁻¹)

X_4 = Mean EC (dS m⁻¹)

D: Village dummy variable (1=affected village)

X_5 = Quantity of Urea + DAP (Kg ha⁻¹) × Mean EC (dS m⁻¹)

4.10. Welfare gains from salinity reduction

Next, the welfare gains are estimated from decreases in salinity. This is equivalent to the welfare losses suffered by villagers as a result of increased salinity. Table 4.12 provides estimates of welfare losses from increased salinity using different methods of estimation. Methods I, II and III reflect the three estimated production functions given in Table 4.11. Method IV provides an estimate of productivity loss by comparing productivity in affected and unaffected villages.

Table 4.12. Estimates of losses per hectare from increased salinity obtained using different methods

Estimate	Per hectare land productivity (Mean EC = 1 In dS m⁻¹)	Per hectare land productivity (Mean EC =3 in dS m⁻¹)	Loss per hectare (kg)	Loss per hectare (INR)
I	2582	2410	172	1008
II	2681	2540	141	826
III	2557	1721	836	4899
IV	–	–	1647	9651

Note: Estimates I, II and III use different production function specifications and the estimate IV is obtained by comparing farm productivity of affected and unaffected villages. Losses in INR are calculated by assuming an average paddy price of 5.86 per kg.

Based on scientific evidence, soil salinity level is considered to be safe if it is equivalent to 1; any higher values of mean EC are considered unhealthy for crops. Table 4.12 (Methods I, II and III) presents productivity levels for salinity equal to 1 and the maximum salinity observed in the affected village, which is 3. Estimates of welfare gains are obtained by comparing predicted yields per hectare corresponding to the salinity levels of 1 and 3, given the sample mean values of all other variables in the production function. The productivity gain with the Cobb-Douglas specification of production function (Method I) is 172 kg of paddy per hectare. With the production function considering the synergistic effects of fertilizers and salinity, the production gain falls to 141 kg per hectare. In the case of the production function that considers the exponential relationship between paddy yield and salinity, a change in salinity from the maximum level of 3 to the safe level of 1 results in a gain of 836 kg per hectare. These estimates show a complicated non-linear relationship between farm productivity and land salinity. It must, at the same time, be noted that these are gains attributed to a decrease in the mean level of salinity from 3 to 1, and that they represent the maximum gains possible.

Method IV estimates the gains that would accrue if salinity decreases by comparing the productivity in the controlled farms with those affected by salinity. The predicted per hectare yield of unaffected and affected farms are 3,252 and 1,605 kg respectively. These estimates are obtained by substituting the mean values of input variables for the unaffected and affected villages into the estimated Cobb-Douglas production function (Method 1). The mean values for the input variables are obtained from Tables 4.9 and 4.10, which provide descriptive statistics for the affected and un-affected villages. Using this method, the average per hectare gain from reducing salinity is estimated to be 1,647 kg.

Table 4.12 suggests that there are indeed welfare gains to be had by reducing soil salinity. These gains can range between INR 1,000 and INR 5,000 per hectare depending on the specification of the production function. Conversely, an examination of affected and un-affected villages at mean input level suggests that the losses could be as high as INR 10,000 per hectare.

The analysis shows the challenges associated with estimating welfare loss for an agricultural community in which paddy cultivation is dominant. These challenges have to do with the underlying assumptions about the physical relationship between salinity and productivity and the methodology used for estimating welfare.

4.11. Conclusion

This study examines the externality effect of shrimp-induced salinity on the productivity of paddy. The data collected shows that the soil salinity status was normal in both Thiruvettakudy and Poovam villages in the period before shrimp farming, which is 1994–1995. Also, an analysis of soil samples taken during 2006 shows that soil salinity is in the normal range in the unaffected village (Thiruvettakudy). In Poovam however, a spatial pattern in soil salinity is observed. In the lands adjoining shrimp farms, the mean EC level is very high and ranges from 4.95 to 15.89 dS m^{-1}, while cultivated lands have an EC range of 0.02 to 3.0 dS m^{-1}.

How have farmers responded to increasing soil salinity? Shifting to direct sown paddy technology has emerged as a coping strategy for dealing with salinity and to manage water scarcity. The shift in paddy production technology is more evident in Poovam, the salinity-affected village. DS paddy constitutes 65 per cent of the total paddy area in this affected village while it accounts for 59 per cent of the total paddy area in Thiruvettakudy. The analysis of farm budgets shows that the returns in Poovam are negative–net losses of INR 5,400 per hectare and INR 4,743 per hectare respectively for transplanted paddy and direct sown paddy. Such losses can certainly not be sustained by Poovam's farmers and their choosing DS over TP is a means to reduce these losses. The comparison with Thiruvettakudy is telling–in this village returns per hectare are INR 4,328 (DS) and INR 6,265 (TP). This situation has forced a few farmers in Poovam to sell their lands.

By estimating paddy production functions with different specifications, it is found that salinity has a negative and statistically significant influence on paddy yield. In the case of the Cobb-Douglas specification, a one per cent increase in EC is associated with a 0.063 per cent decrease in paddy yields. The estimates of gains in paddy yield from reduced salinity increase with the more non-linear specifications of production function.

How can the farmers of Poovam gain from a reduction in soil salinity to safe levels? Data from the cropped areas in Poovam show a maximum salinity level of 3. For those farms that are growing paddy despite being near this salinity level, the average gain would be INR 1,000 to INR 5,000 per hectare depending on the specification of the production function. This average gain is based on an increase in yield of 172 to 836 Kg per hectare. No doubt many farms have not reached this level of salinity, but if conditions do not change then with continued exposure to the effects of being near shrimp farms, they may well reach this level. There is good reason for this expectation, which unfortunately may further burden Poovam's farmers. Some of the lands in Poovam which are not cropped at present may previously have been agriculturally active, with farmers allowing them to lapse into the current state of permanent fallows with high values (6.60) of salinity.

A key agent of change in Thiruvettakudy, the Farmer's Irrigation Society, has been responsible for transforming the village into an agriculturally prosperous community. This institution has brought in farmers' participation in salinity management. This model could serve Poovam, as also other agricultural communities in the coastal tracts of Tamil Nadu and Puducherry well. Salinity control measures like rainwater harvesting, the application of amendments like gypsum based on soil tests, the maintenance and regulation of sluice gates, leaching and drainage can all be employed to lower salinity in Poovam. Monitoring is critical to prevent an increase in salinity over the long term, and will require more frequent and regular soil testing by the authorities.

Is there a case for the region's shrimp farmers to internalize the costs of increased land and water salinity in their neighbourhood? A variety of economic instruments exist that can be used for reducing such externalities. Direct compensation may not be feasible, but a regulatory framework for taxing externalities can be developed which will pull the farmers of Poovam out of a cycle of losses, and bring long-term sustainability to their agricultural efforts.

References

Ahmed, I., 'Why Fishermen Oppose Prawn Farms?' *New Indian Express*, 25th May, 2005, p. 4.

Battacharya, D., Rahman, M., and Khatun, F.A., 'Environmental Impacts of Trade Liberalisation and Policies for the Sustainable Management of Natural Resources: A Case Study on Bangladesh's Shrimp Farming Industry', United Nations Environment Programme, 1999.

Flaherty, M., Vandergeest, P., and Miller, P., 'Rice Paddy or Shrimp Pond: Tough Decisions in Rural Thailand', *World Development*, 27(12), (1999), 2045–2060.

Hattab, K.O., 'Land Use Planning for Management of Agricultural Resources', National Agricultural Technology Project (NATP), Karaikal, PAJANCOA & RI, 2004.

Kolstad, C.D., *Environmental Economics*, (Oxford: Oxford University Press, 2000).

Kumar, A., Birthal, P.S., and Badruddin, 'Technical Efficiency in Shrimp Farming in India: Estimation and Implications', *Indian Journal of Agricultural Economics*, 59(3), (2004), 413.

Naganathan, M., Jothisivagnanam, K. and Rajendran, C., 'Blue Revolution in a Green Belt', *Economic and Political Weekly*, 30(12), (1995), 607–608.

Primavera, J.H., 'Socio-economic Impacts of Shrimp Culture', *Aquaculture Research*, 28, (1997), 815–822.

Statistics of Marine Product Exports: Marine Products Exports Development Authority, (MPEDA), India, 2005.

Thanh, T. B., Canh, L. D., and Brennan, B., 'Environmental Costs of Shrimp Culture in the Rice-growing Regions of the Mekong Delta', *Aquaculture Economics and Management*, 3(1), (1999), 31.

Village Annual Crop Abstracts, Directorate of Economics and Statistics, Karaikal.

5

Evaluating Gains from De-Eutrophication of the Dutch Canal in Sri Lanka

W.R. Rohitha[1]

5.1. Introduction

Farmed shrimp is a cash crop that earns valuable foreign exchange to Sri Lanka, even though it contributes to only two per cent of world production. According to reports of the Department of Customs, shrimp exports accounted for 50 per cent of the total fisheries exports from Sri Lanka in the late nineties. The rapid growth of the industry in Sri Lanka which is concentrated in the North Western Province of Sri Lanka, has been mainly owing to initiatives of the private sector with no government support (Rohitha, 1997). Global shrimp production has grown at a phenomenal rate of 20–30 per cent per year in recent times with countries in Asia contributing to 70 per cent of world production.

The Dutch canal associated wetland system in Sri Lanka has emerged as one of the most economically important wetlands due to shrimp farming. Since the1980s, shrimp farming in the Dutch Canal has rapidly developed without any planning or coordination (Rohitha, 1997). There are more than 1300 farms covering a land area of 3750 hectares (Siriwardena, 1999) while 48 per cent of the farms (covering 40 per cent of the developed area) are illegal and unauthorized. The haphazard development of the industry has resulted in high eutrophication of the lagoon system contributing

[1] Financial support for this study is acknowledged to the South Asian Network for Development and Environmental Economics (SANDEE). I am grateful to Priya Shyamsundar, Herath Gunatilake, Hemasiri Kotagama, Partha Dasgupta, Karl-Goran Maler, and M. N Murty for valuable comments and guidance and to S. Madheswaran for advice on the econometric analysis.

to a decline in the shrimp industry's output as well as a decrease in the lagoon's fish harvest. The shrimp industry faces frequent disease outbreaks resulting in low productivity, which could be mainly attributed to the self-imposed pollution of its source of water. The shrimp industry was in debt to financial institutions for over LKR one billion due to capital investments and LKR 700 million of accumulated loan interest[2] towards the end of the twentieth century. Any further disease outbreaks would jeopardize these investments as well as the employment of over 40,000 people connected directly or indirectly to the industry. The lagoon fishermen are also badly affected by the eutrophication of lagoon water.

In 1999, the Government of Sri Lanka gave in to representations made by the shrimp farmers and prepared a proposal for the resuscitation of the Dutch canal. The main aim of the project was to clean the Dutch canal such that it recovers from the eutrophication and attains normal lagoon conditions. The total cost of this project was estimated at LKR 180 million. However, the project has yet to commence because of uncertainties related to its benefits. Thus, it is quite important to understand and value the output losses in the Dutch Canal that result from the current high pollution level and the possible benefits from resuscitation.

Shrimp farming and its consequences

Shrimp farming though seemingly viable for individual farms, can create significant negative externalities at the overall system level. It is important to analyze the extent of losses incurred as a result of such externalities. Such a study would be particularly important since the shrimp industry is likely to expand to the North Eastern Coast of Sri Lanka, which is considered as a 'high potential' area for commercial shrimp farming. With political peace, this area may witness large scale development in coastal aquaculture. Coastal aquaculture development however needs to be analysed in terms of its ecological impact on the Dutch canal wetland system. This would help the development of guidelines for coastal aquaculture in other parts of Sri Lanka.

The shrimp industry faces water pollution problems because individual producers do not treat their emission before discharge into the Dutch canal, from which fish farms draw raw water. Unfortunately, planning authorities have not analyzed the aggregate impact of untreated effluents emissions

---

[2] The conversion rate is approximately US $1 equals to LKR 100.

by farms on the quality of canal (Neiland et al., 2001). Generally speaking, the production area should be limited by keeping in mind the absorption capacity of the lagoon and the externality that each farm creates by polluting the lagoon. Planning authorities could play an important role by (a) demarcating shrimp production areas, (b) limiting effluent emission to the carrying capacity of the canal, and (c) educating shrimp farmers about the effects of lagoon pollution on their productivity. While techniques to study impacts are available, few such studies appear in the case of shrimp culture literature (Neiland et al., 2001). The study of the environmental effects of wetland use in Sri Lanka is also inadequate (2001). The present study attempts to fill this gap by valuing the environmental services of improved water quality in the Dutch canal wetland system. The value of clean water is assessed as an input to shrimp farming, which is a pointer to the economic viability of rehabilitating the Dutch canal.

5.2. Study area and data

The Dutch canal is a brackish water wetland that connects three lagoons in the Puttalam district in the north-western coastal region of Sri Lanka. The Dutch canal wetland covers a 30 km wide strip at its maximum and is 172 km in length. The climate is tropical with low variation in temperature and high variation in rainfall.[3] The Dutch Canal can be divided into three sections – Wattala/Modera to Negambo lagoon, Negambo lagoon to Madampe and Madampe to Puttalam lagoon. The section of the canal from Madampe to Puttalam lagoon is the focus in this chapter. The length of the Dutch Canal studied is 61 kilometers and the depth of the canal has a high variation and is location dependent.

This Canal, as the name suggests, was constructed during the Dutch colonial period (between 1658 and 1795) to transport goods. The canal connects Colombo to Puttalam and was constructed by linking different water bodies. During the Dutch and British colonial periods, the canal served as a major transport route. However, after the construction of a railway line from Colombo to Puttalam in 1926, this water route was abandoned. After the commencement of shrimp farming in the early part of the 1980s, this area was rapidly transformed into an economically vibrant region.

---

[3] The major part of the study area south of the Mundel lagoon is in the Intermediate Zone, which has an annual rainfall of 1,000 to 1,500 mm while and the area north of the Mundel lagoon is in the Dry Zone with an annual rainfall less than 1,000 mm.

5.2.1. Study area

Shrimp farming is the major commercial activity in this wetlands system. Lagoon fishery and cattle rearing are the other traditional economic activities that provide substantial income to the inhabitants of the region. Mangrove vegetation, salt marshes and sea grass beds are the ecologically important ecosystems associated with the Dutch canal system (Rohitha, 1991 and 1997). The vegetation prior to the development of shrimp farms is reported in the topographic maps of 1984 as being mainly composed of aquatic mangrove habitats, marsh and barren lands, sand dunes and shores. With the expansion of shrimp farms, land use in the area has changed. An estimated 1,500 hectares of mangroves cover have been cleared to construct shrimp farms, adversely affecting the natural balance of the ecosystem.

Shrimp farms use the Dutch Canal and associated water bodies as the principal source of water. A very high concentration of shrimp farms is found along the Dutch Canal, especially from Thoduwawa to Mundel lagoon. The water salinity and soil conditions of this area are conducive to shrimp farming. The supernormal profits in this industry during the 1980s attracted many investors and led, in turn, to a rapid expansion in farms. Most of the lands along the canal are either Crown or government lands and were rented by private companies and individuals to establish shrimp farms. At the time of leasing these lands, the government imposed different conditions with the intention of protecting the natural ecosystem of the area. However, due to the poor supervision and monitoring by authorities, shrimp farms gradually started to violate these conditions.

Shrimp farms in the area can be categorized into two major groups – industrial and backyard systems. Industrial shrimp farms usually cover a large area and have individual ponds of equal size arranged in an orderly way, rectangular in shape with an average dimensions of 30 × 50 meters. Industrial shrimp farms are usually surrounded by high walls or fences. Backyard shrimp farms on the other hand cover smaller areas while the the ponds vary in size and shape. Dykes surrounding individual ponds are less prominent than those in industrial shrimp farms. The shape of the farm is somewhat irregular as it exploits natural contours along creeks and canals.

5.2.2. Survey design and data collection

Both primary and secondary data have been used for this study. Pollution data was collected from the National Aquatic Resources Research and

Development Agency (NARA) which has been collecting water quality data [such as P^H, Dissolved Oxygen, Ammonia, Nitrate, Nitrite, Biological Oxygen Demand(BOD), Total Suspended Solid (TSS), salinity etc.] at ten monitoring points along the Dutch Canal since 1990. Five of these monitoring points, Ambakandawila, Bangadeniya, Chilaw, Karukupone, and Palavi, were purposively chosen for this study. The reason for selecting these sites was that at least five shrimp farms around the monitoring station had written records of feed and production. The farms chosen were those that operated as a company or partnership since they kept records for administrative and accounting purposes. This limited the sample size to 25 farms, even though a large number of shrimp farms presently operate in the Puttalam District. During the field survey it was found that approximately two-thirds of the shrimp farms in the Puttalam District were quite small (averaging between three to five ponds) and operate illegally. These farms usually do not keep written records of any kind.

The primary survey collected data on production and feed from these 25 shrimp farms. These farms typically have 15 to 20 ponds and in certain cases, even 35 to 40 ponds. Records are maintained separately, pond–wise. For purposes of this study, each pond is regarded as a sub-farm and the sample includes 700 observed ponds. Pond-wise data was obtained on shrimp yield or harvest, feed used, number of Post-larvae (PL) seed used per pond per hectare and such other information. In order to determine levels of pollution in the Dutch Canal water, ammonia content was used as a proxy for water quality. Data on ammonia concentration for the period 1995–2003 across the five monitoring points mentioned above was taken from NARA, Sri Lanka and the Aquaculture Service Centre of the Provincial Fisheries Ministry, North Western Province, Sri Lanka.

5.3. Water quality valuation techniques

The economic value of water quality improvements in the Dutch Canal is estimated using the production function method[4]. This technique estimates the value of non-market goods such as environmental quality, which is an input in the production of a marketable commodity, by valuing its physical contribution to the economic output. Production functions are widely used to estimate the impact of deforestation, soil erosion, wetlands and reef destruction, air and water pollution etc., on productive activities such

---

[4] Vincent describes this method in Chapter 3.

as crop cultivation, fishing, hunting etc. (Freeman, 1993; Gunethilake, 2003; Barbier et al., 2002). These have also been used to value the impact of environmental changes on the agricultural sector (Kopp et al., 1985). Shrimp farming is similar to agriculture in the sense that it produces an aqua-cultural crop with water quality as an input. Thus, this approach is similar to the analyses undertaken in the previous chapter on paddy externalities.

Estimation of the value of the water quality in shrimp production has two steps – (a) Estimating the production function, the physical relationship between water quality and shrimp production. Using this function, the change in fish production due to changes in water quality can be predicted, and (b) Imputing a monetary value to this change in production. Since shrimp is a private good, the value of water quality change is obtained by multiplying the change in production of shrimp by its market price (Kotagama, 1998).

Methodology

A generalized neoclassical production function is used for estimating the productivity changes in shrimp farming due to pollution. This production function includes lagoon water quality as an input (representing levels of pollution) along with other conventional inputs like capital and labour. Assuming that there are 'N' numbers of shrimp farms in the Dutch Canal area the production function of the ith farm is given as:

$$Y_i = f_i(K_i, L_i, S_i, M_i, Q) \tag{1}$$

where

$$Q = \sum_{i=1}^{N-1} q_i \tag{2}$$

and

    Y_i: Shrimp production by i^{th} farm

    K_i: Capital investment of ith farm

    L_i: Labour of ith farm

    S_i: Seeds used by i^{th} farm

    M_i: Material inputs of ith farm including feed

Q : Aggregate Pollution level of the canal

q_i : Pollution (effluents) released by the ith farm

The water pollution by one farm affects other farms. Therefore in this model it is assumed that the externality of pollution is of the reciprocal type. The incremental pollution of lagoon at a particular monitoring point is the sum total of pollution from all the neighbourhood farms. This incremental pollution plus the pollution that is already present in the lagoon from the upstream farms will determine the quality of water at the monitoring point.

Typically, one would anticipate, in a Nash type equilibrium, the model to have an interactive pollution component between the ith farm and the other farms. However, it is assumed here that the individual pond's own emission is very small in comparison with the aggregate emission of other ponds and farms in the neighbourhood and is therefore inconsequential for its own production. The farm behaves as a pollution-taker (similar to a perfectly competitive firm who is a price-taker). It is affected by the aggregate pollution of all other farms since that affects the water quality it receives at the pond gate. The ith farm cannot however influence the jth farm's pollution decision by its individual action. The jth farm would not change its own pollution strategy based on what the ith farm does in this period.

As a first step the marginal product (partial derivative of Yield) is derived with respect to pollution (Q), which has a negative effect on the production of the ith farm:

$$\frac{\partial Y_i}{\partial Q}\left(K_i^*, L_i^*, S_i^*, M_i^*, Q\right) \leq 0 \tag{3}$$

Given the level of pollution (Q) in the lagoon at the point where the farm draws the water, the shrimp farmer chooses other inputs so that its profits are maximized. A decline in water quality of the lagoon adversely affects the farm's productivity and profits. If the market price of shrimps is 'P', then the monetary value of environmental quality is the product of P and the marginal productivity of lagoon water quality. This is estimated as below:

Marginal value of clean water

$$= P\frac{\partial Y_i}{\partial Q}\left(K_i^*, L_i^*, S_i^*, M_i^*, Q\right) \tag{4}$$

Estimation of shrimp yield function

The yield function of shrimp farms is estimated in line with the mathematical model set up above. The yield of shrimp farms depends on variable inputs such as feed, seeds (post larvae), and quality of the water intake (pollution level).

According to De Silva and Jayasinghe (1993), the shares of the production cost associated with various inputs in shrimp farming are 55 per cent for feed, 25 per cent for fuel, 12.5 per cent for seed, 4.3 per cent for labour, one per cent for fertilizer, and one per cent for harvesting effort while the rest are miscellaneous expenses. Most of the shrimp farms in Sri Lanka operate as cottage enterprises and maintain proper pond-specific records only for feeding and stocking, which are useful for them to determine the harvesting schedule. The records for labour and fuel expenses are unreliable since they are not recorded systematically by the farms. Therefore, labour and fuel were excluded from the empirical yield function. As the fertilizer and harvesting effort constituted less than one per cent of the production cost, they were also excluded from the empirical yield function. The quality (pollution level) of the water intake in different seasons was included in the yield function as an exogenous variable. Two seasons are considered – the first six months (January–June) are labelled as Season One and the remaining six months (July–December) are labelled as Season Two. Concentration of toxic ammonia, hydrogen sulphide, nitrates and nitrites, and Biological Oxygen Demand (BOD) are the common measures used to assess the pollution level of water bodies. Ideally, a pollution index representing the level of pollution in the lagoon could be constructed but there is no accepted way to determine the weights for each pollutant in this index. However, since shrimp is most sensitive to the concentration of toxic ammonia, ammonia is taken to be representative of the pollution level. As the concentration of ammonia varies along the Dutch Canal, a series of dummy variables is used in this model to pick up the effects of pond location on the shrimp yield.

$$Y_i = f_i(F_i, S_i, Q, T, D) \tag{5}$$

where:

Y_i: Shrimp production by i^{th} farm

F_i: Feed used by i^{th} farm

S_i: Seeds/post larvae used by i^{th} farm

Q: Pollution level (Water quality) in the Dutch Canal

T: Season (Dummy variable)

D: Location (Dummy variable)

The production function is given in equation (5) and the estimated equation in equation (6) below. This is a modified version of the standard Cobb Douglas production function. It considers the possibility of non-linear relationships between seed and shrimp production on the one hand, and between pollution and shrimp production on the other. It presumes that shrimp production is exponentially related to water pollution.

$$LnY_i = \alpha_0 + \alpha_1 LnF_i + \alpha_2 LnS_i + \alpha_3 LnS_i^2 + \alpha_4 Q + \alpha_5 T \qquad (6)$$
$$+ \beta_1 D_1 + \beta_2 D_2 + \beta_3 D_3 + \beta_4 D_4$$

Table 5.1 describes the variables used in the estimation, the expected signs of their coefficients and the sources of data. Table 5.2 presents the descriptive statistics of the variables used in the production function analyses – yield, stocking density and feeding intensity (and level of pollution) at each monitoring site. The highest average yield was recorded at Palavi (2293 Kg per ha) and the lowest yield was recorded at Ambakandawila (1569 Kg per ha). However, the highest and lowest stocking densities were recorded at Bangadeniya (110237 PL/ha) and Karukapone (68716.46 PL/ha). The highest and lowest feed used were at Bangadeniya (3517 Kg/ha) and Ambakandawila (2454 Kg/ha). The findings are within the ranges recorded in other studies (see for example, Corea et al., 1995).

Table 5.1. Description of variables

Variables	Description	Expected sign	Source
	Dependent Variable		
Yield	Harvest from each pond in Kg/ha		Farm Records
	Independent Variables		
Feed	Feed used for entire culture cycle, Kg/ha	Positive	Farm Records
Seeds	Number of Post larvae/seed stocked in the pond per hectare	Positive	Farm Records
Water Quality (pollution level)	Concentration of toxic ammonia at the referral sampling point (ppm)	Negative	NARA and Aquaculture Services Centre –NWP

(Contd.)

(Contd.)

Variables	Description	Expected sign	Source
Season	Dummy variable, T= 1 for the second half of the year (July-December), = 0 otherwise	Unknown	Farm records
Location	Four dummy variables were used to capture location effect on shrimp production. D_1 = 1 if Ambakandawila (Amb), = 0 otherwise; D_2 = 1 if Bangadeniya (Ban), = 0 otherwise; D_3 =1 if Chilaw (Chi), = 0 otherwise; D_4 = 1 if Karukapone (Kar) = 0, otherwise; Palavi (Pal) is the default dummy.	Unknown	

Table 5.2 Descriptive statistics of variables

MONI-TORING STATION	YIELD (Kg / ha)	SEED (Pl/ha)	FEED (kg/ha)	AREA (Hectare)	WQ (ppm)	Number of Obs. (N)
Amb	1569.2 (1107.6)	104948 (20432.9)	2454.6 (1559.3)	6658.3 (1139.2)	.19 (.16)	50
Ban	2152.11 (1548.6)	110237.2 (43776.4)	3517.9 (2284.9)	5659.7 (2752.27)	.12 (8.25E-02)	242
Chi	1796.9 (788.6)	91666.7 (24870.9)	2686.1 (1091.7)	5243.8 (1404.9)	.14 (.10284)	90
Kar	1667.1 (916.3)	68716.5 (30534.2)	2751.5 (1719.9)	5940.8 (9990.08)	9.40E-02 (.11714)	286
Pal	2293.5 (664.4)	90272.7 (23894.7)	3288.8 (1238.4)	5281.8 (1413.65)	.28 (5.18E-02)	33
Total	1873.7 (1188.5)	89595.9 (38937.9)	3011.8 (1884.02)	5774.4 (6617.7)	.12 (.1)	701

Note: Mean and Standard Deviation (in brackets) for all variables

5.4. Analysis of results

The regression results of the production function are presented in Table 5.4. As expected, seed and feed have a positive effect and water pollution has a negative effect on shrimp yield. The coefficients of seed, feed, and water pollution are statistically significant at the one per cent level. The coefficient of seed, i.e., the number of Post Larvae (PL) introduced into a square meter of a given pond (stocking density) is positive while that of its square is negative and both are statistically significsant. This suggests that the shrimp yield (yield per hectare) is increasing at a decreasing rate as stocking density increases. It also confirms a known fact in shrimp farming practice that an increase in stocking densities in turn increases the yield but at a decreasing rate.

Feed, the most important factor of production in the shrimp industry, has a coefficient that is significant at 0.01 level. The elasticity of shrimp yield with respect to feed is 0.83 and the estimated Feed Conversion Ratio (FCR) of the shrimp industry in the study area is 1.6.[5] Though shrimp are not efficient feed converters (Csavas, 1994), the FCR recorded here are high which suggests that there is an un-utilized quantity of feed in the pond. This is the main cause of water pollution. Thus, for every kilogram of shrimp produced, more than a matching amount of organic matter is released to the environment as dry matter content.[6] If 50 per cent of this effluent is assumed to be solid waste, then more than 500 grams of organic matter in dissolved form is released into the environment. According to Edirisinghe et al. (1997), the crude protein content of the shrimp feed is generally 35–40 per cent. This suggests that for every kilogram of shrimp produced, a minimum of 30 grams of Nitrogen (according to standard calculations, the Nitrogen content of crude protein is 16 per cent) is released into the Dutch canal. This is the main cause of eutrophication of the Dutch canal.

The results also suggest that the season has no impact on output though different season have some variations in ambient temperature and rainfall. Four intercept dummy variables were used to distinguish between the five monitoring stations – *Ambakandawila, Bangadeniya, Chilaw, Karukapone and Palavi* (control dummy). The shrimp yield at the first four locations is significantly lower than at *Palavi*. While *Palavi* records the highest yield, *Bangadeniya* had the lowest yield, everything else remaining the same. The results suggest that locational differences such as soil type, salinity levels of the canal, water flow rate of the canal and more importantly the concentration of farms in the particular areas do matter. Bangadeniya area has the highest farm density among the five locations while Palavi has the lowest density.

---

[5] Feed Conversion Ratio is defined as amount of feed required (kg) to gain one kg weight of bio mass.

[6] In the shrimp farms, 1.6 Kg of feed is used to produce one kg of shrimps by the farms. The dry matter content of one kg shrimp is approximately 300 grams. Shrimp feed has about 95 per cent of dry matter. Thus approximately 1.2 kg of dry matter is released when one kg of shrimp is produced.

Table 5.3. Estimated shrimps yield function

Independent Variable	Coefficient	t-Values
Log (seed)	0.1478068***	4.01
Log (seed square)	−0.048780***	−3.24
Log (feed)	0.8343413***	38.45
Water quality	−0.6375154***	−4.16
Season	−0.0139276	−0.57
Ambakandawila (monitoring point 1)	−0.2493378***	−3.28
Bangadeniya (monitoring point 2)	−0.3068635***	−4.92
Chilaw (monitoring point 3)	−0.2329436***	−3.50
Karukapone (monitoring point 4)	−0.2584816***	−4.00
Constant	−0.2287412	−0.62
R-square	0.7389	
Adjusted R-square	0.7145	
F (9, 659)	381.25	
Number of Observation	668	

Note: *** Significant at 1per cent level. Dependent variable = log (yield per hectare)

Table 5.4. Gains from improving water quality to a safe level in the Dutch Canal

	Amount
Predicted value of yield per hectare based on current level of pollution (Y_1 hat)	1874.135 Kg
Predicted value of yield per hectare based on safe level of pollution (Y_2 hat)	2001.529 Kg
Incremental output per hectare due to water quality improvement from current level to safe level (Y_2 hat − Y_1 hat)	127.394 Kg
Incremental revenue per hectare (price x incremental output)	LKR 81,532.16
Incremental profit of water quality improvement for the total extent of shrimp farms in the Puttalam District (incremental profit x total area under shrimp farming, which is 2,000 hectares for both seasons)	LKR 163,064,320

A key result is the statistically significant negative relationship between water pollution and yield. The incremental per hectare yield from improving the water quality of canal can be estimated by comparing the yields with and without water pollution. Before the shrimp industry started operating, the water quality of the Dutch canal is assumed to have been at the safe level of 0.075 ppm. The current average water quality of the canal is 0.125 ppm. The (estimated) yield function can be used to predict the output of shrimp for different levels of pollution in the canal. The predicted per hectare yields at pollution levels of 0.125 ppm and 0.075 ppm are 1874.1 Kg and 2001.5 Kg respectively (see Table 5.4). Therefore, farm productivity per hectare is likely to increase by 127.4 Kg if water quality improves from the current level to the safe level.

Monetary estimates of gains from water quality improvement

The estimates of physical reductions in yield due to water pollution (as obtained above) can be combined with data on shrimp prices to get monetary estimates of damages due to pollution in the Dutch canal. This would enable a Cost benefit Analysis of the proposed De-Eutrophication programme by the government. As a first step, average annual market price, cost of production of shrimp and average of annual shrimp production in the Puttalam District are obtained from published and unpublished data on the shrimp industry for the period 1990 to 2003. The average market price of shrimp was LKR 640 per kg while the average cost of shrimp production was LKR 410 per kg. About 2,000 hectares of area are annually used for shrimp culture in the Puttalam District (this is the aggregate area cultivated in the first and second season). The current production per hectare stands at 1874.1 kg and the predicted output under clean conditions is 2001.5 kg. This would mean an increase in output per hectare of 127.4 kgs. Using this data, the incremental farm revenue per hectare from water quality improvement of canal is estimated at LKR 81,532.16. The extrapolation of incremental revenue from pollution reduction to all ponds covering 2000 hectares in the study area provides an estimate of annual benefits equal to LKR 163.064 million (see Table 5.4).

Since canal pollution in this study is mainly attributable to excessive (more than optimal) use of feed, an awareness programme that incentivizes farmers to use an optimal level of feed could in fact result in additional profits (cost saving) to the farmers. As discussed earlier, the estimated project cost of de-eutrophication of the Dutch Canal is LKR 180 million. The findings clearly show that resuscitation of the Dutch canal is economically feasible and the benefits that the cleaning project would generate could be recovered within two years even at a ten per cent discount rate, without affecting the present profitability of the farmers.

5.5. Conclusion and policy implications

Untreated effluent emission from shrimp farms into the Dutch canal has increased the level of water pollution and adversely affected the survival of the shrimp industry in the Puttalm district of Sri Lanka. Over time the profits of the shrimp industry have declined, and incomes of local fishermen have been affected by the eutrophication of the Dutch canal system.

Sustainable development of aquaculture requires an ecological system with unpolluted water and a continuous supply of post larvae shrimp. This requires controlled and 'cleaner' aqua-cultural practices. This study suggests that a less polluted Dutch canal would increase productivity by 127 Kg of shrimp per hectare.

There is a proposal to rehabilitate the Dutch canal which is expected to cost LKR 180 million. It is found that the benefits from enhanced shrimp production from cleaning the Dutch Canal would help recover the costs of clean up in a short period (less than two years). This may also create opportunities for increased profits in the future and would ensure the continued survival and growth of the shrimp farms. This would ensure continued to employment workers in the industry, in addition to ecological benefits that would accrue from rehabilitating the Dutch Canal.

In order to control further pollution, the government needs to regulate effluent discharge into the Dutch canal. Earlier attempts by the Government were unsuccessful due to the insufficient of resources and authority vested in the regulating institutions. Thus, the Government's monitoring and implementation framework needs to be further strengthened.

A well-managed shrimp industry can also bring much needed infrastructure to backward areas. The government has recently announced that shrimp farming will be introduced to the southern parts of the country. Therefore, there is a pressing to come up with a coherent national policy agreeable to all stakeholders.

There are many stakeholders in the case of the Dutch canal – shrimp farmers, labourers, the general public sharing a concerns for bio-diversity, and the government. The conservation of the Dutch canal will result in a win-win situation for all the stakeholders.

References

Barbier, E., Acreman M., and Knowler, D., *Economic Valuation of Wetlands – A Guide for Policy Makers and Planners* (Ramsar and IUCN: Gland, 1997).

Barbier, E., Strand, I., and SathiraThai, S. 'Do Open Access Conditions Affect the Valuation of an Externality? Estimating Welfare Effects of Mangrove-Fishery Linkages in Thailand', *Environmental and Resource Economics*, 21, (2002), 343–367.

Barbier, E.B., 'Valuing the Environment as Input: Applications to Mangrove-Fishery Linkages', *Ecological Economics*, 35, (2000), 47–61.

Csavas, I., 'Important Factors in the Success of Shrimp Farming, *World Aquaculture*, 25(1), (1994), 34–56.

Corea, A.S.L.E., Jayasinghe, J.M.P.K., Ekarathne, S.U.K., and Johnston, R., 'Environmental Impact of Prawn Farming on Dutch Canal : The Main Water Source for the Prawn Culture Industry in Sri Lanka', *Ambio*, 24 (7–8), (1995).

Corea, A.S.L.E., Jayasinghe, J.M.P.K., Ekarathne, S.U.K., Johnston, R., and Jayawardena, K., 'Self Pollution: A Major Threat to the Prawn Farming Industry in Sri Lanka', *Ambio*, 27(8), (1998).

De Silva, J.A. and Jayasinghe, J.M.P.K., 'The Technology and Economics of Small-scale Commercial Shrimp Farms in the West Coast of Sri Lanka', *Journal of Tropical Aquaculture*, 8, (1993).

Edirisinghe U., Jayasinghe, J.M.P.K., and Wannigama, J.P., 'Evaluation of Presently Practiced Water Exchange Rates on the Black Tiger Prawns and on the Water Quality in Semi- intensive Culture System of Sri lanka, *j. aquat.sci.*, 2, (1997), 55–59.

Freeman, A.M., *The Measurements of Environment & Resource Values: Theory and Methods*, (Washington DC: Resources for the Future, 1993).

Gunethilake, H., *Environmental Valuation: Theory and Applications*, Post Graduate Institute of Agriculture, Sri Lanka : University of Peradeniya, 2003.

Jayasinghe, J.M.P.K., 'Shrimp Aquaculture and Environment', Sri Lanka Study Report, A Regional Study and Workshop on Aquaculture Sustainability and Environment, Beijing, October 1995.

Jayasinghe, J.M.P.K., and Macintosh, D.J., 'Disease Outbreaks in Shrimp Culture Grow-out Systems of Sri Lanka', *Tropical Agricultural Research*, 5, (1993).

Jayasinghe, J.M.P.K., and De Silva, J.A., 'Prawn Culture Development and Present Land use Pattern in Coastal Areas of Sri Lanka', Proceedings of International and Interdisciplinary Symposium Ecology and Landscape Management in Sri Lanka, 1990.

Jayasinghe, J.M.P.K. and Wijesekara, R.G.S., 'Brackish Water Shrimp Culture in Sri Lanka: Technical, Environmental and Social Concepts', National Aquatic Resources Research and Development Agency, Colombo, Sri Lanka, 2000.

Jayasinghe, S., 'An Economic and Environmental Analysis in Sri Lanka', *Energy and Environmental Economic Series No. 9*, Institute of Policy Studies, Colombo, Sri Lanka, 2001.

Kopp, R.J., Vaughan, W.J., Hazilla, M. and Carson, R., 'Implications of Environmental Policy for US Agriculture: the Case of Ambient Ozone Standards', *Journal of Environmental Management*, 20, (1985), 321–331.

Kotagama, H., 'Estimates of Environmental Unit Values in Sri Lanka Applicable to Extended Benefit-cost Analysis of Investment Projects', Postgraduate Institute of Agriculture, Sri Lanka: University of Peradeniya, 1998.

Neiland, A.E., Soley, N., Varley, J.B., Whitmarsh, D.J., 'Shrimp Aquaculture: Economic Perspectives for Policy Development', *Marine Policy*, 25, 2001, 265–279.

Rohitha, W.R., 'Prawn Culture in Arachchikattuwa AGA Division', a dissertation in partial fulfillment of Postgraduate Diploma in regional Industrial Development, RIDE XII, Sri Lanka, NIBM, Sri Lanka and RVB, Netherlands, 1991.

Rohitha, W. R., 'Strengthening the Institutional Framework to Promote Coastal Aquaculture of North Western Province, Sri Lanka', A M.Sc. thesis, AIT, Bangkok, 1997.

Siriwardene, P.P.G.S.N., 'Report on Code of Good Practices for Shrimp Aquaculture in Sri Lanka' (Draft), National Aquatic Resources Research and Development Agency, Colombo, Sri Lanka, 1999.

6

Pesticide Productivity and Vegetable Farming in Nepal

Ratna Kumar Jha and *Adhrit Prasad Regmi*[1]

6.1. Introduction

Vegetable producers around the world heavily rely on the use of chemical pesticides to ensure pest control. Although pesticides do not directly contribute to agricultural yields, there is evidence to suggest that intensive use of pesticides has significantly increased agricultural production (Brethour and Weersink, 2001). However, pesticide use also poses risks to human health and the environment (Travisi et al., 2006). Thus, it is important to examine the trade-offs associated with the costs and benefits of pesticides under different empirical contexts.

Several studies show that there are significant social and environmental costs to pesticide use (Ajayi, 2000; Antle and Pingali, 1994; Antle and Capalbo, 1994, Rola and Pingali, 1993). Some of these studies (Rola and Pingali, 1993; Rahman, 2002) also suggest that indiscriminate pesticide use can lead to larger pest-related yield losses relative to situations where pesticides are not applied. In the absence of pest attacks, pesticide use only results in extra costs and no real benefits. Nevertheless, in the hope of combating the problem of pests, farmers frequently apply high doses

[1] The authors are thankful to the South Asian Network for Development and Environmental Economics (SANDEE) for financial support and expert advice. We are grateful to Priya Shyamsundar, A.K. Enamul Haque, P. Mukhopadhyay, S. Madheswaran and Mani Nepal for their critical encouragement. We record our appreciation of the support of Kavita Shrestha and Anuradha Kafle of the SANDEE Secretariat for providing the administrative support towards completing this study. Finally, we would like to thank all the enumerators and respondents for their endurance and cooperation.

and disproportionate combinations of several pesticides, contributing to a pesticide treadmill in certain areas (Shetty, 2003). Farmers in developing countries in particular continue to use pesticides at increasing rates (WRI, 1998).

Pesticides do not enhance productivity directly like other standard factors of production such as land, labour and capital. Rather, they help farmers compete against pests that would otherwise reduce agricultural output. Thus, pesticides are a class of damage control agents (Babcock et al., 1992), making them different from other inputs in agriculture (Lichtenberg and Zilberman, 1986). This central issue needs to be recognized in developing a pesticide use policy (Chambers and Lichtenberg, 1994). It is also important for empirical studies that seek to evaluate pesticide use.

Given the damage control role of pesticides, it is useful to examine the empirical evidence on the marginal contribution of pesticides to agricultural yield. Marginal productivity estimates reported in different studies differ sharply. In the case of cotton, Ajayi (2000), for example, estimates the Marginal Value Product (MVP) per CFA[2] of pesticide to be in the range from 4.39 to 0.47 for different functional specifications. A marginal value product per unit cost of pesticides greater than unity implies that pesticides are under-utilized and farmers can increase their profitability by increasing the amount of pesticides from the current level (see Figure 6.1). In another study, Prabhu (1985) reports the MVP to be less than unity, i.e., INR 0.13 per rupee cost of pesticide. However, such conclusions on the value of the marginal productivity of pesticides can depend on the functional specification of the model.

In this study, the use of pesticides in Nepal is examined. The use of pesticide on vegetable crops in Nepal has increased dramatically in recent years (Maharjan et al., 2004). However, it is worth noting that the average use of pesticides in Nepal, which is at 142 g/ha (ADB, cited in Dahal 1995) is rather low in comparison to that of India (500 gm/ha), Japan (12 kg/ha), or Korea (6.6 kg/ha) (Gupta, 2004). Pesticide use is heavily concentrated in the cultivation of vegetables, mustard and cotton in Nepal. Its use is more intensive in the Terai[3] region and in the Kathmandu valley and its surrounding areas where agriculture is commercialized.

---

[2] CFA stands for Communauté Financière Africaine (French-speaking African Financial Community): 550 CFA=1 US$.

[3] The flat area in the southern part of Nepal from the Churiya Mountain range to the Indian Border is termed the Terai.

Despite a rapid increase in pesticide use in vegetable farming, no study thus far has evaluated the productivity of pesticides in vegetable farming in Nepal. Two studies that come close in terms of the topic under study are a household survey (Pujara and Khanal, 2002) and a socio-economic study (Shrestha and Neupane, 2002) conducted in the Kavre district of Nepal. These studies have shown that profits from vegetables farming (potato, tomato, bitter gourd and chilli) where pesticides are used, are higher than other crops grown in the same area. But these studies have either adopted a production function approach (considering pesticides as a normal yield-enhancing input) or relied on a partial budget analysis. It is noted that 'productivity' estimates using pesticides as a yield-enhancing input in the production process are suspect because the 'productivity' of pesticides is actually derived only when a crop is infested with pests. Using a conventional production function approach may result in biased estimations of the impacts of pesticides on yields (Lichtenberg and Zilberman, 1986). Thus, the main objective of this chapter is to understand the economics of pesticide use in vegetable crops in Nepal under a damage control framework. The data from a sample of Cole crop[4] growing households in the Bhaktapur district of Nepal is used for the analysis.

One aspect that researchers must take into consideration while studying pesticide use is the Integrated Pest Management (IPM) approach in farming.[5] IPM training, which involves ecological education and information on pesticides, has been promoted in many countries. Irham (2001) and Irham and Mariyono (2001) have found that the IPM programme has significantly reduced the use of pesticides in rice and soybean farming in Indonesia. Similarly, Upadhyaya (2003) reported that the use of pesticides decreased by 40 per cent in almost all National IPM programme areas in Nepal. In Nepal, IPM is introduced through the Farmer Field School (FFS) training programme of the Department of Agriculture.[6] The general understanding

---

[4] Cauliflower and cabbage are the cole crops considered in this study. Cauliflower and cabbage belong to the same species (*Brassica oleracea*) of the *Brassicaceae* family. Both of these crops have more or less similar growing seasons, cultivation practices and pest problems. Farmers apply similar types of plant protection measures for both of these crops.

[5] IPM means the careful consideration of all available pest control techniques and subsequent integration of appropriate measures that discourage the development of pest populations and keep pesticides and other interventions to levels that are economically justified and reduce or minimize risks to human health and the environment (FAO, 2002)

[6] FFS has now become the model approach for educating farmers in Asia and Latin America (Ponitus et al., 2000). IPM education through FFS focuses on the location specific issues of agro-ecology; resisting generalization and blanket recommendation of pesticides use (Dilt, 1990).

is that the frequency of pesticide applications by farmers has decreased after attendance at FFS. These findings are based on case studies and individual FFS reports which mainly focus on the rice agro-ecosystem. In this study, the effect of IPM training on pesticide use in Cole crop production is also examined.

6.2. Pesticide use in agriculture: a review

During the last three decades, a number of empirical studies[7] have attempted to measure the productivity of chemical pesticides in agriculture. These studies can be categorized into two broad groups depending upon the methods used (Ajayi, 2000). One group uses the generic Cobb-Douglas production functions and the other uses a variant of it by taking into consideration the unique characteristics of pesticides. The findings of some of the studies are presented in Appendix 6.1. Almost all of the first generation studies (Headley, 1968; Campbell, 1976; Carlson, 1977), which evaluate the economic performance of pesticides within the production function framework using non-linear functional forms, conclude that the value of the marginal product of pesticides exceeds marginal factor costs implying that the current level of pesticide use is lower than the optimum. However, there are reasons to believe that pesticide productivity may be overestimated because of the choice of functions used in the study. Lichtenberg and Zilberman (1986), for example, argue that first generation studies may have failed to capture the damage control nature of pesticides in the model specification. Furthermore, Fox and Weersink (1995) explain how corner solutions can arise in the use of damage control inputs, meaning that marginal value products may not equal marginal factor costs at optimal use. They also explain why farmers may not be particularly responsive to prices in their use of pesticides.

Lichtenberg and Zilberman (1986) suggest that the contribution of damage control agents to production may be better understood if one conceives of actual (realized) output as a *net* result of two interdependent components – potential yield and potential loss due to pests. Pesticide use needs to be conceptualized in terms of its role in preventing output

---

[7] Headley(1968), Campbell(1976), Carlson(1977), Prabhu (1985), Lichtenberg and Zilberman (1986), Carrasco-Tauber and Moffit(1992), Babcock et al. (1992), Rola and Pingali (1993), Huang et al. (2001), Praneetvatakul and Waibel (2002), and Dung and Dung(2003) are noteworthy among them.

losses. The exact nature of the damage-prevention ability of pesticides is not known, but based on biological science it is realistic to assume that the damage control function takes a value in the range of 0 to 1. Lichtenberg and Zilberman (1986) suggested four separate damage control functions for pesticide use in agriculture. These are:

Exponential: $\quad G(X_p) = \left(1 - e^{-\lambda X_p}\right)$

Logistic: $\quad G(X_p) = \left[1 + e^{(\mu - \sigma X_p)}\right]^{-1}$

Weibull: $\quad G(X_p) = \left(1 - e^{-X_p^C}\right)$

Pareto: $\quad G(X_p) = \left(1 - K^\lambda X_p^\lambda\right)$

where G is the damage prevented by pesticide use, X_p is the quantity of pesticide used and λ, μ, σ, c and k are damage control parameters that need to be empirically estimated.

These functions are integrated into the production function as $Y = f(X)^* G(X_p)$, where Y is output, X's are standard yield-enhancing inputs and X_p is the pesticide amount used in the production.

Carrasco-Tauber and Moffit (1992) and Praneetvatakul and Waibel (2002) compared the conventional approach with these alternative specifications of the damage control function by fitting these to empirical data and found that the exponential function gave the best fit. All other functional specifications provided higher estimates of the marginal productivity of pesticides. Ajayi (2000) found the Weibull specification of the model more plausible for economic interpretation and more congruent with biological processes. The determination of the most useful specification of the function for the economic analysis will partly depend on the nature of the data.

Shankar and Thirtle (2005) point out that most econometric analyses of pesticide productivity are typically handicapped by their failure to incorporate entomological information and detailed, stage-by-stage data on pest infestation and pesticide application. Given this limitation, Shankar and Thirtle (2005) emphasize that Litchenberg and Zilberman's (LZ) framework provides a more accurate framework for the analysis of pesticide productivity than traditional production function analysis. Huang et al. (2001) employe this framework in the analysis of pesticide productivity in rice production in China. A similar strategy here is followed since this study is also limited by the availability of information on pest incidence.

6.3. Study area and data

The data for this study come from a survey of a sample of Cole crop farmers in the Bhaktapur district which has a vibrant group of commercial and intensive vegetable farmers. Bhaktapur produces the largest amount of vegetables among the three districts (Kathmandu, Bhaktapur and Lalitpur) in Kathmandu valley (MoAC, 2006). There are 54 vegetable farmer groups in 11 vegetable production pockets[8]. Since 2004, some 20 IPM Farmer Field Schools have trained a total of 505 farmers (both male and female). Table 6.1 identifies the pocket-wise cultivated area under Cole crop, the number of Cole crop growing households, and the number of trained farmers in each pocket.

Table 6.1. Pocket-wise distribution of cultivated and Cole crop area in Bhaktapur

Production Pockets	Total Cultivated Area (ha)	Cole Crop Cultivated Area (ha)	No. of Households Growing Cole Crop
Bode	323	40	150
Sipadole	401	25	225
Nakhel	905	25	125
Kharipati	778	30	90
Dadhikot	652	35	85
Bhaktapur N.P	414	30	433
Katunje	382	20	153
Balkumari	155	30	287
Balkot	385	25	104
Jhaukhel	523	20	301
Duwakot	476	20	157
	5394	**300**	**2110**

Source: Information obtained from Plant Protection Officer of District Agriculture Development Office, Bhaktapur (2004).

---

[8] The production pocket is a prioritized location for the production of a specific commodity such as vegetables, cereals, etc., and is identified under the prioritized production package strategy of the Agriculture Perspective Plan (1995–2015) of Nepal.

Five vegetable production pockets were selected for this study where Cole *crops* are intensively cultivated from an area. A sample of 211 Cole crop farmers (approximately 10 per cent of the Cole crop farmers in the area) were interviewed over the period of January to May, 2006. First, an inventory was prepared of those farmers belonging to vegetable farmer groups formed by the government's and those planning to grow Cole crop during the study season. Those farmers were then categorized into two groups – FFS farmers[9] and Non-FFS farmers. The respondents for this study were chosen from these two sub-samples of farmers. 67 FFS farmers and 144 Non-FFS farmers were randomly chosen.[10]

In the first phase, basic socio-economic and demographic information was collected from a total of 211 households. In the second stage, data related to input use and output were collected in three to five rounds of successive interviews to cover the duration from transplanting to harvesting of the Cole crop, which varies from three to five months depending on the variety planted. Information on the use of pesticides was collected on every visit from each household in order to improve the reliability of data affected by the length of the recall period.

Table 6.2 presents descriptive statistics on farmer characteristics. Out of the total 211 respondents, 82 per cent (173) were male and 18 per cent (38) were female farmers. The majority of the respondents were illiterate but 35 per cent had studied up to tenth grade. Most of the respondents, about 94 per cent of them, indicated that farming is their major occupation. The average age of the respondents was 43 years and they had an average landholding size of six *ropani*[11] of which they used three *ropani* on average in Cole crop farming. The maximum cropping intensity[12] found in the area was 300 per cent but the mean intensity was 217 per cent. At the end, data could be used from only 201 farmers for this study.[13]

---

[9] FFS farmers are those farmers who have participated in the season long Farmer Field School to learn the skills of integrated pest management.

[10] There are 2110 Cole crop growing households in Bhaktapur, out of which 670 were FFS trained while 1440 were FFS non-trained. To represent this proportion, we randomly selected 67 farmers with FFS training and 144 farmers without FFS training from the inventory of farmers planning to grow Cole crop during the study season in order to make up the total sample size of 211, which is 10 per cent of 2110.

[11] 20 *ropani*= 1 hectare

[12] Cropping Intensity = (Total area under crop in 365 days/Total cultivable Area available for 365 days)*100

[13] We left out two respondents because they suffered complete crop failure while we had to drop seven pesticide non-users during analysis stage.

Table 6.2. Summary statistics of the variables

Variables	N	Min	Max	Mean	S.D
Age of respondent (Years)	201	16.0	85.0	43.0	13.1
Vegetable farming experience(Years)	201	0.0	50.0	14.1	10.3
Cole crop cultivated area (ropani)	201	0.4	13.0	2.6	2.0
Total landholdings (ropani)	201	1.0	17.0	6.0	3.1
Cropping intensity (%)	201	133.3	300.0	217.1	42.2
Production (Kg / ha)	201	450.0	60000.0	23203.7	10285.6
NPK nutrients (Kg / ha)	201	92.0	1135.0	529.0	254.8
Labour (Mandays / ha)	201	240.0	718.8	427.8	105.7
Capital (NPR / ha)	201	7000.0	79000.0	20793.7	11598.9
Pesticide (a.i. gram/ha)	201	53.3	22650.0	2632.8	3571.3
Type of participant (FFS)	201	0.0	1.0	0.3	0.5
Hail storm damage (Hail)	201	0.0	1.0	0.1	0.3
User of NPK in combination (Fc)	201	0.0	1.0	0.3	0.4

Source: Primary Survey

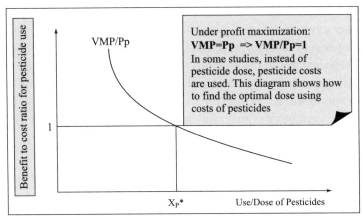

Where,

VMP = Value of Marginal Product

Pp = Unit price of pesticide

X_p^* = Optimal dose of pesticide

Figure 6.1.   Optimal use of pesticides

6.4. Theory and methods

Researchers evaluate the productivity effect of pesticides in terms of the output that a producer obtains due to reduction in potential yield loss from pests. The value of output loss that is prevented by the application of pesticides is a measure of the productivity of pesticide use.

Figure 6.2 presents graphically the impact of changes in pesticide use on production. Y_{max} is the maximum potential output for a given dose of input use without pest infestation. In reality, complete crop loss due to pest attack ($Y=0$) is unlikely to occur because of regulation of pest dynamics by biological and natural processes within the agro ecosystem. As such, the actual minimum level of output that a producer obtains after a pest attack under a natural pest control regime, i.e., without application of pesticides, is Y_{min}. Y_{min} varies depending on the level of natural enemies of pests present and the effect of other agro-ecological phenomena. The difference between Y_{max} and Y_{min} is the maximum potential yield loss abated by pesticide use. This difference is a measure of the destructive capacity of pests that is eliminated by the application of pesticide quantity X_p. It measures the effectiveness of the pesticide $G(X_p)$. The optimal use of the pesticide dose is shown in the diagram as $X_p{}^*$.

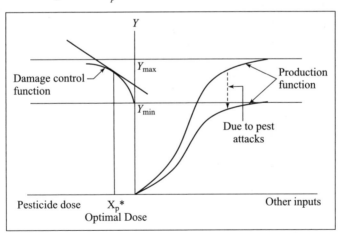

Where,

Y_{max} = Maximum attainable yield by using pesticide
Y_{min} = Minimum yield without pesticide use
X_p = Use of pesticide
$X_p{}^*$ = Optimal level of pesticide

Figure 6.2.   Impact of pesticide on yield loss reduction in a production system.

6.4.1. Model specification

In order to empirically estimate the production impacts of pesticide use, Lichtenberg and Zilberman (1986) specify different non-linear functional forms for the pesticide-yield relationship. The general production function for vegetables is given as:

$$Y = f(Z_i) \tag{1}$$

where Y is the quantity of crop production and Z is a vector of farm inputs including pesticides. However, to accommodate the unique role of pesticides as damage control agents, a distinction is made between pesticides and other inputs and equation (1) is written as:

$$Y = f[Z, G(X_p)] \tag{2}$$

where Z now represents a vector of conventional inputs excluding pesticides and X_p is the amount of pesticides.

Theoretically, the proportion of potential yield loss from pest attacks ranges from zero (i.e., complete loss of the crop) to unity (i.e., perfect control of pests). The value of $G(X_p)$ should be between 0 (meaning no damage abatement) and 1 (meaning 100 per cent damage abatement). $G(X_p)$ follows a cumulative probability distribution with respect to the values of X_p. Combining the standard Cobb-Douglas production function with a logistic function that estimates the damage avoided due to pesticides use, the following joint production function is estimated:

$$Y = \alpha \prod_{i=1}^{n} Z_i^{\beta_i} . G(X_p) \tag{3}$$

where α is the technological shifter, Z_i are inputs ($i=1$ to n) and $G(X_p)$ is the damage control function where $0 < G(X_p) < 1$.

Taking log of both sides in equation (3) gives the following econometric model for estimating pesticide use:

$$\ln Y = \ln \alpha + \beta_i \sum_{i=1}^{n} \ln Z_i + \ln G(X_p) + u_i \tag{4}$$

where u_i is an error term with mean zero and constant variance.

The above equation is estimated for three different specifications of the damage control function – Modified Exponential, Logistic and Wiebull; however, the empirical calculations of optimal pesticide use below are undertaken only for the Modified Exponential form. A Cobb-Douglas production function is also estimated with pesticides treated as a regular input.

Using an exponential specification of the damage function provides the following econometric model:

$$\ln Y = \alpha + \beta_1 \ln(NPK) + \beta_2 \ln(L) + \left(\beta_3 + \beta_4\,(Fc)\right)\ln\left(K_o\right) + \tag{5}$$
$$\delta_1\,(Hail) + \delta_2\,(Fc) + \ln\left(1 - e^{\left(-\lambda_1\left(X_p\right) - \lambda_2\,(FFS)\left(X_p\right)\right)}\right)$$

where,

Y = Crop yield (kg /ha)

NPK = Total Nitrogen, Phosphorous and Potassium nutrients (Kg/ ha)

L = Labour (mandays /ha)

F_c = 1 if farmers use all three major nutrients (NPK), that is the use of fertilizers in combination, or = 0 otherwise

K_o = Capital (NPR/ha); this include the cost of compost, seed and land preparation

$Hail$ = 1 if farmers suffered from hailstorm damage or = 0 if otherwise

FFS = 1 if farmers have participated in farmer field school or = 0 if otherwise

X_p = Total amount of pesticide used (gm / ha)

Equation (5) provides an estimate of the yield loss abated by the use of pesticide. This is used to determine the best or optimum dose of pesticide (X_p). Considering the alternative LZ specifications of the damage control function, this specification provided the best estimates.

6.4.2. Optimal level of pesticide use

An important issue is to identify the level of pesticide use that would optimize yields. As shown in Figure 6.1, the pesticide amount X_p^* represents the level of pesticide which maximizes profit for a producer. In equation 6, the Marginal Product (MP) of pesticide (derived from equation 5) is equated to the ratio of the pesticide and Cole crops prices:

$$MPP\left(= \frac{dY}{dX}\right) = \frac{(\bar{Y})\left(e^{-(\lambda_1 + \lambda_2\,(FFS))X_p}\right)(\lambda_1 + \lambda_2\,(FFS))}{\left[1 - \left(e^{-(\lambda_1 + \lambda_2\,(FFS))X_p}\right)\right]} = \left[\frac{P_P}{P_v}\right] \tag{6}$$

Thus, the optimum level of pesticide (X_p^*) is given by:

$$X_p^* = \frac{\ln\left((\overline{Y})\left(\lambda_1 + \lambda_2\ Type\right) + \left(\dfrac{P_p}{P_v}\right)\right) - \ln\left(\dfrac{P_p}{P_v}\right)}{\left(\lambda_1 + \lambda_2\ FFS\right)} \tag{7}$$

Where,

$\overline{Y}$ = average crop yield (Kg /ha)

P_p = the unit average price of pesticide (NPR/ gm a.i.)

P_v = the seasonal average farm gate price of Cole crops (NPR/Kg)

It is useful to note that in the modified exponential specification, the marginal productivity of pesticide use is directly linked with the participation of farmers in the Farmers' Field School (FFS) training programme, (see equation 6).

6.4.3. Description of variables

In estimating equation (5), the following variables are used. Y, the dependent variable, is the quantity (kilograms or kg) of Cole crops harvested per hectare. The physical quantity of output is taken as the dependent variable as there is no cross-sectional variation in the price of Cole crops.

Fertilizer use is represented by NPK, which is the sum of the quantity (kg) of major nutrient elements, viz. Nitrogen (N), Phosphorous (P) and Potash (K) per hectare used during the study season. The nutrient content of the commercial chemical fertilizers used by farmers are – Urea (46 per cent N), Diammonium Phosphate $(DAP$, 18 per cent N and 46 per cent P) and Muriate of Potash (60 per cent K). The quantity of NPK was calculated taking this into account.[14]

L is the total labour input (person days) used per hectare. This is the sum of all family and hired labour hours used in all the farm operations from land preparation to harvesting. The labour hours are converted into person days assuming a working duration of eight hours per day.

K_o or capital is the monetary value of inputs other than chemical fertilizer, labour and pesticide. It is expressed in Nepali Rupee[15] per hectare. This

---

[14] NPK = Amount of Nitrogen (N) per hectare + Amount of Phosphorous (P) per hectare + Amount of Potassium (K) per hectare; N per ha = (((Amount of Urea*.46) + (Amount of DAP*.18))/Cole crop grown area); P per ha = ((Amount of DAP *.46)/ Cole crop grown area); K per ha = ((Amount of MoP*.6)/ Cole crop grown area).

[15] 1 US $ = 63 Nepali Rupees(NPR)

variable encompasses the costs of compost, land preparation and seed or seedling. The cost of compost covers the monetary value of compost either purchased from the market or farmers own production or borrowed. Similarly, land preparation input (Tractor) and seed or seedling input were valued, whether it is the farmers' own or brought from the market, at the market price in order to calculate its costs.

X_p is the total quantity (grams) of active ingredient (a.i.)[16] of pesticides per hectare used by a farmer during the study season. Here, pesticide indicates the use of both insecticides and fungicides.

Three dummy variables are used in this analyses. *Hail* is the dummy variable that captures the effect of hailstorm that occurred during the study season. The farmers, whose Cole crop were affected by hailstorms were coded as 1 and others whose crops were not affected by hailstorms, as 0. F_c is a dummy variable that captures whether the farmers used all three major nutrients (NPK). It equals 1 for farmers who use all three nutrients in combination and 0 otherwise. *FFS* is a dummy variable which equals 1 for farmers who participated in the Farmer Field School and 0 otherwise.

6.5. Results and discussion

This section describes the types of pesticide used in the study area and the estimation of the production function and marginal products of inputs and pesticides.

6.5.1. Pesticide use and farmer perception

Farmers in Bhaktapur used forty three commercial products from twenty different pesticides. The survey data shows that farmers use 15 commercial products of five different types of fungicide and 28 commercial products of 15 different types of insecticide in Cole crop farming. The most commonly used fungicides are – Carbendazim, Copperoxychloride, Mancozeb, Metalaxy eight per cent plus Mancozeb 64 per cent. Similarly, Chlorpyriphos, Cypermethrin, Dichlorvous, Dimethoate, Endosulfan, Fenvelerate, Parathion-methyl and Monocrotophos are the most commonly used insecticides in Bhaktapur for Cole crops. Most of these insecticides fall under World Health Organization (WHO) categories of IB to III, implying that they belong among the extreme to moderately hazardous

---

[16] Active ingredient (a.i.) means the biologically active part of the pesticide.

classifications. FFS trained farmers generally apply well known commercial pesticides rather than less known formulations.

Out of the total amount of pesticides used in Cole crops, 76 per cent are insecticides and 19 per cent are fungicide. Figure 6.3 shows that farmers used 2373 gm active ingredient of fungicide and 1963 gm of insecticide per hectare on average. Overall, farmers applied 2633 gm of pesticides per hectare. This finding contradicts the findings of an earlier survey report of PPD (2004), which indicated that farmers applied 1224 gm of insecticides and 1295 gm of fungicides per hectare on cauliflower farming in the Bhaktapur District. The numbers suggest that average pesticide use is higher than previously understood.

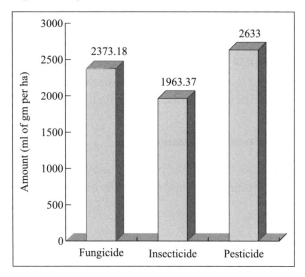

Figure 6.3. Average amount of pesticides used on cole crop (grams a.i./ ha)

6.5.2. Estimation of pesticide productivity

Table 6.2 presents the summary statistics of the variables used in the econometric analyses. In the sample, the average yield per hectare is about 23,000 kilograms. The average pesticide use is 2633 grams active ingredient per hectare. Hailstorms affect approximately 13 per cent of farmers and approximately 27 per cent farmers use all three major nutrient (NPK) fertilizers in combination.

For the empirical analysis, four different models were estimated – the Cobb-Douglas, the modified Exponential, the Logistic and the Wiebull. The results are presented in Table 6.3.

Table 6.3. Results from the non–linear estimation of various production functions

Variables	Cobb-Douglas	Damage Control Specifications		
		Modified Exponential	Logistic	Weibull
Intercept	6.424***	7.163***	7.097***	7.176***
	(5.607)	(6.20)	(6.117)	(6.167)
ln(NPK)	0.174***	0.165***	0.165***	0.160***
	(2.849)	(2.796)	(2.776)	(2.665)
ln(L)	0.349***	0.406***	0.382**	0.383***
	(2.645)	(3.11)	(2.916)	(2.932)
ln(Ko)	0.050	–0.050	–.029	–0.033
	(0.750)	(–0.683)	(–0.392)	(–0.458)
ln(Ko)*Fc		0.465***	0.431***	0.434***
		(2.780)	(2584)	(2.613)
ln(Pesti)	0.005			
	(0.196)			
Hail	–1.514***	–1.492***	–1.516***	–1.514***
	(–15.412)	(–15.430)	(–15.660)	(–15.68)
Fc	–0.130*	–4.693***	–4.364***	–4.392***
	(–1.755)	(–2.852)	(–2.661)	(–2.690)
λ_1		0.012***		
		(2.844)		
λ_2		0.048		
		(0.279)		
μ			1.394	
			(0.064)	
σ		0.061		
		(0.163)		
c				0.218
				(1.50.131)
R^2	0.61	0.63	0.63	0.63
N	201	201	201	201

Absolute values of asymptotic *t*-statistics (for the damage control specification) and *t*-statistics (for the Cobb- Douglas specification) are shown in parenthesis. ***, **, and * refers to significance at 1%, 5% & 10% levels.

Note: λ_1 and λ_2 are coefficients of pesticide use and the interaction of FFS with pesticide use in the modified exponential model respectively; μ and σ are coefficients of pesticide use in the Logistic model; c is the coefficient of pesticide use in the Weibull model.

In all specifications (Table 6.3), fertilizer use, NPK, and labour elasticity coefficients have the expected sign and are highly significant. However, the coefficient[17] for Capital (K_o) is statistically insignificant indicating that the yield is not responsive to capital (compost and land preparation) expenditure. The coefficient for the dummy variable F_c, which shows the use of all three fertilizers, is negative and statistically significant in all specifications. This suggests that farmers may not be using inorganic fertilizers, viz., Urea, DAP and Murate of potash in the proper combination. The coefficient of hailstorm (*Hail*) is negative and significant in all specifications suggesting that hailstorms contribute to crop losses.

The coefficient of pesticide use has a positive sign in all specifications of the production function. However, the coefficient for pesticide use (λ_1) is significant only in the modified exponential form of the production function. In fact, all the parameter estimates of the modified exponential model are significant at the one per cent level except for Capital (K_o) and the interaction of FFS with pesticide (λ_2). The R^2 obtained from this model was 0.63. The signs of the estimated input parameters of this model accord well with agronomic facts. The positive and statistically insignificant coefficient of the interaction of FFS with pesticide (λ_2) indicates that yield is not responsive to FFS training in the case of Cole crop production in the study area.

Figure 6.4 shows the damage abatement resulting from the different levels of pesticide used in Cole crop production in Bhaktapur based on the modified exponential specification (equation 5).

The value of $G(X_p)$ is in the range $0 < G(X_p) < 1$. The minimum amount of Cole crop (Y_{min}) a farmer can produce without using pesticide is 6703 kg per hectare, which is 35 per cent of the average production of Cole crop in Bhaktapur. Table 6.4 provides the results of the calculation of damage abatement and yield increment due to pesticides. The pesticide productivity curve is presented from this data graphically in Figure 6.5.

The yield loss reduction in Cole crop approaches zero as pesticide use (X_p) increases to above 850 gm per hectare. The maximum attainable yield by using pesticide (Y_{max}) is 20,938 kg per hectare. Thus, the maximum abated yield by pesticide use[18] is 14,235 kg per hectare.

---

[17] The coefficient of K_o is $\beta_3 + \beta_4 = .415$ and standard error is calculated as $SE(\beta_3 + \beta_4) = sqrt$ [(variance(β_3) + variance(β_4) - 2 covariance(β_3, β_4)]=0.959. The t-vaue of K_o is 0.433 which is not significant.

[18] The maximum abated yield by pesticide use = $Y_{max} - Y_{min}$

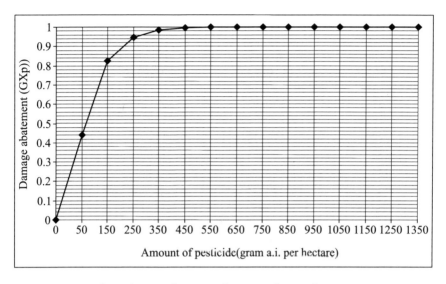

Figure 6.4. Resultant damage abatement function of pesticide

Note: This graph is based on the modified exponential functional specification. All variables are evaluated at mean values.

Table 6.4. Computation of damage abatement and yield increment due to pesticide use (modified exponential functional specification)

Pesticide amount used (X_p)	Damage abatement function $G(X_p)$	Cumulative yield increment (*Kg/ha*)	Yield loss reduction (*Kg/ha*)
50	0.4408	9229	5161
100	0.6872	14391	2887
150	0.8251	17277	1614
200	0.9022	18892	903
250	0.9453	19794	505
300	0.9694	20299	282
350	0.9829	20582	158
400	0.9904	20740	88
450	0.9946	20828	49
500	0.9970	20877	28
550	0.9983	20905	15
600	0.9991	20920	9

(Contd.)

(Contd.)

Pesticide amount used (X_p)	Damage abatement function $G(X_p)$	Cumulative yield increment (Kg/ha)	Yield loss reduction (Kg/ha)
650	0.9995	20929	5
700	0.9997	20934	3
750	0.9998	20937	2
800	0.9999	20938	1
850	0.9999	20939	0
900	1.0000	20939	0
950	1.0000	20940	0
1000	1.0000	20940	0
1050	1.0000	20940	0
1100	1.0000	20940	0
1150	1.0000	20940	0
1200	1.0000	20940	0

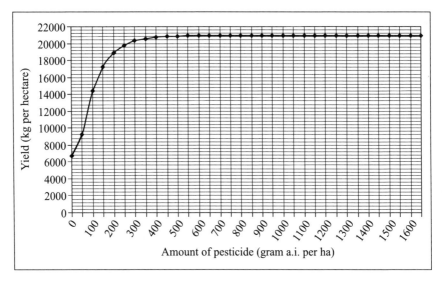

Figure 6.5. Pesticide productivity curve

6.5.3. Marginal productivity of pesticides

At the average pesticide application rate of 2633 gm per hectare, we estimate the marginal productivity of pesticides for the modified exponential specification (equation 6 in page 125) to be close to zero. Thus, this estimate falls below the estimates of Prabhu (1985), Ajayi (2000), and Huang (2001) as mentioned in Appendix 6.1 (see at the end of the chapter). Figure 6.6 shows the significantly declining trend of the marginal value product of the pesticide as its application increases.

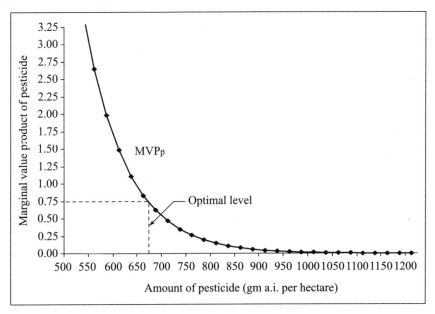

Figure 6.6.   Marginal value product of pesticide use in cole crop production

Note: This graph is based on the modified exponential functional specification. All variables at mean values are evaluated.

Using equation 7 (in page 126), the optimal level of pesticide used is calculated to be 680 gm of a.i. for Cole crops in Bhaktapur (at the mean of the sample). This is based on the average farm gate price of Cole crop in the season, which was NPR 7.5 per kg, and the average price of a gram of active ingredient of pesticides, which was NPR 0.75.[19] The average application of a pesticide dose in the sample was 2633 gm of active ingredient of pesticides per hectare. This clearly shows that farmers overused about 1953 gm of the active ingredient of pesticides per hectare. In other words, farmers lose NPR 1465 (1953 × 0.75) per hectare because of inefficient use of pesticides in their Cole crop farming. Farmers use 3.9 times more pesticides than

---

[19] This is based on the average price of all pesticides used in Cole crops in Bhaktapur in 2006.

they should. Thus, one can conclude that farmers overuse pesticides substantially. It is possible that farmers deliberately apply an overdose of pesticides because they are uncertain of the effectiveness of the dose used, and therefore wish to avert the risk of bigger pest attacks.

It is interesting that the extent of overuse of pesticide differs between farmers trained on IPM at the Farmers' Field School and farmers not trained in FFS. Estimates show that farmers with FFS use 2.7 times the optimal dose as compared to farmers without FFS who use 4.4 times the optimal dose.

Table 6.5 shows that only a small proportion of farmers (three per cent) use the optimal level of pesticides. The majority in Bhaktapur (74 per cent) use more than the optimum amount of pesticides and obtain a very small increase (one to four per cent) in yield relative to the average yield.

Table 6.5. Cole crop production using different level of pesticide by farmer

Participant Category	Level of Pesticide Use	Proportion of Participants	Production Level (Kg/ha)	
			Mean(Y_i)	Difference(D)
Non-FFS farmers	Below Optimal	21%	20891.96	– 11%
	Optimal	4%	19610.71	– 16%
	Above Optimal	74%	24276.49	4%
FFS Farmers	Below	25%	22012.94	– 4%
	Optimal	2%	23600	3%
	Above	73%	23157.45	1%
Overall	Below Optimal	22%	21290.53	– 8%
	Optimal	3%	20180.61	– 13%
	Above Optimal	74%	23923.51	3%

Note:

- Production level difference (D) is calculated as: $\dfrac{\left(Y_i - \bar{Y}\right)}{\bar{Y}} \times 100\%$

- Mean yield ($\bar{Y}$) of non-*FFS* farmers, *FFS* farmers and Overall is 23355, 22878, and 23203 (Kg/ha) respectively.

6.6. Conclusions and policy recommendations

Chemical pesticides play an important role in combating pest problems in agriculture. The production and productivity of agriculture in recent years is largely the result of enhanced use of pesticides as well as increased use of nutrients and water. There are, however, growing public objections to the use of chemical pesticides because of their negative externalities on human health and the environment. In order to balance public concern about chemical residues and ecological damage with food security issues, one need to understand better what the trade-offs are between greater and more limited use of pesticides. Accurate, improved and locally specific information about the productivity of pesticide in agriculture are crucial in the formulation of policy on the issue.

This study investigates the impact of pesticide use on Cole crop production in the Bhaktapur district of Nepal. The economic performance of pesticides is evaluated using non-linear functional forms. The methods used in this study allow to examine the effectiveness of Farmers' Field Schools (FFS) training on potential yield as well. However, the model used in this study carries a limitation. The exponential functional specification used imposes an assumption that there is no output without pesticide application.

It is found that pesticides significantly contribute to Cole crop production by limiting yield losses. As expected, the marginal contributions of pesticide use declines with increased use of pesticides. What is interesting is that the contribution of pesticides is close to zero at the average level at which Cole crop growers currently use pesticides. In the study area, farmers apply pesticides at more than at their profit maximizing or optimum level. The profit maximizing amount of pesticide per hectare for Cole crop production is 680 gms while the average farmer uses pesticides in Cole crops at about four times this optimal level. This is happening despite a perception among a majority of farmers that pesticides are harmful to human health as well as beneficial organisms prevalent in the vegetable ecosystem. The results of this study show that reduction in pesticide use from the current level will not decrease yields significantly.

Wilson and Tisdell (2001) suggests four reasons behind the overuse of pesticides – (a) ignorance regarding the sustainability of pesticide use; (b) the lack of alternatives to pesticides; (c) underestimation of the short and long term costs of pesticide use; and (d) weak enforcement of laws and regulations. These reasons seemed to be equally valid in the case of this study.

Both farmers, who attended and who have not attended, overuse pesticides. However, farmers trained in the farmer field school tend to use a lot less pesticides. Policy makers and planners need to review the IPM programme in Nepal and revise the FFS curriculum. The FFS programme should be designed in such a way that it empowers farmers to make decisions suitable for a locally specific vegetable production system. This ultimately leads to the adaptation of alternative technologies for growing healthy crops.

The study sheds some light on discrepancies between claims by agriculturists and economists regarding pesticide productivity. Though general recommendations based on such a small-scale study cannot be made, the results are still relevant for regulatory decisions. Further empirical studies are required on a wider scale to understand pesticide productivity across Nepal's diverse agro-ecosystems. It would be useful to study the correlations between farmers' perceptions of risk and pesticide use level as well as the implication of any training they may have on integrated pest management.

Appendix 6.1. Empirical findings from pesticide productivity studies.

Source	Functional Specification	Finding
Headely (1968)	Cobb- Douglas Function	The marginal value of one dollar expenditure for chemical pesticides is approximately $4.0
Campbell (1976)	Cobb- Douglas Function	The marginal dollar's worth of pesticides input yielded around $12 worth of output.
Prahbu (1985)	Cobb- Douglas Function with some modifications	The marginal value product of pesticide was less than unity, that is 0.13.
Carrasco-Tauber and Moffit (1992)	Cobb- Douglas Function compared with Damage Function Specifications	All functional specification indicates high marginal productivity of pesticides except the exponential specification.
Ajayi (2000)	Cobb- Douglas Function compared with Damage Function Specifications	The marginal value product per unit cost of insecticides is greater than unity in the Cobb- Douglas model and all the alternative LZ damage specification except Weibull specification.

(Contd.)

(*Contd.*)

Source	Functional Specification	Finding
Huang et al. (2001)	Exponential Damage Control Specification	The Marginal product of pesticide was only 0.07 Kg.
Praneetvatakul and Waibel (2002)	Cobb- Douglas Function compared with Damage Function Specifications	The abatement function, "the exponential form", gave the best fit to the empirical data of rice.
Dung and Dung (2003)	Cobb- Douglas Function	10 per cent increase in total dose of pesticides will contribute to a micro increase of 0.346 per cent of rice yield.

References

Ajayi, O.C., 'Pesticide Use Practices, Productivity and Farmers' Health: The Case of Cotton-rice System in Cote D'Ivoire, West Africa', Pesticide Policy Project, Special Issue Publication Series No. 3, University of Hanover, Germany, 2000.

Antle, J.M. and Pingali, P.L., 'Pesticide Productivity and Farmer Health: A Philippine Case Study', *American Journal of Agricultural Economics*, 76, (1994), 418–430.

Antle, J.M. and Capalbo, S.M., 'Pesticide, Productivity and Farmer Health: Implication for the Regulatory Policy and Agriculture Research', *American Journal of Agricultural Economics*, 76, (1994), 598–602.

Babcock, B.A., Lichtenberg, E. and Zilberman, D., 'Impact of Damage Control and Quality of Output: Estimating Pest Control Effectiveness', *American Journal of Agricultural Economics*, 74, (1992), 163–172.

Baker, S.L. and Gyawali, B.K., 'Promoting Proper Pesticide Use: Obstacle and Opportunities for an Integrated Pest Management Programme in Nepal', in Policy Analysis in Agriculture and Related Resource Management, Ministry of Agriculture/Winrock International, 1994.

Brethour, C. and Weersink, A., 'An Economic Evaluation of the Environmental Benefits from Pesticide Reduction', *Agricultural Economics*, 25, (2001), 219–226.

Campbell, H.F., 'Estimating the Marginal Productivity of Agricultural Pesticides: The Case of Tree-fruit Farms in the Okanagan Valley', *Canadian Journal of Agricultural Economics*, 24(2), (1976), 23–30.

Carlson, G.A., 'Long Run Productivity of Pesticide', *American Journal of Agricultural Economics*, 59, (1977), 543–548.

Carrasco-Tauber, C. and Moffit, L.J., 'Damage Control Econometrics: Functional Specification and Pesticide Productivity', *American Journal of Agricultural Economics*, 74, (1992), 158–162.

Chambers, R.G., and Lichtenberg, E., 'Simple Econometrics of Pesticide Productivity', *American Journal of Agricultural Economics*, 76, (1994), 407–417.

Dahal, L., 'A Study on Pesticide Pollution in Nepal,' National Conservation Strategy Implementation Project, IUCN, Kathmandu and National Planning Commission, HMG Nepal, 1995.

Dilts, D. and Hate, S., 'IPM Farmer Field Schools: Changing Paradigms and Scaling up', Agricultural Research and Extension Network Paper 59b, 1996, 1–4.

Dung, N.H. and Dung, T.T.T, 'Economic and Health Consequences of Pesticide Use in Paddy Production in the Mekong Delta, Vietnam', EEPSEA Research Report no. RR2, International Development Research Centre, Singapore, 1999.

Fox, G. and Weersink, A., 'Damage Control and Increasing Returns', *American Journal of Agricultural Economics*A. 77, (1995), 33–39.

FAO, 'Internation Code of Conduct on the Distribution and Use of Pesticides', Food and Agriculture Organization (FAO) of United Nations, Rome 2002.

Giri, Y.P., Mainali, B.P., Aryal, S., Paneru, R.B., Bista, S. and Maharjan, R., 'Use of Insecticide on Vegetable Crops in Dhading District of Nepal', Proceedings of the Fourth National Workshop on Horticulture', National Agriculture Research Council Nepal, 2004, 431–438.

Gupta, P.K., 'Pesticide Exposure – Indian Scene', *Toxicology*, 198, (2004), 83–90.

Headley, J.C., 'Estimating the Productivity of Agricultural Pesticides', *American Journal of Agricultural Economics*, 50, (1968), 13–23.

Huang, J., Qiao, F., Zhang, L., and Rozelle, S., 'Farm Pesticides, Rice Production, and Human Health in China', EEPSEA Research Report No. 2001-RR3, International Development Research Centre, Singapore, 2001.

Irham, 'Integrated Pest Management Programme, Pesticide Use and Rice Productivity: A Case Study of Yogyakarta, Indonesia', Proceedings of the International Workshop on Environmental Risk Assessment of Pesticides and Integrated Pesticide Management in Developing Countries, Selbstverlag Institut für Geographie und Geoökologie, der Technischen Universität Braunschweig , Kathmandu, Nepal, 2001, 73–81.

Irham and Mariyono, J., 'The impact of Integrated Pest Management Programme on Pesticide Demand for Soybean Farming in Yogyakarta, Indonesia', Proceedings of the International Workshop on Environmental Risk Assessment of Pesticides and Integrated Pesticide Management in Developing Countries, Selbstverlag Institut für Geographie und Geoökologie, der Technischen Universität Braunschweig , Katmandu, Nepal, 2001, 62–72.

Kim, J.M., 'Analysis of Economic and Environmental Effects of Pesticide Application with Special Reference to Vegetable Production', Acta Hort. (ISHS) 524, (2000), 33–38. http://www.actahort.org/books/524/524_3.htm

Lichtenberg, E. and Zilberman, D., 'The Econometrics of Damage Control: Why Specification Matters?', *American Journal of Agricultural Economics*, 68, (1986), 261–273.

Maharjan, R., Aryal, S., Mainali, B.P., Bista, S., Manadhar, D.N., Giri, Y.P. and Paneru, R.B., 'Survey on Magnitude of Pesticide Use in Vegetable Crops', Proceedings of the Fourth National Workshop on Horticulture', National Agriculture Research Council, Nepal, 2004, 291–98.

MoAC, 'Area, Production and Yield of Vegetables', Statistical Information on Agriculture, Agri-business Promotion and Statistics Division, Ministry of Agriculture and Cooperatives, Government of Nepal, 2005, 76.

Paneru, R.B., Giri, Y.P. and Mainali, B.P., 'Status of PoPs in Nepal: Preliminary Inventory of Production, Import, Distribution and Uses', Proceedings of the Inception Workshop on Implementation of the Stockholm Convention on Persistence Organic Pollutants (PoPs) Enabling Activities in Nepal, Ministry of Population and Environment and UNIDO, Kathmandu, Nepal, 2004, 40–59.

Ponitus, J., Dilts, R., and Bartlett, A., 'Ten Years of IPM Training in Asia: From Farmer Field School to Community IPM', FAO Community IPM Program Jakarta, Indonesia, Food and Agriculture Organization of the United Nations, Regional Office for Asia and the Pacific, 2002, Bangkok. *www.communityipm.org.*

Praneetvatakul, S. and Waibel, H., 'The Productivity of Pesticide Use in Rice Production of Thailand: A Damage Control Approach', *Thai Journal of Agricultural Economics,* Thailand, 22, (2002), 73–87.

Prabhu, K.S., 'The Treatment of Pesticides in the Production Function Framework: A Skeptical Note', *Indian Journal of Agricultural Economics,* 40, (2000), 123–139.

Pujara, D.S. and Khana, N.R., 'Use of Pesticides in Jaishidihi Sub-catchment, Jhikhu Khola Watershed, Middle Mountain in Nepal', Proceedings of the International Workshop on Environmental Risk Assessment of Pesticides and Integrated Pesticide Management in Developing Countries, Selbstverlag Institut für Geographie und Geoökologie, der Technischen Universität Braunschweig , Kathmandu, Nepal, 2001, 168–177.

PPD, The Survey Report about The Use of Pesticide in Rice and Vegetable, Plant Protection Directorate, Department of Agriculture, Government of Nepal, 2004.

Rahman, S., 'Farm Level Pesticide Use in Bangladesh: Determinants and Awareness', *Agriculture Ecosystem and Environment,* 95, (2003), 241–252.

Rola, A.C. and Pingali, P.L., 'Pesticides, Rice Productivity, and Farmers' Health – An Economic Assessment', World Resources Institute and International Rice Research Institute, Los Baños, Laguna, Philippines, 1993.

Shanker, B. and Thirtle, C., Pesticide Productivity and Transgenic Cotton Technology: The South African Small Holders Case, *Journal of Agricultural Economics,* 56, (2005), 97–116.

Shetty, P.K., 'Pesticide Stewardship and Food Security in India', Internet publication, (2003). http://www.npsalliance.org/Conf2003/PDF2003/PKShetty.pdf

Shrestha, P.L. and Neupane, F.P., 'Socio-economic Context on Pesticide Use in Nepal', Proceedings of the International Workshop on Environmental Risk

Assessment of Pesticides and Integrated Pesticide Management in Developing Countries, Selbstverlag Institut für Geographie und Geoökologie, der Technischen Universität Braunschweig, Kathmandu, Nepal, 2001, 205–223.

Travisi, C.M., Nijkamp, P., and Vindigni, G., 'Pesticide Risk Valuation in Empirical Economics: A Comparative Approach', *Ecological Economics*, 56, (2006), 455–474.

Upadhyaya, N.S., 'Integrated Pest Management in Nepal', in F. P. Neupane (ed.), Proceedings of the Workshop on IPM through FFS, Plant Protection Directorate, Nepal, 2003, 1–14.

Wilson, C. and Tisdell, C., 'Why Farmers Continue to Use Pesticides Despite Environmental, Health and Sustainability Cost', *Ecological Economics*, 39, 2001, 449–462.

WRI, 'World Resource' 1998/1999', World Resource Institute (WRI), UK, Oxford University Press, 1998.

7

Forests, Hydrological Services, and Agricultural Income: A Case Study from the Western Ghats of India

Sharachchandra Lele, Iswar Patil, Shrinivas Badiger, Ajit Menon and *Rajeev Kumar*[1]

7.1. Introduction

Tropical forest ecosystems generate multiple benefits to society, among which are goods such as fuelwood, fodder, timber, leaf manure, food and medicines, and services such as carbon sequestration, habitat for wildlife, and biodiversity. One important set of benefits from forest ecosystems is watershed services, which include hydrological regulation (groundwater recharge, low-flow augmentation, and flood control) and soil conservation. Thus, changes in forest conditions are likely to have profound implications

[1] This study was part of a larger four-year research project titled 'Land-Use Change, Watershed Services and Socio Economic Impact in The Western Ghats Region' carried out by the Centre for Interdisciplinary Studies in Environment and Development (CISED) in collaboration with the National Institute of Hydrology (NIH), Ashoka Trust for Research in Ecology and the Environment (ATREE) and UNESCO's International Hydrological Programme with support from the Ford Foundation. Additional support was provided by the South Asian Network for Development and Environmental Economics (SANDEE) to strengthen the socio-economic component of this research. The socio-economic analysis reported here pertains to one of the four study sites in the larger project, and uses the results of the catchment hydrology study carried out by ATREE at this site. We are grateful to the residents of the Baragi village in Chamrajanagar district of Karnataka State for their enormous patience and cooperation. Special mention must be made of our field assistant Subbanna who helped us diligently in data collection. Thanks also to Santosh Hegde for GIS support. Comments received from SANDEE resource persons and SANDEE referees at the time of formulation of the study, and from Kanchan Chopra, Seema Purushottaman, a SANDEE referee and the editors of this book on previous drafts of this chapter are gratefully acknowledged.

for society. This is particularly true in the case of river basins in South Asia, where forests as well as water resources are being used intensively by a large population, often under a highly seasonal rainfall regime.

In spite of their importance, the watershed service benefits of tropical forests and associated ecosystems are perhaps the least well understood and the most contentious of all forest-related benefits. Neither are the physical relationships between forest cover and watershed services adequately understood, nor (partly as a consequence) are their socio-economic impacts accurately assessed. As a result, when it comes to the management of forested watersheds, policy making is dominated by conventional wisdom that assumes that 'more forest' of any kind at any location and in place of anything else is 'better' for all watershed services for all communities downstream. Such oversimplifications are no longer scientifically tenable.

As a modest yet empirically grounded contribution aimed at filling this knowledge gap, a four-year research project on the impacts of forest cover change on watershed services in four sites spread over two eco-climatically distinct regions of the Western Ghats of peninsular India was launched, in collaboration with the National Institute of Hydrology, the Ashoka Trust for Research in Ecology and the Environment, and UNESCO's International Hydrological Programme. The economic assessment reported here is from one site in the lower rainfall region (Bandipur in Southern Karnataka). It seeks to predict in economic terms the consequences for agriculture of hydrological change that might result if the forests in a currently heavily used catchment were to regenerate fully. The study, one of the first studies of its kind in South Asia, is also distinctive in its use of detailed hydrological data, in its contextualisation of the community-water relationship in the local techno-institutional arrangements, and its willingness to go beyond 'marginal change' analysis.

7.2. Forest ecosystems, watershed services and social well-being: the existing literature

7.2.1. Forest cover change and hydrological services: the complex and contentious linkages

Popular belief is that forests perform extremely critical watershed functions, as they enhance rainfall, act as 'sponges' that prevent floods during the monsoon and release water during the dry season, and prevent soil erosion. But debates generated by clear-cutting experiments in temperate watersheds have triggered much rethinking amongst forest hydrologists of this reigning orthodoxy over the past few decades. It has been observed that trees actually consume more water (through transpiration) compared to other vegetation, that trees may prevent sheet erosion but not gully erosion, that flood control effects of forests may be significant only in small or medium-sized catchments, that sediment loads in rivers emerging from geologically unstable mountain systems such as the Himalayas may be hardly influenced by the extent of forest cover in the catchments, and that the soil erosion and water infiltration rates of different 'non-forest' land-uses vary quite dramatically. It is therefore now accepted that the effects of forest degradation, loss, or afforestation on watershed functioning will vary with climate, spatial scale, precipitation characteristics (such as rainfall intensity), pedology, soils and, most importantly, with the type of change that actually takes place in the vegetation, whether classified as forest or otherwise (Bruijnzeel, 1993; Bonell, 1993; Bruijnzeel, 2004).

In the Western Ghats region, natural forests have been extensively transformed by state agencies and local communities into various forms such as monocultural forest plantations of Teak, Eucalyptus and Acacia, heavily used but well-managed forests that are more in the form of tree savannas or even grasslands, heavily used open-access forests that have often degraded to scrub, and coffee/tea/rubber plantations. Hydrological studies of these land-cover changes are few and potentially divergent. Findings include significant declines in water yields when grasslands are planted with eucalyptus in the Nilgiris (Sikka et al., 2003), possible increases in overland flow due to planting up of grasslands with *Acacia auriculiformis* in the Western Ghats (Putty and Prasad, 2000), but rapid recovery of soil hydraulic properties when *Acacia auriculiformis* is planted on the highly degraded (laterized) soils of the coastal Western Ghats (Purandara et al., 2001). The hydrology of deciduous forests is poorly understood since most studies are in the evergreen forests.

7.2.2. Links between forest hydrology and human well-being

A detailed review of the literature on economic assessments of the impacts on watershed services of forest conversion is beyond the scope of this chapter (see Lélé and Venkatachalam, 2006). First, it is important to mention that only a few studies are available that look at the hydrological impacts of forest conversion as scholars have focused much more on the soil erosion impacts of forest conversion. Second, many of these studies are not grounded in empirically validated hydrological models, the exceptions being those led by Vincent et al. (1995), Kramer et al. (1997), Pattanayak and Kramer (2001) and Aylward and Echeverria (2001). Others either assume some simple relationships or seek to bypass the problem by adopting a contingent valuation approach in which (implicitly) the consumer is assumed to have full knowledge of the biophysical relationship between forest cover change, hydrology and economic activity (e.g., Chopra and Kadekodi, 1997)[2]. Third, in terms of the nature of forest cover change studied, few studies have looked at the impact of forest degradation, the main focus being on either complete deforestation or forest conversion. Fourth, the regional coverage of the studies, especially of the hydrologically grounded ones, is limited, with studies in South Asia being particularly scarce. We are not aware of any environmental economic assessments of forest-driven hydrological change in the Western Ghats region. Finally, economic analyses tend to focus on aggregate changes in agricultural profits or consumer surplus, but do not include changes in employment generated or wage incomes.

In spite of these limitations, the literature has significantly illuminated the complex relationship between forest cover change, hydrology and local communities. For instance, the impacts can be in different directions. Vincent et al. (1995) show that replacement of natural forests by dense pine plantation can reduce water flows whereas Pattanayak et al. (2001) analyze a situation where loss of forest cover leads to reduced baseflow. The magnitude of the economic impact also varies considerably from study to study. This contextual nature of the impact requires one to better understand the role played by eco-climatic conditions and the techno-institutional variables mediating between the hydrological system and the water use sectors.

This study contributes to the existing literature literature in three ways. First, it is located in a region – the Western Ghats in India – that is of considerable significance in terms of watershed services but has received limited attention so far. Second, it draws upon real hydrological data that have been made available to the researchers because this study is part of a larger interdisciplinary effort. Third, in addition to direct changes in agricultural income of farmers, it estimates changes in usage income received by marginal farmers or landless households due to changes in agriculture.

---

[2] The Chopra and Kadekodi study also highlights the difficulty of separating out, in a contingent valuation approach, the economic value of different elements of the forest ecosystem service 'bundle'.

7.3. Framework and objectives

A modified version of the framework given by Pattanayak (2004) that outlines the links between forest cover change and economic welfare is used in this Chapter (see Figure 7.1). An explicit step is included for highlighting changes in water applied to agriculture even though, as will be seen, it is not always possible to measure this change directly. The influence of location, technology and institutions on how 'available water' gets translated into 'applied water' is also explicitly acknowledged.

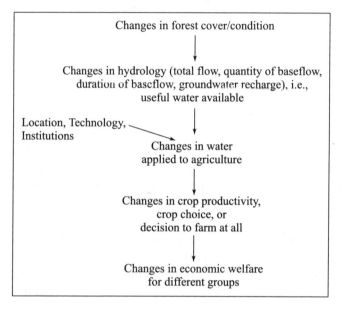

Figure 7.1.   Conceptual framework

It should be clarified that agriculture is not the only sector in which water is used. Obviously, water is also essential for domestic activities and the livestock sector. In the particular context of this study, however, our observations suggest that a combination of government drinking water supply schemes and precautionary practices followed by the communities ensure that water availability for the domestic and livestock sectors will not be significantly affected by changes in hydrology. Focusing on the impacts on agriculture therefore seems reasonable for this study.

The objectives of this economic assessment then are to understand how changes in hydrology translate into changes in water applied to agriculture and thereby to changes in productivity and crop choice and eventually into changes in farmer income and wage employment in the village. Note that this is not a complete benefit-cost analysis of forest cover change impacts across different stakes and stakeholders (see Lélé et al., 2001, for an example of this type of study); nor does it look at other aspects of economic welfare such as distributional issues between small and large farmers. The interest of this study lies in understanding the direction and average magnitude of income impacts caused by changes in hydrological services alone.

7.4. Study site: ecological, social and agro-hydrological characteristics

7.4.1. Western ghats region

The Western Ghats region – a forested region straddling a range of hills running parallel to the western coast of India – is in many ways an ideal region for exploring the links between forest cover, hydrology and local economies. First, virtually all the major rivers in southern India originate in the Western Ghats. Changes in land-use and land-cover in the Ghats are potentially of critical importance to the millions of people depending on these streams and rivers, especially in the drier eastern portion of the Deccan plateau. These changes are also of importance to the communities residing in the Western Ghats themselves, because even in this generally high rainfall region seasonal scarcity of water is ubiquitous. Second, the region has a long history of forest dependence by local communities, so forest degradation has significant implications locally. Third, the region is considered a global biodiversity hotspot, so forest cover change has much wider significance.

7.4.2. The biophysical context

The hills and forests of Bandipur (11°57′02″N, 76°12′17″E to 11°35′34″N, 76°51′32″E) are part of the hilly southern fringe that separates the Mysore region of Karnataka state from the Nilgiris in Tamil Nadu and the Wynaad region in Kerala. The ridges range up to 1400m a.s.l. and the streams emerging from these hills and ridges drain into flat terrain to the north at about 800m a.s.l. The geology is dominated by Gneissic rocks and the soils are dominated by weathered alfisols, acidic and porous, with clay increasing from about 20–30 per cent in the upper 20 cm to over 50 per cent at 50 cm. The surface layers are sandy clay loam with coarse sand and pockets of clay-rich 'black soils'. The region is characterized by a climate classified by the Indian Meteorological Department as 'Tropical Savanna, hot, seasonally dry'. Annual rainfall varies spatially from less than 700 mm in the eastern fringes to over 1200 mm in the south-west. The rain comes both from the south-west monsoon (June–September) and the north-east monsoon (October–December). Pre-monsoon showers in March–May can also periodically cause major rainfall events in the dry season. The forests are tropical dry deciduous of the *Terminalia alata* (Roxb.)-*Anogeissus latifolia* (DC.)-*Tectona grandis* (L.f.) series (Pascal, 1986). The main forested area was declared a National Park in the 1970s. There is significant human use and associated forest cover changes along the entire northern fringe of the National Park. The main occupation in the villages surrounding the National Park is agriculture, with *jowar* (*Sorghum bicolour*), *ragi* (*Eleusine coracana*), maize and, more recently, cotton and tobacco being the principal rainfed crops while paddy and sugarcane cultivation occurs in the irrigated lands. Animal husbandry, agricultural wage labour and forest product collection are important secondary occupations. Village communities are heterogeneous, with hamlets of tribal groups such as *Soligas* located right on the park fringe and more mixed caste hamlets elsewhere.

In a region of 800 mm rainfall, rainfed cultivation is the norm. However, over the centuries, farmers in this area as well as in other parts of peninsular India have devised irrigation tank technology as a solution to the problems of water scarcity (Vaidyanathan, 2001). The plains around the Bandipur forest are dotted with such structures. The tanks, created by earthen embankments, impound the streamflow and, if they are adequately filled, the water is let out through sluices into channels that provide gravity-based irrigation to the lands downhill from the channels. Since the rainfall in this area is somewhat bimodal, occasionally the tanks may fill up twice a year and enable the irrigation of two crops. Although groundwater-based irrigation, mainly through borewells, has begun to spread in this region, most irrigation in villages close to the National Park still comes from irrigation tanks. Surface flows in streams emerging from the National Park are therefore crucial to agriculture, but their use is mediated by the tank systems. A larger research project of which this study is a part involved the selection and monitoring of 'control' (i.e., relatively undisturbed forest) catchments within the core area of the National Park and of 'heavily used' or 'degraded' catchments on the fringe. One of the degraded catchments so chosen was of the Baragi stream, which emerges from the Marigudi ridge and flows eastwards through Baragi village before turning northwards and joining other streams. The Baragi irrigation tank was constructed in the nineteenth century across this stream and then renovated and expanded to its present size in 1982. The tank now has a Full Reservoir Level (FRL) of 31.84 m (104.43 feet) giving a live storage level variation of 6.19 m (20.43 feet) and a corresponding live storage volume of 1.32 M.cu.m, a waterspread area of 106.65 acres (43ha) and an irrigated command of 135 acres (source: Minor Irrigation Department). The catchment area of the tank is 29 sq.km., including 22 sq.km. of heavily used forest, with the rest being agriculture and barren land.

7.4.3. Agrarian context

To understand the manner in which the availability of water in the irrigation tank influences agriculture and incomes in Baragi village, it is necessary to arrive at a picture of the overall agrarian context of the village. Baragi revenue village is a large village, whose boundary includes a significant portion of the forests on the eastern slopes of the Marigudi ridge. The total geographical area of the revenue village is recorded as 2795 hectares, including 1403 hectare that are designated as forest land, mostly subsumed under the National Park.

The Baragi revenue village contains several hamlets, of which the one relevant to this study is the main settlement of Baragi itself that is located downstream of the Baragi irrigation tank. Baragi is a large hamlet, with 392 households drawn from various castes and landholding categories. There is of course a correlation between caste and landholding, with the upper caste households generally owning more lands. The total percentage of landless households is quite significant (19 per cent), but the bulk of the households (59 per cent) are in the small-holder[3] category. It should be noted that the labourers working on agricultural lands in the tank command area are drawn not only from the Baragi hamlet but also from neighbouring hamlets.

Agriculture is the main occupation in Baragi. The important irrigated crops are paddy (cultivated in the tank irrigated area) and sugarcane, turmeric and onion in the borewell irrigated areas. The main dry crops are *jowar, ragi,* cotton and marigold. Livestock rearing (both cattle and goats) and collection of forest produce are important secondary occupations.

---

[3] Landholding classes are defined as per the Government of Karnataka benchmarks: small= <5 acres, medium = 5–10 acres, large>10 acres. Landholding is calculated in terms of equivalent dry acres using the ratio 1 acre of irrigated land = 3 acres of dry land.

Some persons in the Baragi hamlet are engaged in non-agricultural jobs. A significant fraction of adults in the landless and marginal landholding households migrate seasonally in search of wage labour, usually to the coffee growing areas in neighbouring Wynaad and Kodagu districts.

Much of the agriculture in the Baragi village and surrounding areas is rainfed. But the extent of irrigated land is not insignificant, comprising 15 per cent of the cultivated area in 2003.[4] This includes a tank command area of 54.7 hectare (135 acres) and a well irrigated area of 19 hectare (47 acres). Moreover, the productivity of irrigated lands is several times higher than that of rainfed lands, making the irrigated land in general and the tank command land in particular a major asset in the local economy. With landholdings in the tank command being well distributed, the tank irrigation system is of direct concern to a significant fraction of households in the Baragi hamlet (144 out of 392) and of indirect concern to many households among the landless and small landholding classes who engage in wage labour.

Water is important not just for agriculture; households also depend on tank, stream and ground water for domestic use and for use by livestock. However, it was observed that these uses are relatively insulated from changes in tank inflow patterns for two reasons. First, the villagers have followed a tank management system wherein some minimum storage for livestock-related and domestic use is guaranteed. Second, state agencies have implemented drinking water supply schemes that draw upon deep borewells which are not at this point in time sensitive to the catchment hydrological changes that have been examined. Thus, our investigation focused on agriculture and within that on the impact of changes in catchment hydrology on the economic benefits from tank irrigated agriculture.[5]

7.4.4. Link between tank filling, cropping patterns and agriculture, and implications for the study design

The traditional irrigation tanks in peninsular India in general and the Baragi tank in particular are not meant for 'protective' or supplementary irrigation of rainfed crops. They are designed to supply water to cultivate

---

[4] This fraction was ~6 per cent in 1970, but increased substantially when the irrigation tank was renovated in 1982. Additional increases have taken place due to the spread of open well and borewell-based irrigation.

[5] We investigated the possible impact of changes in groundwater recharge in the catchment on groundwater levels in the area upstream of the tank, and found that the groundwater was currently abundant enough to not feel the impact of forest cover change.

water-intensive crops, typically paddy (Shah, 2003). If there is adequate water to irrigate the entire command area during the growing season for an irrigated crop, the command area farmers cultivate the irrigated crop. Otherwise, they do not release water at all and instead cultivate an un-irrigated crop.

Farmers have to decide by the end of June as to whether there is enough water in the tank to irrigate a four-month paddy crop during the *kharif* (June–November) season. If not, they opt to cultivate *jowar* (an un-irrigated crop). Similarly, if the tank is adequately filled by early December, the farmers opt for a six-month long *rabi*/summer[6] (December–June) paddy crop; otherwise they leave the command area largely fallow.[7]

This irrigated tank agricultural system has several implications for the analysis of impacts of hydrological change. First, the irrigation tank system is an almost 'binary' or 'threshold-based' system – there are no partially irrigated crops with productivity that is mid-way between *jowar* and paddy (in the *kharif* season) or between almost nothing and paddy (in the summer). The impacts of changes in the pattern and quantum of inflows would not be felt in any simple proportionate manner but rather in terms of changes in the probabilities of different crops being taken up. The relevant economic variable then becomes the *expected value of annual agricultural incomes*. And the impact of hydrological change has to be in terms of the change in expected value of agricultural income. Further, estimating this requires estimating not just changes in crop production or income, but also changes in crop probabilities, induced by changes in the probabilities of tank fillings.

---

[6] *Rabi* typically refers to the crop immediately after the monsoon (approximately November–February), and summer refers to the third crop (February–June). Since the irrigated paddy crop taken if the tank is full in December straddles these two seasons, we call it the *rabi*/summer crop.

[7] The actual linkages are somewhat more complicated. First, there is some inter-seasonal dependency. The summer paddy crop invariably extends till end of June, by which time they usually miss the sowing window for the *kharif* unirrigated *jowar* crop. They then end up cultivating a smattering of short-duration crops in a few of the agricultural plots that have adequate moisture. Second, not cultivating an irrigated summer paddy crop means the tank remains partially filled till April, increasing the probability of the tank getting filled by the pre-monsoon rains in April–May. Third, occasionally, even if the tank is not full, the farmers immediately below the tank embankment get enough seepage water to be able to cultivate an irrigated crop while others cultivate a rainfed crop. Fourth, the decision about whether or not an irrigated crop should be taken up and water should be released from the tank is not the command area farmers' alone. It requires the approval of the Minor Irrigation Department. This can sometimes be delayed, resulting in missing the season. These complications are not easy to factor into the quantitative analysis, but would have to be kept in mind during policy discussions.

Second, the management of the irrigation tank is a collective one. This means that the irrigation decision applies to the entire command area. For instance, even if there is enough water to irrigate half the command area for a paddy crop, such partial irrigation will not be carried out – either all farmers in the command get the benefit or nobody gets the benefit of the inflows into the tank. In such a situation, the farm-level agricultural production function approach cannot be used to determine the contribution of irrigation to incomes, because the quantity of water applied is not a farm-level decision variable. Consequently, the impacts of the big switches in cropping pattern had to be estimated from an irrigated to an unirrigated one, or vice-versa, for the whole command area.

Third, the significant degree of economic class difference within the community means that agricultural wage labour is an important dimension of the economy. With adults from many landless and small holder households working as wage labourers in the irrigated lands, changes in cropping patterns affect the demand for agricultural wage labour. Economic impact therefore needs to be measured in terms of changes in both farmer incomes and agricultural wage incomes.

7.5. Relationship between rainfall, catchment response and tank filling[8]

Before proceeding to the economic analysis, the understanding of the relationship between rainfall, tank inflows and irrigation events that emerged from the larger research project is presented. The analysis of the relationship between rainfall and irrigation events under present catchment vegetation is first presented. The impact of forest regeneration on this relationship is then predicted.

7.5.1. Rainfall and tank filling

Discussions with the farmers indicated that the tank fills more frequently in the post-monsoon (October–December) period than in the pre-monsoon or monsoon period. This is because a) more rainfall tends to occur in the September–November period than in the April–June period (see Figure 7.2),

---

[8] This section draws heavily upon the larger research Project, reported in LéLé et al., 2007, including the catchment hydrology studies carried out by Krishnaswamy et al. from ATREE and the agrohydrological analysis by Badiget et al. from CISED.

and b) the rains during the monsoon wet the catchment and so there is likely to be higher runoff (per unit rain) in the post-monsoon period.

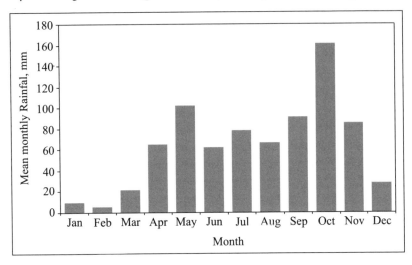

Figure 7.2. Intra-annual variation in rainfall near Baragi Village

Source: 20 years daily rainfall data for Mookahalli rain gauge station, maintained by the Directorate of Economics & Statistics, Government of Karnataka.

Historical data on tank water levels, obtained from the Karnataka Minor Irrigation Department for the period 1994–2005, were plotted along with rainfall (Figure 7.3) and compared with farmer recall of irrigation events. In the graph, sharp rises in the tank water levels refer to events of tank filling which are followed by steady declines in tank water levels corresponding to irrigation releases, in addition to evaporation and seepage losses. It can be seen that, during this ten-year period, there were a total of nine irrigation events resulting from eight full tank fillings and one partial filling in the Baragi tank. Of these, seven irrigation events occurred during the summer or the January–May period (corresponding to December tank filling events), and two irrigations events occurred during *kharif* or June–November period (corresponding to June tank filling events). In other words, December tank filling events are far more common, a point confirmed in the discussions with farmers. Analysis of seasonal rainfall patterns preceding tank filling events suggests that the net rainfall occurring between September and November is the primary determinant of a tank filling by December. A probabilistic analysis of historical rainfall and actual irrigation events suggests that the probability of a three-monthly rainfall event during this period such that the tank fills by early December is 57 per cent, or once in two years, whereas the probability of a similar (tank filling) rainfall happening in the March–June period is 23 per cent.

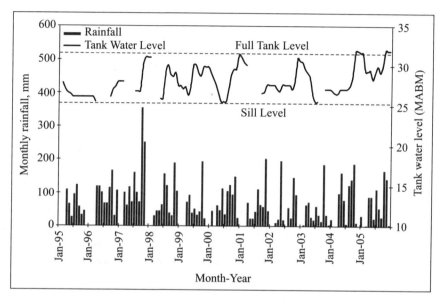

Figure 7.3.   Monthly rainfall and tank level of Baragi irrigation tank for 1994–2005

Source: Weekly water level data collected by Minor Irrigation Department. Discontinuities arise because data were not collected during certain periods.

7.5.2. Rainfall, runoff and vegetation

From the December tank filling events for the years 2002, 2004 and 2005 (the years for which the tank water level data were more reliable), it was found that the average amount of rainfall required during the September–November period for the tank level to rise from dead storage to FRL was 314 mm. Using the relationship between reservoir level and storage capacity for this tank (given in Minor Irrigation Department documents), the weekly changes in tank levels, and estimated values of evaporation and seepage losses, it was estimated that the tank catchment had a gross runoff coefficient[9] of 15 per cent. This tank catchment includes 22.12 sq.km. of

---

[9] Ratio of runoff to rainfall. Here 'runoff' is equated to tank inflows although some of these inflows may be subsurface.

open and degraded forest area (75 per cent of the total area) and 7.26 sq.km. of cultivated, fallow and grassland area (25 per cent of the total area). A one-dimensional soil-water budget model (Raes, 2002) was applied to estimate the runoff from the agricultural areas in the catchment.[10] Subtracting this agricultural runoff from the gross runoff gives the contribution of the forested catchment, from which the runoff coefficient of the forested catchment works out to 18 per cent. This matched broadly with the results of event-specific streamflow monitoring carried out in the forested catchment by our hydrologist collaborators during 2004 and 2005, which gave a September–November runoff coefficient of 23 per cent.

The runoff coefficients for similar rainfall events during the same period (2004 and 2005) in the control catchments monitored inside nearby Bandipur National Park were around 12–14 per cent. It was therefore concluded that regeneration of the forest in the Baragi tank catchment to the density in the control catchment would lead to a decline in the runoff coefficient at least from 18 per cent (the lesser of estimated and measured runoff coefficients) to 12 per cent. This means that more rainfall than the current average of 314 mm would be required for the tank to fill by early December. Specifically 460 mm of rainfall would be required when the runoff coefficient of the forested catchment drops to 12 per cent.

Since rainfall is an exogenous stochastic variable, this means the probability that the rainfall in a given year is enough or more than enough to fill the tank (the 'probability of exceedance') would decline as the runoff coefficient declines, or alternatively the 'return period' of tank filling rainfall will increase. This relationship is plotted in Figure 7.4.

The graph shows that the relationship between return period and runoff coefficient is highly non-linear. The return period increases from its current value of approximately two years (57 per cent probability) to approximately six years (18 per cent probability) when the runoff coefficient declines from the current 18 per cent to 12 per cent. Any further reduction, even by one or two per cent points, results in a sharp increase in the return period to ten years.

For the June tank filling, the current probability is two years in ten, or 20 per cent. An analysis similar to the above, using both historical weekly tank

---

[10] This model combines the SCS-Curve number method with root zone soil-moisture balance to estimate runoff. The SCS curve number method (USDA, 1993) is a simple and widely used method for estimating approximate runoff from a rainfall event or sequence of events, using information such as hydrologic soil group, land use, treatment and transient soil hydrologic conditions.

inflows and field measurements of runoff during the April–June period in the Baragi and the control catchments, indicates that this probability would decline to seven per cent if the Baragi forest vegetation regenerated to reach the density in the control. These changes in tank filling probability (and hence probability of irrigated crop cultivation) are used in section 7.8, after estimating the economic returns under tank filling and no-tank-filling scenarios in the next two sections.

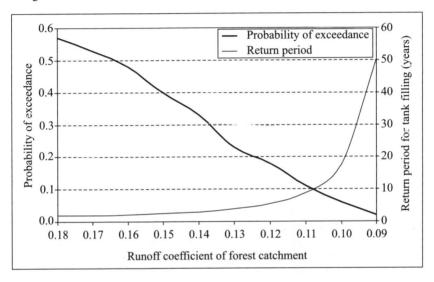

Figure 7.4. Variation in 'Probability of Exceedance' of rainfall required to fill tank with variation in forested catchment runoff coefficient during the northeast monsoon (September–December).

7.6. Socio-economic data collection and sampling

The socio-economic data collection focused on the estimation of agricultural productivity, incomes and wage employment in farms located within the tank command under different cropping scenarios. To reduce errors involved in oral recall data was collected as far as possible through actual monitoring. This could be done during two growing seasons – *kharif* (June–November) 2004 when unirrigated *jowar* was cultivated, and *rabi*/summer (January–June) 2005 when an irrigated paddy crop was cultivated. Data was obtained for these crops through actual monitoring of crop cultivation practices and production for a sample of farmers. The data for the alternate crops (that would have been grown if the tank had filled differently) had to be collected using oral recall.

A total of 144 farmers[11] own land in the tank command, most of them from the Baragi hamlet of Baragi village, and a few from the neighbouring hamlets/villages of Hongahalli and Tenkalahundi. The details of this population of farmers are given in Table 7.1. Note that landholdings in the tank command are typically quite small, averaging 1.0 acres for the entire population of 144 farmers.

Table 7.1. Landholding classes among tank command farmers

Hamlet to which farmer belongs	Land holding category [acres][a]				Total farmers	Plots[c] monitored: unirrigated jowar	Plots monitored: summer paddy
	0–1	>1–2	>2–4	>4			
Baragi	85	23	6	3	117	28	34
Hongahalli	18	4	0	0	22	5	5
Tenkala-hundi	1	4	0	0	5	1	1
All hamlets	104	31	6	3	144[b]	34	40

Note: [a]Refers only to the land held by the farmers within the tank command.
[b]Includes those who got seepage water from the waste weir during the summer of 2005.
[c]Almost all farmers own only one plot in the command, so plot and farm are equivalent. In the three cases where the farmer owned multiple plots in the command, the focus was on a single plot for practical reasons.

The monitoring effort aimed at sample of about 25 per cent of the population data was obtained for 34 farmers (out of 138) during *kharif* (2004) and 40 farmers (out of 144) during the summer of 2005. A stratified random sampling approach was used. Based on the existing literature and preliminary discussions with farmers, it was anticipated that agricultural income might vary depending upon landholding size soil type, as well as soil moisture. Since direct measurement of soil moisture was not possible, two proxy location variables were used – location along the reach (head-end, middle and tail-end, the assumption being that head-enders get more seepage water) and elevation within the command (upland, mid-land, lowland, the observation being that lowland plots get more soil moisture from seepage). Hence the sample was stratified by landholding size, soil type, reach and elevation.

---

[11] Actually 138 farmers own land within the command, and six other farmers get irrigation if the tank fills and overflows.

The data collection was carried out at two levels. Basic socio-economic data on household demographics, education, occupation, and landholdings inside and outside the tank command for the household as a whole was collected. Data on actual labour, other inputs, costs and production was gathered only for land held within the tank command. The data was collected through a combination of the 'diary' method (where farmers maintained daily notes on farming activities and inputs) and verification by field researchers on a weekly basis. The harvest data were gathered through direct observations in the fields.[12] Later on, it was found that during an unirrigated *kharif* season, not all farmers cultivated hybrid jowar; a small number cultivated fodder jowar, marigold or beans. While fodder jowar cultivators were present in the sample, for the other crops, figures had to be used based on discussions with the farmers. Similarly, for the cropping scenarios that could not be covered (mainly irrigated paddy during *kharif*), productivity information based on group discussions with the farmers, and cost data from the summer paddy crop that was monitored, were used.

7.7. Estimating agricultural Incomes and wage employment under alternative hydrological scenarios

Income from agriculture has several components and its estimation involves some definitional and practical issues. The agricultural system is an integration of farming, and animal husbandry, with cattle being maintained primarily for manure and draught power, and milk being produced in small quantities largely for self-consumption. In turn, the crop residue from jowar or paddy is used as fodder. Food crops are also largely self-consumed, but there is an active market in these crops in the neighbouring town. The market for manure is thin, as is also for crop residue. Family labour is often used substantially on the farm, but some farmers also hire out their labour locally. In estimating net returns from agriculture, market prices are used for food crops. Crop residue generated was compensated by the manure provided by livestock, and so no separate estimation of the value of crop residue or input cost of own manure was

---

[12] In most cases, the land was owned as a single parcel or plot and so the data collected pertain to the farmer's entire tank-irrigated landholding. In the few (3) cases where the farmer (typically a big landholder) held multiple parcels within the command, we focused all the data collection on only one parcel for practical reasons. Thus the fraction of plots sampled was somewhat lower (22 per cent) than the fraction of households sampled.

made. Net income from farming was defined as gross income minus paid out costs only, thereby clubbing returns to own labour with the profits from farming and avoiding the question of estimating the shadow price of own labour.

The analyses of gross and net incomes and wage labour hired in the entire command area are presented, first for the cropping scenarios during the *kharif* season and then for the *rabi*/summer season. Extrapolating gross income estimates from the sample farmers to the entire command area is relatively easy (using information on crops cultivated and key physical factors influencing crop productivity, as explained below). Extrapolating net income and wage labour hiring from the sample to the entire command area is complicated because paid out costs (including wage labour hired) depend not on the physical factors influencing crop productivity but on the socio-economic endowments of the household (e.g., landholding, family labour available, livestock holding, etc. – for details, see Lélé et al., 2008). The focus in this chapter being on estimating the *changes* in average values between two hydrological scenarios, simple averages of net income and wage labour hired from the sample farmers to estimate values for the entire command are used. Exploring the factors determining variation in paid out costs would help understand the differential impacts of hydrological change on different farmer groups, but this exercise is not within the scope of this chapter.

7.7.1. Incomes and wage employment under alternative scenarios for the kharif season

As explained in section 7.4.4, the two alternative scenarios for the *kharif* season are cultivation of (mostly) jowar under unirrigated conditions or cultivation of paddy under irrigated conditions. The estimates for unirrigated *jowar* (and other crops) are presented first and in more detail. Then estimates for an irrigated *kharif* crop based on farmer discussions are presented.

Unirrigated jowar in the *kharif* season

The average productivity of *kharif* hybrid jowar for the sample farmers was 1350 kg/acre, and gross income INR 7600/acre. Average net income was INR 4340/acre and average hired labour was INR 1140/acre. However, in extrapolating the results to the entire command area, certain modifications are required. First, eight farmers cultivated fodder jowar in a total of 10 acres. Since four of these were there in the sample, data was used from those sample farmers to extrapolate to all fodder jowar cultivators. Second, several plots close to the tank embankment received so much seepage that jowar cultivation was not possible. Farmers cultivated either marigolds (11.7 acres) or beans (2.8 acres). The economic returns were estimated for these minor crops based on discussions with the farmers. Finally, our observations showed that productivity in upland or higher elevation plots was significantly lower than that in midland or lowland plots due to differences in soil moisture from seepage (see Lélé et al., 2008). As the sample was not proportionate to the distribution of hybrid jowar cultivating farmers across elevations,[13] average values were stratified by elevation and then applied to corresponding elevation-wise areas.

The estimated production, gross income, net income and wage employment generated during the unirrigated *kharif* season of 2004 from all crops are given in Table 7.2.

Table 7.2. Estimated production and income in entire tank command: unirrigated *kharif*

Crop	Elevation	Area (acres)	Average Yield (kg/acre)	Gross Income per acre for sample farmers (Rs.)	Gross income of all farmers in command (Rs.)	Net income of all farmers in command (Rs.)	Wage employment generated in command (Rs.)
Hybrid Jowar	Upland	44.5	710	4190	186,560	60,109	36,956
	Midland/ Lowland	73.3	1450	8137	596,435	353,725	86,372
Fodder Jowar	All	2.0	600	3460	6,747	−13,480	n.a.
Mari-gold	All	11.7	1500	4500	52,538	3503	n.a.
Beans	All	2.8	6000	1800	4,950	825	n.a.

(Contd.)

---

13 Once the fodder jowar cultivators were removed, our sample contained only four upland farmers whereas there were 50 in the population.

(*Contd.*)

Crop	Elevation	Area (acres)	Average Yield (kg/acre)	Gross Income per acre for sample farmers (Rs.)	Gross income of all farmers in com-mand (Rs.)	Net income of all farmers in com-mand (Rs.)	Wage employ-ment gener-ated in com-mand (Rs.)
Fallow	Inside command	0.4	0	0	0	0	0
	Fed by waste weir	4.8	0	0	0	0	0
Total		139.4	–	–	847,229	404,681	123,328

Note: Net income from fodder jowar is negative because the market price of fodder jowar is very low. Presumably, the shadow price of self-consumed fodder jowar is higher.

It is to be noted that the wage employment generated is slightly underestimated because data is not available for wage labour used in the few farms cultivating marigold, beans and fodder jowar.

Estimating income and employment under irrigated *kharif* paddy scenario and the difference

During the period of data collection, there was no irrigated *kharif* crop. Hence, for the alternative scenario of irrigated paddy cultivation during the *kharif* season, productivity estimates were based upon discussions with farmers. The cost data from the summer paddy survey was used. This was adjusted to the shorter duration of the *kharif* crop and tighter supply of wage labour during *kharif* due to marginal farmers being busy with their own crops. These estimates of production, income and employment generation are given in Table 7.3.

As expected, an irrigated *kharif* crop would be more lucrative for the farmers and would generate more employment for wage labourers than an unirrigated *kharif jowar* crop. For instance, net income for farmers in the command increases by almost 50 per cent and employment generated more than doubles. But these are absolute differences, which need to be weighted by the probability of irrigation happening or not happening in *kharif*, to get an expected value of *kharif* incomes. This we do in sec. 7.7.3.

Table 7.3. Estimated aggregate production and income in entire tank command: irrigated *kharif*

Crop	Elevation	Area (acres)	Average Yield (kg/acre)	Gross income of all farmers in command (Rs.)	Net income of all farmers in command (Rs.)	Wage employment generated in entire command (Rs.)
	Upland	46.15	2,850	789,165	208,640	258,278
	Midland	50.05	2,625	788,288	226,271	
Paddy	Lowland	38.425	2,400	553,320	173,716	
	Fed by waste weir	4.8	2,625	75,600	21,700	11,051
Total for all tank irrigated lands		139.4		2,206,373	630,327	269,329

7.7.2. Incomes and wage employment under alternative scenarios for the rabi/summer season

The estimation for the summer cropping scenarios is simpler because cultivation takes place in the tank command only if there is irrigation, in which case the cultivated crop is paddy. The detailed data from monitoring sample farmers during the irrigated *rabi*/summer crop of January–June 2005 enabled us to estimate average productivity and income levels. There being no variation in productivity by elevation (see Lélé et al., 2008, section 7.2.1), average values were applied to the entire command area. Estimates of average and extrapolated gross income, net income and wage employment generated in the entire tank command from summer paddy are given in Table 7.4.

In the no irrigation scenario, there is virtually no cultivation, so there is no income for the farmers. So the totals in the last row of Table 7.4 represent the differences between the irrigation and no irrigation scenarios, at least as far as farmer income is concerned. Thus, for e.g., a tank filling in December means an increase in gross income of INR 14,800 per farmer (total farmers in command area being 144).

The effect on wage employment is not as high as suggested by Table 7.4. Most of those who obtain wage employment in summer paddy cultivation do not sit idle if there is no summer paddy crop. But the discussions with these agricultural labourers suggest that they would get less than half of the employment that is generated by summer paddy. Fifty per cent of the wage employment in summer paddy have been accordingly assumed as the employment obtained in years when no summer crop is taken.[14]

Table 7.4. Estimated aggregate production, income and employment generated in entire tank command: summer paddy

Crop	Elevation	Area (acres)	Average Yield (kg/ acre)	Average Gross income per acre for sample farmers (Rs.)	Gross income for all farmers in command area (Rs.)	Net income for all farmers in command area (Rs.)	Wage employ- ment gener- ated in entire com- mand (Rs.)
Paddy	Tank com- mand	134.6	2,584	15,307	2,060,322	1,507,128	258,230
Paddy	Fed by waste weir	4.8	2,584	15,307	73,474	53,746	9,209
All tank irrigated land		139.4	2,584	15,307	2,133,796	1,560,874	267,439

7.8. Likely impacts of changes in catchment vegetation on agricultural incomes and wage employment in the tank command

We are now in a position to use the estimates of changes in tank fillings due to changes in vegetation derived in section 7.5 and the estimates of incomes and wage employment generated under different cropping scenarios derived in section 7.7 to predict the changes in income and wage employment due to changes in forest vegetation. A detailed calculation for gross income is given in Table 7.5 for gross income.

The gross income (irrigated vs. unirrigated) for a particular season of a particular scenario occurring and summed to get the expected value of gross income for that season. Repeating this for the other season and summing gives the expected value for the entire year. Since the hydrological analysis showed that regeneration of forests would lead to declines in June and

---

[14] Furthermore, this employment is available elsewhere (typically in the neighbouring districts of Wynaad and Kodagu), requiring seasonal migration on the part of the labourers.

Table 7.5. Predicted impact of catchment forest regeneration on gross income of Baragi tank command area farmers

Scenario	Season	Probability of tank filling (and hence of irrigation)	Gross income from irrigated crop	Probability of tank not filling	Gross income from unirrigated crop	Expected value of gross income
Degraded forest in catchment (Current)	Kharif	20 %	2,206,373	80 %	847,229	1,119,058
	Rabi/summer	57 %	2,133,796	43 %	0 (no crop)	1,216,264
Total for entire year						2,335,322
Regenerated catchment forest (Simulated)	Kharif	7 %	2,206,373	93 %	847,229	942,369
	Rabi/summer	18 %	2,133,796	82 %	0 (no crop)	384,083
Total for year						1,326,453
CHANGE in expected value when catchment forest regenerates	In total value					-1,008,869
	In value per acre					-7237
	In value per farmer					-7006
	% Change					-43 %

Note: In US$, the figures for changes in total gross income, gross income per acre and gross income per farmer are $25,222, $181 and $175 respectively.

December tank filling frequencies, this translates into a lower probability of cultivating irrigated crops and therefore a correspondingly lower expected value of gross income. The decline of 43 per cent is quite substantial.

Similar calculations give changes in the expected value of annual net income and annual wage employment that might be predicted from regeneration of the forested catchment. The summary estimates are given in Table 7.6 and, as in the case of gross income, the changes are substantial (–48 per cent and –31 per cent respectively).

Table 7.6. Predicted impact of catchment forest regeneration on the net income of baragi tank command area farmers and wage employment generated in the command area

Scenario	Season	Expected value of net income	Expected value of employment generated
Degraded forest in catchment (Current)	*Kharif*	449,810	152,528
	Rabi/summer	889,698	76,220
	Total for year	1,339,509	228,748
Regenerated catchment forest (Simulated)	*Kharif*	420,476	133,548
	Rabi/summer	280,957	24,070
	Total for year	701,434	157,617
Change in expected value when catchment forest regenerates	In total value	– 638,075	– 71,131
	In value per acre	– 4577	– 510
	In value per farmer	– 4431	– 494
	% change	– 48 %	– 31 %

7.9. Conclusions and implications

The likely impacts of regeneration of a degraded forest catchment on streamflow and the consequent impact on irrigation tank-based agriculture in a downstream village have been simulated, focusing on changes in average incomes and hired labour. It is found that regeneration of the forest will reduce the runoff coefficient of the forested catchment and thereby significantly reduce the probability of the irrigation tank filling in either season. This in turn reduces the probability of the command area farmers being able to cultivate an irrigated paddy crop in either season. Less frequent paddy crop cultivation results in significant reductions in income from, and wage employment generated in, the command area.

This result, that increases in or regeneration of forest cover in the hilly catchment will actually reduce the economic benefits accruing to the community downstream, is perhaps counter-intuitive and certainly contrary to some of the findings in the watershed services literature such as that of Pattanayak and Kramer (2001). This is not because the hydrological relationships in the Western Ghats are topsy-turvy. It is a consequence of the particular way in which streamflows are being managed and utilized by the local community, viz., by impounding wet season flows and using the water in the dry season, and that too for a water-intensive crop which can be cultivated only if the tank fills up completely during the rainy season. This kind of agriculture depends on quick runoff from the tank catchment so that the tank fills more easily and in time for the farmers to start cultivating an irrigated crop. Reduced forest vegetation and soil compaction in the tank catchment due to grazing will ensure early runoff and thus favour this kind of agriculture.

It is to be noted that under somewhat different agricultural water use systems, the impacts may be different. For instance, the decline in streamflow because of regenerating forest vegetation does not mean that this portion of the rainfall is entirely lost to evapotranspiration by the forest. It is possible that a significant portion of this water would end up in the form of an increased contribution to the groundwater aquifer (a partitioning that we were unable to estimate). Agriculture based on open well or bore well cultivation might then stand to gain (although such agriculture is currently not very prevalent in this village). One could also visualize a scenario where the irrigation tank was managed to provide protective irrigation to a much larger area of dry crops (such as *jowar* or *ragi*). Under these circumstances, the farmers would feel the impacts of declining inflows less sharply (although it would still be negative).

A couple of caveats are in order. First, hydrological changes cannot be restricted to a micro scale. Decreased use of irrigation water in the tank command usually means higher availability downstream. But it is not possible to trace these wider scale effects easily. One can also say that further downstream the catchment size is much larger, and so forest cover changes in one small catchment upstream are not going to dramatically affect the users that far downstream. Second, the prediction of decline in benefits is based only on declines in flows. However, improvement in forest condition will also result in declines in upstream soil erosion and consequently reduce the siltation rate of the tank, thereby extending its useful life. That there is substantial sediment entering the tank is obvious to anybody visiting the tank. However, from discussions with local farmers, it seemed that there was enough dead storage capacity in the tank to absorb the current silt load (corresponding to a degraded catchment) for a couple of decades. Thus, the effects of changes in siltation due to changes in forest condition have been deferred in time and are perhaps small in any case. The irrigation tank-dependent community or communities immediately downstream of the Bandipur forests still stand to lose economically in their agricultural incomes and agricultural wage employment if the forests regenerate.

Empirically, the results highlight the point that, under certain circumstances, farmers immediately downstream of a forested catchment may have an incentive to degrade the forest (or to let it degrade) in order to 'harvest' greater streamflows. In other words, the watershed 'service' of forests is a highly contextual phenomenon hence simplistic assumptions about its direction and magnitude should not be made. Methodologically, this study also makes a strong case for a more rigorous and interdisciplinary approach to understanding the phenomenon of watershed services. In addition to the obvious need for substantial analysis of catchment hydrology, this study highlights the importance of understanding the crucial 'agro-hydrological' linkage between standard aggregate hydrological variables such as runoff or recharge and the water applied in the field – a linkage that is both technological and social in nature. Farmers who do not have access to certain technologies do not have a direct linkage with the runoff from the catchment. The functioning of a technology like an irrigation tank is also dependent on social arrangements around it. In this case, since all the tank command farmers agree to a system that is 'all or none' (irrigated water-intensive crop for all or no irrigation at all), the technology generates certain kinds of outcomes. The other modest methodological contribution offered is the illustration of how one may address 'non-marginal' change situations and ones in which relationships are probabilistic. Finally, the study also draws attention to the need to look at impacts in terms of both agricultural profits or incomes and wage employment generated, and the need to be sensitive to the nature of local markets for labour and other inputs.

The idea is not to claim that forest regeneration reduces all benefits from forests. No attempt was made to estimate the value(s) of all other forest ecosystem benefits and how they would change if the forest regenerated (see Lélé et al., 2001). As a part of the larger research project, some qualitative and quantitative data regarding the use of forest produce by local communities were collected. Preliminary analysis indicates that the set of households collecting forest produce for consumption or sale is entirely different from the set of households cultivating land in the tank command. The forest-dependent households live in and cultivate lands upstream of or outside the command area of the tank, and they would certainly stand to gain from a denser forest. This underlines the fact that even within the so-called 'local community' there can be major divergences in the nature of the stakes of different groups in the forest. Policy-makers must therefore move away from simplistic notions of forests being good for everything and everybody in all circumstances, and facilitate context-specific, ecologically and economically informed forest governance mechanisms.

References

Aylward, B. and Echeverria, J., 'Synergies between Livestock Production and Hydrological Function in Arenal, Costa Rica', *Environment and Development Economics*, 6, (2001), 359–381.

Bonell, M., 'Progress in the Understanding of Runoff Generation Dynamics in Forests', *Journal of Hydrology*, 150(2–4), (1993), 217–275.

Bruijnzeel, L.A., 'Land Use and Hydrology in Warm Humid Regions: Where do We Stand?' *Journal of Hydrology*, 216, (1993), 3–34.

Bruijnzeel, L.A., 'Hydrological Functions of Tropical Forests: Not Seeing the Soil for the Trees?' *Agriculture, Ecosystems and Environment*, 104 (1), (2004), 185–228.

Chopra, K. and Kadekodi, G., 'Natural Resource Accounting in the Yamuna Basin: Accounting for Forest Resources', Project Report, Delhi, Institute of Economic Growth, 1997.

Kramer, Randall A., Richter Daniel, D., Pattanayak, S. and Sharma, N.P., 'Ecological and Economic Analysis of Watershed Protection in Eastern Madagascar', *Journal of Environmental Management*, 49(3), (1997), 277–295.

Lélé, S., Krishnaswamy, J., Venkatesh, B., Badiger, S., Purandara, B.K. and Menon, A., 'Forest Cover Change, Hydrological Services, and Socio-economic Impact: Insights from the Western Ghats of India', Final Project Report, Bangalore, Centre for Interdisciplinary Studies in Environment and Development, Ashoka Trust for Research in Ecology and the Environment, National Institute of Hydrology and UNESCO International Hydrological Programme, 2007.

Lélé, S., Patil, I., Badiger, S., Menon, A. and Kumar, R., 'The Economic Impact of Forest Hydrological Services on Local Communities: A Case Study from the

Western Ghats of India', SANDEE Working Paper No. 36–08, Kathmandu, South Asian Network for Development and Environmental Economics, 2008.

Lélé, S., Srinivasan, V. and Bawa, K.S., 'Returns to Investment in Conservation: Disaggregated Benefit-cost Analysis of the Creation of a Wildlife Sanctuary', in Ganeshaiah, K.N., Uma Shaanker, R., and Bawa, K.S., (eds.), *Proceedings of the International Conference on Tropical Ecosystems: Structure, Diversity and Human Welfare*, (New Delhi: Oxford-IBH Publishing Co., 2001), 31–33.

Lélé, S. and Venkatachalam, L., 'Assessing the Socio-economic Impact of Changes in Forest Cover on Watershed Services', in Krishnaswamy, J., Lélé, S. and Jayakumar, R., (eds.), *Hydrology and Watershed Services in the Western Ghats of India*, (New Delhi: Tata McGraw-Hill, 2006), 215–248.

Pascal, J.P., 'Explanatory Booklet on the Forest Map of south India', *Travaux de la Section Scientifique et Technique, Hors Série No. 18: French Institute*, Pondicherry, 1986.

Pattanayak, S.K. and Kramer, R.A., 'Worth of Watersheds: A Producer Surplus Approach for Valuing Drought Mitigation in Eastern Indonesia', *Environment & Development Economics*, 6 (1), (2001), 123–146.

Pattanayak, S., 'Valuing Watershed Services: Concepts and Empirics from Southeast Asia', *Agriculture, Ecosystems & Environment*, 104 (1), (2004), 171–184.

Purandara, B.K., Venkatesh, B., Bonell, M., and Jayakumar, R., 'Hydrological and Soil Impacts of Natural and Anthropogenic Forest Disturbances', in Subramanian, V. and Ramanathan, A.L., (eds.), *Ecohydrology: Proceedings of the International Workshop on Ecohydrology*, (New Delhi: Capital Publishing Co., 2001), 433–444.

Putty, M.R.Y. and Prasad, R., 'Run off Processes in Head Water Catchment – An Experimental Study in Western Ghats in South India', *Journal of Hydrology*, 235, (2000), 63–71.

Raes, D., 'BUDGET – A Soil Water and Salt Balance Model', Reference Manual, Leuven, Belgium, Department Land Management, K.U.Leuven, 2002.

Shah, E., *Social Designs: Tank Irrigation Technology and Agrarian Transformation in Karnataka, South India*, (New Delhi: Orient Longman, 2003).

Sikka, A.K., Samra, J.S., Sharda, V.N., Samraj, P. and Lakshmanan, V., 'Low Flow and High Flow Responses to Converting Natural Grassland into Bluegum (Eucalyptus globulus) in Nilgiris watersheds of South India', *Journal of Hydrology*, 270 (1–2), (2003), 12–26.

USDA, 'National Engineering Handbook, Section 4, Hydrology (NEH-4)', Washington, D.C., Soil Conservation Service, U.S. Department of Agriculture, 1993.

Vaidyanathan, A. (ed.), *Tanks of South India*, (New Delhi: Centre for Science and Environment, 2001).

Vincent, J.R., Kaosa-ard, M., Worachai, L., Azumi, E.Y., Tangtham, N. and Rala, A.B., 'The Economics of Watershed Protection: A Case Study of Mae Taeng,' MANRES Project Report, Bangkok, Natural Resources and Environment Program, Thailand Development Research Institute, 1995.

8

Can Mangroves Minimize Property Loss during Big Storms?: An Analysis of House Damages due to the Super Cyclone in Orissa

Saudamini Das[1]

8.1 Introduction

Mangrove forests provide a range of ecosystem services to humans (Dixon, et al., 1994; MEA, 2003). Among these services, storm protection remains one of the most important regulating services provided by mangroves. During storms, mangroves provide protection to inland properties and lives by reducing wind and storm surge velocity. Given recent increases in the frequency of cyclones and the fear of further increases in frequency and intensity due to climate change (Steffen, 2006), both research and quantification of the storm protection function of mangroves becomes important.

Since the Indian Ocean Tsunami of December 2004, the protection services of coastal forests have been in the limelight. Though some anecdotal reports and studies have concluded that the presence of mangroves reduced the extent of tsunami damage (UNEP, 2005; Danielson et al., 2005; Kathiresan and Rajendran, 2005; Dahdouh-Guebas et al., 2006), critics

[1] I acknowledge with gratitude the financial and academic support from the South Asian Network for Development and Environmental Economics (SANDEE). I wish to thank Priya Shyamsunder, Kanchan Chopra, Enamul Haque, M. N. Murthy, Jeff Vincent and other SANDEE colleagues for their useful ideas, suggestions and comments. I would like to thank the Emergency Officer and staff of the Emergency Offices of Kendrapada and Jagatsinghpur districts of Orissa for the innumerable ways in which they supported this project. I record with appreciation the infrastructure and academic facilities received from the Institute of Economic Growth, New Delhi.

have questioned their validity citing limited sample size and inappropriate statistical analysis (Kerr et al., 2006; Baird, 2006). Some researchers see coastal forests as playing either a marginal or no role in containing tsunami damages and have underscored the need for clearer answers (Kerr and Baird, 2007; Chatenox and Peduzzi, 2007; Cochard, R. et al., 2008). Theoretically, it is well established that mangroves can reduce cyclone impact by dissipating wave energy (Mazda et al., 1997, 2006; Brinkman et al., 1997; Massel et al., 1999; Hamza et al., 1999; Harada and Imamura, 2005; Quartel et al., 2007). But there is little in the way of detailed empirical work (Khazai et al., 2007). Moreover, few studies examine the protection offered by mangroves against wind velocity. This chapter attempts a detailed empirical analysis of the storm surge and wind protection services of the mangrove forests of Orissa State in India during the October 1999 Super Cyclone by analyzing the damage to residential houses.

In October 1999, Orissa was battered by a super cyclone with a landfall wind velocity of 256 km per hour, heavy torrential rain ranging from 400 mm to 867mm, and a storm surge height of approximately seven metres. It devastated 12 of the 30 districts of the state and damaged nearly 19,58,351 residential houses in addition to causing numerous other damages (Gupta and Sharma, 2000).

The state government reported house damages after the Super Cyclone under three different categories, namely, Fully Collapsed (FC) houses, Partially Collapsed (PC) houses and Swept Away (SA) Houses. FC and PC reflected the number of houses damaged by surge and wind whereas SA houses were the result of flooding or storm surge related damages. The number of these damaged houses in Orissa were reported to be 23,620 swept away, 7,46,322 fully collapsed, and 11,87,591 partially collapsed houses. This study focuses on the reduction in fully collapsed and partially collapsed houses in the Kendrapada district as a result of mangrove protection against wind and surge.

Cyclone-related damages are mediated by many factors including cyclone intensity. Cyclone intensity is reflected by wind velocity, velocity of storm surge and the quantum and duration of torrential rain. Factors like elevation, topography, bathymetry, coastal distance, coastal forests, economic and social relations, government efficiency, etc., also influence damage occurrences. Thus, the coastal mangrove forest is one factor among many that play a decisive role in damage that occurs. Consequently, data availability, controls for other factors, and an interdisciplinary approach are critical in understanding the specific role of coastal forests.

In this study, an interdisciplinary model and village level data on in the Kendrapara district of the State of Orissa are used in order to evaluate the storm protection services of mangroves. An analysis of the protection offered to human life is offered elsewhere (Das, 2007b). A spatial analysis of the damages is attempted by using detailed GIS and socio-economic data of the affected areas and examining the roles of multiple factors simultaneously. A cyclone damage function is first estimated while the avoided damages are calculated thereafter.

8.2. Studies on valuing the storm protection role of coastal forests

The storm protection value of mangroves is seen as equivalent to the construction of a sea wall at the coastline (Chan et al., 1993). But rigorous economic analyses of this feature are rather limited. In recent years, a few studies have evaluated the protective services of mangroves using three different approaches – avoided damages (value of damages avoided due to mangrove presence); avoided expenditures (difference in expenditures when it comes to the maintenance and repair of infrastructure in a mangrove protected area as opposed to an unprotected area); or replacement costs (the cost of installing infrastructure that can provide the same protective services as mangroves) (Badola and Hussain, 2005; Tri et al., 1996; Sathirathai, 1998). In a recent study, Barbier (2007) recommended the use of an Expected Damage Function (EDF) to measure the storm protection value of coastal wetlands. Though each of these methods has different advantages, relatively more studies have used the avoided damages approach. The use of the avoided damages approach to value storm protection began with Farber (1987), who modeled wind velocity and valued the protection value of wetlands against wind damages from hurricanes.

One well conceptualized study that uses the avoided damages method to evaluate cyclone protection services of mangroves is by Badola and Hussain (2005). Conducting a primary survey of damages in the aftermath of the Super Cyclone of October 1999, in Orissa, they showed the damages per household to be less in a village sheltered by mangroves as compared to the damages per household in a village with a dike nearby but without mangroves and a village without either mangroves or dikes. Although the authors deserve credit for their attempt to select villages that were similar except for the presence or absence of mangroves and dikes, the attribution of the entirety reduced damages to the presence of mangroves seems to be an overestimate given the economic and geographic heterogeneity of the villages (Das, 2007b). In a more recent publication, Costanza et al. (2008) have also used this approach to measure the value of coastal wetlands for hurricane protection in the USA.

Researchers have also used the avoided damages approach to evaluate the protective role of coastal forests during the Indian Ocean Tsunami of 2004 (Kathiresan and Rajendran, 2005). Others have questioned the accuracy of the statistical analyses of such findings (Kerr et al., 2006; Baird, 2006; Vermaat and Thampanya, 2006, 2007).

This chapter also adopts the avoided damages method. This method takes into account the actual damages suffered in mangrove protected areas in order to estimate in areas not protected by mangroves as opposed to the damages suffered the volume of damages that are averted due to mangrove presence. The method involves two steps. Step 1 estimates a storm damage function linking damages to possible explanatory variables and step 2 calculates the avoided damages with the help of the marginal effects of mangroves. The value of avoided damages being the value of storm protection, the reliability of this measure is dependant on how accurately we account for all the potential factors that might have an impact on the storm damages function. Inflated storm protection values due to the omission of potential variables in the damage function could be a serious limitation of this methodology.

Mangroves or other coastal barriers should never be considered the main decisive players when analyzing the damages due to extreme events. Some of the other recognized important factors are elevation, coastal distance and inundation distances (Bretschneider and Wybro, 1977; FAO, 2006; Baird, 2006; Chatenoux and Peduzzi, 2006, 2007; Dahdouh-Guebas et al., 2006; Cochard et al., 2008).

This study, which evaluates the protective role of mangrove forests in reducing house damage, takes into consideration the roles played by socio-economic, geo-physical, and meteorological factors (such as village level wind velocity and sea elevation i.e., storm surge height), at different coastal points in impacting cyclonic damage.

8.3. Study area

The study area for this research is the Kendrapada district of the State of Orissa in India[2]. The district has eight *tahasils* (administrative units under a district) which are demographically not very different from each other. Kendrapada is the most cyclone prone area in the Indian peninsula and experiences, on average, one cyclone per year (Das, 2007a; IMD, 2000).

The landfall point of the Super Cyclone 1999 was at a place called Ersama lying 20 km south of Kendrapada district and the entire district was severely battered by both cyclonic wind and rain. Four of the eight *tahasils* of the district were affected by storm surge (Gupta and Sharma, 2000). The position of the district was to the north of the cyclone eye track throughout the cyclone period. Thus, the wind direction was from sea to land throughout the study area because cyclonic wind moves anti-clockwise in the northern hemisphere. This provides a good opportunity to test the wind buffering capacity of the mangroves.

In 1999, before the Super Cyclone hit the state, the Kendrapada district had 192 sq. km of mangrove forests located in two different blocks of the district – one in Mahakalpada *tahasil* and the other in Rajnagar *tahasil*. At both locations, mangroves spread continuously for more than 20 km parallel to the coast but the width of the forest, spreading vertically to the coast, varied from 0.5 km to 10 km at different places. More than 93 per cent of the mangroves were densely stocked and well-protected (FSI, 2001). 80 per cent of the total mangrove forests were in Rajnagar *tahasil*. Kendrapada district also has a few patches of casuarina plantation (of 0.2 to 0.4 km width) which were planted in 1974 under the coastal shelterbelt plantation scheme of the state government. The entire coastline of the study area was planted with casuarina trees after a very severe cyclonic storm hit the area in the year 1972. Casuarinas grow on sandy beaches and on sand dunes that are more elevated than areas where mangroves grow and do not get inundated during high tide. But since the coastline of the study area was mostly swampy and low lying, casuarinas could survive only in limited pockets (Mohanty, 1992), and, where they have survived, the width of the forest is nearly uniform (0.2 to 0.4 km).

Available records show that 80 per cent of the district's 60 km long coastline was covered with mangrove forests of nearly 10 km width in the past. Different factors have led to the destruction of these forests over time,

---

[2] The study area also includes 86 coastal villages from an adjoining district.

but maximum destruction seems to have occurred between 1952 and 1980 (Orissa District Gazetteer, 1996). 1952 was the year when ownership of these forests came to be transferred from the *zamindars* (the feudal land owners) to the state government while in 1980 the Wild Life Division Department was created by the state government and the management of the mangrove forests came to be transferred to this division. Mahakalpada *tahasil* witnessed the most destruction where only a thin strand of mangroves was left by 1999. In contrast, the destruction of mangroves in Rajnagar *tahasil* was marginal. It may be that the presence of ferocious animals (crocodiles, for instance) in these forest areas made the conversion of forest to other land uses difficult initially when state protection was inadequate. But the proclamation designating this forest area as the Bhitarkanika Wild Life Sanctuary in 1975 and as a national park in 1988 ensured continued protection.

The study area has a high level of poverty. More than 50 per cent of the population lives below the poverty line. According to the report of the Census of India (2001), 94 per cent of the households in Kendrapada district live in rural areas. With regard to the quality of houses in rural Kendrapada, the census figures show that only 10 per cent of the households have concrete roofs while the number with cemented walls is 17 per cent have cemented walls. Of the 17 per cent, only two per cent have walls with concrete while the rest use either raw brick or mud.

8.4. Methodology

In order to evaluate the storm protection services of mangroves, a cyclone damage function is first estimated using damage data in physical units, then the volume of avoided damages due to mangrove presence is estimated in step 2, and the storm protection value estimated by valuing the avoided damages in the final step. During cyclones, the extent of damage in a particular area depends on the intensity of the cyclone (reflected in wind velocity and storm surge) as well as on the physical and socio-economic features of the area. Physical features like the location of the village vis-à-vis the coastline, the cyclone eye, the presence of mangroves or other cyclone barriers etc., can help reduce the cyclone impact. Similarly, the economic well being and the strength of the community in terms of helping each other also influence the extent of damage. Thus, cyclone damages are expected willingness of the community to help to depend on the wind velocity, the velocity of storm surge water, the population or property at risk, and other socio-economic factors.[3] This is presented in the following equation as:

$$D_i = d(V_i, W_i, P_i, S_i) \tag{1}$$

where i represents the location (villages),

D_i is the damage suffered,

V_i is velocity of wind,

W_i is velocity of storm surge or the severity of flooding due to surge,

P_i is population or property at risk and,

S_i is the group of socio-economic factors at the location

In order to estimate equation 1, data is required on damages suffered as well as all the other independent variables. However, direct measures were not available of either V_i and W_i at the different locations. How these variables are approximated by taking into account their determinants is discussed below. The socio-economic variables that are used are also discussed.

8.4.1. Wind velocity

The wind velocity (V_i) at a place depends on the approximate radial wind *(RWi)* at the location and other factors such as the minimum distance of the location from the coast line *(dcoast_i)* and the type and the width of wind barriers near the village (barrier_i).

$$V_i = v(RW_i, dcoast_i, barrier_i) \tag{2}$$

In order to measure radial wind at a place, one needs to understand its various determinants. Radial wind over a location during a tropical cyclone depends on:

(a) the position of the location vis-à-vis the horizontal structure of the cyclone that consists of the eye, the eye wall, the wall cloud, and the outer storm structure and

(b) the minimum distance of the location from the centre of the eye of the cyclone *(dcypath_i)*. Areas under the cyclone eye and the eye wall face maximum wind *(Vmax)* while wind velocity over other

---

[3] The study ignores flooding due to torrential rain as a cause of damage since it rained almost the same amount everywhere in the study area and there were no spatial differences in rainfall over the locations. Moreover, village-specific rainfall data was unavailable. As the variation in rainfall is expected to be correlated with distance from coast and distance from cyclone path, implicitly, it is controlled for by including these variables in the model.

areas declines with distance away from the center of the eye or as *dcypath$_i$* increases. Since meteorologists estimated the radius of the super cyclone eye to be approximately 15 kilometres (IMD, 2000), the radial wind is assumed to be at its maximum in areas lying within a 15 km radius (*dcypath$_i$* <=15) from the center of the cyclone eye in our analyses. With the help of meteorologists, the radial wind is approximated for areas lying beyond a 15 km radius (*dcypath$_i$* >15) by a power function (*velocitypow*) (Roy Abraham et al., 1995).

$$Velocitypow_i = V_{max} \, (dcypath_i/R)^{-\alpha} \qquad (3)$$

where *R* is the radius of the cyclone eye (15 km in the present case) and α was taken as 0.6 at the suggestion of meteorologists.

The study area is agricultural land with an average elevation less than 10 meters everywhere (District Planning Map for Cuttack, Jajpur, Kendrapada and Jagatsinghpur of Orissa, 2000). The only wind barriers are the coastal forests, i.e., the mangrove and casuarina plantations. Mangroves are represented as the width of the forests in km between the village and the coast. Some coastal tracts also have casuarina forests. Because the width of these planted casuarinas is nearly uniform, casuarinas are represented by a dummy variable, the *casuarinadummy*.

Thus, the wind velocity at the ith location can be re-written as equation (4) below:

$$V_i = v \, [V_{max} \text{ if } dcypath_i \leq 15, \text{ velocitypow}_i \text{ if } dcypath_i > 15,$$
$$dcoast_i, \text{ mangrove}_i, \text{ casuarinadumy}_i) \qquad (4)$$

As the model includes variables *dcoast$_i$* and *mangrove$_i$*, it also implicitly controls for the distance of a village from the mangrove forest boundary that equals *dcoast$_i$ – mangrove$_i$*.

8.4.2. Velocity of storm surge (W$_i$)

Storm surge is the abnormal rise of the sea level in excess of the predicted astronomical tide. It is mainly due to the atmospheric pressure variation and the strong surface wind of a cyclone. It is noted that sea elevation also depends on other features of the cyclone as well as the physical features of the coastline. Due to these features, a coastal point facing high wind may face low sea elevation or vice versa. Thus, the velocity or severity of surge at an interior location depends on the level of sea elevation (*surge$_i$*) facing that location, and physical features of the place such as the minimum distance from the coast (*dcoast$_i$*), the elevation of the place (*topodumy$_i$*), the distance of the place from river channels (*dmajriver$_i$ and dminriver$_i$*), the presence of natural barriers (*mangroves$_i$, casuarindadummy$_i$* sand dunes, etc.) between the village and the coast line, the presence of man-made barriers (*roadumy$_i$* - dikes) near the village, etc. Taking all these factors into account, the following function for the severity of flooding due to storm surge was defined:

$$W_i = \frac{w(surge_i, dcoast_i, dmajriver_i, d\min river_i, topodumy_i,}{mhabitat_i, mangrove_i, casaurinadumy_i, roadumy_i)} \tag{5}$$

Surge$_p$ is the elevation of the sea at the coastline nearest to the location. Sea elevation during the Super Cyclone along the coast line of the study area was measured with the help of a surge envelop curve (Kalsi et al., 2004). This curve identifies the surge at all the locations along the coast affected by the Super Cyclone.

The study area is full of major and minor river channels and their roles during a storm surge are different. The major rivers carry the high velocity surge water to interior areas. As a result, the surge effect on coastal villages near the big river is reduced. But the opposite happens in the case of minor rivers. Hence, the minimum distance from river channels was divided into two, i.e., minimum distance from a major river (*dmajriver$_i$*) and minimum distance from a minor river (*dminriver$_i$*).

Topodumy$_i$ is a dummy variable for low elevation and equals one if the village is located within a mangrove habitat area and 0 otherwise. Elevation data for the study area was unavailable. However, it is known that mangrove forests grow mainly in low lying vulnerable areas that get inundated regularly during high tides. Hence, low and high areas were determined using the present and historical (1950) mangrove forest maps. Villages with *topodumy$_i$* = 1 are likely to be low lying areas and ones with *topodumy$_i$* = 0 are likely to be situated at a higher elevation.

Mhabitat$_i$ is the width of the historical mangrove forests (or the width of the mangrove habitat) that lay between the village and the coast as seen in the 1950 forest map of the area. The study area has had a vast stretch of mangrove forests historically, some of which has been destroyed. The width of the mangrove habitat in a particular location depends on the topographical, hydrological and bathymetric features of the area. Thus, this variable is taken as a proxy to capture the effects of these factors on storm surge velocity or storm damage occurrences. Researchers have also argued that since mangroves come up in sheltered bays, the physical features of the mangrove habitat could be providing the protection which is wrongly ascribed to the vegetation (Chatenoux and Peduzzi, 2007). Hence, there is a need to separate the effect of physical features from the effects of vegetation on storm damages. These two effects are separated by – (a) having both *mhabitat$_i$* and the *mangrove$_i$* variable in the damage equation and (b) by excluding non-mangrove habitat areas (areas with *mhabitat$_i$* = 0) from the analysis (see description of sample areas below).[4] Thus, *mhabitat* is used as a proxy only for the physical features of the mangrove habitat areas, and not for all the physical features of the coastline.

Mangrove$_i$ is the width of the mangrove forest (vegetation) that existed on October 11, 1999, between the ith village and the coast. *Casurinadumy,* as previously explained, is the dummy variable for the presence of casuarina forests between the village and the coast. Lastly, *roadummy* is the dummy variable for the presence of village road or dikes as dikes are also used as village roads in coastal areas.

8.4.3. Socio-economic factors (S$_i$)

The cyclone, like any other natural calamity, is presumed to have a differential impact on people depending on their socio-economic status (FAO, 2000) and the coastal poor are likely to be more vulnerable than their wealthier counterparts. There are perceptible differences between a rich and a poor household when it comes to cyclone preparedness. A wealthy household owns a good quality house, a vehicle to escape in, a transistor radio or television set to listen to cyclone warnings and some educated members of the family who would be quick to react to cyclone warning. In contrast, a poor household is more likely to live in an inferior quality house, which could be located in low-lying vulnerable areas, and may not have access to the same kinds of coping strategies as a rich household. In the case of this

---

[4] There could also be un-vegetated sheltered bays, mud flats, etc., in coastal areas having a significant impact on storm damages. Hence the sample is restricted to areas with mhabitati>0 to exclude the un-vegetated areas from analysis and then both mhabitati (width of mangrove habitat) and mangrovei (width of mangrove vegetation) are retained as explanatory variables so that the former captures the effect of the physical features of mangrove habitat and the latter the effect of vegetation. Exclusion of areas with mhabitati = 0 is also justified on the ground that the paper evaluats the storm protection services of mangroves and these areas can never be protected by them.

study, there was no village level data to capture differences between the economically better off and worse off villages in the study area. Therefore an attempt was made to account for these differences by using the following village level factors – percentage of literates (since responsiveness of people to cyclone warning depends on their level of education (FAO, 2000); percentage of different types of main income earning members; percentage of scheduled caste population; the minimum distance to a metallic road (better scope for economic prosperity); and presence of village road (connectivity to metallic road).[5] In addition, a *tahasildar* (officer in charge of a tahasil) dummy variable was used to capture differences in the efficiency of local administration (*tahasildars* are responsible for cyclone warning, evacuation, relief, etc.) and other locational differences among *tahasils*.

Thus, each village is conceived as defined by a socio-economic index, which is influenced by the factors described above.

$$S_i = \frac{s(tahasildar_i, literate_i, scheduledcaste_i, cultivator_i, aglabor_i,}{hhwor\,ker_i, otwor\,ker_i, m\arg wor\,ker_i, droad_i, roadumy_i)}$$

(6)

where S_i is the socio-economic well-being index of the ith village;

Tahasildar$_i$ is the dummy for both the local administration and other locational omitted variables. It equals one for all villages falling under one *tahasil* and zero for other villages.

Literate$_i$ is the percentage of literate people; *scheduled caste$_i$* is the percentage of scheduled caste people; *cultivator$_i$*, *aglabour$_i$*, *hhworker$_i$*, *otworker$_i$*, and *margworker$_i$* are the percentage of cultivators, agricultural labourers, percentage of workers in own household industries (located either at home or within the village), percentage of other workers (doctors, teachers, engineers, barbers, washermen, priests, etc.), and the percentage of marginal workers respectively in the ith village; *droad$_i$* is the minimum distance of the village from the metallic road; and R*oadummy$_i$* is a dummy variable for the presence of the village road that equals one for a village if village road exists and 0 otherwise.

To sum up, equations 4, 5 and 6 define the three sets of variables determining wind velocity, storm surge velocity and the socio-economic

---

[5] In the absence of data on the availability of mass media (TV, radio) at the village level, the percentage of other workers (otworkers) that includes people with high education, high mobility and in occupations other than agriculture and household industries (that is, doctors, teachers, engineers, barbers, washermen, priests, etc.) is used as proxies for the availability of this commodity.

conditions of a village. Since these equations cannot be estimated as the dependant variables are unobserved, the determinants of equations 4, 5 and 6 are combined to define the cyclone damage function:

$$D_i = d \, (\, mangrove_i, mhabitat_i, topodumy_i, casurinadumy_i, velocit\text{-}ypow_i, surge_i, dcoast_i, dmajriver_i, dminriver_i, droad_i, roadumy_i, pop99_i, literate_i, scheduledcaste_i, cultivators_i, aglabours_i, hhworkers_i, otworkers_i, margworkers_i, tahasildar_i)$$

(7)

where D_i is the house damage suffered in the ith village. The right hand side variables are already defined above and are also explained in Table 8.1.[6] The damage function (7) was estimated for both Fully Collapsed (FC) and Partially Collapsed (PC) houses separately in order to get a correct picture of the sheltering capacity of mangrove forests.

8.4.5. Description of sample areas

The damage equation was estimated over different sample areas in order to correctly assess the storm protection benefits from mangroves. First, the sample was restricted to areas that historically had mangroves between those areas and the coast (or for which $mhabitat_i > 0$). This was done because including the non-mangrove areas is meaningless as these areas can never be protected by mangroves. Moreover, as explained above, by excluding these areas, one can indirectly control for the topographical and bathymetric features.

Table 8.1 List of variables (in alphabetical order)

Variables	Definition of variables (all distances in km)
Aglabour	Percentage of agricultural laborers in a village
Casurindmy	Dummy variable for the presence of casuarina forest in coastal distance of a village
Cultivator	Percentage of cultivators in a village
Dcoast	Minimum distance of a village from the coast

(Contd.)

---

[6] Factors like time and season of occurrence of the cyclone, the number of hours between landfall and the broadcast of the cyclone warning, etc., have been ignored as the analysis is for the damage data of a single cyclone. Moreover, since the present analysis is for damages to static properties, these factors are not likely to have any impact.

(*Contd.*)

Variables	Definition of variables (all distances in km)
Dcypath	Minimum (radial) distance of a village from the path of cyclone eye
Dmajriver	Minimum distance of a village from a major river (directly connected to sea)
Dminriver	Minimum distance of a village from a minor river (a tributary of major river)
Droad	Minimum distance of a village from a metallic road
Hhworker	Percentage of people working in (own) household industries in a village
Literate	Percentage of literate people in a village
Mangrove	Width of existing mangrove forest in coastal distance of a village
Margworker	Percentage of marginal workers in a village
Mhabitat	Width of the historical mangrove forest (as existed in or before 1950) in coastal distance of a village or between a village and the coast
Nonworker	Percentage of non-workers (aged dependants, housewives, students, children, etc.) in a village
Otworker	Percentage of other workers (doctor, teacher, engineer, barber, washerman, priest, etc.) in a village
Pop99	Total population of a village in 1999
Radial wind	The expected wind velocity at different radial distances (dcypath) from the cyclone eye
Roadumy	Dummy variable for the presence of village road (=1, if village road exists, =0, otherwise)
Schdulcaste	Percentage of scheduled caste people in a village
Surge	Level of sea elevation (in meters) at different coastal points
Tahasildar	Dummy variable for local administration
Topodmy	Low elevation dummy (=1 for villages that have or had mangrove earlier and = 0 for others)
Velocitypow	Approximate radial wind velocity (kmh^{-1}) in a village due to cyclone as given by a power function

In step 2, the sample was further restricted by excluding areas that came under the cyclone eye, where wind velocity was greater than or equal to

190 km per hour.[7] This was done because wind direction for areas coming under the cyclone eye is circular (anti-clockwise before the cyclone eye passes and clock-wise afterwards) and no forest can provide any sheltering service, particularly from the wind effects.

In step 3, the sample was further subdivided into areas within 10 km of the coast and beyond 10 km from the coast in order to evaluate the effectiveness of mangrove protection for areas lying within different bandwidths from the coastline. In this case, our attempt was to identify the coastal distance up to which mangrove protection remains effective. Thus, regressions were estimated for four different samples as described below.

Sample 1: Areas with $Mhabitat_i > 0$.

Sample 2: Areas with $Mhabitat_i > 0$ and wind velocity < 190 kmh^{-1}.

Sample 3: Areas with $Mhabitat_i > 0$, wind velocity < 190 kmh^{-1} and $Dcoast_i$ $<= 10$.

Sample 4: Areas with $Mhabitat_i > 0$, wind velocity < 190 kmh^{-1} and $Dcoast_i$ > 10.

An explanation is necessary at this point for the use of the *tahasildars* dummies in the damage equation. It is known that the *tahasildars* cannot impact damage to immovable properties. However, these dummies were included to capture the effect of locational variables or any omitted factors. The *tahasils* are small administrative units under a district and significant locational differences were not expected between them. Thus the damage equations were estimated both with and without these dummies.

8.4.6. Valuing residential damages

After estimating the cyclone damage equations for fully collapsed and partially collapsed houses, the role of mangroves in mitigating house losses is quantified. This is done by estimating the volume of house damages (both for FC and PC) averted by mangroves and then valuing the averted damages at different prices. Total averted damages (DA) in Kendrapada are defined as

$$DA = \sum_i \hat{y}_i - \sum_i \hat{y}'_i = Y - \sum_i \hat{y}' \qquad (8)$$

---

[7] V_{max} is the wind velocity in the eye wall region of a cyclone and areas coming under the cyclone eye face this wind velocity. V_{max} is estimated to be 190.1622 km h^{-1} for the Super Cyclone after landfall using the parameters from meteorologists (Das, 2007b).

where $\hat{y}_i$ is the predicted or the fitted value of the model for the ith unit (village or *gram panchayat*). Thus, its sum equals the actual Y and $\hat{y}'_i$ is the predicted or the fitted value for the same unit with a restriction (like *mangrove_i* = 0).

The averted damages are estimated under two restrictions – (a) if there were no mangroves present before the cyclone (*mangrove_i* = 0), and (b) if the presence of mangroves were as they existed in 1950 (*mangrove_i* = *mhabitat_i*). These averted damages are then compared to damages actually witnessed. Again, as explained before, the protection services of mangroves are expected to be better captured in Sample 2. Sample 1 is the total area that receives storm protection from mangroves. Thus, the averted damages are calculated and the average values for Sample 2 are measured. Next this average value is multiplied by the number of villages of Sample 1 in order to estimate the total storm protection value for the study area[8].

Once the physical volume of house damage avoided is estimated, the next step is to value these damages. This was done by using local construction costs to estimate the value of rebuilding damaged housing.

8.5. Data

The study required four different types of information – information on house damages due to the cyclone, meteorological information on cyclone intensities, geo-physical or locational information, and socio-economic information. This information and their respective sources are described in Table 8.2.

Table 8.2. Description and sources of data

Data Head	Description	Source
Damages due to super cyclone	Number of houses, Fully Collapsed (FC) and Partially Collapsed (PC) in each village or in each *gram panchayat*	Emergency office and *Tahasildar* Office of Kendrapada and only Emergency Office of the District Jagatsinghpur, Orissa.

(Contd.)

---

[8] This hypothesis has been found valid in our earlier analysis where the average value per unit of mangroves was found higher for Sample 2 area than the same value for Sample 1 area for different types of damages analyzed (Das, 2010).

(Contd.)

Data Head	Description	Source
Meteo-rological Information	Landfall wind velocity, radius of cyclone eye, and sea elevation at different coastal points	Cyclone Warning Division, Mausam Bhawan, Government of India, New Delhi, Department of Atmospheric Sciences, Indian Institute of Technology, New Delhi
	Track of the cyclone	National Center for Disaster Management (NCDM), Indian Institute of Public Administration, New Delhi
Geo-physical Information	Distances of different villages or *gram panchayat* from coastline, cyclone track, river channels, metallic roads and width of present and historical mangrove forests	GIS and remote sensing data from Digital Cartography and Services, Bhubaneswar and GIS ARC VIEW Software.
Socio-economic Information	Total population, percentage of literates, scheduled caste, different types of workers and non-workers in different villages or in *gram panchayats* before cyclone	Primary Census Abstract of the State of Orissa for the year 1991 and 2001

House damages due to the cyclone were obtained from three different offices of the Government of Orissa – the Emergency Department of Kendrapada and Jagatsinghpur district and the *tahsildar's* office of Kendrapada district. The Orissa State Government categorized damaged houses into three categories – Fully Collapsed (FC) houses (with more than 80 per cent damage), Partially Collapsed (PC) houses (which includes all damages that come to less than 80 per cent) and Swept Away (SA) houses (where both the wall as well as the roof were completely washed away by water). Both FC and PC reflected mainly wind and partially surge related damages to residential houses while SA houses were mainly due to flooding by the storm surge. SA houses were limited to near coast areas whereas house damages beyond that were either FC or PC. This chapter, as mentioned before, focuses only on FC and PC houses. Since 98 per cent of the houses are expected to have suffered damage in the district and damages were either FC or PC in a major part of the study area, each additional house with partial damage is assumed to be one less house that is fully collapsed.

The *tahsildar* office maintained house damage figures at the *tahsildar* office. However, some *tahasils* had village level information while others had information only at the *gram panchayat* level, i.e., at a higher unit of administration between the village and *tahasil*. Accordingly, the study data includes a mix of 365 villages and 138 *gram panchayats* covering the Kendrapada district and 86 coastal villages of the Kujang-Paradeep *tahasil* of the adjoining Jagatsinghpur district. Kujang-Paradeep *tahasil*, situated south of Kendrapada, is included in the study area as some house damage data was available for this area[9].

Two meteorological variables were used, i.e., *velocitypow$_i$* (a measure of approximate radical wind velocity at different villages) and *surge$_i$* (the height of sea elevation at the nearest coastline for each village) in our damage equation. To calculate *velocitypow$_i$*, detailed information was needed on the cyclone including the landfall point, the landfall wind velocity, the movement of the cyclone eye, the radius of the eye, the formula for calculating radial wind at different radial distances and the rate of decline of the maximum wind. This information was obtained from the Cyclone Warning Division of the Meteorology Department (*Mausam Bhawan*), Government of India, New Delhi; the Department of Atmospheric Sciences, Indian Institute of Technology, New Delhi; and the publications of the National Center for Disaster Management (NCDM), Indian Institute of Public Administration, New Delhi. The NCDM. Report (Gupta and Sharma, 2000) describes the positions of the cyclone eye at different locations. Using these details, the cyclone eye path was demarcated at the level of villages. The minimum distances of villages from this path (the variable, *dcypath$_i$*) were calculated with the help of Arc View GIS 3.2 and we used this distance and other parameters described above to calculate *velocitypow$_i$* for all the locations (villages and *gram panchayats*) of the study area. This was calculated with the help of the formula described by meteorologists (see equation 3 in page 177).

---

[9] To have a data set with uniform units, the villages were grouped according to the *gram panchayats* they belonged to, but this reduced the number of observations to 132 for Sample 1 and 89 for Sample 2. Many villages had to be dropped because data for other villages belonging to that particular *gram panchayat* was not available. Regression results with only 132 and 89 observations did give similar results as the larger data set but the level of significance was comparatively lower. The coefficient of mangrove variable was significant for both the samples but the results for Sample 3 and 4 could not be tried due to very few observations. Hence, in spite of the heteroskedasticity problem, the larger data set was used.

The *surge$_i$* variable, i.e., the approximate height of the sea elevation at different coastal points, was calculated from a surge envelope curve (see Figure 8.1). The Cyclone Warning Division of the Meteorology Department of the Government of India provided the surge envelope curve of the eastern India coast line for the Super Cyclone.

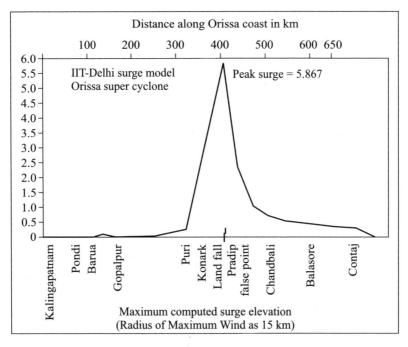

Figure 8.1.   Sea elevations at Orissa coast during 1999 Super Cyclone landfall.

In order to generate the geo-physical and locational variables (*mangrove$_i$*, *mhabitat$_i$*, *casuarinadumy$_i$*, *roadumy$_i$* and different distances), GIS files on village boundary, rivers, roads, coastline and forest cover were used which were purchased from a private source, Digital Cartography and Services, Bhubaneswar, Orissa. Indian Remote Sensing Satellite IRS-1D, LISS III Pan censor images of October 11, 1999, with 23.9 metre resolution, were used to measure the coastal forest cover (both mangroves and casuarinas) before the Cyclone. In order to demarcate the historical (1950) spread of the mangroves in the study area, jpg images (1: 250000 scale) were used from the archives of the US Army Corps (NF 45-14 Series U502, 'Cuttack' sheet). The year 1950 was used as the reference year because mangrove destruction reportedly began after the abolition of the feudal system in 1952 (Orissa District Gazetteer of Cuttack, 1996). The different available digitized data were then combined with the help of Arc View GIS Software 3.2 in order to develop a village-level coastal Orissa digitized physical map. The geo-referencing of all the images was done at the 1:50000 scale.

With the help of the software, different distances were then calculated as required for the analysis. The distances (distance from cyclone path, from coastline, from a major river, from a minor river, from metallic road, etc.) were measured as the minimum distances from the centre of the village (or *gram panchayat*) to the cyclone track, coastline, river, road, etc. The widths (distance between the coast and the interia boundary of the forest) of the 1999 mangrove and the 1950 mangrove for each village and the *gram panchayat* were calculated along the minimum distance between the village and the coast.

The mangrove variable were defined as the width of the forest in km between the village and the coast (not the area of the forest) because the spread of the forest along the coast is continuous in the study area while the breadth is different at different places and this analysis focused on capturing the impact of the spatial features of the villages on damages witnessed. The socio-economic variables (population, share of literates, scheduled castes and different categories of workers) were obtained for each village (or *gram panchayat*) from the Primary Census Abstract of Orissa for 1991 and 2001. The Super Cyclone hit Orissa in 1999 while census data were available for only 1991 and 2001. Therefore the average annual compound rates of growth for the decade 1991–2001 were estimated for different variables, and the 1991 figures extrapolated to the year 1999 using these growth rates.

Male99 was used in place of the total population of 1999 as proxy for the number of households, which in turn was a proxy for the number of properties at risk in the damage equation. Male99 was the total number of males in a village (or *gram panchayat*) in the year 1999. This variable was used because an accurate measure of the total number of houses at risk in each village or *gram panchayat* was not available. It was felt that the total number of males was a more accurate measure of the number of households/properties than the total population as house ownership usually vests with the male member of the house.

8.6. Results and discussion

Table 8.3 shows the summary statistics for the entire study area and Sample 1 areas. As evident from the Table, the study area lies between 0.22 to 72.83

km from the cyclone path and within 0.65 to 51.23 km from the coastline. The width of the mangrove forest varies from 0 to 10 km at different places. Agriculture is the main occupation but nearly 70 per cent of the population are non-workers. Owner farmers (cultivators) constitute 11 per cent of the population while agricultural labourers total five per cent of the population. The number of houses damaged range from 0 to 1885 for FC houses and 0 to 2365 for PC houses.

Table 8.3. Descriptive statistics of house damage model

Variables	Entire Study Area (n = 589)		Sample 1 (n = 516)	
	Mean (std. dev)	Mini (max)	Mean (std. dev)	Min (max)
Fully collapsed (FC)	233.25 (295.2)	0 (1885)	229.31 (297.81)	0 (1885)
Partially collapsed (PC)	206.07 (335.85)	0 (2365)	119.87 (214.67)	0 (2119)
mangrove	0.44 (0.92)	0 (10)	0.46 (0.91)	0 (10)
mhabitat	4.01 (2.30)	0 (13.7)	4.58 (1.85)	0.5 (13.7)
topodmy	0.12 (0.33)	0 (1)	0.13 (0.33)	0 (1)
casurindmy	0.33 (0.47)	0 (1)	0.37 (0.48)	0 (1)
dcypath	21.64 (12.55)	0.22 (72.83)	19.20 (10.98)	0.22 (72.83)
velocitypow	156.73 (32.62)	73.69 (190.16)	163.19 (23.80)	73.64 (190.16)
surge	2.89 (2.03)	0.7 (5.9)	3.14 (2.04)	0.7 (5.9)
dcoast	26.00 (14.18)	0.65 (51.23)	26.65 (14.67)	0.65 (51.23)
dmajriver	3.83 (3.22)	0.06 (16.66)	4.01 (3.32)	0.06 (16.66)
dminriver	3.15 (3.10)	0.08 (15.23)	3.21 (3.21)	0.08 (15.23)
droad	2.44 (2.85)	0.02 (17.55)	2.21 (2.57)	0.02 (15.68)
roadumy	0.80 (0.40)	0 (1)	0.80 (0.39)	0 (1)
Male99	943.37 (995.1)	3 (5340)	768.27 (863.8)	3 (5340)
literate	0.66 (0.09)	0.20 (1)	0.66 (0. 09)	0.19 (1)
schdulcaste	0.21 (0.17)	0 (1)	0.21 (0.17)	0 (1)

(Contd.)

(Contd.)

Variables	Entire Study Area (n = 589)		Sample 1 (n = 516)	
	Mean (std. dev)	Mini (max)	Mean (std. dev)	Min (max)
cultivator	0.11 (0.06)	0 (0.43)	0.12 (0.05)	0 (0.42)
aglabour	0.05 (0.04)	0 (0.25)	0.04 (0.08)	0 (0.25)
hhworker	0.004 (0.006)	0 (0.07)	0.004 (0.007)	0 (0.07)
otworker	0.06 (0.04)	0 (0.36)	0.06 (0.04)	0 (0.36)
margworker	0.08 (0.08)	0 (0.57)	0.08 (0.08)	0 (0.57)
nonworker	0.69 (0.09)	0 (0.83)	0.68 (0.09)	0 (0.83)

Of the different explanatory variables, three sets of variables were found to be significantly correlated with each other in the different sample areas – *Velocitypow$_i$* and *surge$_i$* (r ≈ 0.65, P<0.01); *mangrove$_i$* and *velocitypow$_i$* (r ≈ −0.50, P<0.01), *mangrove$_i$* and *surge$_i$* (r ≈ −0.30, P<0.01). Both *velocitypow$_i$* and *surge$_i$* are dependant on cyclone intensity and, thus it makes sense that they are correlated. However, there is no theoretical justification for the cyclone variables to be correlated with the mangrove variable. It can be taken as a coincidence that there are more mangroves with distances away to the north from the cyclone landfall point. Both *velocitypow$_i$* and *surge$_i$* are important variables in examining the impact of mangroves on houses and therefore, both the variables were chosen to be retained in the estimated model. In order to ensure that the significance of the mangroves is not due to the variables it is correlated with, the results were compared by dropping the variables correlated with mangroves one by one from the estimation which showed that there was no change in the significance of mangrove. A high and significant correlation between *mangrove$_i$* and *mhabitat$_i$* was expected, but this was not the case (r < 0.10, P>0.05) for all the sample areas. This was probably due to the fact that mangrove destruction has been random without a systematic pattern.

8.6.1. Fully Collapsed (FC) Houses

The estimated equation for this model is

$$FC_i = \frac{\alpha_0 + \alpha_1 mangrove_i + \alpha_2 mhabitat_i + \alpha_3 topodumy_i + - - - +}{\alpha_{19} m \arg wor\,ker\,s_i + \alpha_{20} tahasildar_i + v_i}$$

(8)

where v_i is the error term and other variables have been previously defined. Equation 8 was estimated for all four sample areas. The error term was heteroskedastic for all sample areas and the presence of heterogeneous units (villages and *gram panchayats*) in the data set was expected to be the main reason. Assuming error variances to be proportional to the size of the units, weighted least squares estimates were tried, using both area as well as the total population as weights. OLS was also tried with robust standard errors and very similar results were achieved from all the three types of estimates. OLS was retained with robust standard errors since the WLS estimates are based on some assumption about the error variances.

8.6.2. Expected signs

The *mangrove$_i$* variable is expected to reduce the degree of damage to houses and therefore to have a negative coefficient with FC; the same is true for the coefficient of *casurinadumy$_i$*. Negative coefficients for the variables *dcoast$_i$* (that is, more distance from coast implying less intensity of cyclone), *dmajriver$_i$* and *dminriver$_i$* (since villages nearer rivers are likely to suffer more damage) are also expected. Among other variables for which a negative coefficient is expected are *cultivators$_i$*, *hhworkers$_i$* and *otworkers$_i$* (they are the better-off people in the study area) and for *roadumy$_i$* (villages with village road tend to be usually better off and to have better quality houses). The variables, *velocitypow$_i$* and *surge$_i$*, are expected to have a positive coefficient (with high values indicating the higher intensity of the cyclone). The same goes for the following variables – *droad$_i$* (proximity to metallic road means economic well-being), *male99$_i$* (property at risk), *topodumy$_i$* (because low lying areas are more vulnerable and poor), *schedulecaste$_i$*, *aglabour$_i$* and *margworker$_i$* (who tend to be very poor people). A question mark for both *tahsildar$_i$* and *mhabitat$_i$* is used as these variables are likely to capture the effects of unobserved omitted variables among *tahasils* and coastal topographic factors, respectively, with regard to house damage.

Equation 8 is estimated with and without *tahasildhar* dummies. The expected signs and the estimated regressions are presented without the *tahasildar* dummies in Table 8.4 but show the results with the *tahasildar* dummies in Appendix 8.1.

The coefficients shown in Table 8.4, wherever significant, have the appropriate signs. As expected, wind velocity is the main cause of fully collapsed houses. The mangrove variable is significant with a negative sign for Samples 1, 2 and 4 as seen in Table 8.4. Thus, mangroves seem to have reduced the number of fully collapsed houses. But its effect is not visible in areas within 10 km from the coast. It may be that these areas witnessed the maximum number of swept away houses and, consequently, the number of fully collapsed houses was limited. Interestingly enough, mangrove protection is seen to be effective for areas as far as 50 km away from the coast[10]. However, in most equations, the socio-economic variables are insignificant, possibly because of limited variation in house quality and demographics in the entire district.

It is interesting to note that mangrove protection from wind damage is visible only when the cyclone effects are captured in a more disaggregated manner by dropping the *tahasildar* dummies. Appendix 8.1 shows results with the *tahasildar* dummies. All the dummies are significant either with a positive or negative sign depending on the sample area and the *tahasil's* proximity to the cyclone track. At the same time, meteorological and geophysical variables that were expected to capture the cyclone impacts are insignificant. Thus, it can be concluded that the *tahasildar* dummies, being locational variables, are only capturing the cyclonic effects in an aggregate manner. No omitted variables seem to be present among the *tahasils* as the significance of these dummies is completely in accordance with the cyclone impact on the respective *tahasils*. Furthermore, the results with *tahasildar* dummies are less reliable due to high multicollinearity among explanatory variables as reflected by the values of Variance Inflation Factors (VIF).[11] The VIF of some of the tahasils is as high as 60 and the prediction of averted damage due to mangrove presence with these coefficients may not be very reliable. Hence, the results of Table 8.4 are used to calculate averted damages.

---

[10] Interaction between mangrove and wind velocity was tried by including terms like mangrove*velocitypow and velocitypow*exp (mangrove) etc., along with mangrove and mangrove remained significant in both cases. These results are not reported since the scientific evidence on the nature of interaction between mangrove and wind velocity is yet to be established.

[11] The variance inflation factor is defined as $VIF = 1/(1 - r^2_{ij})$, where r^2_{ij} is the coefficient of correlation between the ith and the jth regressor and $var(\hat{\beta}_i) = \sigma^2/\Sigma x_i^2 (1 - r^2_{ij}) = \sigma^2/\Sigma x_i^2 * VIF$. Thus, VIF shows the extent to which the variance of an estimator gets inflated by the presence of multicollinearity.

Table 8.4. Ordinary least squares estimates with robust std. errors for fully collapsed houses

Equation/variable	Exp. signs	Sample-1 Areas with mhabitat>0	Sample-2 Part of sample-1 beyond cyclone eye	Sample-3 Part of sample-2 within 10km from coast	Sample-4 Part of sample-2 beyond 10km from coast
Mangrove	(−)	-84.27 *** (3.83)	-60.11*** (3.12)	-40.39 (1.19)	-56.11 *** (3.48)
Mhabitat	(?)	20.83 *** (3.17)	11.14 * (1.87)	-16.21 (0.73)	21.00*** (3.15)
Topodumy	(+)	-27.86 (0.70)	2.70 (0.10)	-33.50 (0.75)	-13.42 (0.36)
Casurinadumy	(−)	-45.22 (1.19)	-9.77 (0.27)	-37.96 (0.87)	-61.09 (1.22)
Velocitypow	(+)	1.70** (2.55)	2.78*** (3.55)	14.30 *** (4.58)	3.04 *** (3.62)
Surge	(+)	13.17 (1.34)	1.09 (0.11)	-29.97 * (1.97)	7.59 (0.52)
Dcoast	(−)	0.54 (0.59)	-1.28 * (1.69)	-31.69 ** (2.06)	0.64 (0.72)
Dmajriver	(−)	-6.32 ** (2.41)	-8.09 ** (2.71)	-15.12 (0.87)	-8.17 *** (3.10)
Dminriver	(−)	-8.46 *** (2.73)	-5.92 * (1.68)	-29.50 * (1.84)	-3.14 (0.85)
Droad	(+)	-7.37 (1.23)	-0.20 (0.04)	7.40 (0.92)	-0.95 (0.15)
Roadumy	(−)	28.43 (1.41)	9.20 (0.41)	96.87 * (1.68)	-12.65 (0.59)
Male99	(+)	0.26 *** (10.38)	0.21 *** (6.87)	0.22 *** (6.55)	0.25 *** (7.38)
Literate	(−)	-49.35 (0.53)	-63.7 (0.89)	-27.28 (0.17)	65.07 (0.73)
Schdulcaste	(+)	59.77 (1.22)	17.05 (0.41)	42.94 (0.20)	47.06 (1.08)
Cultivator	(−)	35.47 (0.21)	-260.90 * (1.88)	-20.21 (0.07)	-161.66 (0.89)
Aglabour	(+)	-127.96 (0.62)	-1.29 (0.01)	-388.85 (0.80)	2.01 (0.01)
Hhworker	(−)	-622.63 (0.56)	-583.11 (0.76)	6923.27 (1.27)	-441.69 (0.59)
Otworker	(−)	-495.70** (2.13)	-497.08**(2.40)	-1564.66*** (3.65)	-699.03 ** (2.53)
Margworker	(+)	64.59 (0.58)	9.61 (0.08)	-232.05 * (1.66)	84.82 (0.52)
Constant	(?)	-245.98 * (1.79)	-218.92 * (1.68)	-1256.18*** (3.52)	-507.93*** (2.80)
		N=516,R²=0.55,	N=338,R²=0.54,	N=61,R²=0.77,	N=277,R²=0.58,
		F(19,496)=12.56	F(19,318)=7.61, Pro	F(19,41)=4.93	F(19,257)=7.14,
		Pro=0.00	= 0.00	Pro=0.00	Pro=0.00

Notes: ***, **, and * imply 1%, 5%, and 10% level of significance respectively. Figures in parenthesis are the absolute t-values.

Table 8.5. Weighted least squares estimates (weight = area) for partially collapsed houses

Equation/variable	Exp. signs	Sample 1	Sample 2	Sample 3	Sample 4
Mangrove	(+)	61.69 *** (6.81)	63.44*** (4.75)	1.20 (0.03)	29.83 *** (2.68)
Mhabitat	(?)	5.07 (0.81)	23.36** (2.08)	-55.23 ** (2.52)	27.57 *** (3.00)
Topodumy	(-)	-2.31 (0.06)	36.03 (0.64)	92.14** (2.10)	-132.95 * (1.96)
Casurinadumy	(+)	-56.09 (1.60)	-126.26** (2.21)	-25.82 (0.44)	-86.10 (1.56)
velocitypow	(-)	-3.18*** (4.75)	-3.21 *** (2.72)	-1.53 (0.59)	-2.07 ** (2.46)
Surge	(-)	24.84 ** (2.10)	24.19 (1.29)	10.02 (0.44)	2.21 (0.15)
Dcoast	(+)	1.26 (0.88)	-2.45 (1.02)	18.97 (1.18)	-5.55 *** (2.96)
Dmajriver	(+)	13.14 *** (3.25)	22.32 *** (3.86)	41.31 * (1.89)	16.27*** (4.19)
Dminriver	(+)	2.60 (0.45)	8.77 (1.00)	-35.91 * (1.93)	22.39 *** (3.76)
Droad	(-)	-7.42 (1.03)	-2.57 (0.32)	-11.31 (1.15)	5.42 (0.87)
Roadumy	(+)	-89.11*** (2.81)	-99.16 ** (2.35)	52.93 (0.82)	-158.49***(4.79)
Male99	(+)	0.11 *** (10.03)	0.12 *** (6.66)	0.06 *** (2.74)	0.24 *** (15.57)
Literate	(+)	278.32 (1.53)	393.84 * (1.61)	-448.14* (1.77)	64.05 (0.29)
Schdulcaste	(-)	307.97*** (3.42)	463.10***(3.67)	569.49**(2.49)	-7.49 (0.08)
Cultivator	(+)	-159.54 (0.59)	-610.66 (1.58)	-203.29 (0.47)	-1123.81*** (2.77)
Aglabour	(-)	-1546.75 *** (3.81)	-2032.36 *** (3.63)	-2599.18 *** (3.67)	-253.73 (0.60)
Hhworker	(+)	3274.30 (1.44)	3396.18 (0.86)	-6707.80 (0.83)	-1995.19 (0.74)
Otworker	(+)	-792.83 ** (2.21)	-979.39 **(1.94)	-1152.71**(2.04)	-69.60 (0.11)
Margworker	(-)	-291.94 * (1.73)	-347.51 * (1.60)	-600.64 ** (2.37)	265.05 (1.54)
Constant	(?)	-378.56 *** (2.48)	310.45 (1.36)	800.75 ** (2.11)	385.10 * (1.80)
		N=515, F(19,495)	N=337, F(19,317) =22.72,	N=61, F(19,41)	N=276, F(19,256)
		=35.52, Pro=0.00,	Pro = 0.00, $\bar{R}^2$ =0.55	=9.31, Pro = 0.00,	=70.01, $\bar{R}^2$ =0.83
		$\bar{R}^2$ =0.56		$\bar{R}^2$ =0.72	

Notes: ***, **, and * imply 1%, 5%, and 10% level of significance respectively. Figures in parenthesis are the absolute t-values.

8.6.3. *Partially Collapsed (PC) Houses*

The same set of regressors as used for fully collapsed houses was used for partially collapsed houses. Table 8.5 and Appendix 8.2 present the two sets of results, one without the *tahasildar* dummies, and the other with these dummies, respectively, along with the expected signs.

The heteroskedasticity test was significant for all samples for this data set and OLS with robust standard errors resulted in most of the variables being insignificant. The use of Weighted Least Squares estimates with both area and total population as weights produced better results and also gave the expected signs of the coefficients. The estimates with area as weight were retained for the final analysis and for calculating averted damages because of higher $\bar{R}^2$ and F value[12].

In the case of partially collapsed houses, the coefficients were expected to show signs opposite to what they were expected to have in the case of fully collapsed houses. As mentioned earlier, the state government has grouped damaged houses into only two categories, i.e., either fully collapsed or partially collapsed, in the major part of the district (SA houses were limited to the near-coast areas) and the partially collapsed category included houses with a range of house damage varying from 10 per cent to 80 per cent. Mangrove may have reduced the degree of partial damage to houses but there being no data on the severity of partial damage to houses in different areas, this hypothesis cannot be tested. Considering that almost every house in the study area experienced some amount of damage during the Super Cyclone (only two per cent of the houses had both concrete walls and roof), the number of partially collapsed houses are expected to be more in mangrove protected areas because this reflects a reduction in fully collapsed houses. On a cautious note, the correct dependant variable to test this hypothesis would have been the ratio of fully collapsed to partially collapsed houses in each location since it is presumed each additional partially collapsed house to be one less fully collapsed house. To substantiate the argument that mangroves reduce the degree of house damage, models were estimated with the ratio of FC to PC houses as the

---

[12] Since the OLS results were insignificant and WLS estimates are based on the *a priori* assumption that error variances are proportional to the variable used as weight, the Feasible Generalized Least Squares (FGLS) estimates (Wooldrige, 2003) were also calculated for PC houses. FGLS estimates compared to WLS estimates had higher coefficients as well as t values, but because the variance inflation factors of these estimates were very high, they were not used for the final analysis.

dependant variable for different sample areas and *mangrove*$_i$ was found to be significant with negative sign (see Appendix 8.3).

However, interest was more in regressions with FC and PC separately as dependant variables since the aim in the study was the valuation of storm protection. With the ratio of FC to PC as a dependant variable, there was difficulty in interpreting and valuing averted damage. Thus, for the present analysis and the type of data available, the *mangrove*$_i$ variable is expected to be positively associated with partially collapsed houses as mangrove protected areas are likely to see more of these houses.

The effect of mangroves on partially collapsed houses appears to be strong and robust. *Mangrove*$_i$ is significant with a positive coefficient in all the tables (with or without *tahasildar* dummies) for all sample areas and this proves either that mangrove-protected areas have witnessed more partially collapsed houses, or that mangroves have reduced the degree of wind damages to houses[13] by converting full damages to partial damages in the case of houses.

8.6.4. Damages averted due to mangrove vegetation

As mentioned earlier, house damages avoided due to the presence of mangrove forests were defined as

$$DA = \sum_i \hat{y}_i - \sum_i \hat{y}'_i = Y - \sum_i \hat{y}',$$

where $\hat{y}_i$ is the predicted value of the model for the ith unit and $\hat{y}'_i$ is the predicted value assuming that mangroves are currently non-existent (*mangrove*$_i$ = 0).

In this case the mangrove protection is defined as $DA = -\sum_i (\hat{y}_i - \hat{y}'_i)$,

where $\hat{y}'_i$ is the predicted value by replacing mangrove variable by 0. These values are calculated for FC and PC houses and these averted damages are presented for Sample 2 areas only (see Table 8.6) as this sample reflects the wind protection of the forests more accurately (Das, 2010).

These figures are the extra damages that would have occurred if the district had no mangrove forest before the cyclone. This implies that in the absence of mangroves, the presently mangrove protected areas would

---

[13] The mangrove variable remains significant even if the robust option is used with the WLS estimates.

have witnessed less partially collapsed houses as more houses would have collapsed fully.

Table 8.6. Averted house damages and values

Type of House Damage	Averted Damages (no of houses)	Value per km width of Mangrove per Village
	Sample 2	Sample 2
Fully collapsed houses	13,687 (72957–59276)	Rs. 1428.15
Partially collapsed houses	–14,339 (44,528–58,867)	–Rs. 280.18

In the absence of mangrove forests, the villages lying in the Sample 2 area would have witnessed 13,681 more fully collapsed houses and 14,339 less partially collapsed houses (see Table 8.6). The number of fully collapsed houses in these areas was 59,276 during the Super Cyclone. In the absence of mangroves, this number would have risen to 72,957. Thus, without mangroves, the people in these areas would have seen 23 per cent more fully collapsed houses than they actually witnessed. These areas saw 58,867 PC houses. In the absence of mangroves, this number would have been 44,528, implying that the number of PC houses would have been lower by 24 per cent [14].

Another way to think about this is in terms of what the reduction in fully collapsed houses might have been if the 1950 level of mangroves had still remained intact. This is analyzed by estimating the averted damages by historical mangroves (assumption 2). The answer to this is that the area would have witnessed only partially collapsed houses and no fully collapsed houses as the number of FC houses with the presence of the 1950 mangroves is negative while the number of PC houses increases by 78 per cent.

8.6.5. *Storm protection value of mangroves*

The next step is to value the residence protection services of mangroves. In order to do this, it is assumed that a 150 sq meter house has a construction cost of INR 53, 800 in rural Orissa based on estimations by HUDCO

---

[14] The percentage of averted FC houses is not exactly equal to averted (or rather increased) PC houses as the study area also includes areas that had swept away houses though not analyzed here.

(Housing and Urban Development Corporation of India), the largest public sector undertaking engaged in house construction in India. This number is used for valuing avoided FC houses. A negative value of INR 10,000 is also used for each averted (in fact, increased) PC house based on a personal communication with B. K. Mishra, the Emergency Officer of Kendrapada in 2006–2007.

Multiplying the number of averted FC houses by INR 53,800 and the number of averted PC houses by INR 10,000, the total value of house damages averted by mangroves in Sample 2 is estimated as INR 59,26,47,800.[15] However, this is an aggregate measure which is related to the sample size and the sum of the mangrove variable over the sample.[16] The values per unit of mangroves are estimated in the next step where the values for both km widths and per hectare of mangroves are calculated.

8.6.6. Value per km width of mangroves

First the average value per km width of mangrove forest per village of Sample 2 is estimated. As mentioned before, the average per village value of Sample 2 is multiplied by the number of villages of Sample 1 in order to estimate the total storm protection value. The average value per km of mangroves per village for averting FC and PC damages in Sample 2 is defined as:

$$\bar{\beta} = \left[\frac{\sum_{i=1}^{N_2} AD_i}{\sum_{i=1}^{N_2} M_i} \right] / N_2, \tag{9}$$

where $\bar{\beta}$ is the benefit per village from 1 km width of mangrove,

AD_i is the value of averted damages in village i, M_i is the width of mangroves in km for village i, and N_2 is the number of villages in Sample 2.

Next, the benefits to all villages in Sample 1 as $\bar{\beta}^* N_1$ is estimated, where N_1 is the total number of villages in the bigger sample, i.e., Sample 1 (Sample 2 is a subset of Sample 1 or $N_2 \subset N_1$).

---

[15] The averted damage calculation for Sample 1 area shows the averted FC houses to be 17 per cent more and PC houses to be 18 per cent less in the absence of mangroves.

[16] The total averted damages ($\sum_i AD_i$) due to mangroves are equal to $\hat{\beta}_M {}^* \sum_i M_i$ in a linear model where $\sum_i M_i$ is the sum of the mangrove variable over all the observations in the model.

Since the sample included heterogeneous units (both villages and *gram panchayats*) both $\sum_{i=1}^{N_2} M_i$ and N_2 were calculated by the following formulas for the Sample 2 area.

(i) $$N_2 = R + \sum_j a_j v_j \tag{10}$$

where R is the number of villages in Sample 2 for which village level data is available and where the second term represents the total number of villages falling under the *gram panchayats* covered in Sample 2. In the second term, a_j is the average number of villages in a *gram panchayat* in the jth *tahasil* and v_j is the number of *gram panchayats* of jth *tahasil* falling in Sample area 2. Here the summation is over all *tahasils* in Sample 2.

(ii) $$M = \sum_{i=1}^{R} M_i + \sum_j \left(\sum_k M_{kj} \right) a_j v_j \, , \tag{11}$$

where M is the total km width of mangrove in Sample 2, M_i is the km width of mangrove for village i and M_{kj} is the km width of mangrove for the kth *gram panchayat* of the jth *tahasil* and a_j and v_j are the same as above.

These average values / km of forest / village were INR 1428 for FC houses and (–) INR 280 for PC houses. Taking their difference, INR 1148 the average storm protection value / km of forest / village (see Table 8.7) is achieved. To obtain the value of aggregate damages averted, this number needs to be multiplied by the total number of villages that can be protected by the mangroves. As all the villages of Sample 1 area can be protected by mangroves, the unit value calculated from Sample 2 is multiplied by the total number of villages that fall within Sample 1. Thus, INR 9,75,800 (US $23,233) the total storm protection provided by one km width of mangroves in the study area to be is estimated. If the area has a two km wide forest, then this value would be doubled and so on.

8.6.7. *Value per hectare of mangroves*

It is also useful to think about the storm protection benefits in terms of hectares of mangroves. The study area had 30,766 hectares of mangrove forest in 1950 but this was reduced to 17,900 hectares by October 11,

1999.[17] The total value of damages averted by mangroves in Sample 2 was estimated as INR 59,26,47,800. This is the difference in terms of the values of averted FC houses to PC houses. This value is divided by the area of extant mangroves to calculate the storm protection value per hectare of the forest as INR 33,109 for the Sample 2 area. Dividing this by the number of villages of Sample 2 and multiplying by the number of villages of Sample 1, the protection value of hectare of forest is INR 51,168 for the study area. Thus, the mangroves of Kendrapada provided storm protection worth INR 59,26,47,800 by averting house damages in the district. In other words, the study area community benefited by INR 51,168 per hectare of the forests extant before the cyclone. These values are reported in Table 8.7.

Table 8.7. Storm protection values of mangroves

Average storm protection value /km width of forest / village	Rs. 1148 (Rs. 1428 – Rs. 280)
Total storm protection value / km width of forest for the study area	Rs. 9,75,800
Total storm protection value / hectare of forest for study area	Rs. 51,168

8.7. Conclusions and policy recommendations

This chapter assesses the wind and surge protection services afforded by the mangrove forests of the Kendrapada district of Orissa to residential houses during the Super Cyclone of October 1999. This was done by analyzing the number of fully collapsed and partially collapsed residential houses in the study area. The mangrove effect on these houses was calculated by taking into account simultaneously the role of meteorological, locational, physical and socio-economic factors.

Mangrove protected areas witnessed fewer fully collapsed houses and more partially collapsed houses. The house damage averted by mangroves was valued by taking into account the market cost of repairing these damages. It is found that the protection value provided by every km width of the mangroves in reducing residential house damages is about INR 1148

---

[17] The chapter considers only the dense mangroves which are 93% of the total mangrove cover (192 sq km) of the district.

per village and INR 9,75,800 for the entire study area. The protection value per hectare of forest for the study area is INR 51,168.

The next inevitable question is whether mangrove forests should be conserved to avoid these damages. In order to answer this question, one needs to look at the alternate uses to which mangrove land in the area can be put and their value. It is found that the value of a hectare of coastal land in the Kendrapada region is about INR 172,970 (personal communication with Jatindra Das, IANS correspondent, Bhubaneswar, Orissa). Thus, the value of coastal land in alternate uses far exceeds the value provided by mangroves through protecting residential property. If decisions are made based on this information alone, it will not be possible to justify mangrove conservation or rehabilitation. However, the argument for mangrove conservation rests on more complex grounds. Mangroves provide a lot more services than wind and storm surge protection. Furthermore, it has been shown elsewhere that mangroves significantly reduce human and livestock casualties resulting from storm surge (Das, 2007b). Thus, the case for formulating policy to protect mangroves remains strong as long as one is careful to include the multiple services and benefits that mangroves provide. In this chapter, a partial analysis is undertaken mainly to outline the methodological issues that need to be considered in a careful evaluation of the benefits of mangrove conservation.

Appendix 8.1. Ordinary least squares estimates with robust std. errors for fully collapsed houses with *Tahasildar* dummies

Equation/variable	Exp. signs	Sample-1	Sample-2	Sample-3	Sample-4
Kujangparadep	(?)	909.85*** (7.49)	556.26*** (4.24)	686.47 *** (2.38)	99.52 (0.72)
Mahakalpada	(?)	874.58*** (7.07)	460.83*** (5.97)	948.17 *** (4.99)	-132.11 (1.32)
Rajnagar	(?)	Dropped	-523.572*** (3.67)	Dropped	-830.38*** (5.26)
Rajkanika	(?)	315.66*** (3.10)	-139.24 (1.22)	Dropped	-694.83*** (5.73)
Patamundai	(?)	755.16*** (5.71)	268.69*** (2.87)	Dropped	-298.16** (2.41)
Aul	(?)	510.56*** (4.32)	Dropped	Dropped	-598.56*** (5.39)
Garadpur	(?)	1263.88*** (8.11)	Dropped	Dropped	Dropped
Marsaghai	(?)	1162.41*** (7.62)	570.23*** (6.38)	Dropped	Dropped
Kend-derabis	(?)	869.89*** (7.09)	431.25*** (5.91)	Dropped	-147.91 (1.41)
Mangrove	(-)	-16.73 (1.02)	-10.05 (0.58)	-38.16* (1.80)	-13.62 (0.85)
Mhabitat	(?)	6.87 (1.21)	-0.20 (0.05)	-36.76*** (3.19)	3.69 (0.66)
Topodumy	(+)	-17.95 (0.53)	-7.54 (0.35)	45.02 * (1.81)	-49.32 (1.48)
Casurinadumy	(-)	-7.32 (0.23)	19.22 (0.62)	21.27 (0.63)	-11.60 (0.22)
Velocitypow	(+)	-1.31 ** (2.15)	-0.43 (0.64)	4.80* (1.84)	-0.56 (0.59)
Surge	(+)	9.87 (1.19)	-0.79 (0.09)	-10.59 (1.07)	5.59 (0.45)
Dcoast	(-)	-0.73 (0.61)	-0.07 (0.08)	9.03 (0.92)	-0.30 (0.30)
Dmajriver	(-)	1.02 (0.47)	-1.11 (0.40)	-1.66 (0.17)	-0.94 (0.34)
Dminriver	(-)	-0.68 (0.31)	-2.40 (0.90)	-1.37 (0.14)	-2.42 (0.78)
Droad	(+)	-14.24 *** (2.89)	-3.55 (0.86)	-2.49 (0.46)	-0.28 (0.05)
Roadumy	(-)	12.64 (0.74)	-7.20 (0.38)	36.49 (1.01)	-9.30 (0.45)

(Contd.)

(*Contd.*)

Equation/variable	Exp. signs	Sample-1	Sample-2	Sample-3	Sample-4
Male99	(+)	0.26*** (10.34)	0.28*** (10.24)	03C*** (9.79)	0.28*** (7.14)
Literate	(−)	7.70 (0.11)	38.88 (0.68)	−123.41 (1.11)	57.44 (0.80)
Schdulcaste	(+)	86.13** (1.98)	28.80 (0.85)	−25.62 (0.23)	12.52 (0.36)
Cultivator	(−)	−78.74 (0.54)	−266.58 ** (2.37)	−141.38 (0.67)	−234.89 * (1.74)
Aglabour	(+)	−331.12 * (1.87)	−172.52 (1.36)	−527.43 (1.49)	−71.94 (0.48)
Hhworker	(−)	−1415.72 (1.14)	−512.98 (0.79)	2010.21 (0.65)	−694.77 (1.08)
Otworker	(−)	−504.96 ** (2.77)	−635.22 *** (2.91)	−445.53 (0.79)	−539.58 ** (2.11)
Margworker	(+)	−61.78 (0.69)	−69..90 (0.71)	−.1˙3.86 (1.01)	−31.04 (0.22)
Constant	(?)	−588.69 *** (3.70)	−262..08 * (1.87)	−1222.48*** (4.65)	303.56 (1.18)
		N=516,R²=0.66, F(27,488)=12.45, Pro=0.00	N=338,R²=0.71, F(25,311)=missing,	N=61,R²=0.91, F(21,39)=19.35 Pro=0.00	N=277,R²=0.68, F(26,249)=missing,

Notes: ***, **, and * imply 1%, 5%, and 10% level of significance respectively. Figures in parenthesis are the absolute t-values.

Appendix 8.2. Weighted least squares estimates (weight=area) for partially collapsed houses with *Tahasildar* dummies

Equation/variable	Exp. signs	Sample-1	Sample-2	Sample-3	Sample-4
Kujangparadep	(?)	Dropped	-397.24 * (1.75)	Dropped	-503.74** 2.37
Mahakalpada	(?)	145.45 ** (2.26)	-178.43 (1.04)	349.40 * (1.85)	-432.76 *** 3.61
Rajnagar	(?)	433.79*** (3.64)	36.99 (0.18)	1112.86 *** (3.90)	499.46*** 3.72
Rajkanika	(?)	492.46*** (4.36)	78.52 (0.39)	Dropped	28.35 0.24
Patamundai	(?)	726.58 *** (8.82)	367.31 ** (2.10)	Dropped	95.18 0.89
Aul	(?)	655.26 *** (3.83)	234.66 (0.93)	Dropped	Dropped
Garadpur	(?)	251.07 *** (3.40)	Dropped	Dropped	Dropped
Marsaghai	(?)	205.14 *** (2.95)	Dropped	Dropped	-281.08* (1.84)
Kend-derabis	(?)	35.56 (0.47)	-349.99 ** (2.00)	Dropped	-510.61*** (4.39)
Mangrove	(+)	72.17*** (7.63)	66.25 *** (5.35)	33.38 ** (2.00)	21.85** (2.13)
Mhabitat	(?)	-2.70 (0.40)	19.90 * (1.87)	-37.82 ** (2.03)	41.73 *** (4.41)
Topodumy	(-)	45.73 (1.30)	69.55 (1.39)	12.92 (0.32)	-25.77 (0.46)
Casurinadumy	(+)	-64.33 ** (2.10)	-158.33 *** (3.13)	-140.57 ** (2.64)	-163.71 *** (3.54)
Velocitypow	(-)	1.24 (1.23)	-0.70 (0.47)	14.00 *** (3.70)	0.80 (0.77)
Surge	(-)	10.91 (0.89)	-0.09 (0.00)	-26.03 (0.32)	6.27 (0.47)
Dcoast	(+)	0.23 (0.11)	2.02 (0.71)	-14.88 (0.99)	0.04 (0.02)
Dmajriver	(+)	9.27 (2.43)	16.30 *** (2.93)	25.23 (1.41)	13.95 *** (4.06)

(Contd.)

(Contd.)

Dminriver	(+)	11.73 ** (2.12)	21.59 *** (2.64)	-54.55*** (3.49)	19.93 *** (3.90)
Droad	(-)	-12.61 *** (3.06)	-14.32 * (1.95)	15.94 * (1.66)	-2.78 (0.52)
Roadumy	(+)	-20.14 (0.69)	-5.22 (0.13)	91.22 * (1.75)	-43.97 (1.53)
Male99	(+)	0.04 ** (2.41)	0.04* (1.78)	0.03 (1.40)	0.12 *** (6.80)
Literate	(+)	-192.43 (1.14)	-294.51 (1.29)	-327.11 (1.59)	352.13 * (1.81)
Schdulcaste	(-)	114.43 (1.40)	142.18 (1.24)	234.96 (1.17)	110.6 (1.29)
Cultivator	(+)	39.38 (0.16)	43.93 (0.13)	99.02 (0.28)	-310.48 (0.90)
Aglabour	(-)	-718.90 * (1.95)	-908.86 * (1.81)	-1796.35*** (3.03)	-60.86 (0.17)
Hhworker	(+)	2645.87 (1.34)	2567.03 (0.74)	1306.76 (0.20)	-1596.56 (0.73)
Otworker	(+)	-171.08 (0.54)	390.82 (0.71)	-483.83 (0.82)	615.84 (1.15)
Margworker	(-)	185.70 (1.22)	149.75 (0.76)	-426.79** (2.07)	670.23 *** (4.68)
Constant	(?)	-144.27 (0.70)	352.50 (1.11)	-1519.72 ** (2.46)	-234.10 (1.00)
		N=515, F (27,487) =40.35, Pro=0.00, $\bar{R}^2$ =0.67	N=337, F(26,310) =26.82, Pro = 0.00, $\bar{R}^2$ =0.67	N=61, F(21,39) = 14.38, Pro = 0.00, $\bar{R}^2$ =0.82	N=276, F(26,249) =90.00, $\bar{R}^2$ =0.89

Notes: ***, **, and * imply 1%, 5%, and 10% level of significance respectively. Figures in parenthesis are the absolute t-values.

Appendix 8.3. Ordinary least squares estimates with robust std. errors for the ratio of fully collapsed to partially collapsed houses

Equation/variable	Exp. signs	Sample-1	Sample-2	Sample-3	Sample-4
Mangrove	(−)	−0.70** (2.19)	−0.66** (2.30)	−1.22 (0.73)	−0.39* (1.84)
Mhabitat	(?)	0.53 (1.38)	−0.11 (0.45)	−1.94 (1.37)	0.28 * (1.85)
Topodumy	(+)	4.07 (1.27)	4.02 (1.56)	7.28 (1.48)	0.95 (0.66)
Casurinadumy	(−)	3.82* (1.63)	2.36 (1.45)	15.31 * (1.76)	0.81 (0.66)
Velocitypow	(+)	0.02 (0.81)	−0.002 (0.12)	−0.13 (0.48)	0.02 (1.09)
Surge	(+)	0.44 (0.91)	0.04 (0.10)	−0.49 (0.32)	0.37 (1.05)
Dcoast	(−)	−0.18*** (2.78)	0.05 (1.41)	1.94 (1.57)	0.08 ** (1.97)
Dmajriver	(−)	0.55** (2.14)	−0.21** (2.23)	0.75 (0.36)	−0.21***(2.65)
Dminriver	(−)	−0.12 (0.65)	−0.04 (0.27)	0.34 (0.16)	−0.06 (0.46)
Droad	(+)	−0.84***(2.61)	−0.63 ** (2.06)	−2.22 (1.59)	−0.25 ** (2.09)
Roadumy	(−)	0.42 (0.27)	−1.56 (1.17)	−10.16 (1.11)	−0.57 (0.80)
Male99	(+)	−0.001* (1.76)	−0.001 (1.31)	−0.005 * (1.69)	0.0003 (0.77)
Literate	(−)	−8.65 (0.78)	−18.36 (1.33)	−74.96 (1.49)	1.18 (0.28)
Schdulcaste	(+)	−0.55 (0.15)	−7.09 * (1.78)	−20.32 (1.03)	−1.51 (1.03)
Cultivator	(−)	−5.31 (0.53)	−0.22 (0.03)	−68.64 (0.87)	−0.50 (0.10)
Aglabour	(+)	−5.17 (0.28)	6.55 (0.80)	−161.58 (1.17)	7.83 (1.25)
Hhworker	(−)	−48.53 (1.28)	−15.02 (0.40)	193.35 (0.39)	−40.80 (1.20)
Otworker	(−)	−20.51 (0.84)	19.01 (1.25)	−58.61 (0.45)	12.19 (1.12)
Margworker	(+)	−3.05 (0.44)	3.23 (0.97)	5.82 (0.42)	3.80 (1.01)
Constant	(?)	10.84 (1.04)	19.16 (1.36)	102.40 (1.22)	−3.85 (0.86)
		$N=486, R^2=0.11$, $F_{(19,466)}=3.91$, $Pro=0.00$	$N=318, R^2=0.15$, $F_{(19,298)}=2.88$, $Pro=0.00$	$N=48, R^2=0.46$, $F_{(19,28)}=1.02$, $Pro=0.47$	$N=270, R^2=0.15$, $F_{(19,250)}=5.09$, $Pro=0.00$

Notes: ***, **, and * imply 1%, 5%, and 10% level of significance respectively. Figures in parenthesis are the absolute t-values.

References

Badola, R., and Hussain, S. A., 'Valuing Ecosystem Functions: An Empirical Study on the Storm Protection Function of Bhitarkanika Mangrove Ecosystem,India', *Environmental Conservation*, 32, (2005), 1–8.

Baird, A. H., 'Tsunamis: Myth of Green Belts', SAMUDRA Report No. 44, July 14–19, 2006.

Barbier, E. B., 'Valuing Ecosystem Services as Productive Inputs', *Economic Policy*, 22 (49), January (2007), 177–229.

Bretschneider, C. L. and Wybro, P. G., 'Tsunami Inundation Prediction', in Bretschbeider C. L. (ed.), *Proceedings of the15th Coastal Engineering Conference*, 1006–1024, (New York: American Society of Civil Engineers, 1977)

Brinkman, R. M., Massel, S. R., Ridd, P. V. and Furukawa, K., 'Surface Wave Attenuation in Mangrove Forests', *Proceedings of the 13th Australian Coastal and Ocean Engineering Conference*, 2, (1997), 941–949.

Chan, H. T., Ong, J. E., Gong, W. K., and Sasekumar, A., 'The Socio-economic, Ecological and Environmental Values of Mangrove Ecosystems in Malaysia and their Present State of Conservation', in Clough, B. F. (ed.), *The Economic and Environmental Values Of Mangrove Forests and Their Present State of Conservation in South-East Asia/Pacific Region*, 1, 41–81 (Okinawa: International Society for Mangrove Ecosystems, International Tropical Timber Organisation And Japan International Association For Mangroves, 1993).

Chatenoux, B. and Peduzzi, P., 'Analysis of the Role of Bathymetry and Other Environmental Parameters in the Impacts from the 2004 Indian Ocean Tsunami', UNEP / DEWA/ GRID Europe, (Switzerland: 2006) http://www.grid.unep.ch/ product/publication/download/environment_ impacts_tsunami.pdf

Chatenoux, B. and Peduzzi, P. 'Impacts from the 2004 Indian Ocean Tsunami: Analyzing the Potential Protecting Role of Environmental Features', *Natural Hazards*, 40, (2007), 289–304.

Cochard, R., Ranamukhaarachchi, S.L., Shivakoti, G.P., Shipin, O.V., Edwards, P.J., and Seeland, K.T., 'The 2004 Tsunami In Aceh And Southern Thailand: A Review On Coastal Ecosystems, Wave Hazards And Vulnerability', *Perspectives in Plant Ecology, Evolution and Systematics*, 10, (2008), 3–40.

Dahdouh-Guebas, F., and Koedam, N., 'Coastal Vegetation and Asian Tsunami', *Science*, 311, (January, 2006), 37.

Dahdouh-Guebas, F., 'Mangrove Forests And Tsunami Protection', *McGraw-Hill Yearbook of Science & Technology*, (New York: McGraw-Hill Professional, 2006) 187–191.

Dahdouh-Guebas, F., Jayatisa, L.P., Di Nitto, D., Bosire, J.O., Seen, D., Lo, and Koedam, N., 'How Effective were Mangroves as a Defense against the Recent Tsunami?', *Current Biology*, 15, (2005), R443–R447.

Danielson, F., Sorensen, M. K., Olwig, M. F., Selvam, V., Parish, F., Burgess, N. D., Hiralshi, T., Karunagaran, V. M., Rasmussen, M. S., Hansen, L. B., Quarto, A., and Suryadiputra, N., 'The Asian Tsunami: A Protective Role For Coastal Vegetation', *Science*, 310, (2005), 643.

Das, S. 'Storm Protection Values of Mangroves in Coastal Orissa', Kumar, P. and Sudhakara Reddy, B. (ed.) *Ecology and Human Well-Being*, (New Delhi: Sage Publications, 2007a).

Das, S., 'Storm Protection by Mangroves in Orissa: An Analysis of the 1999 Super Cyclone', SANDEE Working Paper No. 25–07, Kathmandu, Nepal, December, 2007b.

Das, S., 'The case for mangrove conservation: Valuing damage averted in Orissa's 1999 Super Cyclone', Draft Manuscript and Paper presented at the World Congress of Environmental and Resource Economics, University of Quebee, Montreal, June (2010).

Dixon, J.A., Louise F. Scura, Richard A. Carpenter, and Paul B. Sherman, 'Economic Analysis of Environmental Impacts', 2nd edn. (London: Earthscan Publication in Association with the Asian Development Bank and the World Bank, 1994).

FAO, 'Reducing Agricultural Vulnerability to Storm related Disasters', COAG 01/6, FAO Corporate Document Repository, Annexure, XI, APDC/01/7 (2000).

FAO, 'Coastal Protection In The Aftermath Of The Indian Ocean Tsunami: What Role For Forests And Trees?' Concept Note, Conclusion and Policy Recommendation, Regional Technical Workshop, Khao Lak, Thailand, August 2006, 28–31.

Farber, S. 'The Value Of Coastal Wetlands For Protection Of Property Against Hurricane Wind Damage', *Journal of Environmental Economics and Management*, 14, (1987), 143–151.

Gupta, M.C., and Sharma, V.K. 'Orissa Super Cyclone, 99', National Center for Disaster Management, Indian Institute of Public Administration, New Delhi, New United Press, 2000.

Harada, K., and Imamura, F. 'Effects of Coastal Forests on Tsunami Hazard Mitigation, a Preliminary Investigation', *Advances in Natural and Technological Hazards Research*, 23, (2005), 279–292.

Hamza, L., Harada, K. and Imamura, F., 'Experimental and Numerical Study on The Effect of Mangrove to Reduce Tsunami', *Tohoku Journal of Natural Disaster Sciences*, 35, (1999), 127–132.

IMD, 'Damage Potential of Tropical Cyclones', Indian Meteorological Department, Govt. of India, 2002.

IMD, 'Tracks of Cyclones in Bay of Bengal and Arabian Sea, 1890–1990', Indian Meteorological Department, Govt. of India, 2000.

Kalsi, S.R., Jayanthi, N. and Roy Bhowmik, S.K., 'A Review of Different Storm Surge Models And Estimated Storm Surge Height In Respect of Orissa Supercyclonic

Storm of 29 October, 1999', Indian Meteorological Department, Govt. of India, January, 2004.

Kathiresan, K. and Rajendran, N., 'Coastal Mangrove Forest Mitigate Tsunami', *Estuarine, Coastal and Shelf Sciences*, 65, (2005), 601–606.

Kerr, A.M. and Baird, A.N., 'Landscape Analysis and Tsunami Damages in Ache: Comment on Iverson and Prasad (2007)', *Landscape Ecology*, 23, (2008), 3–5.

Kerr, A.M., and Baird, A.N., 'Natural Barriers to Natural Disasters', *Bio-Science*, 57 (2), (2007),102–103.

Khazai, B., J. Ingram, C. and Saah, D.S., 'The Protective Role of Natural and Engineered Defence Systems in Coastal Hazards', Report prepared for the State of Hawaii and the Kaulunani Urban and Community Forestry Program of the Department of Land and Natural Resources, Spatial Informatics Group, LLC, 1990 Wayne Ave, San Leandro, CA 94577, USA, 2007.

Kerr, A.M., Baird, A.H. and Camphell, S.J., 'Comments on Coastal Mangrove Forest Mitigate Tsunami by K. Kathiresan and N. Rajendran', *Estuarine, Coastal and Shelf Sciences*, 67, (2006), 539–541.

Massel, S. R., Furukawa, K. and Brinkman, R.M., 'Surface Wave Propagation in Mangrove Forests', *Fluid Dynamics Research*, 24, (1999), 219–249.

Mazda, Magi, Y.M., Ikeda, Y., Kurokawa, T. and Asano, T., 'Wave Reduction in a Mangrove Forest Dominated by Sonneratia Sp.', *Wetlands Ecology and Management*, 14, (2006), 365–378.

Mazda,Y., Magi, M., Ikeda, Y., and Hong, P.N., 'Mangroves as a Coastal Protection From Waves in The Tong King Delta, Vietnam', *Mangroves and Salt Marshes*, 1, (1997),127–135.

MEA (Millennium Ecosystem Assessment), 'Ecosystems and Human Well-being: A Framework for Assessment', Washington, DC, Island Press 2003.

Mohanty, N.C. 'Mangroves of Orissa', Project Swarajya Publication, Nayapalli, Bhubaneswar, 1992.

Orissa District Gazetteer, Cuttuck, The Gazetteers Unit, The Department of Revenue, Bhubaneswar, Government of Orissa 1996.

Quartel, S., Kroon, A., Augustinus, P.G.E.F., Vansanten, P. and Tri, N.H., 'Wave Attenuation in Coastal Mangroves in Red River Delta, Vietnam', *Journal of Asian Earth Sciences*, 29, (2007), 576–584.

Roy Abraham, K., Mohanty, U.C. and Dash, S.K., 'Simulation of Cyclones using Synthetic Data', *Proceedings of the Indian Academy of Sciences, Earth and Planetary Sciences*, (1995), 1044635–1044666.

Sathirathai, S., 'Economic Valuation of Mangroves and the Role of Local Communities in The Conservation of Natural Resources: A Case Study of Surat Thani, South of Thailand', EEPSEA Research Report http: 703.116-43-477/ publications.research1/ACF9E.html, 1998.

Steffen, W., 'Stronger Evidences but New Challenges: Climate Change Science 2001–2005', Department of Environment and Heritage, Australian Green House Office, Australian Government, 2006.

Tri, N.H., Adger, N., Kelly, M., Granich, S. and Nimh, N.H., 'The Role of Natural Resource Management in Mitigating Climate Impact: Mangrove Restoration in Vietnam', CSERGE (Center for Social and Economic Research on Global Environment) Working Paper, GEC 96–06, 1996.

UNEP (1996) 'After the Tsunami: Rapid Environmental Assessment', Report of UNEP Asian Tsunami Task Force, February (2005) (see http://www.unep.org/tsunami/tsunami rpt.asp).

Vermaat, J. E. and Thampanya, U., 'Mangroves Mitigate Tsunami Damage: A Further Response', *Estuarine, Coastal and Shelf Sciences*, 69, (2006), 1–3.

Vermaat, J.E. and Thampanya, U., Erratum to 'Mangroves Mitigate Tsunami Damage: A Further Response' (*Estuarine, Coastal and Shelf Sciences*, 69, 1–3, (2006), *Estuarine, Coastal and Shelf Sciences*, 75, 564, (2007).

Wooldridge, J.M., *Introductory Econometrics: A Modern Approach*, (Ohio: Thomson Learning, 2003).

9

Valuation of Recreational Amenities from Environmental Resources: The Case of Two National Parks in Northern Pakistan

Himayatullah Khan[1]

9.1. Introduction

Natural resource systems such as lakes, rivers, streams, estuaries, forests and parks are used extensively by people for various kinds of recreational activities. From an economic perspective, the services provided by natural resources have two important features. The first is that the economic value of these services depends upon the characteristics of the natural resource system. Knowledge of the values of these services may be important for a variety of resource management decisions. The second important feature is that access to the resource for recreation is typically not allocated through the markets. Rather, access is typically open to all visitors at a zero price or a nominal entrance fee that bears no relationship to either recreational value to the visitor or the cost of resource conservation. And there is no or little variation in these access prices over time or across sites to provide data for estimating the demand for these sites for recreation.

In developing countries, governments are often strapped for resources to protect and conserve the natural resources. In such situations, ecotourism

---

[1] This study is based on data from two different studies conducted by the author earlier (Himayatullah, 2003 and 2004). See also Khan (2006) for further details. I gratefully acknowledge the financial support provided by the South Asian Network for Development and Environmental Economics (SANDEE) and Higher Education Commission, Islamabad. I am heavily indebted to Professors Karl G. Maler, Partha Dasgupta, Enamul Haque and Dr Priya Shyamsundar and Dr Herath Gunathilake, for their valuable criticism, expert comments and suggestions. The study would have never been completed without their help.

can be an important source of income for ensuring both natural resource conservation and economic growth. A growing body of literature stresses the role eco-tourism can play in managing national parks and protected areas. In developing countries, park entry fees are often low, or sometimes non-existent. Further, whatever tourism revenues that exist are frequently merged with other general sources and not earmarked for park maintenance. Because of the ineffective capture of ecotourism revenues, alternative land uses that provide greater short-run returns, such as logging, agriculture, and cattle grazing, seem profitable even on public lands. The result is often deforestation, soil erosion, watershed degradation, and irreversible loss of bio-diversity.

The potential benefits from charging user fees and using differential pricing in national parks are significant. User fees are a mechanism to capture the public benefits of ecotourism, which often accrue primarily to the private sector. They can also be used to reduce visits to areas that suffer from overuse and ecological damage. Developing countries have little experience in guiding natural resource managers to design effective pricing strategies. Assessment of the impacts of user fees and differential pricing is needed so that appropriate policies can be devised and implemented.

Like many other developing countries, Pakistan is seeking to revitalize its tourism sector, including nature-based tourism. Pakistan is one of the poorest among South Asian countries in terms of bio-diversity. Forests cover as little as five per cent of the country and deforestation rates have been high. In recent years, however, the Government of Pakistan has shown an interest in the expansion and proper maintenance of the national park system. But, though the number of national parks and reserves is small in Pakistan, their management is far from satisfactory. This may be partly because of insufficient governmental funds and open access of visitors to these places. Economic valuation of these environmental resources can provide valuable information for the better management of parks.

In this chapter two parks – the Margalla Hills National Park and the Ayubia National Park located close to Islamabad are taken as case studies. There are some similarities and differences between these two parks and they are not too far from each other. The Travel Cost Method (TCM) is used for estimating the consumer surplus and recreational benefits and identifying a revenue-maximizing entrance fee for the parks. Using the results of this study, policy recommendations for improving park services are provided so that benefits can be further increased.

9.2. Studying two parks in Pakistan

Pakistan is very deficient in forest resources with forests covering only five per cent of its area. There are only few national parks in this country and these are threatened by forest fire, soil erosion, human settlement inside the parks encroachment by local villagers, and the pollution. These factors coupled with the insufficient government funding could be responsible for the failure of environmental resource conservation in this country. Two sources of funds are available for park management in Pakistan– (a) federal and/or provincial government budgetary allocations; (b) revenues generated from park entry fees. The government budget allocated for the management of national parks in Pakistan is very limited as it must compete with developmental programmes such as education, healthcare, infrastructure, defense spending, etc., in the country. Therefore, visitor charges are potentially important revenue generating instruments for park management. The entry charges to parks should be based on the recreation benefits visitors get and there is a need for estimating these benefits.

Ayubia National Park (ANP) is a small national park in the Murree hills not far from Islamabad. It is located to the North of Murree in the Himalayas. Ayubia consisting of four hill stations, namely, Khaira Gali, Changla Gali, Khanspur and Gora Dhaka is spread over an area of 26 kilometers. The chairlifts provided at this place are a matter of great attraction. It is an important place from the viewpoint of wild life, nature, ecotourism, and education. There are steep precipices and cliffs on one side and on the other are tall pine trees. The scenery is superb with huge pine forests covering the hills and providing shelter to numerous mammals.[2]

The Margalla Hills National Park (MHNP) is spread over an area of about 15,800 hectares. It includes Margalla Hills, Rawal Lake and Shakar Parian and was given the status of a national park in 1980 after the government recognized the growing threat to its flora and fauna. Of the three distinct units, the largest area, Margalla Hills of approximately 12,600 hectares, is shaped by villagers who depend on the park for timber and non-timber forest products as well as recreation. Margalla Hills consists of mountain wilderness, an urban recreation and cultural centre, and a large reservoir. Rawal Lake of approximately 1,900 hectares represents a man-made park

---

2 The park is home of Asiatic Leopard, Black Bear, Yellow Throated Marten, Kashmir Hill Fox, Red Flying Squirrel, Himalayan Palm Civet, Masked Civet and Rhesus Macaque. Birds in the park are Golden Eagle, Griffin Vulture, Honey Buzzard, Peregrine Falcon, Kestrel, Indian Sparrow Hawk, Hill Pigeon, Spotted Dove and Collared Dove.

environment, which has the appearance of a natural ecosystem. To provide a continuous supply of drinking water, city planners reestablished part of a pre-historic lake, which created a rare opportunity for the population in and around Islamabad to experience a lake environment and enjoy sports in addition to common outdoor recreation activities such as picnics, strolls and jogging. Shakar Parian, covering approximately 1,300 hectares represents an urban recreational and cultural park and provides the urban population facilities for activities such as sports, jogging and picnics. The Park is a habitat for various species of animals and birds. The notable animals here include the Gray Goral, Barking Deer, and Black Partridges. The MHNP is famous for bird watching[3].

9.3. Research methods

9.3.1. Methodology

The Travel Cost Method (TCM) used in this Chapter is basically an extension of conventional Household Production Function (HPF) model (see Chapter 2) that considers the household as maximizing utility based on numerous consumption and production decisions. The TCM enables an assessment of individual preferences for the demand of a non-market good like environmental recreation. It uses the cost of traveling to a recreation site in order to infer recreational benefits provided by the site. TCM studies have consistently shown that as the price of access (cost of travel) increases, the visit rate to the site falls. The TCM is usually estimated as a trip generating function where the visitation rate depends upon the cost of travel to the site, travel costs to substitute sites, and socio-economic characteristics of visitors (Garrod and Willis, 1999).

There are two approaches to TCM, the Zonal Travel Cost Method (ZTCM) (see Chapter 10) and the Individual Travel Cost Method (ITCM). Since the MHNP and the ANP are two substitute parks and are located close to the twin cities of Islamabad and Rawalpindi, and a majority of visitors are

---

3 Other animals in the park include Monkey, Chir Pheasants, Asiatic Leopard, Wild Boar, Jackal, Rhesus Macaque, Leopard Cat, Gray Goral Sheep, Chinkara Gazelle (rare), Red Fox, Pangolin, Porcupine, Yellow Throated Marten and Fruit Bats. Reptiles in the park are Russelles Viper, Indian Cobra and Saw Scaled Viper. Other birds in the park are the Griffin Vulture, Laggar Falcon, Peregrine Falcon, Kestrel, Indian Sparrow Hawk, Egyptian Vulture, White Cheeked Bulbul, Yellow Vented Bulbul, Paradise Flycatcher, Golden Oriole, Spotted Dove, Collared Dove, Larks, Shrikes, and Buntings

from nearby areas, ITCM is used. The ITCM has a distinct advantage over the ZTCM in that it takes into account the inherent variation in the data, rather than relying on zonal aggregate data. For a more practical travel perspective, the ITCM has the advantage that its trip generating function can be estimated using a smaller number of observations than the ZTCM (Garrod and Willis, 1999). However, the former requires more information about individual visitors and is reliant on an expensive questionnaire survey being undertaken to elicit visitor characteristics, preferences, and behaviour. Nevertheless, the ITCM is generally more flexible and applicable at a wider range of sites than ZTCM.

In order to model the travel cost function, following Freeman (1993), it is assumed that the individual's utility depends on the total time spent at the site, the quality of the park, and the quantity of a composite private good. With the duration of the visit fixed for simplicity, the time on site can be represented by the number of visits. The individual solves the following utility maximizing problem[4]:

$$Max: U\,(X,\,r,\,q) \tag{1}$$

subject to the twin constraints of monetary and time budgets:

$$M + p_w \cdot t_w = X + c.r \tag{2}$$

$$t^* = t_w + (t_1 + t_2)r \tag{3}$$

where X = the quantity of composite private good, whose price is the numeraire.

r = number of visits to the park,

q = environmental quality at the site,

M = exogenous income,

p_w = wage rate,

c = monetary cost of a trip,

t^* = total discretionary time,

t_w = hours worked,

t_1 = round-trip travel time, and

t_2 = time spent on site.

---

4 This section draws heavily on Freeman (1993), and Ward and Beal (2000).

It is assumed that r and q are (weak) complements in the utility function, implying that the number of visits will be an increasing function of the site's environmental quality. The time constraint reflects the fact that both travel to the site and time spent on the site take time away from other activities. Thus there is an opportunity cost to the time spent in the recreation activity. It is also assumed that the individual is free to choose the amount of time spent at work and that work does not convey utility (or disutility) directly. Thus the opportunity cost of time is the wage rate. Finally, it is also assumed that the monetary cost of a trip to the site has two components – the entry fee f, which could be zero, and the monetary cost of travel. This cost of travel is $p_d \times d$, where p_d is the price or cost per-kilometer of travel and d is the distance to the site and return from it.

Substituting equation (3) into (2) yields:

$$M + p_w \cdot t^* = X + p_r \cdot r \tag{4}$$

where p_r is the full price of a visit, which is the sum of entry fee (f, which could be zero), p_d is the per/km cost of travel and d is the distance in km as shown in equation 5.

$$p_r = c + p_w (t_1 + t_2)$$
$$= f + p_d \cdot d + p_w (t_1 + t_2) \tag{5}$$

As equation (5) makes clear, the full price of a visit consists of four components – the entry fee, the monetary cost of travel to the site, the time cost of travel to the site, and the cost of time spent at the site. On the assumption that individuals are free to choose the number of hours worked at a given wage rate, the two time costs are valued at the wage rate.

Maximizing equation (1) subject to the constraint of equation (4) will yield the demand function for visits:

$$r = r (p_r, M, q) \tag{6}$$

The data on rates of visitation, travel costs, and variation in entry fees (if any) can be used to estimate the coefficient on p_r in a travel cost-visitation function. Because of the linearity of equation (5), the coefficient on p_r can be used to derive the individual's demand for visits to a site as a function of the entry fee.

It is further assumed that there are substitute sites available. Thus, the demand equation is specified as below:

$$r_{ji} = r_j(p_{rji}, (p_{rki}), M_i, q_i) \tag{7}$$
$$(i = 1,...i,....., s), (k = 1,....., k,...., m), \text{ and } k \neq j$$

where r_{ji} is the number of visits individual i makes to the jth site, p_{rji} is the full price of a visit by i to j, and p_{rki} is the set of substitute prices for visits to other sites. This type of model can be estimated from data on individual observations (see, for example, Freeman 1993 and McConnell, 1985).

9.3.2. Factors that determine recreational demand

As discussed, the number of trips per period made to the two parks by each individual is denoted by r. Various independent variables are used to explain variation in the dependent variable r. Both economic theory and the considerable experience of recreation managers have shown that demographic and other independent variables influence recreation visitation. Apart from demographic variables, the most important variables include travel cost, travel time, substitute sites, and site quality and congestion.

Demographic variables such as age, sex, education, income, employment status, rural versus urban residence and family size affect recreational demand. Intuitively, age would appear to be an important determinant of demand for park visitation and is expected to be inversely related. That is, as age increases, participation decreases. Gender may be another determinant. It is generally expected that men would be more likely to participate than women. With regard to education, people with higher education, it could be said, appreciate outdoor nature-based activities more than people with less formal education. Household income has also, generally, been found to have a positive correlation with participation in many outdoor recreation activities. It is expected that the higher the household income, the higher the number of park visitations. Urban dwellers are likely to participate in recreation more than people from rural areas. Similarly, a better-quality park may attract an individual more often than a degraded-quality park.

The relationship between travel cost and park visitation is expected to be negative. On the question of what costs should be included under travel costs, some researchers have inquired closely into the costs of fuel, oil, tires, repairs and maintenance of vehicles in order to estimate appropriate travel costs. Seller, et al., (1985) used the cost of fuel, accommodation and food costs. Beal (1995) also found that a majority of respondents considered fuel, food, and accommodation costs as relevant to their trip decision.

The value of travel and on-site time is an important issue in TC studies. Numerous attempts have been made to value travel time in different ways.

McConnel (1992), for instance, has argued that the opportunity cost of on-site time should be included in the price variable but agrees that there is no systematic method, conceptually or empirically, for doing so. Cesario (1976) argued that it is more reasonable that a trade-off is made between time for travel and leisure activities rather than between work and travel time. He reviewed a number of empirical studies of commuting and found that the value of time varied between one quarter and one half of the wage rate. While valuing travel time has been addressed in several recent studies, there is still no consensus on a consistent procedure yet (Nillesen, 2002). Thus, in this study, Freeman (1993) is being followed, and full wage is being used to value time.

Generally, the effects of both time costs and transportation costs on the demand for recreation need to be estimated separately. However, since the two may be highly correlated and a separate estimation too difficult to carry out, in this chapter, travel costs include all monetary costs of travel to park as well as time cost. The time spent in traveling to the site and time spent on the site were valued at the prevailing wage rate and were added to the monetary cost of travel, the cost of fuel (in case the visitor was using his own car) or the fare of public transportation, meals, accommodation, etc.

As previously stated, prices of substitute sites also affect recreational demand for park. Some visitors may believe that each national park is unique and has no substitute. Conversely, some people use other forms of outdoor recreation (like going to a movie) as substitutes for nature-based recreation in national parks. Freeman (1993) approached the substitute site dilemma by suggesting that researchers ask visitors which other single site is visited frequently and include only that site's price as the relevant substitute price. He asserted that a next-best site yielding similar characteristics and services (a national park, in this instance) is the appropriate alternative. This approach has been followed in this study. MHNP and ANP are the closest substitute site for each others. The two parks are located at a distance of 40 miles from each other.

9.3.3. Sample size, sampling and data collection methods

The data to undertake this study was collected in 2002–2003. The data for ANP was collected during the summer of 2002 and MHNP data collection took place later in the year and in 2003. For the MHNP, a daily head count at various entry points to the two parks was undertaken for 45 days in order to establish the size of the population visiting the park. Then, one per cent of population of visitors was identified as the sample, which gave a sample size of 1000 respondents. Keeping in view seasonal and geographic variations in park visits, the sample was distributed as identified in Table 9.1. However, for the ANP, because of various constraints, 300 visitors were surveyed. Systematic random sampling was used, where every 10th visitor was interviewed. In case he/she refused, another visitor was interviewed.

Table 9.1. Sample respondents interviewed in different seasons and locations of the MHN park

Seasons	No. of Respondents	Location	No. of Respondents
Summer	220 (22%)	Shakarparian	300 (30%)
Fall	220 (22%)	Rawal lake	200 (20%)
Winter	220 (22%)	Margalla Hills	500 (50%)
Spring	340 (34%)		
All	1000 (100)	All	1000 (100)

The survey questionnaire used in this study consisted of two parts. The first part contained general information about the visitor including gender, education, marital status, age, income, place of living, etc. The second part of the questionnaire related to the visitor's recreational behaviour.

9.3.4. Econometric models

Economic theory does not suggest any particular functional form for TCMs. The most common practice is to statistically test various functional forms such as :

   (a) Linear $r = \alpha + \beta P$

   (b) Log-linear $\log r = \alpha + \beta P$

   (c) Double-log $\log r = \alpha + \log \beta P$

   (d) Negative exponential $r = \alpha + \log \beta P$

Having tried various functional forms, it was decided that the linear functional form was the best fit for the study data. Therefore, only linear regression results are reported.

The basic model used in this study depicts the number of visits to park as a function of factors such as the travel cost, time spent in traveling, substitute sites, income, education, age, gender, rural versus urban residence, family size, site quality, employment status, etc. Thus, the model was specified as follows:

$r_i = \beta_0 + \beta_1$ *travel cost* $+ \beta_2$ *household income* $+ \beta_3$ *travel cost* (*substitute site*) $+ \beta_4$ *age of visitor* $+ \beta_5$ *visitor's highest level of education* $+ \beta_6$ *household size* $+ \beta_7 D_1$ (male dummy)$+ \beta_8 D_2$ (urban dummy) $+ \beta_9 D_3$ (good park quality dummy) $+ e_i$ 　　　　　　　　　　　　　　　　　　　　　　　　　　　　　(8)

where r_i, the dependent variable, stands for the number of visits by the ith individual to the park per period of time, travel cost means round trip total cost from an individual's residence to and from the site and includes the opportunity cost of travel time and stay at park. Travel cost to substitute site means travel cost to and from a residence to a substitute site including travel time costs. $D_1 = 1$ if male and 0 otherwise, $D_2 = 1$ if urban dweller and 0 otherwise, $D_3 = 1$ if the visitor's perception about the site's recreational facilities is good and 0 if bad. Table 9.2 summarizes explanatory variables and hypotheses.

Table 9.2. Explanatory variables and hypotheses

Variables	Expected Sign	Description
Travel cost	−	It includes round trip total cost to and from the park including opportunity cost of travel time and time spent at the site. It is hypothesized that the no. of visits to the site and travel cost are inversely related.
Household income	+	Household average monthly income in Pakistan Rupees (PKR57.50 = US $1). We also hypothesize that household income and the no. of visits to the site are positively related.
Price of substitute	+	Travel cost from a residence (place of living) to and from the next best alternative substitute site including travel time and time spent at that site. It is hypothesized that MHN Park and AN Park are substitutes so that the travel cost of AN Park (for instance) and the no. of visits to MHN Park are positively related.

(Contd.)

(Contd.)

Variables	Expected Sign	Description
Age	−	Age (in years) of the visitor/respondent at the time of interview. The hypothesis is that the visitor's age and the no. of visits to the park are inversely related.
Education	+	Highest level of education (in years) of the respondent. It is expected that the level of education of visitors and the no. of visits are directly/positively related.
Household size	±	Number of family members in a household. The household size may also affect the no. of visits to park but the sign is not certain; it may be positive or negative.
Sex	+	Gender of respondents (D1 = 1 if male and 0 otherwise). We assume males will visit the park more often than females.
Residence	+	Respondent's area of origin (D2 = 1 if urban dweller and 0 otherwise). Visitors from urban areas, especially the twin cities of Islamabad and Rawalpindi, will visit the park more often than those from other areas, including rural areas.
Park Quality	+	Quality of the site/park (D3 = 1 if perception of the visitor is good about the park and 0 otherwise). It is assumed that if the visitors know that the quality of the park is good, then they will visit it more often than those who think that the quality of the park is not good.

9.3.5. *Estimating revenues*

One of the main reasons for estimating the travel cost function is to be able to calculate the consumer surplus, which provides an understanding of the value visitors place on recreational parks. Once the average visitor's travel cost or price is known, one can obtain the consumer surplus in a linear demand curve as the area above this price but under the demand curve. Simple geometry was used to estimate the consumer surplus from the parks.

One of the policy goals was to understand how to introduce an entrance fee for visitors to these national parks. Traditionally, these are not priced and so it has been difficult for the governments in developing countries to ensure sustainable management of these parks. While arbitrary fixation of rates is possible, a thorough study like this one would give policy makers a better set of choices to set the initial rate, which once set, remains sticky for many years, in countries of South Asia. Recognizing that the consumer surplus reflects maximum willingness to pay, an entry fees was identifed that would increase government revenues and at the same time be less than individual consumer surplus.

9.4. Results and discussion

9. 4.1. Descriptive statistics

Table 9.3 provides the descriptive statistics of variables used for estimating demand functions of two parks for recreation.

Table 9.3 Descriptive statistics of the respondents

Variables	MHN Park			AN Park		
	Mean	Min	Max	Mean	Min	Max
N						
No. of Recreation-al Trips	9.00	1.00	20.00	7.00	1.00	14.00
Yearly Spending on Ecotourism (Rs.)	5,500	1,000	10,000	5,300	1800	11508
Household Monthly Income (Rs.)	12,000	4,900	100,500	15,500	7,630	25,000
Distance (Km)	30	1.12	90.45	70	10	250
No. of Trips to the Park	7.00	1.00	15.00	4.00	1.00	10.00
No. Of Trips to Substitute Parks	1.61	1.00	5.00	5.00	0.00	7.00
Age (Years)	38.95	17.00	65.60	43.00	20.65	60.80
Household Size	6.80	4.34	11.35	6.00	3.50	10.20
Male	67%			61%		

(Contd.)

(*Contd.*)

Variables	MHN Park			AN Park		
	Mean	Min	Max .	Mean	Min	Max
Married	60%			60%		
Education:						
None	24%			24%		
Primary	55%			50%		
Secondary	11%			15%		
Technical diploma	3%			7%		
Bachelor's Degree	5%			3%		
Graduate	2%			1%		
Residence:						
Urban (mainly from Islamabad and Rawalpindi	60%			60%		
Do you want improvement in quality? Yes =	62%			60%		
How should the money be raised?						
Increase entry fee	38%			38%		
Govt. budget real-location	40%			40%		
Donation	22%			22%		

Visitors to ANP are a slightly older and richer than those who visit MHNP. The mean annual number of recreational trips per visitor to MHNP was a bit higher at seven relative to four visits to ANP. This may be because MHNP is closer than ANP to Islamabad – the mean distance from the visitor's home to the park was longer in case of ANP. The majority (60 per cent) of visitors in both parks was from urban areas and their annual spending on eco-tourism was almost the same in both cases. More than 76 per cent of park visitors to both parks were literate. The average age of the visitors and size of the households were also almost the same in both cases. The male-female ratio of visitors was marginally higher for MHNP.

More than 62 per cent of the respondents in MHNP and 60 per cent of respondents in ANP wanted improvements in the quality of services of the park. On the question about how more resources should be allocated for the park management, in both cases, 38 per cent of the respondents preferred an increase in entrance fee and 40 per cent chose reallocation of government budget.

In order to find out visitors' perceptions about quality improvements in the park, respondents were asked what kind of improvements they would like to see at the park. Table 9.4 presents details on the kinds of improvements that were identified and preferred. Most visitors indicated that they would increase the number of visits that they would make if park facilities were improved.

Table 9.4. Visitor's perceptions regarding improvements in two national parks

Area of Improvement	Specific Details
Recreational site	Site-seeing, bird-watching, relaxation, walking tracks, exercising, other
Information about parks	Maps, information sign, precaution sign, tourist information center
Traffic	Road conditions, traffic safety, traffic signs, parking
Miscellaneous	Waste disposal, lavatory, food and beverage services, accommodation

Source: Visitor Surveys in 2003 and 2004.

It is clear from Table 9.5 that visitors visit the two national parks for a number of reasons. Recreational activities at the park include sightseeing, bird-watching, walking, relaxation, exercising, eating sea-food, swimming, and water-sports like boating and sailing. The most number of visitors to MHNP come there to eat fish and aquatic food, while sight seeing seems to be the biggest issue drawing visitors to ANP. The majority of the visitors (62 per cent in case of MHNP and 50 per cent in case of ANP) reported a combination of various reasons for visiting these parks.

Table 9.5. Reasons for visiting MHN park by sample respondents

Reasons to Visit Park	MHNP (No.)	ANP (No.)
Sight-seeing	50	60
Walking	40	20
Bird-watching	30	25
Relaxation	40	30

(Contd.)

(Contd.)

Reasons to Visit Park	MHNP (No.)	ANP (No.)
Exercising	60	5
Eating fish and food	100	10
Swimming	40	–
Boating	20	–
Combination	620	150
All	1000	300

Source: Survey.

9.4.2. Estimation of benefits based on the individual travel cost method

Table 9.6 reports the results of the travel cost regression models for MHNP and ANP. As expected, the travel cost incurred by individuals is inversely related to park visitation rates. This implies that the higher the travel cost paid by visitors to reach the park, the less frequently they visit. It can be thus inferred that there is less demand to visit the park from those visitors who live far from it compared to those who live close to the park.

In addition to travel cost, household income has a positive impact on recreational demand. Visitors with high income are willing to pay more visits to the park. This implies that if the income level of visitors increases so would the recreational demand in both parks. The education of visitors bears a positive sign while the age variable has a negative algebraic sign. But both these variables have insignificant coefficients.

The dummy variables for male, urban dweller and good perception of visitors about the environmental quality of the park have positive coefficients. However, only the latter dummy has a statistically significant coefficient. This implies that if the quality of services of the park were improved, visitor would like to pay more visits to the park.

9.4.3. Recreational value of parks

The next step is to estimate the consumer surplus for the parks. This is done for the MHNP but are unable to do it for ANP because of some data limitations.

Table 9.6. Estimated results of linear regression equations for visitation

Variable	MHNP	ANP
Dependent Variable	**No. of Visits**	**No. of Visits**
Intercept	2.35 (3.12)	2.41 (2.32)
Travel Cost	−0.04 (−2.68)***	−0.06 (−2.58)***
Household Income	0.0053 (2.13)**	0.0057 (2.23)**
Price of Substitute	0.0031 (2.19)**	0.00309 (2.19)**
Age	−0.014 (−1.49)	−0.024 (−1.69)
Education	0.0089 (1.37)	0.0059 (1.17)
Family Size	0.0009 (0.15)	0.0029 (0.35)
Male		
Dummy 1 (1 for Male)	0.366 (1.34)	0.332 (1.54)
Dummy 2		
(1 for Urban Dweller)	0.008 (1.20)	0.018 (1.40)
Dummy 3		
1 if Visitor's Perception is Good	0.035 (2.13)**	0.045 (2.33)**
R2	0.534	0.47
F.Statistics	16.7	13.5
N	1000	300

Note: ** and *** indicate significance at 5% and 1% level respectively.

The consumer surplus is based on the estimated recreational demand function for MHNP. For an average visitor who visits the park seven times a year with an average travel cost of PKR 500 per trip, the consumer surplus is the area above PKR 500 but below the choke price[5] of PKR 675 under the recreational demand function. The consumer surplus is found to be PKR 612 per visitor per year. The per visitor consumer surplus is multiplied by an estimated 100,400 visitors per year to obtain a total consumer surplus for the MHNP of PKR 8.7 million per year.

---

[5] The choke price is obtained from the travel cost demand function as the price at which demand is zero.

The total recreational value equals the consumer surplus plus total cost of the visit. The annual monetary recreational value for MHNP is therefore PKR 58.7 million[6]. This equals the generated consumer's surplus, which is approximately PKR 8.7 (US $0.15) million plus travel cost, which is PKR 50.2 million (US $0.88 million). This is the value that the park yields every year for the economy. However, this is not the revenue from the park.

It is noted that the total travel costs include the opportunity costs of time as well as payments by visitors to transportation companies and service providers such as hotels, restaurants, tourist agencies, etc. The consumer surplus indicates the additional amount that the visitors are willing to pay to enjoy the park's environmental resources such as air, water, fish, birds, animals and, in general, scenic beauty. This figure, however, does not show the non-use value of the MHN Park.

9.4.4. Entrance fee

The issue of providing a better understanding to set an entry fee is at the core of this study. In the sample of households from MHN parks, an average visitor spends nearly PKR 3500 per year on visits to the park and his average travel cost is about PKR 500 per visit. Currently, visitors do not pay any entry fee for entry into the park. Since they are frequent visitors, it is possible to set two entry fees – one for regular visitors while the other for single entry visit.

First, if an average visitor derives PKR 612 as consumer's surplus for visits to the park per year then this gives us the maximum value that can be extracted as the entry fee. Given that visitors make an average of seven visits per year, this suggests that for a single entry visit the maximum value that can be set for the entry fees is approximately PKR 87 per visitor. At this fee, the entire consumer's surplus would be extracted by the park authority. However, consumers must retain a portion of the surplus in order to ensure that they continue to visit the park and this gives the transaction a win-win solution. As such, an entry fee of PKR 87 per visit or PKR 612 per year is the upper limit that the Park authority can charge.

Survey data collected through visitor interviews indicates that visitors are voluntarily willing to pay around PKR 20 per visit. Thus, the park authority can set a rate between PKR 20 and PKR 87 per visit or between PKR 140 and PKR 612 per year for visits to the park. Using a rule of thumb of 50

---

[6] We used an exchange rate prevalent when the data were first analyzed of 1 US$=57.63 PKR

per cent of the consumer surplus, the recommended rate per visit for day visitors could be PKR 43 for single entry ticket or PKR 306 for annual fee for a visitor. Since there are about 100,400 visitors to the park each year, if each of the visitors paid an entry fee of PKR 43, the authorities would earn about PKR 4.3 million or approximately US $75000 per year that could be used for park management.

It is to be noted that with introduction of entry fee into the park, there will be demand for better management of the parks by a visitor and so it is also important to recognize that a portion of the entry fee should be designated for maintenance of the park.

9.5. Conclusions and policy implications

In this chapter the individual travel cost model is being used to measure the recreational value of two national parks, MHNP and ANP in Pakistan. It was found that the two parks provide considerable recreational value to visitors. The parks draw their visitors because of a variety of attributes – sightseeing, exercising, good sea food and more.

Using the estimates from the MHN park, it is shown that the annual monetary recreational value for MHNP is PKR 58.7 million. This is the value provided by the park to the economy. On further analyses, it is recommended that some of this value can be captured to increase revenues to the park. By setting an entry fee of PKR 43 per visit, the park authorities could earn about PKR 4.3 million (US $75000) per year, which could be used for a variety of park improvements. This entry fee is feasible given the overall benefits accrued by visitors to the park.

Government planners envision both MHNP and ANP as ecotourism destinations. Keeping in view the large amount of consumer surplus and recreational values from at least one of these two parks, federal and provincial level governments can justify a larger annual budget for managing such parks.

The recreational benefits and entry fees estimated in this chapter underscore the importance of conservation of nature in Pakistan. There are several national parks in Pakistan that require additional investments. This study will hopefully draw attention to the demand for nature and the benefits that accrue from investing in nature. One can also be hopeful that this kind of a study will trigger interest in estimating feasible entry fees and revenue opportunities for different parks.

References

Abala, D. O., 'A Theoretical and Empirical Investigation of the Willingness to Pay for Recreational Services: A Case Study of Nairobi National Park', *Eastern Economic Review*, 3, (1987), 271–292.

Baldares, M. J. and Laarman, J. G., 'Derechos de Entrada a las Areas Protegidas de Costa Rica', *Ciencias Economicas*, 10, (1990), 63–76.

Bateman, I. J. and Willis, K. G. (eds.), *Valuing Environmental Resources: Theory and Practice of the Contingent Valuation Method in the US, EU, and Developing Countries* (New York: Oxford University Press, 1999).

Beal, D. J., 'Sources of Variation in Estimates of Cost Reported by Respondents in Travel Cost Surveys', *Australian Journal of Leisure and Recreation*, 5(1), (1995), 3–8.

Cesario, F. J., 'Value of Time in Recreation Benefit Studies', *Land Economics*, 51(2), (1976), 32–41.

Chase, L., Lee, D., Schulze, W., and Anderson, D., 'Ecotourism Demand and Differential Pricing of National Park Access in Costa Rica', *Land Economics*, 74(4), (1998), 466–482.

Choe, K., Whittington, D. and Lauria, D. T., 'The Economic Benefits of Surface Water Quality Improvements in Developing Countries: A Case Study of Davao, Philippines', *Land Economics*, 72(4), (1996), 519–527.

Cummings, R. G., Brookshire, D. S., and Schulze, W. D., 'Valuing Environmental Goods: An Assessment of the Contingent Valuation Method', (Savage, MD: Rowman and Littlefield Publishers, 1986).

Durojaiye, B. O. and Ipki, A. E., 'The Monetary Value of Recreational Facilities in a Developing Country: A Case Study of Three Centres in Nigeria', *Natural Resources Journal*, 28, (1988), 315–328.

Echeverria, J., Hanrahan, M., and Solorazano, R., 'Valuation of Non-Priced Amenities Provided by the Biological Resources within the Monteverde Cloud Forest Preserve, Costa Rica', *Ecological Economics*, 13, (1995), 43–52.

Farber, S., 'The Value of Coastal Wetlands for Recreation: An Application of Travel Cost and Contingent Valuation Methodologies', *Journal of Environmental Management*, 26, (1988), 299–312.

Freeman, A. Myrick III, *The Measurement of Environmental and Resource Values: Theory and Methods*, (Washington, DC: Resources for the Future, 1993).

Garrod, G. and Willis, K. G., *Economic Valuation of the Environment: Methods and Case Studies*, (Cheltenham, UK and Northampton, MA, USA: Edward Elgar, 1999).

Govt. of Pakistan, *Economic Survey 2000–01*, Finance Division, Economic Advisor's Wing, Islamabad, 2001.

Grandstaff, S. and Dixon, J. A., 'Evaluation of Lumpinee Park in Bangkok, Thailand', in J. A. Dixon and M. M., Hufschmidt (eds.), *Economic Valuation Techniques for the Environment: A Case Study Workbook*, (Baltimore: Johns Hopkins University Press, 1986).

Hadker, N., Sharma, S., David, A., and Muraleedharan, T. R., 'Willingness-to-pay for Borivli National Park: Evidence from a Contingent Valuation', *Ecological Economics*, 21, (1997), 105–122.

Himayatullah, 'Economic Valuation of the Environment and Travel Cost Approach: The Case of Ayubia National Park', *The Pakistan Development Review*, 42, (2003), 537–551.

Himayatullah, 'Demand for Eco-tourism: Estimating Recreational Benefits from the Margalla Hills National Park in Northern Pakistan', Working Paper No. 5–04, Kathmandu, SANDEE, 2004.

Hotelling, H., *The Economics of Public Recreation: The Prewitt Report*, (Washington DC: National Park Services, 1947).

Isangkura, A., *Environmental Valuation: An Entrance Fee System for National Parks in Thailand*, EEPSEA Research Report Series, Economy and Environment Program for Southeast Asia, Tanglin: Singapore, 1998.

Khan, H., 'Willingness to Pay for Margalla Hills National Park: Evicence from the Travel Cost Method', *The Lahore Journal of Economics*, 11, (2006), 43–70.

Kaosa-ard, M., Patmasiriwat, D., Panayotou, T., and Deshazo, J. R., *Green Financing: Valuation and Financing of Khao Yai National Park in Thailand*, (Bangkok: Thailand Development Research Institute, 1995).

Lindberg, K. and Johnson, R. L., 'Estimating Demand for Ecotourism Sites in Developing Nations', *Trends*, 31, (1994), 10–15.

Loomis, J. B. and Walsh, R. G., *Recreation Economic Decisions: Comparing Benefits and Costs*, (State College, PA: Venture Publishing, 1997).

Maraseni, T. N., Maroulis, J., and Cockfield, G., An Estimation of Willingness to Pay for Asparagus (Asparagus racemosus Willd) Collectors in Makawanpur District, Nepal, *Journal of Forest Science*, 54, (2008), 131–137.

McConnell, K. E., 'The Economics of Outdoor Recreation', in Kneese, V.A.L and Sweeney, J.L. (eds.), *Handbook of Natural Resources and Energy Economics, Vol.1*, (Amsterdam: North-Holland, 1985).

McConnell, K. E., 'On-site Time in the Demand for Recreation', *American Journal of Agricultural Economics*, 74, (1992), 918–925.

Moran, D., 'Contingent Valuation and Biodiversity: Measuring the User Surplus of Kenyan Protected Area', *Biodiversity and Conservation*, 3, (1994), 663–684.

Munganata, E. D. and Navrud, S., 'Environmental Valuation in Developing Countries: The Recreational Value of Wildlife Viewing', *Ecological Economics*, 11, (1994), 135–151.

Nillesen, E., 'The Travel Cost Approach: An Application to Bellenden Ker National Park', an unpublished thesis submitted to the School of Economics, University of Queensland, Australia, 2002.

Pearse, P. H., 'A New Approach to the Evaluation of Non-priced Recreational Resources', *Land Economics*, 11, (1968), 135–151.

Riley, E., Northrop, A. and Esteban, N., 'A Willingness to Pay Study for Park Fees: Quill/Boven National Park and St Eustatius Marine Park, St Eustatius, Netherlands Antilles' St Eustatius National Parks Foundation, National Parks Office, Gallows Bay, St Eustatius, Netherlands Antilles, 2006.

Schaeffer, R. L., W., Mendenhall III and Ott., R. L., *Elementary Survey Sampling*, (5th edition), (USA: Duxbury Press, 1996).

Seller, C., Stoll, J. R. and Chavas, J., 'Validation of Empirical Measures of Welfare Change: A Comparison of Non-market Techniques', *Land Economics*, 61(2), (1985), 156–175.

Shultz, S., Pinnazo, J., and Cifunetes, M., *Opportunities and Limitations of Contingent Valuation Surveys to Determine National Park Entrance Fees: Evidence from Costa Rica*, Selected Papers Presented at Annual Meetings of American Agricultural Economic Association, (Toronto: Canada, 1997).

Smith, V. K., Desvousges, W. H. and McGiveny, M. P., 'The Opportunity Cost of Travel Time in Recreation Demand Models', *Land Economics*, 59, (1983), 259–278.

Southgate, D. and Whitaker, M., *Economic Progress and Environment: One Developing Country's Policy Crisis* (New York: Oxford University Press, 1994).

Tobias, D. and Mendelssohn, R., 'Valuing Ecotourism in a Tropical Rain-forest Reserve', *Ambio*, 20, (1991), 91–93.

Ward, F. A. and Diana, D., *Valuing Nature with Travel Cost Models: A Manual – New Horizons in Environmental Economics*, (Cheltenham, UK and Northampton, MA, USA: Edward Elgar, 2000).

Wennergen, E. B., 'Valuing Non-market Priced Recreational Resources', *Land Economics*, 40, (1964), 234–241.

World Resource Institute, *World Resources: A Guide to the Global Environment (The Urban Environment)*, Oxford and New York: Oxford University Press, 1996–1997.

Yaping, Du., *The Value of Improved Water Quality for Recreation in East Lake, Wuhan, China: Application of Contingent Valuation and Travel Cost Methods*, EEPSEA Research Report Series, Economy and Environment Program for Southeast Asia, Tanglin, Singapore, 1998.

10

Valuing the Land of Tigers: What Indian Visitors Reveal

Indrila Guha and *Santadas Ghosh*[1]

10.1. Introduction

In the south-east corner of India's state of West Bengal, the Sundarban is part of the largest riverine delta region in the world. It is a complex ecosystem which is well known for both its mangroves (one of the three largest single tracts of mangrove forest in the world) and for being the home of the Royal Bengal Tiger. It is the only mangrove forest in the world that is inhabited by tigers. The Sundarban was declared a reserved forest in 1926. The Sundarban Tiger Reserve was formed in 1973 by the Government of India under the Project Tiger scheme, to protect this highly endangered animal. In 1987 the Sundarban was recognised a World Heritage Site by UNESCO and in 1992 it was designated a Ramsar site.

The Sundarban is rich in biodiversity, which plays a significant role in physical coastal evolution. The entire riverine delta is a significant habitat for a variety of terrestrial and marine species – birds, spotted deer, crocodiles

[1] Our study is the partial outcome of a research project funded by SANDEE (South Asian Network for Development and Environmental Economics) and hosted by Global Change Programme, Jadavpur University. We are immensely benefited by various Biannual R&T Workshops of SANDEE. We are specifically thankful to Enamul Haque, Priya Shyamsundar, Jeffrey Vincent, Kanchan Chopra, M.N. Murty and E. Somanathan for their detailed discussions and comments at various stages of the work. Our study has also been enriched by the observations and advices of Karl-Goran Maler and Subhrendu Pattanayek. We express our sincere gratitude to Joyashree Roy, Coordinator, Global Change Programme, for providing all the crucial institutional support throughout the study period.

and snakes amongst them. The region has experienced a rapid depletion of forest cover and loss of faunal diversity due to human encroachment. Conservation in recent years has helped slow down such erosion of the Sundarban forest, but threats remain. Presently, the protected area is bounded by the Bay of Bengal in the south and the border with Bangladesh in the east. In the north and the west, the reserve forest is separated from human settlements by numerous lesser rivers and water channels. The present regime of protection is aimed at leaving the tiger habitat insulated from human interventions. Human movements are restricted only to a buffer zone by the issue of priced permits and the issuing authority (the Department of Forests) monitors all human movement in the forest.

The villages bordering the Sunderban forest are located on deltaic islands. Settlements on these islands are relatively recent – almost all have emerged within the last century and by clearing the forest. Residents of these islands are mainly dependent on rain-fed agriculture, but also on forest products and fishing. They are otherwise disadvantaged by their remoteness and lack of infrastructure like electricity.

In the Sundarban, conservation efforts have imposed a cost on the local stakeholders in the form of income that the poor have foregone by being barred from the forest. Thus, it is useful to view development interventions in the region through the lens of social cost benefit analyses. The costs borne by locals as a result of conservation need to be compared to the Total Economic Value (TEV) of the Sundarban, which includes both 'use value' and 'non-use value'. Studies carried out so far on the region estimate values for extractible forest products and its ecological contribution in terms of increased productivity of fish farms (Santhakumar et al. 2005, Chopra 2005).

For a protected area which receives visitors, the 'recreational services' it can provide is a major part of its non-use value. The Sundarban's unique mangrove forest landscapes and its position as a tiger habitat make it a singular tourist attraction. This is proved by the rising number of visitors in recent years despite poor transport options into and within the region, and major infrastructural deficits like little or no electricity. This study aims to provide a baseline estimate of the recreational value of the Indian Sundarban.

Two alternative methodologies exist for estimating the value of a recreational site. The Contingent Valuation Method (CVM), as a 'stated preference' valuation technique, circumvents the absence of markets for environmental goods. This method asks potential visitors to a recreational site what they are willing to pay for the experience there. However, since this method does not record visitors' actual behaviour, literature on such techniques indicates that when there is a market for the service to be valued, CVM should be avoided. That is why the Travel Cost Method (TCM) is chosen, which has emerged as a more acceptable methodology for valuing recreational services. It involves the estimation of recreational demand for the site based on visitors' 'revealed' – as opposed to 'stated' – preferences. Apart from valuing the recreational services, TCM data also help the policy authority fix an entry fee that can either maximize revenue or control the number of visitors.

This study relies on a primary survey of a sample of visitors to the Indian Sundarban from November 2005 to March 2006. Following TCM, the recreational demand for the site is estimated. Literature on the Travel Cost Method recognizes that, other than travel cost, visitors' socio-economic conditions may have significant effects on their demand for recreational services from a site. This study explores survey data as well as data from secondary sources to bring out such determinants and quantitatively estimate their influence on recreational demand. The study also estimates an entry fee level that maximizes revenue.

10.2. Studies estimating recreational value

Both CVM (Kadekodi, 2004) and TCM (Champ et al., 2003; Chopra, 2004; Markandya et al. 2001) have been used to measure recreational values of environmental goods like protected wildlife areas. Some studies have used both methods (Herath & Kennedy 2004; Nam & Son 2001) and attempted a comparison of the two different estimates.

The use of TCM often follows two routes. The Individual Travel Cost Method (ITCM) (see Chapter 9) considers the number of visits a single visitor pays to a site within a specified period. This represents quantity of demand, which is a function of the visitor's travel cost to the site as well as of other economic and qualitative indicators (Xue et al. 2000; Khan 2004). Thus, a survey of visitors yields the number of data points equal to the sample size and the functional relationship between visitation and travel cost can be estimated.

ITCM, however, cannot be applied to sites that receive few multiple visits by the same visitors. In such cases, the Zonal Travel Cost Method (ZTCM) is adopted (Tobias & Mendelsohn 1991; Maille & Mendelsohn 1992). ZTCM estimates the demand for a recreational site in terms of 'visitation rate' from different zones to that site. Visitation for a zone is defined as the number of visitors per thousand population from that zone. The more distant the visitors' zone is from the tourist site, the greater the travel cost which lowers the visitation rate from that zone to the site. The functional relationship between 'visitation' from the zones and their 'average travel costs' to the site is empirically estimated in the form of a Trip Generating Function (TGF). In ZTCM, the number of data points equals the number of zones that can reasonably be constructed with respect to visitors' originating places. The suitable functional form for the TGF varies across studies, with linear and log-linear forms appearing more frequently in the literature (Carr & Mendelsohn 2003, Nam & Son 2001).

10.3. Methodology for ZTCM

The Travel Cost Method has been used for valuation of recreational sites since it was conceived by Hotelling (1947). As discussed in the previous chapter and Chapter 2, the method is based on the assumption that the costs incurred by a visitor for a trip can be used as a proxy for the recreational value placed by him for it. It is his *minimum* demand price for the recreational service the site is seen to possess. As travel cost increases, 'visitation' decreases following the law of demand. An empirical estimation of this demand is crucial for computing the value of recreational services offered by the site. Information on varying travel costs, along with other relevant socio-economic explanatory variables, is used to estimate the 'recreational demand function'.

In ZTCM, 'quantity demanded' is represented by 'visitation from zones' to the site rather than the number of times a single visitor visits the site within a period. For a theoretically consistent negative relation between demand price and visitation, visitors' originating places are categorized into zones depending on their distance from the site. Assuming travel cost to be an increasing function of distance, the primary cause of variation in visitation rate from different zones is traced to their distances from the site. Implicitly, it also assumes that tastes and preferences of visitors across the zones are homogeneous.

Within a given period, a reasonably sized random sample of visitors surveyed at the site is expected to yield the shares of different zones in the total number of visitors. Suppose N_i is the estimated number of visitors from zone 'i' and P_i is its total population. Then visitation V_i (say, per thousand people) for zone 'i' is defined as

$$V_i = (N_i / P_i) \times 1000$$

The average travel cost from each zone is calculated on the basis of information collected from the sample of visitors from that zone. The travel cost is calculated 'per visitor' inclusive of all actual expenses from the visitor's originating point (including the entry fee) as well as his/her opportunity cost of time, taken as potential earnings lost for the duration of the trip. If T_i is the average travel cost from zone 'i', then visitation from zone 'i' (V_i) is supposed to be functionally related as

$$V_i = f (T_i , Z_i)$$

where Z_i is a vector of zonal variables that are expected to influence V_i. The functional form and the components of Z_i are case-specific. These are usually decided by exploring the survey data. The relationship between V, T and Z is known as the Trip-Generating Function (TGF). The demand function for each zone is obtained by using the corresponding value of Z_i in the estimated TGF, and aggregate demand can be obtained as the sum of zonal demands.

The value of the recreational services offered by the site is measured by the difference between the estimated demand prices and the actual expenses that the visitor incurs during the whole trip. In other words, it refers to the Consumer Surplus (CS), estimated as the area under the demand curve and above the price-line representing visitors' actual travel cost. For each zone a 'choke-price' can be calculated using the estimated TGF which represents the maximum of all demand prices from that zone (i.e, that value of T_i for which estimated V_i falls to zero). If T^0 is the average (actual) price paid by visitors and T^C is the choke-price, then consumer surplus (per thousand people, or any other unit used for computing V_i) is

$$CS = \int_{T^0}^{T^C} V \, dT$$

The CS for each zone, thus estimated, needs to be adjusted by an appropriate multiplicative factor to account for the total population in that zone. Aggregate CS can be obtained as the sum of zonal surpluses, which represents the recreational value of the site. However, it should be recognized that this sum measures only the recreational value of the site and not its Total Economic Value.

In practice, ZTCM is beset by problems like 'zero visitation rates' and 'multipoint trips'. In the literature, ITCM has greater theoretical acceptance over ZTCM. yet practical problems render the application of ITCM impossible in specific sites. The low standard of tourist amenities – in many conditions the utter lack of them altogether – and the problems with infrastructure, like little or no electricity, make it rare for a visitor to attempt more than one trip in a year to the Indian Sundarban. Moreover there is little variation in terms of time spent on the spot by visitors. This is why ZTCM was relied upon despite its shortcomings.

Other issues specific to ZTCM, such as deciding the optimum number of visitors' originating zones were confronted. Literature on the method (Nillesen et al. 2000; Font 2000; Nam & Son 2001) has dealt with how to treat foreign tourists, multipoint tourists, the possibility of zero visitation from an originating zone and heteroskedasticity (unequal variance of the random error term across zones in the regression model) in zonal data. An application of ZTCM in measuring biodiversity value in Keoladeo National Park (India) provides a detailed listing of the above mentioned problems that confront such studies (Chopra, 2004).

10.4. Nature of a Sundarban tour

Organized tourism in the Indian Sundarban began in the mid-1980s, after the inception of the nationwide tiger conservation programme Project Tiger[2]. In the absence of any regular publication of visitor statistics, data collected from the office of the Field Director, Sundarban Tiger Reserve, show that visitor arrival in 2005–2006 was 63,900, which increased to 75,000 in 2006–2007. Local tour operators reported a steady increase in visitors' number since the beginning of this decade. Tourism in the delta still does not follow a master plan, but the forest cannot be entered without a permit, which is mandatory. The authority's role in promoting tourism has so far been limited to building and manning five watch-towers inside the buffer zone of the forest, and one Mangrove Interpretation Centre describing the Sundarban's flora, fauna and ecology through models and photographs.

---

[2] http://projecttiger.nic.in/sundarbans.htm

Visitors can apply for their permits at any one of four different issuing offices, but these have to be shown and stamped at a single entry point to the forest. This is the village Pakhiralay where the Forest Range Office is located. There is still no restriction on the number of permits issued to tourists and this may indicate that tourism carrying capacity of the forest is not yet a consideration for the authority.

A Sundarban tour is always a cruise through the water channels within the buffer zone of the reserve forest with halts at riverbank watch-towers. These cruises are conducted in hired private boats that can also house small groups of tourist for the night. However, on-shore accommodation in tourist lodges is also available in and around Pakhiralay village.

Tourism in the Indian Sundarban is still largely unplanned, although it is being slowly organized, and this is why prospective visitors to the Sundarban find little useful information. The area is relatively inaccessible which, combined with the minimal infrastructure, makes it difficult for a visitor to tour independently. This is where a number of small enterprises step in with 'tour packages' catering to visitors' tastes and budgets. Survey data, supported by focus group discussion with the tour operators, suggests that as many as 83 per cent of all visitors in the Sundarban use these tour packages.

Tourist arrival in the Sundarban is concentrated mainly in the winter months. This study found that more than 73 per cent of annual visitors actually spent their trip time within a four-month period in the winter (2005–2006)[3]. This gave rise to a separate problem as a ZTCM study addressing seasonal variation required sufficient visitation from all zones during different seasons. This was not feasible in this study as visitor arrival in other months is very thin and there were time and budget constraints. That is why recreational demand for the whole year was estimated and seasonal effects left out.

10.4.1. The tour packages

Discussions with tour operators identified several common packages offered to visitors. Most operators offer their packages in the winter months only. A broad categorization of these packages was assembled.

---

[3] From (i) survey data on visitor arrival and (ii) data obtained from the office of the Field Director, STR.

(a) Around 25–30 operators, all located in Canning, the nearest
town and rail-link from Sundarban, cater to visitors who are
self-organized in large groups. They offer a return package using
launches (big watercrafts) from Canning to Sundarban. Typically
these trips are of two to three day's duration and visitors stay
overnight in the launch. However, a visitor can also opt for staying
on-shore near Pakhiralay at his/her own cost. These operators
offer services which are almost a perfect substitute to each other
and so the package cost vary within a narrow range only. (Canning
package is Table 10.1)

Table 10.1. Types of tours packages: seven options in the survey questionnaire

Package Code	Tour type/operator
1	Self-made trip for individual or group visitors – with or without any fixed points for starting or ending the trip, no prior deal on food or accommodation or on boats to visit the forest.
2	Canning Package – with launches operated from Canning. 25–30 operators are in operation from Canning. Packages usually target tourist from low to middle-income group
3	Sonakhali Package – operating seasonally from Sonakhali. A handful of seasonal operators; these are usually low-cost packages
4	Kolkata package I – 'All inclusive' package offered by WBTDC (a public sector undertaking) from kolkata, targeting high-income group
5	Kolkata package II – 'All inclusive' package tours offered by 'Help Tourism' from Kolkata. (A private initiative; catering to high-income group)
6	Kolkata package III – 'All inclusive' package tours offered by 'Sundarban Tiger Camp' from Kolkata. (A private initiative; catering to high-income group)
7	Custom-made package – Tour package (may not be all inclusive) offered by some enterprising individuals operating seasonally and offered to tourists, with or without any fixed originating or terminating point.

Note: The seven tour packages were identified using focused group discussions
with four tour operators conducted prior to the survey and were finalized during
pre-testing of questionnaire (in February, 2005).

(b) The West Bengal Tourism Development Corporation (WBTDC, a public sector enterprise) and two other private operators offer round trip 'all inclusive' packages from Kolkata to Sundarban. Visitors can avail these packages without being in a group. The package costs are significantly high and it targets visitors from the high-income group. (Kolkata packages I–III in Table 10.1)

(c) Some enterprising individuals, using their contacts in Sundarban, offer negotiable 'custom-made packages' to small-sized group visitors. These packages may or may not be 'all inclusive' and usually do not have any fixed point of origin or termination. The tour itinerary is also customized fitting the preferences of the visitors' (Custom-made Package in Table 10.1).

(d) In the peak tourist season, a few seasonal operators offer package tours originating from Sonakhali – the nearest road link to Sundarban. These are usually low-cost packages targeting low and middle income visitors. (Sonakhali Package in Table 10.1)

(e) Apart from the four types of packages described above, small groups of visitors also travel to Sundarban on a self-made tour package. In most cases, they arrive at Pakhiralay on their own, choose food and accommodation on their own, and hire a local boat (smaller watercraft) to enjoy the forest. (Self-made trip in Table 10.1)

These visit options can effectively divide the recreational market into segments and in this study the survey questionnaire contained seven options to identify the respondents' tour package. The options were devised to be mutually exclusive and exhaustive.

10.5. Survey design and sampling

A study on ZTCM depends critically on the sample of visitors selected for collecting information on their places of origin and travel cost. This study collected information in two distinct sets. In the Indian Sundarban, every inbound visitor group must produce their entry permits at a single checkpoint. There is one permit issued per watercraft or per group. These permits contain number of visitors, place of origin (address) and the type of watercraft they used. This study collected this data for all visitors between the third week of November (2005) and the second week of March (2006). This was achieved by manning the entry point for all the days during that period and information on place of origin could be recorded for 73 per cent of all visitors in one full year.

The second set of data comprises travel cost and other individual and household level information obtained from the visitor survey conducted simultaneously during the same period. Data was collected from returning tourists after their visit to the forest. Interviews of 906 visitors were completed using a structured questionnaire with a single respondent from each family chosen in the sample[4]. The 'per capita travel cost' and other household level information are assumed to be same for the family members accompanying the respondent. By this count, the total number of visitors on whom information could be collected is 1,948 (based on 906 interviews, including foreign nationals). This total amounts to roughly three per cent of annual visitor arrival.

The first set of data was used to calculate the zonal visitation rates, while the second set was used to estimate zonal averages of travel cost and to determine visitors' socio-economic profiles. Other zonal information relevant for estimating the TGF was collected from secondary sources[5].

The seven options for tour packages (Table 10.1) were arrived at during the pre-testing of the questionnaire (done in February 2005) and focus group discussions with tour operators. It was foreseen that the recreational market could be segmented and therefore a stratified random sample of returning visitors were selected. The proportion of the sample selected from each of the seven tour options was decided based on information collected from operators in the previous year. Interviews were conducted by trained field investigators who were instructed in the random selection of respondents within strata, independent of gender and age.

10.6. Data exploration: descriptive statistics

The first set of data, comprising 73 per cent of annual visitors, showed us that more than half originated from the nearest metropolitan city, which is Kolkata. Of the balance, most had travelled from elsewhere in the state of West Bengal. Only a very few came from the rest of India and abroad. With the second set of data, comprising three per cent of annual visitors, it is found that their distribution by place of origin is similar to the first set (Figure 10.1).

---

[4] In this study, visitors are considered to belong to the same 'family' if they use a common kitchen.

[5] Census 2001: Directorate of Census Operations; Government of India.

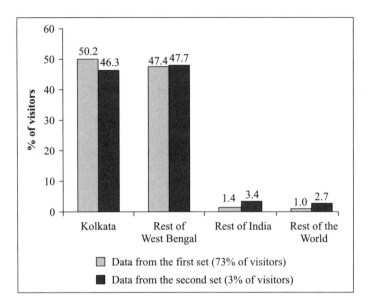

Figure 10.1. Distribution of Visitors to the Sunderban

It was found that visitors were mostly spending for two to three days in Sundarban. Almost half of them are salaried employees who came for the trip in their rest days/ holidays which involved no opportunity cost of time. It was found that very few (around one per cent) visitors reported agriculture as their source of earning. Visitors' education level in general is fairly high with 70 per cent of them reportedly being graduates or above.

10.6.1. Some practical issues

As is the convention with TCM, per-capita travel cost of a trip to Sundarban accounting for all the monetary expenses from visitor's originating point was caluctated. Since responses were elicited only from the returning tourists, the cost of return was assumed to be equal to the cost of arrival to the site and hence was doubled. The visitors were asked about their possible alternative usage of time during the trip and accordingly opportunity cost of time was included.

10.6.1.1. Multi-point tourists

Multi-point tourists create a problem for estimation in the travel cost method. It is customary to take into account only that part of the total arrival cost of multi-point tourists which is incurred for this part of the trip only. This is difficult since cost data may not be disaggregated in this way. In this study, multi-point visitors (those with a tour itinerary that has Sundarban as one amongst several destinations) stayed in the city Kolkata for some duration. The proportion of days spent in Sundarban was used, out of the total days of the trip, to deflate the Kolkata-home portion of travel cost.

However, as the Sundarban is located in one far-end of the country, a trip to Sundarban is usually not part of a multi-point tour circuit. Only visitors coming from distant districts or from outside the state show some evidence of multi-point tourism (Table 10.2). As the southern districts (near the Sundarban) of West Bengal generate the majority of visitors, the overall proportion of multi-point tourists in the sample is found to be a low five per cent.

Table 10.2. Percentage of multipoint visitors across regions: survey-estimate

Origin of visitors	Per cent of visitors from the origin reporting multipoint tour
Five southern districts in West Bengal, including Kolkata	0 %
Seven districts in the west and central West Bengal	1 %
Five districts in north West Bengal	46 %
Rest of India	61 %
International	88 %

Alternatives to travel cost calculation for multi-point tourists may have a significant effect on empirical estimates. However, the effect is assumed to be less significant if such tourists constitute only a small proportion of total visitors, as is the case here.

10.6.1.2. Foreign tourists

Foreign tourists are often treated as a separate segment when their share in the total number of visitors is significant. In the first data set (73 per cent of annual visitors) only one per cent originated from outside India. This is too small a share to be separately treated and this segment was left out. So, the recreational value of Sundarban, arrived at in this study, should be interpreted as the value accrued to Indian tourists only.

10.6.1.3. Duration of stay

In ZTCM, per-capita travel cost is assumed to be related with zonal distances and other zonal characteristics. But travel cost is also greatly affected by visitors' duration of stay. The effect may cancel out while calculating zonal average of travel costs. But it requires that various durations of stay appear in the same proportion in the sample of visitors from each zone. It was found that this is a rather stringent requirement and was not true in this study.

It was found in the survey sample that the durations of stay of different visitors ranged from one-day to six-days. One way of circumventing the problem is standardization of travel costs for a common duration of stay (like 'per day') and estimation of the demand for recreation. However, this would mean a six-day trip to Sundarban, for example, generates six times the value of a one-day trip. In reality, this could lead to over-estimation of the value. So, different durations of stay were considered as different 'recreational services' while estimating the TGF. However, longer durations of stay (above three-days) are rare among visitors in Sundarbans. Also a very short duration (one-day) was found to be an outlier because people usually spend three to six hours in the forest and because of the remoteness of the area it is difficult to return home on the same day. So, separate TGFs were estimated for two-day and three-day trips

10.6.1.4. Market segmentation

To identify the possible market segments from the survey data, each of the respondents is identified with one of the seven tour types (packages) described in Table 10.1. The tour packages were examined for whether they differ in the quality of service they provide to visitors, or whether visitors rate them by the watch-tower visits they include. Any difference on the latter count might relate to the probability of sighting a tiger and the scenic beauty of the sites the towers occupy. To confirm, respondents from each of the tour packages were asked about which of the five watch-towers they visited. It was found that under each of the seven tour packages, there is similar divergence in the coverage of five watch towers. Each package offers different durations of stay in the Sundarban and longer durations cover more of the towers during the forest trip.

The packages do differ with respect to their quality of service and this is picked up by visitors depending on their per capita income (obtained from survey data). Table 10.3 contains the distribution of these average values across the seven tour types. The tour options can be broadly divided into 'high-cost' and 'low-cost' categories which appeal to visitors with different levels of per-capita income. Accordingly a two-segment split of the recreational market we opted for, which is described in Table 10.4.

Table 10.3. Average travel cost and per-capita income across tour packages

Package Code	Average travel cost in INR per visitor (all durations)	Average per capita monthly income of visitors (INR)	Per cent of visitors taking the package
1	1,320	3,280	17.2
2	960	4,240	49.6
3	1,720	3,320	0.6
4	2,400	10,360	5.5
5	6,800	7,200	0.8
6	3,440	10,680	3.5
7	1,680	4,640	22.8

Table 10.4. The two-segment split of the recreational market used in the study

Segment 0 (Low cost)	Segment 1 (High cost)
Package codes 1, 2, 3 & 7	Package codes 4, 5 & 6

This analysis was possible using only the second set of data (three per cent of visitors). However, the first set (73 per cent of visitors) was used to decide zonal visitation rates. The number of visitors in each segment in the first data set was computed by splitting them into two segments using the ratio obtained from second data set.

10.6.1.5. Number of zones

Deciding the number of zones in a ZTCM study is a challenging issue. Firstly, the zones need to be identified in a way such that information on zonal socio-economic statistics is available from secondary sources. Secondly, the number of zones should not be too many so that a 'zero visitations' appears in a zone and at the same time it should not be too few to limit the degree of freedom during estimation of TGF. Keeping these constraints in mind, it was concluded in favour of eight zones comprising one or several districts of West Bengal and Rest of India (ROI). The zones are described in Table 10.5. None of these zones have zero total visitation rates but a few zones showed zero visitation rate from one market segment. This is plausible because all types of tour packages are not picked up by visitors from all zones due to economic viability or convenience. For example, visitors residing in the zone nearest to the site did not avail high cost packages which originate from a farther point (Kolkata).

Table 10.5. Identification of zones used in estimating TGF (excluding foreign nationals)

Zone code	Composition
1	District of South 24 Parganas in West Bengal state, hosting the study site
2	Metropolitan city of Kolkata, itself a district in West Bengal, neighbouring zone 1
3	District of North 24 Parganas (West Bengal) neighbouring zone 1
4	District of Howrah (West Bengal) neighbouring zone 2
5	District of Hooghly (West Bengal) neighbouring zone 3
6	Districts of Nadia, Burdwan & Midnapore (East and West) (West Bengal)
7	Districts Bankura, Birbhum, Purulia, Murshidabad, Maldah, Dinajpur (Uttar & Dakhsin), Jalpaiguri, Coochbihar, Darjeeling (West Bengal)
8	Rest of India (ROI) – All of India excluding West Bengal

Note: The codes for the zones may be interpreted as their ranks with respect to geographical proximity to the recreational site

10.6.2. Zonal explanatory variables

Although variables such as age and sex of the respondents are used very much as the determinants of visitation frequency to a site for estimating TGF in ITCM, in zonal models these variables normally do not appear because such variables remains undefined for a zone. On the other hand, per-capita income of zones may vary and so it stands as a regressor. Using the survey data, per-capita income from the visitors from each zone was calcutated. However, it was found that only richer visitors came from distant zones and the survey estimates of zonal average per capita income were not representative of true zonal averages. The effect of income is supposed to be captured in this study by the dummy variable used for two segments (high-cost and low-cost) of the market.

Information was also collected on the primary occupations and educational qualifications of the respondents. Occupation wise, it was found that maximum number of visitors came from the service sector. A negligible percentage of respondents reported agriculture as their primary occupation implying that the farming community which is among the poorest of all does not spend money on a luxury good like 'nature tourism'. Turning to respondents' educational qualifications, it was found that none of the visitors have failed to complete primary education. While detailed information on educational status at the zonal level are not readily available, 'literacy rates' (in percentage) are available district wise and for the country as a whole.

This exploration of survey data provided a clue that, at the zonal level, 'literacy rate', 'percentage of urban population to total population' and/ or 'percentage of working population engaged in service sector' might be significant determinants for visitation rates. Secondary data show that there is a significant variation with respect to these variables across zones (Table 10.6).

Table 10.6. Zonal data from secondary sources[6]

Zone Code	Total zonal population	Per cent of zonal population living in urban area	Per cent of zonal population employed in service sector	Per cent of zonal literacy
1	6909015	16	52	69
2	4580544	100	96	81
3	8930295	54	72	78
4	4274010	50	73	77
5	5040047	33	56	75
6	21161927	22	41	71
7	29325333	12	36	59
8	948561239	28	35	65

[6] Directorate of Census Operations, Government of India, round 2001

Secondary data on districts were used from Census estimates of 2001. Assuming equal rate of change in identified variables across zones over time, the district level data were projected for 2005–2006. Since some zones comprised of several districts of West Bengal, data for each constituent district was weighted by its population to derive corresponding zonal averages.

10.7. Empirical estimates

10.7.1. The TGF

The summary statistics from survey data (Table 10.7), show the distribution of average travel cost across zones, durations and market segments, and justify the use of dummy variables for segments and durations in estimating the TGF.

The distinction in the market segments and durations is also evident from the scatter plots. Estimation was carried out on the pooled data for eight zones, two durations of stay and two market segments. Zonal visitation was also calculated as the estimated number of visitors 'per 100,000 people' from that zone. The visitation rate data from primary survey showed 28 non-zero entries resulting in the same number of data points. Scatter plot of data also showed evidence of non-linear relationship between them. Experiments with different alternative forms suggested a double-log relationship between visitation and travel cost as the most suitable for linear regression.

Two possible regressors, percentages of service-sector workers and percentage of urban population, were found to be highly positively correlated and one of them had to be dropped to avoid the problem of high multicollinearity. Zero and higher order partial correlations between them suggested 'percentage of workers in service-sector' as the more acceptable explanatory variable against 'percentage of urban population'. Zonal 'literacy', showed a weak correlation with visitation and did not provide statistically significant relationship during various regression runs. Table 10.8 shows the final set of variables used in estimating the TGF.

Judging from the significance of the coefficients, the goodness of fit and other parameters, the final form of the estimated TGF was decided on the basis of adjusted R^2 value (while adding and dropping variables from the function). After taking care of possible heteroskedasticity in zonal data, robust estimates of regression coefficients were obtained which are shown in Table 10.9.

Table 10.7. Summary statistics from survey data: distribution of visitors, travel cost and per-capita income across zones, durations and market segments

	Low Cost Packages					
Zone	Per cent of sample visitors taking ,such packages		Average travel cost per capita (INR)		Average per capita household monthly income (INR)	
	2-days Duration	3-days Duration	2-days Duration	3-days Duration	2-days Duration	3-days Duration
1	3.13	4.19	677	984	2,947	2,452
2	13.95	28.63	923	1,344	5,326	5,137
3	4.58	3.63	892	1,044	3,519	3,185
4	6.98	2.79	1,102	1,294	3,008	3,777
5	2.96	3.13	922	1,249	4,139	3,687
6	4.97	4.52	890	1,702	2,742	3,726
7	4.13	1.17	804	2,351	1,430	3,794
8	0.39	0.67	1,855	2,298	17,250	7,188
	High Cost Packages					
Zone	Per cent of sample visitors taking such packages		Average travel cost per capita (INR)		Average per capita household monthly income (INR)	
	2-days Duration	3-days Duration	2-days Duration	3-days Duration	2-days Duration	3-days Duration
1	0.00*	0.00*	-	-	-	-
2	4.02	1.67	2,306	3,824	8,516	8,440
3	0.11	0.11	2,938	4,727	NA**	5,000
4	0.50	0.00*	2,295	-	3,676	-
5	0.11	0.11	3,100	4,830	NA**	7,500
6	0.33	0.00*	2,796	-	7,708	-
7	0.33	0.39	2,592	5,066	9,732	6,352
8	1.28	1.23	2,768	5,313	22,552	11,560

Note: * No visitors in this category
** Visitors did not reveal their income

Table 10.8. Variables used for estimating TGF

Variable	Description
LNVST	Natural log of visitation (visitation = number of visitors per 100,000 people)
LNTRVCO	Natural log of average travel cost per visitor

(Contd.)

(Contd.)

Variable	Description
PCSRVC	Percentage of working population engaged in service sector – zonal variable
HIGHCOST	Dummy variable for segments = 1 for 'High-Cost Packages' = 0 otherwise
THREEDAY	Dummy variable for duration of stay = 1 if the respondent paid a 3-day visit = 0 otherwise

Table 10.9. Regression results for the trip generating function

Dependent variable: LNVST Number of observations = 28		
Regressor	Coefficient	t-value
CONSTANT	37.902	4.33***
LNTRVCO	-5.762	-4.46***
PCSRVC	0.066	7.49***
HIGHCOST	3.687	2.26**
THREEDAY	2.559	3.57***
$F(4, 23) = 31.57$ Prob $> F = 0.0000$; $R^2 = 0.8503$		

Note: ** significant at 5% level;
*** significant at 1% level

Travel cost and percentage of working population engaged in the service sector in a zone were found to be the two most important determinants of zonal visitation. While travel cost was negatively related with the visitation rate, the percentage of population engaged in the service sector was found to have significant positive effect on the zonal visitation rate.

Both the dummy variables obtained significant positive coefficients implying that demand for a three-day trip would be more than two-day trips and that demand for a high-cost package would be more than the low-cost packages, if they were available at the same 'cost'.

10.7.2. Valuation: the consumer surplus

With the estimated TGF, a recreational value of the site was arrived at by estimating aggregate consumer surplus (CS). The TGF was used to derive the relationship between 'visitor number' (per 100,000 population) and travel cost for each zone (j=1,2....8) and for each segment and duration. As an example, for low-cost (HIGHCOST=0) and two-day duration

(THREEDAY=0) trips, visitor (demand) per 100,000 population was estimated from zone 'j' as:

$$LNVST_j = CONST + \beta_1 LNTRVCO + \beta_2 SRVCj$$
$$= \beta_1 LNTRVCO + Z_j \quad \text{(Say)}$$

or, $VST_j = TRVCO^{\beta_1} . e^{Z_j}$ (1)

In a double-log form, the estimated number of visitors is never truly zero as the demand curve never touches the vertical axis. So, to calculate the choke price for demand given in (1), the travel cost was raised successively until the estimated number of visitors (for the specific segment and duration) from zone 'j' was *rounded off* to zero. Following the methodology described in section 10.3, if T_j^0 and T_j^c are the actual travel-cost and choke-price respectively, then CS (per 100,000 population) for zone 'j' is calculated as:

$$CS_j = \int_{T_j^0}^{T_j^c} VST_j \, d\,(TRVCO)$$

$$= e^{Z_j} \int_{T_j^0}^{T_j^c} TRVCO^{\beta_1} \, d\,(TRVCO)$$

$$= e^{Z_j} \frac{1}{\beta_1 + 1} \left[(T_j^c)^{\beta_1 + 1} - (T_j^0)^{\beta_1 + 1} \right]$$

This estimate was multiplied by the total population (unit of population in 100,000) to obtain the CS for zone 'j' for the specific segment and duration. Similarly, for other segments and durations and for other zones, CS was estimated and the sum of these estimates was considered the value of recreational services of the Indian Sundarban as revealed by Indian visitors.

The aggregate CS is INR 15.1 million (US $ 0.377 million[7]) for the Indian Sundarban during 2005–2006. Table 10.10 shows its distribution across zones, segments and durations. It was found that as a single zone, the city of Kolkata derived the most (34 per cent) of CS followed by the neighbouring

---

[7] Using Exchange rate US $1 = INR 40

district of North 24 Parganas (28 per cent). As for segments and durations, it was found that the three-day visitors under 'low-cost' packages contribute almost 60 per cent of the total CS for the Sundarban.

10.7.3. Revenue maximising entry-fee

A Travel Cost Method study is well suited for a site like the Sundarban to find an entry fee that can maximize revenue collection for the authority. With the TGF, successive changes in per capita travel cost (representing equal changes in entry fee) can be introduced. This will yield sets of estimated number of visitors and corresponding revenue collections. Initially, depending on the elasticity, higher entry fees will raise revenue collection. However, this positive relationship will reverse after some point. In this study, the existing entry fee of INR 15 per visitor per day is found to be grossly sub-optimal. Total revenue collection from domestic visitors is presently estimated at INR 1.39 million (US $ 0.03 million) whereas this study estimates show that it can be raised by over three times to INR 4.96 million (US $ 0.12 million) if revenue maximization is the objective of the authority. The projections of revenue collection against various entry fee levels are shown in Figure 10.2 and it is found the revenue maximising entry-fee is INR 154 (US$ 3.85) per visitor per day.

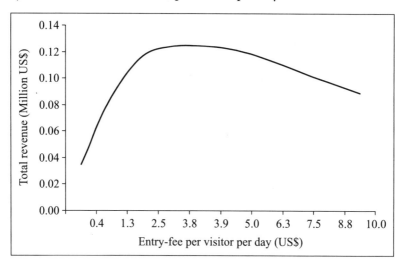

Figure 10.2.   Projection of revenue collection with varying entry-fee rate

Table 10.10. Distribution of aggregate CS across zones, segments and durations (in Million INR)

Zone	2 days; Low cost	2 days; High cost	3 days; Low cost	3 days; High cost	Total
1	0.426	0.000	0.926	0.000	1.352
2	1.228	0.627	2.653	0.729	5.237
3	0.562	0.076	3.429	0.102	4.168
4	0.106	0.128	0.641	0.000	0.875
5	0.091	0.011	0.280	0.017	0.399
6	0.177	0.030	0.104	0.000	0.311
7	0.279	0.042	0.021	0.022	0.364
8	0.158	0.944	0.741	0.546	2.389
TOTAL	3.028069	1.857865	8.794947	1.414615	15.0955

10.8. Conclusion and policy implications

In this chapter, the recreational demand for the Indian Sunderban is estimated. The Indian Sunderban received 63,900 visitors during 2005–2006 and tour operators are unanimous that the number is growing each year. Of these, some 50 per cent are from Kolkata and the rest mainly from various parts of West Bengal. Tourism is highly seasonal and characterized by few multipoint tourists or foreign visitors. A majority of the visitors are educated and employed in the service sector.

The annual recreational value of the Indian Sundarban is estimated to be approximately INR 15 million (US $ 377,000). This estimate of the recreational value of the Indian Sundarban needs to be read with certain provisos. Visitors whose duration of stay is one day and more than three days have been left out in the calculations. Foreign visitors have also been omitted. Though small in number, these categories will push the estimate upward. There is also the impact of the general population increase (data used from the 2001 Census) and the increase in visitors of metropolitan origin, both of which will exert a positive effect on the absolute value of consumer surplus in the future.

The tourism market in the Sunderban is divided into two segments catering to tourists with differential income. It may be useful for park authorities to consider which part of the market they would really like to grow and in what fashion. The number of visitors is likey to swell with increased amenities for tourists and with information dissemination to attract new visitors as well as with the transformation of the Indian economy with more people being engaged in the service sector. Going by the present dynamics of Indian economy, it is not a distant possibility when such an increase will put pressure on the carrying capacity of the site.

An important observation is that the current entry fees to visit the Sunderban are very low and park authorities are able to capture less than 10 per cent of estimated consumer surplus. If the fees are increased from the current value of INR 15 to INR 154 per visitor per day, total revenues can be increased by more than 300 per cent. This would bring nearly INR five million (US $ 0.12 million) per year in revenues to the park. Improved facilities and infrastructure are also likely to lead to both increased visitation and higher revenues. The authorities may need to devise long term plans to cope with potential increase in visitors and may want to use estimates of elasticity of demand in considering future entry fees.

References

Champ, P.A., Boyle, K.J. and Brown, T.C. (eds), *A Primer on Nonmarket Valuation*, (The Netherlands: Kluwer Academic Publishers, 2003).

Chopra, K., 'Economic Valuation of Biodiversity: The Case of Keoladeo National Park', G. Kadekodi (ed.) *Environmental Economics in Practice: Selected Case Studies from India*, (New Delhi: Oxford University Press, 2004).

Chopra K., '*Trade, Environment and Human Well-being in the Sunderbans*', 2005, 'Draft Report 2005'.

Carr, L. and Mendelsohn, R. 'Valuing Coral Reefs: A Travel Cost Analysis of the Great Barrier Reef', *Ambio*, Vol. 32, No. 5, 2003.

Font, A. R., 'Mass Tourism and the Demand for Protected Natural Areas: A Travel Cost Approach', *Journal of Environmental Economics and Management*, Vol. 39, No. 1, 2000, 97–116.

Herath, G., Kennedy, J., 'Estimating the Economic Value of Mount Buffalo National Park with the Travel Cost and Contingent Valuation Models', *Tourism Economics*, Vol. 10, No. 1, 63–78(16), 2004.

Kadekodi, G.K., (ed.), *Environmental Economics in Practice: Selected Case Studies from India*, (New Delhi, Oxford University Press: 2004).

Khan, H., 'Demand for Eco-tourism: Estimating Recreational Benefits from the Margalla Hills National Park in Northern Pakistan', Working Paper No. 5–04; SANDEE, 2004.

Maille, P. and Mendelsohn, R., 'Valuing Ecotourism in Madagascar', *Ambio*, 1992.

Markandya, A., Perelet, R. Mason, P. and Taylor, T., *Dictionary of Environmental Economics;* (Earthscan Publications, London: 2001.

Nam, P. K. and Son., T. V. H., 'Recreational Value of the Coral surrounding the Hon Mun Islands in Vietnam: A Travel Cost and Contingent Valuation Study', EEPSEA Research Report, 2001 Rpt http://www.worldfishcenter.org/Pubs/coral_reef/pdf/section2-6.pdf

Nillesen, E., Wesseler, J. and Cook, A., 'Correcting for Multiple Destination Trips in Recreational Use Values using a Mean-value Approach: An Application to Bellenden Ker National Park, Australia', Discussion Paper No. 7; Mansholt Graduate School,. 2003 http://www.sls.wau.nl/mi/mgs/publications/Mansholt_Working_Papers/MWP_07.pdf

Santhakumar, V., Haque, A.K. E., and Bhattacharya, R., 'An Economic Analysis of Mangroves in South Asia', in Mohsin Khan (ed.) *Economic Development in South Asia,* Tata McGraw Hill: New Delhi, 2005, 369–437.

Tobias, D. and Mendelsohn, R., 'Valuing Ecotourism in a Tropical Rain-forest Reserve', *Ambio,* 1991.

Xue, D., Cook, A. and Tisdell, C., 'Biodiversity and the Tourism Value of Changbai Mountain Biosphere Reserve, China: A Travel Cost Approach', *Tourism-Economics,* December – 6, (4), 2000, 335–357.

11

Estimating Welfare Losses from Urban Air Pollution using Panel Data from Household Health Diaries

Usha Gupta[1]

11.1. Introduction

Air Pollution is a major environmental problem in both developed and developing countries. The harmful effects of air pollution include corrosion of metals and buildings, reduction in visibility, degradation of soil due to acid rain, depletion of the ozone layer, global warming and damages to human health. However, researchers are more concerned with damages to human health as human capital is the primary contributor to economic welfare. The health effects are more intense in urban cities with significant emission sources, unfavourable dispersion characteristics and high population densities. Many health problems like eye irritation, respiratory illnesses etc., may be directly attributable to exposure to air pollution. If not treated in time, acute illnesses may become chronic due to prolonged and continuous exposure to air pollution. Air pollution induced illnesses result in increased expenditures on mitigating activities and a loss in wages to people. Welfare gains would occur if air quality is improved to safe levels.

The link between exposure to air pollution and health-related social costs is well established in the west.[2] Studies in the past have used the benefit

[1] This work was undertaken with the financial support of the South Asian Network for Development and Environmental Economics (SANDEE). I have gained enormously from the comments of resource persons Jeff Vincent, Maureen Cropper, Priya Shyamsunder, M. N. Murty and many other resource persons of SANDEE at various stages of this study. I wish to express my thanks to the SANDEE Secretariat for the encouragement and support for doing this work.

[2] See Dickie and Gerking, 1991; Dockery et al., 1993; Alberini and Cropper et al., 1997; Alberini

transfer approach to estimate the willingness to pay for improved air quality (Alberini and Krupnick, 1997) in developing countries. However, this method, which relies on developed country estimates, does not take into consideration country specific socio-economic characteristics, baseline health, behavioural responses, pollution levels, characteristics of pollutants, weather conditions etc. and therefore may yield misleading results. Therefore, in order to obtain more reliable estimates of welfare gains from air pollution reduction, country/area specific detailed studies are required. Several studies have estimated the economic costs of air pollution. A few of these are discussed below.

One of the early studies in this field was Ostro (1983), who estimated a dose response function to assess the impact of particulates and sulfates on morbidity in the USA. To measure this association the study took into consideration Work Days Lost (WLD) for employed people and Restricted Activity Days (RAD) for the combined sample of adults and other non-workers. The results indicated that a one per cent increase in particulates would increase WLD by about 0.45 per cent and RAD by 0.31 per cent for all people in the age group of 18–65 years. The evidence suggests that an association between air pollution and health is stronger and more severe in developing countries due to poor nutrition, low awareness and unhygienic conditions. As a result, people may have to incur more costs towards health care in these countries (Chestnut, et al., 1997). Such evidence is supported by Lvovsky et al. (1998), who analyzed health damages from exposure to the high levels of particulates in 126 cities worldwide where the annual mean levels exceeded 50 $\mu g/m^3$. Using meta-analytical techniques dose-response relationships were extrapolated to various cities. To assess health damages comprehensively the study included mortality, morbidity and chronic illnesses. The study concluded that India suffered from a disproportionably heavy burden of urban air pollution by international standards. In terms of a share of the per capita GDP, health damages due to exposure to particulates were estimated at nine per cent for India.

Based on the Gerking and Stanely (1986) model and using the dose-response method, Kumar and Rao (2001) measured the economic benefits of air quality improvement in the Panipat Thermal Power Station Colony in India. They estimated a medical care function (a binary response variable based on one month's recall period) in association with the pollution variable

and Krupnick, 1997; 2000; Kumar and Rao, 2001; Murty et al., 2003.

(PM$_{10}$ or small dust particles), monthly income, health status, age, years of schooling, etc. In this study, the estimated medical care cost is supposed to illustrate peoples' Willingness to Pay (WTP) for reduced levels of PM$_{10}$ in the ambient air. Income and health status variables were significant determinants of WTP for improved air quality. The estimated WTP ranged from INR 21 to INR 52.5 per month for a sixty seven per cent reduction in the ambient mean concentration of PM10 level (required to meet World Health Organization standards).

In another Indian study, Murty et al. (2003) estimated a household health production function model for measuring economic benefits from reduced air pollution in the Indian cities of Delhi and Kolkata. Using six months of data relating to sick days, averting, and mitigating activities, they estimated a system of simultaneous equations. The results showed that if the current level of Suspended Particulate Matter (SPM) was reduced to the safe level of 200 μg/m^3, the total per annum monetary gain to the urban populations of Delhi and Kolkata would be INR 4897 million and INR 3000 million respectively.

The present study analyzes welfare gains from reductions in air pollution in the urban city of Kanpur, India. The city is known as the 'Commercial Capital' of Uttar Pradesh. However, over the years it has acquired notoriety as one of the most polluted cities in the country. The maximum weekly average concentration of PM$_{10}$ in Kanpur was 224 (μg/m^3) in 2004[3] whereas the safe levels recommended by the World Health Organization (WHO)[4] and India's National Ambient Air Quality Standards (NAAQS) were 20 (μg/m^3) and 60 (μg/m^3) respectively. This study matches air pollution data from four monitoring stations in Kanpur with household health data in order to examine the health and productivity benefits of reducing air pollution.

11.2. Study site

Kanpur is the largest and most populous industrial city in the state of Uttar Pradesh in India. The area of Kanpur urban agglomeration[5] is 305.27 sq. km and its population density is 9756 per square kilometre (2001 Population Census Data). The annual average growth rate of the population was 3.5 per

---

[3] The year of the present study.

[4] World Health Organization, 2000.

[5] Area of urban agglomeration comprises Kanpur Municipal Corporation, Cantonment, Armapur Industrial Estate, Railway Colony, Chakeri and the Indian Institute of Technology, as reported in Kanpur City Development Plan, 2006.

cent (national average being 1.54 per cent/annum) during 1991–2001. The percentage of the workforce involved in the primary, industrial and service sectors are four per cent, 31 per cent and 65 per cent respectively.

Kanpur is famous for its cotton, woollen and leather industries. Most of the heavy and large-scale industries like fertilizer units, ordinance and gun factories and power plants are located in the southwest part of the city. A cluster of tanneries along the Ganga River in Jajmau Industrial Estate is situated in the Northeast part. These industrial units contribute significantly to air pollution. A thermal power plant of 264 MW capacity has two small boilers operating on obsolete technology producing a large amount of fly ash that causes an increase in the level of particulate matter in the ambient air. Transportation in Kanpur comprises about 0.2 million petrol/diesel driven vehicles which contribute roughly 142 MT of pollutants per day. Another major source of pollution is a long M.G. rail track passing through the city with residential and industrial areas located on either side. The railway line has seventeen manned level crossings. The level of PM10 increases to five or six times the National Ambient Air Quality Standards (NAAQS)[6] on these crossings when trains pass. Households too contribute to air pollution in Kanpur city. Most households living in slum settlements and colonies use inefficient fuel such as coal, wood, kerosene etc. for cooking and space heating generating localized smoke that affects visibility and causes eye irritation.

According to CPCB sources, about 60 per cent of the geographical area, particularly the densely populated central part of Kanpur, is severely affected by air pollution.[7] Kanpur has been identified as one of the air pollution hotspots in India.[8]

Referring to the findings of a World Bank study (2006), the *Time* magazine reported that the industrial city of Kanpur had been ranked the seventh most polluted city in terms of air pollution in the world. Furthermore, a report that listed the most polluted cities in four Asian countries ranked Kanpur number one. The report indicated that this city fared worst among all Indian cities followed by Kitakyushu in Japan, the Indonesian capital Jakarta and the Chinese city of Xiangshan. The growing population in Kanpur was one of the main reasons for the worsening air quality.

---

[6] See CPCB Parivesh Newsletter 2(1), June 1995.
[7] See SANDEE Working Paper – 17-06.
[8] Environmental Management Plan, 2000.

'Eco Friends 2002' reported that in the last decade, there had been a very high incidence of asthma in Kanpur. The burgeoning traffic has increased the levels of carbon monoxide, hydrocarbons, benzene, nitrogen oxides, sulphur dioxide and lead in the air. The dust-ridden city of Kanpur, which was dubbed earlier as the 'Capital of TB' where even monkeys had been afflicted with the deadly disease, has now fast turned into a hotspot of asthma. A Medical College in Kanpur reported, 'In any city, the asthma patients were between two to five per cent of the total population. However, in Kanpur, the number of asthma patients exceeded 10 per cent of the total population....' Experts predicted that every fourth person in the city would be a victim of asthma if air quality in Kanpur kept plummeting at the current rate. Thus, Kanpur is sitting on an environmental time bomb, which can explode any time.

11.3. Data sources and survey design

The pollution parameters considered in the study are PM_{10} (small dust particles) and NOx (Nitrogen Oxides) in order to explore the association between air pollution and health. Data relating to these pollutants were collected from the publications of Central Pollution Control Board (CPCB) and Uttar Pradesh Pollution Control Board (UPPCB) during the year 2004. There were four monitoring stations in Kanpur at the time of our survey. Vikas Nagar (VN), Deputy Ka Parao (DKP) and Kidwai Nagar (KN) are located in residential areas and Fazal Ganj (FG) is located in an industrial area that is surrounded by a large residential area.

The sampling procedure used for the household survey was based on a two-stage stratification – air pollution monitoring stations and the type of dwelling. For the first stage of stratification an area of one-kilometer radius was marked around each monitoring station and a sample of an almost equal number of households was drawn from each monitoring station area. The second stage of stratification followed Kanpur Development Authority's (KDA) classification of households residing in different 'types of dwellings'. These dwellings broadly reflected the households' economic status and variability in their living standards and income levels. According to KDA, 67 per cent of the total population lives in Kaccha houses, which are single rooms or a portion thereof, 21 per cent in two-room dwellings, and 12 per cent in three or more room houses. The final sample consisted of 222 and 163 households residing respectively in one-room and kaccha houses representing the poorest section of the society; 116 households lived in two-room dwellings, representing the lower middle class category; 57 and 47 households resided in three and more than three-room houses respectively and were considered to be economically better off belonging to higher middle and high income levels.

Primary data were collected through a household survey by administering a questionnaire through a face-to-face interview with the head or any other working member of the household. The survey questionnaire had four main sections with detailed subsections to facilitate the collection of relevant data on key variables. Sections 1 and 2 covered various aspects of socio-economic and demographic features such as religion, family background, sex and age of household members, level of their education, marital status, occupation and the size of the accommodation/house. Section 3 provided data on the general awareness of households regarding air pollution induced illnesses, indoor air pollution, drinking water quality, and averting activities undertaken by the households. Its subsections contained information on individuals' past health stock (chronic diseases), their habits and the general awareness of households about air pollution induced illnesses. To collect data on gross annual income, different income brackets were offered to the respondents to select their respective range of income in Section 4. Data on an alternative measure of the wealth of households/individuals in the form of average annual expenditure and inventory of durable consumer items were also collected to cross check the income levels.

A unique feature of this study is the Weekly Health Diary. The health diary was maintained for eighteen weeks (six weeks in each season; summer, winter and monsoon seasons) to capture the impact of seasonal variations on health. Trained enumerators visited all the households, every week in each season, to record information on medical symptoms, mitigating expenses, days of medicine taken, number of sick days, and workdays lost due to air pollution induced sickness. The first phase data covered the winter season (January 2004–February 2004); the second phase the summer season (May 2004–June 2004) and the third phase covered the monsoon season (July 2004–September 2004).

With a health diary for 18 weeks and a total of 3122 household members (consisting of both children and adults), the existing data set resulted in a panel, containing 56,196 observations (3122 × 18). 2098 working and non-working members were identified from this sample in the age group of 15 years and above. The minimum permissible age to work is 15 years in India according to Indian labour law.

Weather data relating to temperature, relative humidity and wind speed were collected from the Department of Meteorology (Chandra Shekhar Azad University of Agriculture, Kanpur) in order to analyze the impact of weather variation and seasonality on health.

11.4. Methodology

Many variants of the Household Health Production Model as originally found in Grossman (1972) have been formulated to explore the health impacts of air pollution. The present study uses Freeman's model (1993)[9] to estimate the economic benefits from reduced morbidity due to a reduction in air pollution in Kanpur city. As noted in Chapter 2, the household health production function and the demand function for mitigating activities that are implicit in the utility maximizing behaviour of an individual are derived as follows:

An individual's utility function may be defined as:

$$U = U(X, L, H, Q) \tag{1}$$

where, X is the consumption of marketed good, L denotes leisure time available per period to an individual, H represents days of sickness or health status and Q shows level of ambient air pollution. Individuals derive utility from the consumption of X and L whereas H and Q result in disutility.

An individual produces good health by combining mitigating activities[10] with the given level of air pollution (Q), health status and other socio-economic characteristics.

The household health production function can be written as.

$$H = H(M, Q, Z) \tag{2}$$

where, H: days of sickness or health status, M: mitigating activities, Q: level of ambient air pollution, Z: a vector of other parameters.

Mitigating activities (M) include the individual's demand for medicines, hospitalization, pathological tests, doctor consultation, etc. The other health characteristics (Z) of an individual are the history of chronic illness, habits etc. The model assumes that individuals could maintain a given

---

[9] Murty et. al., 2003 estimated this model to measure the welfare gains of reduced air pollution and morbidity in the Indian cities of Delhi and Kolkata.

[10] The estimated model does not include averting activities because the survey data reveals that people in Kanpur do not adopt averting activities (such as a.c. car, staying indoors, using heater, mask, diverting to cleaner route, etc.) to avoid exposure to air pollution.

health status even with higher ambient air pollution through the choice of mitigating activities. It means that there are substitution possibilities between mitigating activities and the ambient air quality.

The individual chooses X, L and M so as to maximize utility subject to the budget constraint:

$$I = Y + w(T - L - H) = X + P_M M \qquad (3)$$

where, Y is non-wage income; w is wage rate; (T-L-H) is time spent at work (T is total time and L is leisure time); P_M is the price per unit of mitigating activity.

Given the pollution level (Q), prices of mitigating activities (P_M), wage rate (w), income (I) and other exogenous variables, individuals maximize utility with respect to X, M and L. The maximizing function is given as,

$$MaxG = U(X, L, H, Q) + \lambda[Y + w(T - L - H) - X - P_M M] \qquad (4)$$

where λ is the Lagrange multiplier that can be interpreted in terms of the marginal utility of income. Solving the maximizing function, we obtain an individuals' demand function for mitigating activities (M) and the marginal willingness to pay function for air quality improvement (MWTP) as:

$$M = M(I, P_m, Q, Z) \qquad (5)$$

$$MWTP = w.dH/dQ + P_M.\delta M/\delta Q + (\delta u/\delta H).dH/dQ/\lambda \qquad (6)$$

Expression (6) shows that MWTP for health benefits from the reduction in pollution is the sum of observable reductions in the cost of sick time, cost of mitigating activities and the monetary equivalent of disutility of illness. To obtain MWTP the health production function and the demand function for mitigating activities may be estimated simultaneously, or alternatively, a reduced form 'damage function' (dose-response function) with health as a function of pollution parameters and other variables can be estimated. This can be combined with a seperately estimated demand for mitigating behaviour.[11] Since our estimates of WTP are based on the first two components and do not take into consideration the monetary equivalent of the disutility of illness, these are the lower bounds of WTP.

---

[11] The estimation of damage function in the health production function framework is obtained by substituting the demand function for mitigating activities, M, into the health production function (Freeman 1993).

11.5. Estimating household health production function model

11.5.1. Household health production function

Since pollution parameters (PM_{10}, NOx, etc.) are monitored twice a week in Kanpur, one week has been taken as a recall period to analyze the impact of air pollution on health. The primary data used in the present analysis have two salient features: (a) dependent variables are a count of the total number of sick days in a given week during the three seasons and (b) there are repeated observations for the same individuals, constituting a panel data set.

In this case, using the Poisson regression model for estimating the household health production function is more appropriate because it takes into consideration the preponderance of zeros and the discrete nature of the dependent variable. The Poisson model is given by:

$$prob\left(Y_{it} = {y_{it}}\big/{x_{it}}\right) = \frac{\mu_{it}^{y_{it}} e^{-\mu_{it}}}{y_{it}} ; Y_{it} = 0,1,2 \tag{7}$$

where, Y_{it} is the count of the number of sick days due to air pollution induced illnesses occurring during week t to the i th individual. $\mu_{it} = \exp(\chi_{it}\beta)$ represents both the mean and the variance of illness, χ_{it} is a matrix of covariates of the i th individual and β is a vector of regression coefficients. The predicted count of sick days during week t for i th individual is, therefore, $\hat{y}_{it} = \exp(\chi_{it}\beta)$ or $\ln \hat{y}_{it} = \chi_{it}\beta$. The marginal effect of change in x_{it} is computed as $\hat{y}_{it}$ β. For estimation purposes the model specification is as follows:

$$\ln y_{it} = \alpha_i + \beta_i X_{1it} + \beta_2 X_{2it} + ... + \beta_s X_{sit} + U_{it} \tag{8}$$

The Poisson model estimates were obtained using the maximum likelihood method.[12] However, it is noted that in practice the Poisson regression model is restrictive in many ways. Firstly, it is based on the assumption that events occur independently over time. The independence assumption may break down, as there may be a form of dynamic dependence between the occurrences of successive events. For example, the prior occurrence of an event, such as sick days due to air pollution, may increase the probability of a subsequent occurrence of the same or similar event. Secondly, the

---

[12] To correct the special serial correlation inherent in panel data, the Generalized Estimating Equation (GEE) approach devised by Liang and Zeger (1986) can be used.

assumption that the conditional mean and variance of y_i, given X_i are equal may also be too strong and hence fail to account for over dispersion (the variance exceeds the mean). This restriction may produce larger estimated standard errors of the estimated β. An alternative for the purpose of obtaining accurate estimates of the standard errors, after adjusting for the problem of over dispersion, is to apply the negative binomial distribution model.

11.5.2. Demand for mitigating activity

The dependent variable (M) indicating the demand for mitigating activities is a censored variable, i.e., the dependent variable is zero for corresponding known values of independent variables for part of the sample. To address this problem, the Tobit model[13] is used to estimate the demand function for the mitigating activities. Thus,

$$M_{it} = \alpha = \beta \chi_{it} + U_{it} \text{ if RHS} > 0 \tag{9}$$
$$= 0 \text{ otherwise}$$

where, M_{it} refers to the probability of the ith household incurring positive mitigating expenditure at time t, and X_{it} denotes a vector of individual characteristics, such as chronic diseases, income, age and education, pollution parameters, weather conditions, etc.

11.5.3. Empirical specification

Econometric estimation includes two reduced form equations consisting of the household health production function and the demand function for mitigating activities. The estimated coefficients were used to compute the marginal effect of pollution on H (sick days) and M (mitigating activities). The random effects panel data regression model is used to estimate both of these equations. The results from the fixed effects (fe) estimates of sick days are also presented (Table 11.2).

$$H = \alpha_i + \beta_1 pm_{10} + \beta_2 dtemp + \beta_3 t \max + \beta_4 NO_x + \beta_5 wind +$$
$$\beta_6 age + \beta_7 bcj + \beta_8 asthma + \beta_9 BP + \beta_{10} TB + \beta_{11} heart + \upsilon$$
$$\tag{10}$$

---

[13] Amemiya (1984). While OLS parameter estimates for a Tobit model are biased and inconsistent, the maximum-likelihood estimates are unbiased and consistent (Maddala 1983).

$$M = \gamma_i + \delta_1 pm_{10} + \delta_2 dtemp + \delta_3 t\max + \delta_4 NO_x + \delta_5 wind +$$
$$\delta_6 age + \delta_7 bcj + \delta_8 asthma + \delta_9 BP + \delta_{10} TB + \delta_{11} heart + \varpi$$

(11)

The variables used in the equations are:

Dependent variables

Days of Sickness (H): H shows the number of days of sickness, in a recall period of one week, due to air pollution induced diseases/symptoms. It also represents the health status of individuals.

Mitigating Activities (M): Mitigating activities (M) include expenses on medicines, doctor's fees, diagnostic tests, hospitalization, travel to doctor's clinic etc.

Independent variables

PM_{10}: It is measured for two days per week in Kanpur. The time weighted average concentration of pollutants is recorded for each day for 24 hours at equal intervals of 8 hours. The average of the maximum values for two days' observations was taken. It was measured in $\mu g/m^3$. PM_{10} remains in the atmosphere for longer periods because of its low settling velocity. It can penetrate deeply into the respiratory tract and cause respiratory illnesses in humans.

Nitrogen Oxides (NOx): The average of maximum twice-weekly values of NOx is measured in $\mu g/m^3$. NO and NO_2 are the main components of NOx. It is produced by natural phenomena such as lightning, volcanic eruptions and bacterial action in the soil and by anthropogenic sources such as combustion of fuels in internal combustion engines, thermal power plants, industrial and heating facilities and incinerators. Exposure to NO_x is linked with increased susceptibility to respiratory infection, asthma attacks, and decreased pulmonary function. Short-term exposure is associated with lower respiratory illnesses such as cough, sore throat and runny nose.

Variation in Temperature(DTEMP): This is the weekly average value of the difference between the maximum and minimum temperatures daily.

Maximum Ambient Temperature(TMAX): This is the weekly average of the daily maximum ambient temperature.

Wind: The weekly average of wind speed is measured in meter/second. Wind moves air pollutants from one location to another. The extent of dilution of air pollutants depends on wind speed and its direction.

Age: Years of age of an individual. With ageing the health stock deteriorates increasing thereby both proneness to illness and mitigating activities.

Chronic Illnesses: Chronic illnesses such as Asthma, BP, TB and Heart Disease are included as dummy variables which take the value 1 if an individual has a particular disease; otherwise it takes the value 0. These are control variables, which account for the health stock. An individual with a chronic illness is more susceptible to air pollution exposure and is likely to have higher medical expenses and a higher number of sick days.

BCJ: This variable stands for blue-collar jobs. It takes the value 1 if a person has a blue-collar job, otherwise it takes the value 0[14]. It also represents the work place environment.

Station Dummy (Sd1, Sd2 and Sd3): To capture the location specific effect on health, station dummies have been introduced.

Table 11.1 provides details of descriptive statistics of the variables used in the estimation of the household health production function. The statistics relate to a full longitudinal data set comprising individuals both in working and non-working categories with 37500 observations. The average numbers of sick days (H) is 0.188/week/person. The average medical expenditure incurred on air pollution induced sickness is INR 3.35/week/person. Normalizing BCJ for the working population, 68 per cent of the working population is exposed to higher levels of air pollution at their respective work places. Over eight per cent people in Kanpur have chronic diseases, namely Asthma, TB, BP and Heart. The average level of NO_x concentration is 23.5($\mu g/m^3$). This is well within the permissible limits of NAAQS standards whereas the level of PM_{10} exceeds the limit by 275 per cent.

Table 11.1. Descriptive statistics

Variables		Mean	Std.Dev.	Minimum	Maximum
PM_{10}	($\mu g/m^3$)	224.44	69.55	42.5	462.5
NOx	($\mu g/m^3$)	23.49	4.97	10.5	39.0

(Contd.)

---

[14] In the present study, blue-collar workers are rickshaw pullers, vegetable vendors, rag pickers, factory workers working outside the factory building, and, if inside the building, those exposed to indoor smoke, fumes and dust.

(*Contd.*)

Variables	Mean	Std.Dev.	Minimum	Maximum
Wind (m / sec)	7.39	2.72	3.54	14.66
Dtemp (^{0} C)	9.87	3.21	5.2	15.27
Tmax (^{0} C)	30.50	8.59	15.5	42.9
Age (years)	34.34	15.36	15	100
BCJ	0.26	0.44	0	1
Asthma	0.020	0.14	0	1
Bp	0.033	0.18	0	1
Tb	0.015	0.12	0	1
Heart	0.017	0.13	0	1
Medical expenditure (M) (Rs.)	3.35	24.95	0	1200
Sick days (H)	0.188	0.99	0	7
Ratio of absence days to sick days	0.1424			
Number of observations	37500			

11.6. Results

11.6.1. Estimates of equations

Tables 11.2 and 11.3 present the results of estimated Poisson and Tobit models respectively. In the dose response estimation, the coefficients of pollution parameters, viz., PM_{10} and NO_X are positive and significant at one per cent level of statistical significance. A calculation of the marginal effects of reducing the levels of PM_{10} concentration in the ambient air by one $\mu g/\mu^3$ shows the number of sick days for a representative person in Kanpur to lower by 0.00015 days/week. If the pollution level is reduced to the safe levels of NAAQS standards, the number of sick days would reduce by 0.0249 days/week, or by 1.3 days/annum for an average person. These calculations are based on coefficient estimates from the random effects model in Table 11.2.

Table 11.2. Number of sick days (H): Poisson estimates

Independent Variables	Coefficients(re)	Coefficients(fe)
PM_{10} (+)	0 .0008034 (3.84)***	0.0008024 (3.84)***
NO_x (+)	0.0306 (11.90)***	0.0307 (11.90)***
WIND (–)	–0.0422 (6.57)***	–0.0421 (6.57)***

(*Contd.*)

(*Contd.*)

Independent Variables	Coefficients(re)	Coefficients(fe)
DTEMP	−0.0501 (10.69)***	−0.0502 (10.70)***
TMAX	−0.0002 (0.09)	−0.0001 (0.06)
AGE	0.0066 (1.68)*	
BCJ	0.276 (2.05)**	
ASTHMA	0.933 (2.26)**	
BP	0.548 (1.69)*	
TB	0.982 (2.08)**	
HEART	0.654 (1.45)	
Constant	−2.320 (11.48)***	
Log likelihood	−18811	−14946
Wald chi2 (14)	332.5 (0.000)	301.4 (0.000)
Number of observations	37500	13062
Number of groups	2098	729

Note: Figures in paraentheses are t-values. The Hausman test does not reject the random effects model.

The coefficients of WIND and DTEMP are negative and significant at the one per cent level. The negative signs of the coefficients of TMAX and DTEMP indicate a decrease in the number sick days during clear and warm days. AGE and individuals' health history of suffereing from ASTHMA, TB and BP have positive and statistically significant coefficients. The coefficient of workplace environment BCJ is positive and significant at the five per cent level indicating that people in polluted work environments are likely to have a higher number of sick days.

Table 11.3. Tobit equations of mitigating activities (M) left censored(0)

Independent Variables	Coefficients(re)	Pooled Tobit Coefficients
PM_{10} (+)	0.1032 (2.36)**	0.1035 (2.35)**
NO_x (+)	2.883 (5.14)***	2.891 (5.14)***
WIND	− 4.216 (3.12)***	− 4.229 (3.12)***
DTEMP	− 4.773 (4.79)***	− 4.786 (4.79)***

(*Contd.*)

(*Contd.*)

Independent Variables	Coefficients(re)	Pooled Tobit Coefficients
TMAX	− 0.0375 (0.10)	0.0374 (0.09)
AGE	0.5516 (3.25)***	0.5525 (3.25)***
BCJ	24.41 (4.30)***	24.48 (4.30)***
ASTHMA	79.89 (5.50)***	80.07 (5.51)***
BP	59.80 (4.89)***	59.98 (4.89)***
TB	91.74 (5.83)***	91.99 (5.84)***
HEART	66.54 (4.15)***	66.70 (4.16)***
Constant	− 445.65 (18.66)***	− 447.12 (18.66)***
Log Likelihood	− 14422	−14425
Rho	0.00064	−
Uncensored Obs: 1511	Left censored Obs: 35989	
Number of groups: 2098		

Note: Figures in the parentheses are t-values.

Table 11.3 presents the estimate of the demand function for mitigating activities (medical expenditure). Random effects and pooled (cross-sectional) Tobit coefficient estimates are presented. The similarity between random effects and pooled Tobit coefficients suggests robust results. The rest of the discussion focuses on the random effects model. The coefficients of pollutants PM_{10} and NOx are positive depicting a reduction in mitigating expenses with a fall in the concentration levels of PM10 and NO_x in the ambient air. The coefficients of PM_{10} and NO_x are statistically significant at five per cent and one per cent respectively. Although the level of concentration of NO_x does not exceed the NAAQS limits in Kanpur, even at the lower levels it has significant adverse effects on health as is reflected by the positive sign of the coefficient. The marginal effect of PM_{10} on the demand for mitigating activities of an average person is INR 0.0042/ week which translates to INR 0.684/week reduction if the pollution level is improved to meet the NAAQS standards.

The significant and negative coefficient of DTEMP indicates a reduction in mitigating expenses on sunny days. The coefficient of AGE is positive and significant, indicating a deteriorating health stock with age. All chronic diseases ASTHMA, BP, TB, and HEART have positive coefficients and are significant at the one per cent level, meaning that people with these conditions have significantly higher medical expenditures. The coefficient of blue-collar jobs is positive and significant at the one per cent level, suggesting a higher medical expenditure by blue-collar workers as they are exposed to higher levels of air pollution at their respective work places. The results of pooled Tobit have also been reported to check for autocorrelation in the panel level error term. Since rho is nearly 'zero' the panel estimator is not different from the pooled estimator, thus ruling out the possibility of autocorrelation in the panel error term.

11.6.2. Welfare gains from reduced sick Days (H)

Using the results of the estimated equations (Tables 11.2 and 11.3), welfare gains to the population of Kanpur city from reductions in air pollution to the safe level are measured. The present study attempts to value the sick days in monetary terms by taking into account workdays lost (absent days) and low efficiency days (restricted activity days) for both working and non-working individuals. Figure 11.1 describes these concepts:

	Working Individuals	Non-working Individuals
Workdays lost (WLD) due to sickness	Loss in daily wages	Loss in daily minimum average wage
Sick but not absent from work (Restricted Activity Days-RAD)	One third of the daily wage is lost	One third of the daily minimum average wage

Figure 11.1. Monetary valuation of air pollution–sick days

The amount of daily wages lost due to absence from work may be taken as the cost of workdays lost due to air pollution induced sickness for working individuals. However, to compute the cost of illness of non-working individuals the imputed cost of their non-cash labour needs to be known. This study uses the per day minimum average wage rate of INR 83.51 fixed by the Government of India for the State of Uttar Pradesh as the imputed per day labour cost for non-working individuals. To value productivity loss during the low efficiency days (restricted activity days)[15] in monetary terms, a loss of one third amount of the daily wages is considered.

---

[15] Low efficiency days (restricted activity days) can be the days when work is not completely lost but the routine is inefficiently performed due to sickness.

Welfare gains to working individuals

An improvement in air quality is expected to lower morbidity and thereby reduce workdays lost (WLD) while improving efficiency (RAD). Valuing the reductions in WLD at the daily wage rate of INR 207, a representative individual is estimated to gain INR 38 per annum whereas estimating at one third of the daily wage rate, the monetary value of an improvement in RAD would be INR 77 per annum. Thus, the total economic gain to an individual is estimated as INR 115 per annum if air pollution is reduced to the safe level as per the NAAQS standard. Extrapolating these gains to the entire 'working population' of Kanpur the total gains are estimated as INR 97 million per annum.

Gains to non-working individuals

Following the same procedure, the gain in workdays due to reductions in air pollution has been estimated using the daily average minimum wage rate of INR 83.51. Thus, the annual gains to a non-working representative individual are estimated as INR 15 and INR 31 due to loss of workdays and improved efficiency respectively. By extrapolating this gain to the entire 'non-working' population of Kanpur, the annual gains from reduced sick days are estimated as INR 103 million.

Adding together the gains to working and non-working individuals, the total economic gains due to an improvement in air quality and reduced sick days are estimated as INR 200 million per annum.

11.6.3. Welfare gains from reduced mitigating activities (M)

The gains to a representative person from reduced medical expenditures due to improved air quality is estimated as INR 36 per annum which accounts for a reduction of 20.4 per cent in mitigating expenditure. By extrapolating this gain to the total population of Kanpur, the annual gain from reduced mitigating activities (M) is estimated as INR 110 million. The total welfare gain due to a reduction in sick days and mitigating activities is INR 310 million per annum in Kanpur.

11.7. Conclusion

The analysis undertaken in this chapter presents estimates of health benefits from improved air quality in Kanpur. The estimated household health production function model consists of two functions–the health production function and the demand function for mitigating activities. To estimate this model, individual health diary data was collected. There are already a few studies from the west that use health diary data to estimate household health production function models (Alberini and Krupnick, 1997). However, this study is the first of its kind in India to use panel data from household health diaries. Many more such studies are required for other urban areas in India to provide useful inputs to design policies to control urban air pollution. The results of the study show a total gain of INR 310 million per annum to the population of the city of Kanpur from reduced morbidity if air quality were improved to meet the NAAQS standard.

However, estimates presented in this study are a lower bound because they do not include expenditures on averting activities and the opportunity cost of time associated with medical care (the time spent on traveling and waiting at doctor's clinic and the time of the attendant or accompanying person, etc.). Also the estimated household health production function model in this study does not take into consideration losses that are incurred due to the disutility of discomfort caused by illness. Economic gains would be higher if the benefits of improved visibility, recreation opportunities and reduction in material damages, etc., are taken into account.

In the year 1997–1998 the Central Pollution Control Board (CPCB)[16] developed an Environmental Management Plan (EMP) for Kanpur with a strong focus on air pollution reduction. The plan recommended a wide range of measures such as changes in fuel use, relocating air-polluting industries, improving the road network and increasing the public transport facility. However, the progress so far has been very slow and the city needs to implement the EMP on a priority basis. There are significant costs involved in improving air quality. This would be the case if CNG is introduced for vehicular transportation or if the mode of transport is changed from road to metro rail or if any relocation of polluting industries occurs. The estimates of welfare gains from air pollution reduction obtained in this chapter should help justify these costs.

References

Alberni, A., Cropper, M., Tsh-Tan Fu, Krupnick, A., Jun-Tan-Liu, Shaw, D. and Harrington, W., 'Valuing Health Effects of Air pollution in Developing Countries:

---

[16] See CPCB Environmental Mangement Plan (2000).

the Taiwan Experience', *Journal of Environmental Economics and Management,* 34, (1997), 107–126.

Alberini, A. and Krupnick, A., 'Air Pollution and Acute Respiratory Illness: Evidence from Taiwan and Los Angeles', *American Journal of Agriculture Economics,* 79 (7), (1977), 1620–1624.

Alberini, A., and Krupnick, A., 'Cost of Illness and Willingness to Pay Estimates of the Benefits of Improved Air quality: Evidence from Taiwan', *Land Economics,* 76, (2000), 37–53.

Amemiya, T., 'Tobit Models: A Survey', *Journal of Econometrics,* 24, (1984), 3–61.

Chestnut, L.G., Ostro, B.D., and Vichit-Vadakan, N., 'Transferability of Air Pollution Control Health Benefits Estimates from the United States to Developing Countries: Evidence from the Bangkok Study', *American Journal of Agricultural Economics,* 79, (1997), 1630–1635.

CPCB, 'Air pollution and its control', *Parivesh Newsletter,* 2(1), (1995), Delhi, Indian Central Pollution Control Board.

CPCB, 'Environmental Management Plan (Recommendations), Zonal Office Kanpur, Uttar Pradesh, India, 2000.

Dickie, M., and Gerking, S., 'Willingness to Pay for Ozone   Control: Inferences from the Demand for Medical Care', *Journal of Environmental Economics and Management,* 21, (1991), 1–16.

Dockery, D. W., Pope Arden, C., Xiping, X., Spengler John, D., Ware James, H., Fay, Martha E., Ferris, Benjamin G. and Speizer, Frank E. 'Association Between Air Pollution and Mortality in Six US Cities', *New England Journal of Medicine,* 329, (1993), 1753–1759.

Eco Friends for Environmental Education, Protection and Security, [ecofriends www.org], 2002.

Freeman, III, A. M., *The Measurement of Environmental and Resource Values: Theory and Methods,* (Washington DC: Resources for the Future, 1993).

Grossman, M., 'On the Concept of Health Capital and the Demand for Health', *Journal of Political Economy,* 80, (1972), 223–255.

JNNURM, 'Kanpur City Development Plan', *Jawaharlal Nehru National Urban Renewal Mission,* JPS Associates (P) Ltd., Consultants, Kanpur, India, 2006.

Kumar, S. and Rao, D. N. 'Valuing Benefits of Air Pollution Abatement Using Health Production Function: A Case study of Panipat Thermal Power Station, India', *Journal of Environmental & Resource Economics,* 20(91–102), (2001).

Liang, K. Y. and Zeger, S. L., 'Longitudinal Data Analysis using Generalized Linear Model', *Biometrika,* 73, 13–22 in Stata Cross-Sectional Time-Series Reference Manual Release 8, Stata Press Publication, 1986.

Lvovsky, K., 'Economic Costs of Air Pollution with Special Reference to India', *South Asia Environment Unit World Bank,* Prepared for the National Conference on Health and Environment Delhi, India, July 7–9, 1998.

Maddala, G. S., *Limited-dependent and Qualitative Variables in Econometrics,* (London: Cambridge University Press, 1983).

Murty, M. N., Gulati, S. C. and Banerjee, A., 'Health Benefits from Urban-Air Pollution Abatement in the Indian Subcontinent', Discussion Paper No. 62/2003, Delhi, Institute of Economic Growth, 2003.

Ostro, B., 'The Effects of Air Pollution on Work Loss and Morbidity', *Journal of Environmental Economics and Management,* 10, (1983), 371–382.

Ostro, B., 'Estimating the Health and Economic Effects of Particulate Matter in Jakarta: A Preliminary Assessment', Paper presented at the Fourth Annual Meeting of the *International Society for Environmental Epidemiology, 26–29,* Cuernavaca, Mexico, 1992.

Gupta, U., 'Valuation of Urban Air Pollution – A Case Study of Kanpur City', Environmental and Resource Economics, *Journal of European Association of Environmental and Resource Economics (2008), 41:315-326.* Working Paper Number 17–06, South Asian Network for Development and Environmental Economics (SANDEE) and Discussion Paper Series Number 96/2005, Delhi, Institute of Economic Growth, 2005.

World Health Organization (WHO), 'Quantification of the Health Effects of Exposure to Air Pollution', Report of a WHO Working Group, Bilthoven, Netherlands, 2000.

12

Children in the Slums of Dhaka: Diarrhoea Prevalence and its Implications

M. Jahangir Alam[1]

12.1. Introduction

Diarrhoeal disease is one of the five leading causes of morbidity and mortality among children aged between zero and five years. Global estimates show that deaths due to diarrhoea[2] have declined from 4.6 million in the 1980s (Snyder and Merson, 1982) to 3.3 million in the 1990s (Bern et al., 1992) and to 2.5 million in 2000 (Kosek et al., 2003). Much of the improvement is possibly due to improvement in health treatment and management

[1] I acknowledge with gratitude the financial support from South Asian Network for Development and Environmental Economics (SANDEE). I also appreciate the mentoring by members of the SANDEE advisory board such as Subhrendu K. Pattanayak, E. Somanathan, Enamul Haque, M. N. Murty and Priya Shyamsundar. I am grateful to Anwarul Hoque, Wasiqur Rahman Khan, Minhaj Uddin Mahmud and Mani Nepal and to an anonymous reviewer for their valuable comments. I would like to thank INTERVIDA BANGLADESH for providing data on diarrhoea, which was useful in calculating the yearly cost. Comments from participants at the Australian Health Economics Society Conference 2007 and European Association of Environmental and Resource Economists Conference 2008 are also acknowledged. I wish to express my thanks to the SANDEE Secretariat and to Mohammad Nasir Uddin Khan and Fahim Subhan Chowdhury, who provided excellent research assistance.

[2] A standard definition of diarrhoea could be the passing of three or more liquid stools in a 24-hour period and twelve or more loose or watery stools for breast-fed baby. Diarrhoea is generally characterized as "acute watery", "persistent" or "dysentery". Acute watery diarrhoea has an abrupt beginning and lasts less than 14 days. Persistent diarrhoea lasts more than 14 days, which generally results in significant weight loss and nutritional problems. Dysentery is diarrhoea in which blood is obviously seen in the faeces (WHO).

and increased use of Oral Rehydration Therapy (ORT) in the developing countries (WHO, 2004). However, morbidity has not shown a parallel decline despite the improvement in infrastructural facilities in developing countries. This is possibly because of limited changes in behavioural factors such as hand washing and low levels of awareness. The incidence of diarrhoea attacks among the children per year was at 3.2 episodes per child in 2000 in developing countries (Kosek et al., 2003).

In Bangladesh diarrhoeal diseases cotinue to play a significant role among the causes of death among children below five years of age according to the Interim Poverty Reduction Strategy Paper (PRSP) published by the Government of Bangladesh in 2002. These children are malnourished and therefore vulnerable to diarrhoea related deaths. Around 125,000 children under five die each year from diarrhoea, i.e. 342 children per day as per the PRSP repot.

As Bangladesh is a riverine country, floods are a common natural hazard. Although diarrhoeal diseases are prevalent throughout the year, epidemics of diarrhoeal diseases and cholera mainly occur twice a year – during the hot and humid summer months of April–May, and during and after the monsoon floods in July–September (Luby et al., 2004). For example, from 30 July to 26 August 2007, 104,846 cases of diarrhoea and 20 deaths were recorded in flood affected areas in Bangladesh (Case Fatality Rate = 0.02 per cent) (WHO, 2007). In the same period 19,190 diarrhoea cases were admitted to the specialized hospital, International Centre for Diarrhoeal Disease Research, Bangladesh (ICDDR,B) from flood affected areas across Dhaka (WHO, 2007).

The worst cases of diarrhoea are found in the urban slums[3] of Dhaka. In these slums, overcrowding and poor basic amenities coupled with inadequate attention to personal hygiene result in a great risk of infection. Water quality at the point-of-use is often worse than that at the point-of-source because drinking water can become contaminated by storage and behavioural activities (Alam, 2007). In fact, in Dhaka slums, 27 per cent of all deaths are attributable to diarrhoea (Alam, 2007). Furthermore, dehydration resulting from diarrhoea causes other health related complications in children.

The aim of this study is to understand the prevalence of diarrhoeal diseases among children in urban slums in Dhaka and identify what interventions

---

[3] A slum is cluster of compact settlements of five or more households which generally grow very unsystematically and haphazardly in an unhealthy condition and atmosphere on government and private vacant land.

can improve the situation. The study has two major objectives. The first is to identify the risk and duration of child diarrhoea and how these relate to engineering, behavioural and socio-economic factors. The second objective is to compute the economic costs to slum households from diarrhoea. There are very few studies in the past that have examined the impacts of diarrhoeal disease on slum dwellers. Thus, one can be hopeful that this study will make a contribution to poverty reduction strategies in Bangladesh by examining slum children, their health and the costs borne by slum households. This study also extends the current literature on diarrhoeal costs by examining more carefully the opportunity costs associated with child care.

12.2. Determinants and costs of child diarrhoea

Diarrhoea is usually attributed to ingestion of water or foods contaminated with fecal coliforms or other pathogens, or fecal-oral contamination. Unsafe water supply, inadequate sanitation facilities, and lack of awareness on personal hygiene cause 88 per cent of diarrhoea attacks (WHO, 2004). Age, nutritional status, diet, drugs, immunologic status, use of rehydration fluids, poor water storage and hand feeding are the major factors affecting the duration of diarrhoea episodes (Mirza et al., 1997). With hygiene interventions that reduce contamination of hands, food and water, and better management of water and sanitation facilities, diarrhoea is almost preventable (Fewtrell et al., 2005).

Alberini et al. (1996) uses the terms behavioural and engineering factors for identifying factors linked with the incidence and severity of diarrhoea. The engineering factors mainly include clean water sources and sanitation services (Checkley et al., 2004). Behavioural factors focus on the household behaviours and hygiene practices such as use of soap, hand washing practices by mother and children before meals and after defecation, use of a lid while carrying and storing water and boiling/treating water (Alberni et al., 1996, Han and Hlaing 1989; Knight et al., 1992; Hoque et al., 1999; and Jalan et al., 2003). All these factors lead to changes in the exposure of risks to diarrhoea.

In order to understand the implications of diarrhoeal diseases, it is useful to estimate the costs borne by households. Economic models that take into account behavioural responses of households can be used to carefully estimate the monetary value of cost of diarrhoeal attacks. Using such models, it can be shown that individual's willingness to pay (WTP) for a small reduction in exposure of children to diarrhoea is comprised of lost earnings due to diarrhoea, marginal cost of averting activities, marginal medical expenditures and the monetary value of disutility caused by exposure of children to diarrhoea (Harrington and Portney, 1987). For children, however, sick days during diarrhoeal illness have no real implication in terms of loss of income[4] but during the period of sick days attending parent(s) might lose income and/or leisure, which should be included in the cost estimations. The value of the disutility due to sickness in children and their parents cannot, however, be estimated directly. Thus, in practice, the WTP for diarrhoea reductions or alternatively, the costs associated with diarrhoea, are generally classified into treatment costs, averting costs from actions taken to avoid sickness and opportunity costs in terms of lost time.

The cost of treatment of diarrhoea in developing countries vary considerably because of diverse health care systems, differences in hospital capacity, their scope and sources of funding, pricing policy on drugs and differences in per capita income (Phelps, 1992); Mohaghan and Mohaghan, 1996). There are several studies that estimate diarrhoeal costs. Patel et al., (2003), for instance, estimate that the average cost of treating (direct medical, non-medical and indirect costs) diarrhoea per child in urban India to be US $14 per episode. Two other studies from India have slightly different estimates. Dasgupta (2004) finds the annual cost of illness due to diarrhoea in urban Delhi to be INR 1,094 (US $25.41[5]); while in Pune, Gokhale (2002) estimate costs to be INR 276 (US $5.64) (includes only the direct medical costs) for an average duration of 2.01 days per episode of diarrhoea. In the Philippines, the average medical doctor costs per episode of diarrhoea are estimated at US $9 and US $7 respectively for urban and rural areas when treated in private health centres (WHO, 2001). In Indonesia, diarrhoeal costs are estimated at US $2.27 per child (Lerman et al., 1985). On the other hand, in Peru, the estimated ambulatory visit cost ranges from US $7.49 to US $16.56 per child (Proyecto, 2000). Table 12.1 provides some estimates of the costs of child diarrhoea. From this, it can be seen that the cost per child per episode of diarrhoea ranges from US $1.94 to US $14 in Asia.

---

[4] However children can incur costs from diarrhoea if it leads to stunted growth, physically or mentally. For example, if children that suffer from diarrhoea are weaker, then they might collect lover wages (in terms of field labour) as adults.

[5] US $1 = INR 43.05

Table 12.1. Cost of child diarrhoea per child per episode

Author(Year)	Location	Cost per Episode		Age Group	Cost Components
		Local Currency	US(US$)		
Lerman et al., (1985)	Indonesia	–	US $2.27	Below 5 years	Health centre, hospital, and private expenditure
Gokhale (2002)	India	Rs. 276.23	US $5.64		Direct medical costs
Patel et al., (2003)	India	Rs. 500	US $14	6–59 months	Direct medical (the medical personnel services, the medications, general of incentive care services, the laboratory investigations. Direct non-medical (traveling cost to the physician or the hospital, cost of food to the family and patient, hospitalization and other incidental costs. Indirect costs(wage lost of employed guardians attending to the child)
Dasgupta (2004)	India	Rs. 83.33	US $1.94	Below 15 years	Treatment costs
Gomez et al., (1998)	Argentina	–	US $30	0–23 months	Average cost of a doctor or clinic visit, transportation, parent/guardian time lost from work.
DeSoarez et al., (2006)	Brazil	–	US $53	Below 5 years	Direct costs (cost of medical visit, hospitalization, medications, laboratory tests, extra expenses and travel to obtain medical care) Indirect costs (foregone earnings of caregiver, lifetime productivity loss of a dying child)

Most studies (Lerman et al., 1985; Dasgupta, 2004) calculated the cost of child diarrhoea without valuing the opportunity cost of the care-giving family members. Moreover, studies often do not identify risk factors associated with the prevalence and duration of diarrhoea in urban slums. This study not only identifies these risk factors but also calculates the treatment cost (home and medical) along with the indirect opportunity costs of time associated with child diarrhoea in urban slums in Dhaka, Bangladesh. However, the costs estimated in this study do not include averting costs or the value of disutility from sickness (see Chapter 2). Thus, this study provides a lower bound estimate of household WTP to reduce diarrhoea. Nonetheless, such an estimate of the costs of diarrhoea can be used to justify public investments and education campaigns to prevent and reduce diarrhoeal incidence in slums.

12.3. Study area and sampling

There are a total of 1,925[6] slums with 267,065 households within Dhaka Metropolitan Area (DMA). Approximately 95 per cent of the slums contain fewer than 500 households. In 50 per cent of the slums the primary water source is tap[7]. In the case of the other slum-dwellers, 2.6 per cent rely on tube wells, 0.4 per cent on ponds, 1.3 per cent on rivers, and 0.1 per cent on other sources for drinking water. The remaining 46 per cent of the slums have no specified water source with households from these slums having to search for a water source on a daily basis. With regard to sanitation facilities, 12.3 per cent of the slums possess water-sealed latrines, 21.5 and 22.6 per cent possess open and pit latrines respectively while the remaining 43.6 per cent have no specified sanitation system.

The Dhaka Metropolitan Area (DMA), which was chosen for this study is divided into eight equal zones. Four slums were randomly selected from each zone for undertaking a household survey. On average, each slum had 142 households and 15 households were randomly selected from each slum. A household survey was conducted from 26 May 2007 to 12 June 2007. Data was on a total of 480 households from 32 slums.

---

[6] While the author collected the data on the slum characteristics, water source and sanitation facility from the Local Government Engineering Department, the calculations were his own.

[7] Dhaka Water Supply and Sewerage Authority (DWASA) currently supply water to 75 per cent of the city area. 82 per cent is form of ground water sources which is tapped through Deep Tube Wells (DTW), and the remaining 18 per cent is sourced from the water treatment plants (in Saidabad and Chandnighat) and two other smaller units in Narayanganj (Haque et al., 2006)

A constant skipping factor (k) was used to determine the number of households to be skipped in order to select households for the interview. The value of the skipping factor was obtained by dividing the total number of households within the particular slum by the sub-sample size, which was fixed at 15. The enumerator selected the first household at random on the basis of the completed interview or the unwillingness of the selected household to participate in the survey. The enumerator then skipped k households and selected the next household and subsequently skipped another k households and so on until 15 interviews were completed.

In this study, households are defined as a group of individuals related by blood or marriage living in the same premises and sharing one set of cooking utensils. The principal respondents to questionnaire were women because it was thought that they were more aware of children's health condition compared to the men of the household. Furthermore, households without any child between zero to five years were excluded from the survey.

The household survey was divided into several sub-components. Data was collected on household members, household status, household information on diarrhoea, opportunity cost of diarrhoea, water system, water collection and storage, behavioural factors related to water use, sanitation facility, sanitation use, awareness and hygiene.

Table 12.2 presents summary statistics from our household survey. The average age of respondents (females) and the heads of the household are 27 and 34 years respectively. The 480 households in our sample had a total of 2,142 members. The average, maximum and minimum size of a household is 4.46, 12 and 2 respectively. The average monthly household income is BDT 5,330 (US $76)[8]. On an average each household had more than one child below the age of five years with a maximum of three children.

From the surveyed households 613 children were below the age of five years with an average age of 2.65 years. Out of 613 children in the sample, 298 suffered from diarrhoeal attacks within the recall period of 15 days and the average duration of a diarrhoea episode per child is 3.76 days. Figure 12.1(a) shows the duration of child diarrhoea and the per centage of children with diarrhoea amongst the total number of children. This figure shows that 51 per cent of the total number of children had no episodes of diarrhoea during the recall period. Approximately 12 per cent of the children suffered from diarrhoeal attacks lasting two days, and approximately 13 per cent had an episode lasting for three days.

---

[8] US $1 = BDT 68.87

Table 12.2. Socio-economic conditions of slum households

	Variable	Obs.	Mean	Std. Dev.	Min	Max
House-hold Variables	Age of respondent (Years)	480	27	7	16	60
	Age of household head (Years)	480	34	8	18	70
	Household member	480	4.46	1.31	2	12
	Household monthly income (Taka)$^{\Psi}$	480	5,330	2,468	400	23,500
	Number of Children (28 days to 5 years)	480	1.28	0.49	1	3
Children Variables	Age of child (Years)	613	2.65	1.52	0	5
	Diarrhoea	613	.49	.50	0	1
	Duration of diarrhoea (Days)	298	3.76	2.37	1	15

Figure 12.1(b) shows the duration and the per centage of children with episodes of diarrhoea within the recall period of 15 days. In Figure 12.1(b), it is clearly identifiable that duration of child diarrhoea is mostly between two and three days with 27 per cent of the children having diarrhoea for two days and 28 per cent having it for three days. Approximately 5.7, two and one per cent of the children suffered from diarrhoea respectively for 7, 10 and 15 days.

12.4. Methods of estimation

12.4.1. Econometric model

There are two aspects to the problem of diarrhoea in households. First, there is the occurrence or probability of diarrhoea and factors that influence diarrhoeal occurrence. Following this, one needs to examine how different factors affect the duration of diarrhoea. The probability of having diarrhoea and duration of diarrhoea are generally the result of two different stochastic processes. The two processes, however, can be explained by the same set of explanatory variables, but these variables need to be interpreted differently for each case. In estimating the prevalence and duration of diarrhoea, it is

---

$^{\Psi}$ Exchange rate: US $1 = BDT 68.87

noted that the variable child diarrhoea is binary in nature, while data on duration of diarrhoea needs to be treated as count data. In order to figure out how to estimate the determinants of these two variables a variety of models were considered.

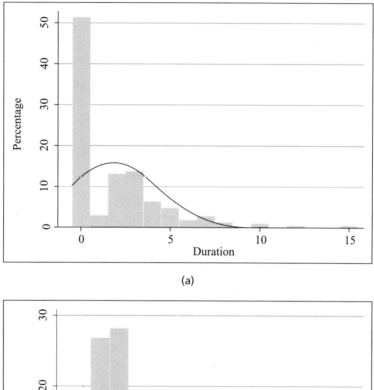

(a)

(b)

Figure 12.1.   Duration of child diarrhoea within the recall period of 15 days.

The probability or prevalence of child diarrhoea is estimated by using a Logit model and the duration of diarrhoea by using count data models. For estimating the duration of diarrhoea, a Poisson regression model is first used and a test for over dispersion is done. This is because if over dispersion is found in the data, it is better to use a Negative Bionomial regression model. However, both the Poisson and Negative Binomial models have a limitation in that they do not consider that the zero outcomes of the data generating process are qualitatively different from the positive ones (Greene, 2007; Mullahy, 1986). An alternative model suggested to overcome this limitation is the Hurdle model (Mullahy, 1986). In this formulation, a binary probability model determines whether a zero or non-zero outcome occurs. In the latter case, a (truncated) Poisson or Negative Binomial distribution describes the positive outcomes (Green, 2007). This approach is followed and a model similar to that of Noronha and Andrade (2002) is used.

Thus, a hurdle or two-part model is constructed where two parametrically independent likelihood functions are specified, each representing a stage in the estimation procedure. The first likelihood function is based on the whole sample, representing the binary process whether the child is affected by diarrhoea or not. This process is determined by the vector of parameters (β_1, α_1) estimated using a Logit model. The second likelihood function is based on the sub-sample having count data of children who suffered from diarrhoea. This process is determined by a vector of parameters (β_2, α_2) estimated using a Negative Binomial model.

12.4.2. Model Specification Test

Specification tests of the different count data models were carried out to justify the use of Negative Binomial Hurdle model against other available models. The likelihood ratio test (LR Test) was used for this purpose (Green, 2007 and Cameron and Trivedi, 2005). The hypotheses testing procedures are as follows. First, the existence of over dispersion in the data is tested so as to select our model specification between the Poisson type count data models (Poisson model or Poisson Hurdle model) and the Negative Binomial type count data models (Negative Binomial model and Negative Binomial Hurdle model). If the over dispersion parameter equals zero, then the Negative Binomial model and the Negative Binomial Hurdle model reduce to the Poisson model and the Poisson Hurdle model, respectively. Hence, LR test is used to test the following – (a) H_0: Poisson model against H_A: Negative Binomial model, and (b) H_0: Poisson Hurdle model against H_A: Negative Binomial Hurdle model.

Second, to choose our model specification between the non-Hurdle count data models (Poisson model or Negative Binomial model) and the Hurdle count data model (Poisson Hurdle model or Negative Binomial Hurdle model) two additional hypotheses are tested. Since the non-Hurdle count data models and Hurdle count data models are not nested with each other in our model specification, the LR test is used to test the following – (c) H_0: Poisson model against H_A: Poisson Hurdle model, and (d) H_0: Negative Binomial model against H_A: Negative Binomial Hurdle model.

12.4.3. Dependent variables

The objective is to identify the determinants of child diarrhoea and duration of diarrhoea. The first dependent variable diarrhoea takes a value of 1 if the child suffers from diarrhoea within the recall period of 15 days and 0 if not. The second dependent variable duration, explaining the number of sick days the child suffers from diarrhoea only if the first dependent variable takes the value of 1. It is assumed here that the factors determining child diarrhoea and its duration may or may not be the same.

12.4.4. Independent variables

As previously stated, factors that influence the incidence of child diarrhoea and its duration are related to behavioural responses such as washing of hands with soap after defecation (Mirza et al., 1997; Han and Hlaing, 1989), using strainers to purify drinking water and level of awareness about advantages of quality of drinking water, hygiene and sanitation (Fewtrell et al., 2005). Diarrhoea is also affected by engineering factors such as water source and sanitation (Fewtrell et al., 2005). From the assessment of the literature, the following independent variables are used.

For an analysis we have considered a set of engineering, behavioural and socio-economic variables. The engineering variables considered are water availability for 24 hours and pit[9] type of sanitation. The behavioural variables are use of narrow-necked container, strainer and cloth, and hand washing after defecation. The variables owning radio and television,

---

[9] Pit type of sanitation has a slab and there stool remains in the pan below most of the times.

mothers' education, age, adult diarrhoea, member, participation in NGO hygiene related awareness activities, semi *pucca* house, perception and location are the socio-economic variables in our model. Table 12.3 presents the hypothesis related to how the various risk factors affect the probability of diarrhoeal occurrence and the duration of diarrhoea. All of the variables used in this analysis are described as follows:

Table 12.3. Variable explanations and expected sign

Independent Variables	Dependent Variables	
	Diarrhoea (=1 if yes; 0 otherwise)	Duration (Duration of child diarrhoea in days)
Water Availability (=1 if water from all sources is available for 24 hours; 0 otherwise)	−	−
Pit (=1 if sanitation type is pit; 0 otherwise)	−	−
Narrow-necked Container (=1 if collection container is narrow-necked; 0 otherwise)	−	−
Strainer & Cloth (=1 if household uses cloth or strainer as straining instrument; 0 otherwise)	−	−
Hand Wash (= 1 if household respondent washed at least one hand after defecation; 0 otherwise)	−	−
Radio & TV (= 1 if household owns a radio and television; 0 otherwise)	−	−
Mother's Education (= 1 if mother's education greater than class five; 0 otherwise)	−	−
Age (=1 if child age greater than 2 years; 0 otherwise)	−	−
Adult Diarrhoea (= 1 if household member having diarrhoea other than the child; 0 otherwise)	+	+
Member (number of household member)	+/−	+/−
Participation (= 1 if household respondent participated in any hygiene related activities taken by NGO; 0 otherwise)	−	−
Semi *Pucca* (=1 if cement wall and tin or cement roof; 0 otherwise)	−	−
Perception (=1 if respondent have the perception that contaminated water causes diarrhoea; 0 otherwise)	−	−
Location (= 1 if the slum is located near river; 0 otherwise)	+	+

12.4.5. Engineering Variables

Water availability is a dummy variable that takes the value 1 if water is available for 24 hours and otherwise zero. The coefficient of this variable is expected to be negative explaining negative association with the occurrence of child diarrhoea and its duration.

The variable pit is a dummy variable that takes the value of 1 if the household has a pit type of sanitation, otherwise zero. This variable is expected to have a negative association with both dependent variables.

12.4.6. Behavioural variables

The variable narrow-necked container takes a value of 1 if the household uses a narrow-necked container to store water, and zero otherwise. It is expected to have negative association with both dependent variables.

Strainer and cloth variable explains whether the household uses a strainer or cloth as a straining instrument, in which case it takes a value of 1, and zero otherwise; and the relationship with the dependent variables is expected to be negative. If the households know the proper way to use the strainer and cloth as straining instrument then we will have a negative association.

To measure the hygiene practice of the household respondent, the variable hand washing is taken, that takes the value of 1 if the respondents wash at least one hand with soap after defecation, and otherwise zero. This hygiene variable is expected to be negatively associated with diarrhoea and its duration.

12.4.7. Socio-economic variables

The variable radio and television is a dummy variable and it takes the value of 1 if household owns both a radio and television, otherwise zero. A negative link is expected between households owning radio and television with diarrhoea prevalence and duration since exposure to media means that the respondents have more knowledge and awareness about hygiene practice and disease.

Mother's education is a dummy variable taking the value 1 if the mother's education is higher than primary level (class five) and otherwise zero. Educated mothers are expected to have their children less exposed to diarrhoea and have their child suffer fewer days.

The age variable is a dummy variable taking the value 1 if the child is older than two years[10] and is otherwise zero. Age is anticipated to be negatively correlated with both of the dependent variables. As children grow, their disease prevention power increases, and thus a negative association is expected.

The adult diarrhoea variable is a dummy variable that takes the value 1 if there is any adult member other than the child suffering from diarrhoea in the household and is otherwise zero. It is expected to be positively related with both diarrhoea and its duration.

The member variable accounts for the total number of people in the household. One is uncertain about its association with diarrhoea and duration. More members in the households could mean that the household tasks can be divided among the members and done properly. On the flip side more members in the household means that there are too many people living in the same room, and if one of the member is sick, he/she may transmit the disease to other members. Again households with a greater number of people may be poorer or may have less time to devote to tasks if there are disproportionately more young children in large families.

The participation variable is a dummy variable taking the value 1 if the mother of the child participated in any hygiene awareness activities undertaken by NGOs and otherwise zero. Participation in hygiene activities indicates that the respondent have sufficient knowledge about hygiene and how certain diseases can be avoided or how to cure certain diseases. Therefore, participation is expected to be negatively associated with the prevalence of diarrhoea and its duration.

The variable semi *pucca* defines the structure of the house and this variable has been used as a proxy to household income or wealth. It takes a value of 1 if the house is made of cement wall and tin or cement roof, otherwise it takes a value of zero. Semi *pucca* is expected to be negatively linked with the dependent variables.

Perception is an awareness measuring variable. It takes a value of 1 if the household respondents perceive that drinking contaminated water causes diarrhoea and zero if they do not have such perception. It is anticipated to have a negative relation with both of the dependent variables.

Location is a dummy variable, which takes a value of 1 when the slum that the household resides in is situated near a river, otherwise it takes a

---

[10] Impact of diarrhoea and malnutrition is greatest for children under two years (Food and Nutrition Bulletin, 1982).

value of zero. It is anticipated that households that are nearer to rivers will be affected more by diarrhoea and the duration will also be longer. The location variable helps one to see slum fixed effects.

12.5. Results and discussion

12.5.1. Mean test between affected and unaffected households

In our sample, 49 per cent of the households were affected by diarrhoea and the average duration of child diarrhoea was 3.76 days. Table 12.4 discusses access to clean water, sanitation and other characteristics of the affected and unaffected households and identify the significant differences. Narrow-necked container, hand washing, owning radio and television, child age, mother education and adult diarrhoea are significantly different between the affected and unaffected households.

As Table 12.4 shows there are differences in a variety of factors between affected and unaffected households. About 40 per cent of the affected households had water available for 24 hours a day while 45 per cent of the unaffected households had the same facility. In terms of behavioural factors that are important, 80 per cent of affected households and 86 per cent of unaffected households used a narrow-necked container. Among households with diarrhoea, 51 per cent of the respondents said that they washed at least one hand with soap after defecation, while the same number was higher at 63 per cent for unaffected households.

About 29 per cent of the affected household had an adult member suffering from diarrhoea, which was significantly different from 21 per cent of the unaffected households. Only two per cent of the respondents from the affected household participated in hygiene related awareness activities taken by NGO, which was higher at five per cent for unaffected households. It should be noted that 10 per cent of unaffected household respondent had the perception that drinking contaminated water causes diarrhoea, while this perception was held by eight per cent of affected households. Of the affected households, 63 per cent were in slums situated near a river.

12.5.2. Empirical results

Figure 12.2 shows results from the specification tests favour the Negative Binomial Hurdle Model against all other specifications considered. The LR test statistic for hypothesis (1) for the Poisson model against Negative

Table 12.4. Descriptive statistics

Variables	Overall (obs. = 613) Mean (Std. Dev.)	With Diarrhoea (obs. = 298) Mean (Std. Dev.)	Without Diarrhoea (obs. = 315) Mean (Std. Dev.)	Equity Mean Test Mean Difference (Std. Error)	t-stat
Diarrhoea	0.49 (0.50	1.00 (0.00)	–	–	–
Duration	1.83 (2.51)	3.76 (2.37)	–	–	–
Water Availability	0.42 (0.49)	0.40 (0.49)	0.45 (0.50)	–0.05 (0.04)	–1.37
Pit	0.39 (0.49)	0.39 (0.49)	0.40 (0.49)	–0.02 (0.04)	–0.44
Narrow-necked Container	0.83 (0.38)	0.80 (0.40)	0.86 (0.35)	–0.06* (0.03)	–1.82
Strainer & Cloth	0.10 (0.31)	0.12 (0.33)	0.09 (0.29)	0.03 (0.02)	1.29
Hand Wash	0.57 (0.50)	0.51 (0.50)	0.63 (0.48)	–0.11** (0.04)	–2.81
Radio & TV	0.10 (0.30)	0.07 (0.25)	0.12 (0.33)	–0.06* (0.02)	–2.39
Mother's Education	0.10 (0.30)	0.08 (0.27)	0.12 (0.33)	–0.05* (0.02)	–1.92
Age	0.56 (0.50)	0.52 (0.50)	0.60 (0.49)	–0.08** (0.04)	–2.08
Adult Diar-rhoea	0.25 (0.43)	0.29 (0.45)	0.21 (0.41)	0.08** (0.03)	2.27
Member	4.64 (1.41)	4.57 (1.28)	4.71 (1.52)	–0.14 (0.11)	–1.27
Participation	0.04 (0.19)	0.02 (0.15)	0.05 (0.21)	–0.02 (0.02)	–1.61
Semi *Pucca*	0.05 (0.22)	0.06 (0.23)	0.05 (0.21)	0.01 (0.02)	0.52
Perception	0.09 (0.29)	0.08 (0.27)	0.10 (0.30)	–0.02 (0.02)	–1.06
Location	0.61 (0.49)	0.63 (0.48)	0.60 (0.49)	0.03 (0.04)	0.86

Notes:

** indicates significance level at 5 per cent, and
* indicates significance level at 10 per cent

Binomial model is $\chi^2_{(1)} = 560.88$, and it rejects the Poisson model at one per cent level of significance. The LR statistic for testing hypothesis (2) for Poisson Hurdle model against the Negative Binomial Hurdle model is $\chi^2_{(1)} = 20.35$. Again the Poisson Hurdle model is rejected at one per cent significance level. Furthermore, the LR test statistic for testing hypothesis (3) for Poisson model against Poisson Hurdle model is $\chi^2_{(15)} = 683.96$, which allows to reject the Poisson model. For testing hypothesis (4) for the Negative Binomial model against Negative Binomial Hurdle model, the $\chi^2_{(15)} = 143.42$, which rejects the Negative Binomial model at one per cent significance level. Given that the specification tests favour the Negative Binomial Hurdle model, the analysis is based on the estimates of parameters of this model.

Presented below are results that show the factors that affect the prevalence of child diarrhoea and those that affect the duration of the disease. Unless otherwise specified, the correlations and associations are shown to be statistically significant if the level of significance is 10 per cent or lower.

The econometric results are shown in Table 12.5. Narrow-necked container, strainer and cloth, hand wash, radio and television, mother education, age, adult diarrhoea, member and perception are found to be significantly associated with the prevalence diarrhoea. For duration of diarrhoea, significant association is found with hand wash, adult diarrhoea, participation in NGO hygiene awareness activities and semi *pucca* house.

12.5.3. Prevalence of child diarrhoea

As expected, use of narrow-necked container to store water, reduces the incidence of child diarrhoea (by 11 per cent), because dirt and flies cannot quickly enter into stored water. Strangely, use of strainer showed a positive relation with child diarrhoeal attacks which is puzzling. But this can possibly be explained by the fact that households did not use strainers appropriately. For example, households using folded-cloth as strainer must ensure that the cloth is cleaned properly and in the case of metallic or plastic strainers, they need to be purified before being used. The qualitative evaluation during the household surveys suggests that this was not being done.

Hygiene practice as represented by hand wash with soap after defecation was found to be negatively associated with the prevalence of diarrhoea. It should be mentioned here that for 97 per cent of the cases, respondents were

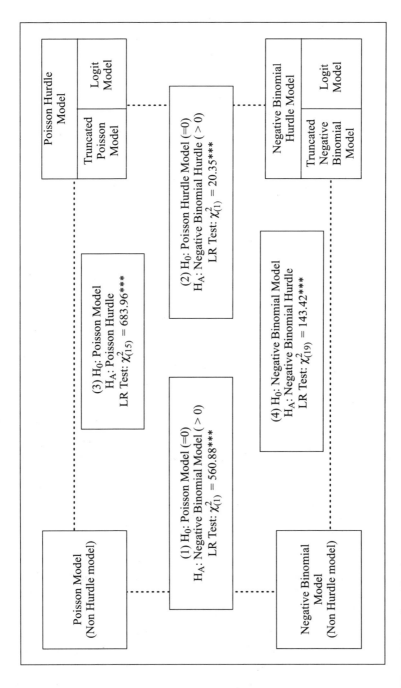

Figure 12.2.   Specification test

the mother of the child in the household. The probability of diarrhoea falls by 12 per cent if the respondents washed at least one hand after defecation with soap.

Table 12.5. Negative binomial-logit hurdle regression of the prevalence of child diarrhoea and duration

Variables	Logit regression (Diarrhoea)		Negative Binomial (Duration)		
	Marginal effect	z	Coefficients	z	Exp (Coef)
Water Availability	−0.068	−1.38	0.057	0.670	1.06
Pit	0.008	0.22	0.101	1.130	1.11
Narrow-necked Container	−0.109*	−1.83	0.046	0.380	1.05
Strainer & Cloth	0.145**	2.19	0.159	1.240	1.17
Hand Wash	−0.122***	−3.03	−0.298***	−3.660	0.74***
Radio & TV	−0.143***	−3.29	−0.088	−0.630	0.92
Mother 's Education	−0.131*	−1.86	−0.080	-0.710	0.92
Age	−0.085*	−1.92	−0.033	−0.400	0.97
Adult Diarrhoea	0.091*	1.80	0.215*	1.830	1.24*
Member	−0.027*	−1.85	−0.021	−0.650	0.98
Participation	−0.213**	−2.00	−0.372*	−1.650	0.69*
Semi *Pucca*	0.073	1.35	−0.223*	−1.900	0.80*
Perception	−0.077	−1.04	−0.074	−0.510	0.93
Location	0.035	0.68	0.061	0.610	1.06
constant			1.336	6.810	3.80
lnalpha			−2.176	−5.560	0.11

Notes:

*** indicates significance level at 1 per cent or lower,
** indicates significance level at 5 per cent, and
* indicates significance level at 10 per cent

Ownership of radio and television reduces the probability of having diarrhoea. This implies that the respondents give importance to the hygiene and health related awareness messages heard and seen over the radio and television, and also practices them in their day to day life. The probability that the child is contracted by diarrhoea falls by 13 per cent if the child's mother has education higher than primary level. This may be because higher level of education helps to develop basic ideas about health and hygiene. Age of the child is also a significant variable suggesting that as age increases children are either careful or develop physical resistance to some diarrhoeal attacks. As expected, the probability of diarrhoeal attack falls by 21 per cent if the respondent (the child's mother) participated in hygiene related awareness activities taken by the NGOs.

12.5.4. Duration of child diarrhoea episodes

To interpret the coefficients of the Negative Binomial model, the following equation is used $(e^b - 1) * 100$ (Cameron et al., 1988). The resulting number is interpreted as the per centage change in the dependent variable for a unit change in the independent variable. Whether the change is an increase or decrease depends on the sign of the resulting number derived from the equation. As an example, the coefficient of water availability is 0.057 and taking its exponential gives the number 1.06. Inputting this number in the equation gives a resulting number of six per cent. This means that as the water availability variable changes from zero to one, the duration of diarrhoea reduces by six per cent. As expected, washing at least one hand with soap after defecation reduces duration of diarrhoea episodes. Duration of diarrhoea reduces by 26 per cent for respondents who wash at least one hand as compared to those who do not.

If the child's mother participates in any NGO hygiene awareness activities, their child's diarrhoea duration is 31 per cent less than in the case of children whose mothers do not participate in such activities. It is also possible that people consider awareness activities only after being affected by diarrhoea.

There are several variables that were expected to be significantly associated with diarrhoea or duration, but were not and it is useful to identify them. These variables are water availability, type of latrine and perception that drinking contaminated water causes diarrhoea. From the econometric estimation one can sequentially identify important variables for reducing child diarrhoea – participation in NGO hygiene activities, owning a radio and television, mother's education and hand washing, and for duration – participation in NGO hygiene awareness activities, hand washing and semi *pucca* houses. From the above econometric estimation it can be clearly stated that behavioural factors reduce the probability of being affected by diarrhoea and duration as compared to engineering factors.[11]

---

[11] An anonymous reviewer suggested that variables such as hand washing, participation in NGO hygiene activities, perception of the water-diarrhoea link and adult diarrhoea were

12.6. Cost and sensitivity analysis of child diarrhoea

For calculation of the cost of diarrhoea, only households which had a child suffering from diarrhoea within the recall period of 15 days (Table 12.6) were considered. Households incurred different type of direct costs once a child had the diarrhoea attack. These were classified into: cost of treatment at home, cost of medical treatment in a hospital and cost of transportation. Home treatment costs included the cost of medicine, cost of Oral Rehydration Saline (ORS) from local shop, and cost of home-made oral saline; medical treatment costs include hospital admission fee, boarding charge, doctor's fee, cost of diagnosis and medication; and transport cost includes costs for traveling to the medical centre.

Adding the direct costs to the costs of work and leisure time given by the care-giver in the house gives the total cost of diarrhoea. The cost of

Table 12.6. Different types of cost of child diarrhoea (BDT) (15 days)

Variable	Obs	Mean	Std. Dev.	Min	Max
1. Home treatment cost (saline, doctor fee and medicine from local store)	261	92	127	3	1,000
2. Medical treatment cost (admission, sit, doctor fee, medicine)	12	140	136	5	450
3. Transport cost	13	56	80	10	300
Direct Cost (1+2+3)	*264*	*100*	*139*	*3*	*1,000*
4. Work lost due to child diarrhoea	72	148	135	6	667
5. Leisure lost due to child diarrhoea	298	152	165	7	1,346
Indirect Cost (4+5)	*298*	*188*	*188*	*7*	*1,346*
Total cost of child diarrhoea (Direct and Indirect Cost)	*298*	*276*	*273*	*13*	*1,790*

potentially endogenous. To check for endogeneity, case by case, we performed a Durbin-Wu-Hausman test on a regression of the original model but in addition included the residuals of each endogenous right hand side variable, which were estimated as a function of all exogenous variables (Davidson and MacKinnon, 1993) and one instrumental variable. We also undertook the endogeneity test jointly by including all four predicted residuals as right hand side variables along with the regular variables of the original model. We used distance between the sanitation and water source for sanitation purpose and occupation of the respondent as instruments for hand washing. For NGO participation the instrumental variable was whether the respondent is a housewife; for perception, the instruments were flood affected slum, distance from market and level of education of household members, and for adult diarrhoea the instrument was total number of day labourers in the household. Results show no endogeneity in any of the suspected variables.

lost work-time and/or leisure-time is the opportunity cost of the person taking care of the child during illness. The opportunity cost of care-giver is calculated by multiplying total hours of work time and leisure-time spent to nurse the affected child and the wage rate of the care-giver in case of an earning member. In case of non-earning members average hourly income of the family is used. This gives us the total cost of a child diarrhoea episode for an average slum household in Dhaka to be BDT 276.

Since a major proportion of the cost of each episode of diarrhoea attack is due to the value assigned to leisure-time of the care-giver a sensitivity analysis of these costs was conducted. The analyses used different weights for the hours spent for diarrhoea care by earning and non-earning members of the family (Table 12.7). The wage rate was taken if the care giver was an earning member, otherwise hourly household income was taken for calculating the opportunity cost of leisure lost.

Table 12.7. Sensitivity analysis of the cost of child diarrhoea (BDT) (15 days)

		Weight of Leisure Hours Lost (Earning Member)				
		1.00	0.75	0.50	0.25	0.00
	1.00	276	269	262	255	249
	0.75	245	238	231	224	218
Weight of Leisure Hours Lost (Non Earning Member)	0.50	214	207	200	193	186
	0.25	183	176	169	162	155
	0.00	152	145	138	131	124

The value of this leisure lost of the care-giver may not be equal to value of work time. If the leisure lost of the care-giver is considered equal to his/her value of working time, the weight given is one; when the leisure time is valued as equal to half the value of working time, the weight is 0.5. When it is assumed that leisure has no value, then the weight is 0. With these different weights for the cost of leisure time, it is found that the total cost of each episode of child diarrhoea attack ranges from BDT 124 to BDT 276 (Table 12.7).

Diarrhoea is common in slum areas throughout the year and households bear these costs at different periods in the year. The annual costs of diarrhoea for a child and for a household can be calculated based on information about monthly diarrhoea attacks and the estimated costs of diarrhoea for the recall period of 15 days using the following equation:

Yearly expected cost of a representative child for diarrhoeal disease

$$= \sum_{i=1...,12} 2W_i(\lambda\alpha_c\beta_c)C_{jk}$$

where, W_i is a weighting factor for each month of a year and for calculating the weighting factor data on monthly prevalence of diarrhoea was obtained from the clinic of Intervida Bangladesh[12]. λ is the probability of observing child diarrhoea in each household surveyed, calculated by dividing the number of affected households by the total number of surveyed households. α_c denotes the probability of being a child of the affected household, which was calculated by dividing the total number of child of the affected household by the total member of the affected households. β_c represents the probability of getting diarrhoea if the individual concerned is a child from an affected household, which was derived through dividing the number of child affected by diarrhoea by the total number of child members of the affected households (Table 12.8). C_{jk} is the weight that is given to the care giving persons leisure lost, with and without job, where j is the weight for non-earning member and k is the weight for earning member.

Table 12.8. Probability of diarrhoeal attack for a child

Variable Name	Explanation	Value
The probability household being affected from diarrhoea (λ)	324/480	0.675
The probability of being a child from affected household (α_c)	416/1479	0.281
The probability of getting diarrhoea if the individual concerned is a child from an affected household (β_c)	298/416	0.716
Average child size in a family (δ_c)	613/480	1.28

Note: 324 – Number of households affected by child diarrhoea.
       416 – Number of child from the affected household.
       479 – Total member of the 324 affected household.
       298 – Number of child affected by diarrhoea.
       613 – Total number of child from the surveyed households.
       480 – Number of households surveyed.

---

[12] Intervida Bangladesh is a NGO primarily providing education in the slum level. They have over thirty educational centres in Dhaka city slums and three primary health care centers. The enrolled students and their family members are entitled to receive treatment absolutely free of cost from these three primary health care centres.

In order to compute the weighting factor (W_i), the average prevalence of diarrhoea is first obtained in May and June (data collection period). For example, the figures for May and June were 21 and 18, and the average of these two month cases is $[(21+18)/2] = 19.5$. From Intervida Bangladesh, it was possible to find out that the average number of child diarrhoea cases for January was 6.85. Thus the weighting factor for January $(W_{i=1})$ was $(6.85/19.5) = 0.35$. This weight $(W_{i=1})$ was then multiplied with $(\lambda \alpha_c \beta_c)$ – a scalar, to compute the 15 days weight. The resulting figure is $[0.35*(0.675*0.281*0.716)] = 0.05$. As the recall period of the survey was 15 days, it was multiplied by two to compute it monthly. Therefore the monthly weight for January is $(0.05*2) = 0.10$.

Using the sensitivity on the value of leisure time of the care-giver for earning and non-earning members, the cost of an episode of child diarrhoea is BDT 276, and multiplying this with monthly weights provides the estimate for each month. Summing these monthly costs for all months gives the annual cost of diarrhoea of a child. Thus, the costs of diarrhoea per child per year is estimated to be BDT 656 (Table 12.9 and Table 12.10), which gives a weight of 100 per cent to both the leisure lost of the earning member and non earning member who takes care of the child during illness. This cost ranges from BDT 296 to BDT 656 depending on the weight given to leisure lost of caregivers (Table 12.10).

Annual cost of diarrhoea attacks on children for a representative household was also estimated. This is calculated by multiplying the monthly costs of diarrhoea per child with the average number of children per household and then summing this monthly cost over all months in the year. Thus the annual cost of diarrhoea attacks for each household is estimated to be BDT 837 (Table 12.9 and Table 12.11) with 100 per cent weight to both working member and non-earning members leisure lost. The yearly cost of diarrhoea for a representative household varied between BDT 378 to BDT 837 depending on the weights given to the leisure lost of the earning member and non earning member (Table 12.11).

Table 12.9. Yearly cost of child diarrhoea

Month	Number of Children Affected by Diarrhoea[Φ]			Average Case	Weighting Factor (W_i)	15 Days Weight	Monthly Weight	Cost of a Representative Child[Ψ]	Cost of a Representative Household for Children[Ψ]
	2005	2006	2007						
January	6	5	10	6.85	0.35	0.05	0.10	26	34
February	7	10	6	7.49	0.38	0.05	0.10	29	37
March	9	13	11	10.87	0.56	0.08	0.15	42	54
April	9	17	26	17.52	0.90	0.12	0.24	68	86
May	17	15	31	21.21	1.09	0.15	0.30	82	104
June	21	16	16	17.73	0.91	0.12	0.25	68	87
July	24	14	21	19.67	1.01	0.14	0.27	76	97
August	10	9	20	12.98	0.67	0.09	0.18	50	64
September	24	8	14	15.07	0.77	0.11	0.21	58	74
October	20	20	10	16.39	0.84	0.11	0.23	63	81
November	11	13	19	14.39	0.74	0.10	0.20	55	71
December	17	8	5	9.98	0.51	0.07	0.14	38	49
Yearly								656	837

Note:

[Φ] Data collected from health clinic in the slums of Intervida Bangladesh. Data corresponds to two slums for 2005 and 2006 and three slums for 2007. The data corresponding to the months shows the number of child seeking treatment from the health clinic suffering from diarrhoea in the respective years

[Ψ] 100 per cent weights to leisure lost

Table 12.10. Yearly expected cost (BDT) of a representative child diarrhoea

		Weight of Leisure Hours Lost (Earning Member)				
		1	0.75	0.5	0.25	0
Weight of Leisure Hours	1	656	639	623	607	591
Lost	0.75	582	566	549	533	517
(Not Earning Member)	0.5	508	492	476	459	443
	0.25	434	418	402	386	370
	0	361	344	328	312	296

Table 12.11. Yearly expected cost (BDT) of a representative household for children

		Weight of Leisure Hours Lost (Earning Member)				
		1	0.75	0.5	0.25	0
Weight of Leisure Hours	1	837	817	796	775	754
Lost	0.75	743	722	702	681	660
(Not Earning Member)	0.5	649	628	608	587	566
	0.25	555	534	513	493	472
	0	461	440	419	398	378

12.7. Conclusions and policy recommendations

In this study, the presence of child diarrhoea in the slums of Dhaka is first examined. It is found that socio-economic variables such as owning a radio and television, education of the mother and participation in NGO hygiene awareness activities reduce the probability of diarrhoea prevalence. Participating in NGO hygiene awareness activities and semi *pucca* houses contribute to a reduction in the duration of childhood diarrhoea. Behavioural factors, such as use of narrow-necked container reduces the probability of child diarrhoea, while hand washing with soap after defecation reduces both the probability of diarrhoea and the duration of child diarrhoea. For example, the probability of diarrhoea in children falls by 12 per cent if the respondents washed at least one hand after defecation with soap. Thus, this study suggests that NGO and media campaigns should focus on water storage and hand washing issues.

The role of the mother is very important in stemming childhood diarrhoea. This is a result that emerges from many studies but is worth strongly reinforcing. This study suggests that primary education of mothers contributes to a 13 per cent reduction in the prevalence of diarrhoea, participation of the respondent (in 97 per cent of the cases respondents were the mother of the child) in NGO hygiene awareness reduces the average duration of diarrhoea by 31 per cent and diarrhoea prevalence falls significantly if they practise good hygiene and washes her hands after defecation.

It should be noted that on average only 10 per cent of the unaffected household respondents perceived that drinking contaminated water causes diarrhoea. There is clearly an urgent need to increase awareness about the link between water contamination and diarrhoea. Health and hygiene awareness campaigns by the NGOs and the media should get this message out swiftly to reduce the burden of diarrhoea on children.

The study estimates that the average duration of an episode of child diarrhoea in Dhaka slums is 3.76 days. The direct cost per episode of child diarrhoea, which includes cost of home treatment, medical treatment and transport costs, is BDT 100. However, if the opportunity cost of the time of the care giver who takes care of the sick child during an episode of diarrhoea is taken into account, then the average cost per episode of child diarrhoea is BDT 276 (US $4).

The cost of diarrhoea per episode varies according to assumptions made about the value of leisure time. It is therefore estimated, that the costs could vary between BDT 124 (US $1.81) to BDT 276 (US $4) per episode of child diarrheoa. Using the same set of assumptions, the expected annual cost of child diarrhoea attacks ranges from BDT 296 (US $4.29) to BDT 656 (US $9.52), and the annual cost of child diarrhoea for a representative household ranges from BDT 378 (US $5.49) or about 0.6 per cent of household income to BDT 837 (US $12.15) or 1.31 per cent of household income.

How do these costs compare to child diarrhoea cost estimates from other studies? As indicated in the initial literature review, few studies take into account the opportunity cost of time. Dasgupta (2004) found the direct cost of child diarrhoea to be US $1.94 per episode in India, Gokhale (2002) found it to be US $5.64 per episode in India, while in Indonesia it was estimated to be US $2.27 (Lerman et al., 1985). Simply taking the direct costs and opportunity cost of work lost by the care giver, the current study estimates the cost of child diarrhoea to be US $1.81 (BDT 124) per episode, which falls only slightly below this range. However, if the cost of leisure lost of the care giver is taken into account, the cost of child diarrhoea comes to US $4, which falls in the range from previous studies.

The analyses of factors that affect diarrhoea prevalence suggest that behavioural factors have more influence on the risk of child diarrhoea attacks and the duration of diarrhoea than the engineering factors. Therefore, policy measures should focus on specific issues such as the use of narrow-necked containers, hand washing with soap after defection and promoting hygiene related awareness activities.

References

Alam, M. J., 'Water Quality Tests and Behavioral Factors of Child Diarrhoea in Dhaka Slums', *BRAC University Journal*, Vol. IV No. 1, (2007), 103–109.

Alberini, A., Eskeland, G.S., Krupnick, A. and McGranahan, G., 'Determinants of Diarrhoeal Disease in Jakarta', Policy Research Working Paper No. 1568, The World Bank, Policy Research Department, Public Economics Division, 1996.

Bern, C., Martines, J., de Zoysa, I. and Glass, R.I., 'The Magnitude of the Global Problem of Diarrhoeal Disease: A Ten-Year Update', *Bulletin of the World Health Organization*, 70, (1992), 705–714.

Cameron, A.C., and Trivedi, P. K., '*Supplement to Microeconometrics: Methods and Applications*', (New York: Cambridge University Press, 2005).

Cameron, A.C., and Trivedi, P. K., 'Econometrics Models based on Count Data: Comparison and Applications of some Estimators and Tests', *Journal of Applied Econometrics*, 1, (1986), 29–53.

Cameron, A.C., Trivedi, P.K., Milne, F. and Piggott, J. 'A Microeconometric Model of the Demand for Health Care and Health Insurance in Australia', *Review of Economics Studies*, Vol. 55, (1988).

Checkley, W., Gilman, R.H., Black, R.E., Epstein, L.D., Cabrera, L., Sterling, C. and Moulton, L., 'Effect of Water and Sanitation on Childhood Health in a Poor Peruvian Peri-urban Community', *Lancet*, 10, 363(9403), (2004), 112–118.

Country Profile of India. http://72.14.235.104/search?q=cache:mbv5YjItPLsJ:lcwe b2.loc.gov/frd/cs/profiles/India.pdf+indian+exchange+rate+in+2004&hl=bn& ct=clnk&cd=20&gl=bd , visited 18.02.08.

Dasgupta, P., 'Valuing Health Damages from Water Pollution in Urban Delhi, India: A Health Production Function Approach', *Environment and Development Economics*, 9, (2004), 83–106.

Davidson, R. and Mackinon, J.G., '*Estimation and Inference in Econometrics*', (New York: Oxford University Press, 1993).

De Soárez, P.C., Valentim, J., Sartori, A.M.C. and Novaes, H.M.D. 'Cost-effectiveness analysis of routine rotavirus vaccination in Brazil', *Rev Panam Salud Publica*, 23(4), (2008), 221–230.

Fewtrell, L., Kaufmann, R.B., Ray, D., Enanoria, W., Laurence, H. and MColford, J.M. Jr., 'Water, Sanitation, and Hygiene Interventions to Reduce Diarrhoea in

Less Developed Countries: A Systematic Review and Meta-Analysis', *Lancet Infect Dis.*, 5, (2005), 42–52.

Food and Nutrition Bulletin, 'The Prevention and Control of Diarrhoeal Diseases', The United Nations University Press, 4 (1), 1982.

Gokhale, 'Cost Analysis of Diarrhoea Treatment in the Infectious Diseases Hospital in Pune city', *Indian Journal of Community Medicine*, (2002).

Gomez, J.A., Nates, S., De Castagnaro, N.R., Espul, C., Borsa, A. and Glass, R.I., 'Anticipating Rotavirus Vaccines: Review of Epidemiologic Studies or Rotavirus Diarrhoea in Argentina', *Rev Panam Salud Publica*, 3(2), (1998), 69–78.

Greene, W.H., *Econometric Analysis*, 5th Edition, (New York: Pearson Education, 2007).

Han, A. and T. Hlaing, 'Prevention of diarrhoea and dysentery by hand washing', Transactions of the Royal Society of Tropical Medicine Hygiene 83, (1989), 128–131.

Haque, A.K.E., Chaudhury, M. and Abbasi, P.K., 'Demand for Water in DWASA Zones (2005–2030)', Research Monograph, Institute of Water Modelling, Dhaka, 2007.

Harrington, W. and Portney, P.R., 'Valuing the Benefits of Health and Safety Regulation', *Journal of Urban Economics*, 22(1), (1987), 101–112.

Hoque, B.A., Chakraborty, J., Chowdhury, J.T., Chowdhury, U.K., Ali, M., Arifeen, S. and Sack, R.B., 'Effects of Environmental Factors on Child Survival in Bangladesh: A Case Control Study', *Public Health,* 113(2), (1999), 57–64.

Jalan, J. and Ravallion, M., 'Does Piped Water Reduce Diarrhoea for Children in Rural India?', *Journal of Econometrics*, 112, (2003), 153–173.

Knight, S.M., Toodayan, W., Caique, W.C., Kyin, W., Barnes, A. and Desmarchelier, P., 'Risk Factors for the Transmission of Diarrhoea in Children: a Case-control Study in Rural Malaysia', *International Journal of Epidemiology* , 21(4), (1992), 812– 818.

Kosek, M., Bern, C. and Guerrant, R., 'The Global Burden of Diarrhoeal Disease as Estimated from Studies Published Between 1992 and 2000', *Bulletin of the World Health Organization,* 81, (2003), 197–204.

Lerman, S.J., Shepard, D.S. and Cash, R.A., 'Treatment of Diarrhoea in Indonesian Children: What it Costs and Who Pays for It', *Lancet*, 21, (1985), 651–654.

Luby, S.P., Thorpe, P. and Molla, M.S.I., 'Documenting effects of the July-August floods of 2004 and ICDDR,B's response', *Health and Science Bulletin*, 2(3), (2004), 1–6.

Mirza, N.M., Caulfield, L.E., Black, R.E. and Macharia, W.M., 'Risk Factors for Diarrhoeal Duration', *American Journal of Epidemiology*, 146(9), (1997).

Mullahy, J., 'Specification and Testing of Some Modified Count Data Models', *Journal of Econometrics,* 33, (1986), 341–365.

Mohaghan, M.J. and Mohaghan, M.S., 'Do Market Components Account for Higher U.S. Prescription Prices?', *Ann Pharmacother*, 30, (1996), 1429–1494.

Noronha, K.V.M., and Andrade, M.V., 'Social Inequality in the Access to Healthcare Services in Brazil', CEDEPLAR/FACE/UFMG, BELO HORIZONTE (2002).

Patel, A.B., Dhande, L.A., Rawat, M.S., 'Economic Evaluation of Zinc and Copper Use in Treating Acute Diarrhoea in Children: A Randomoized Controlled Trial', *Cost Effectiveness and Resource Allocation*, 1(7), (2003).

Perú, Ministerio de Salud, *Seminario Modernización del Sistema de Financiamiento de Salud 1997: análisis de costos de los servicios de salud*, (Lima: MINSA, 1997).

Phelps, C.E., 'International Comparison of Health Care System', *Health Economics*, (New York: Harper Collins Publisher Inc., 1992), 234–235, 483–509.

Pohlmeier, W. and Ulrich, V., 'An Econometric Model of the Two-Part Decisionmaking Process in the Demand for Health Care', *The Journal of Human Resources*, 30(2), (1995), 339–361.

Poverty Reduction Strategy Paper, 'A National Strategy for Economic Growth, Poverty Reduction and Social Development (PRSP)', Economic Relations Division, Ministry of Finance, Bangladesh, 2002.

Pramanik.http://rdgs.itakura.toyo.ac.jp/ORC/actprog/sympojium_20030704/Pramanik.pdf visited 05.02.08.

Soarez, P., et al., 'Cost of Rotavirus and Nonrotavirus Diarrhoea among young children in Brazil', Paper presented at the Annual Meeting of the Economics of Population Health: Inaugural Conference of the American Society of Health Economists, TBA, Madison, WI, USA, June 04, 2006.

Snyder, J.D. and Merson, M.H., 'The Magnitude of the Global Problem of Acute Diarrhoeal Disease: A Review of Active Surveillance Data', *Bulletin of the World Health Organization*, 60, (1982), 605–613.

'Water, Sanitation and Hygiene Promotion: A National Strategy for Economic Growth, Poverty Reduction and Social Development', Poverty Reduction Strategy Paper, March 5, 2003.

World Health Organization WHO, 'WHO SITREP Floods in Bangladesh', 26 August, 2007.

World Health Organization WHO. http://www.who.int/topics/cholera/en/

World Health Organization WHO, WHO/V&B/01.22, (2001).

World Health Organization WHO, 'The World Health Report 2004', WHO, Geneva, Switzerland, 2004.

World Health Statistics, (2007), 23.

13

Red Wells, Green Wells and the Costs of Arsenic Contamination in Bangladesh

M. Zakir Hossain Khan and A.K. Enamul Haque[1]

13.1. Introduction

Bangladesh, along with Nepal and the state of West Bengal in India, is facing a major disaster because of arsenic contamination of groundwater aquifers. Arsenic is a natural mineral that is present in the soil and aquifers of these countries. Where it is present in concentrations above the safe level[2] in drinking water, it can cause significant health risks. In Bangladesh, the Bangladesh Arsenic Mitigation Water Supply Project estimates that nearly 30 per cent of all tube wells in the 258 *Upazilas* of Bangladesh have an arsenic content higher than the recommended safe limit.[3] This means that an estimated 27 per cent to 60 per cent of the population is at risk from arsenic exposure (Smith, Lingas and Rahman, 2000).

Historically, Bangladesh has been a forerunner in South Asia in terms of providing its population with access to safe drinking water. It had achieved safe access to water for 97 per cent of its population and had been successful

---

[1] This study has been conducted with financial support from the South Asian Network for Development and Environmental Economics (SANDEE) and was part of Zakir Hussain's M.S. thesis. A.K. Enamul Haque was his supervisor. Priya Shyamsundar, SANDEE Program Director, significantly improved this work through her meticulous reading and questions. Authors remain grateful to Sajjad Zohir (the executive director of the Economic Research Group) for his insightful comments throughout the period of the study. Furthermore feedback from Jeff Vincent, Maureen Cropper, and M. N. Murty enriched the study at various stages.

[2] Recommended safe limit for Bangladesh is 50ppb (parts per billion) but the WHO safe limit is 10ppb.

[3] Department of Public Health and Engineering, Bangladesh, December 2005.

in containing the cholera outbreaks which had plagued the country for centuries. This was possible because the government of Bangladesh with assistance from organizations like UNICEF worked in the seventies and eighties to shift existing sources of drinking water to tube wells in most parts of rural Bangladesh. However, since the discovery of arsenic in ground water in the nineties, Bangladesh has been struggling once again with the problem of delivering safe water. As a quick-fix, the government launched an awareness campaign to inform people about the presence of arsenic in their drinking water sources (tube-wells, in most cases) through a binary colour-coding system. All tube-wells that were safe, i.e., where the water in them was safe for drinking and cooking, were given a green colour while those coloured red were proclaimed to be unsafe. Red-coloured tube-wells are designated as appropriate for other uses. However, it appears that either due to limited alternative safe sources of water or for other reasons, many households continue to use water from the 'unsafe' red-coloured tube-wells.

Interventions to supply arsenic-free drinking water require varying investments at the community level as well as at the level of the household. So one needs to know, how much households would be willing to pay for arsenic-free water. The aim of this chapter is to address this question by estimating the costs that households bear as a result of their exposure to arsenic contaminated water. Using the cost-of-illness approach, the total expenditure that households incur due to sickness is assessed and the benefits of switching from red to green wells are thereby identified.

13.2. Background

Much of Bangladesh is a deltaic plain crisscrossed with huge rivers such as the Ganges, Brahmaputra, Megna and the Teesta. The total population of Bangladesh is 129 million (Census 2001) which makes it one of the most densely populated countries in the world. The per capita Gross Domestic Product (GDP) of Bangladesh is US $444 (BER, 2005) and has been growing between four and six per cent in the past decades. Access to clean water has been a major development target of the Government of Bangladesh. Until the discovery of arsenic, it was thought that 97 per cent of households had access to clean water – this number is now reduced to 74 per cent.[4]

---

[4] http://lcgbangladesh.org/prsp/docs/257,2, an overview.

According to the Bangladesh Arsenic Mitigation and Water Supply Project (BAMWSP) – a major World Bank-funded government project – out of four million tube-wells installed in Bangladesh, 1.2 million have been found contaminated with arsenic (www.bamwsp.org). What is startling here is that the arsenic concentration level in 30–40 per cent wells of the affected area is over 50 µg/liter (World Bank, 2001), much above the safe limit of 0.5µg/liter. In terms of people being affected, DPHE estimated that 38,380 individuals have symptoms of *arsenicosis* or other variant arsenic-affected diseases in Bangladesh (DPHE, 2005). However, this might be just the tip of the iceberg because screening done by BAMWSP reveals nearly 1.1 cases of *arsenicosis* per thousand people (World Bank, 2002).

Several studies exist on arsenic contamination and related geological, scientific, epidemiological, technological, and health aspects. Smith, et al. (1999), for example, show that arsenic contamination may be responsible for bladder and lung cancer rather than other types of cancer. Zaldiver and Guiller (1977) discuss, in the context of Taiwan and Argentina, how 'poor nutrition in children favors toxicity to arsenic.' Likewise, Rahman, Quamruzzaman and Dash (2000) have found incidences of *arsenicosis* in children to be as high as 17 per cent in Bangladesh.

The primary pathway to *arsenicosis* is prolonged exposure through drinking arsenic-contaminated water.[5] It usually takes five to twenty years to develop and, because of its slow process of development, the evolution of the disease is divided into several stages:

(a) *Primary Stage – Melanosis, Keratosis, Conjunctivitis, Gastroenteritis.* In the primary stage, an *arsenicosis* patient may develop several symptoms, sometimes simultaneously, such as the blackening of some parts of the body or the whole body (*Melanosis*); thickening and roughness of the palms and soles (*Keratosis*); redness of the conjunctiva (*Conjunctivitis*); inflammation of the respiratory tract; and nausea and vomiting (*Gastroenteritis*).

(b) *Secondary Stage – Lekonelanosis, Hyper-keratosis, Non-pitting Edema.* If a patient continues to be exposed to arsenic-contaminated water, and if adequate preventive measures are not adopted, then the symptoms advance and become more visible including white intermittent dots within blackened areas (called *Leukonelanosis* or Rain Drop Syndrome), nodular growth on the palms and soles (*Hyper-keratosis*),

---

[5] Absorption of arsenic through the skin is minimal. Thus hand-washing, bathing, laundry, etc., with water containing arsenic do not pose human health risks.

swelling of the feet and legs (Non-pitting *edema*), and peripheral neuropathy as well as liver and kidney disorders.

(c) *Final or Tertiary Stage* – At the tertiary stage, an *arsenicosis* patient's physical condition deteriorates rapidly and the condition becomes irreversible. Gangrene of the distal organs or other parts of the body, cancer of the skin, lungs and urinary bladder, and kidney and liver failure become manifest at this stage.

The National Institute of Preventive and Social Medicine (NIPSOM), Bangladesh, estimates that 50 million people are at risk of developing *arsenicosis*, with *melanosis* and *keratosis* as the most common. According to them, people who are already diagnosed with *arsenicosis* are reported to be either in the primary or in the secondary stage and the number of such patients is increasing.

13.3. Methods

13.3.1. Valuation of benefits of arsenic water

As discussed in Chapter 2, economists have attempted to estimate the costs associated with a decline in environmental quality or alternatively the benefits accruing from an improvement in environmental quality in a number of different ways and for numerous pollutants. A frequently used technique is the cost of illness approach, which generally includes the wage losses associated with sick days and the medical expenditures undertaken to recover from sickness resulting from pollution. For example, Tolley and Fabian (1994) used the cost of illness approach to estimate Willingness-To-Pay (WTP) for reductions in human health problems and risks, while Dickie and Gerking (1991) and Gerking and Stanely (1996) studied the value of air quality improvements based on household expenditures on medical care. Alberini's (1997) study on air pollution related impacts in Taiwan, a well-known empirical assessment, uses the cost of illness method.

Another approach seen in the literature estimates the costs associated with avertive actions or the economic loss incurred by the household in attempting to avoid exposure to pollution. Abdalla, Roach and Epp (1992), for example, estimated averting expenditures to assess the costs of contaminated groundwater.

In Bangladesh, Ahmad et. al., (2002), estimated WTP for piped water supply projects using the Contingent Valuation (CV) method. This study estimated that WTP for a community water stand post is Bangladesh Taka (BDT) 51 per month plus an additional BDT 960 towards capital costs. For domestic connections, the mean estimate is BDT 87 per month plus BDT 1787 for capital expenses. For poor households, the costs are BDT 44 per month and BDT 838 towards capital costs for a stand post and BDT 68 per month and BDT 1401 in capital costs for a home connection. There is, however, a general concern against using the CV method because it uses stated preferences and so is affected by several types of biases inherent in such studies[6].

This study begins by adopting the cost of illness plus the avertive expenditure approach to measure the private cost of arsenic exposure in rural Bangladesh. These costs are in addition to public costs both in terms of public health interventions by the government of Bangladesh and by thousands of NGOs working in rural communities to find safe drinking water sources. The private costs measured in this study should be viewed as the minimum WTP for people in rural areas who live in the contaminated zones. The basic theory relates to the household health production function discussed in Chapter 2 of this book.

A household is assumed to maximize utility subject to a full-income budget constraint:

$$U\left(\cdot\right) = U\left(X, L, S; H_i\right) \tag{1}$$

where, X is the amount of consumption of private goods and services, L is the amount of time spent in leisure, S is the number of sick days and H_i is a vector of characteristics of the individual like education, health status, wealth, etc.

Following Freeman (1993), it can be shown that an individual determines his/her choice of consumption of goods and services and mitigation/averting activities based on income, cost of medical and averting activities, level of contamination of water, health status, and household characteristics. The marginal willingness-to-pay for a reduction in pollution (or an improvement in environmental quality) is given by:

$$MWTP = w\frac{dS}{dR} + P_A\frac{\partial A^*}{\partial R} + P_M\frac{\partial M^*}{\partial R} - \frac{\partial U\!\!\Big/\!\!\partial S}{\lambda}\frac{dS}{dR} \tag{2}$$

where, S is the number of work days lost due to sickness, A is the averting activity undertaken, M refers to mitigating activities (illness and medicine

---

[6] See Chapter 2 of this book.

related), R is the level of contamination, w is the wage, and P_A and P_M are the price of averting and mitigating activities and λ refers to the marginal utility of investment in mitigating and averting expenses to get rid of sickness. It should be noted that variables with asterisk (*) are measured at the optimal level.

Because of difficulties in estimating the last term in equation (2), which measures disutility from sickness, valuation studies often estimate a lower bound for the MWTP, as given in equation (3),

$$MWTP = w\frac{dS}{dR} + P_A\frac{\partial A^*}{\partial R} + P_M\frac{\partial M^*}{\partial R} \tag{3}$$

where MWTP is the sum of a) cost due to work days lost, b) cost due to adoption of averting activities, and c) cost of mitigating activities. Note that all these are expenses or losses incurred at individual or at household level and hence are private costs. The true cost of arsenic contamination, however, will include both public and private cost. In Bangladesh, health services are provided free or at a nominal fee at the local level since most of the hospitals are funded through bilateral or multilateral donor agreements and by the government. Therefore, the true cost of illness due to arsenic contamination in water for Bangladesh is likely to be much larger than this.

Estimating the MWTP from the equation (3) requires resolving several empirical problems, which are presented in different chapters of this book (see for example, Gupta in Chapter 11) and Bogahawatte and Herath (in chapter 14 of this book). This chapter uses probit models to estimate the probability of sickness (a dose-response function) and the probability of incurring mitigating (medical) costs. This information is used to empirically estimate the MWTP. The avertive activities component of MWTP is not included for reasons discussed in section 13.4.3.

13.3.2. Data

The data for this study comes from a survey of 5563 individuals from 878 households, which was undertaken in two *Upazilas* (sub-districts), Matlab and Lakshan, in 2005. These *Upazilas* are located in the southeastern part of Bangladesh, which is the most arsenic prone region. To determine the sample frame, the database of the Department of Public Health Engineering (DPHE) was used and households were randomly chosen for the survey. Although the two *Upazilas* are located within a 50 km distance from each other, one of them, Matlab, is an area where health-related interventions are very high due to its historic linkage with the International Centre for Diarrheal Diseases Research, Bangladesh (ICDDRB).

In terms of the level of contamination by arsenic, the two *Upazilas* are very similar. According to DPHE data, nearly 0.159 per cent of the people in Laksham are affected by at least one of the variants of *arsenicosis* while 0.106 per cent of the people are affected in Matlab. Only 24 per cent tube-wells in Matlab and 32 per cent tube-wells in Lakshan are labeled safe (DPHE, 2005).

A two-step procedure was used to select the households for the survey. In the first stage, 900 tube wells were randomly chosen (450 from each *Upazila*) for the survey from seven Unions[7]. Since the same tube well is shared by several households, at the second stage, one household from each tube well user group was selected randomly. The total number of households ultimately used in this study was 878.

The data collected for this study includes three general classes of information – (a) household level information to determine the general characteristics of the household in terms of income and wealth; (b) health, demographic, and socio-economic characteristics by individuals (each enumerator was trained to identify different variants of *arsenicosis* based on the symptoms of arsenic diseases); and (c) work days lost, income loss, sick days, and averting and mitigating activities both at household level and at the individual level. Avertive activities here refer to actions taken by the households to avoid the use of contaminated water. Mitigating activities refer to doctor and hospital visits.

Tables 13.1 and 13.2 provide a brief summary of statistics at the individual and household levels. The average age of the individuals in the sample is 28 years and the average year of schooling is five years[8] while height and weight of the individuals are 55.10 inches and 41.66 kg respectively. Fifty per cent of the sample individuals are male.

To determine the wealth status of the household, a list of assets for each household was collected. Using this list, a wealth index was developed, which provides a relative scale on wealth for each household. The maximum value of the index was 100 and the minimum value was 0. A total of 43 types

---

[7] Administratively, Bangladesh is divided into several tiers: Division, District, *Upazila,* Union, Ward and Village. Unions are the second tier of local government institutions.

[8] Households use several sources of water for drinking, cooking, bathing, and washing purposes. Based on their responses, this per centage was calculated keeping in view that households using shallow aquifers for drinking and cooking purposes are likely to be at risk.

of assets were included in the calculation of the wealth index. Of the 43 assets, 32 were listed as household assets and the other 11 were listed as productive assets.

Table 13.1. Household level information

Household Information	Mean	SD	N=878 Remarks
Wealth index[9]	51.64	12.40	Index
Family size	6.33		Number of persons
Family size (adult >= 14 years)	4.53		
Technology adoption (averting)	19.88	0.40	Per cent
Cost of technology (averting)	3217	3279.44	Taka
Medicare bills (annual)	11618 116	7844	Taka per year
Operation and maintenance cost (averting technology)	13.04	75.53	Taka per year
Participation in NGO activities	32.00	0.71	Per cent
Highest educational achievement in the family	9.4	3.1	Years of schooling
Per cent of families reported sickness	19.36	0.40	Per cent
Per cent of families drinking water from shallow aquifer sources	86.23	0.345	per cent

Source: Survey Data

Since Bangladesh is a hotspot for NGO activities, there are many non-governmental organizations in the area are involved in raising people's level of awareness against drinking water from arsenic-contaminated sources. Survey data shows that 32 per cent of households had attended such programmes organized by NGOs. In Bangladesh, NGOs cover nearly 50 per cent of the rural population in terms of their activities (Haque, 2005).

---

[9] Based on the information found in the survey, the study also constructed a wealth index for each household based on the HDI of UNDP.

$$WI_i = \left[\frac{\sum_1^{43} a_{ij} - \min(a_{ji})}{\max(a_{ji}) - \min(a_{ji})} \times 100 \right]$$

where, j refers to the holding of i number of assets (a) and a_{ij} = 1 if the ith household has the jth asset, and 0 = otherwise, i = 1,2,3, … m representing households, and j = 1,2,3, … n representing the assets available at the household. The minimum of a_{ji} means holdings by j[th] household of the lowest number of i assets

In terms of drinking water sources by the household, 46 per cent of households in the sample use either a tube well or hand pump as the primary drinking water source. Only 11.5 per cent people use water from deep tube wells as the source of drinking water. Less than 0.5 per cent people use filters and only 0.2 per cent use water from Arsenic Removal Plants (ARP). This clearly shows the extent of vulnerability of the local people in terms of *arsenicosis*.

Table 13.2. Individual level information

Individual Level Information	Mean	SD	N = 5563 Comments
Age	27.49	20.251	Years
Male	50.40 per cent		Male
Education	5.17	4.150	Years
Per cent mitigating	12.21		Per cent
Sick days (non working days [WDL])	5.29	2.016	Days per year
Melanosis (incidence)	3.52		Per cent
Keratosis (incidence)	2.77		Per cent
Conjunctivitis (incidence)	1.76		Per cent
Inflammation of RT (incidence)	1.87		Per cent
Hypo-pigmentation (incidence)	2.88		Per cent
Hyper Keratosis (incidence)	1.10		Per cent
Non-pitting *Edema* (incidence)	0.43		Per cent
Liver and Kidney failure (incidence)	0.068		per cent

Source: Survey 2005. SD = Standard Deviation.

In the study area, a large number of tube wells (though not all) have been marked red (unsafe for drinking) or green (safe) by the government. Survey data shows that 56 per cent of households still drink water from red-labeled tube wells. Further, since all the tube wells are not colour-coded, it is possible that 86 per cent of the households (see Table 13.1), who state that they drink water from shallow aquifer sources, may also be exposed to arsenic.

The survey also collected data on individuals, which is presented in Table 13.2. The survey suggests that five per cent of all the people surveyed have at least one of the various types of *arsenicosis* – four per cent have black spots or *Melanosis*, three per cent have thickening or roughness of palms and soles (*Keratosis*), two per cent have redness in eyes or *Conjunctivitis*, two per cent have inflammation of respiratory tract, 0.43 per cent have swelling of the feet and legs and .068 per cent suffer from liver and kidney failure.

Table 13.3 shows the percentage of cases found with variants of *arsenicosis* amongst people who reported that they were sick from arsenic. Most of the individuals with arsenic-related diseases report their diseases to be in the primary stage. Fifty seven per cent of sick individuals' symptoms related to *Conjunctivitis*, while 34.3 per cent were suffering from *Keratosis*, 45.7 per cent from respiratory problems and 46.4 per cent people from gastrological problems. These figures suggest that the extent of *arsenicosis* is much more severe than is commonly thought.

Table 13.3. Distribution of arsenic related diseases among sick households

Different Arsenic Diseases	Arsenic-Related Diseases	Per cent of Cases
Primary Stage	Melanosis or black spots in the body	8.6
	Keratosis or thickening of the palms and soles	34.3
	Redness of the eye or conjunctivitis	58.6
	Inflammation of the respiratory system	45.7
	Gastrointestinal problem	46.4
Secondary Stage	Hypo-pigmentation or white spots	5.7
	Hyper-keratosis or nodular growth	15
	Swelling of the feet and legs	12.1
	Peripheral Neuropathy	17.1
	Liver or kidney disorder	7.1
Tertiary or Final Stage	Gangrene of the distal organs	3.6
	Cancer of the skin, lung or urine	2.9
	Liver or kidney failure	2.1

Source: Survey 2005

13.3.4. *Empirical model*

In order to estimate the marginal willingness-to-pay for arsenic-free water given in equation (3), three functions need to be estimated. Freeman's (1993) model provides the basis for estimating a dose-response function for sickness and two demand functions for mitigating and avertive activities.

The demand for mitigating activities is given by:

$$M^* = M^*(y, w, P_M, P_A, R, A_W, H_S, H_i) \qquad (4)$$

The demand for averting activities is given by:

$$A^* = A^*(y, w, R, P_M, P_A, A_W, H_S, H_i) \qquad (5)$$

The dose-response function for workdays lost[10] (S) is:

$$S = S(R, M^*, A^*, A_W, H_S, H_i) \qquad (6)$$

Where, w is wage income, y is non-wage income, P_M is cost (price) of mitigating activities, P_A cost (price) of averting activities, R is level of arsenic contamination, Aw is level of awareness, H_S is health status, and H_i is household characteristics. Mitigation activities, M, refer to actions undertaken to reduce the effects of arsenic related sickness and include medical expenses, fees paid to doctors or pharmacists, and travel costs. Averting activities, A, include adoption of different measures to reduce exposure to arsenic. These included switching the source of water to another 'safe' surface or ground water source, harvesting rain water, or using technologies such as the three pitcher method to purify water.

Survey data showed that households with arsenic-affected patients did not have significant amount of either averting or mitigating expenses, probably due to their poor income status. Consequently, instead of using continuous data on mitigating or averting actions, binary variables were used. Thus, mitigating activities take the value 1 if an individual has any medical expenditure and 0 otherwise. Similarly, avertive activities are a binary variable that takes the value 1 if the individual undertakes any avertive actions and zero otherwise.

Only 82 individuals out of more than 3260 individuals with some form of sickness reported Work Days Lost (WDL) due to sickness. The actual number of work-days lost was 5.29 per year. It is possible that perhaps due to poverty, people could not afford to absent themselves from work. Thus in the empirical analyses of this study, sickness is also treated as a binary variable, which takes the value of 1 if the individual reported arsenic-related sickness and 0 otherwise.

The empirical model of equation (3) for estimating marginal willingness to pay (for an individual i) is thus modified as below:

$$MWTP_i = w_i \times \overline{WDL_i} \times P_i(S \,|\, \Delta R) + \overline{M_i} \times P(M \,|\, \Delta R) + \qquad (7)$$
$$\beta_A \times P(S \,|\, \Delta R) \times P(A > 0)/z$$
$$= (A) \quad + \quad (B) \quad + \quad (C)$$

---

[10] Work days lost is equal to or less than the sick days.

where $P(S|\Delta R)$ is the marginal effect or change in the probability of sickness (related to arsenic poisoning) for an individual due to changes in exposure to arsenic poisoning, ΔR is expected changes in the dose of arsenic poisoning in water; w is the average wage of the adult working population, $\overline{WDL}$ is the mean workdays lost, $\overline{M}$ is the mean mitigating expenditure per individual when he/she is affected with arsenic-related diseases and $P(M|\Delta R)$ is the changes in the probability of incurring mitigating expenses due to changes in the level of exposure at the individual level. β_A is the estimated co-efficient of averting expenses when the level of exposure to arsenic changes and measures the marginal changes in the averting expenses due to changes in the level of exposure; $P(A>0)$ is the probability of taking averting measures at the household level; the subscript i refers to individual member-based information; z refers to the number of members in a household.

(a) $w_i \times WDL_i \times P_i(S|\Delta R)$ measures the marginal impact in terms of income loss due to changes in the level of exposure to arsenic (ΔR);

(b) $\overline{M}_i \times P_i(M|\Delta R)$ measures the marginal change in mitigating expenditure due to changes in the exposure to arsenic poisoning; and

(c) $\beta_A \times P_i(S|\Delta R) \times P(A>0)/z$ measures the marginal effect on averting activities at the individual level due to changes in the exposure. The first two terms measure the effect on averting expenses due to changes in exposure to risk.

13.4. Results

13.4.1. Estimating the sickness dose-response function

The first step in the empirical analysis is to estimate the probability of sickness defined in equation (7). The probability estimates in equation (7) are derived using a probit model by maximizing the following log-likelihood function.

$$L = \sum (Y_i LnF(x, \beta) + (1 - Y_i) Ln(1 - F(x, \beta)))$$ (8)

where x is a vector of independent variables and βs are the coefficients. x includes: (a) individual level information such as age measured in years (AGE and AGESQ), sex measured as a binary variable (MALE), and education measured in years (EDUC); (b) household wealth index (WINDEX); and (c) a binary variable indicating the presence of arsenic in drinking water (ARSCODE = 1 means the tube well is labeled 'red' while 0 means the tube well is labeled 'green'). The summary statistics of the variables used are presented in Tables 13.1 and 13.2 F( ) is the cumulative probability function for a probit model. The dependent variable Y_i =1 if an arsenic related disease is prevalent and = 0 if absent for the ith individual.

Using the probit model, the marginal effect due to a change in the source of drinking water (from red to green) is determined.[11] The marginal effect of arsenic, for example, is $\Delta \hat{F} = (\hat{F}|_{ARSCODE=1}) - (\hat{F}|_{ARSCODE=0})$, which shows the effect on changes in the probability of reducing the incidence of an arsenic-related disease when a red source of water is replaced by a green source. Table 13.4 shows the reduction in the probability of sickness to be 4.6%. This measures the benefit in terms of disease prevalence reduction by switching the source of water to a 'safe' mode.

Table 13.4 also shows the coefficient values and the change in the probability of sickness (marginal effects) associated with the age, gender and education of the individual. Since arsenic is a bio-accumulative element, the probability of *arsenicosis* increases with age up to 55 years for both men and women (see Figure 13.1). In terms of impact on the probability of sickness, the model shows that a male has a lower probability (by 0.86 per cent) of getting sick than a female. This is probably caused by – a) the poor health status of the female in a poor household; b) food habits where men often get more nutritious food than women, and c) men

Table 13.4. Estimating the probability of sickness (Probit Model)

	Coeff	Std error	z-value		Marginal effects	Std error	
AGE	0.0516074	0.0053757	9.6	***	0.0041361	0.0004057	***
AGE SQ	−0.0004610	0.0000634	−7.27	***			
Male	−0.1049217	0.0610308	−1.72	*	−0.0085767	0.0049977	*
EDUC	−0.0337094	0.0076790	−4.39	***	−0.0027508	0.0006418	***
ARSCODE	0.4561030	0.0630928	7.23	***	0.0467376	0.0077768	***
CONSTANT	−2.5410500	0.1121453	−22.66	***			

Note: *means significant at 10% level, ** means significant at 5% and *** means significant at 1% level.
Number of observations= 5554, LR chi-square (5) = 240.28, Prob > chi-square = 0.0000, Pseudo R^2=.1039
Log Likelihood = −1035.6753

---

[11] For detailed derivation see Greene (2003, p. 674).

are more mobile because of their work and may not drink water from the same sources whereas women consume most of the water from a single source as they stay at home.

The estimated model further shows that the number of years of schooling is negatively related with the probability of sickness, i.e., higher the level of education lower is the probability of getting sick (which could be caused by more awareness level). Each year of additional education reduces the probability of sickness by 0.27 per cent. Finally, the probability of switching from red to green source of water reduces the probability of sickness by 4.6 per cent, by far the largest gain in terms of reducing sickness. These observations are valid for households using water from red tube wells only.

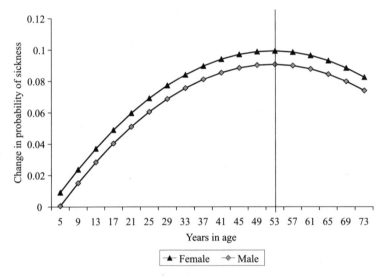

Figure 13.1.   Marginal effect by age

13.4.2. *Medical expenses from arsenicosis*

Mitigating activities include expenditures incurred due to sickness when any individual member in the household is affected by arsenic-related diseases. In the sample of 5563, only 88 reported medical expenditure related to arsenic, whereas 296 were suffering from arsenic-related diseases. Using the probit model, the probability of incurring mitigating expenditure due to exposure to arsenic is estimated. The estimated probit equation and the marginal effects are shown in Table 13.5.

Table 13.5 shows that the probability of incurring mitigating expenses is also influenced by the age of the individual, the square of his/her age, and the level of arsenic in drinking water (ARSCODE). It shows that the probability of incurring health expenditure will be 1.36 per cent higher for households using water from red tube-wells relative to those using green tube-wells. The co-efficients of gender and education are not significant. In Table 13.6 the coefficient value of AGE is positive. This implies that the individual's probability of incurring medical expenditure will increase with age or time. The coefficient of 'male' dummy is not significant.

Table 13.5. Estimating the probability of incurring medical costs (Probit Estimates)

	Coeff	std error	z value		Marginal Effects	std error	
AGE	0.044283	0.008252	5.37	***	0.001092	0.0001850	***
AGE SQ	−0.000355	0.000091	−3.89	***			
FEMALE	0.053080	0.093393	0.57	NS	0.001331	0.002344	NS
EDUC	−0.031557	0.011711	−2.69	***	0.000791	0.000306	***
ARSCODE	0.409407	0.094356	4.34	***	0.013621	0.003980	***
CONSTANT	−3.113758	0.188855	−16.49	***			

Note: * means significant at 10% level, ** means significant at 5% level, and *** means significant at 1% level, NS means not significant. Number of observation= 5554, LR chi-square (5) = 92.03, Prob > chi-square = 0.0000, Pseudo R2=.1018, Log Likelihood = -406.03703

Table 13.6. Calculation of cost of illness or welfare gain

Indicators	Estimated Value	Comments
Average wage	50.623	Weighted Average of Wages
Average sick days lost per individual per year	5.289	Days per year
P(S| ∆R)	0.0467	Marginal effect from Table 13.4
Mitigating expenditure	11,618.12	Average Per year
P(M| ∆R)	0.0136	Marginal effect from Table 13.5

13.4.3. *Averting expenditure at the household level*

Avertive expenses are incurred when adopting any alternative technology to reduce the impact of contamination. It is a precautionary step on the part of the household and expenses are often incurred at the household level rather than at the individual level. Aftab, Haque and Khan (2006) have shown that raising awareness on arsenic-related health risks leads to the adoption of averting technologies.

In this study, only 196 households (out of 878 households in the sample) adopted at least one type of technology (the choice ranging from individual level to community level interventions) and reported operating and maintenance costs or installation costs or both. As a result, a majority of the households did not have any expenditure on averting technologies. Hence, when the demand for avertive activities was estimated, no statistical relationship was found between the adoption of averting technology at the household level and the type of well used. Thus, information on avertive actions was not used for estimating the MWTP.[12]

13.4.4. *WTP for switching water source from red to green*

Using the calculation given in equation (7), and the coefficients of the Tables 13.4 and 13.5, the mean cost of illness for an individual is calculated as BDT 170.51 or US \$2.89 per annum. This is equivalent to BDT 1056.82 or US \$17.91 per household per year. This means that households currently using water from red sources incur these costs. This includes costs in terms of a) loss of income due to sickness (BDT 12.5 per annum for adults only) and b) mitigating expenditures for sick members in the family (BDT 158.01 per annum[13]). This can be interpreted as the minimum benefit for households who make a switch from red to green water sources.

Table 13.7. Lower bound of willingness to pay to avoid arsenicosis

	Lower Bound of WTP (In BDT)	Lower Bound of WTP (US \$1 = BDT 59)
Individual per annum	170.51	2.89
Loss of income due to lost work days	12.50	0.21
Mitigating expenses	158.01	2.68
Household level expenses	1056.82	17.91
Loss on income due to lost work days	56.64	0.96
Mitigating expenses	1000.18	16.95

Source: Calculation done by the Author
Note: Averting expenditure is not included since it has not been found statistically significant.

---

[12] It is to be noted that several other types of functional forms and variables were tried in order to determine the suitability of this function. In no case was the ARSCODE found to be statistically significant.
[13] See Table 13.7

Table 13.8. Comparison of WTP from other studies

Issue for WTP	Method/Approach	Value per House-hold per year	Source
WTP for arsenic free water	Cost of Illness (Work-day loss + Mitiga-tion expenses) (per household)	BDT 1056.82 or (US $17.91)	This study
WTP for Arsenic Free Drinking Water in Rural Bangladesh	Contingent valuation method (home con-nection)	BDT 2,831.00 or (US $48.27)	JK Ahmad, JK, et al., (2002)
	Contingent valuation (standpost)	BDT 1572 or (US $26.73)	Ahmad, JK, et al., (2002)
WTP for urban clear air in Kanpur, India	Cost of illness	INR 850.97 (US $21)	Gupta, Usha (2005)
WTP for faecal coliform free drink-ing water in Delhi, India	Cost of illness	INR 1094.31 (US $26)	Dasgupta, P (2005)

Table13.8 presents the comparative analysis of WTP estimates from different studies. Among them, the study of Ahmad, et al. (2002), is the most relevant. This study used the CV method to estimate the WTP for arsenic-free water at the household level and gives households a choice of either a home water pipe connection or a standpost. However, in this study, WTP was not measured for any specific arsenic-free water technology at the household level. The estimate in this chapter shows that even when a) costs due to lost working days, and b) the cost of mitigation during sickness, are included the cost is lower than that by Ahmad, et al. (2002). The difference is expected given the fact that this study used a revealed preference method of estimation while Ahmad used a stated preference model to estimate the cost of damage.

13.4.5. Total welfare loss due to arsenic exposure

As stated earlier, mitigation of this problem will ensure the health and well-being of about 28–50 million people who are at risk. In financial terms, as estimated from willingness-to-pay, this is substantial. It is estimated that the total medical expenditure from arsenic exposure is potentially in the range of BDT 207 million to 369 million per year. In addition, there are costs in the range of 350 million to 625 million in terms of workday losses.

Thus, the total marginal willingness to pay lies between BDT 557 million and BDT 994 million per annum or nearly 0.6 per cent of the income of households (based on an average per capita income of US $480). This means that if it is possible to mitigate this problem using suitable technologies, there is likely to be a net social gain of US$ 9 to 17 million per annum (see Table 13.9).

Table 13.9. Total WTP or welfare loss for Bangladesh

Extent of Affected	Population at risk in Bangladesh (In Million)	Probable Number of People Affected (In Million)	Total Number of Sick Days (In Million)	WDL (million Taka)	Mitigating Expenditure (million Taka)	Welfare Loss (million BDT)	Welfare Loss (million US $)
(1)	(2)	(3)	(4)	(5)	(6)	(7)	(8)
LOW	28	1.3076	6.92	350.10	206.61	556.71	9.44
AVERAGE	35	1.6345	8.64	437.62	258.26	695.89	11.79
HIGH	50	2.335	12.35	625.18	368.94	994.12	16.85

Notes:
Col 3 = P (S | ΔR) × Col (2) where P (S | ΔR) = 0.0467
Col 4 = Mean [WDL] × Col (3), where mean[WDL], Table 13.2, row 5.
Col 5 = Col 3 × mean[WDL] × Mean[wage], mean[wage=50.62[14]]
Col 6 = Mean [Medical expenses] × P (M | ΔR) × Col 3, where Mean[Medical exp] from Table 13.1, row 6, P(M| ΔR) = 0.0136.
Col 7 = Col 5 + Col 6
Col 8 = Col 7 / 59 where 1 US$=59 Taka at the time of survey.

13.5. Discussions and conclusions

This study has provided a set of key results in terms of risks and costs related to *arsenicosis* caused by drinking water from arsenic-contaminated sources. Some of the key findings of the study are reiterated in the following paragraphs.

In sample area 1, the Matlab *upazila*, nearly 80 per cent of the coded tube-wells are currently labeled red, and in sample area 2, the Laksham

---

[14] Calculated using a weighted average for manufacturing, agriculture and construction wage rates from the national labour survey.

upazila, 70 per cent of the coded tube-wells are red. Fifty-six per cent of households currently drink water from contaminated sources. Nearly 19 per cent of the sample households are affected with at least one variant of *arsenicosis.* This sample further shows that the number of days lost in work due to sickness is 5.28 days per year per sick person. Clearly most households did not report a large number of workdays lost[15]. Nonetheless, in terms of benefits, if a household switches to a green source of water, then it can avoid only about US $1 per year per household in terms of work days lost. The low value implies that adult members of households continue to work while they are sick. It also reflects their low wage earnings.

The study shows that the probability of illness rises with age because arsenic cannot be drained out of the human body and the accumulation of arsenic will increase the probability of sickness in the future. Hence, the current estimate is a lower bound in terms of medical expenditure. The actual cost will rise each year as the incidence of sickness increases by nearly 4 for every 1000 population each year (see Table 13.4).

The study shows that currently households spend nearly BDT 1057 (or US $18) per year to deal with arsenic related ailments and income loss. This is nearly 0.73 per cent of the income of the household (based on US $480 per capita income and a household size of 5.1). Considering that this burden comes from arsenic contamination, which is one among many other diseases, and considering the fact that a large majority of Bangladheshis live with less than US $1 a day, this is a significant burden.

It is important to note that while using a green source of water is a much simpler solution, it may be difficult to find aquifers that are not contaminated. As a result, establishing a community level solution may not be feasible on a large scale. There are two other types of arsenic mitigation options available in Bangladesh. In the first category, there are community based mitigation techniques, which include arsenic and iron removal plants, pond sand filters, deep tube wells and piped water supply. These mitigation options require the involvement of institutions (like NGOs, Government agencies, etc.) to bear the initial cost of investment, which can range from US $2,000 to US $240,000 for 100 households (see Table 13.10). The dynamics of establishing institutions to run these community-based mitigation options is not simple and needs to be taken into consideration when assessing the feasibility of such investments.

---

[15] Only applicable for adult individuals in the household.

Table 13.10. Unit cost of different types of arsenic removal/mitigating technologies

Name of Technology	Type	Capital Cost/Unit (US$)	Operation and Maintenance Costs (Family/ Year) (US$)	Unit Cost* (US $)
Sono 45 – 25 Filter	Household	13	0.5 to 1.5	14
Shapla Filter	Household	4	11	15
SAFI Filter	Household	40	6	46
Bucket Treatment Unit	Household	6 to 8	25	35
Sidko	Community (75 Household)	4250	10	66.67
Alternative water supply				
Iron-Arsenic Removal Plant	Community (10 Household)	200	1	21
Rain Water Harvesting		30	5	0.151
Deep Tube Well		120	4	0.151
Pond Sand Filter		117	15	0.161
Dug Well		102	3	0.256
Piped Water Supply		5872	800	0.375
Arsenic Removal Unit for Urban Water Supply	6000 Household	240000	1–1.5	40.00

Source: worldbank.org/INTSAREGTOPWATRES/Resources/ArsenicVolII_PaperIV.pdf

Note: * calculation by author

The second category includes household level mitigating options such as the three pitcher method and *Shapla* or *Sono* filters. These options cost between US $4 to US $4250 (initial capital) plus US $0.5 to US $25 annually for operation and maintenance. This study suggests that the less expensive of these options, i.e., those that cost less than US $18 annually may be acceptable to households if the initial costs are low or subsidized.

The question still remains why more households do not switch to green tube wells. They are clearly bearing a minimum cost of BDT 1057 (US $18) by not switching. There may be social issues associated with switching or some households may incur time and travel costs if they were to collect water from green wells. Better campaigns and advertising with clear information about the health costs of continuing to use red wells may be useful in persuading people to make the switch.

References

Abdalla, C.W., Roach, B.A. and Epp, D.J., 'Valuing Environmental Quality Changes using Averting Expenditures: An application to Groundwater Contamination', *Land Economics*, Vol. 68 (May), (1992), 163–169.

Aftab, S., Haque Enamul, A.K. and Zakir Hossain Khan, M., 'Adoption of Arsenic-Safe Drinking Water Practice in Rural Bangladesh: An Averting Behavior Model', *Journal of Bangladesh Studies*, Vol. 8, No. 1 (2006), 48–59.

Ahmad, M.F. and Ahmed, C.M., Study on Area Wise Concentration of Arsenic in Bangladesh, Dhaka, ICDDRB, 2004.

Alberini, A. and Krupnick, A., 'Cost-of- Illness and Willingness-to-Pay Estimates of the Benefits of Improved Air Quality: Evidence from Taiwan', *Journal of Land Economics*, 76(1), (2000), 37–53.

Asia Arsenic Network Report, 2004 (www.asiaarsenic.net).

Bangladesh Economic Review 2005, Govt. of Bangladesh.

Department of Public Health and Engineering (DPHE) Bangladesh (2005), 'Supplying Safe Water and Preventing Arsenic'.

Dickie, M. and Gerking, S. , 'Valuing Reduced Morbidity: A Health Production Approach', *Southern Economic Journal*, Vol. 57, No. 3 (1991), 690–702.

Freeman, A. M. III., 'The Measurement of Environmental and Resource Values: Theory and Methods', Washington, D. C., Resources for the Future, 1993.

Greene, William H., *Econometric Analysis*, 5th ed., Prentice Hall, 2003.

Haque, Enamul, A.K., 'Results of a Gender-Disaggregated National Household Survey on Public Expenditure of Bangladesh', Dhaka Gender Budget Secretariat, Institute of Development, Environment and Strategic Studies, North South University, 2005.

Gerking, S. and Stanely, L., 'An Economic Analysis of Air Pollution and Health: The Case of St. Louis', *The Review of Economics and Statistics*, Vol. 68, No. 1, 1996, 115–121.

Rahman, M., Quamruzzaman, Q., Das, R., 'Health Hazards of Arsenic Poisoning', Bangladesh Environment 2000 – A Compilation of Papers of the ICBEN-2000, Feroze Ahmed, M. (ed.), a publication of Bangladesh Poribesh Andolan (BAPA), Dhaka, Bangladesh, 135–150.

Smith, A., Biggs, M.L. and Moore, L., 'Cancer Risks from Arsenic in Drinking Water: Implications for Drinking Water Standards', *Arsenic Exposure and Health Effects*, 1999, (ed.) W.R. Chappell, CO Abernathy and Rebecca L. Calderon,

Proceedings of the Third International Conference on Arsenic Exposure and Health Effects, 1998, San Diego, California.

Smith, A.H., Lingas, E.O. and Rahman, M., 'Contamination of Drinking Water by Arsenic in Bangladesh: A Public Health Emergency', *Bulletin of WHO*, Vol. 78, 2000, 1093–1103.

The National Institute of Preventive and Social Medicine (NIPSOM), (2001), 'The Study on Arsenicosis Patients', NIPSOM, Dhaka, Bangladesh.

Tolley, G. and Fabian, R., 'Future Directions for Health Value Research', *Valuing, Health for Policy*, (ed.) G. Tolley, D. Kenkel and R. Fabian, Chicago, University of Chicago Press, 1994.

Zaldivar, R. and Guillier, A., 'Environmental and Clinical Investigations on Endemic Chronic Arsenic Poisoning in Infants and Children', Zbl. Bakt. Hyg. I. Abt. Orig. B, 2, (1997), 226–234.

14

Air Quality and Cement Production: Examining the Implications of Point Source Pollution in Sri Lanka

Cyril Bogahawatte and *Janaranjana Herath*[1]

14.1. Introduction

Although air pollution is commonly associated with metropolitan areas, the problem is not uncommon in industrial locations of the peri-urban and rural areas. With industrial expansion, increased employment opportunities motivate people to settle down close to factories. Even though some such jobs are risky and hazardous, poverty driven households have no option other than to accept them.

The cement industry in Puttalam, Sri Lanka, could be described as one such industry. It is an expanding localized industrial operation concentrated basically in areas with easy access to the basic raw materials, i.e., limestone and clay. These raw materials are found in abundance in the Northwestern coastal belt from Palavi in the Puttalam district up to Murugan in the Jaffna district. The demand for cement is increasing with rapid developments in the services and construction sector, and about 35 per cent of the demand is met with domestic production. The Puttalam cement factory, which is the biggest of the two functioning factories, produces 80 per cent of the local production of 542,000 MT (Economic and Social

[1] This study was undertaken with the financial support of the South Asian Network for Development and Environment Economics (SANDEE). The resource persons, Professors M.N. Murty, Jeffrey Vincent, A.K. Enamul Haque, Dr Priya Shyamasundar, Dr Subhrendu Pattanayak of SANDEE contributed much to the outcome of this chapter. We wish to thank Ms Kavita Shrestha and the SANDEE Secretariat for their continued encouragement and support.

Statistics, 1998). However, the processes of cement production, which comprise mining, pulverizing, grinding and clinkering, generate air dust particulates, fumes, and gases consisting of Nitrous oxide (NO), Nitrogen dioxide (NO_2), Sulfur dioxide (SO_2) and Carbon monoxide CO. These emissions degrade the air quality of the local area, spreading to around a 3–4 km radius periphery of the factory. Such emissions can contribute to a wide range of health effects, especially respiratory diseases, brain damages, lung cancer, heart diseases, skin irritations, fatigue, headache, and nausea (The World Development Indicators 2004). Further, failing eyesight due to fumes is common in the operational area of the factory.

The magnitude of any health impacts of air pollution depends on the density of population, volume and concentration of emissions, temperature, wind direction, rainfall pattern, geographical conditions, and bio-diversity in the area. It also depends on the health stock of the people and their responses to pollution. It is also generally possible to improve existing emission-controlling systems or to introduce eco-friendly technologies in production. But reduction of emissions may result in an increase in the cost of production of cement. On the other hand, it could also result in the improvement of labour and agricultural productivity as well as the living standards of the local population. Hence, accurate information pertaining to the magnitude of the impacts of air pollution and the costs of air pollution abatement of the cement industry could contribute to more efficient pollution abatement policies.

The main objective of this chapter is to estimate the health benefits of reducing air pollution from cement production in Sri Lanka. This is done – a) by estimating dose response functions for Lower Acute Respiratory Illnesses(LRI), Upper acute Respiratory Illnesses (URI) and All Acute Respiratory Illnesses (ARI) for households living within 3 km from the cement factory; b) by calculating the mitigation cost functions for Lower Respiratory Illnesses, Upper Respiratory Illnesses and All Respiratory Illnesses for the same households; and c) by measuring the welfare benefits to these households of reducing cement air pollution to a lower level.

14.2. Air pollution and health impacts

Exposure to polluted air can contribute to pre-mature mortality (World Development Indicators, 2004; Quah & Boon, 2002; , Cropper et al., 1997; Ostro, et al., 1996; Dockery et. al., 1993; Ostro, 1995; Pope, et al., 1993).

Dockery, et al. (1993), for example, showed that in Kingston, TN, the risk of early deaths in areas that have a high concentration of particulate air pollution (TSP) was 26 per cent higher as compared to areas with lower concentrations. Similarly, Pope, et. al., (1993) identified an association between exposure to particulate air pollution and premature mortality due to cardiopulmonary diseases. In another study in six US cities, Schwartz (1996) found that the exposure to fine particulates ($PM_{2.5}$) was strongly associated with premature mortality while exposure to coarse particulates had little independent effect. In a study in Delhi, India, Cropper, et al., (1997) found that the impacts of air pollution on deaths were particularly high among middle-aged (15–40 years) people. A study which was done in Santiago, Chile (Ostro et al., 1996) revealed that deaths from respiratory diseases and cardiovascular diseases were more prominent with exposure to small particles (PM_{10}). Such results are reinforced by recent studies in the air pollution epidemiological literature – for example, Quah and Boon (2002) show that an increase in the ambient concentration of particulate matter (PM_{10}) is associated with an increase in the risk of premature mortality.

There is considerable evidence of morbidity associated with air pollution. Many studies show consistently higher rates of bronchitis and its symptoms among children in polluted areas with higher exposure to total suspended particulates. Aunan et al., (1998) found in Hungary, for example, that the main benefits from reducing pollutants were the reduction of chronic respiratory diseases and maintenance costs for building materials. Recent studies in India (Gupta 2006; Murthy et al. 2003) show the link between air pollution and respiratory health.

The health effects imposed by air pollution have tangible costs that individuals and households bear. The total economic cost of air pollution in Singapore, for example, was estimated at US $3662 million, i.e., about 4.31 per cent of the country's GDP in 1999 (Quah and Boon, 2002). A World Bank Study in China (1997) estimated that air pollution costs China's economy more than seven per cent of GDP (in 1995), largely in health damages. Murty, et al. (2003), analyzing the impact of higher SPM levels on respiratory diseases in the cities of Delhi and Kolkata, estimated the annual marginal benefits to a household as INR 2086 (US$ 42) in Delhi and INR 950 (US$ 19) in Kolkata from a reduction in current SPM to a safe level. These studies are useful for assessing costs and benefits of pollution prevention policies.

In valuing environmental quality changes, economists prefer to use direct or indirect market values that reveal people's health preferences. There are many approaches to valuing health costs, which include methods such as the defensive expenditure approach, cost of illness approach, health production function, productivity change method and the human capital approach. Each method has its advantages and disadvantages based on how available and good the underlying data are. In valuing the health impacts of air pollution, the Cost-Of-Illness (COI) approach is used by many researchers (Alberini and Krupnik, 2000). The method first establishes cause-effect or dose-response relationships and then values the impacts of environmental change. Many researchers (Alberini, Anna, et al. 1997; Ostro, 1995; Cropper, et al., 1997; Lvovsky, 1998; Quah, et al., 2002) have used dose response functions in estimating morbidity and mortality impacts of air pollution.

In this study, dose response functions are used to estimate the respiratory illnesses caused by cement air pollution in Puttalam district. Mitigation cost functions are estimated to assess the welfare gains from a reduction in cement air pollution.

14.3. Study area

Puttalam district is in the northwestern province of Sri Lanka and the climate in the district is tropical with a marked dry season with an average temperature of 27^0 C and an average annual rainfall less than 1000mm. Administratively, there are 16 Divisional Secretary Divisions (DSD) and 548 Grama Niladhari Divisions (GND) in Puttalam district while the cement factory is situated in Palaviya G.S. division, 8 km away from Puttalam town. It could be described as the only industry that affects ambient air quality in the locality.

The Puttalam cement factory was established in the 1970s due to the availability of raw material. The population density of the area was low at the time of establishment. However, due to infrastructure development and increased employment opportunities with the factory, the population increasesd. According to Department of Census and Statistics (2005) the increment is about seven fold since the 70s. The factory produces more than 30 per cent of the cement demand of the country and contributes to more than 80 per cent of local production, i.e. it is the largest cement producer in the country. The Swiss company, Holcim Group, owns the factory at present and employs about 2000–2500 workers mostly on a contract basis. The factory management assists the locals of the area when it comes to certain social issues such as education, health and community welfare.

The local population claims that cement dust poses a health hazard to them (Reports–2003, 2004–Wayamba Environmental Authority and Central Environmental Authority, GN officers[2]). Further reports indicate that people protested a few times during 2001–2005 against the factory for dust impacts. Although a certain level of visible dust was mitigated with new technology introduced a few years ago, the severity of respiratory illnesses appears to persist. This is the primary motivation for undertaking this study.

14.4. Data

As the study aims at measuring the impacts on respiratory illness of cement air pollution and at estimating welfare gains, data needed to be collected on household information, pollution measurements and certain abatement costs associated with the cement factory. For collecting household data and pollution data, the affected area was first demarcated within a 3 km radius distance area around the factory. Here, the help of National Building Research Organization (NBRO) was utilized. This is a government organization involved in measuring the air pollution levels in major towns and chemical industries in the country. The 3 km area was then divided into six strata of 0.5 km distance each from the cement factory.

Based on the total population of the demarcated study area (1058 households), 500 households were randomly selected for a household survey (see Table 14.1). Household interviews were conducted using a pre-tested questionnaire through personal visits to the selected households by the co-investigator and research assistants in two seasons – wet and dry.

Table 14.1. Sampling of households for the socio-economic survey

Distance from cement factory (Km)	0–0.5	0.5–1	1–1.5	1.5–2	2–2.5	2.5–3
Total Households	09	29	84	133	297	506
Sample size	05	15	40	62	140	238
Sample % of total Households	47	47	47	47	47	47

---

[2] Personal communications with government Officers of the area.

Household data were collected during the months of December 2005 for the wet season and June, 2006 for the dry season. Data were collected on household characteristics, socio-economic factors and health and medical information especially on respiratory illnesses and symptoms for each individual in the household. Respiratory illnesses were recalled by households on the basis of the previous year's illnesses and illnesses within the last two weeks. The data based on 'two weeks recall' were used as a dependent variable for the econometric analyses that follow. The impact of the previous year's illness appears as an independent lag variable.

Pollution data were obtained by measuring air quality at 0.5 km distance from the factory in 10–12 locations during the wet and dry seasons. Measurements of pollutants were done using a measurement device, which was located and operated for 24 hours under NBRO's supervision. Pollution levels of SPM, NO_2, SO_2 and CO were measured (see Table 14.2) taking wind direction into account.

Table 14.2. Air pollution levels within 3Km distance of the cement factory, Puttalam district (National Building Research Organization)

Dis. From CF (km)		Wet Season			Dry Season		
Location	Ave. time (hours)	SPM $\mu g/m^3$	SO_2 $\mu g/m^3$	NO_2 $\mu g/m^3$	SPM $\mu g/m^3$	SO_2 $\mu g/m^3$	NO_2 $\mu g/m^3$
1. (L1-0.5km)	24	144	14	24	107	22	22
2. (L2-0.75km)	24	219	13	50	121	20	23
3. (L3-1km)	24	112	17	32	098	24	23
4. (L4-1.5km)	24	095	19	02	094	47	34
5. (L5-2km)	24	076	45	23	073	22	24
6. (L6-2km)	24	057	14	20	047	23	24
7. (L7-2km)	24	055	32	29	068	17	21
8. (L8-2.5km)	24	130	09	29	045	15	14
9. (L9-3km)	24	126	01	33	025	33	19
10. (L10-3km)	24	125	14	29	039	14	32

All the pollution measurements were taken over two consecutive days to minimize variance. The pollution data were assigned to each household in the analyses based on proximity to the particular location. Measuring pollution levels for each household was impossible as the cost of measurement is high due to constraints of time and apparatus. Thus, in the absence of household specific pollution information and regular government monitoring of air quality, air pollution data had to be generated for specific points and seasons around the factory. Data related to the abatement efforts of the factory could not be obtained despite repeated discussions, meetings and telephone conversations with the senior management of the factory.

Air pollution results showed that the pollution levels were below the ambient air standards of Sri Lanka in 1994 (these standards are controversial), but are high compared to the WHO standards and Indian standards. The SPM level was the most significant, especially in the wet season when SPM was significantly higher than the WHO standards. The average SPM, SO_2 and NO_2 levels of the study area were 80.8, 20.2 and 24.7 µg per cubic meter. There was no specific pattern of SPM levels or other pollutants in relation to wind direction – perhaps due to wind circulation in the area.

The general characteristics of the households indicate an average family size of four persons per household in the area with a mean age of 32 years and an education level of grade four. Nearly 23 per cent of the households reported no schooling and another 77 per cent reported only primary education levels. These education levels are poor compared to many districts and to national indicators (Department of Census and Statistics, 2005). The three main occupations in this area were working for private or government sector, farming and temporary sundry labour. Nearly six per cent of the households have at least one individual working in the cement factory. Of the total households, about 24 per cent was employed in government or private sector enterprises, while the majority of the others were engaged in agriculture, and some others in temporary labour.

The average monthly income of an average household was around SLR 10,910. Since the average household income in 2004 in Sri Lanka was SLR 15,405 (Central Bank, 2004) this result suggests that the households in this area are relatively poor. The average monthly family expenditure was around SLR 7200, of which food expenditure amounted to 88 per cent of the total. The mean value of all assets owned by a household was around SLR 121,900 of which the value of land contributed to around 77 per cent (see Table 14.3). Nearly 67 per cent of the households used firewood, 13 per cent kerosene and 15 per cent LPG as a source of energy for cooking. Of these, 72 per cent households ventilate through kitchen windows; 21 per cent by means of kitchen chimney and nearly seven per cent of households did not have any form of kitchen ventilation (see Table 14.4).

Table14.3. General characteristics of the surveyed households

Item	Mean	Std. Deviation	Min	Max
Average family size	4.0	1.06	2	6
Household size (m²)	29.5	8.09	0	60
Average age of households (yrs)	31.99	17.28	0.3	88.0
Education level (grade)	4.09	1.04	0	11.0
Private and public sector employment (%)	24			
Public sector employment (%)	2.0			
Own farm agriculture (%)	1.1			
Off farm agriculture (%)	3.9			
Size of home garden (perches)	0.678	0.576	0	9.50
Total value of household assets (SLR)	121909	27020	0	250501
Land value per household (SLR)	94289	198101	0	300,000
Wealth (SLR)	67646.4	199675.3	0	3227000
Smokers (%)	12.26			
Expenditure for smoking/month (SLR)	465			
Alcohol consumers (%)	4.52			
Expenditure for alcohol/month (SLR)	236.7			

Table 14.4. Kitchen characteristics (indoor air pollution)

Fuel Type (% of Total)				Type of Ventilation (% of Total)		
F/W	LPG	Kerosene	Other	Window	Chimney	None
67.67	12.66	14.66	5.00	71.60	22.00	7.30

Numerous health related questions were asked. Medical information of the previous year (2005) indicated that Bronchitis, Pleurisy, high blood pressure, and heart trouble were significant in the sample households. Nearly 15 per cent of individuals indicated that they had suffered from these diseases in the last year. Data on symptoms and illnesses related to respiratory illnesses based on 'two weeks recall' showed that nearly 10.1 per cent of individuals suffered shortness of breath, 11.1 per cent cough/phlegm, 1.3 per cent Asthma and 0.8 per cent heart problems (see Table 14.5). The average individual in our sample incurred a total medical cost as a result of all respiratory symptoms of SLR 3402 over a 12 months period.

Table 14.5. Respiratory and related diseases among surveyed households

Illness over last 12 months	% of individuals reported	Mitigation cost/person SLR/year
Bronchitis	3.26	2473
Pleurisy	2.69	6185
High Blood pressure	2.12	4535
Chronic Bronchitis	0.17	1933
Pneumonia	0.12	2510
Heart Trouble	3.95	3137
Other Lung Diseases	0.12	3000
Illness /Symptom over last two weeks		
Shortness of breath	10.14	
Cough/Phlegm	11.11	
Asthma	1.26	
Heart injuries	0.8	

The data also showed that the smoking habit among men is quite significant with the average age of a smoker being 20 years, with daily consumption ranging from 4–5 cigarettes and incurring a monthly expenditure of SLR 465 per household.

14.5. Methodology and estimation

The study uses the household production function model to estimate the economic benefits from reduced morbidity due to reduction in air pollution in Puttalam district in Sri Lanka. The household health production function and the demand for mitigating activities are based on Freeman's (1993) derivations (see also Chapter 2 and 11).

An individual's utility function may be defined as,

$$U = U(X, L, H) \tag{1}$$

Where, X represents consumption of market goods; L denotes leisure; and H represents the health condition due to air pollution. Here, $\delta U/\delta X > 0$; $\delta U/\delta L > 0$; and $\delta U/\delta H > 0$.

The health production function is given by:

$$H = H(A, Q, B) \tag{2}$$

where A = Avertive activities; Q = Pollution and B = Medical or Mitigating treatment.

Avertive activities refer to actions taken by the individual to avert the impacts of air pollution on health. Mitigating activities include medical costs and are actions taken to decrease impacts.

The individual's utility maximization problem therefore is:

$$\max U = U\,(X,\,L,\,H) \text{ subject to } I + w\,(T{-}L) = X + P_a\,.A + P_b\,B \quad (3)$$

where, I is non wage income; T is total available time; Pa is the price (unit cost) of pollution avertive activities; and Pb is the price (unit cost) of medical treatment. Here X is treated as a numeriare (i.e. a good with the price of one). The individual selects X, L, A and B to maximize his/her utility.

The simultaneous solution to the first order conditions of this utility maximization problem establishes the demand for the market commodity, leisure, mitigation activities and medical treatment. For example, the demand functions for avertive activities (A) and medical treatment (B) are given by,

$$A = A^*(\,I,\,w,\,P_a,\,P_b,\,Q) \quad (4)$$

and

$$B = B^*\,(\,I,w,\,P_a,\,P_b,\,Q) \quad (5)$$

It can then be shown that the marginal willingness to pay for reduction in air quality improvements (Freeman, 1993) is:

$$\text{MWTP} = w.\,dH\,/\,dQ + Pa\,\delta A/\,\delta Q + Pb\,\delta B/\,\delta Q + (\,\delta U/\delta H)^* dH/dQ/\lambda \quad (6)$$

Equation (6) shows that MWTP for health benefits from a reduction in pollution is the sum of observable reduction in time cost of illness, cost of avertive and mitigating activities and the monetary equivalent of the disutility of illness.

In this study, the data allows estimation of two equations – the health production function or dose response function (4) and the mitigating expenditure or medical costs function (5). Avertive costs are not estimated because credible and adequate information on avertive costs could not be obtained. The disutility generated from sickness could not be estimated – this is difficult information to assess accurately. Thus, a lower bound of the marginal willingness to pay for reductions in air pollution is estimated.

14.5.1. Estimation of dose response functions

The dose response function indicates the extent to which different diseases respond to various pollutants after controlling for other factors.

In this study, the dependent variable used in the dose response function is presence of upper or lower respiratory illnesses (Pr =1) or not (Pr= 0) among individuals during a two week period prior to the 2005/2006 household survey.

A Logit model (Greene, 2003) is used to estimate the parameters of the dose-response function or the probability of sickness.

The dependent variables are types of respiratory illnesses (upper and lower), which were identified based on a series of symptoms. Upper Acute Respiratory Illnesses (URI) was identified based on symptoms of sore throat, running or blocked nose/sinusitis, ear infection (ear ache), sudden high fever, cough while lying down, headache, irritability and fatigue. Lower Acute Respiratory Illnesses (LRI) were identified based on persistent cough with mucus, pneumonia, chest congestion, wheezing in chest, chest pain while breathing and asthma. By combining both the LRI and URI, All Respiratory Illnesses (ARI) were considered. The dataset is based on individual data and covers 3490 individuals in 500 households over two seasons.

14.5.2. Estimation of mitigation expenditure functions

The mitigating expenditure function represents the relationship between medical and other mitigating expenditures undertaken by individuals and air pollution, with controls for other variables. The dependent variable, mitigating expenditure is a censored variable in this study. Censoring occurs when the dependent variable corresponding to known values of independent variables is zero for part of the sample. Because of the large number of zero values in the dataset for medical expenditures, the Tobit model is used for estimating the demand function for mitigating activities.

The independent variables include a vector of individual characteristics, such as income, age and education, pollution parameters, weather conditions, etc.

Data used refers to mitigation expenditures incurred by 508 individuals in 500 households. Mitigating expenditures include doctors' fees, medicine costs, costs of transportations to the dispensary or hospital, and the time cost of the caretaker. Time cost was based on the caretaker's profession. When the caretaker is unemployed, the time cost was not considered. The data for estimating mitigating expenditure for upper or lower respiratory diseases comes from the 2005/2006 wet and dry season surveys. The data cover 3490 individual observations over the two seasons.

14.5.3. Empirical specifications

The following reduced form equations of the dose response and mitigating cost functions are estimated for Upper Respiratory Illnesses (URI) and Lower Respiratory Illnesses (LRI) as well as All Respiratory Illnesses (ARI) for the wet and dry seasons of 2005/2006.

The dose response function is:

$$Pr\,(1,0) = \gamma_1 + \alpha_1 SME + \alpha_2 Ed + \alpha_3 Age + \alpha_4 NHS + \alpha_5\,In + \alpha_6 S + \alpha_7 SPM + \alpha_8 SO_2 + u \tag{7}$$

The mitigation cost function is:

$$MC = \alpha_1 + \beta_1 SME + \beta_2 Ed + \beta_3\,Age + \beta_4 NHS + \beta_5\,In + \beta_6 S + \beta_7 SPM + \beta_8 SO_2 + v \tag{8}$$

The independent variables are identical in both equations. The definitions of the dependent and independent variables are as follows:.

Probability of a disease Pr (1,0): This represents the incidence of URI, LRI, and ARI ($Pr = 1$) or not being infected with any respiratory illness ($Pr = 0$) amongst individuals;

Mitigation Cost (MC): Mitigation cost represents the amount of expenditure incurred by the individuals in the households for treatment of URI, LRI, and ARI (SLR/person).

The dependent variables are in two clusters: a) individual data; and b) pollution data;

Smoking Expenditure (SME): This represents the smoking expenditure incurred by an individual in the household in SLR/month.

Education Level (Ed): The education level is measured as grade of education received by each individual. Education levels vary from no schooling (grade 0) to grade 12.

Age (Age): Dummy variable representing age = 1 for individuals when the age is higher than 55 years or less than 15 years; age = 0 for the individuals of age in between 15–55 years.

Negative Health Stock of last year (NHS): Dummy variable representing the occurrence of respiratory diseases by each individual of the household in 2005. Here NHS = 1 if the individual suffered from any respiratory diseases and NHS = 0 if there was no occurrence of a respiratory disease.

Income (In): This refers to the total monthly income of the individuals of the household in SLR. When an individual is not earning it was put as zero.

Season (S): Dummy variable representing the wet (September–March, 2005) and dry (April – August, 2006) seasons of the year in the district. Here S = 1 for the wet season and S = 0 for the dry season.

Suspended Particulate Matter (SPM): This is the value of SPM closest to the household residence in microgram/m³ as measured by NBRO for wet and dry seasons separately. SPM that is released during cement manufacture remains in the atmosphere because of its low settling velocity. It can penetrate deeply into the respiratory system and cause upper and lower respiratory illnesses to humans.

Sulphur Dioxide (SO₂): This is the value of the SO_2 gas emission during cement production as measured by the NBRO at a point closest to the household residence in microgram/m³ for wet and dry seasons separately. This emission is included in the equations as interactions with the levels of SPM.

14.5.4. Calculation of welfare gain

The welfare estimates of the impact of air pollution are based only on the medical expenditures incurred by individuals and do not include sick day wage losses. While the dose-response function is estimated, there were no sick days lost as a result of air pollution. Thus, these numbers were not included in the analyses.

Based on the results of the ARI, LRI and URI estimates of the SPM coefficient, the annual welfare effect of various reductions of current SPM can be calculated.

First, the marginal effect of the change in SPM on MC is calculated as follows:

$\partial MC / \partial SPM$ (marginal effect) $= P_r^* \beta_7$, where P_r = Prob Yi > 0 (number of observations of MC which are non-zero/total number of observations in the sample)

The reduction of MC by reducing SPM to a safe level from the current level is:

$\Delta MC = P_r^* \beta_7^* \Delta SPM$ where ΔSPM is the difference between the two season average of SPM and the safe level.

The reduction of MC *per annum* by reducing SPM to a safe level from the current level: $= P_r^* \beta_7 * \Delta SPM * 26$

14.6. Results and discussion

14.6.1. Results of the reduced form equations for dose response equations

Table 14.6 shows the summary statistics of the variables regressed in the dose response equations and Table 14.7 shows the results of the reduced form equations for the dose response equations for ARI, URI and LRI among households in the Puttalam district. The probability of diseases was fitted as a function of pollution and socio-economic variables for Logit estimation of the ARI, URI and LRI equations. In all three estimations, SPM, smoking expenditure, lagged health stock, and income were significant with the expected signs. Other variables were with expected signs. The key variable of interest to us is SPM. SPM has a significant effect on all three respiratory illnesses. An increase in SPM contributes to an increase in the probability of ARI, LRI and URI.

Table 14.6. Summary statistics of the Regression Variables

Variable	Obs	Mean	Std. Dev.	Min	Max
Smoke exp (SLR)	3490	133.46	378.07	0	3000
Edu (grade)	3490	4.08	1.409	0	11
Age (dummy)	3490	0.2993	0.4556	0	1
Health Stock (dummy)	3490	0.1535	0.3600	0	1
M. income (SLR)	3490	3126.33	5456.17	0	80000
Season (dummy)	3490	0.5	0.5000	0	1
SPM (mg/m³)	3490	0.080	0.042	0.025	0.219
SO_2 (mg/m³)	3490	0.0202	0.0109	0.001	0.057

Table 14.7. Estimated coefficients for dose response functions for ARI, LRI and URI
Dependent Variable: Probability of diseases (1,0) Logit function
Mean Probability: ARI = 0.141, URI= 0.126, LRI = 0.024

Independent variable	ARI	LRI	URI
Smoking exp (SLR/month)	0.0005***	0.0003*	0.00058***
	(0.0001)	(0.0002)	(0.0001)
Education (grade)	0.0084	(0.0991)	0.01692
	(0.0359)	(0.0734)	(0.0386)

(Contd.)

(*Contd.*)

Independent variable	ARI	LRI	URI
Age (dummy)	−0.1457	0.2605	−0.2047*
	(0.1165)	(0.2367)	(0.1260)
Negative Health Stock of last year (dummy)	1.2174***	1.1617***	1.2086***
	(0.1142)	(0.2324)	(0.1203)
M.Income (SLR)	0.00002***	0.00004***	0.00001*
	(8.07e-06)	(0.0000)	(8.36e-06)
Season (dummy)	−0.1657	−0.0656	−0.1593
	(0.1755)	(0.3727)	(0.1887)
SPM (mg/m³)	**4.4019***	**6.5021***	**3.7651****
	(1.8414)	**(3.6961)**	**(1.9743)**
SO2 (mg/m³)	5.7020	14.5920	2.7128
	(5.5272)	(11.5165)	(5.9837)
Constant	−2.5227***	−5.4121***	−2.6361***
	(0.2479)	(0.5308)	(0.2664)
Log likelihood	−1396.65	−411.81	−1254.59
N	3490	3490	3490

Note: * Sig @ 10%, **sig @ 5%, ***sig @1%, figures in parentheses are the standard errors

Smoking expenditure, as expected, has a significant positive effect on ARI, LRI and URI. The lagged negative heath stock variable was significant for all illnesses. As the variable measures the presence of disease in the previous year the probability of occurrence of respiratory illnesses in the current period increases if individuals had a respiratory problem in the previous year. The negative sign of the seasonal dummy indicates that the higher probability of respiratory illnesses was in the wet season. As expected, SO$_2$ has a positive impact on the presence of respiratory illnesses in all three groups.

14.6.2. *Results of the reduced form equations of mitigation cost functions*

The estimated coefficients for selected mitigation cost functions for ARI, LRI and URI (after checking for all possible independent variables like rainfall, wind direction, household characters, etc.) models are shown in Table 14.8.

Table 14.8. Estimated coefficients of the mitigation cost functions for ARI, LRI and URI (Tobit analysis)

Dependent Variable: Mitigation cost of ARI, LRI and URI in (SLR)
Mean (SLR/month): ARI = SLR 115.05, URI= SLR 103.58, LRI = SLR 12.83

Independent variable	ARI	LRI	URI
Smoking exp (SLR/month)	0.6137*** (0.1500)	0.2506** (0.1235)	0.6433*** (0.1589)
Education (grade)	15.2965 (44.8375)	62.1696* (36.4562)	14.5839 (48.1866)
Age (dummy)	−114.5835 (146.4894)	102.1859 (124.245)	−134.0764 (156.2598)
Negative Health Stock of last year (dummy)	1368.96*** (159.9084)	547.04** (138.2153)	1365.55*** (170.07)
M.Income (SLR)	0.0260*** (0.0101)	0.0177*** (0.0071)	0.0237** (0.0108)
Season (dummy)	−228.5362 (226.077)	−299.049 (211.10)	−94.4145 (238.105)
SPM (mg/m³)	**5639.58*** (2398.18)**	**4375.43** (2113.88)**	**4833.41** (2532.92)**
SO2(mg/m³)	10111.85 (7161.08)	4591.81 (6255.42)	10102.07 (7624.98)
Constant	−3708.66*** (336.6049)	−3161.25*** (406.948)	−3938.18*** (363.16)
Log likelihood	−5423.77	−1027.02	−4921.58
N	3490	3490	3490

Note: * Sig @ 10%, **sig @ 5%, ***sig @1%, figures in parentheses are the standard errors

Table 14.9. Welfare gains from various reductions in current SPM levels per annum

Distance from the cement factory (Km)	Reduction levels of current SPM (%)	Welfare gain per individual (SLR)	Welfare gain to the community (SLR million)
0–1.5	25	523	0.25
	50	1048	0.51
	75	1,571	0.77
	100	2,095	1.02

(Contd.)

(*Contd.*)

Distance from the cement factory (Km)	Reduction levels of current SPM (%)	Welfare gain per individual (SLR)	Welfare gain to the community (SLR million)
1.5–3.0	25	349	1.30
	50	628	2.35
	75	942	3.52
	100	1,256	4.71
0–3.0	25	349	1.47
	50	**699**	**2.96**
	75	1,048	4.35
	100	1,398	5.91

In the results for the three equations, coefficients of independent variables SPM, smoking expenditure, monthly income and lagged negative health stock were significant with expected signs.

As expected, the mitigation cost of ARI, URI and LRI increases with an increase in the SPM pollution level. Similarly, a higher expenditure for smoking increases the mitigation costs of all respiratory diseases. The significant and positive relationship between income and costs of ARI, LRI and URI suggest that richer individuals obtained more medical treatment. The negative health stock of the previous year has a significant influence on mitigation cost for the current year. The expected sign of the seasonal dummy indicates that mitigation costs for all diseases is higher in the wet season (when there is more sickness) compared to the dry season. As expected mitigation cost of all the diseases seems to increase with the increase of SO_2 level.

14.6.2. *Welfare gain of community through MC with various reductions of current SPM Level*

Table 14.9 shows the welfare effect for the study area by reducing the current SPM level by various levels. For instance, if the SPM level is reduced by 50 per cent (i.e., to 0.040mg/m^3), a family living within 3 km from the cement factory, would benefit by about SLR 2796 (US $28) per year. The welfare gain through reductions in ARI for all the 1058 households living within 3 km of the factory is SLR 2.96 million (US $29,600) per year. Here it is assumed that the average family has four members. This gain would be higher if the costs of lost working days and missing activities as well as other impact through pain and discomfort could be included. Since there was no data collected on lost working days of an individual due to air-pollution-related illnesses, savings in wage losses could not be estimated. The welfare estimates are therefore very conservative estimates of the gains of reduced air pollution.

14.7. Conclusions and policy implications

The study indicates that there are significant health impacts due to cement air pollution on the locals living with in 3km around the cement factory in the Puttalam district. Susceptibility to respiratory illness and costs associated with it seem to be higher in the wet season due to higher SPM levels.

Reducing the current SPM levels of cement air pollutants in significant margins could reduce the mitigation cost of respiratory illnesses immensely, which would in turn lead to welfare gains for the entire society. For instance reduction of SPM levels by 50 per cent would lead to a gain of SLR 699 (US $7) per representative individual while the annual welfare gain to all people within the 3 km region would be SLR 2.96 million. With a 100 per cent reduction in SPM levels, which would mean that the WHO standard would be met, the annual gain per individual would be SLR 1398 (US $14) and the annual gain to the community would be more than SLR 5.91 million.

Compensating affected individuals for their health losses would be one option in overcoming the damages to the households. It might also be less expensive for the factory to bring in technological changes to abate the air pollution. Studies such as this also suggest that Sri Lanka needs to revise its air pollution standards. Informing policy makers about the tangible health costs individuals bear may help them make reasonable decisions about these standards.

This study is a first attempt to bring together socio-economic and pollution data to understand the links between air pollution and health in Sri Lanka. It therefore suffers from some limitations that could be improved in future research. For example, the inclusion of lost working days in the surveyed population could improve the estimations of mitigation cost. With information on abatement costs from the factory, the net benefits of abating pollution could be determined; but this information was un-available. The data on air quality was also limited – with daily data on air quality, the estimations would be more credible. This study, on the other hand, is an example of how health costs can be assessed in developing countries even with limited data.

References

Alberini, A., and Krupnick, A., 'Cost-of-Illness and Willingness-to-Pay Estimates of the Benefits of Improved Air Quality: Evidence from Taiwan', *Land Economics*, 76, (2000), 37–53.

Alberini, A., Cropper, M., Tsu-Tan Fu, Jin-Tan Liu, Shaw, D., Harington, W., 'Valuing Health Effects of Air Pollution in Developing Countries: The Case of Taiwan', *Journal of Environmental Economics and Management*, 34, (1997), 107–126.

Annual Report, Central Bank, Colombo, Sri Lanka, 2004.

Aunan, K., Patzay, G., Aaheim, H. A., and Seip, H. M., 'Health and Environmental Benefits from Air Pollution Reductions in Hungary', *Science of the Total Environment*, 212, (1998), 245–268.

Cropper, M.L., Simon, A. M., Alberrini, A., and Sharma, P. K., 'The Health Benefits of Air Pollution Control in Delhi', *American Journal of Agricultural Economics*, 79(5), (1997), 1625–1629.

Dockery, D.W., Pope, C. A., Xu, X., Spengler, J. D., Ware, J. H., Fay M. E., An Association between Air Pollution and Mortality in Six U.S. Cities', *New England Journal of Medicine*, 329, (1993), 1753–1759.

Economics and Social Statistics, Department of Census and Statistics, Colombo, Sri Lanka, 1998.

Freeman, A.M., III, *The Measurement of Environmental Resource Values: Theory and Methods*, (Washington D.C: Resource for the Future, 1993).

Greene, William H., *Econometric Analysis*, Fifth Edition, (Singapore: Pearson Education, 2003).

Gupta, U., 'Valuation of Urban Air Pollution: A Case Study of Kanpur City in India', *Environmental and Resource Economics*, published online at: www.springerlink.com/content/3226744v320 1kh52/, (2008).

Lvovsky, K., 'Economic Cost of Air Pollution with Special Reference to India', South Asia Environment Unit, World Bank, Washington DC, 1998.

Murty, M. N., Gulati, S. C. and Banerjee, A., 'Health Benefits from Urban Air Pollution Abatement in the Indian Subcontinent', Discussions Paper No. 62/2003, Delhi: Institute of Economic Growth, 2003.

Ostro, B., 'Fine Particulate Air Pollution and Mortality in Two Southern California Countries', *Environmental research*, 70, (1995), 98–104.

Ostro, B., Sanchez, J. M., Aranda, C., and Eskeland, G. S., 'Air Pollution and Mortality, results from Santiago, Chile', *Journal of Exposure Analysis and Environmental Epidemiology*, 6(1), (1996), 97–114.

Pearce, D., 'Economic Valuation and Health Damage from Air Pollution in the Developing World', *Energy Policy,* 24(7), (1996), 627–630.

Pope, C. A., and Kanner, R. E., 'Acute Effects of PM_{10} Pollution on Pulmonary Function of Smokers with Mid to Moderate Chronic Obstructive Pulmonary Disease', *American Review of Respiratory Diseases,* 147, (1993), 1336–1340.

Quah, E. and Boon, T. L., 'The Economic Cost of Particulate Air Pollution on Health in Singapore', *Journal of Asian Economics,* 14, (2002), 73–90.

Schwartz, J., 'Air Pollution and Child Mortality: A Review and Meta Analysis', *Environmental Research,* 64, (1996), 36–52.

Statistical Pocket Book, Department of Census and Statistics, Colombo, Sri Lanka, 2005.

World Bank, China's Environment in the New Century: Clear Water, Blue Skies, The World Bank, Washington DC, 1997.

The World Development Indicators, The World Bank, Washington DC, 2004.

15

Revisiting the Need for Improved Stoves: Estimating Health, Time and Carbon Benefits

Min Bikram Malla Thakuri[1]

15.1. Introduction

Indoor Air Pollution (IAP), especially smoke generated from burning solid biomass fuel in kitchens, is a major environmental health issue in Nepal. Some 85 per cent of Nepalese households are dependent on biomass fuels for cooking energy (CBS, 2004). Biomass fuels such as animal dung, crop residues and wood, which are considered the most polluting fuels, lie at the bottom of the energy ladder, and are used mostly by very poor people. In Nepal these fuels are typically burnt in open fires or poorly functioning stoves and more often with inadequate ventilation creating a dangerous cocktail of hundreds of pollutants to which women and young children are exposed on a daily basis. According to WHO (2007a, based on) estimates, IAP from solid fuel burning was responsible for the deaths of 7,500 people, 204,400 Disability-Adjusted Life Years (DALY) loss and 2.7 per cent of the national burden of diseases in Nepal 2002 data. According to NDHS 2006,

[1] I am grateful to Subhrendu Pattanayak, Priya Shyamsunder, M. N. Murty, Mani Nepal and other resource persons, including SANDEE associates, who provided guidance at various stages of this study. I am thankful to 'Practical Action Nepal' for providing a conducive environment and support for engaging in this research. I also thank Liz Bates from 'Practical Action UK' and to Nigel Bruce from the University of Liverpool, UK, with whom I got an opportunity to work on a similar project and to learn about household energy, indoor air pollution and health. I would also like to thank Rashila Shrestha, Pratap Tamang and Karbo Tamang who supported me in data collection and pollution monitoring. Likewise, I would like to thank Ramjee Prasad Pathak for his support in questionnaire formulation and in the analysis of health related information. I am thankful to Jun Hada, Practical Action, and Ajay Pillarisetti, US Fulbright Fellow, for their feedback. Last but not least, I acknowledge with gratitude the financial support from SANDEE.

Acute Respiratory Infection (ARI) has contributed to 23 per cent of the total deaths in the year 2006 among children below five years of age. In Nepal, Acute Lower Respiratory Infections (ALRI), Chronic Obstructive Pulmonary Disease (COPD) and Tuberculosis are among the top 10 causes of death. There is strong evidence to suggest the role of IAP in the occurrence of such illnesses. Responses to such illnesses so far have focused on treatment rather than on prevention. However, an increasing number of international health professionals and policy makers are beginning to recognize indoor air pollution as a serious problem. While much work has been done on improving stove design, their focus has been on energy efficiency and fuel saving; lifting the burden on women's time and effort; and saving forests. Attention has turned to the issue of indoor air pollution and health only in the last few years (ITDG, 2004).

The economic valuation of health and environmental interventions is becoming increasingly important (WHO, 2004). In light of limited funding, such valuations can provide an important tool to – (a) demonstrate the economic returns to investments in interventions; (b) compare the effectiveness of one intervention against another; and (c) help policy-makers decide on how to allocate their limited resources. With household energy playing such a central role in people's lives, interventions to reduce indoor air pollution could potentially deliver a wide range of benefits in the areas of health, environment and poverty reduction.

A number of technologies and alternatives are available to solve the indoor air pollution problem. However, due to lack of information on the costs and benefits of such technologies, wide-scale adoption is not taking place at a satisfactory pace in Nepal. Given this information gap, this research aimed to analyse the viability of investment in smoke alleviating products. To meet this goal, a survey in 400 households in Rasuwa district, Nepal was administered. The results of the analysis show that the average indoor air pollution level in traditional stove user households is 15 times higher than the recommended safe level. The benefit-cost analysis suggests that investment in IAP mitigating interventions is viable from a household as well as a societal point of view.

15.2. Indoor air pollution problem in developing countries: a review

More than three billion people worldwide depend on solid fuels, including biomass (i.e., wood, dung and agriculture residues) and coal, to meet their basic energy needs such as cooking, boiling water and heating (WHO, 2006). However, inefficient burning of biomass fuel creates a dangerous cocktail of hundreds of pollutants. In general, people in developing countries use solid fuels because of their availability and affordability. Since the use of poor quality fuels decreases with development, the least developed areas are the most likely to experience the highest levels of indoor air pollution (Smith, 1993). In general, cook-stove efficiency is 20 per cent, 30 per cent, 50 per cent, and 70 per cent respectively for wood, charcoal, kerosene, and Liquid Petroleum Gas (LPG) stoves. Such fuel efficiency seems to be inversely correlated with the amount of health damaging pollutants it emits per joule of energy (Smith, 1994).

There is abundant evidence supporting the relationship between IAP and health endpoints such as acute respiratory infections, chronic obstructive pulmonary disease, and lung cancer in women (Smith, 1999; Ezzeti and Kammen, 2001). Inhaling indoor smoke doubles the risk of pneumonia and other acute infections of the lower respiratory tract among children under five years of age. Women exposed to indoor smoke are three times more likely to suffer from Chronic Obstructive Pulmonary Diseases (COPD), such as chronic bronchitis or emphysema, than women who cook with electricity, gas or other cleaner fuels. Use of coal doubles the risk of lung cancer, particularly among women. Moreover, some studies have linked exposure to indoor smoke to asthma, cataracts, tuberculosis, adverse pregnancy outcomes, in particular low birth weight, ischaemic heart disease, interstitial lung disease, and nasopharyngeal and laryngeal cancers. Globally, IAP is responsible for 1.6 million deaths annually and 2.7 per cent of the global burden of disease (WHO, 2006).

As women cook and small children (usually below five years of age) spend most of their time in the kitchen area with their mothers, these two groups are the most vulnerable to indoor air pollution. Smoke inside the house is one of the world's leading child killers, claiming nearly one million children's lives each year (ITDG, 2004). A Gambian study (Schwela, 1997) found that children under the age of five, who were carried on their mother's backs during cooking (in smoky cooking huts), increased their risk of developing Acute Respiratory Infection (ARI) up to six times. This was significantly higher than if their parents smoked. Qin et al. (1991) and Peng et al. (1998) find that more women and children from families using coal for household energy suffer from respiratory symptoms than those from families using natural gas. There is also evidence to support possible associations of IAP with tuberculosis, blindness and prenatal effects (Smith, 1999). The smoke from biomass combustion is also associated with reduced birth weight (Misra et al., 2004). Pokharel et al. (2005) established a strong correlation between the use of solid fuel in traditional stoves and the increased risk of cataract in women who do the cooking. M. R. Pandey (1984) found a significant correlation between the prevalence of chronic bronchitis and exposure to domestic smoke pollution in rural Nepal. Time loss in firewood collection is also very high in Nepal. On average, a household collects 18.3 bharis (i.e., headloads) or bundles of firewood per capita per year. On average, a household spends 5.01 hours for collecting one bhari firewood (Baland et al., 2008).

Studies (ITDG, 2004, for example) suggest that IAP is strongly associated with income level. It is the poor who rely on the lower grades of fuel and have the least access to cleaner technologies. Millions of people would lead a healthier life if their exposure to lethal levels of smoke were reduced. The most effective interventions and the most beneficial to the user and society as a whole would be a shift from wood or charcoal to kerosene, LPG, biogas or grid electricity for cooking energy. Other more progressive alternatives may be ethanol (gel) fuel and biomass gasification (Ballard-Tremeer and Mathee, 2000). But the current energy use and availability trends in developing countries indicate that solid fuel will continue to dominate fuel use in developing countries for the next several years. However, even taking this fact into consideration, there are possible interventions that could potentially reduce exposure to indoor air pollution. These interventions can be classified under three headings (Ballard-Tremeer and Mathee, 2000) – source (fuel, type of stove); living environment (housing, ventilation); and user behaviour (fuel drying, protection of child).

Bluffstone (1998) suggests that for a developing country like Nepal, where agriculture is the major form of livelihood and villagers depend on forests for important economic inputs, interim demand-side policies should be seriously considered to protect forests. According to him, promoting improved stoves is a more efficient and equitable instrument than subsidizing the major alternative fuel (kerosene) in order to reduce firewood demand. He therefore emphasizes provision of subsidies for improved stoves.

A Guatemalan study (McCracken and Smith, 1998) shows that the Plancha stove (an improved stove made of cast concrete) emits 87 per cent less $PM_{2.5}$[2] and 91 per cent less CO (carbon monoxide) per kJ of useful heat delivered as compared to an open fire during the water boiling test. Dasgupta et al. (2004) find the ventilation factor to have a strong effect on the level of Particulate Matter (PM). The study of Pitt et al. (2006) in Bangladesh suggests that chimneys are significantly effective in reducing the health impacts of stove proximity when biomass fuels are in use. The study also reports that proximity to stoves adversely affects the respiratory health of women and young children.

In order to evaluate the effectiveness of interventions, it is important to first value the changes that occur as a result of stoves and other interventions. A big part of this is valuing the health impacts. There are many studies already on valuing the health effects of outdoor air pollution (e.g., Alberini et al., 2000; Cropper et al., 1997; Ostro et al., 1998; Krupnick et al., 2000, 1999, 1996; Murty et al., 2003; and Gupta, 2006). But valuation of IAP is a relatively new area of research. Larson and Rosen (2000) have done some work on this subject while Habermehl (2007) analyses the benefits and costs of the Rocket Lorena Stove dissemination programme in Uganda. Further, WHO reports by G. Hutton, E. Rehfuess, (2006) and G. Hutton et al., (2006) describe the methods and data sources that form the basis for the cost benefit analyses of household energy and health interventions and present the results for eight intervention scenarios of relevance to energy policy in the context of Millennium Development Goals. The report concludes that the health and productivity gains far outweigh the overall cost of interventions to alleviate kitchen smoke.

According to Bruce (2000), households could adopt a new technology, such as an improved stove, if the perceived benefits of adoption are greater than the costs. A study (Parikh, 2000) on the impact of rural energy on the health impacts of poor rural communities in the three Indian states of Rajasthan, Himachal Pradesh and Utter Pradesh finds that the cost to poor families due to days lost collecting fuelwood, lost earnings and cost of medical treatment of adults is 85 billion rupees ($1.84bn) per year. Days lost due to illness and due to time spent on collecting fuel came to one billion days for a population of 226 million.

---

[2] These are very small particles less than 2.5 micrometers in diameter that can enter and penetrate the lungs.

15.3. Study area and data

Our study area consisted of five Village Development Committees in Rasuwa: Galtlang, Goljung, Chilime, Haku and Dhunche. The Rasuwa district lies in the northern part of Central Nepal, about 80 miles from Kathmandu. In 2001, there were 8696 households with a population of 44731 in the district (CBS, 2002). The main ethnic group (about 84 per cent) of the area are Tamang. Most of the households (91.3 per cent) in the area are totally dependent on biomass energy for cooking and room heating. Among this number, most households undertake cooking activity on inefficient traditional stoves in poorly ventilated kitchens. However, some households have installed smokehoods and undertaken changes in the traditional stove in order to mitigate the problem of indoor air pollution with the financial and technical support of Practical Action Nepal.

'Practical Action Nepal', an INGO, has been facilitating villagers in Rasuwa[3] to adopt appropriate technologies to alleviate indoor air pollution since 2001. It has facilitated village communities to select and develop efficient, appropriate and sustainable technological solutions to reduce the IAP problem in Rasuwa district. They used a participatory approach[4] to identify appropriate technology to solve the IAP problem. After experiments, the customers chose the smokehoods technology with stove modification. Under the 'Practical Action Nepal' project in Rasuwa, the smokehood is the major intervention, which is built against the wall with an improved tripod stove beneath it constructed with a mud base. The protective base around the back and the two sides of the tripod stove are made with mud. Likewise, a bar is set across the front of the stove to allow air to pass beneath it to improve combustion. The smokehood drafts away the smoke produced during the incomplete combustion of fuelwood while cooking. The organization took into consideration the special needs of the high hill region where room heating is one of the prime requirements besides cooking while designing the smokehood. Moreover, by incorporating a grill rod inside the smokehood, they made provisions for smoking meat and agro-based products. Users preferred the technology because of its practicality and appropriateness as it reduces the level of pollution, radiates

---

[3] The author works for the 'Practical Action Nepal' Office.

[4] The participatory approach adopted by 'Practical Action Nepal' includes working with communities, discussing with the households about the risks of indoor air pollution, and working with them to find solutions. By applying technical know-how to potential solutions identified by the community, they designed acceptable technology which proved to be effective.

heat inside the room, and allows them to cook the way they want using different types and sizes of pots[5].

Five local entrepreneurs trained by Practical Action Nepal are actively involved in the supply and installation of the smokehoods. A smokehood costs about NPR 5000. There are about 15 revolving fund groups supported by Practical Action Nepal. The local revolving fund groups provide loans to customers to buy smokehoods. The interested household becomes eligible for a loan from the revolving funds after paying the initial membership fee and a down-payment, which is 20 per cent of the total product and installation cost. The customer pays back the loan within two years in monthly instalments. The entrepreneurs had been able to install approximately 450 smokehoods in Rasuwa up to July 2007.

This study is based on primary data collected from household surveys and indoor air quality monitoring. In 2006, household surveys were administered to 400 households (80 with and 320 without intervention). Under the household survey, an attempt was made to collect information on demographic characteristics, resources, skills, climate, household characteristics, energy use, income, health status, etc. A range of confounding factors that might influence pollution levels and exposure, were assessed so their potential effect could be accounted for in the analysis. Information on kitchen size, ventilation, stove type, cooking practices and fuel type were also collected. The main cook was asked about symptoms associated with stove use, including coughing, wheezing, phlegm, eye irritation, headaches, symptoms associated with COPD, etc., and about symptoms of respiratory illness in children. The questionnaire included questions on burns in order to establish whether the interventions were helping to reduce the levels of burns in small children. In addition, individual data were also collected from the household head on household members regarding their annual treatment cost for respiratory problems. First the treatment cost per incident that year was calculated and added up the treatment cost for the particular household. The recall period for most variables was one year. But with respect to fuel use, it was just 24 hours (that is, for fuel use during smoke monitoring).

Indoor air quality monitoring (CO and Particulates, two key emissions harmful to health) in the sample households was conducted. In 60 (30 user

---

[5] Details about the intervention can be found in Practical Action's website (www.practicalaction.org).

and 30 non-user) households, PM_{10}[6] was monitored using Buck S.S. pumps, which is a low-flow sampling pump that draws in air, spins off the larger particles and deposits the lighter, more dangerous ones on a small circular disc of filter paper. The filter is weighed before and after monitoring; the difference in weight indicates the levels of the pollutants in the room. The pumps were calibrated prior to each 24-hour monitoring session using a Buck bubble calibrator.

To measure carbon monoxide, the Industrial Scientific ISC T82 real-time, single gas monitor was utilized. The machine gives real time monitoring results. Once monitoring takes place, the data can be downloaded to a computer. The monitoring of CO was conducted in 203 households (123 without and 80 with intervention). In the survey kitchen, a particulate pump and a CO monitor were set close together. 1.3m vertically and 1.3m horizontally away from the stove. The monitoring was conducted close together for 24 hours.[7]

15.4. Methodology

The collected data was analysed to identify the linkages between IAP and health for the purpose of assessing the viability of investments in IAP mitigating technologies and programmes. In order to do this, the study establishes the link between the IAP level and technological interventions. The marginal health costs associated with IAP are estimated and a Cost Benefit Analysis (CBA) of the intervention undertaken.

15.4.1. Determinants of IAP

Several studies (e.g., Dasgupta et al., 2004; World Bank, 2002; Brauer and Saxena, 2002; Moschandreas et al., 2002; Freeman and de Tejada, 2002) have identified the potential determinants of exposure to indoor air pollution – Fuel type, time spent on cooking, structural characteristics of houses, cooking locations, and household ventilation practices (i.e., opening of windows and doors, etc.) affect exposure. WHO (2002) reports

---

[6] Fine particles that are small enough to penetrate deep into the lungs and potentially pose significant health risks. They can cause inflammation and worsen the condition of people with heart and lung diseases. In addition, they may carry surface-absorbed carcinogenic compounds into the lungs.

[7] Details of smoke monitoring methods are available online at: http://www.hedon.info/goto. php/HouseholdSmokeMonitoring

that indoor air quality may vary depending on the type of cooking devices, type of fuel, hours of burning fire, ventilation, location of kitchen and stove, and user's behaviour (for example, fuel drying, use of pot lids, good maintenance and sound operation of the stove and food preparation style). From the literature and understanding of the local situation, the different factors which might have an effect on indoor air quality determination in rural Nepalese households were identified. These factors include stove and fuel type, housing structure, behavioural factors, family factors, weather factors and other sources of IAP like tobacco smoke, lighting, etc. With regard to fuel type, the dryness of the solid biomass fuel was considered in the analysis. Under housing structure, the size of the kitchen and the number of windows were considered. Behavioural factors include stove use for room heating. Family factors include the number of family members, the use of the stove to prepare foods other than regular food and the number of hours of cooking. Weather factors include temperature and rain. Other sources of IAP such as tobacco smoking and lighting fuel were also taken into consideration. To find the determinants of IAP, a regression is estimated with the following equation:

$$CO_i = \beta_0 + \beta_1 \text{ interven} + \beta_2 \text{ rain\_d} + \beta_3 \text{ avg\_temp} + \beta_4 \text{ k\_size} + \beta_5 \text{ win\_n} + \beta_6 \text{ family} + \beta_7 \text{ heat\_hrs} + \beta_8 \text{ ofood} + \beta_9 \text{ cook\_ses} + \beta_{10} \text{ light} + \beta_{11} \text{ smoking} + \varepsilon_1 \tag{1}$$

where CO is a proxy measure of IAP including PM_{10}. McCracken and Smith (1998) and Naeher et al. (2001) find a strong correlation between CO and PM_{10} indicating the usefulness of CO measurements as an inexpensive and accurate way of estimating PM_{10} concentrations. The right hand side variables were chosen based on existing IAP literature while ε_1 is the random error. The main variable of interest is 'interven', which refers to the smokehood and stove improvement intervention. Other independent variables include rain dummy (rain_d), average temperature in the monitoring day (avg_temp), size of kitchen (k_size), number of windows (win_n), family size (family), use of stove for room heating (heat_hrs), preparation of food other than regular foods (ofood), number of cooking sessions (cook_ses), type of fuel for lighting (light) and tobacco use in kitchen (i.e., smoking). The variables presented in Table 15.1 are defined. Equation (1) is estimated using Ordinary Least Squares method.

Table 15.1. Household characteristics: descriptive statistics

	Unit	Minimum	Maximum	Mean	Std. Deviation	N.*
Total family size	Nos.	1	13	5.17	1.904	400
Intervention	Dummy	0	1	0.20	0.401	400
Income	Rs. '000/year	2.50	354.0C	70.10	59.71	400
CO level – 24 hrs average	ppm)	0.24	74.69	6.58	7.97	203
PM_{10} – 24 hrs average	$\mu g/m^3$	79	2,755	509	482	60
Annual fuel consumption	Kg./Year	900	8,258	2,744	841	400
Annual time spent for firewood collection	Hours/Year	180.00	1,650.00	585.18	219.63	400
Use of dry fuel	Dummy	0	1	0.97	0.18	400
Total hours of cooking a day	Hours/day	0.50	7.25	3.28	1.07	400
Children's day loss due to illness	days/year	0.0	30.0	1.8	3.6	400
Days lost of economically active patients due to illness	Days/Year	0.0	97.0	8.4	9.7	400
Days lost of caretakers	Days/Year	0.0	97.0	4.9	8.4	400
Total household expenditure in treatment (cash)	Rs./Year	0	10,600	331	998	400
Frequency of illness	Frequency /Year	0.0	8.0	3.1	1.4	400
Total days lost of patient and caretakers excluding the children's day loss	Days/year	0.0	194.0	13.3	16.4	400
Subsidized medicines and check-ups received from health post	Rs.	0	1482	375	333.38	400

*Number of observations

(Contd.)

(Contd.)

	Unit	Minimum	Maximum	Mean	Std. Deviation	N.*
Rain	Dummy	0	1	0.35	0.478	400
Size of kitchen (m³)	Meter	2.46	56.00	21.05	10.27	400
Number of windows in the kitchen	Nos.	0.00	3.00	1.30	0.97	400
Number of children below 5 years	Nos.	0.00	5.00	0.91	0.97	400
Number of adults above 60 years	Nos.	0.00	3.00	0.27	0.54	400
Number of cooking sessions	Events	1.00	6.00	3.57	0.85	400
Preparation of food other than regular	Dummy	0	1	0.04	0.196	400
Type of fuel for lighting (clean = 1, No = 0)	Dummy	0	1	0.37	0.483	400
Smoking	Dummy	0	1	0.43	0.495	400
Stove used for heating purpose	Hours	0.00	7.00	0.24	0.64	400
Chronic illness	Dummy	0	1	0.02	0.140	400
Distance from nearest health facilities	Hours/visit	0.03	2.50	0.55	0.76	400
Distance from motorable road head	Hours/visit	0.05	4.00	1.66	1.62	400
Sex ratio	Ratio	0	7	1.335	0.990	394
No. of family members having secondary level education or more	Number	0	1	0.295	0.457	400

*Number of observations

15.4.2. Valuation of benefits

Four types of post-intervention economic benefits are considered in this analysis – (a) health benefits leading to a reduction in treatment cost and savings in days lost due to ill health; (b) fuel savings; (c) cooking time saving; and (d) global environmental benefits due to greenhouse gas reduction. The first three benefits are considered mainly from the household perspective while the environmental benefit is important from a societal perspective.

Total health cost is calculated by adding treatment costs and the value of working days lost due to indoor air pollution. Respiratory infections, mainly ALRI and Upper Respiratory Infections (URI) is considered, for the analysis. There is strong evidence from previous epidemiological studies that air pollution contributes significantly to the occurrence of ALRI (WIIO, 2007b) and URI (Mutius, 1995). Since the intervention had been available in the study area for only a short period of time, only the immediate acute health impacts were considered while chronic diseases resulting from long term exposure were ignored.

The total Treatment Costs (TC) include the cost of treatment and diagnosis (hospital/doctor's fee), lab charge, dietary expenses, and transportation costs and food expenses of the patient and caretakers. Days Lost (DL) refers to the cost associated with the loss of productivity and days of work lost due to illness. It is the sum of time loss of the patient and his/her attendants. During illness the patients need to travel for treatment, stay in hospital or rest at home while the attendants are responsible for giving proper care to the patient. To estimate the marginal effect of interventions on treatment costs and day loss, the following regression equations were used:

$$TC_i = \beta_0 + \beta_1 \text{ interven} + \beta_2 \text{ smoking} + \beta_3 \text{ health\_dist} + \beta_4 \text{ road\_dist} + \beta_5 \text{ lincome} + \beta_6 \text{ family} + \beta_7 \text{ below5} + \beta_8 \text{ above60} + \beta_9 \text{ chronic} + \varepsilon_2 \qquad (2)$$

$$DL_i = \beta_0 + \beta_1 \text{ interven} + \beta_2 \text{ smoking} + \beta_3 \text{ health\_dist} + \beta_4 \text{ road\_dist} + \beta_5 \text{ lincome} + \beta_6 \text{ family} + \beta_7 \text{ below5} + \beta_8 \text{ above60} + \beta_9 \text{ chronic} + \varepsilon_3 \qquad (3)$$

where TC (lcost_rs, log of total treatment cost) refers to the treatment cost and DL (loss_day) refers to the days lost. The explanatory variables are intervention (intervene), smoking in the kitchen (smoking), distance to health facilities (health_dist), distance to road head (road_dist), log of income level (lincome), size of family (family), number of children below five years (below5), number of the old above 60 years (chronic) in the household. These variables are in Table 15.1. In the sample, the treatment cost is zero for several households. In view of the truncated nature of the dependent variable, the Tobit regression is used for estimation of the treatment cost. As the Day Loss (DL) is count data, a negative binomial regression is estimated.

In order to estimate the marginal firewood savings from kitchen interventions, the following firewood consumption regression equation is also estimated:

$$fuel\_q_i = \beta_0 + \beta_1 \text{ interven} + \beta_2 \text{ ofood} + \beta_3 \text{ family} + \beta_4 \text{ lincome} + \beta_5$$
$$\text{ofuel} + \beta_6 \text{ rain\_d} + \beta_7 \text{ heat\_tim} + \beta_8 \text{ cook\_ses} + \beta_9 \text{ fuel\_tim}$$
$$+ \varepsilon_4 \qquad\qquad\qquad (4)$$

where fuel_q is the quantity of firewood used at the household level. The explanatory variables are intervention (intervene), type of prepared food (ofood), family size (family), log of income level (lincome), rain (rain_d), use of stove for heating purpose (heat_tim), number of cooking sessions (cook_ses) and fuel collection time (fuel_tim).[8]

The marginal saving in firewood due to the kitchen intervention is calculated from the above firewood consumption equation (4). Household data from the survey on hours spent per unit of fuelwood collected is also used. With this information and the marginal fuelwood saved, the annul firewood collection time savings is estimated. The monetary value of time savings is calculated by multiplying the time saved in fuel collection by the wage rate (NPR 100/day).

Similarly, based on data from the household survey, the time saved in average cooking time after the intervention is calculated. The mean difference in cooking time between households with and without the intervention is the time savings from the intervention. From this the monetary value of time saved in cooking activity is derived. The monetary value of cooking time saved is the total cooking time saved multiplied by the shadow wage rate[9].

---

[8] As the households collect firewood freely from nearby forests, we did not include the price of firewood in the demand function of firewood. Similarly, since the time to collect the firewood is the same for all households, we ignored it in the analysis.

[9] We used the shadow wage in the economic analyses. This was considered to be 50 per cent of the going wage rate.

The intervention in the study area may have a small but positive impact on global climate change through the reduction in firewood consumption. The burning of solid fuels leads to the emission of many different greenhouse gases (GHGs) such as carbon dioxide (CO_2), methane (CH_4), nitrogen dioxide (NO_2), etc. The CO_2 emission is the most important GHG from fuelwood burning, which is well recognized under the Clean Development Mechanism (CDM) of the Kyoto Protocol. Therefore, in this analysis, CO_2 emission is considered. Based on Habermehl (2007), it is assumed that each kg of non-renewably harvested firewood burned will generate 1500g CO_2. The monetary value of the global environmental benefit is the total CO_2 that is not released into the environment due to firewood that is not used, multiplied by the unit international market price of carbon.

15.4.3. Cost estimates

The initial capital investment for a household is calculated as the sum of the market price of the smokehood, the installation cost of the hood, and stove improvement costs. Similarly, the recurrent fuel costs, operation, repair, and maintenance costs have also been taken into consideration in this analysis. For the CBA from a societal perspective, the programme cost has been included, i.e., the direct programme cost of 'Practical Action Nepal'.

15.4.4. Benefit cost analysis

We have conducted the benefit cost analysis from two perspectives – (a) an economic analysis to assess the social benefit from a societal perspective, and (b) a financial analysis to assess private benefits from a household perspective.

All the prices in the analyses are based on 2006 market prices. A shadow wage was applied for time saved in the economic analyses in order to calculate the true economic price. The shadow wage rate used is 50 per cent of the going wage rate for women. This is based on the assumption that women would use only 50 per cent of their saved time on income generating activities, farming and home-care-related activities.[10]

The life of the intervention is assumed to be 10 years and, therefore, the annual benefit and cost cash flow is calculated for a 10 year period. From the net cash flow, the Benefit-Cost (B/C) ratio, Net Present Value (NPV)

---

[10] Habermehl (2007) also uses the same rate.

and Internal Rate of Return (IRR) are calculated. We calculate the B/C ratio and NPV using the standard discount rate of 12 per cent in the financial analysis (analysis from a household perspective). Some of the benefits of investments to improve indoor air quality will be visible in the long run only. These interventions also have long term environmental benefits for future generations which will not be limited to a single household. Therefore, a lower social discount rate of three per cent is applied in the economic analysis. In addition, in order to check the robustness of the results and the risk associated with the benefit and cost, a sensitivity analysis is performed. The sensitivity of investment was checked in case of cost increase, benefit decrease, or both.

The NPV and B/C ratio (BCR) are calculated using the following equations:

$$NPV = \sum_{t=1}^{T} \frac{(\text{Benefit}_t - \text{Cost}_t)}{(1+r)^t} \tag{5}$$

$$BCR = \frac{\displaystyle\sum_{r=1}^{r} \frac{B_t}{(1+r)^t}}{\displaystyle\sum_{r=1}^{r} \frac{C_t}{(1+r)^t}} \tag{6}$$

where r is the discount rate, t is the year, B_t is the benefit in time t and C_t is the cost in time t and IRR is the rate for which NPV equals zero.

15.5. Results and discussion

15.5.1. Indoor air pollution problem in rural Nepal

All the households use firewood for cooking in the surveyed area. Only a few (1 per cent) households use clean fuels (biogas, LPG, etc.) along with firewood. The average annual firewood consumption is 2,744 kg (see Table 15.1). Due to the high use of firewood (solid fuel), the pollution in the kitchen is very high. Table 15.2 shows that the twenty-four hour average PM_{10} level is 764 $\mu g/m^3$ in households without intervention (control group), which is about 15 times higher than the WHO recommended safe level of 50$\mu g/m^3$. In the sample households with intervention, the 24 hour average PM_{10} level is 255$\mu g/m^3$ which is 66 per cent less than for the control group (see Table 15.2).

The WHO recommends maximum 9 ppm CO level for eight hour average. The findings of this study indicate that the 24 hour average CO level is 9.39 ppm in households with traditional stoves compared to 2.26 ppm (that is, 76 per cent less) in households with smokehoods. The results show that the difference in the levels of pollution (PM_{10} and CO) in the intervention and control groups is statistically significant (see Table 15.2). The results of the study suggest that there is a strong correlation (r = 0.813) between CO and PM_{10}. McCracken and Smith (1998) and Naeher et al. (2001) report similar results. Such high correlation indicates that CO measurements can be an inexpensive and approximate way of estimating PM_{10} concentrations. On the basis of this evidence, CO is used as a proxy measure of PM_{10} in this analysis.[11]

Table 15.2. Characteristics of intervention and control households

Description	Unit	Without Intervention	With intervention	t-stat
Number of HHs	Nos.	320	80	
Total Family Size	Nos.	5.07	5.60	−2.256**
Per cent of population (0–5 Years)	%	16.5%	21.2%	2.928***
Per cent of population (6–15 Years)	%	24.1%	25.9%	−1.499
Per cent of population (16–60 years)	%	55.6%	50.4%	−0.037
Per cent of population (60 years over)	%	5.7%	3.1%	1.717*
Dependency ratio	%	27.85%	31.85%	
Land holding (ropani)	Ropani	9.51	12.16	−3.156***
Income	(Rs./year)	64,630	91,995	−3.725**
PM_{10} Level – 24 hrs average	(μg/m3)	764	255	4.78***
CO level – 24 hrs average	(ppm)	9.39	2.26	6.91***
Annual fuel consumption	(kg/year)	2,886	2,174	7.19***

(*Contd.*)

---

[11] With the use of the filter and buck pump, the PM_{10} monitoring process was quite lengthy. Therefore, we were able to monitor it in 60 HHs only.

(*Contd.*)

Description	Unit	Without Interven-tion	With interven-tion	t-stat
Annual trip for fuel collection	trips	96	73	7.17***
Average fuel collection time per bhari	Hours	6.41	6.33	0.473
Annual fuel collection time (in hours)	Hours/year	617	454	6.23***
Daily cooking hours	Hours/day	3.32 (3 hours 19 minutes)	3.09 (3 hours 5 minutes)	1.70*
Carbon dioxide (CO_2) emission	(kg/year/HH)	4329	3261	7.19***
Frequency of illness due to IAP	Episodes/year	3.3	2.5	4.35***
Days lost due to IAP generated health problems				
Days lost of economically active population due to illness (days/year)	Days/year	9.55	3.84	4.82***
Days lost of children below 15 years	Days/year	2.00	0.74	2.39***
Days lost to caretakers	Days/year	5.63	1.94	3.53***

*** Significant at 1% level, ** significant at 5% level and * significant at 10% level
Note: The number in the parentheses is the standard deviation of the variable
Source: Household Survey, 2006

A range of factors that might influence indoor air pollution levels, known as confounding variables, is assessed in order to analyse their potential effects on CO. Equation (1) is estimated using the Ordinary Least Squares (OLS) method for that purpose. The results are presented in Table 15.3. The results of this study indicate that the coefficient of intervene (smokehoods and stove improvement) is negative and significant (−6.74) indicating that interventions are effective in reducing the indoor air pollution level significantly. Likewise, the size of the kitchen significantly reduces the IAP level – the larger the kitchen area the lower the IAP level. On the contrary, the use of the stove for purposes other than cooking regular food, such as making alcohol, preparing animal feed and for room heating has a significant positive effect on CO concentrations. A positive and significant effect on IAP levels of the number of cooking sessions and smoking is also found. Other variables such as use of polluting fuel for lighting, the total family size, the number of windows in the kitchen have no significant effect on IAP levels.

15.5.2. Measurement of economic benefit from intervention

There is a significant difference among the cooks (Table 15.4) and children (Table 15.5) between the intervention and control groups with regard to the occurrence of respiratory illnesses such as cough, phlegm and wheezing symptoms. The probability of reduction in respiratory illness in women cooks and children below five years after the intervention is significantly high (see Table 6).

The OLS results suggests that the intervention contributes to a reduction in treatment costs by about NPR 603/year per household (see Table 15.7). The Government provides medical check-ups and medicines at subsidized rates in the area through public health facilities. On average, the subsidy on medicines and health check-ups is approximately NPR 375/HH/year (see Table 15.2). If we factor in this cost, the marginal savings due to the intervention would come to about NPR 978/year per household. Likewise, there were savings in sick days after the intervention due to fewer occurrences of diseases. As Table 15.8 shows, the saving in annual sick days for people in the economically active age (patient and caretaker) totals approximately 10 days/HH due to the intervention, which is equivalent to NPR 1000/year (or NPR 500/year in economic price[12]).

Table 15.3. OLS and IV regression results (Dependent Variable: CO level)

	OLS		IV Estimates	
Variables	**Coefficient**	**t-stat**	**Coefficient**	**t-stat**
Intervention	−6.74	−5.35***	−8.82	−2.24**
Rain Dummy	−0.65	−0.51	0.17	0.12
Average Temperature	0.32	2.14**	0.20	0.91
Size of kitchen	−0.11	−2.20**	−0.12	−1.82*
Number of windows in the kitchen	0.26	0.50	0.26	0.47

(Contd.)

---

[12] Economic price includes direct, indirect, and hidden costs like opportunity cost. For the time saving, we assume that only 50 per cent of the saved time would be used productively so it is less than the financial price. The average daily wage rate in the study area is NPR 100/day.

(Contd.)

Variables	OLS Coefficient	t-stat	IV Estimates Coefficient	t-stat
Total family size	0.26	1.02	0.35	1.16
Hours used for heating purposes	1.93	2.78***	2.11	2.83***
Foods other than regular food prepared	4.88	2.23**	4.65	1.97*
Number of cooking sessions	1.34	2.44**	1.57	2.67***
Use of polluting fuel for lighting	0.04	0.03	−0.49	−0.38
Smoking Dummy	3.32	3.41***	2.96	2.83***
Constant	−3.25	−0.82	−2.57	−0.43
R Square	0.337		0.257	
Adjusted R Square	0.299		0.213	
Number of observations	203		203	
F-value	8.083***		5.84***	

Note 1: Dependent Variable: CO level – 24 hrs average
Note 2: *** significant at 1% level; ** significant at 5% level; * significant at 10% level
Source: Household Survey, 2006

The impact of the intervention on fuel consumption is also analysed. Table 15.9 presents the regression result on the determinants of firewood consumption. It is clear that the intervention results in a significant decline in firewood consumption. In the case of OLS, the average firewood saving per day due to the intervention is 3.15 kg per household (roughly 1150 kg/year). The households in the study area do not purchase fuelwood but collect it from nearby forests. In this study area average amount of firewood collected per person per trip is approximately 30 kgs on average. The average time per trip comes to about 6.41 hrs. The results indicate that approximately 31 workings days (the equivalent of NPR 1550 in economic price) are saved per household annually with the installation of the improved stove with smokehood.

In addition, improved stove efficiency and changes in cooking practices lead to significant savings in cooking time. The analysis suggests that intervention saves 14 minutes/day (or approximately 84 hours/year, as seen in Table 15.2) of cooking time. If converted into monetary terms, this saving is equivalent to approximately NPR 525/HH in economic price per year.

Table15.4. Symptoms of illness in main cook (Woman) over 12 months period

Symptoms	Without intervention		With intervention		Difference	t- stat
	%	SD	%	SD	%	
Cough						
Cough first thing in the morning or at other times of the day	93.4%	0.25	67.5%	0.47	25.9%	6.790***
Cough for more than 3 months	48.1%	0.50	18.8%	0.39	29.4%	4.886***
Cough at least 3 months for 2 or more years	45.0%	0.50	17.5%	0.38	27.5%	4.607***
Cough most days, at least 3 months, for 2 more years	24.1%	0.43	15.0%	0.36	9.1%	1.745*
Phlegm						
Had phlegm during last 12 months	89.1%	0.31	65.0%	0.48	24.1%	5.466***
Usually phlegm on most days	86.3%	0.34	65.0%	0.48	21.3%	4.526***
Phlegm for at least 3 months last year	47.5%	0.50	16.3%	0.37	31.3%	5.237***
Phlegm at least 3 months, for more than 2 years	43.8%	0.50	15.0%	0.36	28.8%	4.865***
Phlegm most days, at least 3 months, for more than 2 years	41.6%	0.49	15.0%	0.36	26.6%	4.521***
Episodes of cough and phlegm						
Episodes of both cough and phlegm continue for 3 weeks	60.9%	0.49	12.5%	0.33	48.4%	8.389***
Cough and phlegm for more than 2 years	40.6%	0.49	1.3%	0.11	39.4%	7.108***
Wheezing	20.3%	0.40	7.5%	0.27	12.8%	2.700***
Sore/watering eyes most of the days	28.8%	0.45	5.0%	0.36	23.8%	4.552***
Headaches for most of the days	30.0%	0.46	7.5%	0.27	22.5%	4.210***
Smokers	66.0%	0.474	65.0%	0.480	1.0%	0.211

Note: Total sample for without intervention was 320 compared to 80 with intervention case
*** significant at 1% level; ** significant at 5% level; * significant at 10% level

Source: Household Survey, 2006

Table 15.5. Symptoms of illness in children below five years over last 12 months period

Illness Symptoms	Without		With		Difference	t- stat
	Mean	SD	Mean	SD		
Cough during last two weeks	81.0%	0.39	20.4%	0.41	60.7%	9.663***
Breathe rapidly during coughing	75.8%	0.43	16.7%	0.38	59.2%	8.973***
Coughs and Colds of Children over last 12 months period	86.9%	0.34	64.8%	0.48	22.1%	3.670***
Burn or scalds over last 12 months period	5.2%	0.25	0.0%	0.00	5.2%	1.528
Pneumonia over last 12 months period	6.5%	0.25	5.6%	0.23	1.0%	0.254
Average number of children below 5 years	0.69	0.84	1.04	0.82		3.24***

Note: 153 non-user and 53 user households reported they had children below 5 years.

Note: *** significant at 1% level; ** significant at 5% level; * significant at 10% level

Source: Household Survey, 2006

Table 15.6. Probability of reduction in illness in women cooks and children below five years after intervention

Symptoms	Probability of reduction in illness after intervention (marginal effect)	z-statistics
Symptoms in Women Cooks		
Chronic cough	−0.279	−4.31***
Chronic phlegm (phlegm for more than 3 months)	−0.302	−4.66***
Cough and phlegm symptom regularly for 3 weeks	−0.503	−7.24***
Wheezing	−0.104	−2.14**
Sore/Watering Eyes	−0.237	−4.16***
Symptoms in Children below 5 years		
Cough	−0.607	−7.55***
Breathing rapidly during coughing	−0.592	−7.20***

Note: (i) The results were derived from separate Probit Regression Analyses
(ii) *** significant at 1% level; ** significant at 5% level; * significant at 10% level.

Table 15.7. OLS, IV and Tobit results (Dependent variable: log of treatment cost)

	OLS		IV- Estimates		Tobit regression	
	Coef.	t-stat	Coef.	t-stat	Coef.	T
Intervention	-1.824	-5.61***	-2.986	-2.37**	-2.160	-5.57***
Smoking by a household member (Dummy)	-0.003	-0.01	-0.014	-0.05	-0.085	-0.28
Distance from health facilities (in hours)	0.822	4.74***	0.999	3.87***	0.848	4.14***
Distance from motorable road head (in hours)	0.136	1.69*	0.156	1.79*	0.129	1.36
Total family size	-0.004	-0.06	-0.014	-0.19	-0.005	-0.07
Log of income (Rs. '000/year)	0.834	4.68***	1.000	3.95***	0.944	4.50***
Number of children below 5 years	0.128	0.94	0.213	1.35	0.199	1.25
Number of adults above 60 years	-0.426	-1.92*	-0.521	-2.05**	-0.431	-1.66*
Chronic illness (Dummy)	2.367	2.72***	2.771	2.82***	2.757	2.73***
(Constant)	-0.314	-0.42	-0.877	-0.89	-0.960	-1.08
R square	0.1422		0.0856	Log likelihood	-874.114	
Adjusted R square	0.1224		0.0641	Sigma	2.708849	
F	7.18***		3.99***	Pseudo R2	0.0302	
				Number of observation	400	
Number of observations	400		400			

Note: *** significant at 1% level; ** significant at 5% level; * significant at 10% level

Table 15.8. Marginal effects: negative binomial estimates (Dependent Variable: days lost due to illness)

	Regression		IV Estimates	
	dy/dx	z	dy/dx	z
Intervention	−10.491	−9.86***	−19.157	−2.86***
Smoking by a household member (Dummy)	0.314	0.24	0.696	0.46
Distance from health facilities (in hours)	1.707	1.95*	2.873	2.14**
Distance from motorable road head (in hours)	−0.440	−1.07	−0.281	−0.57
Total family size	−0.217	−0.58	−0.448	−1.05
Log of income (Rs. '000/year)	2.399	2.63***	3.341	2.50**
Number of children below 5 years	0.767	1.12	1.216	1.42
Number of adults above 60 years	−0.539	−0.51	−1.486	−1.13
Chronic illness (Dummy) (Constant)	7.045	1.04	13.371	1.25
Log likelihood	−1418.6568		−1424.5889	
Lnalpha	−0.1492762		−0.0088178	
Alpha	0.8613312		0.991221	
Pseudo R2	0.0215		0.0045	
Number of observations	400		394	

Note: *** significant at 1% level; ** significant at 5% level; * significant at 10% level

Finally, due to the significant reduction in the use of firewood at 1150kg/year, it is estimated that there would be about 1,700kg/hh/year less of CO_2 emission which contributes to an improvement in the global environment. If it is assumed that the economic value of one tonne of CO_2 avoided is approximately US $6.00[13], the saving in firewood use results in a saving of NPR 724/HH/year in terms of a reduction in the level of CO_2 emission.

15.5.3. Issue of endogeneity

The intervention has been treated up to now as an exogenous variable. However, when selecting households for indoor smoke alleviating

---

[13] In this study, the exchange rate between the US$ and Nepalese currency was taken as US $1.00 = NPR 70.00.

technology adoption, the project provided the technology to interested households. The project created a revolving fund to address the credit constraints of low income households and provided loans to interested customers, who then used the loans to buy the kitchen improvements. The adoption of the new technology, however, may depend on the degree of air pollution in the kitchen, the quantity of firewood needed for cooking and heating, and the health impacts of the polluted air coming from the kitchen. The potential dependency of technology adoption (interven) on the dependent variables (CO, TC, DL and fuel_q) in equations (1) through (4) creates an endogeneity problem.

Table 15.9. Determinants of firewood consumption – OLS and IV estimates

	OLS		IV Estimates	
	Coeff.	t-stat	Coeff.	t-stat
Intervention	–3.148	–10.39***	–4.815	–3.82***
Food other than regular food prepared (Dummy)	6.808	11.92***	6.497	9.69***
Total family size	0.511	8.47***	0.540	7.63***
Income (Rs. '000/year)	–0.103	–0.66	0.058	0.27
Use of other fuel (Dummy)	–2.325	–2.06**	–1.657	–1.24
Rain (Dummy)	–0.285	–1.16	–0.694	–1.65*
Stove used for heating purpose (Dummy)	–0.023	–0.13	0.142	0.62
Number of cooking sessions	1.743	13.25***	1.776	11.99***
Fuel collection time	0.049	0.58	0.005	0.05
(Constant)	–0.768	–0.81	–0.954	–0.89
R square	0.6045		0.5162	
Adjusted R square	0.5954		0.5048	
F	66.24***		45.52***	
Number of observations	400		394	

[a] Dependent Variable: Total use of fuel a day (in kg.)

Note: *** significant at 1% level; ** significant at 5% level; * significant at 10% level

Source: Household Survey, 2006

In order to address the possible endogeneity issue, an instrumental variable (IV) approach is used while estimating equations (1) through (4). The adoption of new technology may depend on the household income and the knowledge of the person making decisions on adoption about the link between indoor air pollution and health outcomes of family members. It is possible to take the education levels of household members as proxy for knowledge about the effects of indoor air pollution on health. Household income and education level are therefore used as instruments for intervention (intervene). The sex-ratio is also used as an additional instrument for intra-household decision making capacity when it comes to adopting the improved stove. The decision to adopt an intervention may depend on the bargaining power of the female who generally spends more time on cooking and therefore is more affected by the polluted air.

The contribution of intervention (interven) goes up in all cases when corrected for endogeneity. The results from IV estimates indicate that the effect of intervention on reduction in indoor air pollution is even stronger when corrected for endogeneity. The reduction in CO levels goes up from 6.74 ppm to 8.82 ppm if the results are compared from the OLS and IV methods (see Table 15.3). An alternative model is aso estimated with an alternative set of instruments, where income is replaced by land holding. But the results are not sensitive to the alternative set of instruments.[14] For example, the reduction in treatment cost increases to NPR 987 from NPR 603 (see Table 15.7) while the marginal saving (which includes government subsidies) is NPR 1352. The saving in annual sick days also goes up to 19 days/HH/year (the equivalent of NPR 1900/year in financial terms and NPR 950/year in economic terms) in the case of IV estimates (see Table 15.8). The average firewood saving per day due to the intervention is 4.82 kg for each household (about 1527kg/year, see Table 15.9). This translates into a saving of 40 working days per year per household (the equivalent of around NPR 2000 in economic price).

The analysis indicates that there would be 1725–2290 kg/hh/year less CO_2 emission due to the reduction in firewood use (approximately, 1150–1527 kg/year) based on the OLS or IV estimation method. The reduction in firewood use results in savings of NPR 724–NPR 962/hh/year in terms of a reduced level of CO_2 emission.

15.5.7. Cost of intervention

The intervention costs to the households as well as to society. The initial investment cost for the intervention per household is approximately NPR 5000/HH with a maintenance requirement of NPR 100/year (see

---

[14] This particular set of results is not reported here but is available upon request.

Table 15.10). This cost is estimated as net costs based on the costs of smokehoods plus stove modification minus the cost of the traditional stove. Similarly, the programme cost was calculated based on Practical Action Nepal's direct programme cost in Rasuwa in order to calculate the cost to society. The total programme cost was approximately NPR 4.76 million (1.12 million for seed money, 0.79 million for grants and 2.85 million for other programme costs) during the three years of the project period (see Table 15.10).

Table 15.10. Summary of cost and benefits (in Rs.)

Headings	Perspectives	
	House hold (in Rs.)	Societal (in Rs.)
Costs		
Cost of a smokehood	5000	$(5000+150) \times 640$
Annual maintenance cost	100	100×640
Programme cost (excluding support for smokehoods)	–	2,850,870
Benefits		
Treatment cost saving	987	$(987+375) \times 640$
Day loss due to illness saving	1900 (19 days)	950×640
Annual fuel collection time saving (Rs./Year)	4000 (40 days)	2000×640
Annual cooking hour saving (Rs./Year)	1050 (10.5 days)	525×640
Carbon dioxide (CO_2) emission saving (Rs./Year)	–	962×640

15.5.8. Cost benefit analysis

A household's decision to install a smokehood depends on the direct costs and benefits to the household. Hence, a cost benefit analysis is carried out to assess the viability of the investment for intervention. For a household, the total investment includes the price of intervention (smokehood installation and stove modification cost) which comes to about NPR 5000 with a maintenance requirement of about NPR 100/hh per year (see Table 15.10). The annual financial benefit of the intervention is NPR 987/HH from treatment costs and NPR 1900/HH (19 days) from health care related time savings. Similarly, there is a NPR 5050/HH (or 50.5 days) saving from indirect time savings (i.e., time savings in cooking and firewood collection).

Thus, the total annual financial savings come to about NPR 7,937/HH/year (see Table 15.10). A benefit cost analysis from the household perspective suggests that the investment in a smokehood is highly viable on economic grounds with the estimated Financial Internal Rate of Return (FIRR) being 156 per cent, which is about thirteen times higher than the cut-off discount rate (12 per cent). If only the health benefits of the intervention (ignoring other benefits) are considered, the IRR comes to about 55 per cent. If only the monetary cost saving (that is, the treatment cost saving in cash) is considered, the IRR comes down to 12 per cent (see Table 15.11).

A sensitivity analysis is performed in order to check the robustness of the results and the risk associated with the underlying benefit and cost assumptions. The results of the sensitivity analysis show that the investment in smokehoods is viable even in the case of an increase in the product cost by 20 per cent or a decrease in associated benefits by 20 per cent. Even in the combined case, the BC ratio is greater than the unity, indicating the viability of the investment.

In order to check the viability of the indoor air pollution alleviation programme from a societal perspective, an economic cost benefit analysis is undertaken. Because of increased awareness, a smooth flow with regard to supply, and availability of loan facilities through revolving funds, approximately 640 households are expected to benefit from the intervention in the project area. The CBA analysis from a societal perspective shows that the investment in scaling up the programme on indoor smoke alleviating technologies is economically viable with an EIRR of 71 per cent. Similarly, the analysis shows that over a 10 year period, the NPV will come to NPR 20.1 million with a B/C ratio of 4.7 at the three per cent discount rate (see Table 15.11). The results of the sensitivity analysis indicate that the investment in kitchen smoke alleviation programmes is viable even if programme costs increase by 20 per cent or benefits decrease by 20 per cent. Even if the project costs increase by 20 per cent and the benefits decline by 20 per cent, the BC ratio remains greater than the unity (2.2). Moreover, even in the absence of financial benefits from CO_2 savings, the programme seems viable with an IRR of 57 per cent.

15.6. Conclusions and recommendations

In rural Nepal, most of the households are totally dependent on solid biomass fuel for cooking energy. The biomass reliance has been

Table 15.11. CBA analysis – the results

Scenarios	Present Value (NPRs)		NPV @ 12% Discount rate (Rs.)	IRR	B/C Ratio
	Cost	Benefit			
From Household Perspective					
With treatment cost (cash) saving only	5565	5577	12	12.06%	1.00
With health benefits only	5565	16312	10747	55.05%	2.93
Base Results (with total benefits)	5,565	44,846	39,281	156.73%	8.06
Sensitivity Results					
Total Project cost increase by 20%	6,678	44,846	38,168	130.25%	6.72
Total Project benefits decrease by 20%	5,565	35,877	30,312	124.95%	6.45
Total cost increase & benefits decrease by 20 % each	6,678	32,713	26,035	94.37%	4.90
From Societal Perspective					
Base Results	5,446,465	25,619,447	20,172,982	71.39%	4.70
Sensitivity Results					
Total Project cost increase by 20%	6,535,758	28,270,192	21,734,434	64.59%	4.33
Total Project benefits decrease by 20%	5,446,465	22,616,153	17,169,688	61.51%	4.15
Total cost increase & benefit decrease by 20 % each	6,535,758	22,616,153	16,080,395	49.32%	3.46
Without CO_2 saving benefits	5,446,465	21,369,420	15,922,955	57.46%	3.92

contributing to external economic cost such as deforestation, green house gas emission, drudgery and ill health of rural women and children. The research findings of this study show that the indoor air pollution level is very high (15 times higher than the recommended safe level) in the study area where households use solid biomass fuel for cooking on traditional inefficient stoves. Indoor air pollution is one of the key contributory factors of major health problems, mainly ALRI, and results in high expenditure in terms of treatment and loss of productivity. There is an urgent need to increase access to cleaner fuels and improved technologies to overcome these problems.

The smokehood with improved stove designs has proved to be very effective in reducing the indoor air pollution levels. The benefit-cost analysis suggests that it is viable to invest in this product and its scaling up programme. Yet, the adoption of these interventions is very limited. There are several reasons why scaling up is not taking place. The three most obvious ones are – (a) the information gap – i.e., households not aware of the benefits; (n) expenditure incurred in the intervention and the lack of credit facilities; (c) the absence of a regular supply of intervention technologies because there is no established market. It is imperative for policy makers to deal with these challenges if the problem of indoor air pollution is to be seriously addressed.

References

Baland, J.M., Bardhan, P., Das, S., Mookherjee, D. and Sarkar, R., 'The Environmental Impact of Poverty: Evidence from Firewood Collection in Rural Nepal', CRED WP 2008/01, Centre for Research in the Economics of Development, (Namur, Belgium: University of Namur, 2008).

Ballard-Tremeer, G. and Mathee, A., 'Review of Interventions to Reduce the Exposure of Women and Young Children to Indoor Air Pollution in Developing Countries', Paper prepared for USAID/WHO International Consultation on Household Energy, Washington, DC: Indoor Air Pollution and Health, 2000.

Bluffstone, Randall A., 'Reducing Degradation of Forests in Poor Countries when Permanent Solutions Elude us: what Instruments do we really have?', *Environment and Development Economics* 3 (03), (1998), 295–317.

Brauer, M. and Saxena, S., 'Accessible Tools for Classification of Exposure to Particles', *Chemosphere* 49, (2002), 1151–1162.

Bruce, N., Perez-Padilla, R. and Albalak, R., 'Indoor Air Pollution in Developing Countries: a Major Environmental and Public Health Challenge', *Bulletin of the World Health Report* 78 (9), (2002), 1078–1092.

CBS (2002), 'Population Census 2001', Central Bureau of Statistics, National Planning Commission Secretariat, Government of Nepal, Kathmandu, Nepal.

CBS (2003), 'District Level Indicators of Nepal for Monitoring Overall Development', Central Bureau of Statistics, National Planning Commission Secretariat, Government of Nepal, Kathmandu, Nepal.

CBS (2004), 'Nepal Living Standards Survey', Central Bureau of Statistics, National Planning Commission Secretariat, Government of Nepal, Kathmandu, Nepal.

Dasgupta, S., Huq, M., Khaliquzzaman, M., Pandey, K. and Wheeler, D., 'Indoor Air Quality for Poor Families: New Evidence from Bangladesh', World Bank Policy Research Working Paper 3393, September 2004, World Bank, Washington D.C., 2004.

ESMAP/World Bank, 'India: Household Energy, Indoor Air Pollution, and Health', South Asia Environment and Social Development Unit, Joint UNDP/World Bank Energy Sector Management Assistance Program, November 2002, Washington D.C., 2002.

Ezzati, M. and Kammen, D.M., 'Household Energy, Indoor Air Pollution, and Public Health in Developing Countries', Issue Brief, 02–26, Resources for the Future, Washington D.C., 2002.

Freeman, N. C. G. and Saenz de Tejada, S., 'Methods for Collecting Time/Activity Pattern Information related to Exposure to Combustion Products', *Chemosphere* 49, 2002, 979–992.

Gupta, U., 'Valuation of Urban Air Pollution: A Case Study of Kanpur City in India', SANDEE Working Paper No. 17-06, South Asian Network for Development and Environmental Economics (SANDEE), Kathmandu, Nepal, 2006.

Habermehl, H., 'Economic Evaluation of the Improved Household Cooking Stove Dissemination Programme in Uganda', German Development Cooperation (GTZ), February 2007, Eschborn, Germany.

Hutton, G. and Rehfuess, E., 'Guidelines for Conducting Cost–benefit Analysis of Household Energy and Health Interventions', World Health Organization, Geneva, 2006.

Hutton G, Rehfuess, E., Tediosi, F. and Weiss, S., 'Evaluation of the Costs and Benefits of Household Energy and Health Interventions at Global and Regional Levels', World Health Organization, Geneva, 2006.

ITDG (2004), 'Smoke – The Killer in the Kitchen: Indoor Air Pollution in Developing Countries', ITDG Publishing, London, UK.

Larson, B. A. and Rosen, S., 'Household Benefits of Indoor Air Pollution Control in Developing Countries', A paper prepared for the USAID & WHO Global Technical Consultation on the Health Impacts of Indoor Air Pollution and Household Energy in Developing Countries, Washington, D.C., 2000.

McCracken, J. P. and Smith, K. R., *Emissions and Efficiency of Improved Woodburning Cookstoves in Highland Guatemala*, (Maryland Heights, USA: Elsevier Science Ltd., 1998).

Ministry of Health and Population Nepal (2006), Nepal Demographic and Health Survey Report 2006, Kathmandu, Nepal, New ERA and Macro International.

Mishra, V., Xiaolei Dai, Kirk R. Smith and Lasten Mika, *Material Exposure to Biomars Smoke and Reduced Birth Weight in Zimbabwe*, (New York: Elsevier Inc. 2004).

Moschandreas, D.J., Watson, J., D'Aberton, P., Scire, J., Zhu, T., Klein, W. and Saxena, S. 'Methodology of Exposure Modelling', *Chemosphere* 49, (2002), 923–946.

Murty, M. N., Gulati, S. C. and Banerjee, A., 'Health Benefits from Urban Air Pollution Abatement in the Indian Subcontinent', 236 /2003, Institute of Economic Growth, Delhi, India, 2003.

Mutius, E. von, Sherrill, D.L., Fritzsch, C., Martinez, F.D. and Lebowitz, M.D., 'Air Pollution and Upper Respiratory Symptoms in Children from East Germany', European Respiratory Journal, 8(5), (1995), 723–728.

Naeher, L. P., Smith, K.R., Leaderer, B.P., Neufeld, L. and Mage, D.T., 'Carbon Monoxide as a Tracer for Assessing Exposures to Particulate Matter in Wood and Gas Cookstove Households of Highland Guatemala', *Environmental Science & Technology*, 35, (2001), 575–581.

Pandey, M.R., 'Domestic Smoke Pollution and Chronic Bronchitis in a Rural Community of Hill Region of Nepal', *Thorax*, 39, (1984), 337–339.

Parikh, J., 'Rural Energy and Health Impacts', Report for the Ministry for Environment and Forest, Indira Gandhi Institute of Development, Mumbai, India, 2000, http://www.irade.org/jp/rural.htm [Accessed on January 2007]

Parikh, J., Balakrishnan, K., Sankar, S., Padmavathi, R., Srividya, K., Venugopal, V., Swarna, P. and Pandey, V.L., 'Daily Average Exposures to Respirable Particulate Matter from Combustion of Biomass Fuels in Rural Households of Southern India', *Environmental Health Perspectives*, 110(11), (2002), 1069–1075.

Peng, R., Wang, L., Wang H., He K., Xu X., 'Indoore Air Pollution from Residential Energy Use in China' in McElroy, M.B., Nilesh, C. P., Lyolon, P., (eds.), *Energizing China: reconciling Environmental Protection and Economics Growth*, (Harvard University Press, Boston, 1998), 287–298.

Pitt, M. M., Rosenzweig, M.R. and Hassan, M.N., 'Sharing the Burden of Disease: Gender, the Household Division of Labour and the Health Effects of Indoor Air Pollution in Bangladesh and India', CID Working Paper No. 119, March 2005, Center for International Development, Harvard University, Cambridge, Massachusetts, 2006.

Pokhrel et al. Case-control Study of Indoore Cooking Smoke Exposure and Cataract in Nepal and India, *International Journal of Epidemiology*, 34, 702–708.

Qin Y. et al. (1991), *Indoor Air Pollution in Four Cities in China: Journal of Environment and Health*, 8(3).

Schwela, D. H., Cooking Smoke: A Silent, People and the Planet, 6(3), 1–2.

Smith, K. R., 'Indoor Air Pollution', Pollution Management in Focus, Discussion Note Number 4, The World Bank, Washington D.C., 1999.

Smith, K. R., 'Indoor Air Pollution in Developing Countries: Recommendation for Research', *Indoor Air*, 12, (2002), 198–207.

Smith, K. R., 'National Burden of Disease in India from Indoor Air Pollution', *Proceedings of the National Academy of Sciences*, 97, (2000), 13286–13293.

Smith, K.R., 'Fuel Combustion, Air Pollution Exposure, and Health: The Situation in Developing Countries', *Annual Review of Energy and Environment*, 18, (1993), 529–566.

WHO (2002), 'The World Health Report 2002: Reducing Risks, Promoting Healthy Life', WHO, Geneva.

WHO (2004), 'Measurement and Health Information', World Health Organization, Geneva. http://www.who.int/entity/healthinfo/statistics bodgbddeathdalyestimates.xls [Accessed on July 2007]

WHO (2006), 'Fuel for Life, Household Energy and Health', World Health Organization, Geneva.

WHO (2007a), 'Indoor Air Pollution: National Burden of Disease Estimates', World Health Organization, Geneva.

WHO (2007b), 'Indoor Air Pollution and Lower Respiratory Tract Infections in Children', World Health Organization, Geneva.

16

Benefits from Reduced Air Pollution in Delhi and Kolkata: A Hedonic Property Price Approach

M.N. Murty, S.C. Gulati and *Avishek Banerjee*[1]

16.1. Introduction

There are a number of empirical studies[2], mainly in the developed country context, that use the hedonic property prices approach to estimate the value of environmental goods. The study reported in this chapter is the first of such studies in South Asia. Hedonic prices models (property prices or wages) can be used to estimate a variety of benefits from environmental improvements while other valuation methods like household health production function methods or travel cost methods are specially designed to estimate health benefits or recreational benefits. For example, a generalized hedonic price

[1] The work reported in this chapter forms part of a detailed study sponsored by South Asian Network of Economic Institutions (SANEI). We gratefully acknowledge the generous financial support provided by SANEI. We are grateful to Dr Priya Shyamsundar for detailed comments contributing to the substantial improvements. An earlier version of this chapter was presented at 40th Annual Conference of the Indian Econometric Society, 2004, Bangalore, India and appears in the proceedings of the conference. We are grateful to the participants of the conference for their comments.

[2] Ridker (1967) and Ridker and Henning (1976) provide the first empirical evidence that air pollution affects the property values. The early studies include Freeman (1974a; 1974b), Anderson and Crocker (1971; 1972), Lind (1973), Pines and Weiss (1976), Polinsky and Shavell (1976), Nelson (1978), Portney (1981), Horowitz (1986), Murdoch and Thayer (1988), and Kanemoto (1988). The most recent studies include the following – Michaels and Smith (1990), Parsons (1992), Lansford and Jones (1995), Kiel (1995), Kiel and McClain (1995), and Mahan, Polasky, and Adams (2000). Rrecent studies in India are Parikh (1994), Sen (1994) and Murty, Gulati and Banerjee (2003).

model analysing house prices, travel costs and wages in an urban area can be used to comprehensively measure the benefits from air pollution reduction[3].

Hedonic property price models consider the property price as an increasing function of environmental quality, given house characteristics. Similarly, the individual's marginal willingness-to-pay is a decreasing function of environmental quality – this is the inverse demand function for environmental quality[4]. Obtaining estimates of these functions with these required properties depends upon – (a) good quality data and (b) estimation of appropriate functional forms. This chapter uses data collected through two carefully designed household surveys in Delhi and Kolkata, to show the importance of using appropriate functional forms in the estimation of hedonic property value models. It also provides estimates of consumer surplus benefits to households in both the cities from reducing air pollution to a safe level.

South Asia houses some of the urban conglomerations in the world that are worst affected by air pollution. Delhi and Kolkata are two major urban areas in India with air pollution levels much higher than safety standards. The pollution levels especially that of Suspended Particulate Matter (SPM) are much higher than the Minimum National Standards (MINAS) for India or the WHO standards in these two cities. Figures 16.1 and 16.2 show pollution levels recorded in seven monitoring stations in Delhi and 19 monitoring stations in Kolkata. Pollution concentrations of SPM, SO_2 and NO_x reported in these figures are six monthly average concentrations during October–March, 2001–2002.

Recently, several environmental policy changes aimed at reducing air pollution in these urban areas[5] have been made, and these changes have significant social costs. The socio economic background of people can vary across cities. For example, people in Delhi have a higher per capita income while Kolkata has higher educational levels than Delhi. City-specific estimates of benefits of reducing air pollution may be required given that people live in different urban areas under different socio economic conditions and geographical regions in a big country like India. This is needed to justify the costs of reducing pollution and expanding pollution reduction interventions to different parts of the country.

---

[3] See Murty (2009).

[4] Some studies have failed to obtain inverse an demand function for environmental quality for example, Mahan, Polasky, and Adams (2000).

[5] Examples are introducing Compressed Natural Gas (CNG) as a fuel in the transport sector, changing mode of transport from road to metro rail and relocation of some air polluting industries.

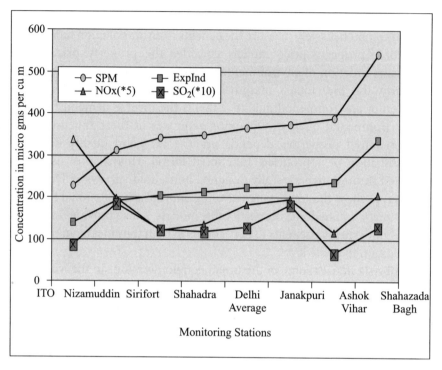

Note: NOx and SO$_2$ are given in multiples of 5 and 10 respectively for bringing uniformity in scale.
Source: CPCB, Delhi

Figure 16.1.   Average concentrations of SPM, NOx, SO$_2$ and the exposure index for the 7 monitoring stations in Delhi for the period October 2001 to March 2002.

16.2. The hedonic price model and choice of functional forms

Hedonic Price Model

Different commodities can be distinguished by the characteristics they possess and their prices are functions of these characteristics. From the point of view of the owner, land and property can be distinguished in terms of location, size, and local environmental quality, while from a worker's perspective, a job is a differentiated product in terms of the risk of on job accidents, working conditions, prestige, training and enhancement of skills, and the local environmental quality at the work place. Environmental characteristics like air or water quality affect the price of land either as a producer good or as a consumer good. Hedonic models exploit this link. Ridker (1967) and Ridker and Henning (1976) provided the first empirical evidence that air pollution affects property values. Freeman (1974) and Rosen (1974) then used hedonic price theory to interpret the derivative of hedonic property price function with respect to air pollution as a marginal implicit price and therefore the marginal willingness-to-pay of individuals for air pollution reduction. Thaler and Rosen (1976) also suggested that the labour market could be viewed as a hedonic market. The derivative of the hedonic wage function with respect to any job characteristic, say exposure to air pollution at the workplace, can be interpreted as a marginal implicit price or workers' marginal willingness to accept increased exposure to pollution.

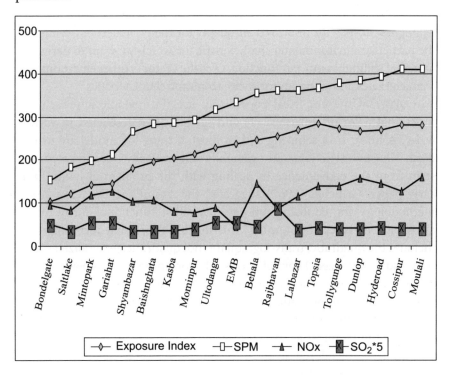

Source: WBPCB, Kolkata

Figure 16.2. Average concentrations of SPM, NOx, SO$_2$ and the exposure index for 19 monitoring stations in Kolkata for the period October 2001 to March 2002.

In a hedonic price model therefore there are two equations to be estimated – The hedonic price function and the individual's marginal willingness-to-pay function for improved environmental quality[6]. In the model of hedonic property prices estimated in this chapter, these equations are given as:

$$P_{hi} = P_h(S_i, N_i, Q_i). \tag{1}$$

$$b_{ij} = b_{ij}(q_j, Q_i^*, S_i, N_i, G_i). \tag{2}$$

Equation (1) is the hedonic price equation where P_{hi} is the property price[7] of the ith house vectors, S_i consists of the structural characteristics of the house, N_i contains the neighborhood characteristics of the house and Q_i stands for the environmental characteristics of the house. Equation (2) is the individual's marginal willingness to pay function where b_{ij} is the marginal willingness-to-pay for improved air quality for the ith household, while q_j is the particular environmental characteristic for which we want to derive the marginal willingness-to-pay function, Q_i^* is the vector of other environmental characteristics and G_i stands for socio-economic characteristics.

In many of the empirical papers that use the hedonic approach, the functional form of equations (1) and (2) are often restricted in various ways[8]. A linear or a semi-log and, at most, a trans-log model are usually used. These restrictions are generally theoretically unwarranted and stem from the convenience in dealing with the problem at hand. In an early paper, Griliches (1967) suggested the use of the Box Cox (1964) methodology for choosing among alternative functional forms under a relevant statistical framework. This flexible functional form approach includes the quadratic, trans-log, square root quadratic, generalized square root and generalized Leontief forms. Halvorsen and Pollakowski (1981) provide a lucid discussion on using a combination of the Box Cox and the flexible functional form approaches. They specify a generalized functional form, namely the quadratic Box Cox functional form, which yields all other functional forms as special cases. In this chapter, the quadratic Box-Cox model is considered the most suitable because of its flexibility, and use in the estimations. Trans-log models are also estimated.

---

[6] See Freeman (1974a) for the derivation of these equations using models explaining consumer choices of private goods, house property, jobs and environmental quality.

[7] Here the monthly rental value of the house is taken as a proxy for the property price.

[8] Michaels and Smith (1990), Parsons (1992), Lansford and Jones (1995), Kiel (1995), Kiel and McClain (1995), and Mahan, Polasky, and Adams (2000).

16.2.2. The quadratic Box-Cox model

The general quadratic Box-Cox functional form for the hedonic property price equation (1) incorporating all other functional forms as special cases is given by:

$$P^{(\theta)} = \alpha_0 + \sum_{i=1}^{m} \alpha_i X_i^{(\lambda)} + \frac{1}{2}\sum_{i=1}^{m}\sum_{j=1}^{m}\gamma_{ij}X_i^{(\lambda)}X_j^{(\lambda)} \qquad (3)$$

where P is the price of property, X_i's are the characteristics of the house including structural, neighborhood and environmental features, α_i and γ_{ij}' are regression coefficients with coefficients $\gamma_{ij} = \gamma_{ji}$, for all i and j (i,j = 1,2,3,...m) and $P^{(\theta)}$ and $X^{(\lambda)}$ are Box-Cox transformations as given below:

$$P^{(\theta)} = \left(P^\theta - 1\right)/\theta, \qquad \text{for all } \theta \neq 0$$

$$= Ln\, P \qquad \theta = 0$$

$$X_i^{(\lambda)} = \left(X_i^\lambda - 1\right)/\lambda \qquad \text{For all } \lambda \neq 0$$

$$= Ln\, X_i \qquad \lambda = 0$$

The transformations are continuous around $\theta = 0$ and $\lambda = 0$ since the limit for the $\theta \neq 0$ case as $\theta \rightarrow 0$ is Ln P and similarly the limit for $\lambda \neq 0$ case as $\lambda \rightarrow 0$ is Ln X_i. It is easy to see that by imposing appropriate restrictions on θ and λ one can arrive at the more specific functional forms of interest.

Imposing zero restrictions on θ and λ one can obtain the trans-log form attributed to Christensen, Jorgenson and Lau (1971, 1973) given by:

$$LnP = \alpha_0 + \sum_{i=1}^{m}\alpha_i LnX_i + \frac{1}{2}\sum_{i=1}^{m}\sum_{j=1}^{m}\gamma_{ij}LnX_i LnX_j. \qquad (4)$$

Similarly, imposing the restriction $\theta = \lambda = 1$ yields the quadratic form attributed to Lau (1974), imposing $\theta = 2$ and $\lambda = 1$ we obtain the square root form, (Diewert, 1974), and with $\theta = 1$ and $\lambda = 1/2$ we can attain the generalized non-homogeneous version of the generalized Leontief form[9]. Adding a stochastic term to equation (3) one gets:

---

[9] For the derivation of these functional forms refer to Halvorsen and Pollakowski (1981)

$$P^{(\theta)} = \alpha_0 + \sum_{i=1}^{m} \alpha_i X_i^{(\lambda)} + \frac{1}{2} \sum_{i=1}^{m} \sum_{j=1}^{m} \gamma_{ij} X_{i=1}^{(\lambda)} X_{j=1}^{(\lambda)} + \varepsilon_i \qquad (5)$$

It is assumed that the true values of θ and λ are distributed normally and independently with zero mean and constant variance. The values of θ, λ, α_0, $\alpha_{i's}$, γ_{ij} and σ^2 (where σ is the standard error of the regression) are estimated jointly by the maximum likelihood technique. The choice of θ and λ are such that they maximize the log likelihood function for the sample observations[10]. Most econometric packages[11] have routine programmes to compute these estimates.

In the following empirical estimation, the significance of θ and λ in the respective regressions are tested by the Chi-Squared test of the Wald-statistic. The same test of significance is performed on the rest of the parameters of equation (5). The Likelihood ratio test is then employed to test the null hypothesis of different standard values of θ and λ (viz. $\theta = 0 = \lambda$, $\theta = 1 = \lambda$, and $\theta = -1 = \lambda$) against the alternative hypothesis of an unrestricted maximum likelihood estimate of θ and λ.

16.3. Data sources and design of household survey

In this study, primary data on house characteristics and socio-economic conditions is used. The data are from a household survey undertaken during October 2001 to March 2002 in the cities of Delhi and Kolkata. 1250 households were surveyed from each city expecting that information could be obtained completely for at least 1000 households per city. The sample size was divided equally around functioning air pollution monitoring stations in the two cities. For illustration, the sample size of 1250 in Delhi was divided into a sub-sample size of 180 around each of the seven pollution-monitoring stations of the Central Pollution Control Board (CPCB). In Kolkata a sample size of 65 was fixed around each of 19 of air-pollution monitoring centres monitored by the West Bengal Pollution Control Board (WBPCB). Ultimately, full information was obtained only for 1187 households in Delhi and 1204 households in Kolkata. Thus, the first stage of stratification was geographic, which was purposive in the sense that the localities around the monitoring stations were the selection criterion.

---

[10] It may be noted that the Box-Cox transformation increases the chances for obtaining normally distributed residuals even though the maximum likelihood estimate does not try to choose θ and λ that make the residuals normally distributed, Box-Cox (1966).

[11] Stata 8 has been used for the current estimation and analysis.

In the second stage, the localities around the monitoring stations were stratified according to the standards of living of the inhabitants which in turn were identified by size of the houses, types of the houses such as bungalows/ independent houses or flats, type of conveyances used in general. The localities were stratified in this form through physical verification by visiting the areas. At this stage, three localities one each from the high, medium and low income category were identified to draw a sample comprising a whole range of households in terms of socioeconomic status. The identification and mapping of localities selected for the survey provided the framework for selecting the households in the third stage. The selection of the targeted number of households was done by adopting a circular systematic sampling procedure in each selected locality.

The household survey included information about socioeconomic characteristics of household members such as educational levels of adult members, occupational status, size, sex and age composition of the family members, and incomes. Information was elicited on type of house, structural characteristics, and neighborhood characteristics comprising distances from highways, bus stops, schools/colleges, industrial complexes, and public parks. Further, information on community characteristics like majority religion, dominant professional group, and crime rate in the locality was collected. Information on the respondent's perception of environmental conditions such as air quality, water quality, extent of green cover, etc. was also collected. Detailed information on prices of properties was also elicited from the respondents. To cross check the property prices obtained from the respondents in the survey, data on property prices were also collected from the property dealers in the surveyed areas.

16.4. Model for estimation and measurement of variables

The hedonic property value model consists of a set of two equations, one representing the hedonic price function, and another representing the marginal willingness-to-pay function for estimation. The two equations of the hedonic property value model estimated in this chapter with Box Cox transformations of both dependent and independent variables are given in the next page:

16.4.1. Hedonic property price function:

$$(Y_1)^{(\theta)} = \alpha_1 + \beta_1(X_1)^{(\lambda)} + \beta_2(X_2)^{(\lambda)} + \beta_3(X_3)^{(\lambda)} + \beta_4(X_4)^{(\lambda)} + \beta_5(X_5)^{(\lambda)} +$$
$$\beta_6(X_6)^{(\lambda)} + \beta_7(X_7)^{(\lambda)} + \beta_8(X_8)^{(\lambda)} + \beta_9(X_9) + \beta_{10}(X_{10})^{(\lambda)} +$$
$$\beta_{11}(X_{11}) + \beta_{12}(X_{12})^{(\lambda)} + \beta_{13}(X_{13})^{(\lambda)} + \beta_{14}(X_{14})^{(\lambda)} + \beta_{15}(X_{15})^{(\lambda)} +$$
$$\beta_{16}(X_{16})^{(\lambda)} + \beta_{17}(X_{17})^{(\lambda)} + u_1$$

(6)

16.4.2. Inverse demand function[12] or individual marginal willingness-to-pay function for environmental quality

$$(Y_2)^{(\theta')} = \alpha_2 + \gamma_{19}(X_{19})^{(\lambda')} + \gamma_{20}(X_{20})^{(\lambda')} + \gamma_{13}(X_{13})^{(\lambda')} + \gamma_{21}(X_{23})^{(\lambda')} +$$
$$\gamma_{10}(X_{10})^{(\lambda')} + \gamma_{18}(X_{18})^{(\lambda')} + u_2$$

where θ and λ are the transformations used in the hedonic price equation and θ` and $\lambda$` are the transformations used in the marginal implicit price function. Since these transformations apply only to positive values of Y and X, the constants and dummy variables are not transformed. The model used in the empirical estimation contains only those variables that provided significant Wald statistics.

The above two equations are estimated in this chapter for three datasets – Delhi, Kolkata and pooled data from both cities. The empirical estimations are done for the unrestricted quadratic Box Cox functional form and the trans-log functional form. The variables used in an estimation of the above two equations are described as follows:

---

[12] It might be noted that the literature on the hedonic property value model suggests the use of all the independent variables in the hedonic property price function also as independent variables in the willingness-to-pay function. We have two reasons for using the functional form with only subset of variables reported in equation (7). Firstly, it is the only one that satisfies the required curvature property of the inverse demand function for the entire relevant range of the atmospheric quality, given by the current average concentration of SPM to the safe level prescribed by WHO and the MINAS. The estimated willingness-to-pay function with full set of variables satisfies the curvature properties of the inverse demand function only in a very limited range of the atmospheric quality. Secondly, the Box Cox transformation, as evident from the chi-square test, is relevant only for the function with subset of variables and not for the function with full set of variables. Thus the transformed Box Cox function with a subset of variables is the best fit in our search for an appropriate functional form for the willingness-to-pay function that has all the properties of the inverse demand function and is also robust to all statistical tests of significance.

Variables for the hedonic property price function:

Monthly rent (Y₁): Information on the monthly rents for the house was collected from each household. Imputed monthly rental values were used for owner-occupied houses in Delhi and Kolkata.

Structural characteristics of the house

Covered area (X₁): Data for total covered area of the houses were collected directly from the households and the figures were reported in square yards. In the case of independent owner occupied or rented houses care was taken to exclude any uncovered area. For flats, of course no such problems were encountered. In the case of multistoried buildings, the covered area was scaled for the number of floors.

Number of rooms including drawing rooms (X₂): The total number of rooms including drawing room were considered as a control variable for the monthly rental value of the house.

Indoor sanitation (X₃): An index for indoor sanitation was constructed out of the following information–separate kitchen, separate bathrooms and toilets, and condition of indoor ventilation. The index ranges from zero to six and has two components. Whenever a separate kitchen, bathroom or toilet was found, the house was given a value of one for each separate facility and otherwise zero. Thus the first component of the index carries a maximum value of three and is obtained for houses where separate kitchen, toilet and bathroom facilities are available. Similarly, for ventilation, a scale of one to three was used with the higher number denoting better ventilation. These values were then added to arrive at a composite scale of zero to six.

Distance characteristics:

Distance from business centre (X₄): The distance from any common business centre in the city was calculated for each household.

Distance from national highways (X₅): The distance of the house from national highways was calculated. Then, an average distance was computed, which proxies for the overall distance of the house from multiple national highways.

Distance from slum (X₆): Distance from the closest slum was calculated for areas around each monitoring station.

Distance from industry (X₇): Distance from nearby industries for each monitoring station in each city was used to control for extreme conditions of pollution in certain parts of the cities.

Distance from shopping centres (X_8): The distance from the nearest local shopping complex was calculated for each monitoring station in the cities.

Environmental Variables:

Perception about air quality (X_{10}): This is an ordered variable in the range of one to three, which is used to rank the locality in terms of the air quality as perceived by households; the higher the rank, the higher the air quality available.

Perception about water quality (X_{12}): This is an ordered variable in the range of one to three, which is used to rank the locality in terms of the water quality as perceived by the residents of that area; the higher the rank, the higher the water quality.

Dummy for adequacy of green cover (X_{11}): This is a one, zero binary dummy variable, which is used to ascertain the perception of a household about the adequacy of the green cover (tree cover) in its location.

SPM (X_{13}): The average daily concentration of Suspended Particle Matter (SPM) in μ gms/m^3 in the last six months from the month of survey for a particular locality is used as a pollution variable.

SO_2 (X_{14}): The average daily concentration of SO_2 in μ gms/m^3 in the last six months for a particular locality is used as a pollution variable.

NO_x (X_{15}): The average concentration of NO_x in μ gms/m^3 in the last six months for a particular locality is used as a pollution variable.

Water supply (X_{16}): The hours of water supply in the particular locality.

Other variables:

Business or salaried class (X_9): A dummy variable is used where one refers to households that own a business and zero to other households.

Variables for the marginal willingness-to-pay function:

Marginal willingness-to-pay (Y_2): The linear transformation of the marginal implicit price for a unit change in the concentration of SPM or the implicit marginal price for environmental quality is estimated using the following expression:

$$\frac{\partial Y_1}{\partial X_{13}} = \frac{X_{13}^{\lambda-1}}{Y_1^{\theta-1}}(\beta_{13}) \tag{8}$$

where linear predicted household-specific values of Y_1 and observed values of X_{13} were used in the computation of the household-specific marginal implicit price. The modulus value (value neglecting sign) of the above expression is used as the dependent variable in the marginal willingness-to-pay function. This variable was constructed only for the most significant pollutant, SPM.

Square of SPM (X_{20}): The square of SPM is used in the second equation keeping in mind the necessary curvature property of the willingness-to-pay function.

City dummy (X_{23}): All observations belonging to Delhi are marked as one and all observations belonging to Kolkata are marked as zero.

Socio-economic variables

Education in years (X_{18}): The education variable is constructed by adding the years of education undertaken by the first five adult members of the family and dividing by five.

Annual gross family income (X_{19}): This is based on the gross annual family income of the household. In the absence of any concrete figures for actual incomes for certain households, certain income brackets were offered to the respondents to choose from.

Tables 16.1 and 16.2 provide the summary statistics of some of the important socioeconomic variables from the household survey. The data shows significant differences in the socio economic characteristics of households between Delhi and Kolkata. The economic status of households measured in terms of annual household incomes, house rent and size of the house indicate that on the average households in Delhi are better off than those in Kolkata. Delhi households have on average annual income, monthly house rent and house size of INR 179565, INR 9537 and 137 square yards respectively in comparison to corresponding values of INR 158930, INR 3903, and 129 square yards in Kolkata. Interestingly Kolkata households have higher level of education in comparison to Delhi households. Households also differ significantly in terms of perception of air quality, drinking water quality and green cover between the two cities. There are also significant differences in ambient air quality with Delhi having higher Particulate Matter (SPM) concentrations and Kolkota having higher NO_x concentrations in relative terms. The levels of SPM concentrations are found to be higher than national or WHO standards in both the cities while it is not so with respect to NO_x and SO_2. Therefore, SPM is taken as a pollution variable for the analysis that follows in this chapter.

Table 16.1. Descriptive statistics of variables used for estimation of the hedonic property value model: location Delhi

	Rent (INR/ month) (Y_1)	Covered area (Sq yards) (X_1)	Number of rooms (X_2)	Indoor sanitation Index (X_3)	Distance from Business Centre (Km) (X_4)	Distance from National Highway (Km) (X_5)
Mean	9536.612	136.9534	4.096040	4.462511	4.992334	1.279174
Std. Dev.	13725.58	342.6036	2.527597	1.148752	4.975135	1.397169
Observations	1187	1187	1187	1187	1187	1187

	Distance from Slum (Km) (X_6)	Distance from Industry (Km) (X_7)	Dummy for Nearby Slums (X_8)	Dummy for Business Community (X_9)	Perception of Air Quality Index (X_{10})	Index for Adequacy of Green Cover (X_{11})
Mean	1.594302	1.330526	0.571188	0.541702	0.144903	0.622578
Std. Dev.	1.217707	1.317624	0.495115	0.498468	0.623511	0.547041
Observations	1187	1187	1187	1187	1187	1187

	Perception about drinking water (X_{11})	SPM (X_{13})	SO_2 (X_{14})	NO_2 (X_{15})	Water Supply (Hours / day) (X_{16})	Distance from Nearest Shopping Centre (Km) (X_{17})
Mean	2.127211	366.3136	12.96807	36.45013	5.998678	2.788031
Std. Dev.	1.113989	86.42897	4.088191	13.13383	5.958350	3.247169
Observations	1187	1187	1187	1187	1187	1187

	Education Index (Years) (X_{18})	Gross annual Family Income (Rs) (X_{19})	SPM*SPM (X_{20})
Mean	12.29264	179565.3	141649.4
Std. Dev.	4.238082	127156.2	69776.29
Observations	1187	1187	1187

Table 16.2. Descriptive statistics of the variables used for estimation of the hedonic property value model: Location Kolkata

	Rent (INR/ month) (Y_1)	Covered area (Sq ft.) (X_1)	Number of rooms (X_2)	Indoor sanitation Index (X_3)	Distance from Business Centre (Km) (X_4)	Distance from National Highway (Km) (X_5)
Mean	3902.831	1169.304	4.324751	4.889535	5.157973	1.137949
Std. Dev.	4288.262	1284.462	3.041145	1.356095	6.775391	1.062752
Observations	1204	1204	1204	1204	1204	1204

	Distance from Slum (Km) (X_6)	Distance from Industry (Km) (X_7)	Dummy for Nearby Slums (X_8)	Dummy for Business Community (X_9)	Perception of Air Quality Index (X_{10})	Index for Adequacy of Green Cover (X_{11})
Mean	0.330133	0.627816	0.553156	2.095515	1.830565	0.347176
Std. Dev.	1.167176	0.789318	0.497373	0.761728	0.785062	0.483201
Observation	1204	1204	1204	1204	1204	1204

	Perception about drinking water (X_{12})	SPM (X_{13})	SO_2 (X_{14})	NO_2 (X_{15})	Water Supply (Hours / day) (X_{16})	Distance from Nearest Shopping Centre (Km) (X_{17})
Mean	2.182724	331.3123	8.892027	123.3310	8.711379	1.243937
Std. Dev.	0.807179	83.98949	2.018197	37.08074	6.359156	1.309642
Observation	1204	1204	1204	1204	1204	1204

	Education Index (Years) (X_{18})	Gross annual Family Income (Rs) (X_{19})	SPM*SPM (X_{20})
Mean	14.28763	158930.1	116816.2
Std. Dev.	3.165503	102890.3	53862.82
Observation	1204	1204	1204

16.5. Estimates of hedonic property value model with alternative functional forms

In this section, the estimated models are discussed for Delhi and Kolkata. Estimates are obtained using both trans-log and Box-Cox models. The estimates based on Box-Cox models provide inverse demand functions for air quality with the required curvature properties. These, therefore, are used for the analysis of welfare gains from the reduction of air pollution.

16.5.1. Delhi

Estimates of the hedonic property price function for Delhi under the general quadratic Box Cox estimation and the trans-log functional forms are provided in Table 16.3. In both the estimates, coefficients of structural variables like Covered area (X_1), Number of rooms (X_2), and Indoor sanitation (X_3) have the correct sign and are significant at the one per cent level. Among the distance characteristics variables, the coefficients of distance from business centre (X_4), distance from industries (X_7) and distance from national highway (X_5) are also significant at one per cent and bear the correct sign. The coefficient of distance from slums (X_6) is significant at the one per cent level. The variable measuring the distance from shopping centre (X_8) has a positive coefficient and it is also significant in the unrestricted (Box-Cox) model.

Table 16.3. Estimates of hedonic price equation for Delhi

Variables (Expected Signs)	Dependent variable Monthly House Rent	
	Trans log Model $\theta = 0$ $\lambda = 0$	Box Cox Transformation $\theta = 0.0765446***$ $\lambda = -0.1064827*$
	Coefficients (t-statistics)	Coefficients (Chi² statistics)
Constant	10.23759*** (11.37)	19.53819
Covered Area: X_1 (+)	0.183950*** (3.95)	0.5438875*** (19.883)
No. of Rooms: X_2 (+)	0.646681*** (9.30)	1.466924*** (167.047)
Indoor Sanitation: X_3 (+)	0.464654*** (4.39)	1.023839*** (25.667)

(Contd.)

(*Contd.*)

Variables (Expected Signs)	Trans log Model $\theta = 0$ $\lambda = 0$	Box Cox Transformation $\theta = 0.0765446$*** $\lambda = -0.1064827$*
	Coefficients (t-statistics)	**Coefficients (Chi² statistics)**
Distance from Business Centre: X_4 (+)	0.143340*** (4.59)	0.2859844*** (16.481)
Distance from National highways: X_5 (+)	0.051224*** (3.36)	0.0948012*** (16.481)
Distance from Slums: X_6 (+)	0.202827*** (3.22)	0.4425801*** (13.032)
Distance from Industries: X_7 (+)	0.144710*** (3.03)	0.3456081*** (12.303)
Dummy for Slums: $^\$X_8$ (–)	−0.257561*** (−4.17)	−0.5026985*** (16.009)
Dummy for Business or salaried class: $^\$X_9$ (+)	0.173580*** (3.43)	0.3713925*** (15.379)
Perception about Air Qlty: X_{10} (+)	0.089259 (1.22)	0.1493541 (1.040)
Adequacy of Green Cover: $^\$X_{11}$ (+)	0.044258 (0.89)	0.0933311 (1.213)
Perception about water Qlty: X_{12} (+)	0.060599 (0.86)	0.1530054 (1.364)
SPM: X_{13} (–)	−0.658795*** (−5.59)	−2.644776*** (38.595)
SO_2: X_{14} (–)	0.142859* (1.62)	−0.922619*** (9.604)
NO_x: X_{15} (–)	−0.268090*** (−2.63)	0.446201** (4.034)
Water Supply in Hrs: X_{16} (+)	−0.033733 (−1.23)	−0.091236 (2.264)
Distance from Shopping Centre: X_{17} (–)	0.019048 (1.30)	0.0406528* (3.303)
Uncentred R²	0.4504	Sigma = 1.421134 LR chi² (18) = 733.67
Adjusted R²	0.4424	Probability > Chi² = 0.000 Uncentred R² = 0.618 Log Likelihood = −11585.625

Likelihood ratio test

Test H_0	Restricted Log likelihood	Chi² Statistics
$\theta = -1 = \lambda$	−14875.305	6579.36***
$\theta = 0 = \lambda$	−11599.854	28.46***
$\theta = 1 = \lambda$	−12809.207	2447.16***

It is also noted that the presence of business class as residents (X_9) affects house rents significantly in both the model estimates. Environmental variables like perception about air quality (X_{10}), adequacy of green cover (X_{11}) and perception about water quality (X_{12}) have coefficients with expected signs in both the models but they are not significant. Even hours of water supply (X_{16}) does not seem to affect house rents significantly. The coefficient of the pollution variable, SPM concentration (X_{13}) is highly significant and has the expected sign in both the Box Cox and trans-log models.

The uncentred R^2 is computed for both the models and it is much higher in the unrestricted model. Other standard diagnostic tests were performed on these models and both the models are free from any serious problem[13]. The likelihood ratio test was performed on each of the independent variables and there was no problem of convergence encountered in the process[14].

The Likelihood ratio test is employed to test the null hypothesis of standard values of θ and λ (viz. $\theta = 0 = \lambda$, $\theta = 1 = \lambda$ and $\theta = -1 = \lambda$) separately against the alternative hypothesis of unrestricted maximum likelihood estimates of θ and λ. The tests reject the null hypothesis of θ and λ being of any of the above standard forms against the alternative of unrestricted θ and λ in all the models estimated in the paper. Thus the quadratic Box Cox estimation is superior when compared to the parametric estimates of the trans-log model (or any other restricted model). This result highlights the importance of the appropriate choice of the functional form for estimating the hedonic price equation.

The linear predictions of house rents Y_1, were computed from the model estimates of the hedonic price equation using the appropriate reverse transformation and these were used to compute the house specific estimates of the marginal implicit prices as shown by equation (8) above. The expression for Delhi is given by[15]:

$$| \frac{\partial Y_1}{\partial X_{13}} | = | \frac{X_{13}^{\lambda-1}}{Y_1^{\theta-1}} (-2.644776) | \tag{9}$$

The household marginal willingness-to-pay function for the reduction in SPM is estimated by regressing the implicit marginal prices on income,

---

[13] The White's heteroscedasticity corrected standard errors are reported.

[14] For a detailed discussion in the estimation method consult Stata 8 Reference Manual (Vol. 1, A to F).

[15] For the trans log model theta and lambda are zero and hence equation (13) reduces to the ratio of X_{13} to Y_1 times the coefficient (–0.658).

education and other socioeconomic variables and SPM concentration and its square. Table 16.4 provides the parametric estimates of the marginal willingness-to-pay function under the two models (Box Cox and trans-log). For this function, the standard Z test does not reject the null hypothesis that lambda is equal to zero even at the 10 per cent level of significance. This means that Box Cox transformation is not required for independent variables in the equation. Therefore the Box-Cox transformation was employed only on the dependent variable for which the standard Z statistic is significant at the five per cent level.

Table 16.4. Estimates of Marginal Willingness-to-pay Equation for Delhi.

Log Values of Variables (Expected Sign)	Dependent Variable Marginal Rent	
	Trans log Model $\theta = 0$	**Box Cox Transformation** $\theta = 0.0736085$**
	Coefficients (t-statistics)	Coefficients (Chi² statistics)
Constant	−43.17935*** (−3.61)	−0.5406424
Education X_{18} (+)	0.430238*** (5.87)	0.0316471*** (53.814)
Income X_{19} (+)	0.538860*** (13.76)	2.6e-06*** (294.164)
SPM X_{13} (+)	14.32783*** (3.51)	0.0117879*** (71.954)
Sq SPM X_{20} (−)	−1.336191*** (−3.89)	−0.0000166*** (90.493)
Perception about Air Quality X_{10} (+)	0.270875*** (3.46)	0.1780826*** (43.498)
		Sigma = 0.5686012
Uncentred R^2	0.357199	LR chi ² (5) = 658.27
Adjusted R^2	0.354477	Probability > Chi² = 0.000
		Uncentred R^2 = 0.555
		Log Likelihood = −3707.6189
	Likelihood ratio test	
Test H_0	Restricted Log likelihood	Chi ² Statistics
$\theta = -1$	−4350.042	1284.85***
$\theta = 0$	−3710.2565	5.28**
$\theta = 1$	−4070.3201	725.40***

Note: *(**) and (***) denotes significance at (10), (5) & (1) % levels.

In the estimated marginal implicit price function for Delhi,[16] socio-economic variables like Education (X_{18}), Gross annual household income (X_{19}) and the Perception for air quality variable (X_{10}) bear expected positive signs and are significant at the one per cent level for both the model estimates. There is a notable distinction in the signs of pollution variables X_{13} and X_{20} in the two models. Only parametric estimates of the unrestricted Box-Cox estimation satisfy the required curvature property of the marginal willingness-to-pay function.

16.5.1. Kolkata

Table 16.5 provides the parametric estimates of hedonic property price function for Kolkata. In the case of Kolkata, the Box-Cox transformation is undertaken only on the dependent variable in the hedonic price equation as the transformation of the independent variables does not produce any significant change in the regression as is evident by the Chi^2 test. The likelihood ratio test rejects the H_0 for all the standard values of θ tested against the unrestricted value of θ.

---

[16] The marginal implicit price for each household derived from the hedonic property price function using equation 9, is not an observed variable. In the context of regression on derived variables Feenstra and Hanson (1997, 1999), Haskel and Slaughter (2001, 2002) and Dumont et al. (2003) suggest different methods of correcting the standard errors of the parametric estimates. All the methods suggest a reduction of the standard error of the parametric estimate for gaining efficiency. Since our parametric estimates are highly significant with this enlarged standard error (uncorrected) bands, we can safely expect them to be significant with further reduction in the standard error. Thus this correction seems redundant in our case. On the other hand, Noboru Hidano (2002) suggests that the problem of identification in case of the marginal implicit price function can be avoided by using higher order functional forms for the hedonic price function than the marginal implicit price function. In this context it may be noted that since the Box Cox transformation uses different functional forms for the two sets of equations this problem of identification is also overcome. Further, in the case of the hedonic price function, in all the cities and in the pooled model as well, a both side transformation with separate parametric values of theta and lambda has been found statistically suitable whereas in the marginal implicit price function only the right hand side transformation is statistically significant. So it is evident that a different functional form has been assumed for estimating the two equations and the problem of identification does not arise.

Table 16.5. Estimates of hedonic price equation for Kolkata.

Variables (Expected Signs)	Dependent variable Monthly House Rent	
	Trans log Model $\theta = 0$ $\lambda = 0$	**Box Cox Transformation** $\theta = 0.3681178$***
	Coefficients (t-statistics)	Coefficients (Chi² statistics)
Constant	10.58682*** (14.39)	35.29286
Covered Area: X_1 (+)	–0.026117 (–1.06)	–0.000507* (2.716)
No. of Rooms: X_2 (+)	0.955376*** (14.82)	2.488142*** (294.673)
Indoor Sanitation: X_3 (+)	0.291560*** (3.12)	1.817918*** (29.506)
Distance from Business Centre: X_4 (+)	0.137361*** (5.57)	0.2563974*** (12.624)
Distance from National highways: X_5 (+)	0.061320 (0.94)	0.974085** (6.240)
Distance from Slums: X_6 (+)	0.150310 (1.34)	–0.0110185 (0.001)
Distance from Industries: X_7 (+)	0.051119 (0.70)	–0.1726866 (0.096)
Dummy for Slums: X_8 (–)	–0.379371*** (–5.59)	–4.930523*** (31.733)
Dummy for Business or salaried class: $^\$X_9$ (+)	0.056327* (1.62)	1.455582*** (7.164)
Perception about Air Qlty: X_{10} (+)	0.050404 (0.78)	0.5017189 (0.709)
Adequacy of Green Cover: $^\$X_{11}$ (+)	0.087828* (1.74)	2.303671** (5.546)
Perception about water Qlty: X_{12} (+)	0.173977** (2.33)	–0.5017189 (0.823)
SPM: X_{13} (–)	–0.719903*** (–7.13)	–0.0587933*** (71.564)
SO_2: X_{14} (–)	0.174656 (1.13)	0.4905682** (5.461)
NO_x: X_{15} (–)	–0.177321* (–1.88)	0.014077 (0.738)
Water Supply in Hrs: X_{16} (+)	0.034463 (0.95)	0.1109009* (2.888)

(Contd.)

(Contd.)

Variables (Expected Signs)	Dependent variable Monthly House Rent	
	Trans log Model $\theta = 0$ $\lambda = 0$	**Box Cox Transformation** $\theta = 0.3681178***$
	Coefficients (t-statistics)	Coefficients (Chi² statistics)
Distance from Shopping Centre: X_{17} (–)	–0.044881 (–0.71)	0.9406537*** (7.249)
Uncentred R²	0.3873	Sigma = 13.44937 LR chi ² (17) = 526.88
Adjusted R²	0.3786	Probability > Chi² = 0.000 Uncentred R² = 0.4376 Log Likelihood = –10836.371
	Likelihood ratio test	
Test H_0	Restricted Log likelihood	Chi ² Statistics
$\theta = -1$	–13365.004	5057.26***
$\theta = 0$	–11022.034	371.33***
$\theta = 1$	–11462.206	1251.67***

Note: *(**) and (***) denotes significance at (10), (5) and (1) % levels. $ denotes variables without transform

In the unrestricted model for Kolkata, the regression coefficient for SPM (X_{13}) is quite small when compared to the same for the Delhi model. However it is highly significant and bears the correct negative sign. Among the structural characteristics, the coefficients of number of rooms (X_2) and indoor sanitation (X_3) have required positive signs and are highly significant while the coefficient of covered area (X_1) bears the opposite sign and is insignificant in the trans-log model and significant in unrestricted model at 10 per cent level. The dummy for Slums (X_8) is significant and negative in both the Box-Cox and trans-log models, while the distance characteristics produce mixed results for Kolkata as a whole[17].

Similar to the model for Delhi, the linear predictions for (Y_1) are computed using expression (8) to get the household specific marginal implicit prices. In this case, however, since the exogenous variables are not transformed, the expression for the marginal implicit price is:

$$\left| \frac{\partial Y_1}{\partial X_{13}} \right| = \left| \frac{1}{Y_1^{\theta-1}} (-0.0587933) \right| \tag{10}$$

---

[17] They are still more effective in case of the unrestricted model (e.g. X_5 and X_{17}).

The estimates of marginal willingness-to-pay function for Kolkata are given in Table 16.6. The coefficients of all the explanatory variables except Income (X_{19}) bear the correct sign and are highly significant. As with Delhi, even in the case of Kolkata, the unrestricted model shows household diminishing marginal willingness-to-pay for the atmospheric quality.

Table 16.6. Estimates of marginal willingness-to-pay equation for Kolkata

Log Values of Variables (Expected Sign)	Dependent Variable Marginal Rent	
	Trans log Model $\theta = 0$	Box Cox Transformation $\theta = 0.4792194**$
	Coefficients (t-statistics)	Coefficients (Chi^2 statistics)
Constant	−22.96979** (−2.48)	3.069313
Education X_{18} (+)	0.796318*** (6.94)	0.0119188*** (22.779)
Income X_{19} (+)	0.571237*** (11.52)	−2.42e-07*** (9.191)
SPM X_{13} (+)	6.737927** (2.07)	0.0021936*** (10.354)
Sq SPM X_{20} (-)	−0.693091** (−2.42)	−3.63e-06*** (11.905)
Air Quality X_{10} (+)	0.173072*** (3.30)	0.0336502*** (10.415)
		Sigma = 0.5686012
Uncentred R^2	0.333585	LR chi ^{2} (5) = 61.23
Adjusted R^2	0.330727	Probability > Chi^2 = 0.000
		Uncentred R^2 = 0.50
		Log Likelihood = -3707.6189
	Likelihood ratio test	
Test H$_0$	Restricted Log likelihood	Chi ^{2} Statistics
$\theta = -1$	−1421.3999	49.53***
$\theta = 0$	−1399.136	5.01**
$\theta = 1$	−1399.4891	5.71**

Note: *(**) and (***) denotes significance at 10 (5) & (1) % levels.

16.5.2. Pooled model

In this section, an estimate of the marginal willingness-to-pay function is made considering segmented house markets for Delhi and Kolkata. The implicit marginal prices for SPM reductions are computed for each city market using estimated hedonic property price equations and then pooled. The pooled implicit marginal prices are regressed on SPM levels and the socioeconomic characteristics of households in both the cities along with a city specific dummy variable (X_{23}). This is one way of dealing with the econometric problem of identification in the estimation of the household marginal willingness-to-pay function in the hedonic property value model as discussed in Freeman (1993).

Table 16.7 presents results from this estimation using Box-Cox and translog models. The coefficients of variables of willingness to pay function have the proper sign and are highly significant. In this case also, the curvature property is satisfied by the unrestricted Box-Cox model only. The likelihood ratio test rejects H_0 for all standard forms of θ and thus the unrestricted model is unambiguously superior to the trans-log counterpart[18]. The welfare gains obtained from a reduction of air pollution in two cities have been computed using this estimate of the inverse demand function or marginal willingness to pay function from the pooled model reported in Table 16.7.

Table 16.7. Estimates of marginal willingness-to-pay equation for the Pooled Model

Log Values of Variables (Expected Sign)	Dependent Variable Marginal Rent	
	Trans log Model $\theta = 0$	Box Cox Transformation $\theta = 0.4792194**$
	Coefficients (t-statistics)	Coefficients (Chi² statistics)
Constant	−30.62877*** (−5.25)	0.4782014
Education X_{18} (+)	0.558753*** (9.23)	0.013794*** (88.590)
Income X_{19} (+)	0.554709*** (18.01)	8.87e-07*** (325.828)
SPM X_{13} (+)	9.689258*** (4.77)	0.0052934*** (228.374)
Sq SPM X_{20} (−)	−0.950415*** (−5.42)	−7.7e-06*** (258.450)

(Contd.)

---

[18] All standard transformations are rejected in favour of the unrestricted quadratic Box Cox transformation.

(*Contd.*)

Log Values of Variables (Expected Sign)	Dependent Variable Marginal Rent	
	Trans log Model $\theta = 0$	Box Cox Transformation $\theta = 0.4792194**$
	Coefficients (t-statistics)	Coefficients (Chi² statistics)
Perception about Air Quality X_{10} (+)	0.221595*** (5.05)	0.0477618*** (40.216)
City Dummy X_{23} (+)	0.790453*** (21.48)	0.214818*** (327.223)
		Sigma = 0.2530792
Uncentred R²	0.42295	LR chi² (6) = 1096.25
Adjusted R²	0.42148	Probability > Chi² = 0.000
		Uncentred R² = 0.46372
		Log Likelihood = −6373.6493
Likelihood ratio test		
Test H_0	Restricted Log likelihood	Chi² Statistics
$\theta = -1$	−7116.5125	1485.73***
$\theta = 0$	−6400.8154	54.33**
$\theta = 1$	−7502.4537	2257.61**

Note: *(**) and (***) denotes significance at (10), (5) & (1) % levels.

16.6. Inverse demand functions for environmental quality and welfare gains from reduced air pollution

The inverse demand function[19] for clean air was derived by fixing variables X_{18} (education) X_{19} (annual gross family income) and X_{10} (perceptions of air quality) in the estimated[20] equations of marginal willingness-to-pay at their sample mean values, and treating the pollution variable SPM (X_{13}) and its square (X_{20}) as the only variables. After applying the appropriate reverse transformation, the linearized[21] predicted values of Marginal Willingness-to-Pay (MWP) in the inverse demand functions for Delhi, Kolkata and the Pooled model are given by equations (11), (12) and (13). The reverse transformation is necessary in order to express predicted values of marginal willingness-to-pay obtained from the Box-Cox transformed variables, in rupee values.

---

[19] This is also the marginal willingness-to-pay function for clean air.
[20] Given in Tables 16.2, 16.4 and 16.6 for Delhi, Kolkata and the Pooled model, respectively.
[21] The reverse linear transformation refers to the $Y = (1 + \theta\alpha_0 + \theta\Sigma\alpha_i X_i)^{1/\theta}$ in which anything other than X_{13} and X_{20} are set at their mean values.

$$MWP = [1.051322 + 0.0008677 \, X_{13} - 0.0000012 \, X_{20}]^{13.585} \quad \text{[Delhi] (11)}$$
$$MWP = [2.560514 + 0.0010512 \, X_{13} - 0.0000017 \, X_{20}]^{2.0867} \quad \text{[Kolkata] (12)}$$
$$MWP = [0.826114 + 0.0009079 \, X_{13} - 0.0000013 \, X_{20}]^{13.585} \quad \text{[Pooled] (13)}$$

From the above estimates of the inverse demand function, the MWP of a typical household (for a reduction in SPM concentration by one micro gram per metre cube from the current average level of pollution) is computed as INR 12.63 for Delhi and INR 8.06 for Kolkata. The marginal willingness to pay of a representative household from Delhi and Kolkata is estimated as INR 10.21 using the demand function obtained from the pooled model. From the pooled model (using suitable dummies for the cities and the city-specific SPM concentrations) the willingness-to-pay for reduction in SPM concentration by one micro gram per meter cube from the current average level of pollution is computed as INR 12.01 in Delhi and INR 8.74 in Kolkata. The MWP estimated from the individual estimates is thus very close to the estimates obtained from the pooled model. This shows that the pooled model can be used for extrapolation of consumer surpluses for any representative city in India using the benefit transfer method. The graphs of inverse demand functions are shown in Figures 16.3, 16.4 and 16.5, respectively for Delhi, Kolkata and the pooled model. The SPM concentration is shown in reversed scale on the X-axis to represent ambient air quality and MWP is shown on the Y-axis.

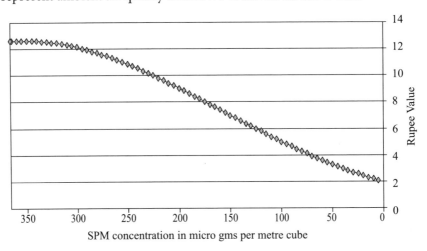

Note: The graph is generated from the Current average level of SPM of 366.31 μ gm/m³ to zero SPM, while the safe limit for SPM concentration is 200 μ gm/m³.

Figure 16.3. Inverse demand function for clean air in Delhi

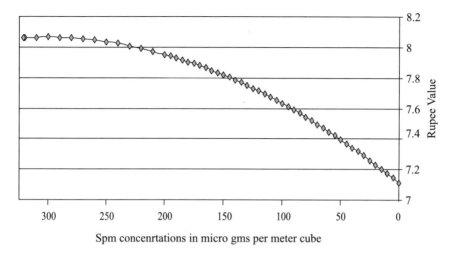

Note: The graph is generated from the Current average level of SPM of 321.39 μ gm/m³ to zero SPM, while the safe limit for SPM concentration is 200 μ gm/m³.

Figure 16.4.   Inverse demand function for clean air in Kolkata

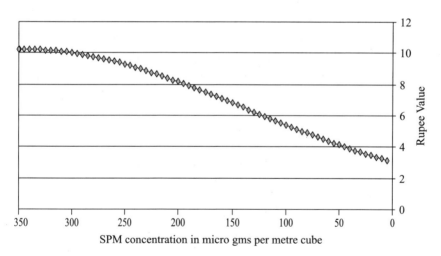

Note: The graph is generated from the Current average level of SPM of 349.09 ∝ gm/m³ to zero SPM, while the safe limit for SPM concentration is 200 μ gm/m³.

Figure 16.5.   Inverse demand function for the Pooled model of Delhi and Kolkata

The consumer surplus generated by a reduction of SPM concentration from the current average to the safe level of 200 μ gm/m³ (MINAS standards)

is computed by integrating the inverse demand function given by equations (11) to (13) with 200 µ gm/m³ as the lower limit[22] and the current average level of pollution in the respective cities as the upper limit. Integration of the inverse demand functions were carried out in Mathematica[23] 4.1 and the results of the consumer surpluses are provided in Table 16.6. The estimated consumer surplus measures the average willingness-to-pay by a representative household for reduction in the ambient air pollution from the current average to the safe MINAS[24] standards.

The annual welfare gains to a typical household from reducing SPM concentration from the current level to the MINAS standard of 200 µ gms/ m³ in Delhi, and Kolkata are respectively, INR 23354 and INR 11727 at 2002 prices. According to the 2000 census, Delhi and Kolkata have urban populations of 12.8 millions, and 14.4 millions with sample average household sizes of 5.46 and 4.56, respectively. Thus, there are 23,47,942, and 31,57,452 estimated urban households in Delhi and Kolkata. The annual benefits from reducing the SPM concentration to safe level in Delhi and Kolkata are respectively estimated as INR 54,833 (US $1142.354) million and INR 37,026 (US $771.375) million. The estimates of welfare gains to the two cities as computed from the Pooled model are also given in Table 16.6. These estimates are very close to the individual estimates of gains in these cities. This shows the robustness of the pooled model. The welfare gains are not computed from the trans-log model, as the required curvature properties are not satisfied by the inverse demand function.

16.7. Conclusion

In this chapter an inverse demand function or marginal willingness-to-pay function for environmental quality is derived based on an examination of housing market. In some cases, hedonic price studies fail to estimate demand functions because of poor quality of data because an inappropriate functional form is used for estimating the hedonic price and willingness-to-pay functions. It has been shown that given reliable data, the inverse demand function with the required properties can be derived. The choice of appropriate functional forms for the hedonic property price and the marginal willingness-to-pay equations is clearly important. Thus, starting

---

[22] 200 µ gm/m³ is the safe WHO and MINAS standard for residential area in India.

[23] Software for Mathematical Solutions.

[24] MINAS: Minimum National Standards for Environmental Pollution in India.

Table 16.8. Estimates of welfare gains in INR to urban households in Delhi, Kolkata and for Pooled model

Nature of Gains to Households	Gains to Household Based on Individual Estimates from Cities		Gains to Household Using Market Segmentation Approach[25]		
	Delhi	Kolkata	Delhi	Kolkata	Pooled
Monthly gains in Rental value due to reduction of SPM concentration by 1 μ gms/m^3	Rs. 12.63	Rs. 8.06	Rs. 12.01	Rs. 8.74	Rs. 10.21
Monthly gains in Rental value due to reduction of SPM concentration from the current average to the safe level corresponding to 200 μ gms/m^3	Rs. 1946.14	Rs. 977.22	Rs. 1887.65	Rs. 980.69	Rs. 1420.61
Annual gains in Rental value due to reduction of SPM concentration by 1 μ gms/m^3	Rs. 151.56	Rs. 96.72	Rs. 144.12	Rs. 104.88	Rs. 122.52
Annual gains in Rental value due to reduction of SPM concentration from the current average to the safe level corresponding to 200 μ gms/m^3	Rs. 23353.68	Rs. 11726.59	Rs. 22651.80	Rs. 11768.28	Rs. 17047.32
Annual gains in Rental value due to reduction of SPM concentration from the current average to the safe level corresponding to 200 μ gms/m^3 to total Urban Households[26].	Rs. 54833.08 Million	Rs. 37026.16 Million	Rs. 53185.10 Million	Rs. 37157.78 Million	Rs. 92612.69 Million[27]

[25] The estimates of individual cities are calculated by using the city-specific dummy and the city's average level of pollution.

[26] The total urban population is obtained from Census 2001 data and deflated by the average size of household in the respective cities which is 5.46 for Delhi and 4.56 for Kolkata.

[27] The total urban population of Delhi and Kolkata is used to evaluate the total gains

from a more general quadratic Box-Cox functional form for the hedonic price function, a number of functional forms need to be considered and tested for their appropriateness.

The hedonic property price function in this study is estimated using primary data on housing characteristics from carefully designed household surveys in Delhi and Kolkata. Estimates of consumer surplus benefits to a representative household from each city are obtained by integrating the inverse demand function for air quality in the range of current average quality and the quality corresponding to a safe level.

Reducing air pollution to meet current safe standards would provide a representative household an annual benefit of INR 23,354 (US \$486.54) in Delhi and INR 11,727 (US \$244.31) in Kolkata. When the benefits are extrapolated to all urban households in each city, the households in Delhi get benefits worth INR 54,833 million (US \$1142.354) while those in Kolkata get benefits worth INR 37,026 million (US \$771.375). Though these benefits appear to be high, it should be noted that these numbers represent a 'comprehensive' value households place on air quality improvements. Thus, they represent benefits from reduction in morbidity and mortality, as well as recreational and aesthetic values and reduced discomfort. It is worth assessing, however, if these estimated benefits justify the cost of environmental policy changes such as introduction of CNG operated vehicles, substituting the metro rail for road transport and relocation of polluting industries in the cities.

References

Anderson, Robert J., and Crocker Thomas D., 'Air Pollution and Residential Property Values' *Urban Studies* 8, (1971), 171–180.

Anderson, Robert J., and Crocker Thomas D., 'Air Pollution and Property Values: A Reply', *Review of Economics and Statistics,* 54, (1972), 470–473.

Blackley, P., R. Follain James, and Jr. Jan Ondrich., 'Box-Cox Estimation of Hedonic Models: How Serious is the Iterative OLS' *The Review of Economics and Statistics,* 66, (1984), 348–353.

Box, G., and Cox D., 'An Analysis of Transformations', *J. Roy. Statist. Soc. Ser. B.,* 26, (1964), 211–252.

Christensen, L., Jorgenson D., and Lau L., 'Conjugate Duality and Transcendental Logarithmic Production Function', *Econometrica,* 39, (1971), 255–256.

Dales, J.H., *Pollution, Property and Prices,* (Toronto: University of Toronto Press, 1968)

Diewert,W., 'Functional Forms for Revenue and Factor Requirement Functions', *International Economic Review,* 15, (1974), 119–130.

Dumont, M., Rayp G., Willeme P., Thas O., 'Correcting Standard Error in Two-Stage Estimation Procedures with Generated Regressands', Working Paper No. D2003/7012/10, Universitiet Gent, 2003.

Feenstra R.C., and Hanson G.H., 'Productivity Measurement and the Impact of Trade and Technology on Wages: Estimates for the US 1972–1990', Working Paper No. 6052, NBER,1997.

Feenstra R.C., and Hanson G.H., 'The Impact of Outsourcing and High-technology Capital on Wages: Estimates for the United States, 1979-1990' , *Quarterly Journal of Economics* 114 (3), (1999), 907–940.

Freeman, A. Myrick, III, 'Air Pollution and Property Values A Further Comment', *Review of Economics and Statistics* 56, (1974a), 454–456.

Freeman, A. Myrick, III, 'On Estimating Air Pollution Control benefits from Land Value Studies' , *Journal of Environmental Economics and Management* 1, (1974b), 74–83.

Freeman, A. Myrick, III., *The Measurement of Environmental and Resource Values Theory and Methods,* Washington D. C. Resources for the Future, 1993.

Goodman, C. Allen, 'Hedonic Prices, Price Indices and Housing Markets', *Journal of Urban Economics.* 5, (1978), 471–484.

Griliches, Z., 'Hedonic Price Index Revisited: Some Notes on the State of the Art', in *1967 Proceedings of the Business and Economic Statistics Section,* 324–332, USA American Statistical Association, 1967.

Halvorsen, R., and Pollakowski H.O., 'Choice of Functional Form for Hedonic Price Equation', *Journal of Urban Economics* 10 (1981), 37–49.

Haskel, J., and Slaughter M.J., 'Trade Technology and UK Wage Inequality', *The Economic Journal* 111, (2001), 163–187.

Haskel, J., and Slaughter M.J., 'Does the Sector Bias of Skill-biased Technical Change Explain Changing Skill Premia?', *European Economic Review,* 46, (2002), 1757–1783.

Hidano, Noboru, ' The Economic Valuation of the Environmental and Public Policy: A Hedonic Approach', (UK : Edward Elgar Publishing Limited, 2002).

Horowitz, Joel, L., 'Bidding Models of Housing Markets', *Journal of Urban Economics,* 20, (1986), 168–190.

Kanemoto, Y., 'Hedonic Prices and the Benefits of Public Projects', *Econometrica.*56, (1988), 981–989.

Kiel, K.A., 'Measuring the Impact of the Discovery and Cleaning of Identified Hazardous Waste sites on House Values', *Land Economics,* 71, (1995), 428–435.

Kiel, K.A., and McClain K.T., 'The Effect of an Incinerator Sitting on Housing Appreciation Rates', *Journal of Urban Economics,* 37, (1995), 311–323.

Lansford, N.H., and J. Lonnie, 'Recreational and Aesthetic Value of Water via the Hedonic Price Analysis', *Journal of Agricultural and Resource Economics,* 20, (1995) , 341–355.

Lau, L., 'Application of Duality Theory: A comment', in M. Intriligator and D. Kendrick (ed.), *Frontiers of Quantitative Economics,* Vol. 2, (Amsterdam: North Holland, 1974).

Lind, Robert C., 'Spatial Equilibrium, the Theory of Rents, and the Measurement of Benefits from Public Program', *Quarterly Journal of Economics,* 87, (1973), 188–207.

Linneman, P., 'Some Empirical Results on the Nature of Hedonic Property Functions for the Urban Housing Market', *Journal of Urban Economics,* 8, (1980), 47–68.

Mahan, B.L., Polasky S. and Adams R. M., 'Valuing Urban Wetlands: A Property Price Approach', *Land Economics,*76, (2000), 100–113.

Markandya, A. and Abelson P. W., 'The Interpretation of Capitalised Hedonic Prices in a Dynamic Environment', *Journal of Environmental Economics and Management* , (1985),12195–12206.

Mendelsohn, R., 'A Review of Identification of Hedonic Supply and Demand Functions', *Growth and Change* ,18, (1987), 82–92.

Michaels, G.R. and Smith, V.K., 'Market Segmentation and Valuing Amenities with Hedonic Models: The case of Hazardous Waste Sites', *Journal of Urban Economics,* 28(2), (1990), 223–242.

Murdoch, J., C., and J. Thayer Mark, 'Hedonic Price Estimation of Variable Urban Air Quality', *Journal of Environmental Economics and Management,* 15(2) (1988), 143-146.

Murty, M. N., Gulati S.C., and Banerjee A., 'Hedonic Property Prices and Valuation of Benefits from Reducing Urban Air Pollution in India', Working Paper No. E 237/2003, (Delhi: Institute of Economic Growth, 2003).

Murty, M.N., 'Environment, Sustainabale Development and Well-Being: Valuation, Taxes and Incentives', (Delhi: Oxford University Press, 2009).

Nelson, Jon P., 'Residential Choices, Hedonic Prices and the Demand for Urban Air Quality', *Journal of Urban Economics,* 5(3), (1978), 357–369.

Parikh, K.S., 'Economic Valuation of Air Quality Degradation in Chembur', (Bombay: IGIDR Project Report, 1994).

Parsons, G.R., 'The Effect of Coastal Land Use Restrictions on Housing Prices: A Repeat Sale Prices', *Journal of Environmental Economics and Management,* 22, (1992), 25–37

Pines, D., and Weiss Y., 'Land Improvement Projects and Land Values', *Journal of Urban Economics,* 3, (1976), 1–13.

Polinsky, S, Mitchell A., and Shavell S., 'Amenities and Property Values in a Model of an Urban Area', *Journal of Public Economics* 5, (1976), 119–129.

Portney, P. R., 'Housing Prices, Health Effects and Valuing Reduction in Risk of Death', *Journal of Environmental Economics and Management*, 8, (1981), 72–78.

Ridker, Ronald G., '*Economic Costs of Air Pollution Studies in Measuremen*', (New York: Praeger, 1967).

Ridker, Ronald G. and Henning John, A., 'The Determinants of Residential Property Values with Special Reference to Air Pollution', *Review of Economics and Statistics*, 49, (1976), 246–257.

Rosen, S., 'Hedonic Prices and Implicit Markets, Product Differentiation in Pure Competition', *Journal of Political Economy*, 82, (1974), 34–55.

Sen, Akshay, 'Determinants of Residential House Price: A Case Study of Delhi', M.Phil Dissertation, Delhi School of Economics, 1994.

Thaler, R. and Rosen S., 'The Value of Life Savings', in N. Terleckyi (ed.), *Household Production and Consumption*, (New York: Columbia University Press, 1976).

17

The Value of Statistical Life

K. R. Shanmugam and S. Madheswaran

17.1. Introduction

Economic development can have significant environmental impacts. This is true of projects in all major such as power and energy, industry, transportation, and sanitation and sewage. Exposure to environmental contaminants may cause risks to human life and health. To regulate these risks, governments undertake a wide variety of environmental policy projects that involve costs. Since resources are scarce, it is essential to pursue only those proposals that have equal benefits relative to those proposing alternative uses of these resources. A necessary condition for a project to pass the test of economic efficiency is that its costs do not exceed its benefits.

In such a benefit-cost analysis, all relevant benefits must properly be assessed and discounted, taking into account the time of their occurrence[1]. Improvements to human health resulting from better environment standards is a key component of benefits that provides justification for many environmental policies. The health benefits of environmental policies include reductions of accidents and the incidence of environment-related diseases.

The evaluation of such benefits is a straightforward extension of the public finance principles of valuation, in which the appropriate estimation is society's Willingness To Pay (WTP) for environmental risk

---

[1] The benefits of policies often have quite different time incidence. For instance, a programme such as mandatory airbags in automobiles which will begin to save lives immediately will save lives over a span of time. The benefits of greenhouse gas abatement accrue over decades and may even continue into the future.

reduction[2]. Programmes for environmental safety reduce the risk to death/health. Given the public nature of reductions in environmental risk, a programme contributing to a small reduction in risk could contribute large health benefits to the society. The literature shows that these benefits have to be estimated as the sum of the WTP for reduced risk to all affected individuals[3].

In a free market, prices paid by people represent their WTP for goods and services. Prices paid for preventing health and death risks cannot directly be obtained because prevention of these risks is not directly purchased in the market. However, there are instances where WTP of people for these services can be measured indirectly by analyzing the prices observable in markets of goods that are either complements or substitutes to the environmental risk reduction. For example, when people purchase smoke detectors (or seat belts) for their homes (or automobiles), they are making a judgment that the reduction in risk of death and other losses associated with fire (or traffic accidents) is worth at least as much as the cost of the smoke detector (or seat belt). In the literature, several revealed preference methods of environmental valuation such as hedonic prices, travel cost and the household health production function are developed by exploiting the possible relationship between an individual's demand for environmental risk reduction and certain goods with observable market prices (see Chapter 2 in this volume).

In the case of the hedonic pricing method of valuation, there are a number of studies analyzing housing markets and labour markets in order to estimate the WTP of people for environmental risk reduction. The hedonic property price model considers that demands for houses and environmental quality are complements (see Murty and Gualti's chapter) while the hedonic wage model considers that the environmental risk at the work place and wages are substitutes. This chapter uses the hedonic wage model of valuing risks to human life and health. The chapter is organized as follows. Section 17.2 presents the methodology. Section 17.3 provides the econometric specification of the hedonic wage function while Section 17.4 discusses various estimation issues. Section 17.5 provides the empirical analysis using data from a survey of industrial workers in the State of Tamil Nadu, India. The final Section 17.6 provides the concluding remarks.

---

[2] Several methods have been proposed in the literature to estimate the implicit prices for life and health. They include the cost of illness approach, human capital approach, insurance approach, court awards and compensation approach, and portfolio approach. See Linnerooth (1976) and Viscusi (1986) for a review.

[3] The basis for this approach is the broader maxim in the public finance literature that the value of the benefits of a public policy consists of WTP for these benefits by the affected people.

17.2. Methodology

17.2.1. Conceptualizing value of life issues

Valuing risks to life is a sensitive and controversial area in economics. Much of the controversy arises due to misunderstandings about the meaning of this terminology. There are two principal value-of-life concepts. The first one is the amount that is optimal from an insurance standpoint while the second one is the optimal deterrence amount.

The basis for purchasing optimal insurance is that it is preferable to the continued transfer of money to the post-accident (ill health) state until the marginal utility of money in the ill health state equals the marginal utility of money in the health state. This is perfectly valid in the case of property damages. But in the case of severe health outcomes such as fatalities that affect an individual's utility function, which decreases both the level and marginal utility for any given level of income, making a lower level payment after a fatality is desirable from an insurance viewpoint.

For severe health outcomes, the optimal deterrence amount will exceed the optimal level of compensation. The economic measure of optimal deterrence is the risk-money trade-off for very small risks of death. Risk regulation policies will always prevent some expected number of adverse health outcomes, but these effects are usually probabilistic. Therefore, the appropriate issue for policy evaluation is not how much we value preventing certain adverse health effects, but what value we should place on small reductions in the probabilities of these outcomes for a large number of affected individuals.

This distinction is important for at least two reasons:

(a) Society's attitude towards saving identified lives seems to be quite different from the attitude towards saving statistical lives. The value society places on an identified life such as a trapped coal miner is likely to be substantially greater than the implicit valuations of life and health status of individuals who cannot be identified, such as the prospective beneficiaries from improved traffic signals or flood control programmes.

(b) An individual's relative valuation of risk reduction is likely to be greater for small changes in the risk. Since an individual's WTP per unit of risk reduction decreases with his/her wealth, he/she will be willing to spend relatively more for initial than for subsequent reductions of risk as his/her wealth becomes depleted with each successive purchase of a decrease in risk. When extrapolated, this relationship indicates that the individual will spend less per unit of risk to prevent certain death and injury than to bring about small changes in these risk levels.

In this instance, what is at issue is not the value of life itself but rather the value of small risks to life/health. Specifically, one needs to understand the amount that individuals are willing to spend to prevent a small risk of death. For small changes in risk, this amount will be approximately equal to the amount of money that they should be compensated to incur such a small risk. It thus serves as a measure of the deterrence amount of the value (to the individual at risk) of preventing accidents and as a reference point for the amount the government should spend to prevent small statistical risks (Viscusi, 2008).

If improvements in safety can be obtained for, say US $5 million per statistical life in project A as opposed to US $10 million and US $15 million per statistical life in project B and project C respectively, then it is desirable to spend on the most cost effective option (i.e., project A) that has the lowest cost per life saved. In reality, there is no such comparable market process at work. As a result, the government uses value-of-life estimates from the market in making its deliberations concerning risk reduction policies.

17.2.2. Economic foundations

The theory of compensating differentials originally conceived by Adam Smith forms the basis of the hedonic approach. He suggests that 'the whole of the advantages and disadvantages of the different employments of labor and stock must, in the same neighborhood, be either perfectly equal or continually tending to equality.... . The wages of labor vary with ease or hardship, the honorableness or dishonorableness of employment'. If non-pecuniary advantages and disadvantages of different employments are unequal then the pecuniary rewards must be unequal in the opposite direction to preserve the equality of total advantages.

Smith (1776) lists five principles for compensating non-pecuniary characteristics of employment–agreeableness or disagreeableness of employment, difficulty and expense of learning, constancy or inconstancy of employment, degree of trust required, and probability or improbability of success. These principles have inspired the development of two applied economic models, namely, the human capital model and the hedonic wage model. While the former considers the length of training (formal schooling and informal training) as the principle explaining compensating wage differentials the latter focuses on quality variations in both worker and job attributes as an explanation for wage differences.

The hedonic approach treats jobs as bundles of characteristics such as working conditions and levels of risk of accidental injury. Employees are described by the amount they require as compensation for different risk levels while firms (employers) are characterized by the amount they are willing to offer workers to accept different risk levels. An acceptable match occurs when the preferred choice of an employee and that of an employer are mutually consistent. Thus, the actual wage embodies a series of hedonic prices for various job attributes including accidental risk and other prices for worker characteristics.

Suppose that there are m such indicators of a worker's personal and job attributes other than job risk level (p), denoted by a vector $c = (c_1, c_2, ..., c_m)$. Let w represent the schedule of annual earnings. Then, $w(p, c)$ reflects the market equalizing differential function. Controlling for other aspects of the job would provide an estimate of the wage premium that workers receive for job risk. Thus the theory considers both sides of the market and examines equilibrium risk choices and either the wage levels or the price levels associated with these choices.

The firm's demand for labour decreases with the total cost of employing a worker. Since providing greater workplace safety is costly to the firm, it must pay a lower wage to offset the cost of providing a safe work environment in order to maintain the given level of profits along the iso-profit or wage-risk offer curve. Figure 17.1 shows wage offer curves for two firms, with wage as an increasing function of risk, OC_1 for firm 1 and OC_2 for firm 2.

Labour supply is characterized by several mild restrictions on preferences. Following a von Neumann-Morgenstern expected utility approach with state dependent utility functions, $u(w)$ represents the utility of a healthy worker at wage w and $v(w)$ represents the utility of an injured person at wage w. A worker's compensation after an accident is a function of the worker's wage. It is assumed that the relationship between a worker's compensation and wage is subsumed into the functional form of $v(w)$ and that workers prefer health to injury, (i.e., $u(w) > v(w)$) and that the marginal utility of income is positive (i.e., $u'(w) > 0$ and $v'(w) > 0$).

For any given risk level, workers prefer the wage risk combination from the market offer curve with the highest wage level. The outer envelop of these curves is the market opportunities locus w (p). That is, workers choose from potential wage-risk combinations along market opportunities locus w (p) to maximize expected utility. In Figure 17.1, the tangency between the constant expected locus EU_1 of worker 1 and firm 1's offer curve OC_1 represents his optimal job risk choice. Worker 2 maximizes his expected utility when EU_2 is tangent to OC_2.

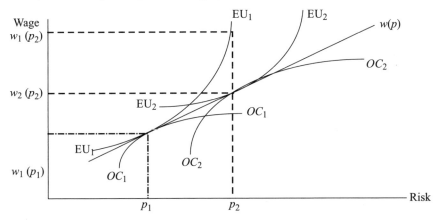

Figure 17.1.   Wage-Risk Trade-off

All wage-risk combinations associated with a given worker's constant expected utility locus must satisfy:

$Z = (1-p) u (w) + p v (w)$ and the wage-risk trade-off along this curve is:
$$\frac{dw}{dp} = \frac{-Z_p}{Z_w} = \frac{u(w)-v(w)}{(1-p)u'(w)+pv'(w)} > 0$$ so that the required wage rate is increasing in the risk level.

The estimated $d\,w/\,d\,p$ is a local measure of the wag-risk trade-off for marginal changes in risk. This estimated slope is both the worker's marginal Willingness To Accept (WTA) risk and his marginal WTP for more safety and the firm's marginal cost of more safety and its marginal cost reduction from an incremental increase in risk. That is, it reflects the marginal supply as well as the marginal demand price of risk.

It is noted that the estimated wage-risk trade-off curve w (p) does not show how a particular employee is compensated for non-marginal changes in risk. In Figure 17.1, worker 2 has revealed a WTA risk p_2 at wage w_2 along EU_2. If risk exposure to employee 1 changes from p_1 to p_2, he will require a higher compensation to keep his utility constant. Thus, with large changes in risk, a worker's wage-risk trade-off will not be the same because the relevant trade-off must be made along the worker's expected utility locus and not the estimated market wage-risk trade-off (Viscusi and Aldy, 2003).

Since each point on the hedonic wage function w (p) represents the slope of the expected utility curve, this function is used to estimate the welfare effect of a marginal change in job risk. If all employees have homogenous preferences, then there will be only one expected utility curve, and the observable points on the $w(p)$ will represent the constant expected utility locus. Likewise, if all firms are homogenous, $w(p)$ will approximate the firm's offer curve. Ideally, one needs to estimate the constant expected utility curve in order to estimate the WTP/WTA for risk reduction. However, most studies use the hedonic function as it is the locus of tangencies that are observable in labour market data.

17.3. Econometric specification of the hedonic wage function

Thaler and Rosen (1976) carried out the first empirical study to estimate the value of life using the hedonic wage approach. Currently there are many studies providing life value estimates for developed as well as developing countries. Basically, these empirical studies specify a wage equation of the type given in equation (1)

$$w_i = \alpha + \beta_1 p_i + \beta_2 q_i + \sum_k \gamma_k X_{ki} + \varepsilon_i \tag{1}$$

where w_i is the worker's wage rate, X is a vector of a worker's personal characteristics variables (such as age or job experience, education, union and marital status, and caste or racial indicators) as well as job characteristics variables (which include indicators for supervisory status, job security, irregular work hours, pleasant worksite, etc.). p_i and q_i represent the probability of work-related fatal and non-fatal injury risks faced by worker i (in some studies the risk variables p and q are allowed to interact with other X variables), and ε_i is the regular random error term reflecting unmeasured factors influencing a worker's wage rate. α (a constant term), β_1, β_2, and $\gamma_k s$ are parameters to be estimated using a regression analysis.

17.4. Estimation issues

Various issues arise in estimating the hedonic wage equation. Some important issues are as follows.

17.4.1. Functional form of the dependent variable

A main issue is whether the wage equation should take the linear or log-linear (semi-log) form. The theory is silent on this issue. It does not specify any specific functional form for linking wage and job risks. In order to choose the right specification with the greatest explanatory power, the flexible functional form given by the Box-Cox transformation can be employed. The Box-Cox transformation modifies the dependent variable such that the estimated wage equation takes the form:

$$\frac{w_i^{\lambda} - 1}{\lambda} = \alpha + \beta_1 p_i + \beta_2 q_i + \sum_k \gamma_k X_{ki} + \varepsilon_i \tag{2}$$

This approach assumes that a λ exists such that the model is normally distributed, homoskedastic, and linear in the regressors. The functional form is dictated by the parameter λ, which is estimated as the value that maximizes the log-likelihood function. The case where $\lambda \to 0$ represents the semi-log form, while the case where $\lambda \to 1$ represents the linear functional form. The flexibility allowed under the Box-Cox transformation can be used to test the appropriateness of these two restrictions on the form of the model.

Studies such as Moore and Viscusi (1988) and Shanmugam (1996/7) employ this procedure. Using the maximum likelihood methods, these studies rejected both specifications based on a likelihood ratio test. However, they found that the semi-log form generates results closer to those found with the unrestricted flexible form. The wage-risk trade-off based on the Box-Cox transformation can be computed by totally differentiating (2) with respect to wage and risk (p or q) and rearranging the terms as:

$$\frac{dw}{dp} = \frac{\hat{\beta}_1}{w^{\lambda-1}} \text{ and } \frac{dw}{dq} = \frac{\hat{\beta}_2}{w^{\lambda-1}} \tag{3}$$

If the dependent variable is in log form, the wage-risk premium is computed by:

$$\frac{dw}{dp} = \hat{\beta}_1 . \bar{w} \text{ and } \frac{dw}{dq} = \hat{\beta}_2 . \bar{w} \tag{4}$$

17.4.2. Risk measures

Since the market opportunity locus reflects both workers' preferences over wage and risk and firms' preferences over costs and safety, an ideal measure of on-the-job risk should reflect both the workers' perception and the firms' perception of the risk. Only a few studies such as Viscusi (1979), Gerking, de Hann and Schulze (1988), and Liu and Hammitt (1999) have used workers' subjective preferences regarding risk. Up to now, no study has compiled data on firms' perception. Several other studies, including Shanmugam (2000), have used a qualitative (subjective) measure to study the on-the-job risk. The subjective measure utilizes a danger perception dummy indicator that takes the value 1 if the worker believes that his job exposes him to dangerous or unhealthy conditions and 0 otherwise.

Moreover, some studies have also included non-pecuniary job attributes such as whether the job provides good security or whether it has irregular work hours, or a pleasant worksite. Inclusion of these factors control for a variety of job attributes, and reduce the bias in the estimated coefficient of the job risk variable. Further they provide an additional test of the validity of the theory.

However, the majority of the studies have constructed an objective index of job risk such as the probability of fatal or non-fatal risk for workers by industry or by occupation from secondary sources. Several papers on the US labour market in the 1970s and early 1980s used actuarial data (Thaler and Rosen, 1976; Leigh, 1981 and Arnold and Nichols, 1983). These studies used a job-related risk measure based on data collected by the Society of Actuaries for 37 occupations in 1967. Studies such as Butler (1983), Leigh (1991), and Cousineau, Lacroix and Girard (1992) used workers' compensation records to construct risk measures. Almost all recent studies on the US labour market have used fatal and injury risk data collected by the US Department of Labour Bureau of Statistics. In India, Shanmugam (1996/7, 2000, 2001) and Madheswaran (2007), for example, have used risk data from the Office of the Chief Inspector of Factories in Chennai. Marin and Psacharopoulos (1982) and Sandy and Elliott (1996) employ data provided by the Office of Population Census and Survey (UK). A well-known problem with the use or average or aggregate industry data on risk to measure individual risk is that workers in different jobs in the same industry face the same probability of risk. Further, the objective measure does not necessarily reflect the worker's perception about the riskiness of his employment.

17.4.3. Wealth effects

An objection raised against the validity of the theory underlying the hedonic wage function is that the most attractive jobs in the economy also pay more. To resolve the apparent paradox, examining the wealth effect is useful. Viscusi (1981) argues that a rich person will prefer to work in a safe job and earn more. Studies such as Viscusi (1978), Garen (1988) and Shanmugam (2001) estimate a risk equation in which the wealth variable enters as an explanatory variable and show that the wealth variable gets a negative and significant parameter estimate.

17.4.4. Workers' behaviour and habits

Another objection is that workers differ in their attitudes towards risks. Therefore, they demand different compensation amounts per unit of risk. The worker with a low value on safety will accept a risky job and receive a low premium per unit of risk while the worker placing a high value on safety will prefer to work in a safe job as they require a high premium per unit of risk. Garen (1988) also argues that workers may differ in unobserved characteristics which affect their productivity and hence their earnings in risky jobs. For instance, some worker may possess unobserved attributes such as cool heads that make them more productive in a risky job than in a safe one. This suggests a cross equation correlation of disturbances in wage and risk equations and OLS will lead to biased estimates of the wage equation.

The availability of certain instruments that determine the choice of the risk level, while not directly affecting wages, allows consistent estimation of the effects of risk variables on wages via a simultaneous and modified selection bias technique proposed by Garen (1988). In his method, (1) is modified as:

$$w_i = f(\alpha + \beta_1 p_i + \beta_2 q_i + \Sigma_k \gamma_k X_{ki} + \varepsilon_i + \phi_1 p_i + \phi_2 q_i) \tag{5}$$

In (5), the disturbance term ε captures the effect of unobservable factors, which influence w regardless of p and q. Disturbances ϕ_1 and ϕ_2 represent unobservables whose effects on wages depend on p and q. If a worker is more productive in a risky job due to unobserved factors, he will have larger values of either ϕ_1 or ϕ_2. p and q are choice variables and are correlated with ε, ϕ_1 and ϕ_2. Therefore, OLS will provide biased estimates.

Higher values of ϕ_1 and ϕ_2 raise the marginal gain in earnings for p and q respectively and raise earnings for given values of p and q. If safety is a normal good, higher values for ϕ_i create offsetting income and substitution effects on choices of p and q. Although it is not known which effect is dominant, the choice of job risks depends on ϕ_1 and ϕ_2. Higher values of ε have an income effect, as does any non-wage income (Y) and workers' degree of risk aversion (say V). Variables that raise the wage (i.e., X_{ki}) also have an income effect on the choice of job risk. The first order approximations to p and q can be written as:

$$p_i = \pi_0 + X_{ki}'\pi_1 + \pi_2 V + \pi_3 Y + \eta \tag{6}$$

$$q_i = \delta_0 + X_{ki}'\delta_1 + \delta_2 V + \delta_3 Y + \mu \tag{7}$$

In (6–7), the disturbance terms η and μ are unobserved heterogeneity that may depend on ε, ϕ_1 and ϕ_2. Higher values for Y, X, and V are expected to reduce the chosen levels of risk. Thus, the entire econometric model consists of equations (5–7). As heterogeneity affects the return w, the OLS estimation of the earnings function is biased. Further, p and q depend on ϕ_1 and ϕ_2 implying that $E\left(\varepsilon + \phi_1 p + \phi_2 q\right) \neq 0$. The selection bias corrected earnings equation will take the following form:

$$\ln(W_i) = \begin{array}{l} \alpha + \beta_1 p_i + \beta_2 q_i + \sum \gamma_{ki} X_{ki} + \rho_1 \hat{\eta} + \rho_2 \hat{\mu} + \\ \rho_3 \hat{\eta} p + \rho_4 \hat{\mu} p + \rho_5 \hat{\eta} q + \rho_6 \hat{\mu} q + \theta \end{array} \tag{8}$$

In (8), $\hat{\eta}$ and $\hat{\mu}$ are the predicted residuals from the OLS estimates of equations (6) and (7) respectively while θ is the error term. As the variance of θ depends on p and q and the model is heteroskedastic, a Weighted Least Squares (WLS) procedure will yield consistent estimates. The terms accompanying $\hat{\eta}$ and $\hat{\mu}$ make explicit the effect of worker heterogeneity and the endogeneity of job risks on wages. The sign pattern of theses terms will provide an estimate of the hypothesis that unobserved factors will have a strong effect on the marginal returns to job risk. Almost all existing studies have estimated the risk compensation without accounting for such unobserved heterogeneity among workers with a few exceptions such as Garen (1988), Sandy and Elliott (1996) and Shanmugam (2001).

17.4.5. *Effect of insurance benefits*

Since the employer can compensate the workers for employment risks either through ex-ante compensation (i.e., wage premium) or ex-post compensation (insurance benefit), the failure to control for ex-post compensation could bias the estimation of the wage-risk trade-off of workers. In India (Tamil Nadu), the Employees State Insurance Act, 1948, provides for certain benefits to employees in the case of sickness, maternity and employment injury. With respect to employment injury, persons covered by the scheme or their dependents are entitled to receive disablement or dependent benefits. The wage limit in order to be covered by this Act was INR 1600 per month (in the early nineties). The employees' contribution was INR 2.25 per cent of the wages (if the daily wage exceeded INR 6) and the firms' contribution was exactly double the employees' share. The schedule of daily wages and the corresponding Standard Benefit Rates (SBRs) are shown in Table 17.1.

Table 17.1. Wages and standard benefit rates

S. No.	Wage ranges	Daily SBRs
1	Below Rs. 6	Rs. 2.50
2	Rs. 6 and above but below Rs. 8	Rs. 3.50
3	Rs. 8 and above but below Rs.12	Rs. 5.00
4	Rs. 12 and above, but below Rs. 16	Rs. 7.00
5	Rs. 12 and above but below Rs. 24	Rs. 10.00
6	Rs. 24 and above but below Rs. 36	Rs. 15.00
7	Rs. 36 and above	Rs. 20.00

Source: Shanmugam (1999)

By including the workers' insurance benefit variable in the hedonic wage equation, this bias could be avoided. An issue in this regard is whether an additive term of workers' insurance benefits or an interactive term with job risks should be incorporated into the wage equation. Viscusi and Moore (1987) argue that insurance benefits affect wages only at positive risk levels. At zero risk, no risk occurs and so no benefits. Therefore, using an interactive model is theoretically appropriate. With this suggestion, the hedonic wage equation in (1) takes the form:

$$\ln w_i = \alpha + \beta_1 p_i + \beta_2 q_i + \sum_k \gamma_k X_{ki} + \varphi WC_i \cdot q_i + \varepsilon_i \qquad (9)$$

where WC_i is the workers compensation benefits payable for a job injury suffered by worker i.

17.4.6. Life-cycle issues

The hedonic wage equation (1) includes the probability of job related death risk, p (or injury q) as a measure of risk, but this ignores life-cycle issues such as variations across individuals in potential losses resulting from death (or injury). A young worker faces a more substantial loss from a given fatality risk relative to an old worker. Thus, there may be age-related differences in proclivity towards risk-taking. Thaler and Rosen (1976) and Viscusi (1979) address this issue by including the death risk-age interaction term. However, this approach does not correctly capture changes in life expectancy with age or the role of discounting with respect to the years of life at risk.

17.4.7. Discount rate for health benefits and the value of life

As mentioned earlier, the health benefits of various environmental policies may have quite different time patterns of incidence. Economic analyses of such policies often require the use of an appropriate discount rate for estimating long term health benefits. Various suggestions emerge from the literature – a zero rate (treating the future and the present equally), the opportunity cost of capital (since funds might be invested in alternate projects with appreciable expected returns) and the real interest rate on low risk (e.g. government) bonds (because such risk free returns, net-of-tax rates best reflect the social rate of time preference). The choice of the discount rate powerfully affects the net present value of alternate policies/proposals.

Economists in general argue that long term health benefits do not differ from other benefits in terms of the principles that are applied in valuing them (Moore and Viscusi, 1990). If capital markets are perfect, one can simply use the society's risk free rate of time preference as the appropriate discount rate for all benefits. In the presence of capital market imperfections that are common in many developing countries, the issue becomes more complex, particularly since health is not traded directly in an inter-temporal market. Some economists have also expressed doubts as to whether the capital rates accurately reflect the trade-offs individuals make with respect to health status over the years.

The question is whether the same rate of time preference can be used for any other benefit component or whether a different rate for health impacts needs to be found. The choice between these two perspectives is not simply a theoretical issue (Moore and Viscusi, 1990). Therefore, many studies have attempted to resolve this issue empirically. These studies have estimated the time preference rate for health impacts and compared the estimated rate with the interest rate for trading financial resources. These studies are broadly grouped as experimental studies and field studies [see Frederick et al., (2003) for an excellent survey].

In the former, people are asked to evaluate the stylized inter-temporal prospects involving real or hypothetical outcomes. In the latter, discount rates are inferred from economic decisions that people make in their ordinary life. That is, discount rates are estimated by identifying the real-world behaviours that involve tradeoffs between the near future and a more distant future. The hedonic wage approach falls into the field studies category. Early field studies have examined consumers' choices among different models of electrical appliances that present purchasers with a trade-off between the immediate purchase price and the long-term costs of running the appliance (as determined by its energy). In these studies, the rates implied by consumers' choices vastly exceeded market interest rates and varied widely across product categories (for example, 17–20 per cent for air conditioners (Hausman, 1979) and 45–300 per cent for refrigerators (Gately, 1980).

Hedonic wage studies have imputed the discount rates from wage risk trade-offs in which, as shown above, workers decide whether to accept a risky job with a higher wage. These studies have used three approaches – discounted life years lost approach (Moore and Viscusi, 1988 and Shanmugam, 2006), the Markov decision model (Viscusi and Moore, 1989) and the life-cycle model (Moore and Viscusi, 1990).

The discounted expected life years approach includes the Expected Discounted Life Years Lost (ELYL) variable (instead of job risk) in the hedonic model to estimate the impact of changes in the expected remaining lifetime on wages. Future health risks are discounted at a rate of time preference, r, so that the ELYL of a worker with T years of remaining life who chooses the risk level p is– $\text{ELYL} = p \ x \int_{0T} (1-e_{-rT}) \ dT = p \ x \ (1-e_{-rT})/r$, where r is the parameter (and not a variable collected from the sample workers). r is an estimate of the workers' implicit rate of discount that they reveal through their choices of job risks and is computed as part of estimation process. The discounted duration of life at risk is also known as the quantity-adjusted death risk and is useful to calculate the quantity-adjusted value of life.

The quantity-adjusted value of life differs from the conventional estimates of the value of life in that the trade off is not between wages and death risk probabilities but between wages and death risks that have been weighted by the discounted number of potential years of life lost. A consideration of duration of life lost makes it possible to estimate the value of each year of life lost. Although this model is simple to estimate, its structure has no formal theoretical basis. However, the Markov decision and life-cycle consumption models have a formal theoretical basis.

In the former, workers select the optimal job risks from the wage offer curve where this risk affects the probability of death in each period. In selecting their optimal occupational risks, workers determine their life expectancy. The latter model recognizes that there is a probability in each period that the consumption stream may be terminated. Thus, the wage responses to the variation in life years at risk provide direct estimates of the discount rate that workers apply to their future utility in all these models.

Using the discounted expected life years lost approach and the Markov decision approach, Moore and Viscusi (1988) and Moore and Viscusi (1990) found that the estimated rate of time preference was 11 per cent for US workers. Adopting the life-cycle approach, Viscusi and Moore (1989) found that the real discount rate for US workers was 2 per cent. Thus, in the labour market studies, the estimated discount rates range from 1 to 14 per cent, a more plausible range than the consumers' implicit rate of discount range of 17 to 300 per cent gauged from appliance purchases. In the Indian context, Shanmugam (2006) estimated the implicit discount rate (ranging from 7.6 to 9.7 per cent) for workers using the discounted life years lost approach.

17.5. Empirical analysis

(i) *Data sources*: The empirical analysis is based on the data collected through a survey of industrial workers in Tamil Nadu (a southern state of India). The sampling procedure adopted for the study was the multi-stage random sampling technique. First, the Madras district of Tamil Nadu was selected as the study area. In the second stage, only blue-collar male employees in manufacturing industries were chosen since they alone faced employment related death risks in the study area from 1987 to 1990. Then, these workers were straitified into 17 groups according to their industrial codes at the 2-digit National Industrial Classification (NIC) level. Fixing one per cent from each stratum, the total sample size was fixed at 522. Then, 522 workers were randomly selected for the interview. A maximum sample of four workers from each randomly selected factory was drawn. The collected data set consists of information on workers' personal as well as enterprise characteristics.

The source of data pertaining to job risk is the Administrative Report of the Chief Inspector of Factories, Madras. The report provides data pertaining to the total number of male workers and the number of death and injury accidents among them on an annual basis at the 2-digit NIC level. These risks may vary substantially over years and can be particularly high when there is a major catastrophe resulting in multiple deaths. Therefore, the average probabilities of fatal risk (p) per 100,000 workers (FATAL) and injury risk (q) per 100 workers (INJURY) over the years 1987–90 were computed. Table 17.2 shows the distribution of workers, and the probabilities of fatal and injury risk by industry. The means and standard deviations of the study variables are provided in Table 17.3.

Table 17.2. Risk measures and workers by industry

NIC	Name of the Industry	P	q	No. of Workers
20–21	Manufacture of food products	16.14	2.66	22
22	Manufacture of beverages & tobacco products	0.00	2.64	6
23	Manufacture of cotton textiles	26.52	59.15	48
24	Manufacture of wool and synthetic fibre textiles	0.00	0.61	1
26	Manufacture of textile products	7.36	0.27	45
27	Manufacture of wood, furniture and fixtures	0.0	2.81	5
28	Manufacture of paper, printing and publishing	17.12	1.24	60
29	Manufacture of leather and leather products	19.94	0.46	17
30	Manufacture of rubber, plastic and petroleum	0.00	0.61	24
31	Manufacture of chemical and chemical products	21.90	0.96	26
32	Manufacture of non-metallic mineral products	17.75	3.11	6
33	Manufacture of basic metal and alloys	21.53	3.55	34
34	Manufacture of metal products and parts	0.00	2.64	50
35	Manufacture of machinery and tools	0.00	2.35	70
36	Manufacture of electric machinery and apparatus	8.58	1.53	39
37	Manufacture of transport equipments and parts	5.97	3.76	64
38	Manufacture of other products	0.00	2.01	5
All	Total	10.44	7.29	522

Source: Shanmugam (1993)

Table 17.3. Variable definitions and descriptive statistics [a]

Variable	Definition	Mean (S.D.)
WAGE (w)	After tax hourly wage rate (in Rs.)[b]	5.3032 (2.248)
FATAL (p)	Job related fatal risk per 100,000 workers	10.4407 (9.256)
INJURY (q)	Job related injury risk per 100 workers	7.2958 (16.553)
DANGER	Indicator for job hazard perception	0.9000 (0.290)
HIGH	Indicator for high school education	0.2624 (0.440)
HSC	Indicator for higher secondary education	0.3984 (0.4900)
DEGREE	Indicator for college degree	0.0766 (0.266)
AGE	Age in completed years	34.142 (6.687)
BC	Indicator for backward community	0.6456 (0.478)
UNION	Indicator for union representation	0.5249 (0.499)
PRIVE	Indicator for the job private factory	0.8697 (0.336)
OWNHOME	Indicator for owning a house	0.4348 (0.496)
WSPOUSE	Indicator for having a working spouse	0.2222 (0.4161)
DISABILITY	Indicator for work limiting disability	0.0747 (0.263)
MARRY	Indicator for being married	0.8122 (0.3908)
TENURE	Job tenure (in months)	128.460 (73.671)
SUPER	Indicator for supervisory status	0.270 (0.444)
IRREGULAR	Indicator for irregular work hours	0.408 (0.492)
SECURITY	Indicator for good job security	0.622 (0.485)
PLEASANT	Indicator for pleasant worksite	0.523 (0.499)
DECISION	Indicator for decision making	0.462 (0.499)
CRR	Worker's insurance replacement rate	0.480 (0.042)

Note:

[a] The sample size is 522

[b] computed by assuming 2000 annual hours worked

Source: Estimated as explained in the text

(ii) *Flexible functional form analysis of the wage equation*: In order to resolve the functional form issue, the maximum likelihood estimation (MLE) technique is employed to estimate the Box-Cox wage transformation wage equation (2) with the following X factors which influence wages – age, age square and education level (human capital variables), and dummy indicators for backward community, union status and employment in a private concern. Maximization of the likelihood function yields a value of λ_u (unrestricted value) that equals 0.3072. The likelihood ratio test statistics which is defined as twice the difference between a null and alternative hypothesis [$\psi=-2(L(\lambda_R)-L(\lambda_u))$] for the restriction against the unrestricted value rejects both linear and semi-log forms[4]. Table 17.4 presents the Box-Cox non-linear regression estimates of the earning function for λ equal to 0, 0.3072 and 1.

Table 17.4. Box-Cox non-linear regression model estimates of wage equations.

Variables	$\lambda = 0$ (semi-log)	$\lambda = 0.3072$	$\lambda = 1$ (linear)
FATAL	0.0097 (4.816)	0.0171 (5.041)	0.0625 (4.977)
INJURY	0.0046 (4.282)	0.0082 (4.539)	0.0324 (4.638)
AGE	0.0752 (4.962)	0.970 (4.104)	0.1242 (1.651)
AGE x AGE	−0.0007 (3.280)	−0.0007 (2.247)	−0.0003 (0.288)
HIGH	0.0746 (2.160)	0.1033 (1.875)	0.2481 (1.380)
HSC	0.1569 (4.620)	0.2396 (4.386)	0.6760 (3.729)
COLLEGE	0.2035 (3.851)	0.3060 (3.619)	0.8261 (2.984)
BC	0.0703 (2.707)	0.1107 (2.659)	0.3308 (2.412)
UNION	0.2306 (6.368)	0.3798 (6.254)	1.234 (5.621)
PRIVATE	−0.0285 (0.774)	−0.0568 (0.963)	−0.2256 (1.168)
Constant	−0.5691 (2.093)	−0.9782 (2.275)	−2.2681 (1.664)
Lambda (λ)	0 (0.000)	0.3072 (4.321)	1.000 (12.456)
σ^2	0.0721 (4.744)	0.1841 (4.282)	1.9545 (3.351)
Log-likelihood	−880.983	−871.416	−951.588

Note: Figures in parentheses indicate absolute t values
Source: Estimated as explained in the text

As expected, both fatal and injury risk variables have a positive and significant influence on the wage rate in all cases. These results are consistent with the hypothesis that the workers receive higher wage compensation for the disadvantages of higher job risks ceteris paribus. Substituting $\lambda, \hat{\beta}_1$, and $\hat{\beta}_2$ values in (3), and multiplying by 2000 to annualize the figure and by the scale of the risk variables, the value of statistical life and injury can be estimated as INR 10.86 million and INR 5207, respectively when $\lambda = 0.3072$. The corresponding values are INR 10.28 million and INR 4876 when $\lambda = 0$ and INR 12.5 million and INR 6480 when $\lambda = 1$. These results imply that although the semi-log form is different from unrestricted estimates in a statistical sense, it yields comparable estimates of the value of life and value of injury. Therefore, the semi-log form is considered throughout the analyses below.

---

[4] The estimated $L(\lambda)$ corresponding to $\lambda_u (=0.3072)$, $\lambda=0$ and $\lambda =1$ are −871.416, −880.983 and −951.588 and the test statistics yield the value equal to 19.134 for the test of λ_R and 160.344 for the test of $\lambda_R=1$. Since the critical $\chi^2(1)$ for 95 per cent confidence level is 3.841, we can consequently reject both linear and semi-log forms.

Column 1 of Table 17.5 provides the OLS estimation results of the semi-log wage equation. Most of the non-risk variables performed well with the expectation of the wage equation in the literature both in terms of magnitudes and direction of the coefficients. The age earnings profile exhibits an inverted-U shape as predicted by the human capital theory. Education dummies are positive and statistically significant at five per cent level. The union differential is approximately 24 per cent. Backward community workers tend to earn more, indicating that they are more productive in blue collar risky occupations. Private firms pay less, but it is not supported by the *t* statistics.

Table 17.5. OLS and WLS estimates of Log wage equations

Variables	1	2	3	4 (WLS)	5	6
FATAL	0.0097			0.0639	0.0111	0.0105
	(6.038)			(1.900)	(7.261)	(6.965)
INJURY	0.0046	0.0077		−0.0380	0.0039	0.0139
	(5.103)	(10.044)		(1.640)	(4.445)	(6.374)
DANGER			0.2593			
			(5.639)			
INJURY x CRR						−0.0306
						(4.985)
AGE	0.0752	0.0763	0.0672	0.0812	0.0650	0.0658
	(5.153)	(5.053)	(4.148)	(4.050)	(4.649)	(4.814)
AGE x AGE	−0.0007	−0.0006	−0.0005	−0.0008	−0.0006	−0.0006
	(3.265)	(3.143)	(2.403)	(2.970)	(3.249)	(3.435)
HIGH	0.0746	0.0695	0.0827	0.1941	0.0674	0.0645
	(2.162)	(1.950)	(2.187)	(2.880)	(2.054)	(2.010)
HSC	0.1569	0.1473	0.1929	0.3713	0.1289	0.1418
	(5.056)	(4.597)	(5.720)	(3.310)	(4.294)	(4.818)
COLLEGE	0.2035	0.2261	0.2485	0.2559	0.1551	0.1700
	(4.058)	(4.373)	(4.531)	(3.370)	(3.201)	(3.582)
BC	0.0703	0.0653	0.0452	0.0748	0.0826	0.0782
	(2.782)	(2.503)	(1.630)	(2.130)	(3.392)	(3.287)
UNION	0.2306	0.2000	0.2101	0.5252	0.2126	0.1935
	(8.829)	(7.549)	(7.440)	(3.200)	(8.144)	(7.502)
PRIVATE	−0.0285	−0.0690	−0.0748	0.1956	−0.0195	−0.0378
	(0.772)	(1.839)	(1.878)	(1.200)	(0.547)	(1.080)
SUPER					0.0806	0.0717
					(2.306)	(2.098)

(Contd.)

(*Contd.*)

Variables	1	2	3	4 (WLS)	5	6
DECISION					0.1289	0.1159
					(4.193)	(3.843)
PLEASANT					−0.0308	−0.0197
					(1.307)	(0.853)
SECURITY					0.0895	0.0847
					(3.456)	(3.343)
IRREGULAR					0.0300	0.0203
					(1.223)	(0.844)
Error−1				−0.0692		
				(2.020)		
Error−2				0.0489		
				(2.260)		
Error−1x FATAL				0.0007		
				(2.220)		
Error−1 x IN-JURY				0.0007		
				(2.750)		
Error−2 x FATAL				−0.0011		
				(2.490)		
Error-2 x INJURY				0.0001		
				(0.700)		
Constant	−0.5691	−0.4724	−0.4942	−1.3569	−0.3956	−0.3515
	(2.162)	(1.739)	(1.713)	(2.530)	(1.550)	(1.408)
R-square	0.583	0.554	0.497	0.567	0.631	0.648
F-statistics	71.540	70.551	56.184	56.150	57.695	58.191

Note: Figures in parentheses are absolute t values

Source: Estimated as explained in the text

In Column 2 of Table 17.5, the fatal risk variable has been excluded. The injury coefficient increases from 0.0046 (in Column1) to 0.0077 and the statistical value of injury risk increases to Rs. 8162.

(iii) *Subjective Measure of Risk*: In Column 3, injury, the objective measure is replaced with a subjective measure namely DANGER. It influences the wage rate positively and significantly, indicating that workers on jobs which they perceive as being dangerous earn an earnings premium of Rs. 2749. It is noted that the value implied by INJURY is roughly three times larger than that implied by DANGER. This discrepancy might be due to imperfect information received by the workers.

Table 17.6. Regression estimates of job risk equations

Variable	Fatal Risk		Injury Risk	
	Coefficient	t-Statistic	Coefficient	t-Statistic
C	4.0310	0.443	−18.4048	−1.127
AGE	0.4885	0.974	1.1368	1.265
AGE*AGE	−0.0042	−0.614	−0.0144	−1.167
HIGH	0.3953	0.346	2.5203	1.232
HSC	0.9319	0.915	5.6940	3.119
COLLEGE	3.1172	1.879	2.2243	0.748
BC	−1.2387	−1.473	−1.6588	−1.101
UNION	−1.1666	−1.368	5.5254	3.614
PRIVATE	−4.0587	−3.375	0.0978	0.045
WSPOUSE	1.5522	1.550	3.9161	2.181
OWNHOME	−2.9582	−3.625	−3.7403	−2.557
R-squared	0.0756		0.0711	
F	4.1818		3.9128	

Source: Estimated as explained in the text

(iv) *Wealth Effect*: Before the selection bias issue is considered, the issue of the wealth effect is taken up. Viscusi (1978) demonstrates that within the context of the health state dependent model of job choice, the optimal job risk will decrease with a worker's wealth. This hypothesis can be tested by estimating a risk equation which includes the wealth variable or some proxy for wealth. Therefore, the task here is to estimate equations (6) and (7). The left side variables are risk measures, p and q, and right side variables are: X = age, age square, education dummies, backward community dummy, union dummy and dummy for private job. V represents risk aversion variables, namely, a dummy indicator for working spouse (which serves as a measure of stability in the risk equations) and Y a wealth variable (= a dummy indicator for owning a house)[5]. Table 17.6 shows the regression results of job related fatal risk and injury risk equations.

Contrary to expectations, human capital variables have positive effects on both the risk measures. However, their effects are not statistically significant at the five per cent level, except HSC in the injury risk equation. The effect of the backward community variable is also slight in both cases. The effect of unions on the job risks is puzzling. It is expected that the impact of unions on risks would be negative as unions provide a forum for workers to

---

[5] Finding proxies for the degree of risk aversion is a difficult task as there is no direct measure of this available. Following Garen (1988) we use a working spouse dummy.

raise their voices for better working conditions. But Viscusi (1980) argues that if unions negotiate only wages, there is an incentive for firms to allow working conditions to deteriorate. He finds a positive association between union status and job risks. In contrast, studies such as Garen (1988) found a negative association. In this case, the union impact is negative (but not significant at the five per cent level) in the fatal risk equation and positive (and significant) in the injury risk equation, indicating that unions play a role in reducing fatal risk but are less worried about the injury risk at worksite.

The coefficient of PRIVE variable is negative and significant in the fatal risk equation, indicating that the fatal risk is relatively less in private sector factories. In the injury equation this variable is not statistically significant. The impact of the working spouse is positive in both equations but significant only in the fatal risk equations, contrary to the proxy for risk aversion. Perhaps, rather than revealing an income effect for the husband, this variable may reflect unusually low family wealth or unusually higher expenses. As expected, the impact of home dummy is negative and significant at the one per cent level in both cases. This result provides strong evidence in favour of the hypothesis that the demand for safety rises with income. The estimated results of these job risk equations are utilized to estimate the selectivity bias of the corrected wage equations below.

(v) *Removal of Self Selection Bias*: As argued above, the self-selection by workers results in biased estimates of the wage premium for job risks. Therefore, the modified self-selection bias technique is used. Using results in Table 17.6, the predicted residuals of η (error-1) and μ (error-2) are constructed and they are allowed to interact with the fatal and injury risk variables to estimate the equation (8). As the model is heteroskedastic, the WLS method is employed. Initially the squared residual [from the OLS estimation of wage equation (8)] is regressed on both risk measures and their quadratic and interaction terms and then the predicted values from this regression are used as weights. The exclusion of homeownership and working spouse variables which are included in the risk equations from the wage equation satisfies the identification conditions.

Column 4 of Table 17.5 reports the WLS estimation results of the wage equation[6]. The estimated coefficient of the fatal risk is 3.88 times larger than

---

[6] The coefficient of $\eta.p$ depends on the correlation of ϕ_1 and η, holding μ constant and that of $\mu.p$ depends on the correlation of ϕ_1 and μ, keeping η constant (see Garen, 1988). In column (8) of Table (17.5), the first term is positive while the second is negative. They are also statistically significant at the five percent level. Notice that the negative effect of $\mu.p$ outweighs the positive effect of $\eta.p$. The net negative effect implies that workers who

what OLS indicates (in Column 1). Garen (1988) also finds that the risk coefficient in WLS is 6.59 times larger than the OLS estimates (in the case of US data) and concludes that the OLS estimation with the assumption of the exogenous risk results in a downward bias in the estimates of the risk premium. The increase in the fatal risk parameter using WLS is consistent with the argument that safety is a normal good. However, the effect of INJURY is negative but not significant at the five per cent level. Almost all the terms involving the risk residuals-error-1, error-2, error-1 x p, error-2 x p and error-1 x injury (except error-2 x injury)–are significant, indicating that unobserved factors (ϕ_1 and ϕ_2) have significant effects on returns to job risks.

Using results in Column (4) and $\eta=\mu=0$ for the average sample worker, the implicit value of life is estimated as INR 67.73 million (3.748 million US $1990). The implicit value of injury is negative. However, these computations vary among workers because η and μ differ for each individual. Workers with very risky jobs tend to have larger η's and μ's and have a higher fatal risk premium and a lower non-fatal risk premium. This is because a dominant substitution effect induces workers with a high return to non fatal risk (ϕ_2) to choose safer jobs and those with a high return to fatal risk (high ϕ_1) to obtain a riskier job, generating the above pattern of compensating differentials.

(vi) *Inclusion of Other Non-pecuniary Job Attributes*: Some other non-pecuniary job attributes could now be added – whether the job provides good security, or whether it has irregular work hours or a pleasant worksite or whether it requires the worker to do the decision-making or to supervise co-workers. The inclusion of these factors will control for a variety of job attributes, and reduce the bias in the estimated coefficient of the job risk variables. The OLS estimation results of wage equation with these additional variables are shown in Column 5 of Table 17.5. The results indicate that earnings are higher if the worker is a supervisor or decision maker or if the job has full security. It is noted that the inclusion of these variables has slightly raised the fatal risk coefficient and reduced the injury risk coefficient (shown in Column 1 of Table 17.5).

---

experience unexpectedly low job risk have an unexpectedly high ϕ_2. Apparently, workers with a larger unobserved return to non-fatal risk choose safer jobs. This suggests that the substitution effect of a higher ϕ_2 towards a risky job dominates the income effect. The positive coefficients of both $\mu.q$ and $\eta.q$ have the reverse interpretation. Workers with an unusually high job risk (larger η and μ) have an unusually high ϕ_1. Therefore, the substitution effect of a larger ϕ_1 towards a risky job dominates the income effect. Also, a large negative coefficient of η implies a negative association of unexpected earnings level (ε) and unexpected job risk. This implies that workers with greater earning capacity or with unexpectedly high returns to fatal risk select safer jobs.

(vii) *Insurance Benefit Effect*: Using the average daily wage rate of the workers (w_i) in the sample and the standard benefit rates given in Table 17.1, the daily benefit rate for each worker (b_i) is computed. Then, the compensation (insurance) replacement rate R_i is calculated as $-R_i = w_i / b_i$. Since this variable is derived from wage rates, the endogeneity issue arises. To overcome that issue, this is first regressed on a worker's personal and job attributes and the estimated value of R_i namely CRR_i is used as a measure of a worker's ex-post compensation component. As benefits affect wages only at the positive risk level, this variable is allowed to interact with injury variable q.

The estimated results are shown in Column 6 of Table 17.5. The injury coefficient is 0.0039 in Column 5 and the corresponding value of statistical injury is INR 4134. As expected, in Column 6, the CRR x q term is negative and statistically significant at five per cent. Due to the inclusion of the CRR variable, the magnitude of the injury parameter changes to 0.0139. Due to the interaction form, the net effect of injury on the log wage is 0.0031 and the value of injury is computed at INR 3286 which is less than the value of the injury estimated in Column 5. It is understood that the failure to control for ex-post compensation has biased the estimates of the value of injury.

(viii) *Rate of Time Preference and the Value of Life*: In order to estimate the quantity adjusted life values and the implicit discount rate that workers use in making their life-cycle employment, the wage equation of the following form is used:

$$\text{Ln } w_i = \alpha + \alpha \, ELYL_i + \gamma \, INJURY_i + \Sigma_k \gamma_k X_{ik} + u_i \tag{10}$$

Information on the worker's age, sex and the remaining life data from the life expectancy tables are used to calculate the remaining life of sample workers (T) which is used to define the discounted life years lost variable ($(1-e_{-rT})/r$). Weighting this variable by the probability of fatal risk (p) yields the discounted expected life years lost variable (ELYL). Since this particular risk variable ELYL is a non-linear function of the discount rate parameter, it is essential to estimate the model using non-linear regression techniques. The discount rate, r, is computed in the estimation process.

Table 17.7 displays the non-linear least square results of wage equation (10). Signs and magnitudes of the coefficients of almost all control variables are largely as expected. Educational dummies are positive and statistically significant at the five per cent level. Wages increase with job tenure (this variable replaces age as age is used to calculate ELYL). The union differential is approximately 23 per cent. Backward community workers and supervisors tend to earn more. Workers in jobs providing good security receive somewhat more, which is unexpected. However, the higher wage of employees with job security is quite consistent with the greater security associated with upper blue-collar positions. Thus, this variable may be capturing the relative ranking of the worker's job rather than any particular job attribute that is not appropriately compensated. Workers who make on the job decisions also receive more. The indicators for pleasant worksite, private job, and irregular work hours have not been included as they are not statistically significant.

Table 17.7. Non linear estimates of Log wage equation

Variables	Coefficient	t value
ELYL	0.0022	2.882
R (discount rate)	0.0763	2.010
INJURY	0.0002	0.147
TENURE	0.0038	17.161
HIGH	0.3278	9.146
HSC	0.3755	10.775
COLLEGE	0.5889	9.883
BC	0.2450	8.753
UNION	0.2231	7.012
SUPER	0.0903	2.078
DECISION	0.1707	4.483
SECURITY	0.1994	6.497
R-squared	0.4153	

Source: Estimated as explained in the text

The results which are of primary interest are the estimated effects of the injury risk variable and ELYL variable and the estimate of real discount rate-r. As expected, the effect of injury risk is positive but not significant at the five per cent level[7]. The estimated r is 0.0763 (i.e., 7.63 per cent) and is statistically significant at the five per cent level. Therefore, both extreme alternative hypotheses that workers exhibit a zero discount rate or an infinite rate (i.e., workers are myopic) when making their occupational choices could be rejected. The bank interest rate on fixed deposits by private people was 12 per cent in 1990. However, the interest rate India has

---

[7] This result is not surprising because many studies that attempt to estimate jointly the effects of fatal and non-fatal injury risks on workers' wages do not find the effect of risk on wages to be significant for at least one of the risk measures (Viscusi and Aldy, 2003).

to pay on the external loans (i.e., the average interest rate on debt to Private Creditors such as the World bank) was only eight per cent in the same year. Thus, the estimated rate is closer to the interest on the external debt. These private values suggest that the appropriate social rate of discount for policies that affect health status over time is the market rate on debt.

The ELYL is positive and significant at the five per cent level. The implicit value per additional expected year of life is INR 1.04 (US $0.058) million. Using the discounted number of life years as the denominator in the calculation yields the average value of a year of life of INR 2.332 (US $0.129) million. These values represent the average WTP for an additional year of life in present value terms. However, the marginal value of a life year is more important for policy purposes.

Since the value of life extension also depends on r, additional life years increase in value for a decline in r. The worker in the sample with 25 years of life remaining (T) who values an extra year approximately at INR 0.35 (US $0.019) million when r is 7.6 per cent will value his marginal year of life at over INR 0.67 (US $0.037) million if r is five per cent. An older worker with five years of life remaining will value an extra year approximately at INR 1.6 (US $0.09) million if r = 7.6 per cent and INR 1.8 (US $0.1) million if r = 5 per cent.

17.6. Concluding remarks

In this chapter, an attempt has been made to value job-related environmental health risks using the hedonic wage approach, taking into account various issues including the wealth effect, self-selection, insurance benefits, life-cycle issues and the rate of discount for health benefits. The empirical estimates of this chapter strongly support the hypotheses that (a) workers demand higher wages for facing job-related fatal and injury risks; (b) higher insurance benefits decrease the wage compensation; and (c) workers are not myopic when making their occupational choices.

The statistical value of life and injury are estimated to be INR 10.28 million and INR 4876 respectively. In order to compare the numbers in this study with those obtained in other studies, a conversion rate provided by the Reserve Bank of India of INR 18.07 = US $1 in 1990 is used, leading to a VSL and VSI of US $0.569 million and US $270. After removing endogeneity and heterogeneity bias, the value of life increases to INR 67.73 million (= US $3.748 million). The estimated values can be compared with those from other countries. Table 17.8 summarizes past (selected) studies on value of life and injury. The estimated life values vary dramatically among these studies. Dillingham (1985) argues that values vary either due to specification errors or errors in variable problems. Viscusi (1993) and Viscusi and Aldy (2003) listed almost all the major studies and found that the range of values per statistical life (in 1990 dollar) was US $0.6 million to US $16.2 million in the United States, Britain, Canada, Australia, and Japan.

Table 17.8. Summary of labour market studies on the value of life and injury

Study (year)	Sample	Source of Risk Variable	Value of Life (US $million)	Value of Injury
Cousineau et al. (1992)	Labor Canada Survey, Canada, 1979	Quebec Compensation Board	3.6	Not reported
Garen (1988)	Panel Study of Income Dynamics (PSID), USA, 1981–82	Bureau of labor Statistics (BLS)	13.5	21021
Herzog and Schlottman (1990)	U. S. Census, 1970	BLS	9.1	–
Kniesner and Leeth (1991)	2 digit manufacture Data, Japan, 1984; 2 digit manufacture data, Australia, 1984; and Current Population Survey, USA, 1978.	Year book of Labor statistics; Industrial Accident Data; and National Traumatic Occupation Fatality Survey (NTOS)	7.6 3.3 0.6	77547 8943 47281
Leigh and Folsom (1984)	PSID, 1974 and Quality of Employment Survey, USA, 1977	BLS	9.7 and 10.3	
Liu et al. (1997)	Taiwan Labor Force Survey , 1982 to 1986	Labor Insurance Agency, Taiwan	0.135 and 0.589 (5 years mean is 0.413)	
Marin and Psacharopoulos (1982)	Population Census and Surveys, U.K., 1977	Occupational Mortality Tables	2.8	–
Moore and Viscusi (1988)	PSID, USA, 1982	BLS and NTOS	2.5 and 7.3	–

(Contd.)

(*Contd.*)

Study (year)	Sample	Source of Risk Variable	Value of Life (US $million)	Value of Injury
Thaler and Rosen (1976)	Survey of Economic Opportunity, USA	Society of Actuaries	0.8	-
Viscusi (1981)	PSID, USA, 1976	BLS	6.5	46200

[Values of life and injury are in 1990 US dollars; all these values, except Liu et al. (1997), are taken from Viscusi (1993)].

Table 17.9. Summary of (selected) studies estimating implicit discount rates

Study/Year	Category	Good (s)	Real/ Hypothetical	Elicitation Method	Annual Discount rate
Chapman (1996)	Experimental	Money & Health	Hypothetical	Matching	Negative to 300 %
Dreyfus and Viscusi (1995)	Field	Life years	Real	Choice	11–17 %
Ganiats et al (2000)	Experimental	Health	Hypothetical	Choice	Negative to 116 %
Johannesson and Johansson (1997)	Experimental	Life years	Hypothetical	Pricing	0–3 %
Loewenstein (1987)	Experimental	Money and pain	Hypothetical	Pricing	−6 to 212 %
Moore and Viscusi (1988)	Field	Life years	Real	Choice	10–12 %
Moore and Viscusi (1990)	Field	Life years	Real	Choice	2 %
Van Der Pol and Cairns (1999)	Experimental	Health	Hypothetical	Choice	7 %
Van Der Pol et al. (2001)	Experimental	Health	Hypothetical	Choice	6–9 %
Viscusi and Moore (1989)	Field	Life years	Real	Choice	11 %

Source: Frederick et al. (2002)

The estimates from this study, ranging from INR 10.28 million to INR 67.73 million (US $0.569–3.748 million), are lower than values from developed nations. The only study from another developing country that compares with the estimates of this study is Liu et al. (1997). They estimated the value (without accounting for the unobserved heterogeneity of workers) for Taiwan as ranging from US $0.135 million to US $0.589 million in 1990 dollars. Viewed in this light, the estimates of this study seem reasonable.

Finally, the estimated discount rate from this study can be compared with those from past (selected) studies that consider health or life years (Table 17.9). The discount rates implied in many experimental studies (using hypothetical choices) vastly exceed market interest rates and differ substantially across studies – negative to 300 per cent (Chapman, 1996; Ganiats et al., 2000; Loewenstein, 1987). However, the rates provided in studies such as Johannesson and Johansson (1997) and Van der Pol and Cairns (1999) are closer to the market rate. Interestingly, the rates provided in studies that consider life years are broadly consistent with the real market interest rate. Thus, the rate estimated in this study, 7.6 per cent, seems reasonable as it falls in the range (1–17 per cent) estimated in existing field studies. Thus, there is no empirical support for utilizing a separate rate of discount for the health benefits of environment policies in developing countries.

One is hopeful that these estimates can aid policy makers, international agencies and researchers in evaluating health projects in India and other developing countries. They can also be used to carry out comparisons with values obtained for developed countries.

References

Alberini, A., Cropper, M., Fu Tsu-Tan, Krupnick, A., Liu, J.T., Shaw, D. and Harrington, W., 'Valuing Health Effects of Air Pollution in Developing Countries: the Case of Taiwan', *Journal of Environmental Economics and Management*, 34, (1997), 107–126.

Arnold, R.J. and Nichols, L.M., 'Wage Risk Premium and Workers Compensation: A Refinement of Estimates of Compensating Wage Differential', *Journal of Political Economy*, 91(2), (1983), 332–340.

Butler, R.J., 'Wage and Injury Rate Responses to Shifting Levels of Workers' Compensation', in *Safety and the Workforce: Incentives and Disincentives in Workers' Compensation* (ed. J.D. Worrall), ILR Press, Ithaca, (1993), 61–86.

Chapman, Gretchen B., 'Temporal Discounting and Utility for Health and Money', *Journal of Experimental Psychology: Learning, Memory and Cognition*, 22, (1996), 771–791.

Cousineau, Jean-Michel, Lacroix, R. and Girard, A.M., 'Occupational Hazard and Wage Compensating Differentials', *Review of Economics and Statistics*, 1992, 166–169.

Dillingham, A.E., 'The Influence of Risk Variable Definition on Value of Life Estimates', *Economic Inquiry*, 24, (1985), 277–294.

Dreyfus, Mark and Viscusi, W. Kip. 'Rate of Time Preference and Consumer Valuations of Automobile Safety and Fuel Efficiency', *Journal of Law Economics*, 38, (1995), 79–103.

Frederick, Shane, Loewenstein, George and O'Donoghue, 'Time Discounting and Time Preference: A Critical Review', *Journal of Economic Literature*, 2002, 351–401.

Ganiats, Theodore, Richard, G., Carson, T., Hamm, Robert M., Cantor, Scott B., Sumner, Walton, Spann, Stephen J., Hagen, Michael and Miller, Christopher, 'Health Status and Preferences: Population-based Time Preferences for Future Health Outcome', *Medical Decision Making: An International Journal*, 20, (2000), 263–270.

Garen, John E., 'Compensating Wage Differentials and Endogeneity of Job Riskiness', *The Review of Economics and Statistics*, 70(1), (1988), 9–16.

Gately, D., 'Individual Discount Rates and the Purchase and Utilization of Energy-using Durables: Comment', *Bell Journal of Economics*, 11, (1980), 373–374.

Gerking, Shelby, Haan M. De and Schulze, William, 'The Marginal Value of Job Safety: a Contingent Valuation Study', *Journal of Risk and Uncertainty*, I(2), (1988), 185–199.

Hausman, Jerry, 'Individual Discount Rates and the Purchase and Utilization of Energy-using Durables', *Bell Journal of Economics*, 10 (1), (1979), 33–54.

Herzog, Henry, W. and Schlottmann, Alan, M., 'Valuing Risk in the Workplace: Market Price, Willingness to Pay and the Optimal Provision of Safety', *The Review of Economics and Statistics*, 72(3), (1990), 463–470.

Johannesson, M. and Johansson, P., Olov, 'Quality of Life and WTP for an Increased Life Expectancy at an Advanced Age', *Journal of Public Economics*, 65, (1997), 219–228.

Kniesner, Thomas J. and Leeth, John, D., 'Compensating Wage Differentials for Fatal Injury Risks in Australia, Japan and United States', *Journal of Risk and Uncertainty*, 4(1), (1991), 75–90.

Leigh, Paul J., 'Compensating Wage for Job related Death: The Opposing Arguments', *Journal of Economic Issues*, 23, (1989), 823–842.

Leigh, Paul, J. and Folsom Roger, N., 'Estimates of Value of Accident Avoidnace at the Job Dependent on the Concavity of the Equalizing Difference Curve', *Quarterly Review of Economics and Business*, 24(1), (1984), 56–66.

Linnerooth, J., 'The Value of Human Life: a Review of Models', *Economic Inquiry*, 17 (1979), 52–74.

Liu, J.T., Hammitt, J.K. and Liu., L.L., 'Estimated Hedonic Wage Function and Value of Life in a Developing Country', *Economics Letters*, 57, (1997), 353–358.

Lowenstein, G., 'Anticipation and the Valuation of Delayed Consumption', *Economic Journal*, 97, (1987), 666–684.

Madheswaran, S., 'Measuring the Value of Statistical Life: Estimating Compensating Wage Differentials among Workers in India', *Social Indicators Research*, Vol. 84, (2007), 83–96.

Marin, Alan and Psacharopoulos, G., 'The Reward for Risk in the Labor Market: Evidence from the United Kingdom and a Reconciliation with Other Studies', *Journal of Political Economy*, 90(4), (1982), 827–853.

Moore, Michael J. and Viscusi, W. Kip, 'The Quantity-Adjusted Value of Life', *Economic Inquiry*, 26, (1988), 369–388.

Moore, Michael J. and Viscusi W. Kip, 'Discounting Environmental Health Risks: New Evidence and Policy Implications', *Journal of Environmental Economics and Management*, 18, (1990), 381–401.

Sandy, R. and Elliott, R.F., 'Union and Risk: Their Impact on the Level of Compensation for Fatal Risk', *Economica*, 63, (1996), 291–309.

Shanmugam, K.R., 'An Econometric Study on the Compensating Differentials for Job Risks', an Unpublished PhD Thesis, University of Madras, 1993.

Shanmugam, K.R., 'The Value of Life: Estimates from Indian Labor Market', *Indian Economic Journal*, 44(4), (1996/7), 105–114.

Shanmugam, K.R., 'Insurance Benefits, Wage Premiums and the Value of Injury Risks', *Manpower Journal*, 35(1), (1999), 1–11.

Shanmugam, K.R., 'Valuations of Life and Injury Risks: Empirical Evidence from India', *Environmental and Resource Economics*, 16, (2000), 379–389.

Shanmugam, K.R., 'Self Selection Bias in the Estimates of Compensating Differentials for Job Risks in India', *Journal of Risk and Uncertainty*, 22, (2001), 263–275.

Shanmugam, K.R., 'Rate of Time Preference and the Quantity Adjusted Value of Life in India', *Environment and Development Economics*, 11, (2006), 569–583.

Smith, A., 'The Wealth of Nations', (Reprint Ed.), (New York: Modern Library, 1776).

Thaler, R. and Rosen, S., 'The Value of Saving a Life: Evidence from the Market', in Nestor E. Terlecky (eds.), *Household Production and Consumption*, NBER, 1976, 265–298.

Van der Pol, Marjon, M. and Cairns, J.A., 'Individual Time Preferences for Own Health: Application of a Dichotomous Choice Question with Follow Up', *Applied Economics Letters*, 6, (1999), 649–654.

Van der Pol, Marjon, M. and Cairns, J.A., 'Estimating Time Preferences for Health Using Discrete Choice Experiments', *Social Science Medicine*, 52, (2001), 1459–1470.

Viscusi, W. Kip., 'Wealth Effects and Earnings Premiums for Job Hazards', *Review of Economics and Statistics*, 60, (1978), 408–418.

Viscusi, W. Kip., *Employment Hazards: An Investigation of Market Performance*, (Cambridge: Harvard University Press, 1979).

Viscusi, W. Kip., 'Union, Labor Market Structure and the Welfare Implications of the Quality of Work', *Journal of Labor Research*, (1980), 175–192.

Viscusi, W. Kip., 'Occupational Safety and Health Regulation: Its Impact on Policy Alternatives', in *Research in Public Policy Analysis and Management*, ed. J.Crecine (ed.), (Greenwich Conn: JAI Press, 1981) 281–299.

Viscusi, W. Kip., 'The Valuation of Risks to Life and Health: Guidelines for Policy Analysis' in (ed. J.D. Bentkover, Vincent Covello and J. Mumpower), *Benefit Assessment: The State of the Art*, (Dordrecht: Reidel, 1986) 193–210.

Viscusi, W. Kip., 'The Value of Risks to Life and Health', *Journal of Economic Literature*, 31(4), (1993), 1912–1946.

Viscusi, W. Kip., 'Value of Life', *The New Palgrave Dictionary of Economics*, Steven N. Durlauf and Lawrence E. Blume (ed.), (The New Palgrave Dictionary of Economics Online, Palgrave Macmillan, 2008).

Viscusi, W. Kip and E. Aldy Joshep, 'The Value of a Statistical Life: A Critical Review of Market Estimates Throughout the World', *The Journal of Risk and Uncertainty*, 27, (2003), 5–76.

Viscusi, W. Kip and Gayer, T., 'Quantifying and Valuing Environmental Health Risks' in *Handbook of Environmental Economics*, Vol. 2, K.G. Maler and J.R. Vincent (ed.), Elsevier Science B.V., (2005) 1029–1103.

Viscusi, W. Kip and Moore, M.J., 'Workers' Compensation: Wage Effects, Benefit Inadequacies, and the Value of Health Losses', *The Review of Economics and Statistics*, 69, (1987), 249–261.

Viscusi, W. Kip and Moore, M.J., 'Rate of Time Preference and Valuations of the Duration of Life', *The Journal of Public Economics*, 38, (1989), 297–317.

18

An Assessment of Demand for Improved Household Water Supply in Southwest Sri Lanka

Herath Gunatilake, Jui-Chen Yang, Subhrendu Pattanayak,
and *Caroline van den Berg*[1]

18.1. Introduction

The Asia-Pacific region accounts for about 57 per cent (635 million) of the global population without safe drinking water and 72 per cent (1.88 billion) of the global population without proper sanitation (UNDP, 2006). Even among the urban households which have access to Water Supply and Sanitation (WSS) many receive low-quality services. The global agenda for poverty reduction stated in the Millennium Development Goals (MDGs) aims to halve the number of people without proper water supply and sanitation by 2015 (United Nations, 2005, ADB, 2005). Large amount of investment on WSS projects is required to achieve this goal. Mobilizing public and private sector financial resources and designing and implementing WSS projects are important tasks trusted upon the developing country governments and their development partners to achieve water related MDGs.

Willingness To Pay (WTP) data on improved water supply and sanitation services constitute the basis for assessing effective demand and benefits of WSS services projects. The WTP concept generally refers to the economic value of a good to a person (or a household), under given conditions. Net economic benefits of improved water services, in simple terms, are estimated as the difference between the consumers' maximum WTP for

[1] This study was funded by the Water and Sanitation Programme for South Asia and the World Bank-Netherlands Water Partnership, respectively. The opinions reflected in this chapter do not represent the views or policies of the Asian Development Bank, RTI International, or the World Bank – Netherland Partnership for Water and Sanitation.

better services and the actual cost of the services. In addition to providing crucial information for assessing economic viability of projects, WTP data are useful for setting affordable tariffs, evaluation of policy alternatives, assessing financial sustainability, as well as designing socially equitable subsidies (Brookshire and Whittington 1993, Whittington 2002, Carson 2003, Gunatilake et al. 2006, van den Berg et al. 2006).

Economists generally prefer to use observed or revealed behaviour in markets in estimating the economic values of goods and services rather than directly questioning respondents. This is because direct questioning may result in many errors (Gunatilake 2003, Boardman et al. 1996, Hausman and Diamand 1994, and Hanemann 1994). However, when direct revealed preference information (information on market demand) or indirect revealed preference information (information on surrogate markets) are not available, project economists are left with two choices – either to confine to cost effectiveness analysis or estimate benefits using the Contingent Valuation (CV) method.

Water supply and sanitation services are not generally traded in the markets. Thus, only limited information on market demand or competitive market prices[2] is available to value benefits. In situations where a considerable amount of time is spent in collecting water, time savings can be used to approximate the benefits of water supply projects. However, this is applicable only to certain situations. Benefits from WSS projects may also be reflected in land values of the project area. But the prevalence of distorted land markets in many developing countries and the lack of reliable data to value land can prevent the use of surrogate market methods such as the hedonic pricing method. WSS projects often constitute improvements to existing systems, for which information on market demand is generally not available. Thus, the use of the CV method is inevitable in the economic analysis of WSS projects.

This chapter presents selected results of a CV study undertaken in 2003, which was intended to facilitate the design of a Public–Private Partnership (PPP) to provide WSS services in southwest Sri Lanka. The study was undertaken in two areas – the Greater Negambo area and coastal strip from Kalutara to Galle. The study was part of a larger effort by international development organizations funding WSS services in Sri Lanka.

---

[2] Information on market for bottled drinking water and other forms of traded water is sometimes available. However, information on such markets in developing countries are often incomplete. Moreover, bottled water or other forms of traded water do not represent all its domestic uses such as cooking, cleaning, and bathing.

The chapter is organized as follows. Section 18.2 briefly discusses the appropriateness of the CV method to estimate WTP in the WSS sector given that the possibility of this method generating unreliable results under certain circumstances. Section 18.3 discusses the study design issues focusing on the measures taken to reduce potential biases. Section 18.4 presents the findings of the paper and section 18.5 provides concluding comments.

18.2. Use of the CV method to measure WTP

The Contingent Valuation Method (CV method) is a survey-based elicitation technique to estimate WTP values of a good which is not traded in the conventional market. The CV method is often referred to as a stated preference method, in contrast to revealed preference methods, which use actual revealed behaviour of consumers in the market. The CV method directly asks consumers' WTP for a non-marketed good under a given condition or a prescribed circumstance. To elicit consumers' WTP values for non-marketed goods, a hypothetical market scenario is formulated and described to the survey respondents. Thus, the elicited WTP values of a good are 'contingent upon' the hypothetical market prescribed in the survey instrument.

Despite its wide use for practical policy purposes, the CV method's ability to reliably estimate WTP is not universally accepted. While some economists have expressed skepticism on the use of direct questioning[3] to estimate WTP, one of the early verdicts on the soundness of the CV methodology came from a group of world renowned economists–Kenneth Arrow, Robert Solow, Roy Radner, Edward Leamer and Howard Schumann. Their Blue-Ribbon NOAA[4] Panel report, states:

> "CV studies convey useful information. We think it is fair to describe such information as reliable by standards that seem to be implicit in similar contexts, like market analysis for new and innovative products and the assessments of other damages normally allowed in court proceedings." (Arrow et al. 1993, p. 4610)

The CV methodology has improved significantly during the last 50 years. One of the pioneers in the field of CV method, V. Kerry Smith (2006),

---

[3] Many cast doubt about the direct questioning method (stated preferences) vis a vis the use of more reliable revealed preferences data, i.e., actual market data. The authors endorse this view and encourage the use of revealed preference data whenever possible.

[4] NOAA stands for National Oceanic and Atmospheric Administration.

argues that CV research has witnessed robust progress, enabling the researchers to better understand consumer preferences. More specifically, the progress on econometric analyses, survey research methods, sampling and experimental design, and policy applications in the last 50 years has been remarkable. In Smith's assessment, concerns relating to measurement bias in estimating non-use values can be excessive.[5] In the case of WSS, however, similar measurement bias is of a lesser concern since direct use values are estimated. As Smith further elaborates, hypothetical bias can also be large because of the nature of CV surveys. Careful development of survey instruments (through initial preparatory work, focus groups, cognitive interviews, and pre-tests), conscientious implementation of field work, and rigorous econometric analysis that link the data to underlying theoretical models (e.g., utility functions) can help reduce hypotheticality in a CV study.

Another important reason behind the expressed reservations about the CV method is the potential divergence between responses[6] and actual behaviour. The emerging evidence shows that predictions from 'hypothetical' CV scenarios seem to compare well with actual behaviour (Cameron et al. 2002, Vossler and Kerkvliet 2003). Griffin et al. (1995) show similar predictable behaviour in the case of WSS improvements. Moreover, Choe et al. (1996) show that WTP values from a CV method is as robust as those from a revealed preference models such as travel cost method. Finally, Smith (2006) contends that the CV methods 'will remain a significant part of efforts to assess consumer preferences for non-market (and new[7]) goods'. Adamowicz (2004), Whitehead (2006), and Whitehead and Blomquist (2006) essentially endorse this view and maintain that CV studies remain a key tool in generating data on new (non-market) goods and services for policy analysis.

The above excerpts do not mean to assert that doubts on the CV methodology amongst some economists have completely disappeared. Despite significant improvements in methodology, debate on the ability of

---

[5] Smith (2006) contends that some of the confusion and apprehension on the CV method arises from the misplaced attention on the use of CV method for natural resources damage litigation.

[6] CV questions ask about future actions of the respondents for hypothetical scenarios.

[7] 'New' in the case of WSS refers to different service quality attributes such as number of hours of service, water quality, customer service, and perhaps the service provider (private and public provision, for example). These attributes which make the service a new commodity are easy to comprehend by a CV respondent; therefore the potentially excessive hypothetical biases may not necessarily occur in WSS sector CV studies.

the CV method to meaningfully measure WTP continues. The authors' view on this matter relates to two characteristics of water supply and sanitation services. The first is the often experienced data deficiencies that prevent meaningful application of revealed preference methods to estimate the demand for WSS services. The second is the familiarity of the respondents on the WSS services which makes it easy to respond to CV questions on WSS services. In comparison to some environmental goods/service such as biodiversity or climate change impacts, WSS is a tangible commodity for the households, so they can understand any proposed improvements and respond to the CV questions reasonably. The first reason leaves no option other than using CV method while the second provides confidence to use the CV method in assessing demand for WSS. However the authors emphasize that it is imperative to use the CV method meticulously, applying the improved methodology to ensure generation of reliable estimates of WTP.

18.3. Planning, design and administering the survey

This section provides details as to how this study was designed and conducted. Over the last two to three decades, the CV method has been used increasingly in developing countries to assess demand for improvements in WSS services. However, applying the CV method in developing countries requires careful adaptation of the method to account for local conditions and cultural differences (Whittington 1998 and 2002b). This study benefited a lot from the above cited studies and consciously used the Whittington (1998 and 2002b) suggestions to improve CV studies in developing countries together with authors own experience in conducting CV studies. In particular Whittington (2002b) identifies three major problematic aspects that need to be addressed to improve CV studies in developing countries – (a) poorly crafted CV scenarios (poor study design); (b) poor survey implementation; and (c) failure to undertake a variety of tests to examine the validity of responses to different CV scenarios. The following section describes how the present study carefully managed the design implementation issues. The validity of the responses is discussed later on.

18.3.1. Initial preparatory work

In conducting a CV study, number of initial steps need to be undertaken to organize the CV study. Among these tasks, reviewing the literature, forming a study team, initial scoping visit to the study area and preparation of the preliminary sampling frame are important. These activities generally help in characterizing the existing WSS situation and to develop credible CV scenarios. In this study, the prior characterization of the existing WSS services in the study area was accomplished based on review of exiting literature, field observations, unstructured open ended interviews, participatory community meetings, and small focus groups. In characterizing the existing WSS situation, attention was given to physical characteristics, economic factors, environmental and health factors and institutional aspects. These activities helped the study team to properly define the commodity in the contingent market.

Description of the commodity or scenario development primarily involves – (a) defining precisely the type of WSS services offered; (b) clarifying how it differs substantively (e.g., quantity and quality) from current options; and (c) explaining the institutional setting for providing the service. Identifying and defining the appropriate commodity requires a careful review and thorough understanding of existing levels of service and alternatives. These aspects were carefully studied using the findings of the above mentioned initial preparatory activities. The preliminary evidence suggested that a certain per centage of the population was connected to the piped water network. Therefore the commodity in question could be 'an improvement in existing services' for this subsample, in contrast to 'a new service connection' for unconnected households. These two subgroups needed different CV market versions as well as elicitation questions, because unconnected households need to pay a connection charge in addition to the water consumption bills.

18.3.2. Study design issues

The CV method directly questions individuals as to how much they are willing to pay for a change in quantity or quality (or both) of a particular commodity. A CV analyst has to resolve a number of issues in designing a CV study such as selecting a survey method, payment vehicle, elicitation question type, design of appropriate bid distribution and sampling method. This section describes these design aspects of the study. Different types of survey methods can be used in a CV study. Given various practical difficulties, face-to-face interviews are preferred in developing countries compared to other methods such as telephone interviews and postal surveys. Telephone interviews are not feasible given that many household do not have access to telephones whereas personal interview can be conducted in developing countries without prior appointments. The number of households refusing to participate in face to face interviews is generally low in developing countries. Therefore, the in person interview method was used in this study.

Selection of the CV elicitation question is a somewhat difficult task. A host of different elicitation questions such as open-ended questions, iterative bidding questions, contingent ranking questions, dichotomous choice questions, and payment card method are available to the analyst. Choosing among these question types is difficult as neither economic theory nor empirical evidence provides clear guidelines in selecting elicitation questions. Researchers[8] frequently recommend the dichotomous choice method (Portney, 1994) and its application in WSS projects has provided reliable results so far (Pattanayak et al., 2006). The present study used the closed ended elicitation method. Closed ended elicitation method are also known referendum methods, therefore these terms are used interchangeably. In this study, a single bounded closed ended CV question was used which offered a single monthly water bill after describing the service improvement and sought acceptance (yes) or rejection (no) for the improved service.

A credible method of payment is required to elicit WTP values for the commodity in question in CV studies. In the case of WSS this is not a major issue as monthly water bills and one time connection charges serve the purpose.

The closed ended elicitation method requires selecting a set of bids to be offered to the households as the monthly water bills and one time connection charges. In selection of the bids, a number of factors need to be considered. First, they should be realistically close to the actual costs and current bills[9]. If some prior knowledge is available on future tariff increases, these new rates should be within the range of bids. The ranges of the connection charge and monthly bill should be sufficiently wide to assess demand and to capture relevant policy alternatives. The number of bids

---

[8] For example, the US National Oceanic and Atmospheric Administration panel appointed to evaluate the appropriateness of CV methods to design compensations for environmental damages, which consists of four world-renowned economists (three of them were Nobel laureates), recommended the dichotomous choice method.

[9] Current water bills can serve as the lower bounds in the bid distribution. Actual cost of provision of improved services should be in the middle of the bid distribution and there should be higher bids that will be rejected by most respondents. Appropriateness of these bids however should be checked during the pre-tests as we did in this study.

included in the study is usually dictated by the study budget because more variations in the bids require larger sample sizes since each bid should be administered to a minimum number of households. Moreover, too many bids and too large a sample may also be logistically challenging during survey implementation. Based on the secondary information collected through initial preparatory tasks, it was initially decided that the range of bids would be LKR 100–1500 and these values were modified based on the focus group discussions and pre-tests.

The study area within Sri Lanka was Greater Negombo and a coastal strip from Kalutara to Galle. The Water Sector Reform Unit (WSRU) in the Ministry of Housing and Plantation Infrastructure, and National Water Supply and Drainage Board (NWSDB) defined the Private Sector Participation (PSP) areas in terms of a list of Grama Niladhari (GN)[10] divisions. The list of households in these GN divisions was the study population. This list was verified with Sri Lanka Department of Census and Statistics (DCS) data to rule out any typographic errors in GN labels. The PSP areas stretched across three districts – Gampaha, Kalutara, and Galle–covering 17 Divisional Secretariat (DS) divisions. The phase I study area was Greater Negombo in Gampaha district that has 2 DS divisions, Negombo and Katana, which include 114 GN divisions. The phase II site was the coastal strip from Kalutara to Galle that includes 15 DS divisions.

Having considered the available budget, different split sample tests, two service areas, the number of bids and other important features of the study, the sample size was decided to be 1800 households. In order to be able to extrapolate the survey findings to the total population of the two PSP service area, it was decided that 1000 and 800 households will be interviewed, respectively, from the two PSP areas – Greater Negombo and Kalutara to Galle coastal strip.

Stratified random sampling approach was used to select the sample. First the strata to be the GN division was determined so that one would have sufficient geographical coverage and spatial representation of the project area. Then, the number of households to be surveyed from each GN based on its population was calculated. To determine the number of households per GN division, the GN division population was divided by the total population in the PSP area multiplied by the sample size of the each study area. Finally the specified number of households were randomly picked from a pre-listing of households in every GN division. The random

---

[10] GN division is the smallest unit of administration in Sri Lanka. A number of GN divisions are administrated by DS divisions. A district include number of DS divisions.

selection of these households ensures that the sample is representative and allows one to generalize the findings to the total population of the two PSP service areas.

Household listings by GN was obtained from the DCS. The DCS maintains the Pre-Listing forms (also called F1 forms) for the 2001 Census of Population and Housing. Each F1 form represents a census block that consists of about 80 houses and/or other buildings in the urban area and 60 in the rural area. On average, each GN division has 10–12 census blocks depending on population density. Each F1 form has summary statistics on population and housing units, lists household heads' name and address, and contains a sketch map of the census blocks. The DCS arranged four personnel to help the study team select the census blocks/F1 forms, photocopy the pages selected, and assemble the photocopies by DS division. It took about four weeks to obtain all photocopies of the F1 forms that were selected. Once all the F1 photocopies were obtained, households from the forms for each GN were randomly selected and households' information was entered into an Excel file after translating the data from Sinhalese to English.

These selected households constituted the survey sample and were contacted by the enumerators by using their names and addresses. A geographical replacement rule was devised for situations in which it was impossible to interview the selected household after repeat attempts. Such situations could arise if the selected household had moved, the DCS had recorded the address incorrectly or the household refused to participate in the interview. The pre-selected household was replaced with one of the five neighbours using a counterclockwise rule. That is, interviewers would start with neighbour 1, then neighbour 2 and so on until one had tried to replace with all five neighbours. If none of these five replacements was available or willing to participate in the interview, interviewers went to the next pre-selected household from the DCS household listings in the same GN. The enumerator guideline document provided additional suggestions for using judgment to maintain the random sampling process. That is, enumerators were asked to replace households with 'similar socio-economic characteristics'.

18.3.3. Survey instrument

The next important task is the preparation of the survey instrument. In this section the following are discussed: how a preliminary survey instrument is developed, focus groups and pretests are conducted, how the survey instrument with input from technical and policy experts is finalized. A survey conducted in Nepal was used as a starting point (Pattanayak et al., 2001) in preparation of the instrument. This survey is based on a selected set of modules from an exhaustive list described in the World Bank's Guidelines for Living Standard Measurement Surveys. The initial preparatory work provided a comprehensive overview of the local conditions at the study sites, including – (a) description of primary water supply options, (b) existing and potential levels of water supply services, (c) financial data on current charges and costs, (d) role of sanitation and hygiene in prevention and control of water borne diseases, and (e) basic economic and social profile of the respondent population.

Based on the findings of the initial reviews and field work the questionnaire of the Nepal study was modified to suite the local conditions. The preliminary questionnaire comprised the following six modules – (a) Introductory Section and Environmental Priorities; (b) Water Sources - Quality and Quantity; (c) Water Treatment and Storage; (d) Sanitation and Sewerage; (e) Contingent Valuation Elicitation Questions; (f) Debriefing Questions and Socio-Economic Profile.

Focus groups are structured brainstorming exercises using individuals from the target population to learn about their opinions, perceptions, and reactions to the overall goals and specific contents of the survey. Individuals were recruited from the target population and individuals with and without a house connection and with varying economic and demographic background (e.g., age, gender, education, and socioeconomic status) were included. Unlike typical contingent valuation studies in developing countries that start with limited background information, this study benefited from several previous engineering and economic studies that had assessed the water supply conditions and/or local people's WTP for improved water supply in this study area. Consequently, the necessary adjustments to the questionnaire were made with only three focus group discussions.

In all three sessions, participants were asked to react to the descriptions and questions drawn from various parts of the survey instrument, particularly the contingent valuation section. The first focus group was conducted in Unawatuna Grama Niladhari (GN) division of Galle district, towards the southern tip of our study area with the participation of three households. The second focus group was conducted in Pilimatalawa GN in Kandy district that was attended by an office clerk, a school vice-principal, a student at University of Peradeniya, a retired businessman, and three housewives. A third focus group was conducted in Kalutara North GN of Kalutara district that was attended by two pre-school teachers, one retired army officer, an elderly person, a young man and a young woman. The three focus groups were supplemented with several purposive discussions with households and government officials. The final survey instrument reflects the insights from the focus groups. Here some of the main findings relevant to the elicitation questions and corresponding refinements made in the instrument are summarized:

> It was clear that wells were a primary and popular source of water supply in the coastal belt that served as a substitute for piped water. Non-traditional alternatives to water from house connections include small-diameter mini-grids and metered stand posts.

> Distance to the network is a key reason for not connecting and this distance was often correlated with distance to a permanent road.

> Respondents were willing to look ahead and earnestly consider the contingent commodity–improved water supply service. The credibility of the scenario could stem from the fact that many households seemed to have heard about plans to expand the water supply network in their area.

> Four features that were of particular concern to participants were–hours of service, health risk, regularity and predictability of billing, and efficient customer service. These features were included in defining the contingent commodity.

> Focus groups suggested that about 100 liters per person per day is adequate and useful. Water Board engineers confirmed that this was a reasonable assumption. Assuming an average family size of five, it was decided to offer 500 liters per day as part of the proposed water supply improvement.

> There were no strong reactions – in favor or against-the range of monthly bill amounts (from LKR 75–1,500 for a private connection) used in the focus groups. Similarly, the proposed connection cost of LKR 6,000–12,000 seems appropriate.

> Some participants drew attention to credit and finance needs, claiming that more people would connect if there were installment plans to cover the connection costs.

The discussion on the institutional context for improved water supply elicited suggested that there is likely to be an institutional effect in the measurement of WTP. Thus, the sample was split between the two major kinds of institutions - private and public sector.

Based on the above mentioned findings of the focus group discussions, the survey instrument was refined and the refined instrument was pre-tested on about 120 respondents drawn from the target population to identify any previously undetected problems. Pretests were conducted in three areas – Negombo, Peradeniya, and Kalutara. Pretests help the study team identify any problems with the content, length, and flow of the preliminary survey instrument. Equally importantly, pretests allowed to further train the enumerators. It also helps set up the logistics of implementation such as formation of groups, assignment of field supervisors, plans for travel etc. The interviews averaged 60 minutes with the most recent ones being considerably shorter (minimum was 40 minutes and the maximum was 180 minutes), mostly because once the enumerators are familiar with the instrument, could navigate through the various sections quickly. In general, a mix of households with and without connections were interviewed in the pretests. The data gathered through the pretests were used only for the refinement of the survey instruments. The following refinements were made based on the pretest results:

The most important contribution of the pretests was to set the range for the monthly bills for the contingent valuation part of the final instrument. Basically we had to find a low bill that was accepted (for connection) by all households who were confronted with that amount. This was determined to be LKR 100 per month for house connections. On the upper end the task was to find a monthly bill that is rejected by all who confront it. The high end pretest bill (LKR 1500) was found to be too high and the upper bound was determined to be LKR 1,000 per month. Based on the pretests, the bids were finalized to be 100, 200, 300, 400, 500, 600, 800, 1000[11]. The monthly water bill was used here as bids because the existing increasing block tariff system would have confused the respondents, if per liter rates were used instead.

---

[11] The eight bids were randomly allocated amongst the households. For example 225 households received the 100 as their water bill in the survey and another 225 households receives 1000 as the bids. When the connection charges were given as additional bids, suitable combinations were applied to prevent lowest monthly bills were associated with lowest or highest connection charges.

The pretest revealed that the description of the CV scenario was too dense and detailed. So (a) it was shortened, (b) the description was made more focused, and (c) identified opportunities for conversation and asking enumerators to use such opportunities to break the monotone.

In response to NWSDB suggestions, the water treatment questions asked reasons from the households who said they were not treating their water.

Based on the pretest responses, the alternative options for a private water connections identified were (a) small-diameter mini-grids, (b) metered stand posts, (c) publicly subsidized dug wells, and (d) small scale independent retailers.

Improvements were made to the instructions within the survey to direct the enumerators to the four different versions of the contingent valuation section.

There were no major changes to the basic structure of the instrument as used in the pretests, other than the splitting of the socio-demographic module into (a) family and health, and (b) socioeconomic. Several changes were made to the wording, structure, and location of questions in the survey. Every translation requires a couple of passes before the ideas are communicated simply. Following is a sample elicitation question for a connected household under private provision:

Suppose your household receives 24-hour water supply service of 500[12] liters per day, with water that is safe to drink directly from the tap, accurate billing of the water, with reliable and responsive customer service by a private service provider, are you willing to pay Rs 200 water bill per month? (1) Yes (2) No

The sample was split between connected and unconnected households and both groups were further subdivided to public and private sector provisions in the CV question. The unconnected households were given two elicitation questions – one on monthly bills and the other on connection charges. The sample was also split between the two study areas.

---

[12] Specifying the quantity of water might confuse the respondent when he/she currently consumes less or more than that. However, in most of the cases, including this study, water availability is less than what households desire to consume. In such situations if the CV question is asked without specifying the quantity under the improved services, that may lead to higher level of confusion as well as incomplete description of the improved service.

18.3.4. Enumerator training

Enumerators for the study were selected from a pool of recent graduates (Bachelor's degree) from University of Peradeniya. Some of these graduates have background in agricultural economics and economics, while others were agricultural science graduates. As expected, most of the enumerators were not experienced in large-scale survey administration, particularly one that involved contingent valuation questions. Therefore, training enumerators became a critical element of the project and benefited the project in two additional ways. First, it allowed the enumerators to become familiar with the survey instrument, especially the intricate details in each section. Second, it served as a form of focus group for the instrument to help the study team refine the wording and flow of the questions.

A 10-day, two-stage training sessions were conducted with a mix of lectures, role-plays and field trials happened. The first stage of the training was undertaken primarily on Peradeniya campus. Classroom sessions over several days introduced the enumerators to the basic elements of the study and its relevance, economic concepts underlying the study, the importance of key questions and how the data would be interpreted. In addition, the principal investigators (Pls) introduced the enumerators to the first four modules – 1) Introduction, 2) Current Water Sources, 3) Water Treatment, Storage and Hygiene Practices, and 4) Household Sanitation Service. After reviewing and discussing key questions; role play of the modules was conducted between sets of two enumerators – i.e., one enumerator would administer the survey to the other and vice versa. These sessions perhaps generated the most intensive learning. The enumerators then conducted two sample interviews in the Kandy area with the first four modules.

The second stage of the training was conducted in Negombo so that the enumerators could get a feel for the study area. The entire team (including the Pls, field coordinators and enumerators) moved to Negombo for four days, and followed a similar pattern of class room lecture, discussion and role play for the remaining modules. These included the following modules – 5) Contingent Valuation of Improved water Supply, 6) Family Roster, and 7) Socioeconomic Profile. Enumerators then conducted two days of trial interviews with randomly chosen subjects in the Negombo area and one day in the Kalutara-Galle strip (around the town of Wadduwa). Care was taken to expose all enumerators to a range of interviewees including at least one specially sampled poor household. The early training interviews lasted between one to three hours.

The questions raised during lectures, role-plays, discussions and the feedback from training interviews was used to develop guidelines for survey implementation. The guidelines discussed the purpose of specific questions and helped develop a common understanding of how to ask certain questions and preferred ways of coding the responses in the questionnaire. In addition to guidance on how to interpret certain questions, the guidelines reiterated the intent of and the critical questions in each module. For example, in the section in the guidelines on WTP, it was emphasized that enumerators should read out the complete scenario for the question, not offer their own version of what they thought. This would ensure that all respondents received identical descriptions of the proposed service, allowing one to compare their responses.

Besides training on the survey instrument, a separate session was held in Negombo to orient both the field coordinators and enumerators to the collection of spatial data. Interviewers were introduced to the rationale behind mapping household locations as well as infrastructural and environmental amenities and disamenities. Another important element of the training focused on developing standards for concepts such as volume of water collected and distance travelled. Accordingly, enumerators were trained to visually assess water container volume. Actual water volumes in a range of sizes of buckets and pots, commonly used for water storage, were calibrated. Estimates were also made of the reasonable quantity of water that was likely to be carried in buckets of certain sizes, as opposed to their full nominal values (e.g., a 20-liter bucket was unlikely to hold more than 17 liters when used for ferrying water). Distance estimates were similarly calibrated with the actual distances – in travel time by foot and in kilometers.

The final element of the training involved working with the enumerators to develop the split sample design for the monetary and non-monetary attributes of the contingent service. For example, eight monthly bill amounts used in the contingent valuation question had to be distributed across the 1800 surveys in a randomized manner. Each enumerator was given a list of monthly bills corresponding to the questionnaire numbers and they were explained how the allocation was done. In the questionnaire, all the eight bids were included and the enumerators marked the correct bid amount in their questionnaires. One of the goals of involving the students in this exercise was to show how split samples are designed and the importance of randomizing the patterns.

18.3.5. Survey administration

One Principle Investigator (PI) served as the overall in-charge of survey implementation and he was assisted by three field coordinators. The 15 enumerators were divided in to three groups and each group was assigned to a field coordinator directly responsible for all logistical aspects of survey implementation. In addition to the daily quota of surveys, each enumerator was given a set of guidelines that covered the following aspects of administering the survey – enumerator code and supervisors contact information; pick-up and drop-off schedule; review of the contingent v 'uation section; and do's and don'ts for each of the 7 sections of the survey. The entire survey team, including the Pls, was based in Negombo for Phase I of the survey implementation. Phase II was staged from two towns – Northern Kalutara in Kalutara district and Hikkaduwa in Galle district–in order to optimize travel times and better facilitate field operations.

The field coordinators were integral to the survey implementation. They handed out blank surveys each morning, facilitated field operations, periodically and randomly monitored interviews for quality purposes, and collected each day's completed surveys after dinner. In rare cases, they rescheduled the interview with a Tamil speaking enumerator when the household does not understand Sinhalese. Besides these responsibilities, the field coordinators also checked each survey for completeness and accuracy according to a quality check list prepared for this purpose. If any discrepancies were detected, the enumerators had to return to the households to correct the errors or fill the missing information. In addition to the reviews conducted by the field coordinators, Project Pls conducted a second round of reviews of surveys. The team also maintained a log of completed surveys on a daily basis. This provided a quick overview of the progress of the survey administration. The graph is a proxy to understand the effective demand for the CV Commodity at a given price. These measures avoid the need for repeated visits to the same households as the survey progressed. On average, the enumerators completed about 65 surveys per day, and the interviews ran around 45 minutes. Therefore the findings of the CV survey can be used for project design and policy analysis.

18.3.6. Data entry and quality checks

While the survey is progressing in the field, a coding sheet and template for data entry was prepared. The data recorded on the paper questionnaires was transferred into the selected data management software, using codes developed during the survey design. Three quality assurance and quality control procedures were employed to ensure that data is transferred without errors – range checks, intra-record checks, and final consistency check. Range and intra-record checks were undertaken during data entry. By building a proper data entry template, the operators were allowed to proceed to the next question if and only if the data for the current question fall within the allowable range of responses for each question. An intra-record consistency check was administered immediately after entry of each questionnaire. A final scan for overall consistency was conducted when all questionnaires have been entered. This final consistency check ensured that values from one question are consistent with values from another question. In addition, spot checks on the data entry operation conducted and 10 per cent of the surveys were double-entered. In addition, 100 per cent of critical modules such as WTP elicitation response were double-entered to ensure that there are no discrepancies between the hard copies and the electronic data set.

As an additional quality assurance measure, the descriptive statistics of the key variables were estimated and examined. Particular attention was paid to identify anomalies, outliers, and improbable values. It would be useful to identify subpopulations of policy interest for further estimation of descriptive statistics. In the present study the subpopulation of the following is used – (a) WSS user type (e.g., private water connection or public tap); (b) socioeconomic group (e.g., households in different consumption quintiles); and (c) subregions of the study area (e.g., administrative units). Data on household consumption expenditures were validated against income, wealth and assets, caloric intakes, demographics, and housing quality to validate the quality of the data. Cross-tabulations by socioeconomic, geographic, and current use status were calculated for all important variables including demand for WSS improvements, water quality perceptions, and consumption. This process helped further assess the quality of data.

18.4. Results

This section presents some of the selected results from the study. As mentioned earlier, this study has broader objectives, which goes beyond estimating the WTP for improved water supply services in the study area. However, given the limited focus of this chapter, only the findings related to assessment of demand for improved services are presented.

18.4.1. Validity tests

To establish the accuracy of CV studies, the analyst may evaluate the survey responses by examining three characteristics – validity, reliability, and precision. Validity refers to whether survey respondents have answered the question the interviewer attempted to ask. If respondents answered the right question, reliability refers to the size and direction of bias that may be present in the answers. Precision refers to the variability in responses. Variability can result from heterogeneity of the population as well as from small or non representative samples. In a study like this the researchers can control only the variability arising from sampling issues. The present study uses systematic sampling strategy and a very large sample, therefore precision errors arising due to sampling problems is not an issue.

Validity can be of two types – convergent validity and construct validity. Convergent[13] validity generally refers to the temporal stability of WTP estimates. It can be assessed by examining the consistency of WTP estimates over time through repeated surveys of the same individuals. From a practical point of view, examining convergent validity is not practically feasible during a project preparatory CV study like this. Construct validity refers to how well the measurement is predicted by factors that one would expect to be predictive a priori. Here the analyst can examine the consistency of CV results with the predictions of economic theory. In a study of this nature, construct validity can be readily checked by estimating a WTP function[14] that relates, a respondent's WTP to the individual's characteristics and to the characteristics of the commodity. Hypothesis testing can be performed using this WTP function to examine construct validity. A multivariate

---

[13] Convergent validity can also be assessed when different estimates of WTP are obtained using different methods for the same sample at the same time.

[14] The type of econometric models used in developing WTP function varies with the type of elicitation question. For example, the open-ended WTP format models WTP function with Tobit models, while dichotomous choice models use probit or logit models.

probit regression model was estimated for this purpose and to estimate the mean WTP. In this regression model, the household's reply (Yes = 1, No = 0) to the dichotomous choice elicitation question of WTP serves as the dependent variable. The independent variables consist of the bid; a set of economic variables (poverty status, connection cost); household data including location and distance to the road; availability of alternative sources of water; occurrence of diarrhoea in the family; education level of the household head; and household perception-related variables such as perception on water pollution in the area and seriousness of water supply shortages.

The regression results in Table 18.1 shows that demand for improved water services will decrease as the monthly water bill increases. Similarly, higher connection costs reduce WTP. Moreover, the results show that WTP is lower among the poor compared to non-poor households, which confirms the positive income effect on WTP. Those who receive remittances from abroad are willing to pay more while Samurdhi (the Sri Lankan Government's flagship poverty alleviation programme) recipients show lower WTP. Those who consume more water are willing to pay more. As economic theory predicts, the availability of water substitutes, mainly wells with good quality water in this case, resulted in low WTP. The aforementioned results are consistent with economic theory. The other findings also agree with the conventional wisdom of human behaviour. For example, distance to the road is positively related to WTP, which may be due to the fact that water is scarcer for households located far from the roads. The dummy variable related to location indicates that there are location differences in WTP. All the perception-related variables including education showed expected relationship to the WTP. The negative and significant dummy variable on ethnicity suggest that there is a difference of WTP for improved WSS service between Sinhalese and Tamil communities. These test results provide a high level of confidence about the construct validity and consequently, about the estimated WTP values. Therefore the findings of the CV survey can be used for policy project design and analysis purposes with confidence.

18.4.2. Assessment of demand

WSS services are generally provided by the public sector. However, public sector goods/services provision is generally decided through political processes rather than as a response to market signals. Politically driven supply of public services frequently shows the characteristic of decoupling of burdens and benefit.[15] Frequently, single-source production (natural monopoly) prevents competition. Moreover, lack of an exit mechanism, as in the case of market-driven economic activities, results in continuation of the provision despite poor performance. These characteristics together make WSS projects prone to huge inefficiencies. Therefore, investigating the effective demand for WSS services is of paramount importance before launching a WSS project. In this section, how the CV results can be used to assess effective demand for WSS service is shown.

Demand generally shows the relationship between the marginal WTP (price) for different quantities of a good. A similar relationship as shown in Figure 18.1 can be directly obtained from the responses to the elicitation question.[16] The information contained in the figure is capable of answering questions related to the demand for the WSS service – Are the beneficiaries willing to pay for access to improved service? How will demand be affected by changes in price? How will demand be affected by income of the consumers? Have the changes in price, income, and other variables been properly accounted for in predicting the demand for project output? As shown in Figure 18.1 the price–quantity relationship can be directly obtained from WTP data. The graph can be a good proxy to understand 'what is the effective demand for the CV commodity given price at LKR 200 per month?' For example, if the monthly water bill is LKR 200, about one third of those households currently without individual taps will be connected. If the water bill goes up to LKR 400, then almost 30 per cent of households without individual taps would be connected. With such a simple figure, the analyst can further examine how different tariff settings would affect the cost recovery of investment on newly proposed services as deliberated in the CV market scenario. This could also be a useful tool to predict effective demand on the proposed WSS services with varying price schemes.

---

[15] When users do not pay directly for public services, the cost of provision is borne by taxpayers. Because everybody may not pay taxes in developing countries, beneficiaries may be a different category of people. This leads to decoupling.

[16] Note that the y axis here represents the per centage of households accepting a bid, and is therefore slightly different from the usual quantity. However the per centage of households accepting the bid is a very good proxy for the quantity. If every household consume the same quantity of water, the curves in the graph become true demand curves.

Table 18.1 Impact of household characteristics and related variables on demand for improved piped water service-probit regression

Variable	MEAN	COEFFICIENT	P-VALUE
Regression constant		1.119	0.000
Monthly consumption charge (Rs.)	487	−0.002	0.000
One-time connection cost (Rs.)	5,534	−0.00003	0.004
Monthly per capita consumption (Rs.)	6,044	0.00003	0.004
Household receives remittance (1 = yes; 0 = no)	0.10	0.276	0.013
Household is a Samurdhi recipient (1 = yes; 0 = no)	0.19	−0.245	0.012
Household head is employed in private sector (1 = yes; 0 = no)	0.41	0.213	0.002
Distance to road (kilometers)	0.32	0.112	0.134
Household resides in Greater Negombo (1 = yes; 0 = Kalutara or Galle)	0.45	−0.484	0.000
Household resides in Kalutara (1 = yes; 0 = Greater Negombo or Galle)	0.23	−0.326	0.000
Per cent of households with access to private wells in Greater Negombo	0.79	−0.329	0.014
Per cent of households that consider water quality of their alternative sources as excellent or good in Greater Negombo	0.59	−0.312	0.013
Household believes that there is a water contamination problem (1 = yes; 0 = no)	0.10	0.248	0.023
Household thinks government should give connection subsidy to low-income households for improved water supply services (1 = yes; 0 = no)	0.30	0.025	0.731
Household is particularly conscious of institutional issues (1 = yes; 0 = no)	0.01	0.570	0.040
Private sector will provide improved service (1 = yes; 0 = public sector will provide)	0.55	−0.116	0.085
Household is particularly conscious of health issues (1 = yes; 0 = no)	0.02	0.648	0.003
Household has experienced a case of morbidity event (1 = yes; 0 = no)	0.02	0.649	0.006
Household is Tamil (1 = yes; 0 = no)	0.03	−0.475	0.047
Household owns the house (1= yes; 0 = no)	0.94	−0.322	0.025
Education of household head (years)	9	0.021	0.090

Number of observations 1735
Likelihood Ratio Statistic 2 (20) 389 0.000
per cent Responses that are Correctly Predicted 73
Log likelihood - 942

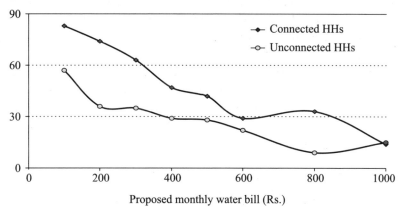

% Households want
improved water service

Figure 18.1. Household demand for improved water service in Sri Lanka

In order to understand the impact of income on effective demand, the estimated WTP function can be simulated for different income levels. Sometimes, a proxy for income is incorporated in the regression models when accurate income data is difficult to obtain. For example, this study uses poverty as a proxy in the regression equation. When reasonable data about future income or any change in related variables are available, these data can be used to predict future demand for improved services. Household characteristics of the subpopulation of interest and attributes of a WSS service (reliability, charges, quality, etc.) can be used to predict acceptance of improved services by the respondents.

The estimated model based on CV data also generates probabilities of connection, given different combinations of consumption charges and service attributes. Therefore, they can be used as a tool to estimate probabilities of acceptance under different policy options. This prediction exercise could be repeated for alternative scenarios to generate a series of probability maps of coverage under service alternatives (Pattanayak et al., 2006). Such simulations will help the analyst predict the service coverage and output of the WSS plant with reasonable accuracy under the most probable future scenarios. This information can then be fed back to engineering designs to avoid under capacity/excess capacity issues in designing water supply plants. Table 18.2 shows predicted rates of acceptance (uptake rates) for different groups. Gunatilake et al., (2007) provides a step by step procedure for predicting the acceptance rates. The predicted uptake rates with most plausible policy scenario answer the effective demand question directly and provide additional information on financial sustainability, and overall viability of the WSS project. The predicted uptake rates given in Table 18.2 show that effective demand is less than that is anticipated by the PSP designers. In this study the designers assume universal coverage (95 per cent of the households in the study area) under the PSP. Note that the predicted rates in Table 18.2 are for unconnected households with a one-time connection charge of LKR 7500.00. As shown in this study, uptake rated significantly increase if there is a subsidy or other financial attunement to pay the connection charge in installments.

Table 18.2. Predicted uptake rates of improved WSS for different groups

Service area	Uptake Rates (per cent)	
	Poor	Non-poor
Greater Negombo		
Connected	49	64
Unconnected	32	47
Kalutara-Galle		
Connected	44	59
Unconnected	27	42

In this study, WTP data gathered from the CV survey measures the amount of monthly income that the household is willing to give up to obtain improved water services, while remaining as well-off as before. Willingness-to-pay, estimated in this manner, is a measure of the economic value (benefit) derived by the household from improved water services. The study used a single bound, closed-ended CV question to elicit household preferences. More specifically, households currently connected to piped water services were asked to consider an increase in monthly consumption charges for improved water supply service. Service improvement was accurately described as providing 500 liters of clean and safe water, 24 hours a day, with regular and fair billing based on metered use together with prompt repairs and efficient customer services. Based on this description, the survey sought consumer responses, either 'yes' or 'no', to different water bills for improved water services.

Table 18.3 provides WTP estimates by sub-groups with a connection, based on the regressions results in Table 18.1. The probit regression results do not provide WTP directly. Mean WTP can be estimated using the coefficients of this regression model as described by Hanemann (1994),

Cameron and James (1987), and Cameron (1988). Gunatilake et.al (2007) provides the step by step procedure for estimating mean WTP using probit regression results. Using this method, the mean WTP for the entire sample is estimated at LKR 234 per month. The method also allows calculating the mean WTP for selected subsamples, which in this case is LKR 357 per month for the non-poor and LKR 106 per month for the poor. The mean WTP for those connected to piped water is about three times higher than that of the unconnected. Given the pre-existing average tariff of LKR 75 per month for a household, the mean WTP for improved service is much higher. However, the analyst should not rely exclusively on the mean WTP values because mean values may provide wrong policy directions.

Table 18.3. WTP estimates by sub-groups with connection fees of Rs. 0 for connected and Rs. 6000 for unconnected households

District	First Quintile (n = 365)		Fifth Quintile (n = 362) Median		Overall (n = 1818)	
Gampaha (Greater Negombo)	105		250		150	
Connected		215		515		425
Unconnected		10		145		55
Kalutara – Galle	180		470		310	
Connected		255		490		405
Unconnected		120		385		200
Overall	160		390		250	
Connected		245		500		410
Unconnected		100		215		115[#]

The estimated WTP values have a number of important uses such as calculating the benefits of the proposed improvements to the water supply system, tariff setting, and making informed decisions on related policy issues of the WSS project. Once the analyst gets reasonable confidence about the estimated mean WTP value, it can be readily used in project economic analysis. The mean WTP multiplied by the number of households served by the project provides the total gross benefit of the project.

The use of WTP estimates in setting tariffs is also reasonably straightforward, but some understanding is required to avoid its misinterpretation and misuse. CV surveys provide measures of the maximum WTP for

---

[#] The simulation was performed with a different, simplified regression model. Therefore the WTP value are only indicative.

proposed improvements in WSS in the context of the existing or proposed institutional regime. The WTP is related but not equal to the future demand or monthly bill paid by the households to the water utility. Although the future demand and WTP contain similar behavioural information on household preferences, WTP is different because it is an ex-ante measure of welfare change associated with the improved WSS. It will not show how much water will be consumed when services are improved, or how many households will be connected to the improved service with a revised tariff structure and connection charges.

WTP cannot be used to estimate revenue directly, because households will pay only a proportion of the maximum WTP expressed in the CV study. Moreover, basic economic principles suggest that monthly charges should be equal to or less than WTP. Therefore, a tariff that charges above WTP will lead to welfare losses and may discourage households from connecting to the water services. Therefore the WTP should be treated as the upper bound of tariff. Furthermore, tariff setting requires additional information because tariffs setting require to meet a set of social, economic, and financial goals such as good governance, financial sustainability, economic efficiency, and distributive justice/fair pricing (Dole, 2003, Dole and Bartlett, 2004, Dole and Balucan, 2006). In addition to WTP therefore, information on the cost of delivery, capital replacement requirements, and various social considerations should be used in setting tariffs.

The estimated WTP functions can also be used to analyze policy issues related to designing WSS projects such as the institutional provision of the service, design of spatially based pro-poor service delivery, affordability and characterizing the low WTP groups. In this study, WTP estimation was triggered by the government's proposal to introduce private-public participation to improve water and sanitation services. The study implicitly assumed that households prefer the private sector as the service provider believing they can benefit more through efficient operation and maintenance. In order to assess households' preference toward the provider, the study used a split sample approach (described in Pattanayak et al., 2006). About half of the sample was told that the improved service will be provided by the private sector, while the rest was told that the reformed public sector will improve the service. A dummy variable was used to analyze households' attitude toward the service provider. A statistically significant negative coefficient (see Pattanayak et al., 2006) indicates that, holding everything else constant, households will have a lower probability of connecting to the improved service if the private sector provide the service. This shows that households' perceptions are against generally held beliefs about the desirability of private sector provision of WSS.

The study also explored the possibility of designing pro-poor service delivery. Towards this end, the WTP for each household in the sample was calculated using the regression model. This study mapped all the surveyed households using Geographic Positioning Systems (GPS).[17] Mapping allowed the investigation of any low WTP clusters or any other type of spatial patterns of clustering of WTP. Two poverty maps for the two service areas were drawn using the survey data and sample-specific poverty definitions. These maps were overlaid with WTP maps to examine whether there is any particular pattern that could be used to design spatially based, targeted pro-poor service delivery designs. The maps did not show any distinct spatial clustering, thus there was no basis to identify localities with high intensity of poverty and low WTP. Therefore, the design of pro-poor special delivery on the spatial clusters was not feasible in this case.

The study also performed simulations to assess the affordability of the poor, using one-time connection charge as the policy lever. The impact of connection charges on WTP was evaluated by simulating an econometric model with different levels of connection charges. The simulation results in Table 18.3 assume zero connection fees for currently connected households and a LKR 6000 one-time fee for unconnected households, while Table 18.4 assumes zero connection fees for all the households.

Thus, the differences in WTP of the two tables are due to connection charges. Comparing these tables clearly shows that WTP is significantly higher if the connection charge is set to zero (i.e., connections are subsidized). WTP is very low among unconnected households when they have to pay connection charges. In the absence of any subsidy, unwillingness to connect to the new system will have serious implications on the viability of the proposed PPP.

The simulation exercises also showed a number of characteristics pertaining to subgroups that have a lower WTP, namely that they are – (a) currently unconnected, (b) poor, (c) happy with the quality of existing water source, (d) house owners, and (e) less educated. Underlying these characteristics is mainly the issue of affordability. In addition, this subgroup

---

[17] Every enumerator was given a GPS unit and instructed to locate the household using the GPS unit after the interview. The simulation was performed with a different, simplified regression model. Therefore the WTP value are only indicative.

has reliable system of self provision of water. Their low WTP for improved water service is also influenced by lower incidence of water-related diseases, lack of perceived link between personal health and water quality, and overall satisfaction with the current supply. Overall, these findings show that there is much less demand for improved WSS in the study area than anticipated by the PPP designers. The above analyses indicate quite a different picture about the feasibility of the proposed project, compared to that indicated by the mean WTP.

Table 18.4. WTP estimates by sub-groups without connection

District	First Quintile (n = 365)		Fifth Quintile (n = 362) Median		Overall (n = 1818)	
Gampaha (Greater Negombo)	215		505		400	
Connected		215		515		425
Unconnected		210		500		385
Kalutara – Galle	310		550		440	
Connected		255		490		405
Unconnected		320		745		480
Overall	290		520		425	
Connected		245		500		410
Unconnected		300		570		430

18.5. Conclusion

The purpose of this chapter is twofold – (a) to show how one can design and conduct a CV study to generate reliable WTP values for improved WSS services; (b) to show the usefulness of reliable WTP values in preparation of WSS projects.

Careful design of the contingent market scenarios and all the measures described in this chapter for ensuring the quality of CV data are paramount in conducting a CV study. Once the validity and reliability of such studies are established, the study findings can be used to make informed decisions on number of aspects of project design, besides provision of project benefit estimates as illustrated in the chapter. The chapter also shows how to generate useful supplementary information on household institutional preferences, affordability and uptake rates with different connection charges and feasibility of pro-poor service delivery. The chapter illustrates the use of WTP study findings together with other reliable secondary information for assessing overall viability of WSS projects.

References

Adamowicz, W., 'What's it Worth? An Examination of Historical Trends and Future Directions in Environmental Valuation', *Australian Journal of Agricultural and Resource Economics* 48(3), (2004), 419–443.

Arrow, K., Solow, R., Portney, P. R., Leamer, E. E., Radner, R., and Schuman, H. , 'Report of the NOAA Panel on Contingent Valuation', *Federal Register* 58(10), (1993) 4601–4614.

Asian Development Bank, 2005, 'Country Water Action: Asia: Are Countries in Asia on Track to Meet Target 10 of the Millennium Development Goals?', November., Available: http://adb.org/Documents/Books/Asia-Water-Watch/asia-water-watch.pdf. Downloaded 10 November 2006.

Boardman, A. E., Greenberg, D. H., Vining, A. R., and Weimer, D.L., 'Cost-Benefit Analysis: Concept and Practice', (New Jersey: A. Simon & Schuster Company 1996).

Brookshire, D., and Whittington, D., 'Water Resource Issues in the Developing Countries', *Water Resources Research* 29(7), (1993), 1883–1888.

Cameron, T.A., Poe G.L., Ethier, R.G. and Schulze, W.D., 'Alternative Non-market Value-Elicitation Methods: Are the Underlying Preferences the Same?' *Journal of Environmental Economics and Management* 44(3), (2002) 391–425.

Cameron, T. A., 'A New Paradigm for Valuing Nonmarket Goods Using Referendum Data: Maximum Likelihood Estimation by Censored Logistic Regression', *Journal of Environmental Economics and Management* 15, (1988), 355–379.

Cameron, T. A., and James, M. D., Efficient Estimation Methods for 'Closed-Ended', Contingent Valuation Surveys', *Review of Economics and Statistics* 69(2), (1987), 269–276.

Carson, R.T., *Contingent Valuation: A Comprehensive Bibliography and History*, (Cheltenham, UK and Northampton, MA: Edward Elgar, 2003).

Choe, K., Whittington, D. and Lauria, D. T., 'The Economic Benefits of Surface Water Quality Improvements in Developing Countries: A Case Study of Davao, Philippines', *Land Economics* 72(4), (1996) 519–537.

Dole, D., 'Setting User Charges for Public Services: Policies and Practice at the Asian Development Bank', *ERD Technical Note No. 9*, Economics and Research Department, Asian Development Bank, Manila, (2003).

Dole, D., and Balucan, E., 'Setting User Charges for Urban Water Supply: A Case Study of the Metropolitan Cebu Water District in the Philippines', *ERD Technical Note No. 17*, Economics and Research Department, Asian Development Bank, Manila 2006.

Dole, D., and Bartlett, I., 'Beyond Cost Recovery: Setting User Charges for Financial, Economic and Social Goals', *ERD Technical Note No. 10*, Economics and Research Department, Asian Development Bank, Manila, 2004.

Griffin, C., Briscoe, J., Singh, B., Ramasubban, R. and Bhatia, R., 'Contingent Valuation and Actual Behavior: Predicting Connections to New Water Systems in the State of Kerala, India', *The World Bank Economic Review*, 9(3), 1995, 373–395.

Gunatilake, H., *Environmental Valuation: Theory and Applications*, (Sri Lanka: Postgraduate Institute of Agriculture, University of Peradeniya, 2003).

Gunatilake, H., Yang, J.C., Pattanayak, S.K. and van den Berg., C., 'Willingness to Pay Studies for Designing Water Supply and Sanitation Projects: A Good Practice Case Study', *Asian Development Bank Technical Note No. 17*, Manila, ADB, 2006. Available: http://www.adb.org/documents/erd/technical_notes/tn019.pdf.

Gunatilake, H., Yang, J.C., Pattanayak, S. and Choe., K., 'Good Practices for Estimating Reliable Willingness-to-Pay Values in the Water Supply and Sanitation Sector', *Asian Development Bank Technical Note No. 23*, Manila, ADB, 2007. Available: http://www.adb.org/Documents/ERD/Technical_Notes/TN023.pdf

Hanemann, W. M., 'Valuing the Environment through Contingent Valuation', *Journal of Econometric Perspectives*, 81, (1994), 635–647.

'Discrete/Continuous Models of Consumer Demand', *Econometrica*, 52, (1984), 541–561.

Hausman, J.A. and Diamand, P.A., 'Contingent Valuation: Is Some Number Better than No Number?' *Journal of Economic Perspectives*, 8(4), (1994), 45–64.

Pattanayak, S., van de Berg, C., Yang, J. and Van Houtven, G., 'The Use of Willingness to Pay Experiments: Estimating Demand for Piped Water Connections in Sri Lanka', *World Bank Policy Research Working Paper No. 3818*, (Washington DC: The World Bank, 2006).

Pattanayak, S.K., Yang, J.C., Whittington, D., Kumar, B., Subedi, G., Gurung, Y., Adhiraki, K., Shakya, D., Kunwar, L. and Mahabuhang, B., 'Willingness to Pay for Improved Water Services in Kathmandu Valley', Prepared for the World Bank, Water and Sanitation Program. Research Triangle Institute, North Carolina, 2001.

Portney, P.R., 'The Contingent Valuation Debate: Why Economists Should Care?', *Journal of Economic Perspectives*, 8(4), (1994), 3–17.

Smith, V.K., 'Fifty Years of Contingent Valuation', in Alberini, A. and Kahn., J.R. (eds.), *Handbook on Contingent Valuation 7–56* (Cheltenham, UK: Edward Elgar Publishing, 2006).

United Nations, The Millenium Development Goals Report, New York.

UNDP, 2006, 'Beyond Scarcity: Power, Poverty and the Global Water Crisis: Human Development Report 2006', United Nations Development Programme, New York.

Berg van den, Pattanayak, C.S., Yang, J. and Gunatilake, H., 'Getting the Assumptions Right: Private Sector Participation Transaction Design and the Poor in Southwest Sri Lanka', *Water Supply and Sanitation Sector Board Discussion Paper No. 7*, (Washington, DC: The World Bank, 2006).

Vossler, C.A. and Kerkvliet, J., 'A Criterion Validity Test of the Contingent Valuation Method: Comparing Hypothetical and Actual Voting Behavior for a Public Referendum', *Journal of Environmental Economics and Management*, 45, (2003), 631–649.

Whitehead, J.C., 'A Practitioner's Primer on Contingent Valuation', in Alberini, A. and Kahn, J.R. (eds.), *Handbook on Contingent Valuation*, (Cheltenham, UK: Edward Elgar Publishing, 2006).

Whitehead, J.C. and Blomquist, G., 'The Use of Contingent Valuation in Benefit-Cost Analysis', in Alberini, A. and Kahn, J.R. (eds.), *Handbook on Contingent Valuation*, (Cheltenham, UK: Edward Elgar Publishing, 2006).

Whittington, D., 'Behavioural Studies of the Domestic Demand for Water Services in Africa: A Reply to Stephen Merrett', *Water Policy*, 4, (2002), 83–88.

Whittington, D., 'Administering Contingent Valuation Surveys in Developing Countries', *World Development*, 26(1), (1998), 21–30.

Whittington, D., 'Improving the Performance of Contingent Valuation Studies in Developing Counties', *Environmental and Resource Economics*, 22(11), (2002b), 323–367.

Index